The Complete Book of
TOOLS

Albert Jackson and David Day

The Complete Book of TOOLS

Michael Joseph, London

Also by Albert Jackson and David Day
Good Housekeeping Do-it-Yourself Book

The Complete Book of Tools was conceived, edited and designed by Dorling Kindersley Limited, 9 Henrietta Street, London WC2

Illustrations Albert Jackson, David Day, Robin Harris

Historical text W. L. Goodman

Managing Editor Amy Carroll

Art Director Stuart Jackman

Editor Viv Croot

Designers Debbie MacKinnon, Paul Chilvers

Editorial Assistant Elizabeth Driver

Authors' Note

Although we have covered the field of tools used in and around the house as completely as possible, inevitably some of the more uncommon varieties will have been omitted. We have also deliberately exluded craft tools unless they are used to make or repair furniture and fittings in the home. For each tool we have given the common range of sizes and materials, but some tools may be found in other sizes and materials according to local tradition and availability.

First published in Great Britain in 1978 by Michael Joseph Limited, 52 Bedford Square, London WC1B 3EF

ISBN 0 7181 1737 9

Typesetting by Filmtype Services Limited, Scarborough
Printed in Italy by A. Mondadori, Verona

Contents

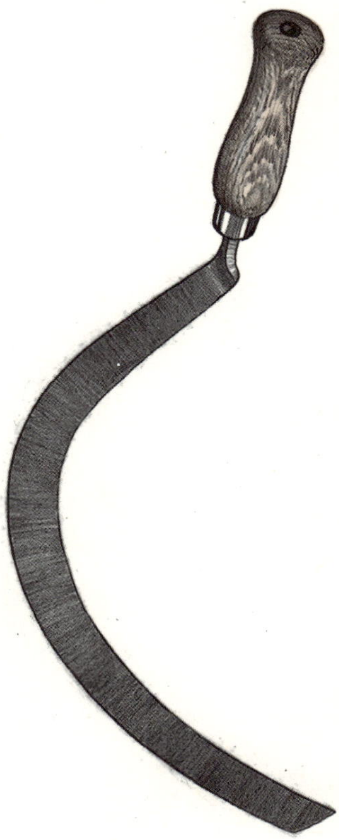

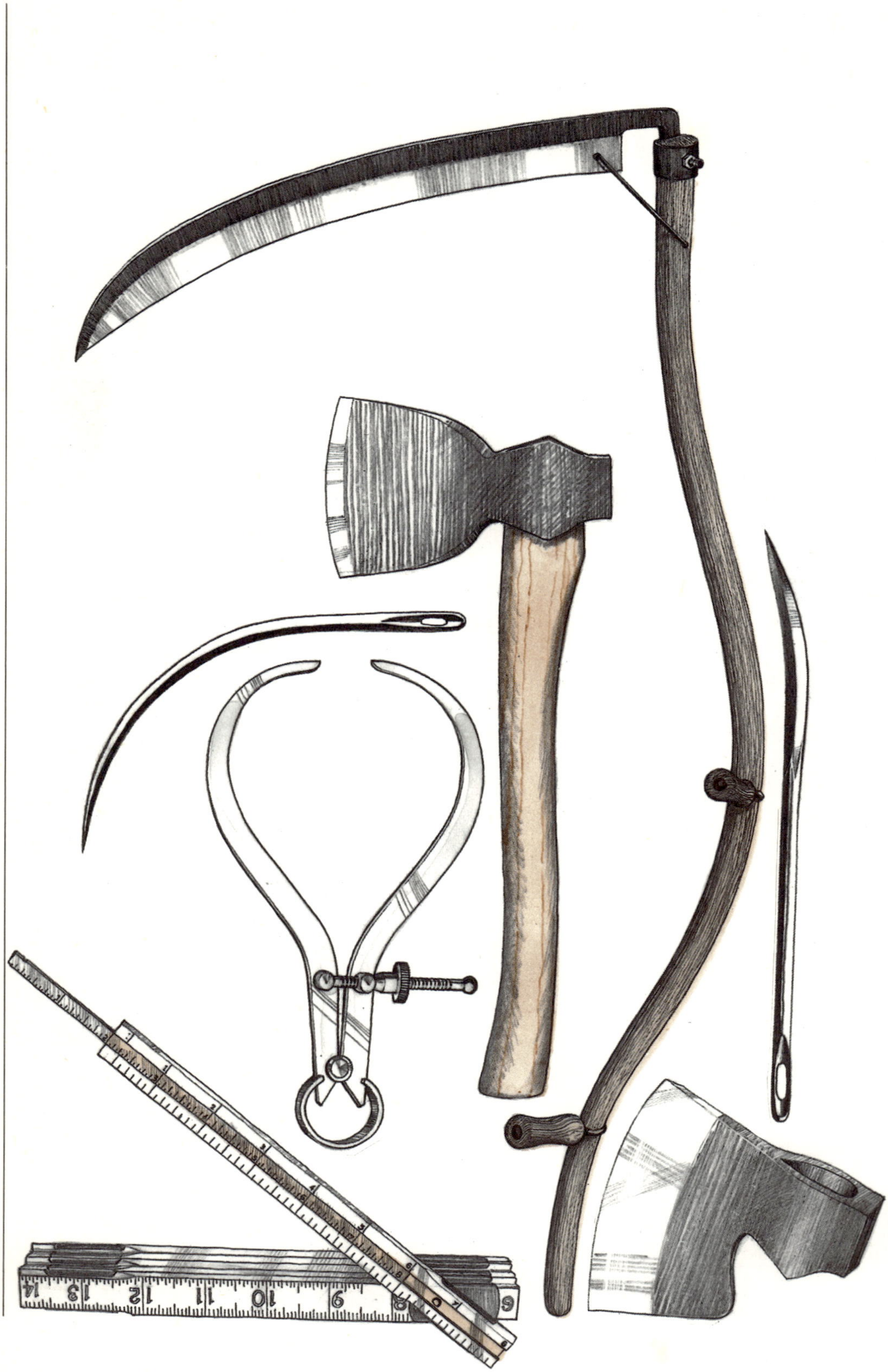

Foreword

Man's progress has been largely a matter of inventing new tools and improving the old ones. Indeed, most of our prehistory is defined by the materials used for them–the Stone, Copper, Bronze and Iron Ages. Recently, in fact during my own lifetime, this progress, as far as tools are concerned, has been explosive; many if not most of the tools I was using as a carpenter and joiner fifty or so years ago are now obsolete and only valued as antiques.

Some of the older basic tools are still, of course, very widely used; in certain circumstances the old things can still be done quite adequately in the old way. A modern tool-kit still contains hammers, axes, chisels, planes and so on, but in many cases the new powered hand tools do the job quicker with much less effort and if handled properly, more effectively than the old. Craftsmen of an earlier generation sometimes complain that the introduction of the new tools has resulted in a loss of skill. This is not the case: new tools need as much skill as old, established ones; what is different is the kind of skill or skills required.

One of the outstanding merits of Albert Jackson's and David Day's book is that they not only devote a good deal of their text to describing and illustrating very carefully the proper way to handle the basic tools, but they also treat the new power tools in an equally detailed and helpful manner, stressing in particular their proper sharpening and safety precautions, which, as any craftsman knows from experience, are closely related.

As a student of the history of tools, I wish a book like this had been written two or three hundred years ago. At that time the men who wrote the books neither knew nor cared very much about the tools used by those who were, to them, the lower orders. Those who did know and care, the tradesmen themselves, could not write the books or in many cases even read them. When occasionally the scholar did meet the craftsman, further difficulties arose. In the Middle Ages a craft trade was often known as a "mystery" and right down to our own times this attitude of secrecy on the part of the skilled artisan was not uncommon. A stranger entering the workshop was a signal for men to put their tools away and when any questions were asked about them it was not unusual to offer frivolous or totally misleading answers. As a rule, the men of learning were in no position to disbelieve what they were told and very often the more unexpected the answer the more impressed they were; after all, it was coming straight from the horse's mouth as it were. There are, in fact, several cases where the exact purpose of some tools in common use only a few generations ago are not now known for certain and can only be a matter of more or less informed argument. There is no risk of this with the tools dealt with by Jackson and Day in this book. They have studied them closely with a keen eye for their possibilities and limitations, knowing that the true fascination of tools lies in using them.

To paraphrase Dr Johnson: there are few ways in which a person can be more innocently employed than in making something useful himself. This book tells you the tools you should have to do what you want to do and how to use them. The rest is up to you.

W. L. Goodman

Rules

The standard Egyptian rule was a cubit (forearm) long, about 20.7in., divided into seven palms, each palm subdivided into four digits (fingers). It was a strip of wood about 2 × 1in. in section with a 45° chamfer on one edge. The Romans used the foot as the unit for practical purposes, about 11.6in. long, divided into four palms and then into either three *unciae* (inches, originally the width of the thumb) or four digits. These were marked on flat strips of wood one or two feet long, the palms being indicated by circles or crosses. Apparently the Romans guessed anything smaller than a finger-width.

Medieval rules were graduated wooden strips. The earliest known two fold rule is dated to 1613. The four fold pocket rule was developed in the late eighteenth century and the two foot length became the standard type.

Bench Rule

SIZE: 1 to 6ft., 300mm to 2m
MATERIAL: Hardwood
USE: To measure a workpiece

Bench rules are straight wooden rules made in one piece. They normally have simple imperial or metric graduations. Stand the rule on its edge for accuracy. Laid flat, its thickness can lead to errors.

Straight Edge

SIZE: 1 to 6ft., 300mm to 2m
MATERIAL: Steel
USE: To test flatness and help cut a straight line

The straight edge is a parallel sided strip of heavy steel, which is beveled on one edge. The bevel is used to cut or scribe against while either edge can be used to test for flatness.

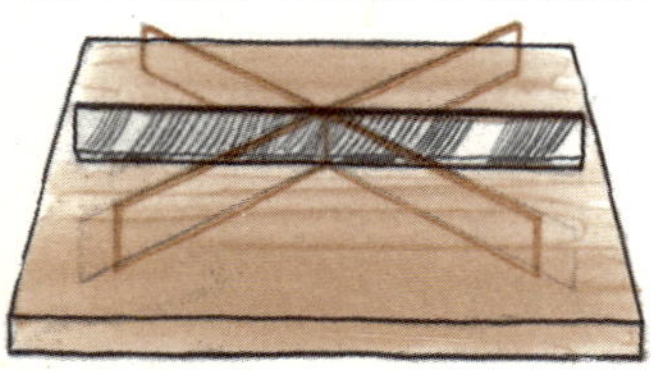

Check flatness by turning the edge to various angles. If there are gaps, the surface is not flat.

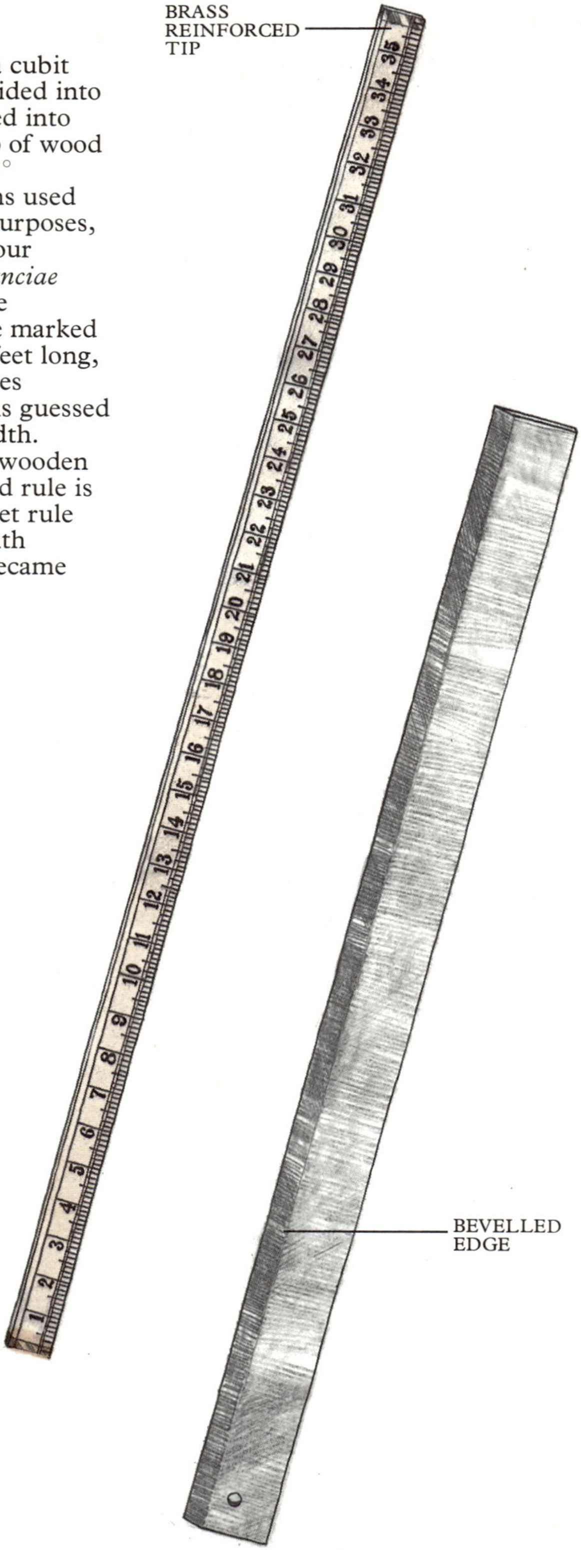

Steel Rule

OTHER NAME: Engineer's steel rule
SIZE: 6 to 72in., 150mm to 2m
MATERIAL: Steel
USE: To determine the size of a workpiece

A good quality steel rule is a very accurate tool for measuring and laying out work. Not only are the graduations very precise, but being steel the rule can be very thin and therefore reduce errors in marking out produced by parallax. A steel rule is essential for any kind of metal work and is also a useful tool in the woodwork shop.

Steel rules have metric or imperial graduations or a combination of both. The rules will usually be graduated on two edges and often on both sides with increasingly smaller divisions of the basic measure. A combined metric and imperial rule is the most useful.

The steel rule can also be used as a straight edge.

Store steel rules carefully. If the edges and ends are damaged, there will be inaccuracies. Many rules have a hole in one end so they can be hung up out of harm's way.

Measuring diameters

The diameter of round stock can be measured with a steel rule. Rest the edge of the rule on the end of the workpiece and locate the squared end against your thumb to line it up with the circumference of the workpiece. Swing the rule backward and forward to obtain the exact diameter.

A reasonably accurate measurement of the bore of a tube can be made in the same way. Locate the squared end of the rule on the inside face of the tube. Swing the rule backward and forward to obtain the internal diameter.

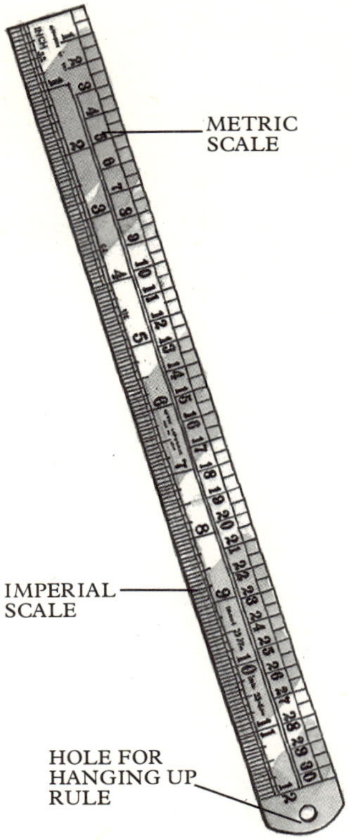

Measuring from a corner

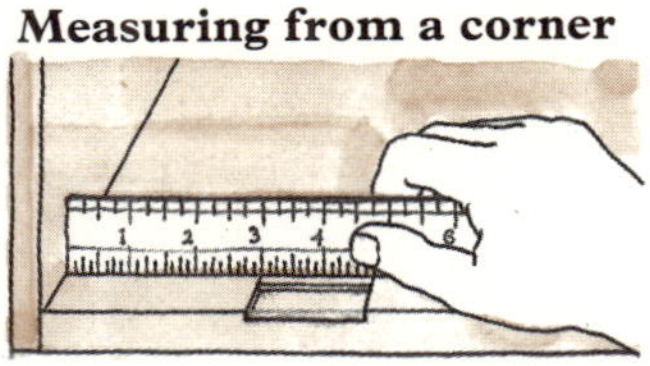

Measure from inside a 90° joint by butting the squared end of the rule against the right angle.

Measuring a diameter

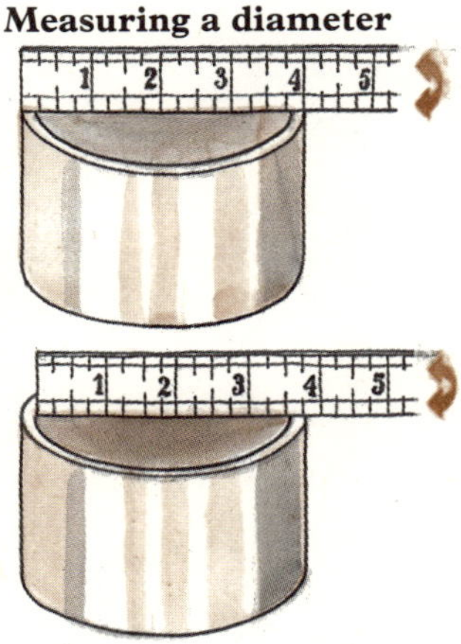

Measure round stock (top) from the outer edge of the piece and bores from the inside face.

Circumference Rule

SIZE: 36 to 48in., 900mm to 1.2m
MATERIAL: Steel
USE: To calculate the circumference of round stock

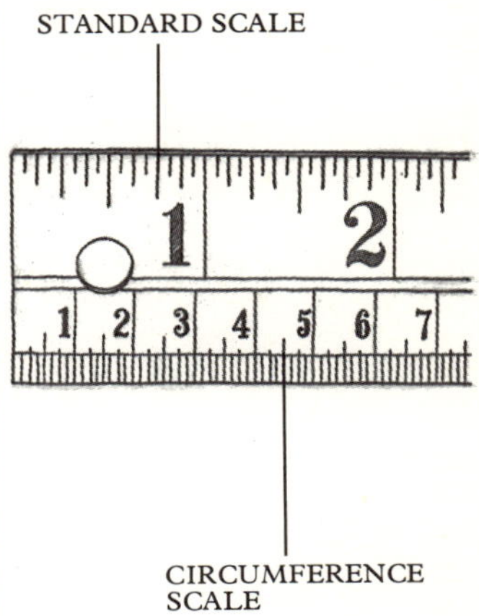

The circumference rule can be used as a standard steel rule, but it is also used to automatically calculate the circumference of a disc or cylinder. One edge of the rule has the standard numerical graduations, which are used to measure the diameter of the workpiece. The corresponding circumference measurement is shown on the other edge.

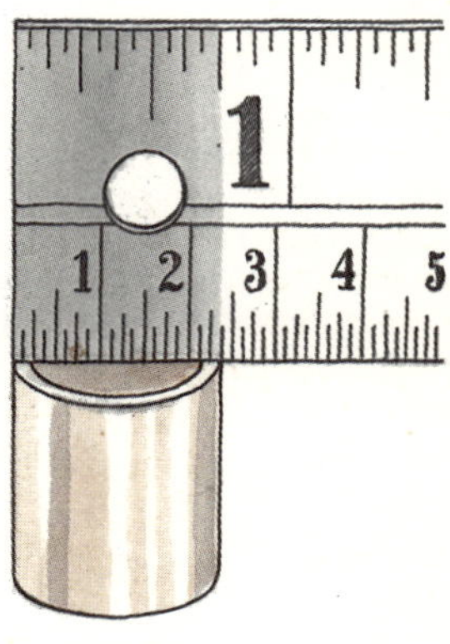

Using the rule

Measure the diameter then read off the circumference measure on the lower edge. A pipe with a diameter of $\frac{3}{4}$in. will have a circumference of $2\frac{3}{8}$in.

Folding Rule

OTHER NAMES: Zig-zag rule, jointed rule, surveyor's rods
SIZE: 1 to 6ft., 300mm to 2m
MATERIAL: Boxwood, alloy steel, plastic
USE: To determine the size of a workpiece, or survey an area

The folding rule can be used in a confined space where a long rule would be inconvenient. It also overcomes the problem of carrying a long measuring rod to the worksite. Both metric and imperial graduations are available on folding rules.

A single folding rule is made from two pieces, which overlap each other and are jointed at one end to swing apart, thus extending the rule. The four fold rule is the traditional carpenter's folding rule. It is made from hardwood and reinforced at the ends with brass. The rule is made from four strips, hinged in pairs to fold back on one another. These hinged sections are jointed at one end with a brass rule joint, made by a disc on one end locating between two discs on the other with a rivet passing through the center of all three. This allows each section of the rule to lay side by side when the rule is closed.

The other common variety of folding rule is the zig-zag rule, which is really an extension of the single fold principle. In this case several sections of the rule are jointed together. Well-made rules have a catch which holds each unfolded section in line with the next.

A folding rule should be protected from damage. Once a joint hinge becomes strained or loose the rule will be inaccurate.

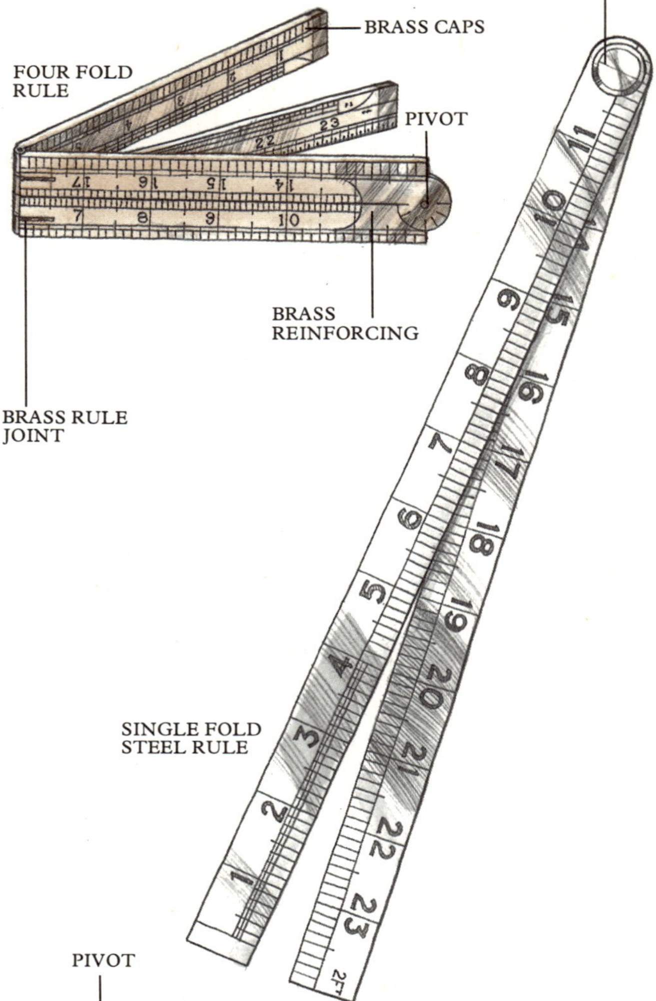

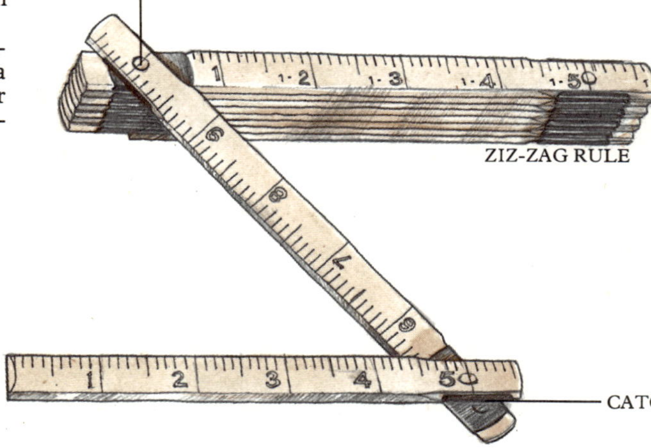

Extension Rule

SIZE: 6 to 8ft., 2 to 2.5m
MATERIAL: Hardwood
USE: To determine the size of a workpiece

The extension rule is a zig-zag rule which includes a brass slide for making internal measurements. The slide extends from the first section of the rule.

To measure the internal width of a frame, open the sections of the rule to fit the gap as closely as possible. Place one end of the rule against one side of the frame and extend the slide to touch the other side.

The slide can also be used as a depth gauge.

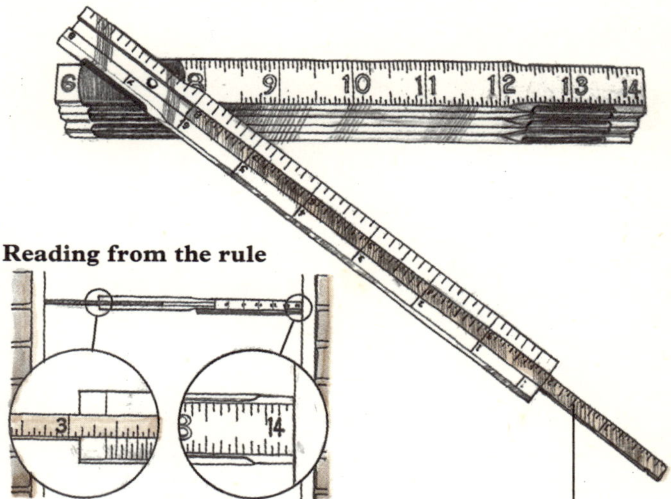

BRASS SLIDE

Reading from the rule

Add the measurement shown on the slide indicating the distance between the frame and the end of the rule to that shown on the rule itself.

Mason's Rule

SIZE: 6ft., 2m
MATERIAL: Hardwood, plastic
USE: To regulate the thickness of mortar joints between masonry units

Mason's rules are used to check accurate progress during wall-building. A wall must be exactly the same height at both ends and the brick courses regulated to correspond with standard window and door frames. There are two types of mason's rule, the "modular" rule and the "spacing" rule. The modular rule determines how many courses of a modular brick or block, plus its mortar joint, will exactly reach a required height. The spacing rule gives the spacing of standard bricks to reach a required height with equal joints between. Both rules have standard numerical graduations on the reverse.

Improvised mason's rule
A home made gauge rod or story pole can be manufactured by calculating the number of courses required, plus the mortar joints, and transferring these calibrations on to a length of softwood. The rod is placed alongside the wall as the work progresses to insure the evenness of each course.

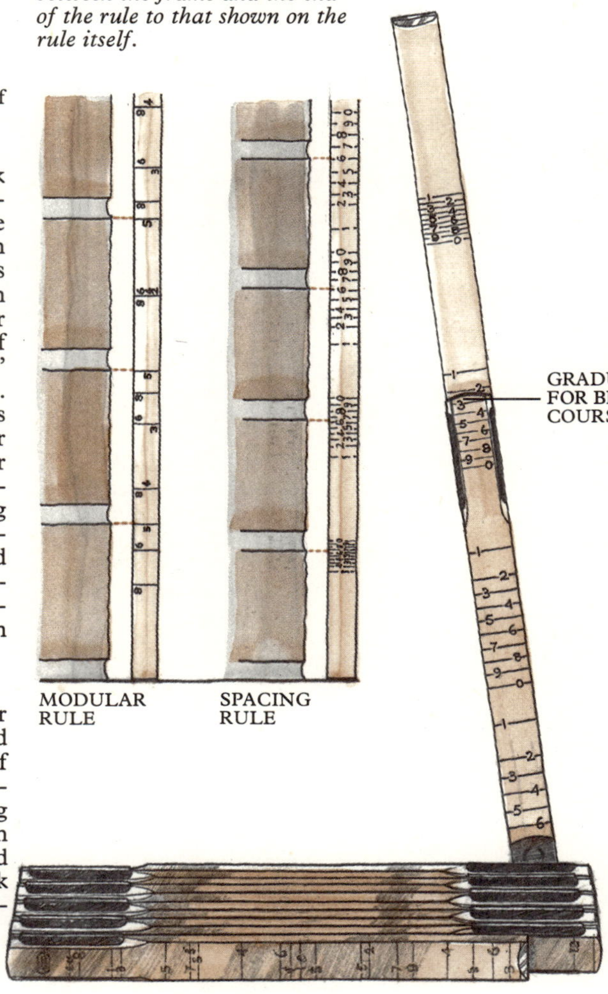

MODULAR RULE

SPACING RULE

GRADUATIONS FOR BRICK COURSES

Push-Pull Steel Tape

OTHER NAME: Flexible rule
SIZE: 3 to 16ft., 900mm to 5m
MATERIAL: *Tape:* steel, fibre glass; *Case:* steel, plastic
USE: To determine the size of a workpiece or survey an area

The push-pull steel tape measure is an extendable steel strip coiled into a container. The tape is spring-loaded, so that as soon as it is released it will automatically return to the case. On some cases a lock is provided to hold the tape when extended. A hook is riveted to the end of the tape to locate on the end of the workpiece so that even a long dimension can be measured single handed. This hook is loosely riveted to the tape and is free to move in and out for a fixed distance. When hooked over an object, it extends by its own thickness so that the measurement can be accurately taken from the end of the tape itself. Similarly when taking an internal measurement the hook retracts so that the measurement is taken again from the end of the tape. Check periodically that the hook has not become too loose, or you will get a false reading. For external measurements, some cases are fitted with a device which indicates the exact measurement including the case.

Tapes are available with both metric and imperial graduations or a combination of both.

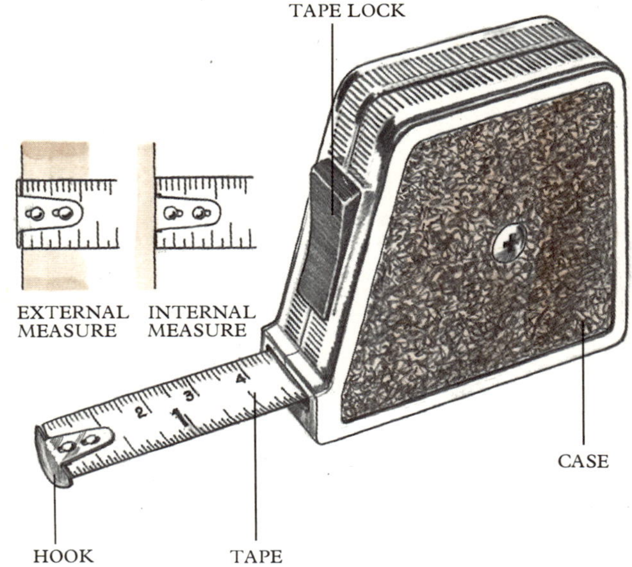

Taking an external measurement

Locate the hook over one end and pull the case to extend the tape, keeping it flat on the work. Read off against the other edge of the workpiece.

Taking an internal measurement

With the back of the case touching one surface, extend the tape. Read off the measurement where the tape enters the case and add 2in. for the case itself.

Measuring a cylinder

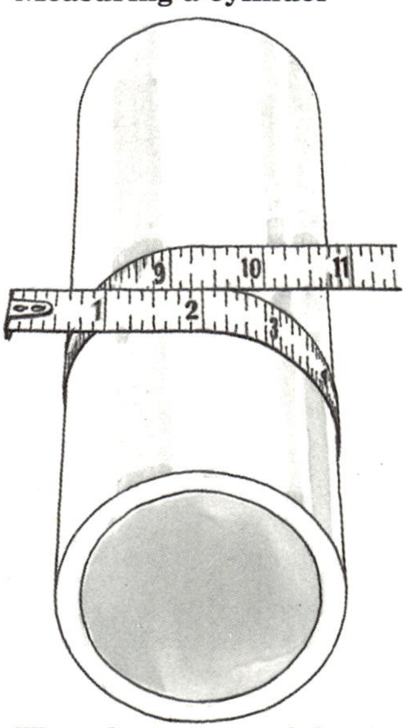

Wrap the tape around the workpiece and align the two meeting edges. Take the 2in. graduation as your reference point and read off the measurement alongside it. To calculate the circumference deduct 2in.

Wind-Up Tape Measure

SIZE: 33 to 100ft., 10m to 30m
MATERIAL: *Tape:* steel, linen; *Case:* steel, plastic, leather
USE: To determine the size of a workpiece or survey an area

The wind-up tape measure is primarily designed for measuring large dimensions, such as the size of a room.

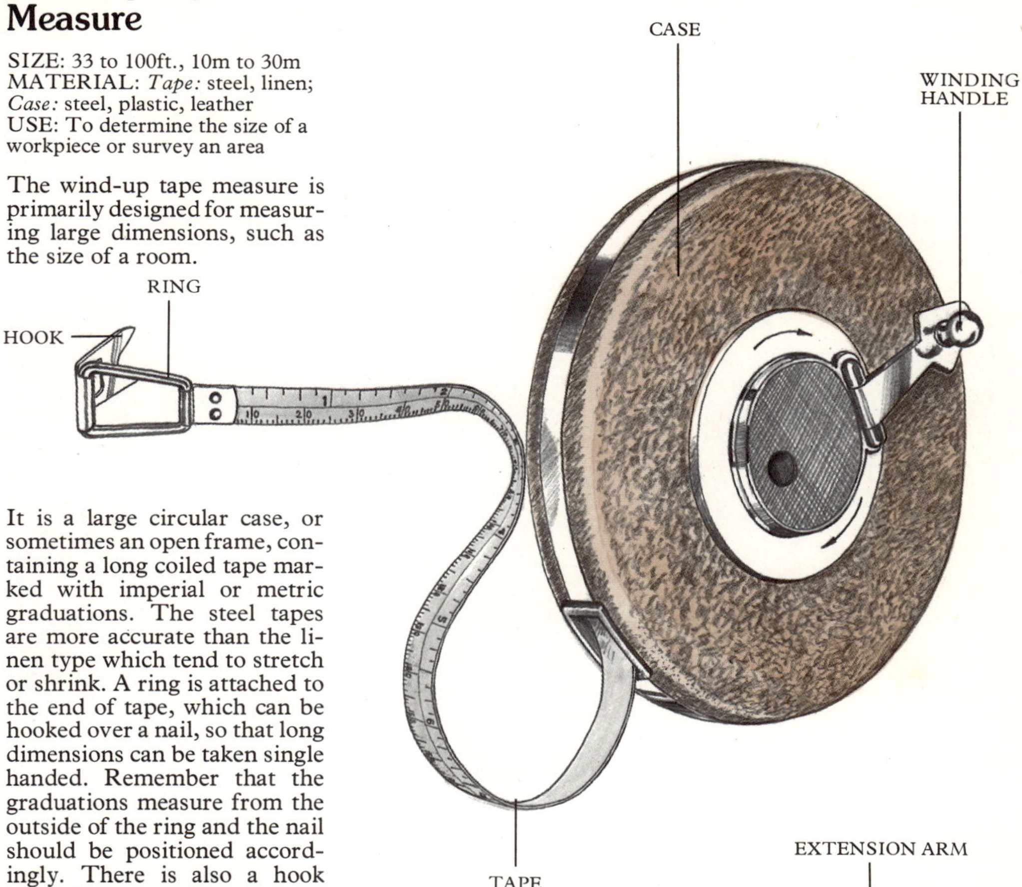

It is a large circular case, or sometimes an open frame, containing a long coiled tape marked with imperial or metric graduations. The steel tapes are more accurate than the linen type which tend to stretch or shrink. A ring is attached to the end of tape, which can be hooked over a nail, so that long dimensions can be taken single handed. Remember that the graduations measure from the outside of the ring and the nail should be positioned accordingly. There is also a hook which hinges out from the ring. This locates over a convenient edge and will automatically align the end of the ring with it. To retract the tape, hinge the winding handle to the open position and crank it clockwise.

Digital Rule

SIZE: Capacity: 999ft., 300m
MATERIAL: Various
USE: To determine the size of the workpiece or survey an area

As the digital rule is run over a surface, the display will indicate the length. It measures curved surfaces as easily as flat. The display is returned to zero by depressing the reset button. By fitting an extension arm the rule can be used to measure ceilings and the height of walls. Digital rules are available with metric and imperial displays.

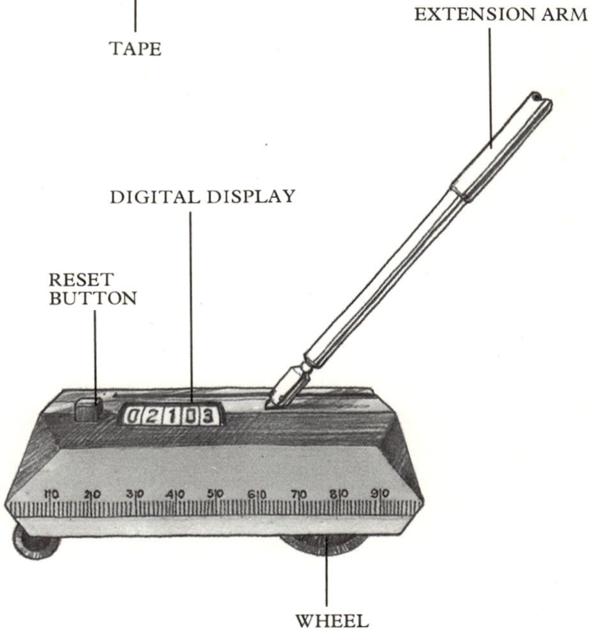

Squares and Bevels

Until quite recent times, all woodworkers made their own squares and similar tools, using suitable pieces of hard, well-seasoned wood. The most common types were large, L-shaped squares for testing the work and smaller tools for setting-out, marking mitres and so on, the latter usually having a stop or fence along the shorter stock.

Tools of this type remained in general use until about the middle of the eighteenth century, when the carpenters' tool makers of London and Sheffield introduced try squares with steel blades and ebony or rosewood stocks edged with brass and fancy inlaid riveting, borrowing the methods of their colleagues, the cutlers and pocket-knife makers.

Try Square

SIZE: *Blade:* 150 to 300mm; *Stock:* 25 to 200mm
MATERIAL: *Blade:* steel; *Stock:* cast iron, hardwood, plastic
USE: To mark out or check the work for square

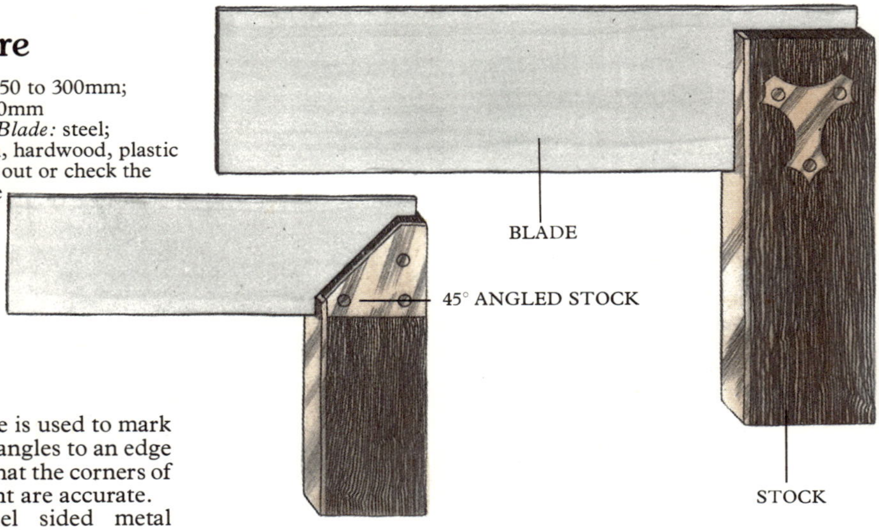

The try square is used to mark a line at right angles to an edge and to check that the corners of a frame or joint are accurate.

The parallel sided metal blade is mounted at one end in the centre of a wider stock and secured by rivets. A superior try square has an L-shaped blade which extends down the length of the stock, which is riveted on either side. This type of square is always accurate, whereas the accuracy of those mounted at the top only can be affected by rivet wear.

The tool forms an accurate 90° both on the inside and outside edges and on some squares the top inside corner of the stock is cut to an angle of 45° for marking a 45° line. The effective length of the blade can be extended by resting a steel rule against the edge when the tool is in position.

You can also use a try square to check work being planed square. Before you begin, plane one face true, mark it as the "face side", so that all measurements can be taken from it. Once the edge is established as true mark it as the "face edge".

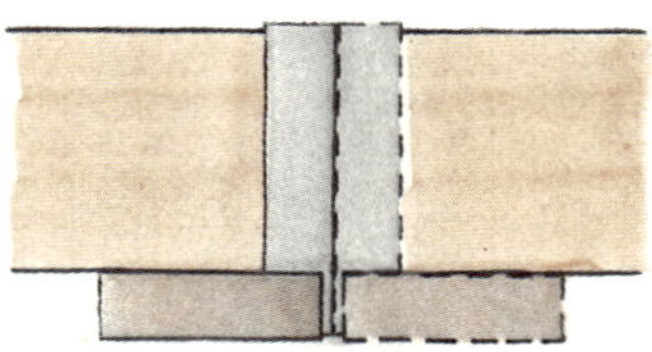

Testing accuracy
Mark a line at 90° to a true edge. Turn the stock over to see if the blade coincides with the line from the other side.

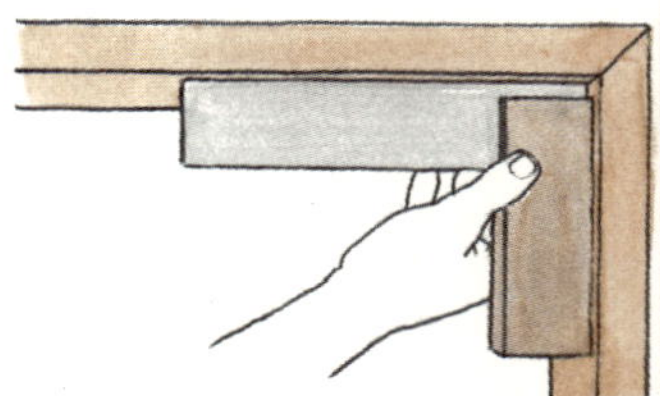

Measuring internal angle
Place the heel of the square into the angle. The edge of the blade should touch the other half of the joint along its entire length.

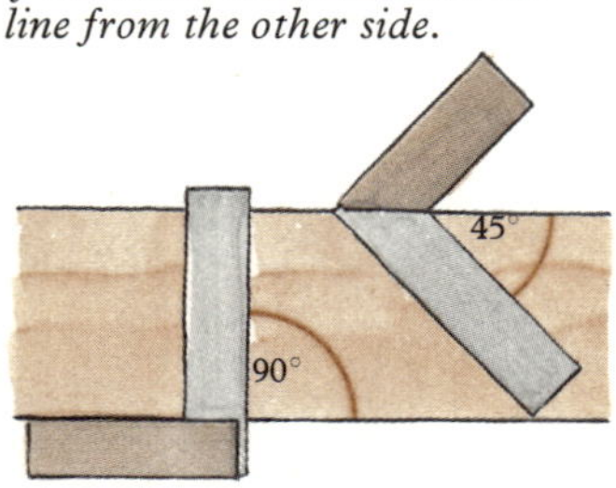

Checking angles
For 90° line hold stock against edge and mark along blade. For 45° line, align angled stock against edge.

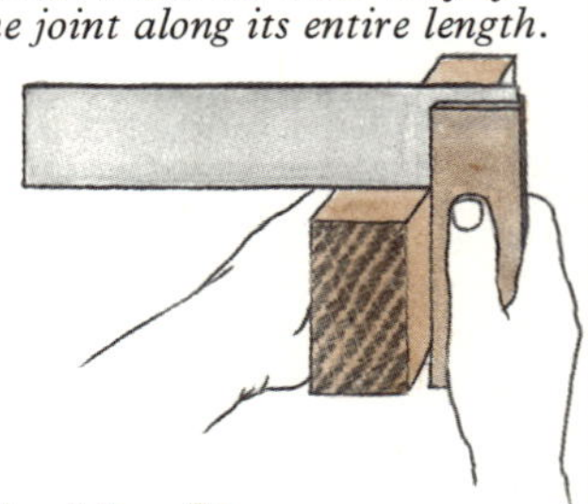

Checking for square
Press stock against face side to see if inside edge of blade completely touches face being planed at right angles to it.

Carpenter's Steel Square

OTHER NAMES: Flat square, rafter square, framing square, roofing square
SIZE: *Blade length:* 300 to 600mm; *Tongue length:* 200 to 400mm
MATERIAL: Steel
USE: To mark out the work for squaring and to check the angles used in the construction of roof framing

A standard carpenter's steel square is marked out in inches or millimetres and is used to set out a job on building boards or to check the squareness of a large frame. Being made from one piece of steel, it is extremely accurate. Standard metric and imperial numerical markings run outward from the right angle. Many squares are also marked with various tables which enable the carpenter to set out staircases or rafters and to calculate areas or, given the other dimensions, the hypotenuse of a triangle.

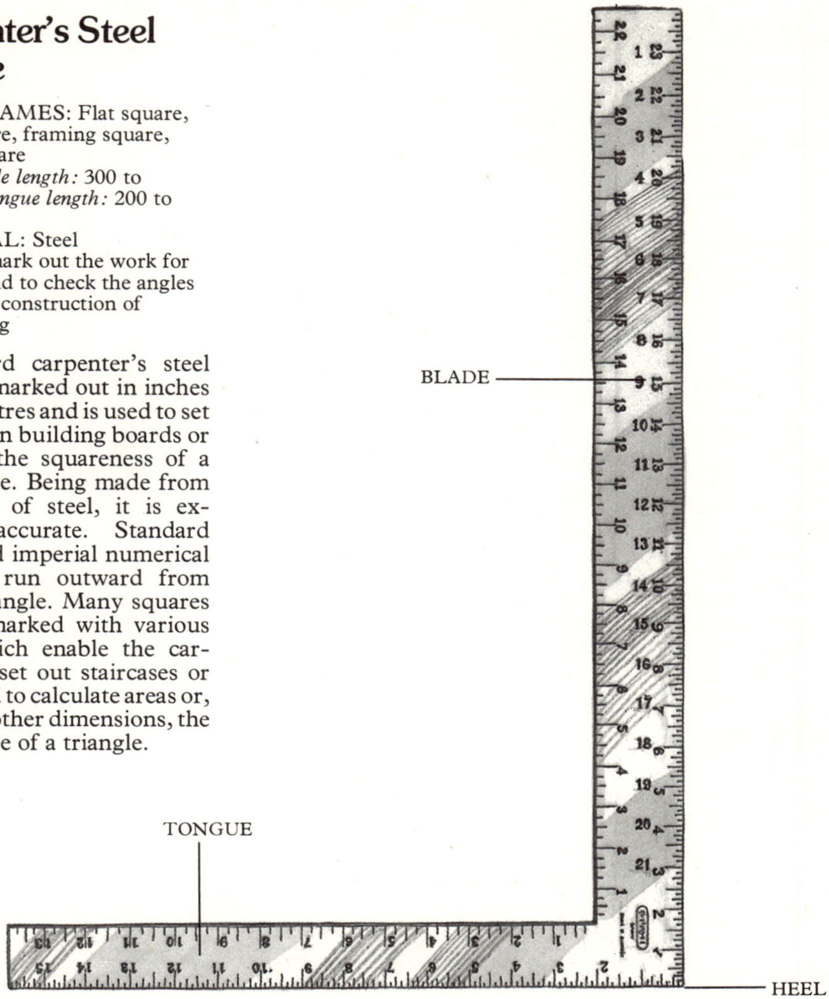

Mitre Square

SIZE: Blade length: 200 to 300mm
MATERIAL: *Blade:* steel; *Stock:* hardwood
USE: To mark out both halves of a mitre joint at 45°

A mitre square is constructed like a try square, but the blade projects from both sides of the stock to form internal angles of 45° and 135°. A line can be marked to 45° to a true edge by pressing the stock against the edge and aligning the blade with the mark. In this way two halves of a mitre joint can be marked out. The mitre square can also be used to check the accuracy of the angle when the joint has been cut.

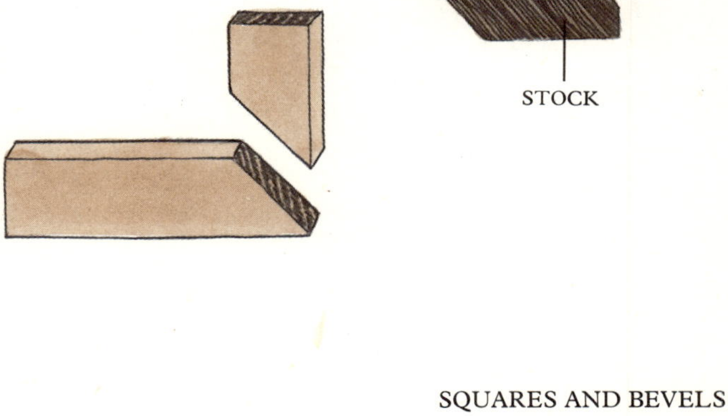

Sliding Bevel

OTHER NAME: "T" bevel
SIZE: Blade length: 190 to 330mm
MATERIAL: *Blade:* steel; *Stock:* hardwood, plastic
USE: To mark out or check angles on the work

The sliding bevel has a parallel sided steel blade, which can be adjusted to form any angle with the stock. Extending approximately half the length of the blade is a slot which enables the blade to be projected or retracted to suit the circumstances. A locking lever secures the blade finger tight at any angle. Other patterns have a slot head screw, which must be tightened with a screwdriver.

Set the bevel to the required angle with the aid of a protractor. Alternatively, set up the required angle from a true edge of a board, or a bench top and align the bevel to that.

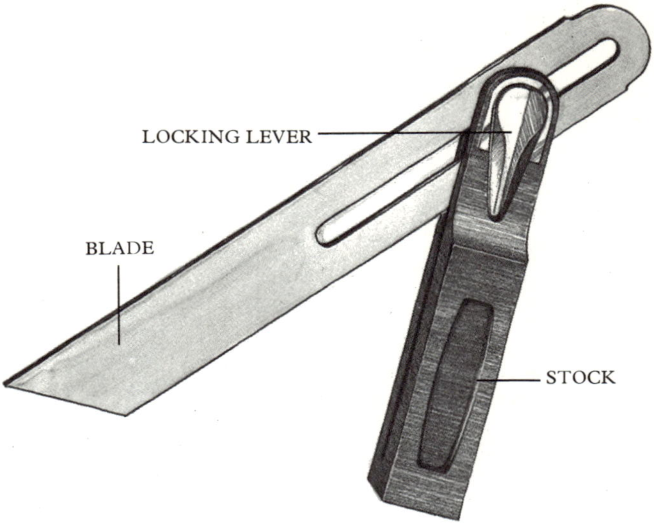

Setting to a protractor
Slacken the locking lever just enough to allow the blade to be moved. Hold the stock against the base of the protractor, set the blade to the required angle and tighten the screw.

Centre Finding Gauge

OTHER NAMES: Centre square, radial square
SIZE: For work up to 150mm in diameter
MATERIAL: Steel
USE: To mark the centre of round stock

The centre finding gauge is a simple tool which enables you to rapidly and accurately locate the centre of a round metal bar or turned wooden section. The tool has a 90° notch cut in one side, and a blade which bisects the notch with its straight edge. The centre finding gauge is rotated approximately one third of the circumference of the work and a second mark made, intersecting the first. For absolute accuracy the tool should be rotated once more and a third mark made. The centre of the work is indicated by the intersection of the lines.

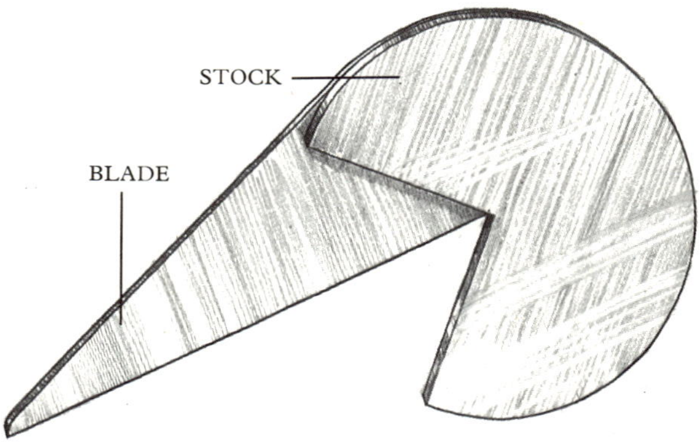

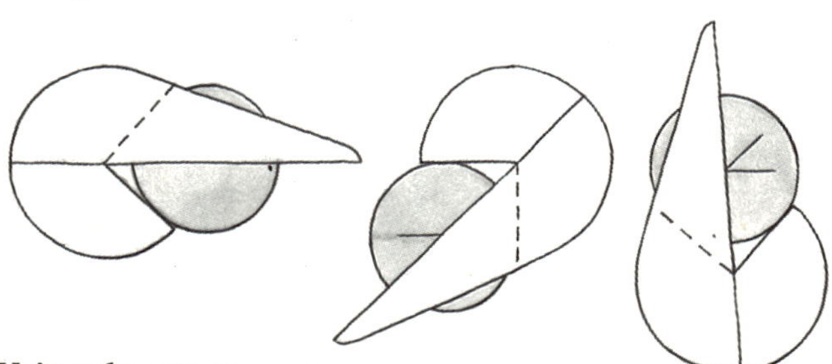

Using the gauge
Push the stock into the notch, and mark a line across the end against the edge of the blade. Repeat if necessary.

Combination Square

SIZE: *Blade length:* 300mm; *Head length:* 110mm
MATERIAL: *Blade:* steel; *Head:* steel, cast iron
USE: To work as a steel rule, try square, mitre square and level

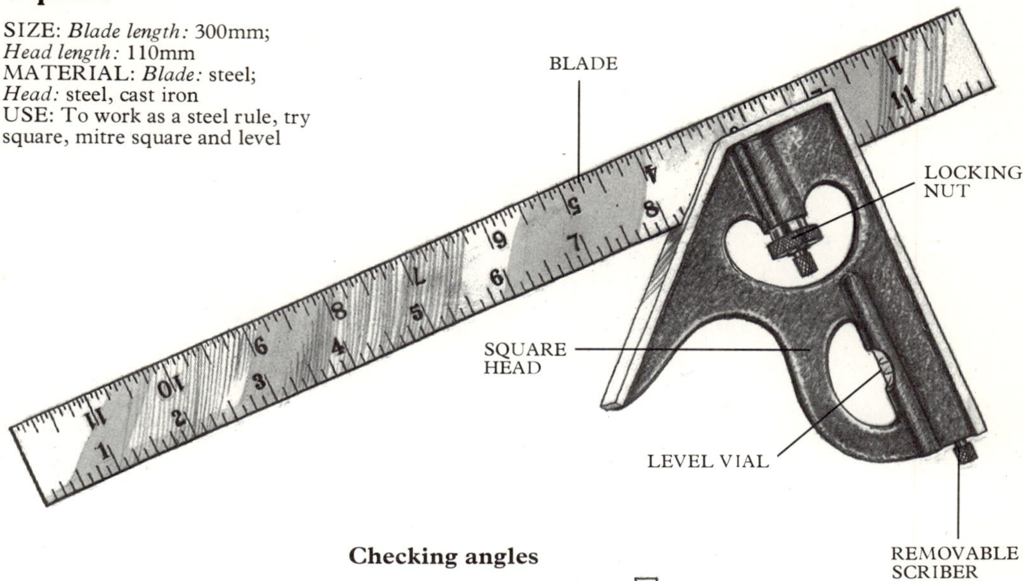

The combination square is a steel rule, securely clamped in a square head. A rounded groove runs along the centre of one side of the rule. When the rule slides into the head, the groove then engages a spring-loaded pin which is locked in place by tightening a knurled nut. The head can be adjusted to any position on the rule.

The tool can be used as a try square with a blade length of up to 250mm while the 45° face on the head transforms the tool into a mitre square. It can also be used as a depth gauge to measure the depth of a mortice for instance. (The measurement is read where the rule enters the head).

The square head is also fitted with a level vial and a removable scriber may be provided with the square head.

Checking angles

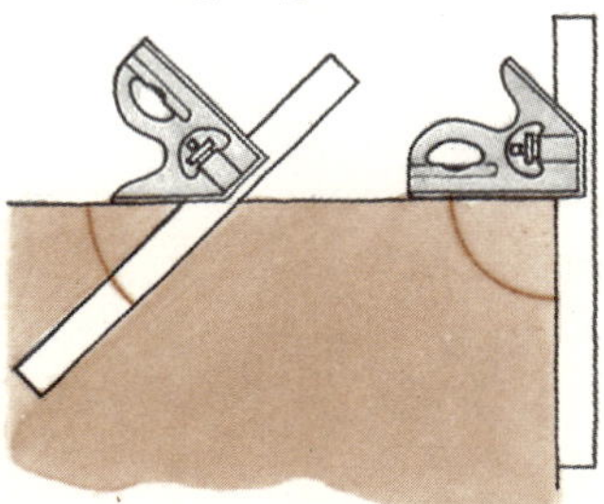

Rest the tool on its square face to check a 90° angle and on its angled face to check 45°.

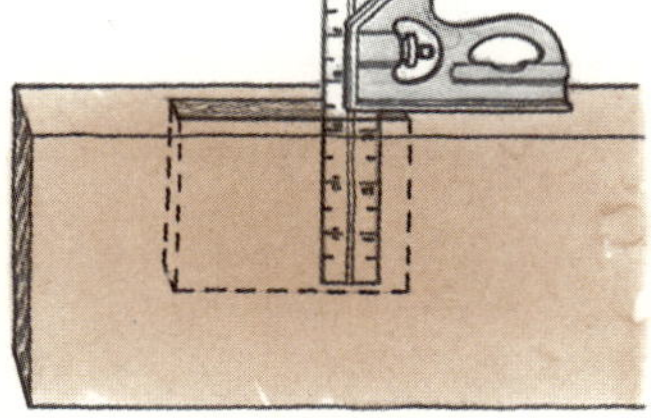

Depth of mortice
Slacken the locking nut, rest the square face flat on the surface of the rail and push the rule into the mortice. Tighten the locking nut, remove the rule and read the depth.

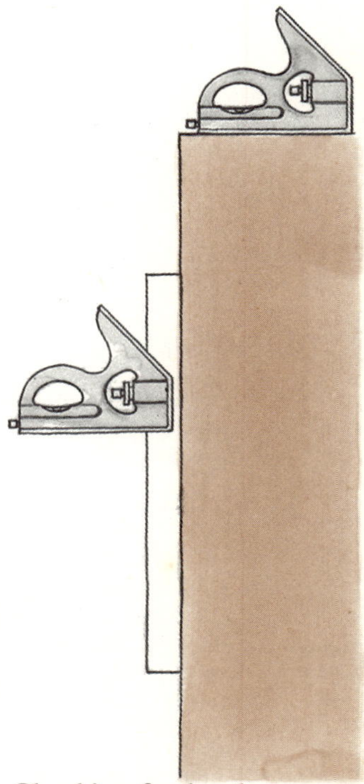

Checking for level
Check for horizontal by resting the square face on the surface and for vertical by holding the attached rule against the vertical member.

Combination Set

SIZE: Blade length: 300 to 600mm
MATERIAL: *Blade:* steel; *Heads:* steel, cast iron
USE: To work as a try square, mitre square, protractor, centre square, level and rule

Although the combination square is commonly sold with a square head only, combination sets are available which clamp to the steel rule in the same way to form a centre square or protractor.

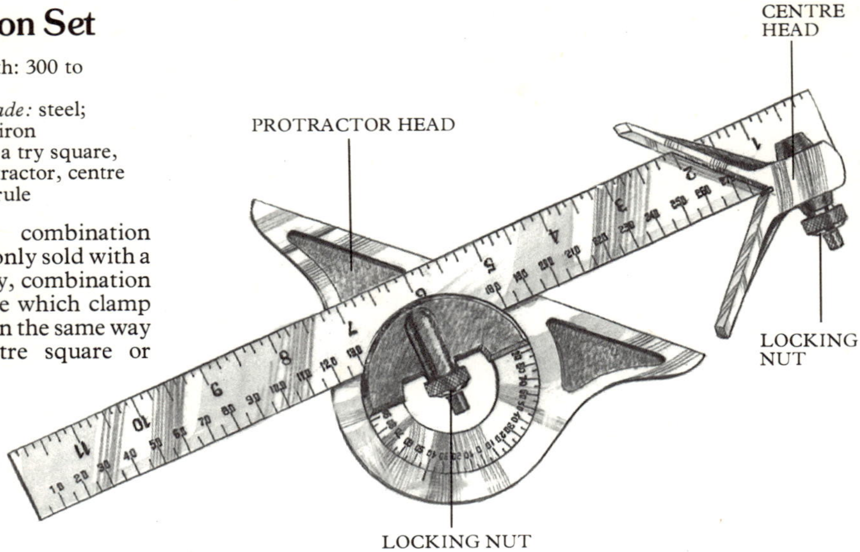

The tool can also be placed over a bevelled edge to measure the exact angle.

The centre head is slipped onto the rule and locked in any position. It can be used to find the centre of a disc of up to 460mm in diameter.

The protractor head can be used to mark off or measure any angle through 180°.

When the protractor head is fitted with a level vial it can measure the level of any vertical or horizontal surface.

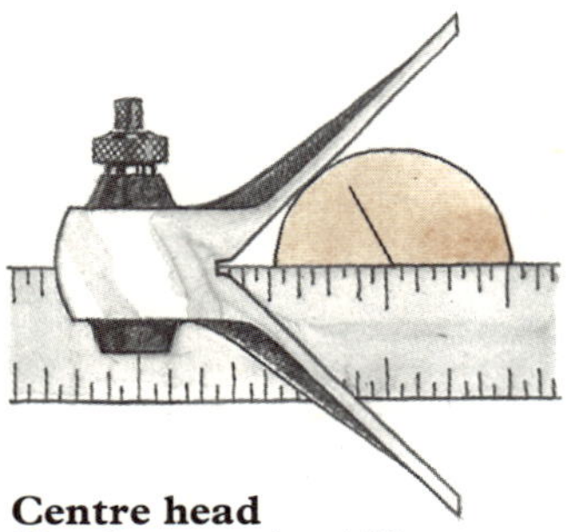

Centre head
Use the centre head like a centre square, wedging the round stock between the jaws and marking off with the rule.

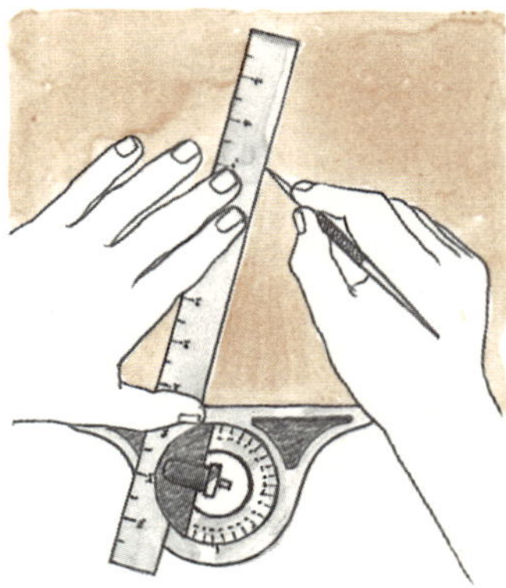

Protractor
Press the flat face of the protractor head against a true edge and mark off the angle.

Engineer's Try Square

SIZE: *Blade length:* 75 to 1000mm; *Stock length:* 65 to 535mm
MATERIAL: Steel
USE: To mark out or check metal for square

Engineer's try squares are made entirely from metal to guarantee constant accuracy. Although larger squares with long blades are used in engineering workshops, the smaller tools with blades up to 150mm in length are more common in home workshops.

A notch is cut in the stock in line with the inside edge of the blade for accurate measurement even when there is a burr on the edge of the work.

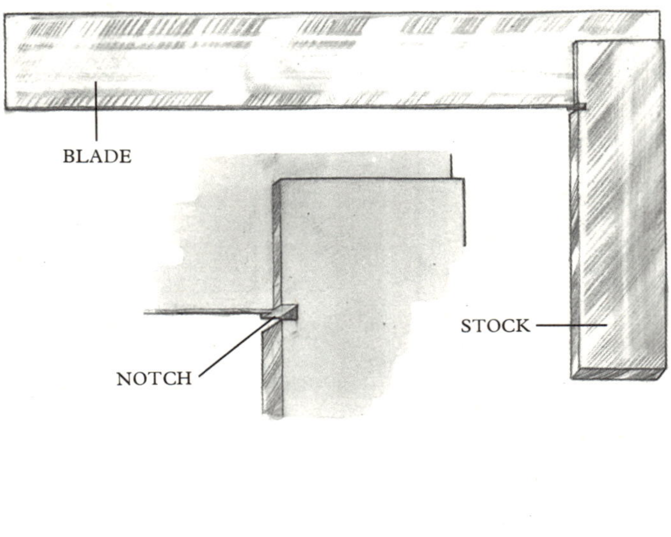

Engineer's Sliding Bevel

SIZE: *Blade length:* 75mm; *Stock length:* 75mm
MATERIAL: Steel
USE: To mark out or check angles on metal

The engineer's bevel is a small, accurately machined tool, which is used to mark out or measure various angles on metal work. Once the blade has been adjusted to the required angle it is locked in place by a knurled nut.

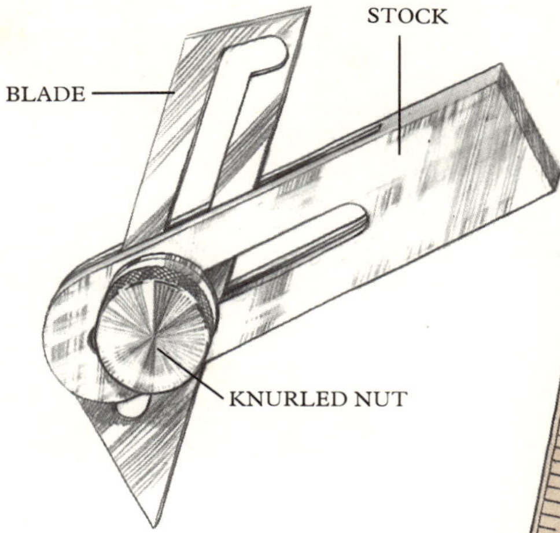

Dovetail Template

OTHER NAME: Dovetail marker
SIZE: As required
MATERIAL: Hardwood, brass
USE: To mark out dovetail joints

Dovetail templates, which are used to set out dovetail joints, are often homemade tools. The shoulder locates over the end of the wood and the sides of the tail are marked against the edge of the template.

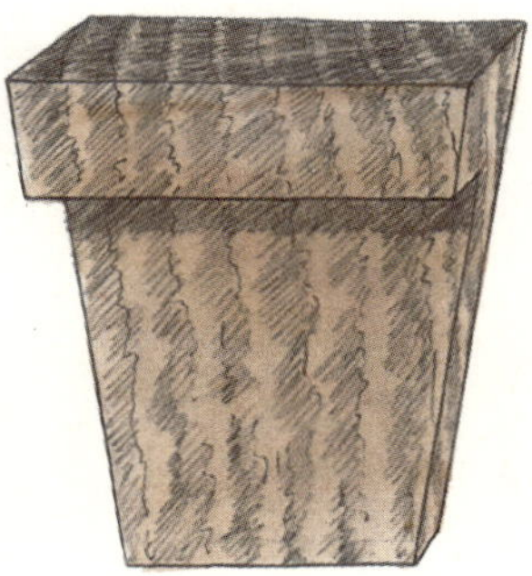

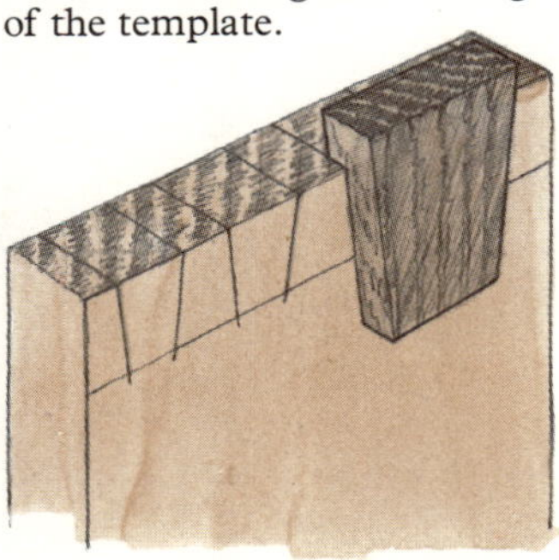

Use the template when you have a series of identical joints to cut to save repeated setting out.

Glazier's "T" Square

SIZE: 600 to 1800mm
MATERIAL: Boxwood
USE: To guide a glass cutter square across a sheet of glass

The glazier's "T" square is in effect a wooden rule morticed at 90° into a stock. The stock is pressed against the edge of a sheet of glass and a glass cutter is used to score a line against the rule.

Plumb and Level

Tools used to test for vertical and horizontal have always worked on the same principle. The essential features were a heavy bob and line. Egyptian levels used the bob and line suspended from the apex of an A-shaped wooden frame. This type was in general use up to the Middle Ages. A later form, common until the mid nineteenth century, was a short plumb rule and bob set at right angles to a straight edge.
Levels had been known and used in surveying and navigating instruments before 1800, but they were adopted by carpenters and others at about that time. They are now also used in plumb rules. The main advantage of an air bubble in a curved glass tube is that it is virtually dead still, which a plumb bob never is.

Spirit Level

OTHER NAMES: Level, plumb rule
SIZE: 75 to 2000mm
MATERIAL: Aluminium, hardwood, plastic
USE: To determine the accurate level of a surface

The important part of any level is the vial. This is a curved or barreled glass or plastic tube containing a clear liquid which may be alcohol, oil or chloroform. There is a bubble of air in the liquid which floats to the highest point of the curve, where two lines are marked on the vial. When the level is "true" the bubble will come to rest between the two marked lines. The vial is protected by a transparent cover and can be replaced if necessary.

Vials are fitted in levels of various kinds. The simplest is a small pocket level, which contains one vial. A "line" level is similar in size, but is fitted with a hook at either end to locate it on a taut cord. This insures that the levelling line is truly horizontal. Standard levels are parallel top and bottom, ranging in length from approximately 225mm up to 2000mm. The shorter 225mm levels are often tapered at both ends. These are known as "torpedo", "canoe" or "boat-shaped" levels. The longer the level, the more accurate the reading. Longer levels contain several vials for measuring horizontally and vertically. Some are set at 45° for angled surfaces.

Before buying check that the level is true by setting it up on a surface already established as truly horizontal.

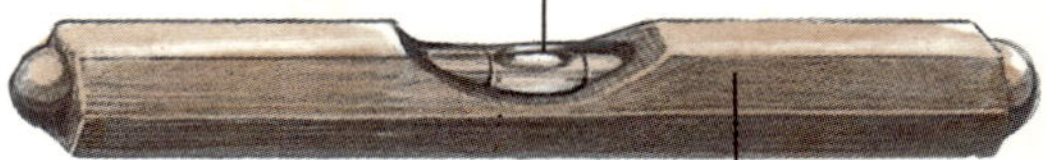

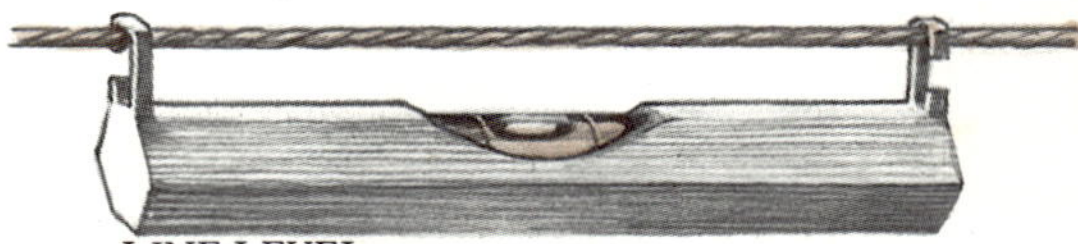

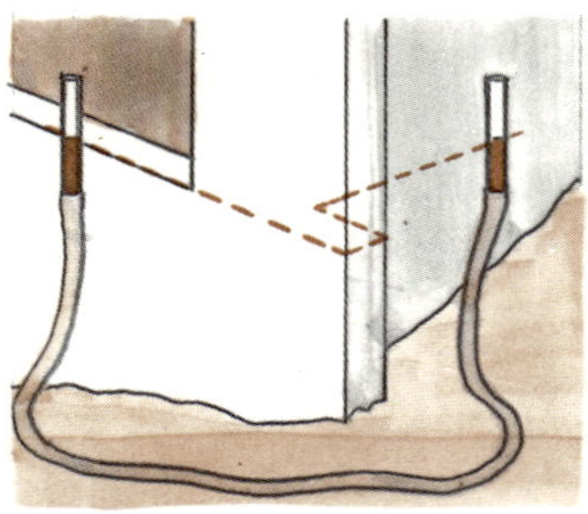

Water level
Make a water level to determine the evenness of two points that are separated by distance or obstruction. Fit short lengths of transparent plastic tube at each end of a hose pipe. Fill the pipe with water until it appears in the tubes. The water will automatically level itself.

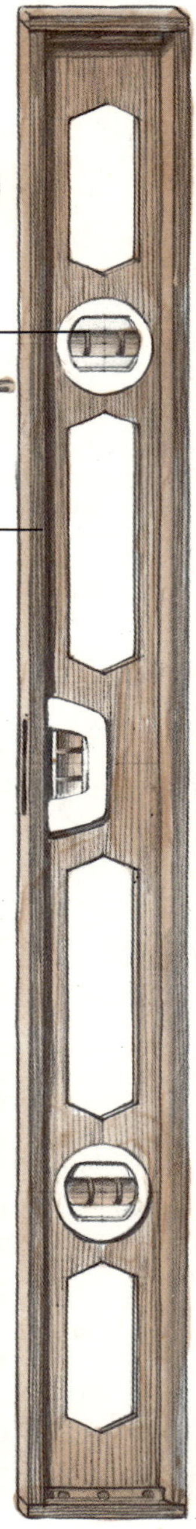

Chalk Line

OTHER NAME: Chalk box
SIZE: 5.5 to 30m
MATERIAL: Cotton, plastic
USE: To snap a marked line

A chalk line is used to mark a straight line on a surface. This may be a plumbed line on the wall for hanging wallpaper vertically, or perhaps a centre line on a ceiling for the application of tiles.

In the best models, the line is contained in a case with coloured chalk powder (white, red or blue). As the line is withdrawn from the casing, a felt gasket distributes an even chalk coating. The line has a hook and ring at one end for attaching to a nail or catching between floor boards.

Marking an accurate line

Attach the hook to one end of the surface and extend the chalk line to the other. Pull it taut and flat and "snap" the centre of the line sharply against the surface to transfer the chalk to the surface.

Plumb Bob

OTHER NAME: Plumb line
SIZE: Weight: 43 to 1800g
MATERIAL: *Bob:* brass, plastic, lead, steel; *Line:* nylon, silk
USE: To determine a vertical line

The plumb bob is used to make sure that a structure such as a door frame is truly vertical, or that an object is directly under a point on a ceiling. This helps in the siting of a light fixture.

The plumb bob is a pointed weight attached to a length of line which is contained in the bob itself and fastens in a slot in the cap. If the hardened point on the bob end becomes bent it will no longer give a true reading, so must be replaced.

Hold the end of the line at the required point and allow it to settle out of its natural swing. Make sure that it is hanging free, and mark the point below the plumb bob or the edge of the line.

Bricklayer's Line and Pins

OTHER NAME: Mason's line and pins
SIZE: Length: 9 to 18m
MATERIAL: *Pins:* steel; *Line:* cotton, plastic, nylon, hemp
USE: To make sure that a course of bricks is straight and true

The line is stretched along a wall and secured at either end by flat bladed steel pins.

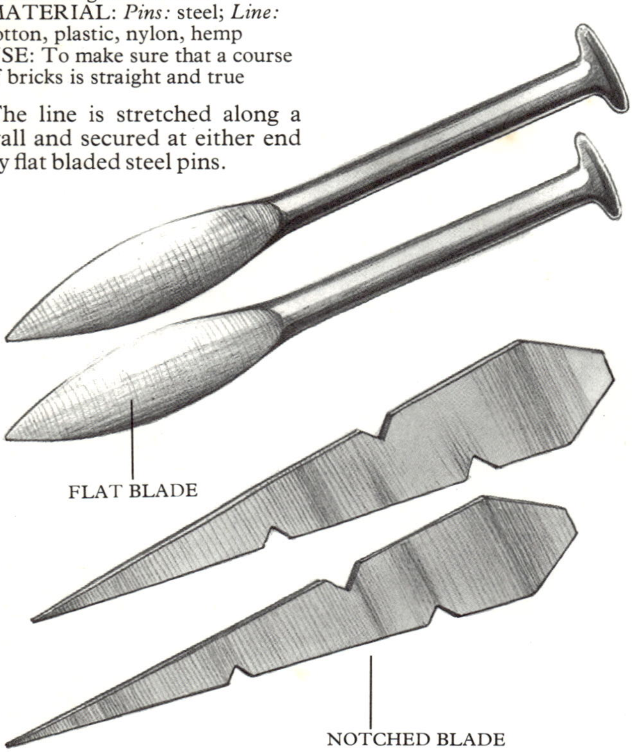

As you lay the bricks take care that the line is not being pushed out of true.

Small flat metal pins known as trigs are pushed into the mortar joints to support the middle of a long line and prevent it sagging out of true.

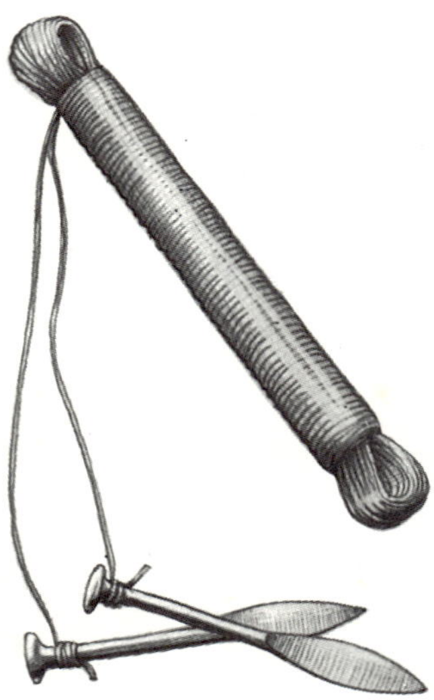

Fix one pin around the corner of a wall, locating the flat section in the nearest vertical joint. Stretch the line and fix it to the other pin.

Line Block

SIZE: Approximately 100mm
MATERIAL: *Block:* wood, plastic; *Line:* cotton, plastic, hemp, nylon
USE: To make sure that a course of bricks is straight and true

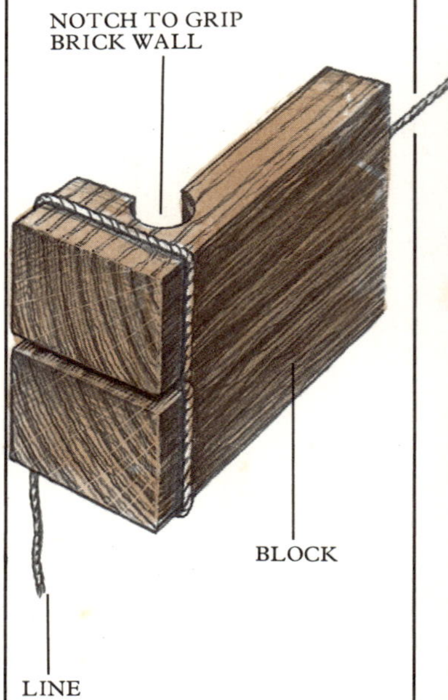

This is the same device as the line and pins but uses plastic or wooden L-shaped blocks in place of the pins. The line passes through a slot in the block and is tied off at each end. As the line is pulled tight the blocks hold their position by friction on the bricks.

Fixing the block
Attach the block to one corner of the wall. Pull the line taut and attach the other block at the next corner.

Dividers and Calipers

Compasses or dividers and calipers are frequently shown among the tools of Roman carpenters, masons, wheelwrights and shipwrights. They are all "firm joint" compasses; in some cases one leg appears to have been slightly longer than the other, so they may have been used as gauges, a tool which the Romans do not seem to have known.

The earliest example of a pair of wing dividers occurs on Jost Ammann's picture of the *Compass-maker's Shop* of 1568. The modern cooper's pattern of spring compasses, made of ash bent in a "U" shape, held together and regulated by a crossbar with a screw of opposite hand at each end, is illustrated on the shop sign of John Jennion of London, dating to about 1730, but may have been in use both in England and France well before this. The earliest beam compass, said to have been six to twelve feet long, with a fixed point at one end and a single moving trammel head, is shown in Roubo's book.

Outside Calipers

OTHER NAMES: Bow calipers, egg calipers
SIZE: *Spring joint calipers:* Up to 300mm; *Firm joint calipers* to 900mm
MATERIAL: Steel
USE: To transfer measurements from a rule to the work or to match two elements to fit

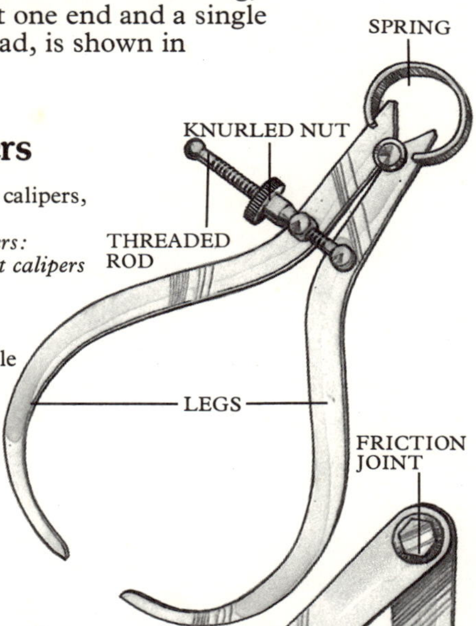

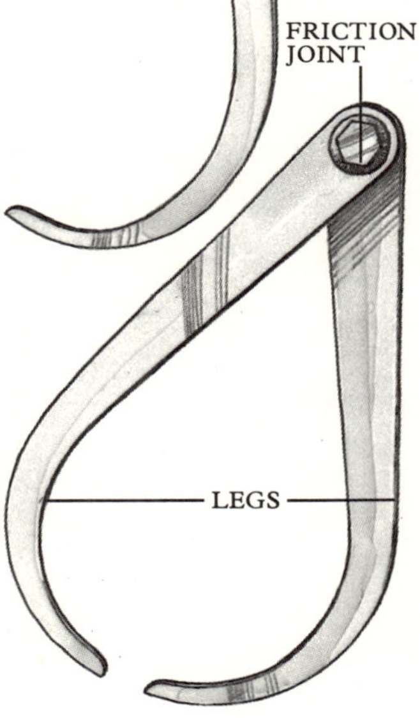

Bowlegged outside calipers which clear the work are used to take outside measurements. Two kinds of calipers are available: firm jointed calipers, which are free to move but are held firmly in any position by friction between the two legs, or spring-jointed calipers which are controlled by a knurled nut on a threaded rod. Within limits, it is possible to take inside measurements with firm joint calipers.

Inside Calipers

OTHER NAME: Straight calipers
SIZE: As outside calipers
MATERIAL: Steel
USE: As outside calipers

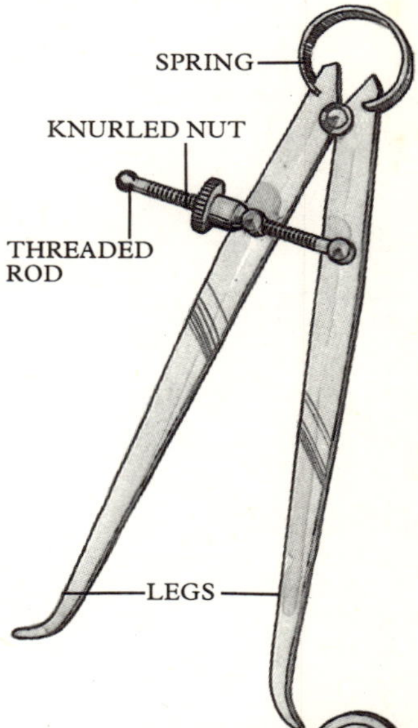

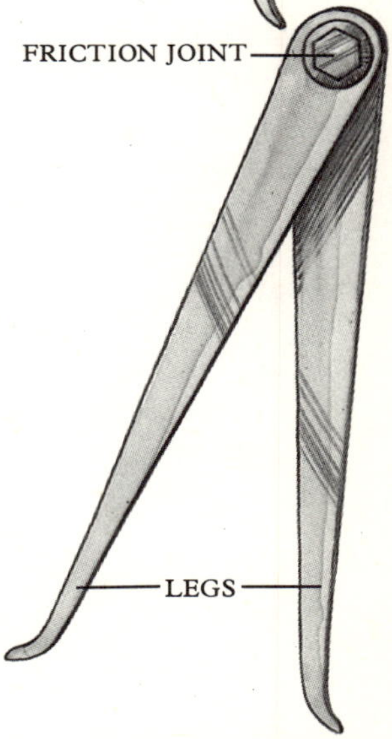

Inside calipers are available in the same size range as outside calipers. They have straight legs, turned out at the top and are used to take inside measurements. They are available with firm or spring joints. As with outside calipers, it is possible within limits to measure external dimensions with firm joint inside calipers.

Adjustment

Adjustment is different depending on the type of caliper. For firm joint calipers close or open the legs to approximate the required measurement.

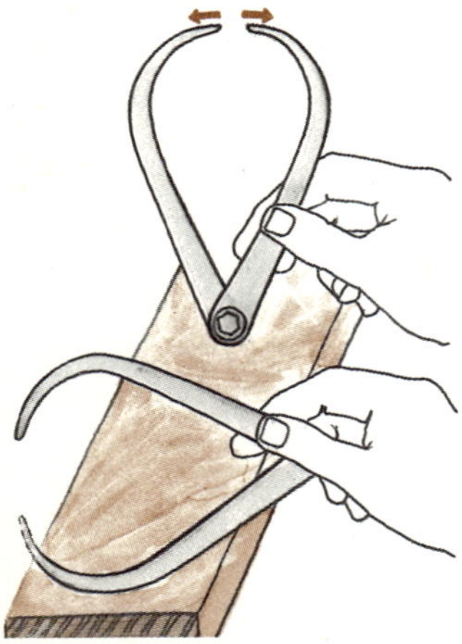

Make fine adjustments by either tapping one leg on a hard surface to close the gap or by tapping the jointed end of the tool to open the legs slightly.

Spring joint calipers are adjusted by the knurled nut. Close the legs against the spring to take the load off the nut, which can easily be adjusted to the approximate position required. Fine adjustment is made by a slight turn on the nut.

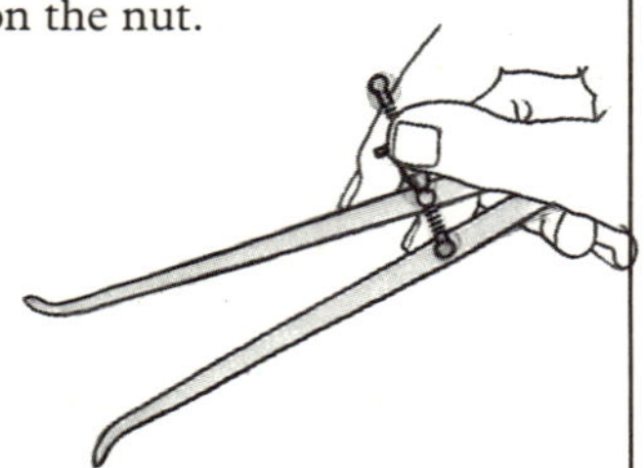

Practise fine adjustment of calipers with one hand; this will leave you a free hand to steady the work.

Care and maintenance

Unless they are misused, calipers require little attention other than an occasional oiling of the moving parts. Take care not to over-oil firm joint calipers. Avoid using them to measure moving parts of machinery, as this can wear down the points of the tool.

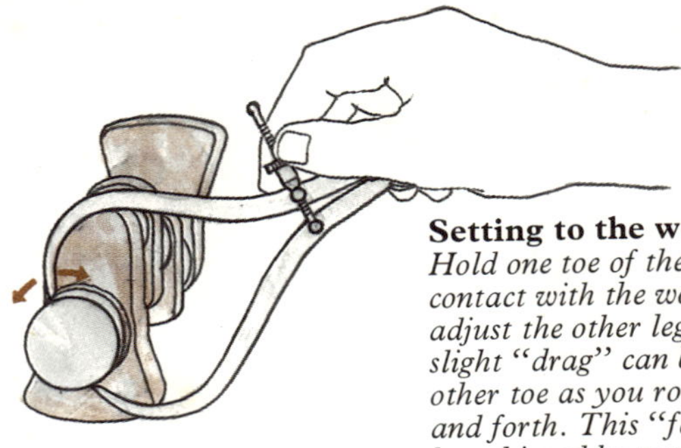

Setting to the work

Hold one toe of the caliper in contact with the work and adjust the other leg until a slight "drag" can be felt on the other toe as you rock it back and forth. This "feel" can only be achieved by practice.

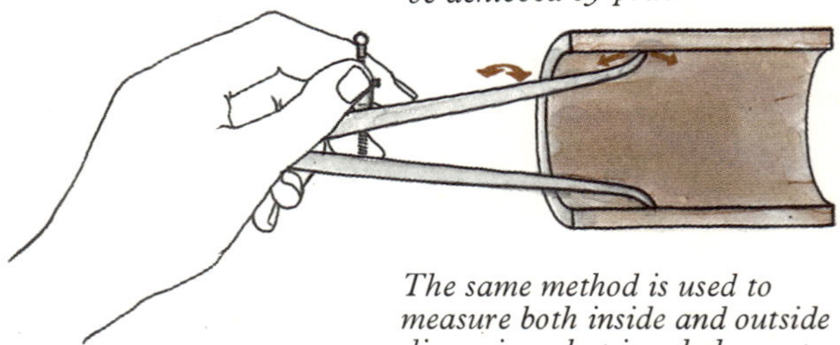

The same method is used to measure both inside and outside dimensions, but in a hole, centre the calipers by rocking them sideways as well as from front to back.

Setting calipers to a rule

For accuracy when setting any calipers to a rule, it is important to read off the measurement at eye level.

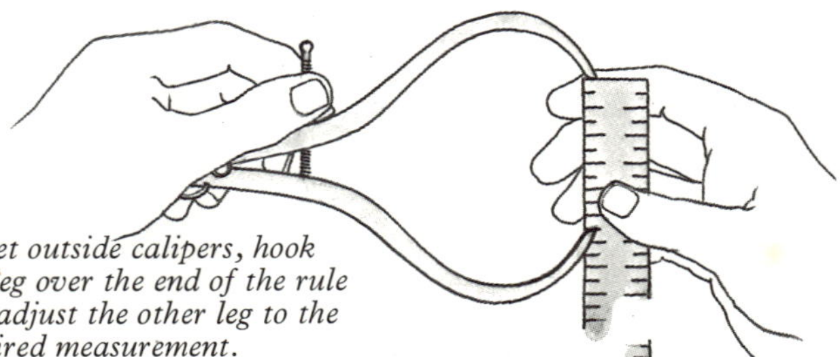

To set outside calipers, hook one leg over the end of the rule and adjust the other leg to the required measurement.

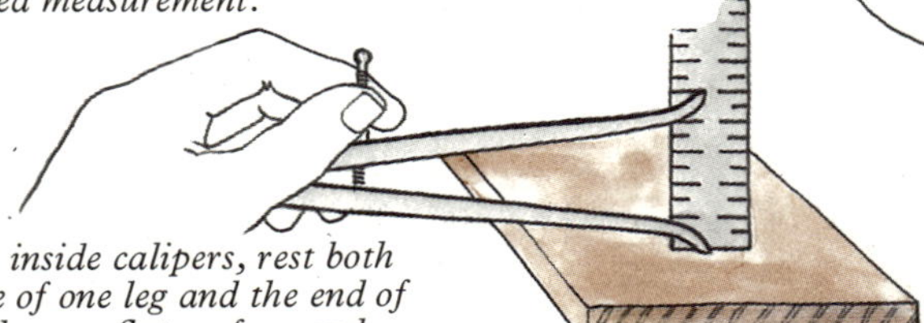

To set inside calipers, rest both the toe of one leg and the end of the rule on a flat surface and adjust the other leg as before.

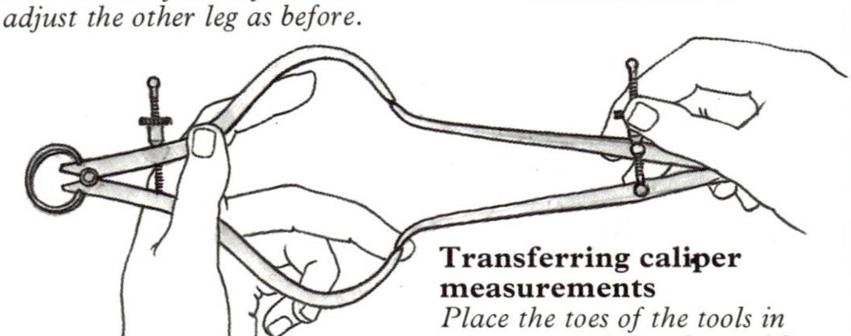

Transferring caliper measurements

Place the toes of the tools in contact, steadying them with a finger of one hand and adjust to match.

Transfer Calipers

Sometimes it is necessary either to open or close the legs of the calipers to remove them from the work, thus losing the measurement. In this case use transfer calipers which have a secondary leg locating on a lock nut situated on one of the primary legs. Lock the secondary leg in position and obtain the required setting. Release the lock nut and remove the tool.

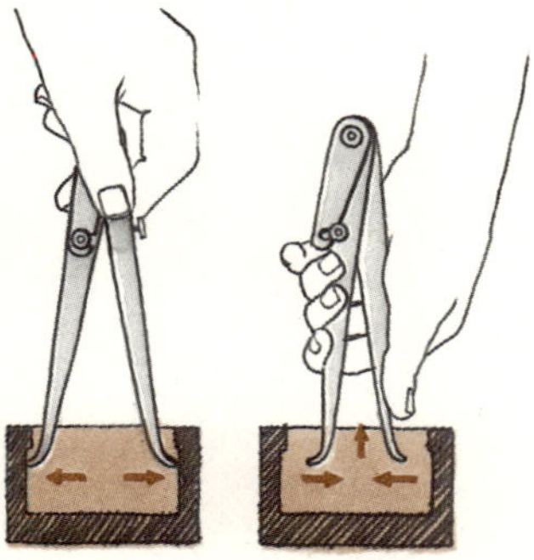

Replace it in contact with the work with the secondary leg, secure the lock nut and read off the measurement.

A spring joint inside caliper can be used for this job by closing the legs by hand, taking care not to disturb the adjusting screw nut when removing the tool from the work.

Odd Leg Calipers

OTHER NAMES: Jenny calipers; hermaphrodite calipers
SIZE: Up to 150mm
MATERIAL: Steel
USE: To scribe lines parallel to an edge

Odd leg calipers can be used to find the centre of round or square section metal stock.

They have two hinged legs. One has either a hardened steel, or a replaceable point, and the other has a toe which runs against the edge of the workpiece.

Be careful not to let the toe slip otherwise the line will wander. Some calipers have a toe which locates over the edge of the work. This is particularly useful when marking sheet metal.

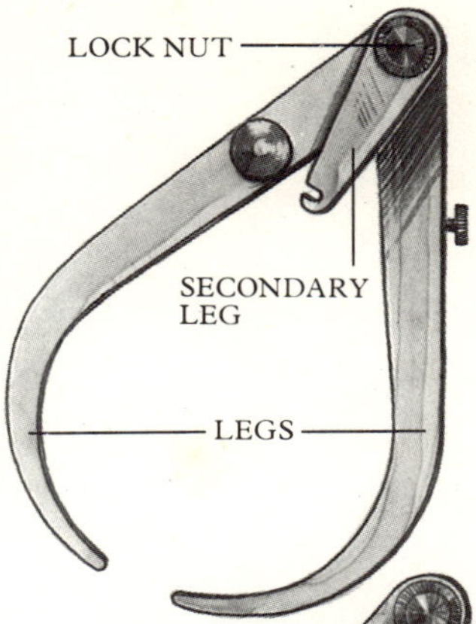

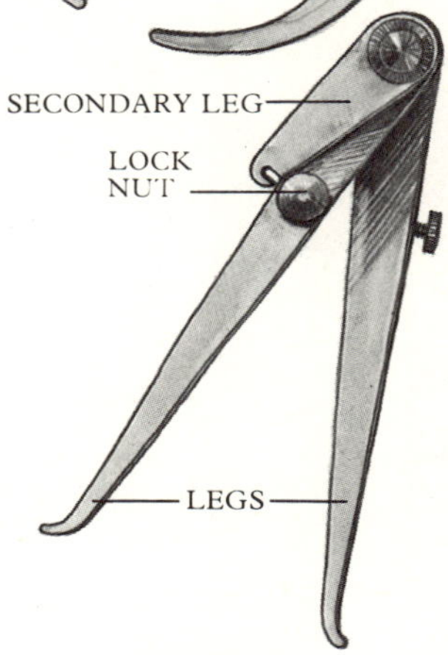

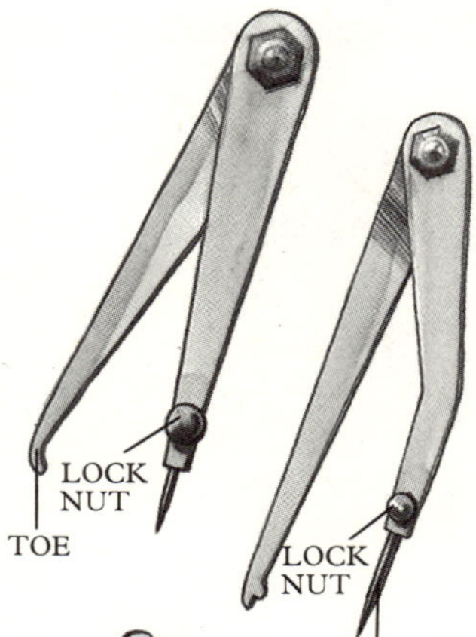

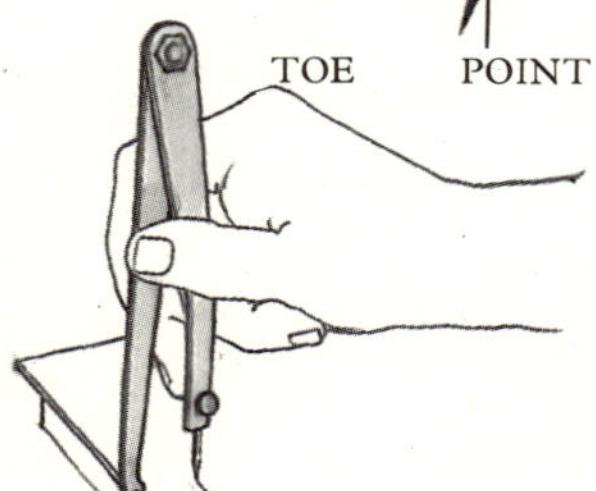

Odd leg calipers have a prehensile toe for positive location on the work edge.

Spring Dividers

OTHER NAMES: Spring compass, bow compass.
SIZE: Up to 300mm measured from centre of roller to the point of the leg
MATERIAL: Steel
USE: To scribe arcs and circles on metal, or to "step off" divisions on a line

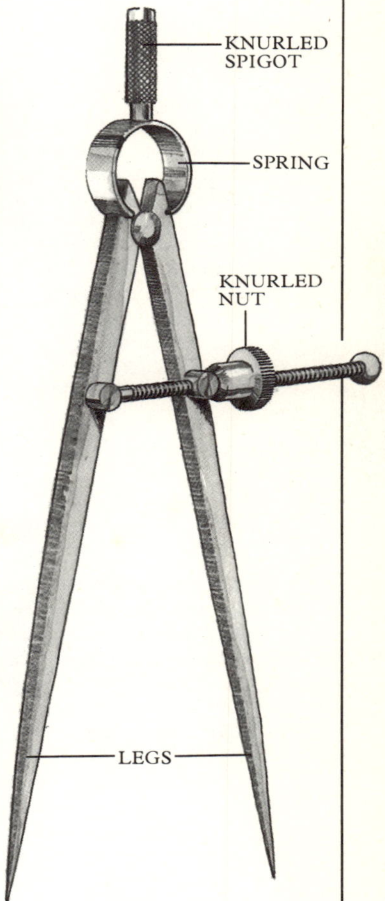

Spring dividers are similar to spring calipers, except they have a small knurled spigot to facilitate the scribing of circles. Adjustment is made by means of a knurled nut on a threaded rod. Dividers normally have two identical flat legs with hardened points. They are sometimes fitted with removable points which can be adjusted for equal length and be replaced when worn.

Wing Compass

OTHER NAME: Wing dividers
SIZE: Up to 450mm
MATERIAL: Steel
USE: To scribe arcs and circles on metal or to "step off" divisions on a line

Wing compasses have solid, square section legs for approximately half their length. Hinged at the joint they are adjusted by means of a curved wing attached to one leg and passing through a slot in the other. The legs are locked in position by means of a knurled screw bearing on this wing. On some patterns, fine adjustment is provided by means of a knurled nut which operates on a screw thread attached to the end of the wing. The leg is moved by the operation of a flat spring riveted to it.

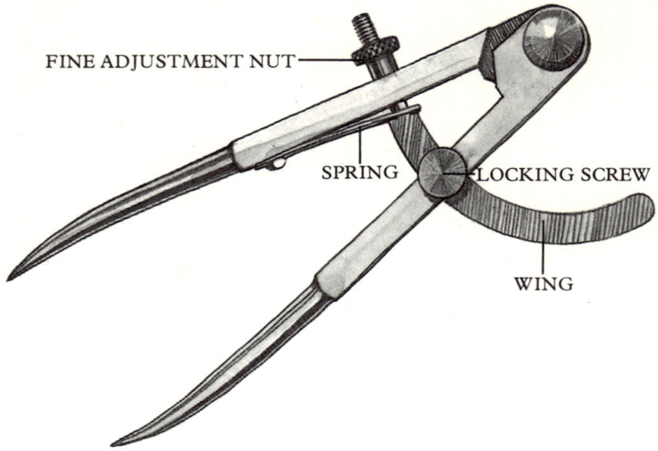

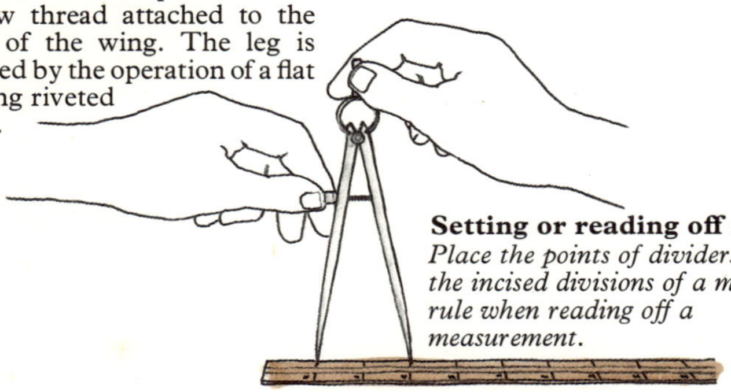

Setting or reading off a rule
Place the points of dividers in the incised divisions of a metal rule when reading off a measurement.

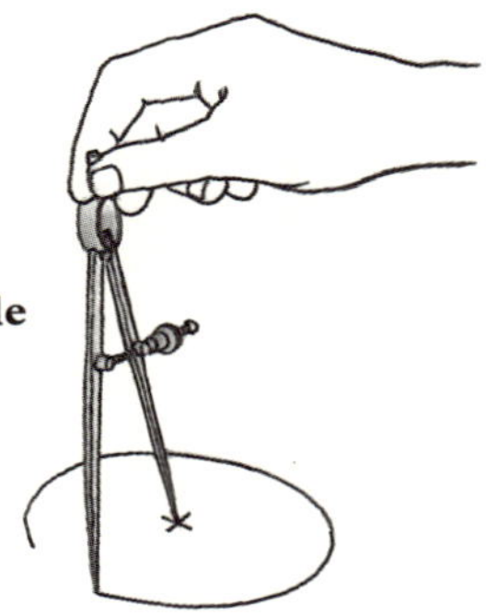

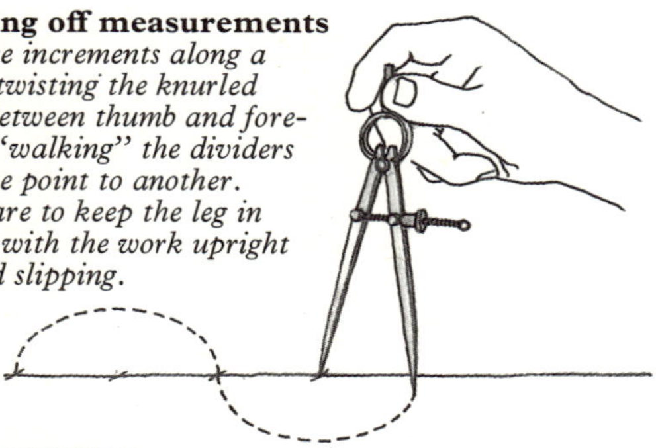

Stepping off measurements
Measure increments along a line by twisting the knurled spigot between thumb and forefinger, "walking" the dividers from one point to another. Take care to keep the leg in contact with the work upright to avoid slipping.

Scribing arcs and circles
To scribe metal, mark the centre point with a punch to hold the point. If the finish is important, first patch the centre with masking tape. Lean the tool in the direction of movement and scribe the circle or arc by revolving the spigot between thumb and forefinger.

Beam Compass

OTHER NAME: Trammel
SIZE: 120 to 180cm measuring capacity
MATERIAL: *Heads:* steel
Beam: aluminium or wood
USE: To scribe large arcs and circles

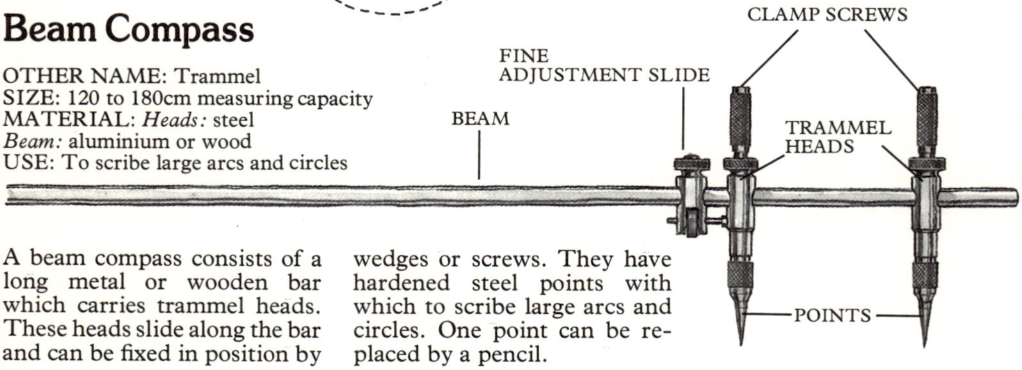

A beam compass consists of a long metal or wooden bar which carries trammel heads. These heads slide along the bar and can be fixed in position by wedges or screws. They have hardened steel points with which to scribe large arcs and circles. One point can be replaced by a pencil.

Slide Caliper

OTHER NAME: Caliper rule
SIZE: To measure up to 81mm
MATERIAL: Steel
USE: To measure internal and external dimensions

One jaw of the slide caliper is fixed to the main part of the tool. The other jaw is part of a slide, which moves in or out until both jaws come into contact with the work. The slide is fixed with a knurled clamp nut and has imperial or metric graduations.

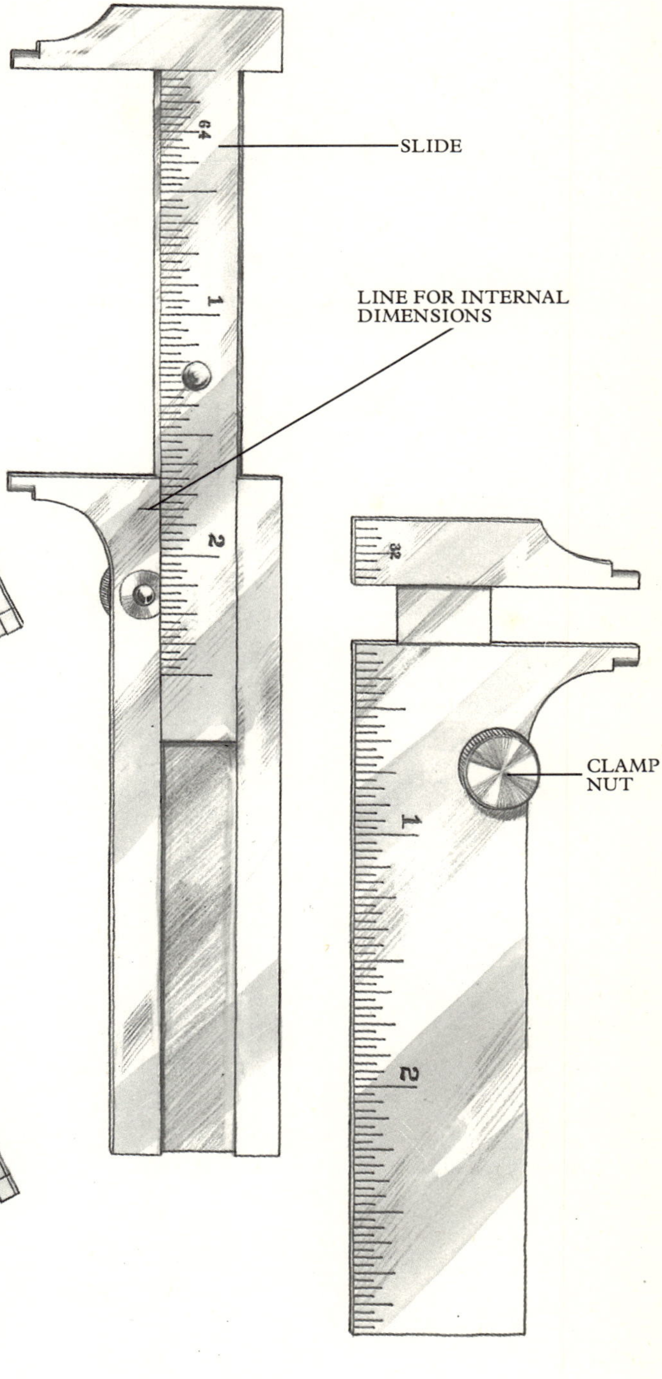

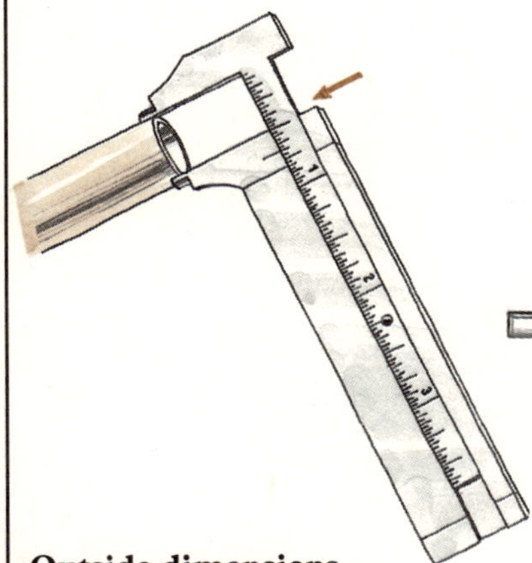

Outside dimensions
Locate the inside edges of both jaws on the work and read off the scale against the edge of the fixed jaw.

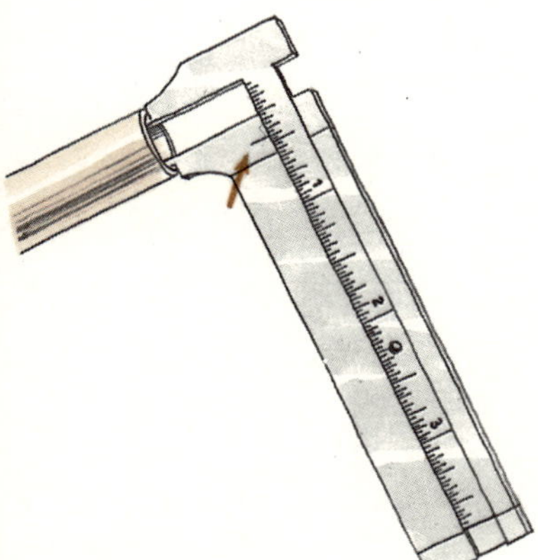

Inside dimensions
Locate the tips of the jaws on both sides of the work and read off against the special line marked on the body of the tool against the scale.

Vernier Caliper

SIZE: Measuring capacity: 6 to 72in.; 150 to 1,800mm
MATERIAL: Steel
USE: To obtain very fine measurements

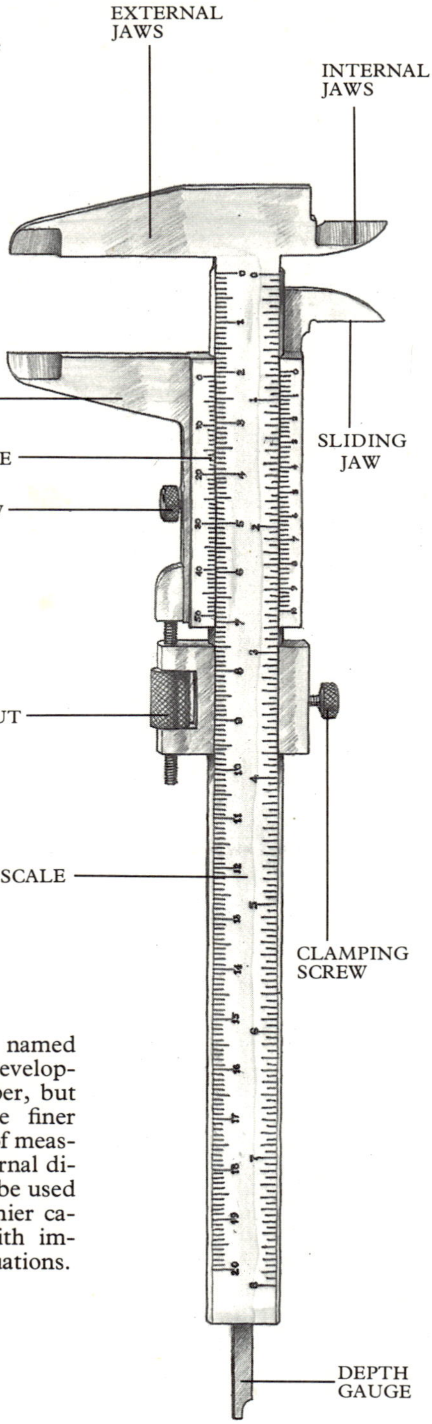

The Vernier caliper, named after its inventor, is a development of the slide caliper, but is graduated to make finer readings. It is capable of measuring internal and external dimensions and can also be used as a depth gauge. Vernier calipers are available with imperial and metric graduations.

Reading a Vernier caliper
Imperial

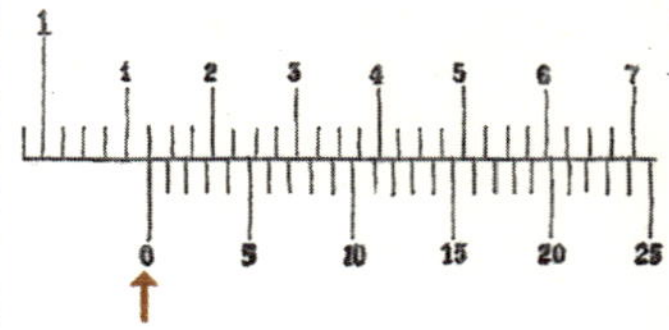

1.00
0.1
0.025
1.125in.

The main scale is graduated in inches which are subdivided into 0.1in., which in turn are subdivided into 0.025in. The Vernier scale runs beneath it. Each Vernier graduation represents 0.001in. Read off the measurement in the main scale indicated by the zero mark on the Vernier scale.

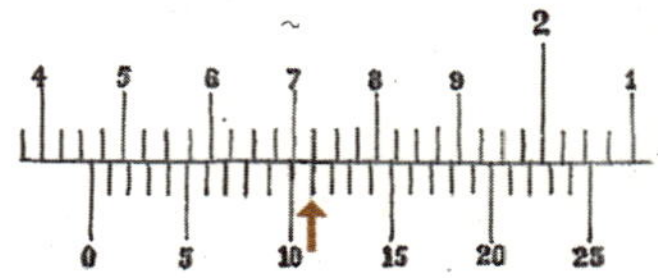

1.00
0.4
0.050
0.011
1.461in.

When the zero mark does not coincide with a line on the main scale, note which line on the Vernier scale does. Add whatever line is indicated on the Vernier scale to the total for an accurate reading.

Metric

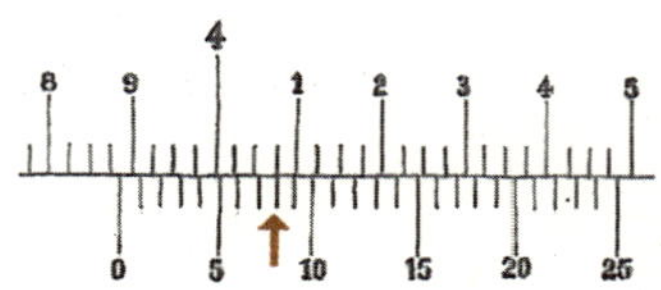

38.00
0.75
0.08
38.83mm

The metric main scale is graduated in 1mm and subdivided into 0.25mm. Each metric Vernier section represents 0.01mm. Read off as for imperial. When the Vernier zero line does not coincide with a main scale line, find a line that does and add the Vernier measure to the total.

Micrometer Caliper

SIZE: Range: 0 to ½ to 6 to 12in.; 0 to 13 to 150 to 300mm; specials up to 24in., or 600mm
MATERIAL: Steel
USE: To obtain very fine measurements

Micrometers are designed to produce the extremely fine measurements required in engineering, so that parts of a machine will meet with the minimum tolerance.

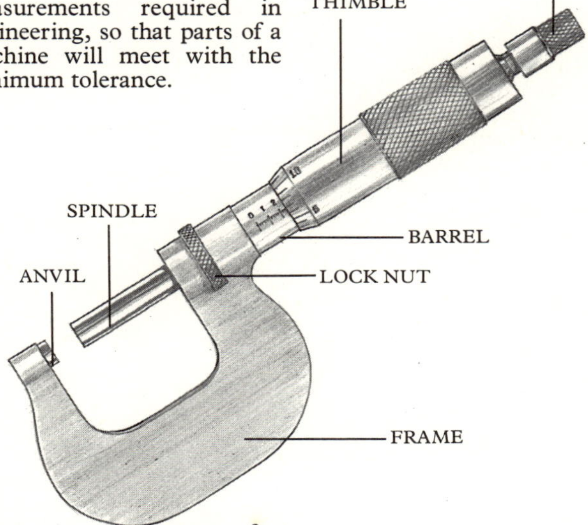

There are micrometers for measuring depth, across screw threads, inside dimensions and, most commonly, outside dimensions. The size range varies, but the most popular micrometer measures outside dimensions of 0 to 1in. (25mm).

The micrometer has a U-shaped frame with an anvil on one side and an adjustable spindle extending from the other. The knurled thimble adjusts the spindle to the required setting, which is then fixed by the lock nut. A ratchet stop is sometimes fitted to the end of the spindle. If the ratchet is used to adjust the spindle it will click or slip when the anvil and spindle contact with the work.

The latest development in micrometers is expensive, but extremely easy to use. When the spindle and anvil come in contact with the workpiece, the measurement can be read directly from a digital display. It is very accurate and does not involve the computations needed by a standard micrometer.

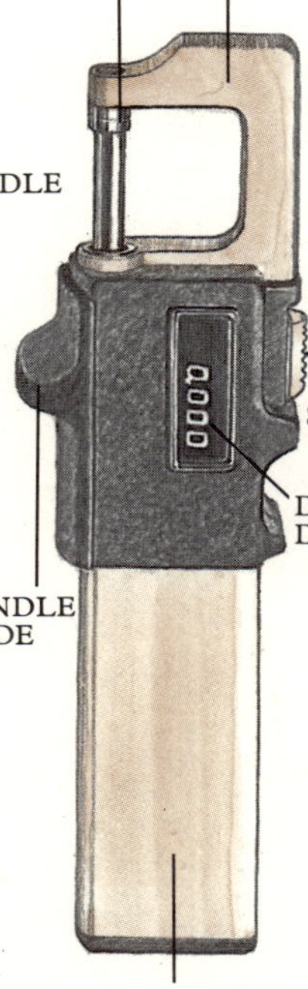

Reading a micrometer
Micrometers are marked in imperial or metric graduations.

Imperial

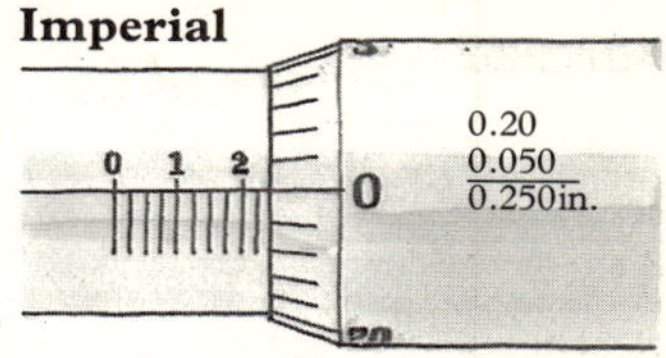

The sleeve scale on an imperial micrometer has major divisions representing 0.1in., subdivided into four equal parts, each representing 0.025in. When the anvil and spindle are in contact with the work, read off the measurement on the sleeve against the edge of the thimble.

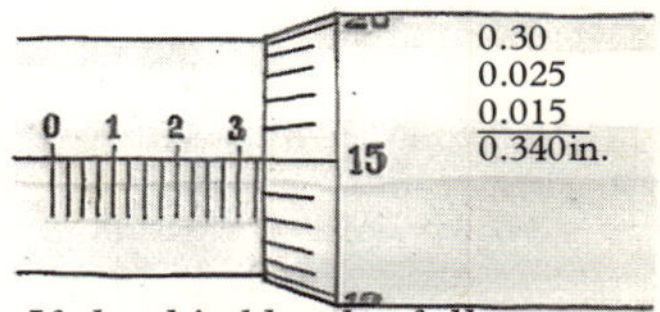

If the thimble edge falls between graduations on the sleeve scale, use the thimble scale. This is graduated in 0.001in. and is numbered every 0.005in. Read off these measurements against the centre line of the sleeve scale and add them to the sleeve scale reading.

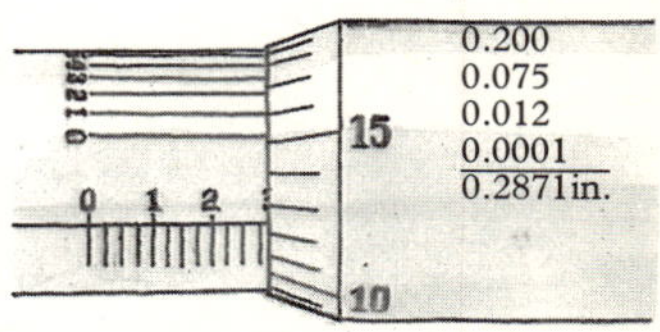

Some micrometers have a Vernier scale marked along the sleeve. This is graduated in 0.0001in. If the centre line on the sleeve falls between two graduations on the thimble scale, read off the Vernier scale to see which graduation coincides with the line on the thimble scale and add the Vernier reading to the total.

Metric
The sleeve scale on the metric micrometer is graduated in 1mm above the line and subdivided into 0.5mm below the line. The thimble scale is graduated in 0.01mm. Read off and calculate the total measurement as for imperial.

Handling the micrometer

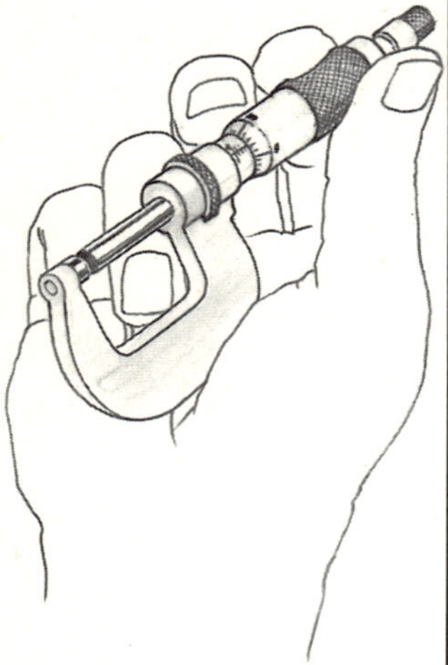

Hold a small micrometer conveniently in one hand by resting the frame in the palm of the hand and supporting it with the ring finger. This leaves the other fingers and thumb free to adjust the tool.

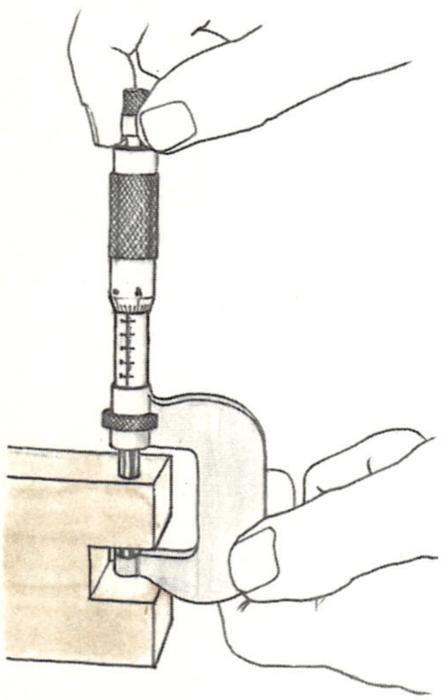

Alternatively hold the frame between the fingers of one hand and adjust the micrometer with the other.

Keep the micrometer free from dust and grease and store it carefully when not in use.

Depth Gauge

SIZE: To measure up to 15in. or 375mm
MATERIAL: Steel
USE: To measure the depth of holes and mortises

A depth gauge is a graduated rule with a sliding head which has a machined flat base.

The flat base is placed on the surface of the workpiece, the rule adjusted to touch the bottom of the recess, and locked by a clamping screw. Remove the gauge and read off the measurement from the rule.

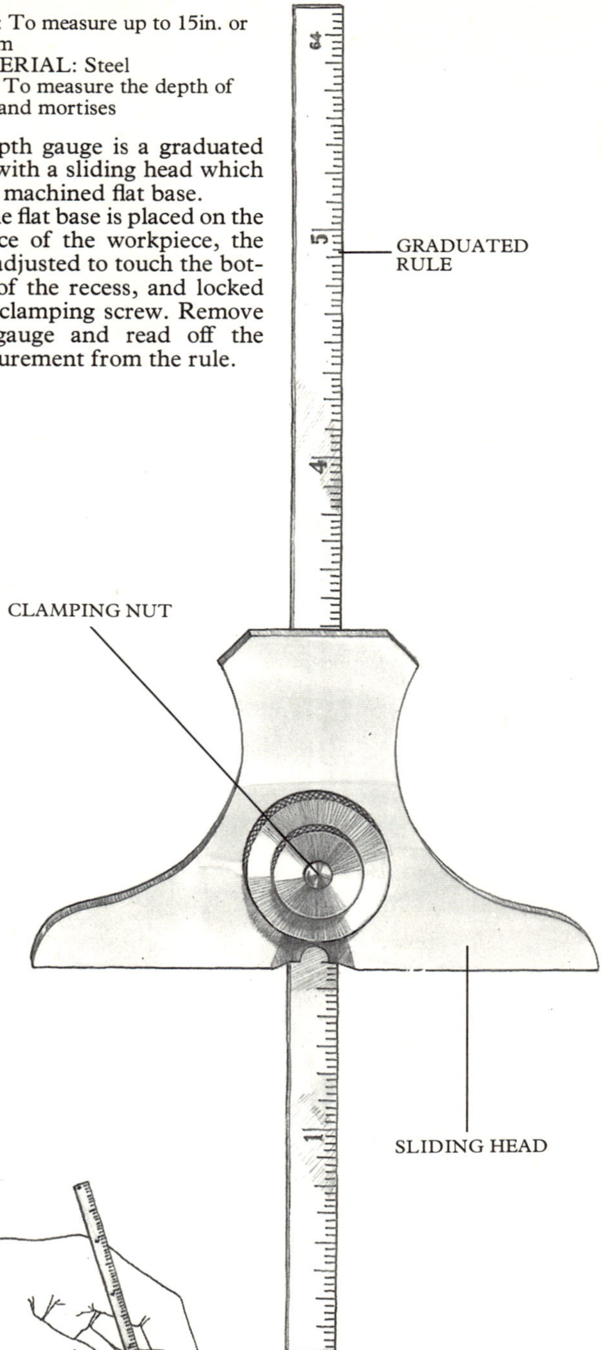

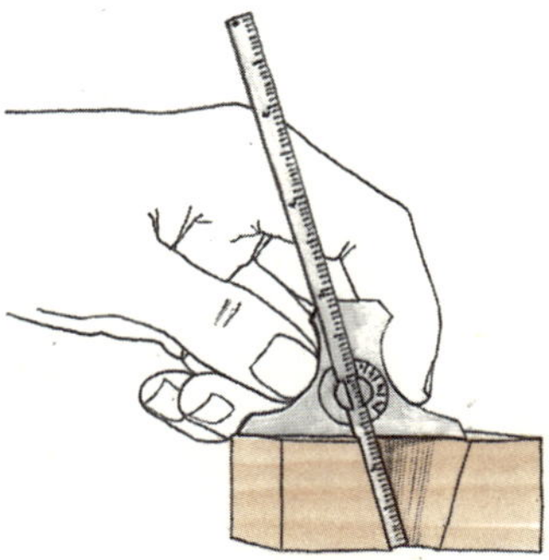

Measuring at an angle
You can use the depth gauge to measure the sloping side of a tapered hole.

Wire Gauge

SIZE: To measure imperial standard: 1 to 36in.; Metric: 0.2 to 10mm
MATERIAL: Steel
USE: To measure the gauge of wire and thickness of sheet metal

The wire gauge is a template which is used to measure the gauge or thickness of sheet metal or wire. Around the edge are graduated, numbered slots which fit wire or sheet metal. The metal or wire is tried in the various slots until it just fits without being forced.

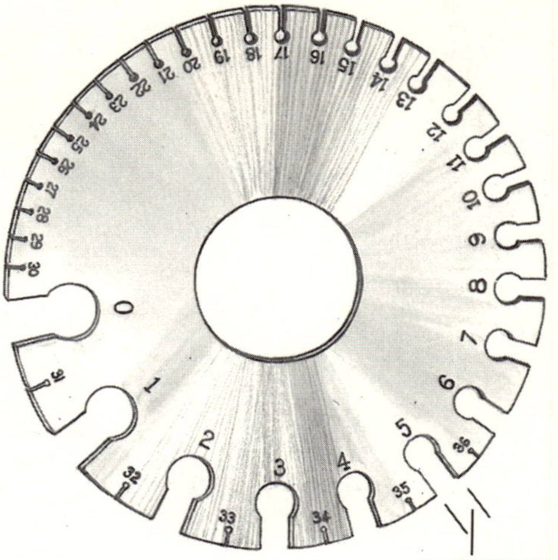

Feeler Gauge

OTHER NAME: Thickness gauge
SIZE: To measure 1½ to 25in. in 0.001in.; 3 to 100mm in 0.001mm
MATERIAL: Steel
USE: To measure very fine gaps

A feeler gauge has a number of thin metal blades of various thicknesses that fan out from a steel case, which protects them from damage when not in use. Each blade is marked with its thickness. The blades are used to measure small gaps, such as between a shaft and its bearing or between electrical contacts.

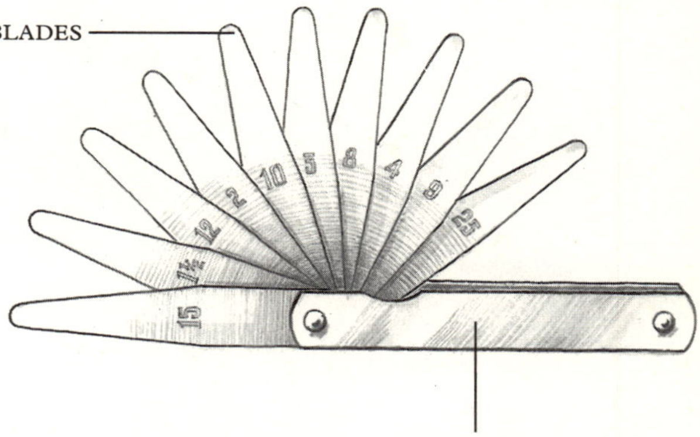

Screw Pitch Gauge

SIZE: To fit a range of threads
MATERIAL: Steel
USE: To measure the pitch of a machined thread

Like the feeler gauge, the screw pitch gauge consists of a series of metal blades in a metal case. The edge of each blade is notched to match the shape and spacing of a range of threads cut in bolts or holes.

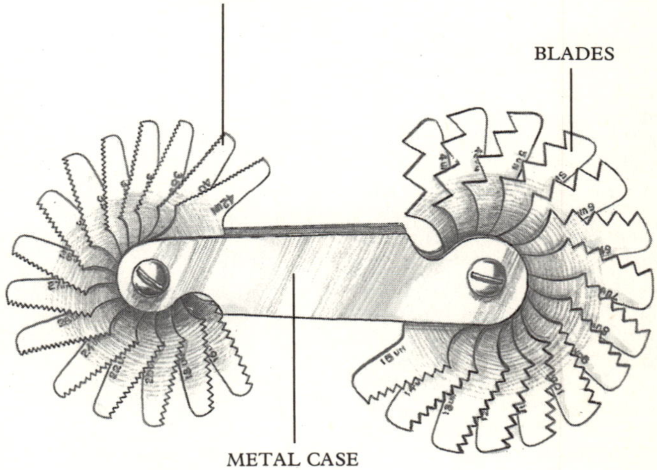

Measuring a screw thread
Hold the edge of the notched blade against the screw thread to see if it fits snugly.

Marking Gauge

SIZE: 162 to 237mm
MATERIAL: Hardwood, steel
USE: To mark a line parallel to an edge

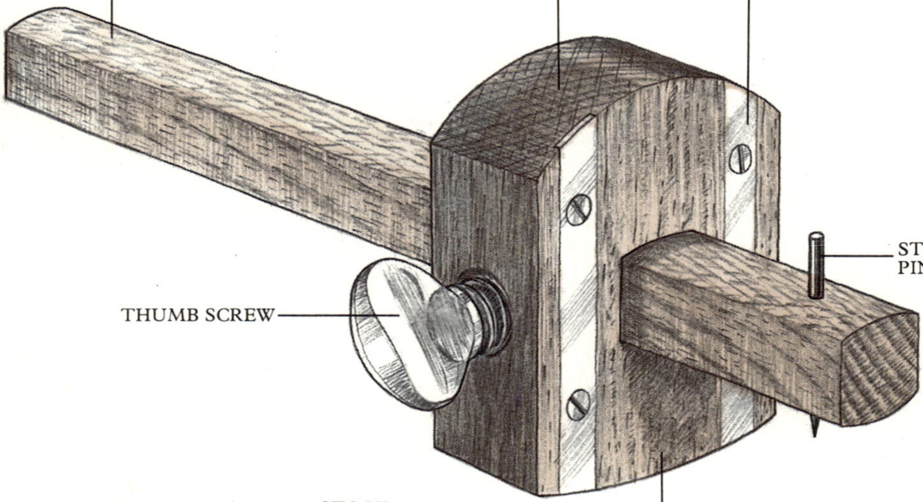

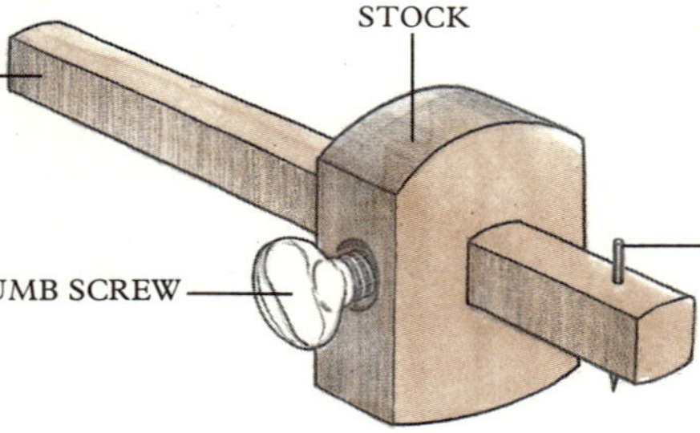

A marking gauge is a beam of hardwood or steel upon which slides a stock, that acts as a fence to guide a pointed pin a set distance from the edge of a workpiece. The steel pin is permanently fixed near one end of the beam and projects approximately 1mm from the underside. The stock is fixed in the required position by a thumb screw on one side. The guide face of the stock can be reinforced with brass facing strips let in flush with the surface. Sometimes the beam is graduated for setting the stock the required distance from the pin. If it is not, simply use a steel rule.

Using a marking gauge

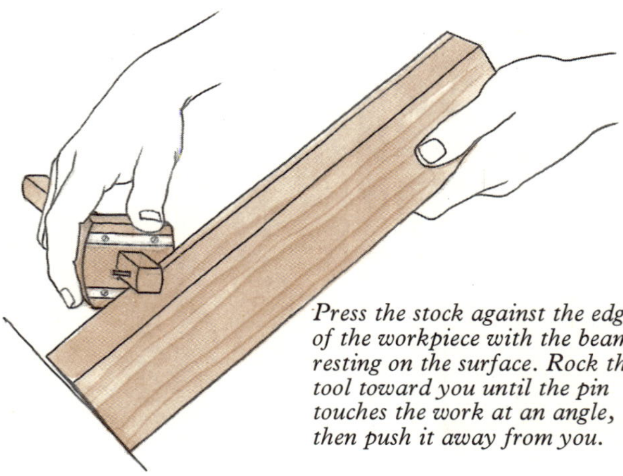

Press the stock against the edge of the workpiece with the beam resting on the surface. Rock the tool toward you until the pin touches the work at an angle, then push it away from you.

Finding centre of rail
When setting out a dowel joint you need to mark out the centre of the rail. Set the pin as near as possible to the centre line and prick a hole in the work. Turn the work around and make a second mark alongside the other. If they do not correspond exactly make slight adjustments by tapping the end of the beam on the bench. Tapping the end nearest the pin will shorten the gap between the stock and pin; tapping the other end increases the gap. Adjust the pin until the two marks meet from both sides of the work.

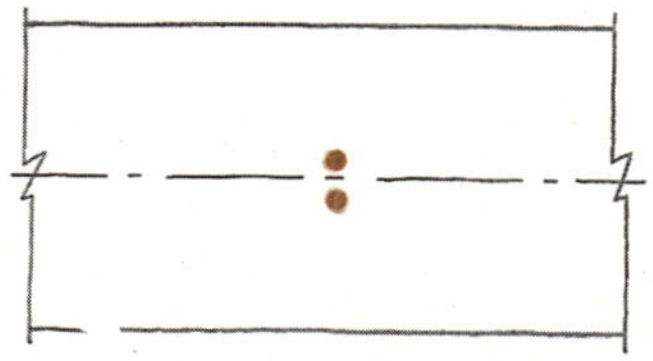

If the marks fall short of the line, lengthen the gap between the stock and the pin.

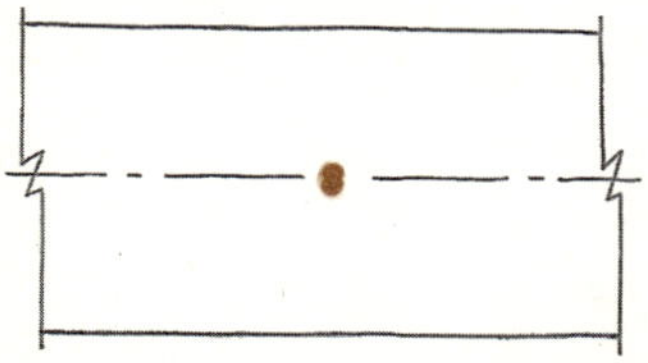

If the marks overshoot the line, shorten the gap between the stock and the pin.

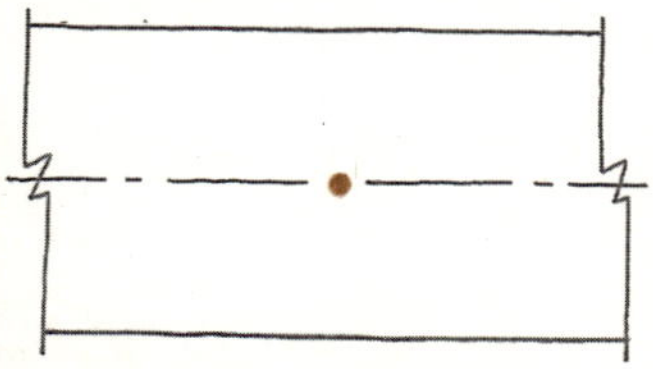

When the two marks correspond exactly on the centre line, the gauge is set correctly.

Cutting Gauge

SIZE: 237mm
MATERIAL: Hardwood
USE: To mark a line parallel to an edge across the grain of timber

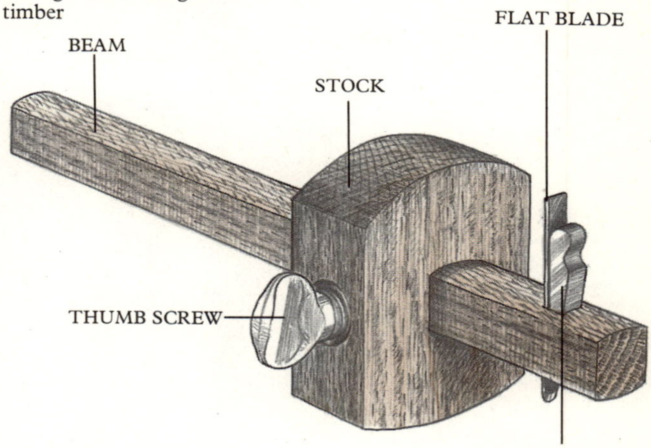

The cutting gauge is constructed and operated in exactly the same way as the marking gauge, but instead of the pointed pin it has a flat blade secured with a small wedge. This is designed to cut across the grain of timber to mark a line where a standard marking gauge would tend to tear the grain. The blade must be periodically removed and honed to a sharp edge.

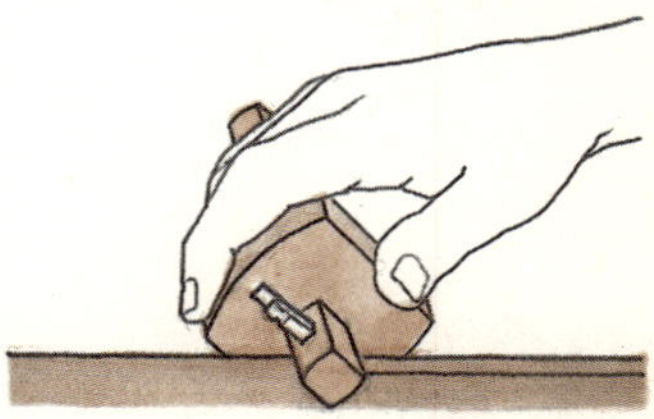

Marking across the grain
Use the cutting gauge as you would a marking gauge to mark across wood grain.

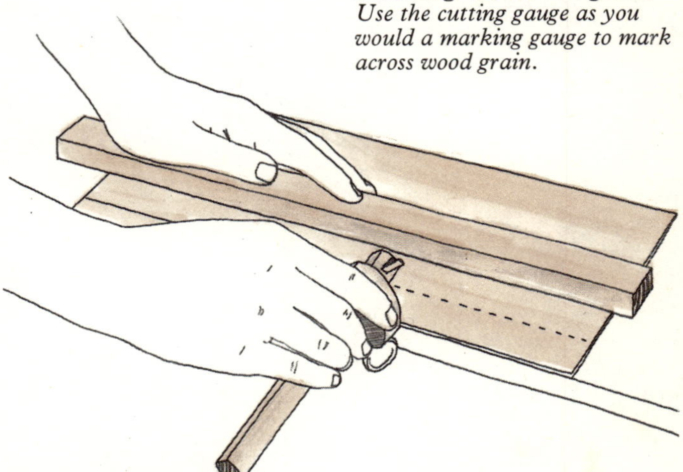

Cutting wood veneer
To cut parallel strips of veneer shoot the edges square on a shooting board and align the edges with a straight edged board. Hold the veneers down firmly with a batten and run the cutting gauge against the edge of the board.

Mortice Gauge

SIZE: 237mm
MATERIAL: Hardwood
USE: To mark two parallel sides of a mortice and tenon

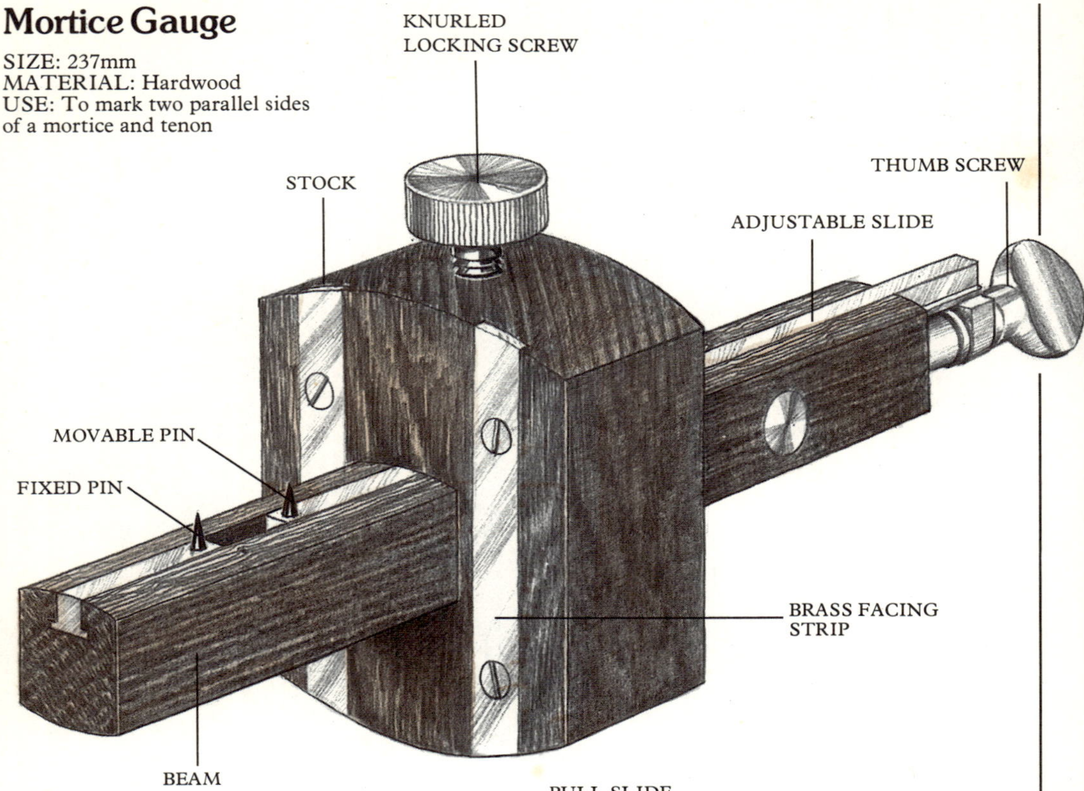

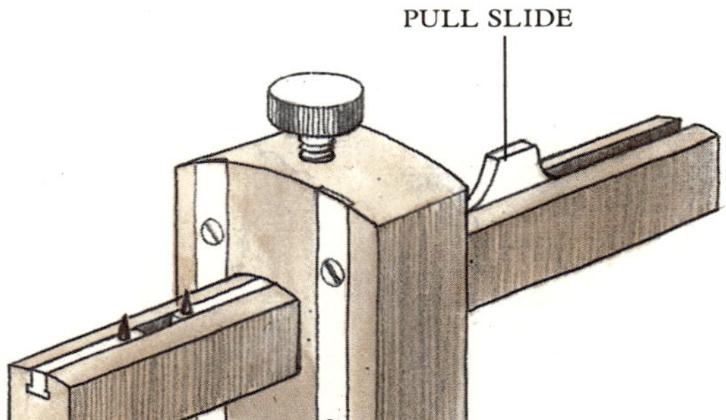

The mortice gauge, like the marking gauge, has a beam and an adjustable stock. However, it has two pins to mark both sides of a mortice simultaneously. One pin is fixed and the other is attached to an adjustable slide. On some tools this is a simple pull slide, on others it may be adjusted by a thumb screw mounted at the end of the beam. Most mortice gauges have another pin mounted on the underside of the beam so that they can be used as a standard marking gauge.

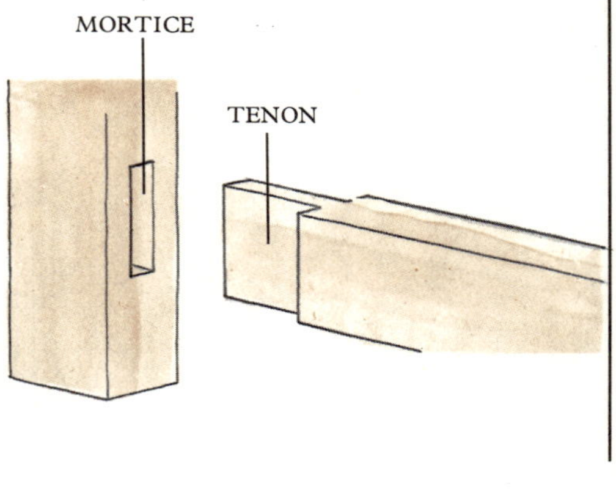

Marking out a mortice and tenon

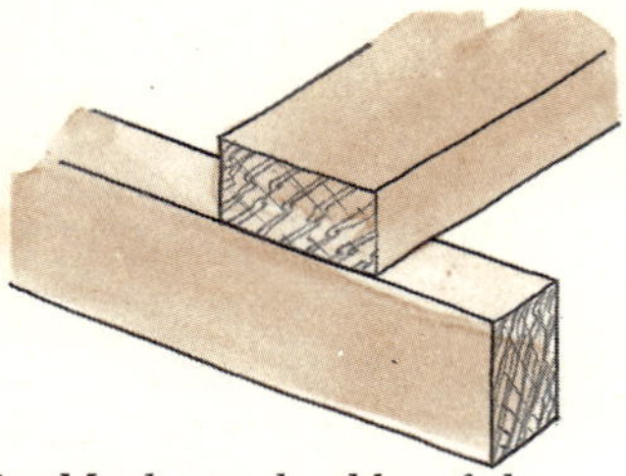

1. *Mark one shoulder of the mortice with a try square, Position the side of the rail against this line and mark the mortice width against the other.*

2. *Square across with a try square. Set the pins and the gauge to correspond with the width of the chisel blade.*

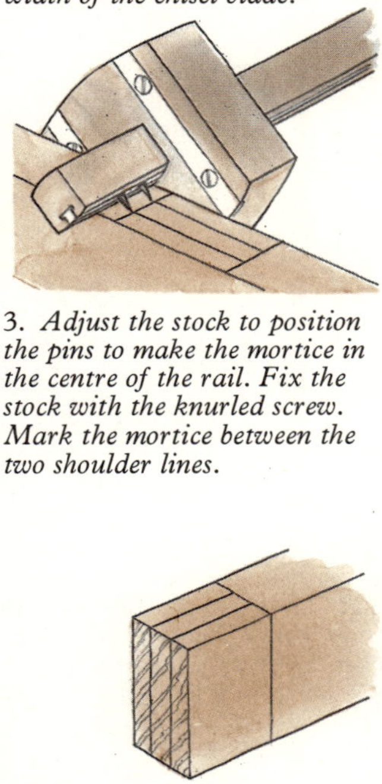

3. *Adjust the stock to position the pins to make the mortice in the centre of the rail. Fix the stock with the knurled screw. Mark the mortice between the two shoulder lines.*

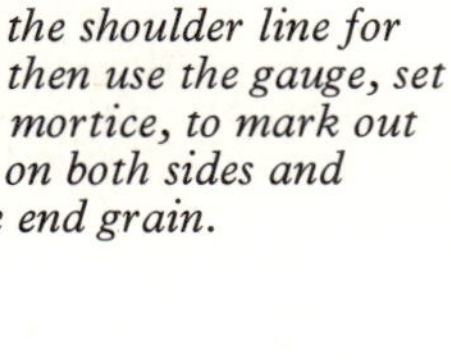

4. *Mark the shoulder line for the tenon then use the gauge, set as for the mortice, to mark out the tenon on both sides and across the end grain.*

Leather Creaser

OTHER NAME: Leather crease
SIZE: 200mm
MATERIAL: *Handle:* hardwood; *Blade:* steel
USE: To mark a line on leather

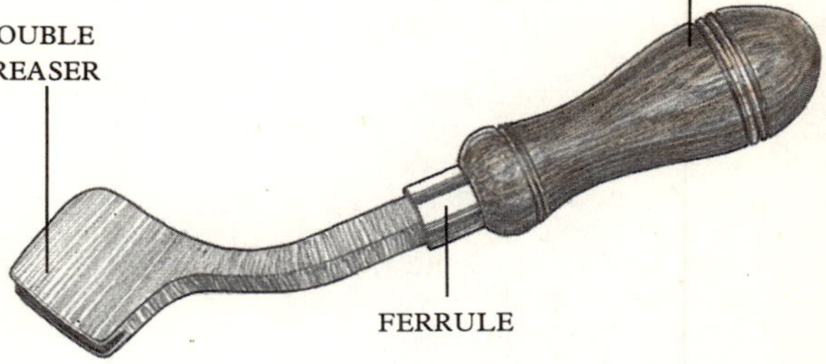

A leather crease has a blade with a blunt edge which is used to mark a dark line on leather as a decorative motif. The creaser is often used cold, but if heated produces a darker line.

A tool with a simple blade is known as a "single creaser" while, a "double creaser" has two parallel edges.

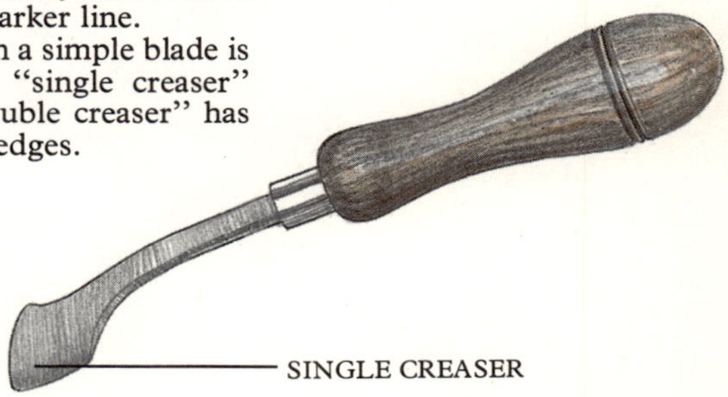

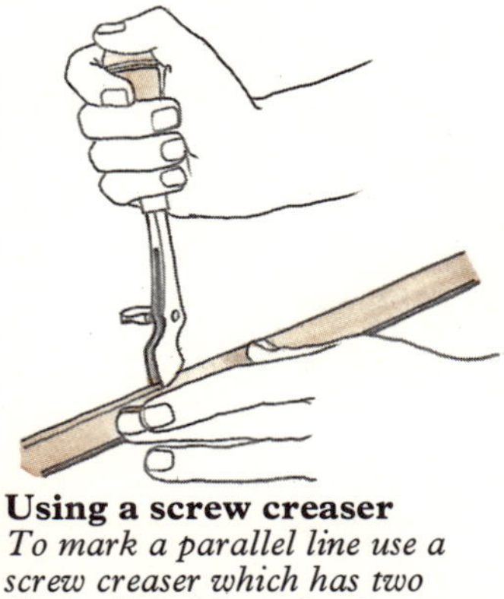

Using a screw creaser
To mark a parallel line use a screw creaser which has two blades linked by a thumb screw. One blade runs against the edge of the workpiece to guide the progress of the other.

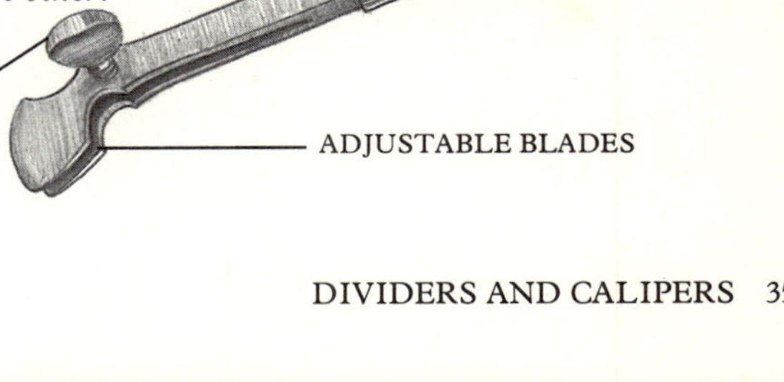

Scriber

OTHER NAME: Scratch awl
SIZE: 87 to 187mm
MATERIAL: Steel
USE: To scribe a line when marking out metal

The scriber is a sharpened steel tool used for scratching marking lines on metal. The simplest scriber has a single point and a knurled shaft for a positive grip. More elaborate scribers are double ended, with fixed or detachable points, or they may be like mechanical pencils, with detachable tungsten carbide points, stored conveniently in the body of the tool. Double ended scribers sometimes have a knife edge at one end for marking wood as well as a pointed end for metal.

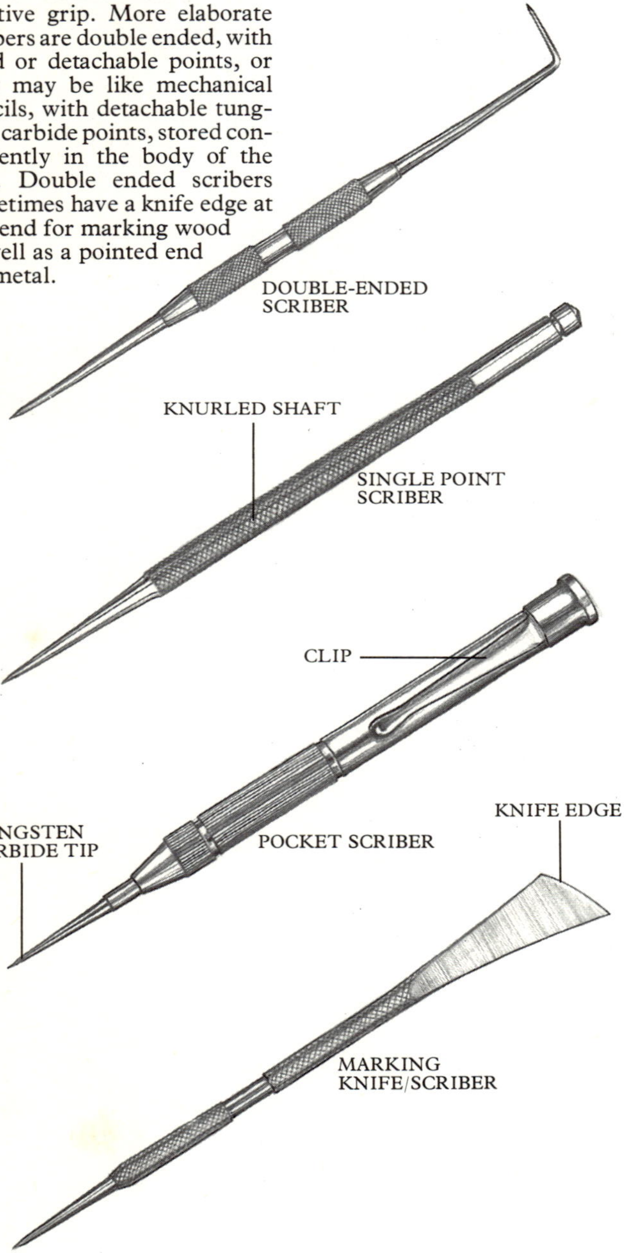

Using a scriber

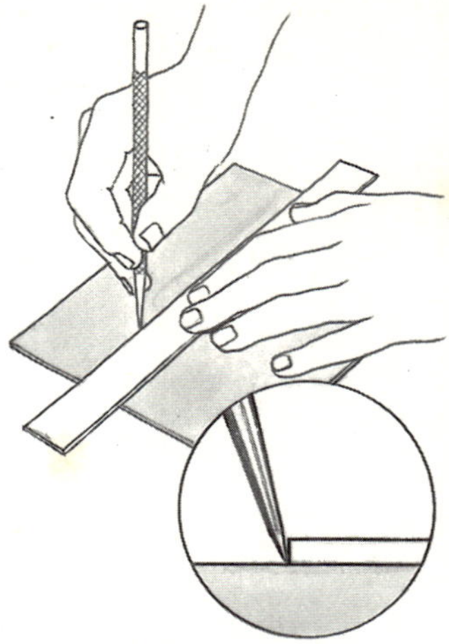

Mark each end of a line to be scribed on metal and join them by a steel rule. Make sure that the actual point of the scriber runs against the rule. Use an engineer's try square to mark a line square to an edge. Position the scriber on the mark and carefully butt the square up against it. Holding the try square firmly with one hand, pull the scriber toward you.

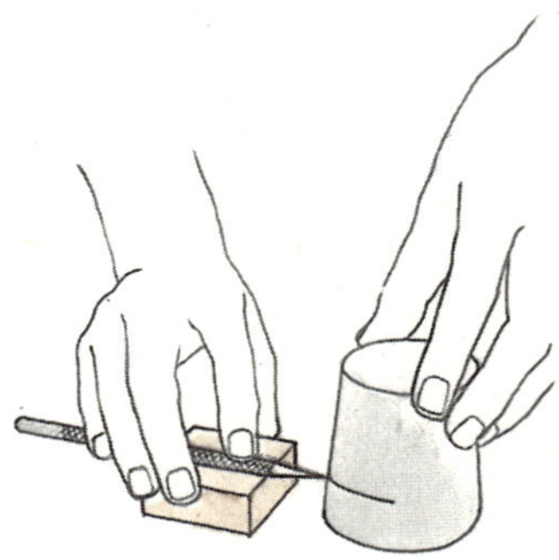

To mark a line parallel to a surface, improvise a surface gauge on a flat surface such as a sheet of glass or chipboard. Pile up blocks of wood or metal to position the scriber at the required height when it is laid flat on top. Small adjustments can be made by adding strips of cardboard or sheet metal.

Place the workpiece on the surface aligning the mark with the point on the scriber. Hold the scriber firmly in place with one hand and rotate the object against the point to mark a line.

Glass Cutter

SIZE: Various
MATERIAL: *Cutter:* steel, diamond; *Holder:* zinc, glass fiber, hardwood
USE: To scribe glass for cutting

A glass cutter is a hardened steel wheel or a chip of industrial diamond mounted in a holder. Better quality tools have replaceable wheels. It is used to score a line across a sheet of glass; bending or shocking the glass on this line encourages it to split along it.

Before you begin to cut glass, lay a blanket or a sheet on chipboard to make a cutting table. Clean all grease from the surface of the glass with paint thinner – greasy glass will not cut evenly – and lubricate the cutting wheel with oil.

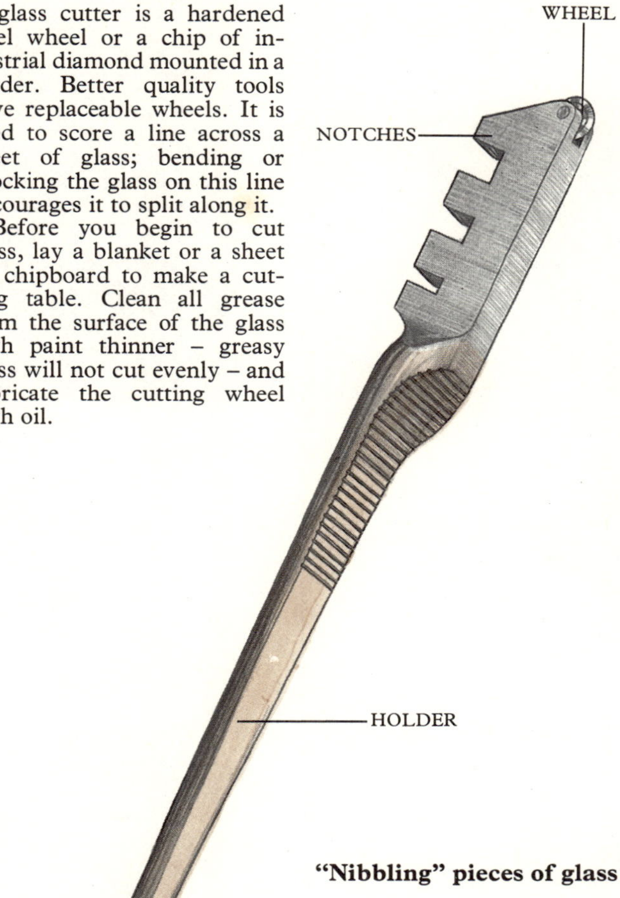
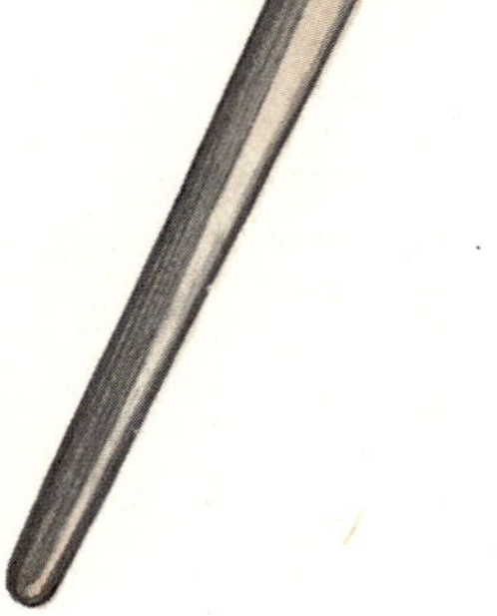

"Nibbling" pieces of glass

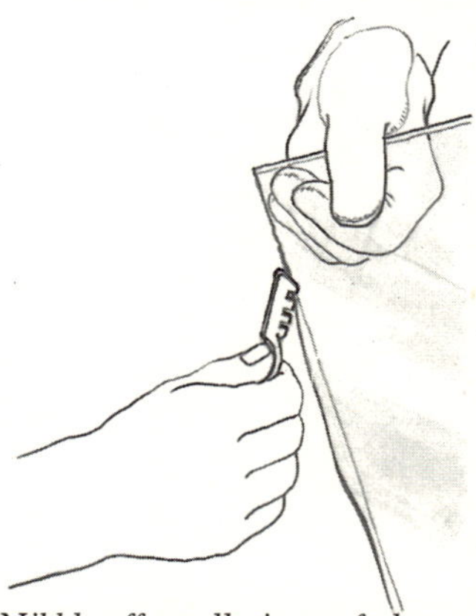

Nibble off small pieces of glass back to the scored line with the notches on the cutter.

Cutting glass

Hold the cutter between forefinger and middle finger and support it with the thumb. Nick the glass at the edge to mark the line and align a glazier's "T" square or wooden straight edge. Place the cutter in position and butt the rule against it. Holding the cutter at an angle to the glass score across the glass. (A sharp cutter will make a grinding noise.) Make sure the cutter runs from the far edge, but lessen pressure as it runs off the near end to avoid chipping.

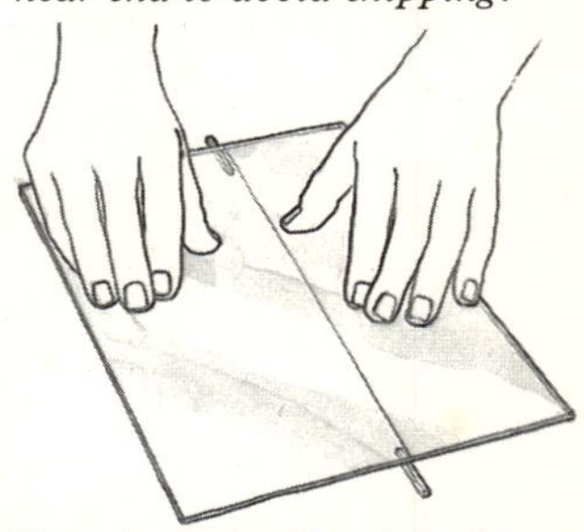

Tap the underside of the line with the back of the cutter. Lay the glass on strips of wood aligned with the scored line and press down firmly on each side of the line to split the glass.

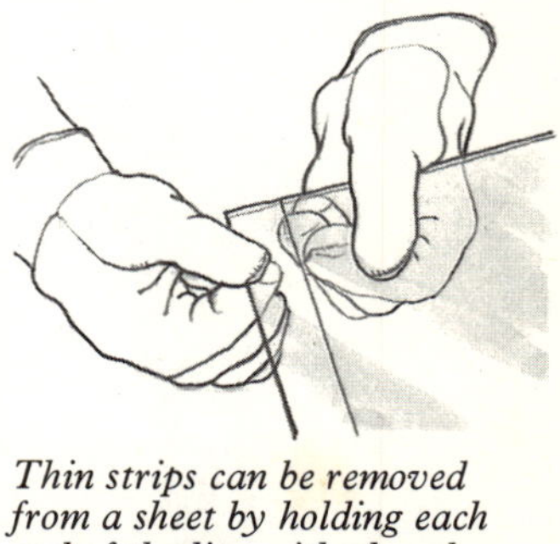

Thin strips can be removed from a sheet by holding each end of the line with gloved hands and snapping along the line. Where necessary finish the sharp edges with an oilstone.

Circle Glass Cutter

SIZE: To cut circles up to 250mm diameter
MATERIAL: *Shaft/base:* brass; *Cutter:* steel
USE: To scribe a circle on glass

The cutting head of the circle glass cutter can be screwed on at right angles to the axis of the shaft for cutting circles, or in line for cutting straight lines. The shaft runs in a swivel base which is held on the glass by a rubber suction pad. A knurled clamp screw locks the shaft in position. Notches on the shaft can be used to nibble the glass.

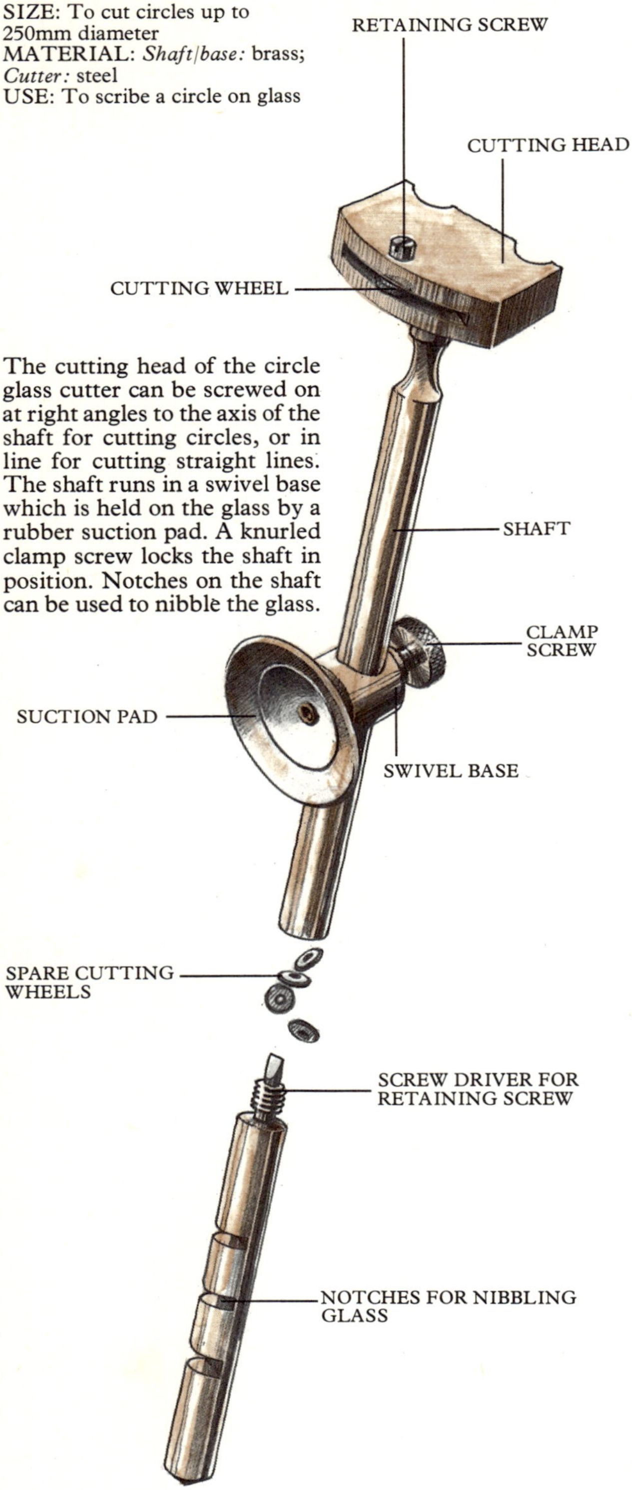

Cutting a round hole

1. *Stick the base in the centre of the intended circle and with the cutter lubricated with oil revolve the cutting head to scribe the circle in the glass.*

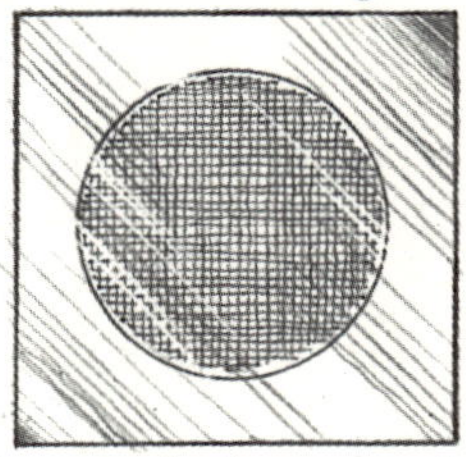

2. *Remove the base, reposition the cutting head and scribe lines approximately 3mm apart across the circle. Tap the back of the glass behind the cut until a crack starts all around.*

3. *Lay the sheet on a flat table, scribed surface down, and tap the centre of the circle until it breaks. With the notches in the cutter shaft break a channel across the circle and then take out the rest of the glass.*

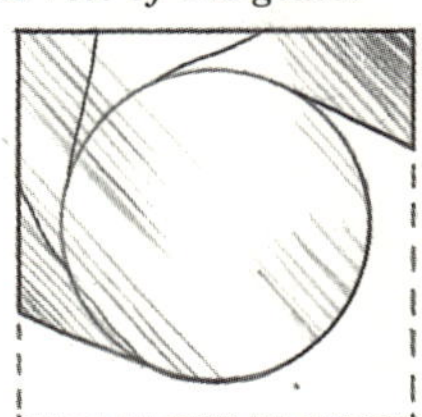

Cutting a disc

Scribe the circle as above and tap the back of the glass to generate a crack all around. If necessary, scribe tangential cuts on the face of the glass and remove the waste.

Tile Cutter

SIZE: Various
MATERIAL: Steel
USE: To scribe tiles for cutting

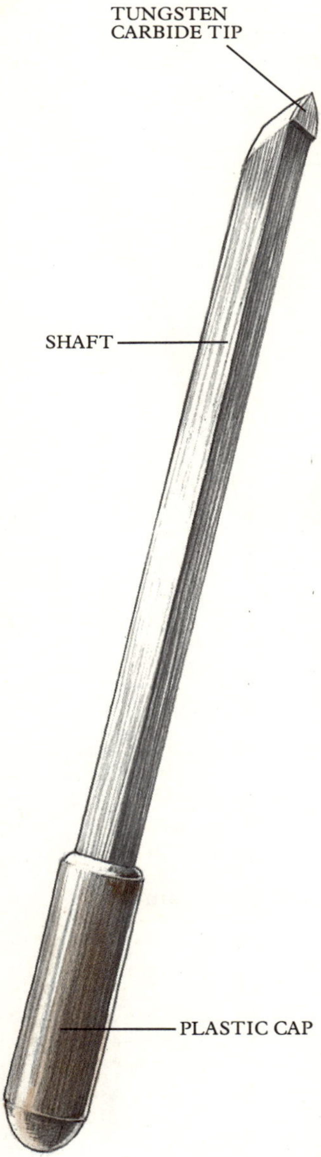

The simplest tile cutter is a square sectioned steel shaft with a pointed tungsten carbide tip. It is used to score a line on the glazed surface of a ceramic wall tile prior to snapping it off.

Cutting tiles

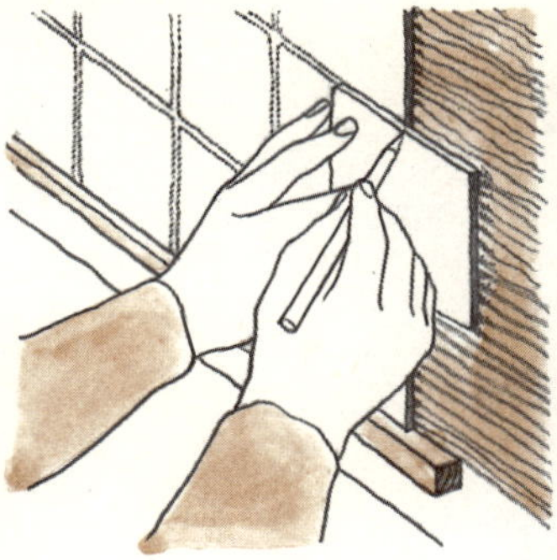

1. *Where a gap occurs at the end of a run of tiles, set another tile against the wall and mark the reverse allowing for the joint between.*

2. *Score across the glazed surface with the tile cutter against a steel rule. Run the scribed line across both edges.*

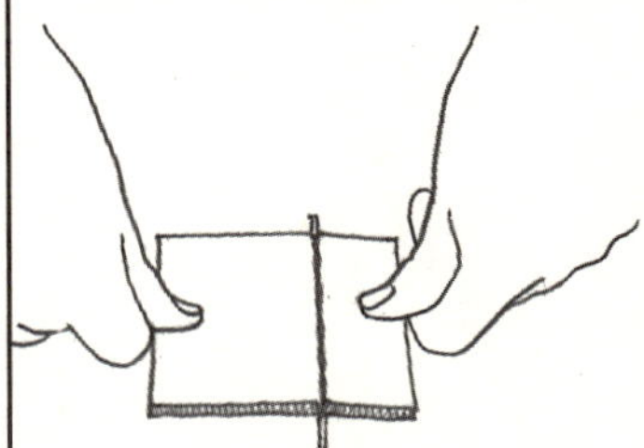

3. *Place the tile, glazed side up, on matchsticks aligned with the scored line. Press on each side of the line to snap along it.*

"Plier" cutters

Plier cutters have jaws with angled faces which press evenly on both sides of the line to make a crack.

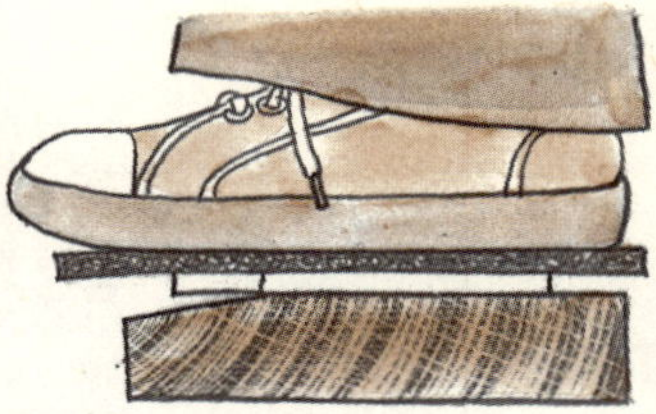

Cutting thin strips
To insure a clean line, plane a shallow angle on a softwood block. Rest the underside of the scored line on the marked line on the block and stand on the tile, using a cloth or cork tile to spread the weight.

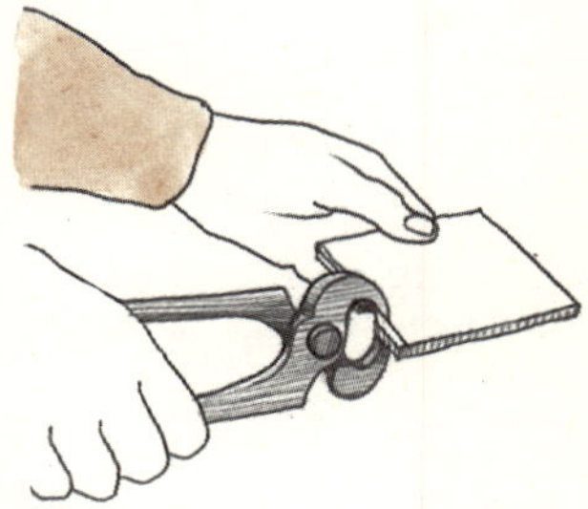

Nibbling edges
Nibble a very narrow strip off a tile with a pair of pincers.

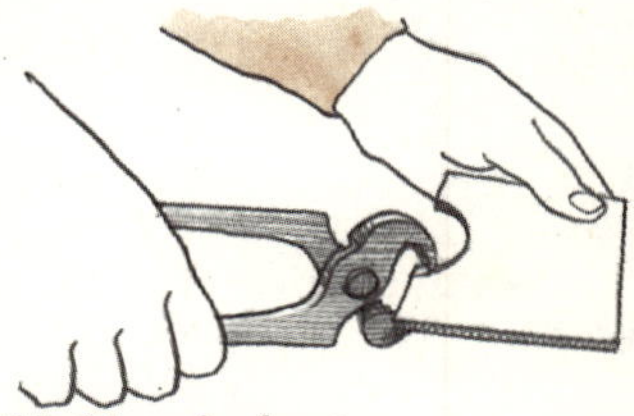

Making indents
To cut an indent from the edge of a tile score with the cutter and snip away the waste with a pair of pincers.

Cutting jig

The jig is graduated to position the required cut line below the slot in the adjustable hinged arm. Holding the tile down with the arm, score the glazed surface by running the cutter along the slot. Press on the arm to snap the tile along the line.

Punches

Punching tools are made in various weights and patterns and are designed to do any kind of piercing or penetrating work, varying from punching location marks for nails or calipers to making holes in sheet metal. Most punches are held in one hand (the shaft is usually knurled to prevent it slipping) and driven, but there are automatic punches and one that can be used by hand only. The anvil or striking part of the standard punch is shaped to be driven either with a mallet (for woodwork) or a hammer (for metalwork). Anvils that are damaged must be reground to their original shape for efficient usage. When using the heavier punches, back up the work with lead cake or blocks of end grain wood. Lever and revolving punches, which are mostly used for leatherwork, incorporate their own back-up.

Nail Set

OTHER NAME: Nail punch
SIZE: *Length:* 100mm; *Point diameter:* 0.5 to 4.5mm
MATERIAL: Steel
USE: To drive the heads of nails below the surface of wood

When a nail is driven flush with the surface of wood, the last few hammer blows often dent or bruise the wood around the nail itself. To avoid this, drive the nail to within 1mm of the surface and then "sink" it below the surface with a nail set. The nail set has a knurled shaft to provide a better grip and a long tapered point, the actual tip of which is ground square, or in some cases slightly concave, to help grip the head of the nail. The tip of the set should match the size of the nail head. A larger tip will leave an unnecessarily ugly hole.

Hold the nail set between fingers and thumb, guiding the tip of the punch on to the head of the nail with the tip of the third finger. Strike the set with a hammer, using short sharp blows, until the head of the nail is about 1mm below the surface of the wood. Fill holes with putty or wood filler before finishing.

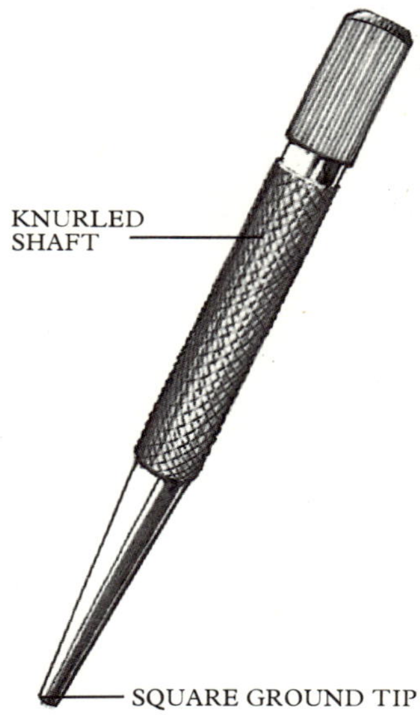

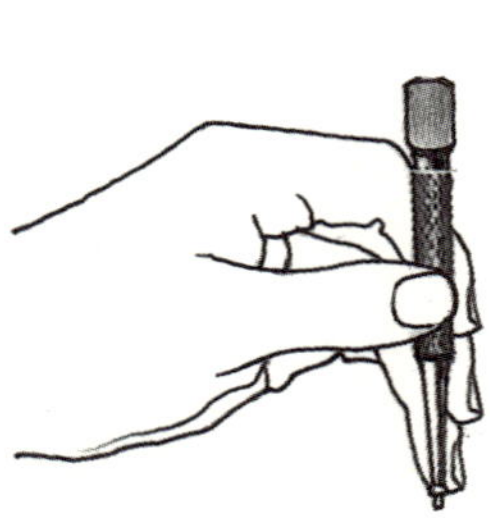

Holding the nail set
The set is held perpendicular to the wood between fingers and thumb of one hand.

Catapunch

SIZE: 103mm
MATERIAL: Steel
USE: To mark centres on metal or wood without the use of a hammer

The catapunch can be used to mark centres on metal or screw positions on wood. It consists of a pointed head mounted on a coiled spring shaft.

Using the catapunch

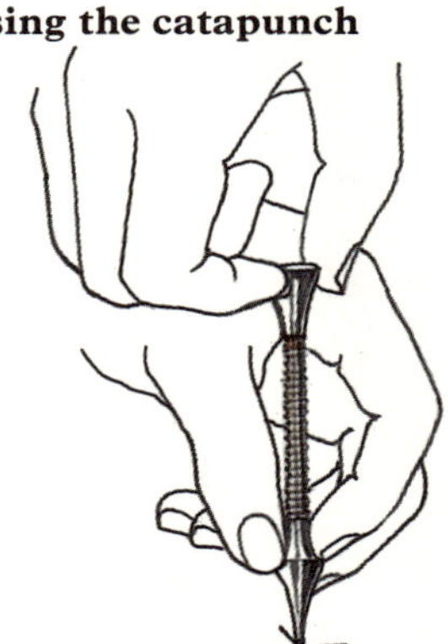

Hold the pointed end of the tool against the work with one hand. Extend and release the spring to mark the surface.

Prick Punch

OTHER NAME: Dot punch
SIZE: *Length:* 100 to 125mm
MATERIAL: Steel
USE: To clarify marked out metal work, identify intersections, and mark hole centres prior to centre punching

The prick punch is similar to the nail set, but it has a sharp conical point with an included angle of 30°. It is used for the final marking out of the cutting lines on metal work. It does this by accentuating the lines with a series of small punched indentations. It can also accurately mark out a hole centre before the mark is enlarged with a centre punch prior to drilling. Moreover, the punch mark made by a prick punch is ideal for setting the point of a pair of dividers.

Using the punch
Hold the punch as you would a nail set and position the point on the mark. Lean the punch away from you to see the point clearly. When accurately centred stand the tool upright and strike the anvil end lightly with a hammer.

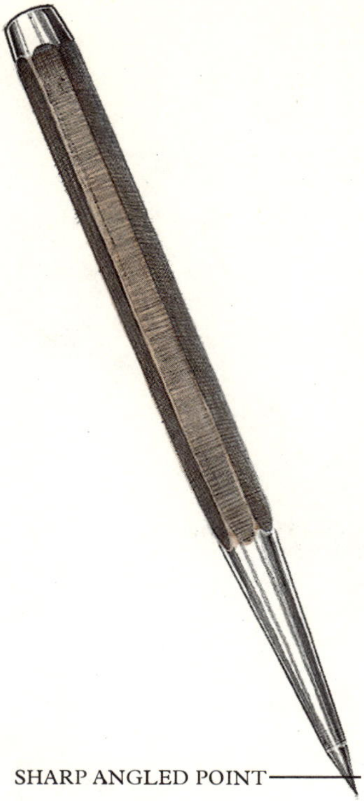

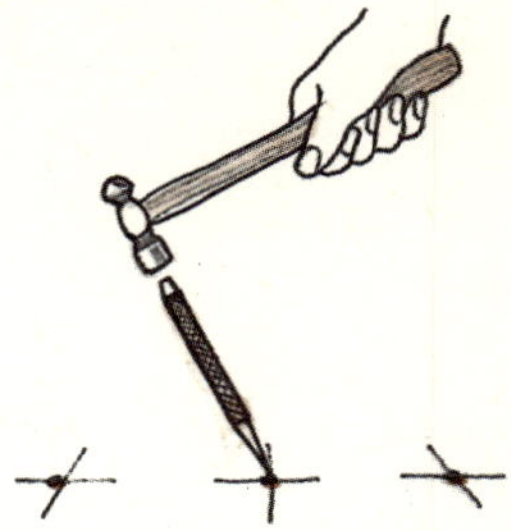

Correcting the centre point
If your first attempt at making the mark does not exactly correspond with the intersection, angle the punch toward the centre and strike again: this will move the punch mark to the exact centre. Even up the punch mark by holding the tool perpendicular and striking it again.

Centre Punch

SIZE: *Length:* 100 to 175mm; *Point diameter:* 3 to 6mm
MATERIAL: Steel
USE: To mark hole centres or enlarge the prick punch marks to guide the point of a drill

The centre punch is exactly the same as a prick punch except that it has a blunter point, ground to an included angle of between 60° and 90°. It may have a round or square sectioned anvil.

Use the centre punch in the same way as the prick punch.

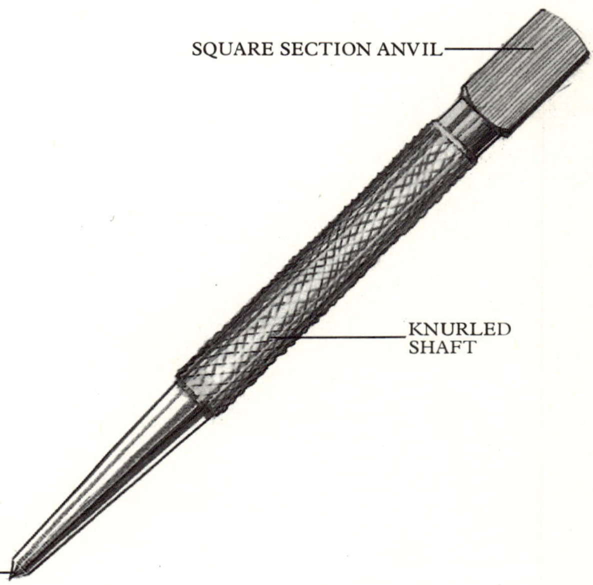

Automatic Centre Punch

SIZE: *Length:* 112 to 150mm; *Pressure:* 2.2 to 22.6kg
MATERIAL: Various
USE: To mark centres on metal without using a hammer

The automatic centre punch does exactly the same job as the normal centre punch, but works in a different way. The point is positioned on the required intersection and the tool pushed down. This automatically releases a striking block which punches the point into the metal. On some models the force can be adjusted. The points are interchangeable.

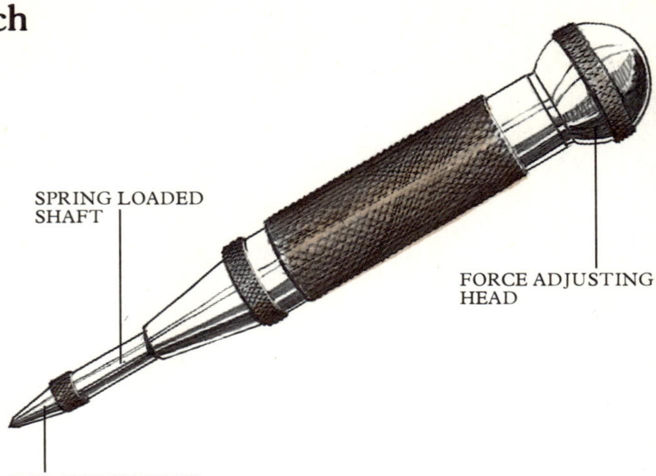

Starting Punch

OTHER NAMES: Drift punch, drive punch, motor and reaper punch
SIZE: *Length:* 150 to 200mm; *Point diameter:* 4 to 6mm
MATERIAL: Steel
USE: To start the removal of a pin from an assembly

The starting punch has a strong tapered point capable of resisting the force applied to it in order to free a pin from its housing. The end of the point should be just smaller than the diameter of the pin. Set the point on the pin and strike the "anvil" with the hammer. Drive the freed pin from its housing with a pin punch.

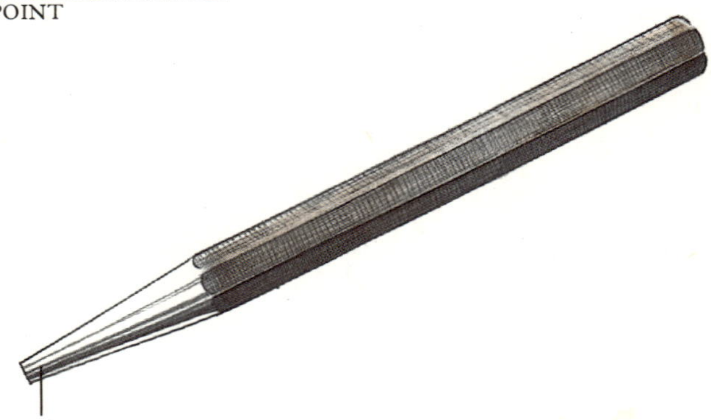

Sheet Metal Punch

OTHER NAMES: Stop punch, screw nail punch, corrugated iron punch
SIZE: *Length:* 175mm; *Diameter:* to suit fastening
MATERIAL: Steel
USE: To punch holes through sheet metal to take fastenings

These punches produce the appropriate holes required by various fastenings such as self-tapping screws and screw nails. They are quicker to use than a drill. Some have a straight cylindrical point matched in size to the fastening and a shoulder, which stops against the metal. Other punches taper to a sharp point and must be struck to produce the hole.

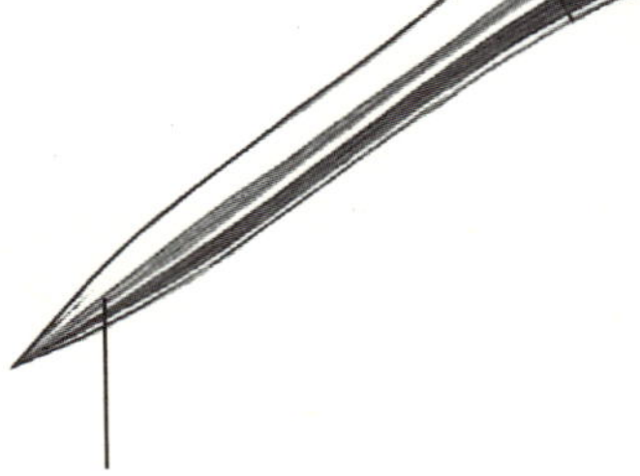

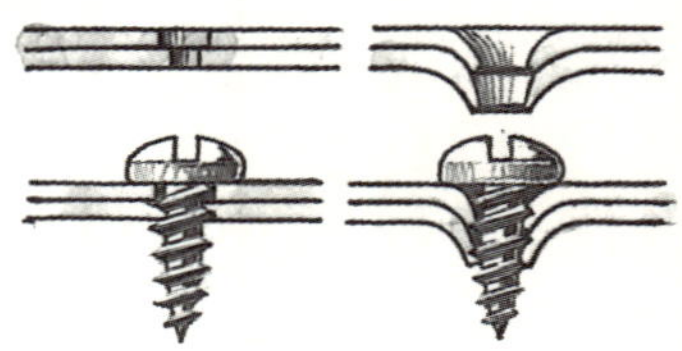

Making holes in sheet metal
You can use a drill to make the holes (left) but a sheet metal punch produces a stronger fixing which gives the screw thread more purchase.

Pin Punch

SIZE: *Length:* 100 to 150mm; *Point diameter:* 1.5 to 9mm
MATERIAL: Steel
USE: To drive out a pin from an assembly

The pin punch has a straight cylindrical shaft with a square end. Match the punch as near as possible to the size of the pin to be removed. If the pin is tapered, check which is the smallest end and choose a pin punch to match it. To remove a pin, center the punch on it and tap the end with a hammer. Do not apply too much force until the pin has begun to move. If the pin has frozen in the housing do not attempt to free it with a pin punch, but go back to a starting punch.

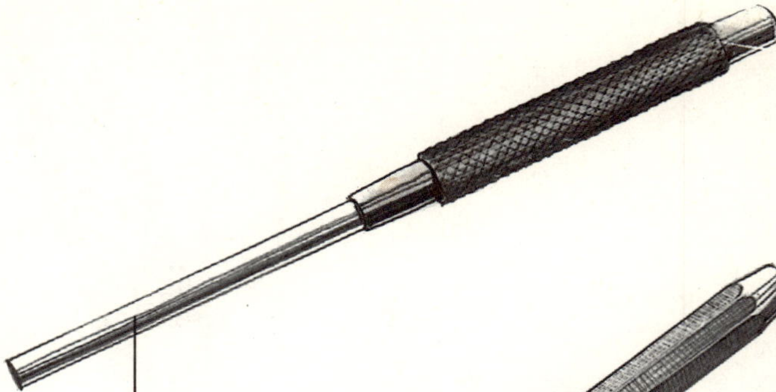

Lining Up Bar

OTHER NAME: Aligning punch
SIZE: *Length:* 300mm; *Point diameter:* 6mm
MATERIAL: Steel
USE: To line up holes to take a fastening

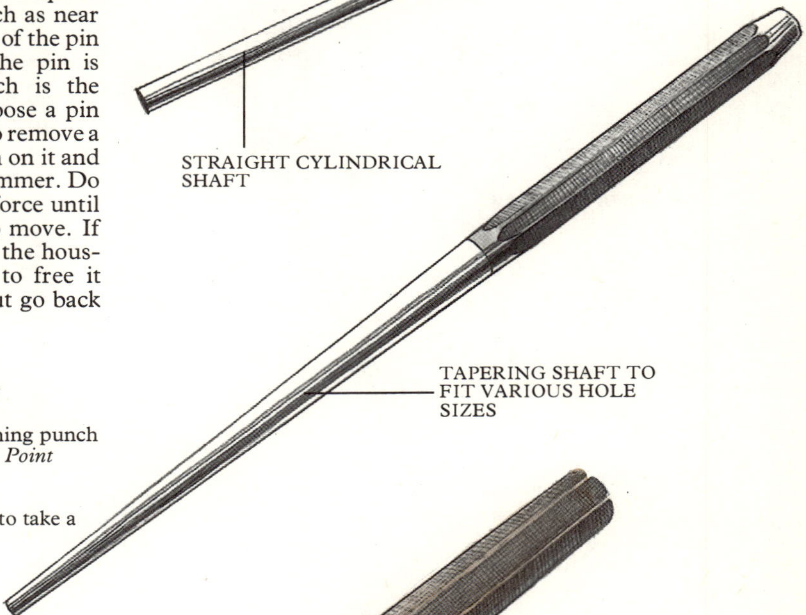

The lining up bar is not a punch in the normal sense. Its long tapered point is inserted in the holes which need to be lined up to take a pin or bolt.

Tinmen's Hollow Punch

SIZE: Hole diameter: 4.5 to 25mm
MATERIAL: Steel
USE: To punch holes through thin sheet metal

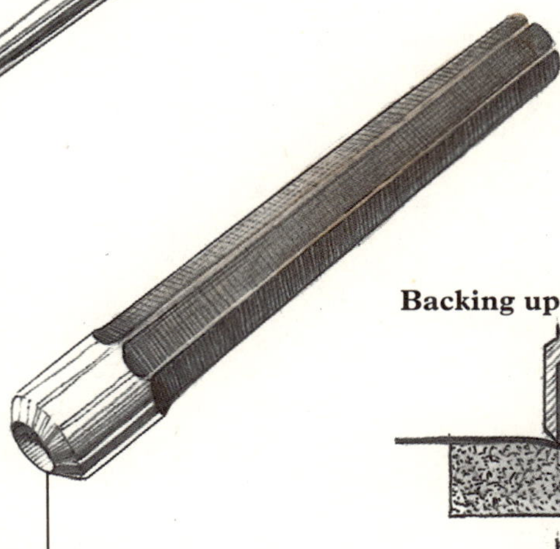

The hollow punch has a solid metal shank terminating in a sharpened, hollowed end. Back up the work, mark the center of the hole with a prick punch and use dividers to scribe the diameter to be punched. Centre the hollow punch on this mark and lightly tap the end with a heavy hammer. Adjust the position of the tool if necessary and strike it again with a heavier blow to cut through the metal. Correct any distortion with a hammer rather than a mallet.

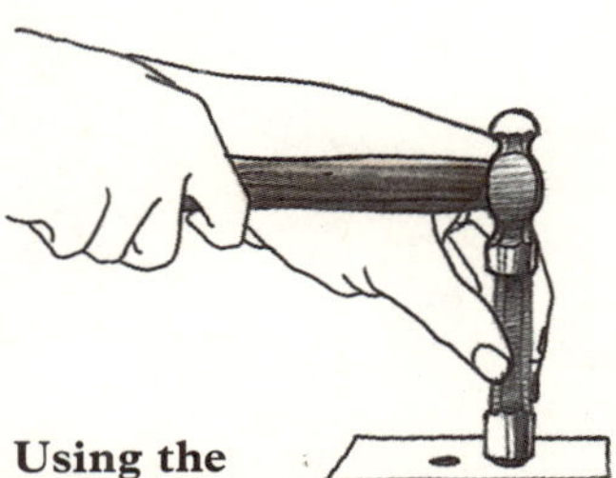

Using the hollow punch
Strike the end with a heavy hammer. Thicker materials may need more than one blow.

Backing up the work

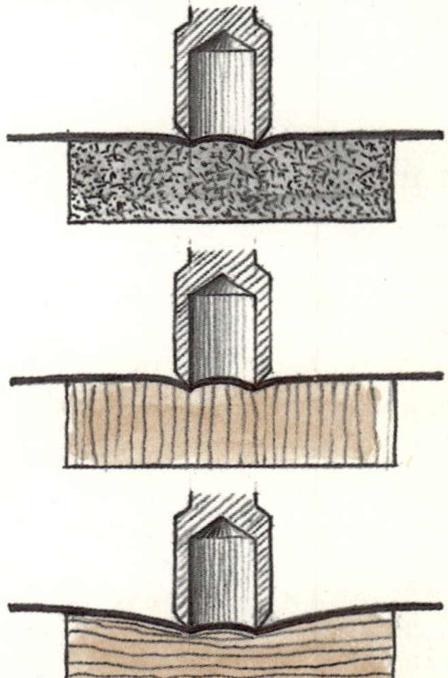

Use a thick material such as lead cake or an end grain wood block to prevent distortion.

Solid Punch

SIZE: *Length:* 150 to 168mm; *Point diameter:* 1.5 to 6mm
MATERIAL: Steel
USE: To punch small holes in thin gauge sheet metal

A solid punch makes it easy to punch a hole in thin sheet metal up to 6mm diameter. You could use a drill, but this is more difficult: the end of the drill has to be ground to a shallow point to avoid heavy burring on the underside of the metal and to reduce the risk of snatching.

The work must be backed up by material thick enough to prevent too much distortion of the metal sheet when cutting. A professional metal workshop might use a lead cake, but an amateur would be better advised to use the end grain of a block of timber.

Using the punch
Mark the centre of the hole with a prick punch, place the solid punch over the mark and tap it lightly with a heavy hammer. Check that the resulting mark is centred over the prick punch mark, replace the punch and strike a heavy blow to cut through the metal. There will be a slight conical depression around the hole, which could be useful if a countersunk head screw is to be inserted. Otherwise, flatten the depression with a mallet.

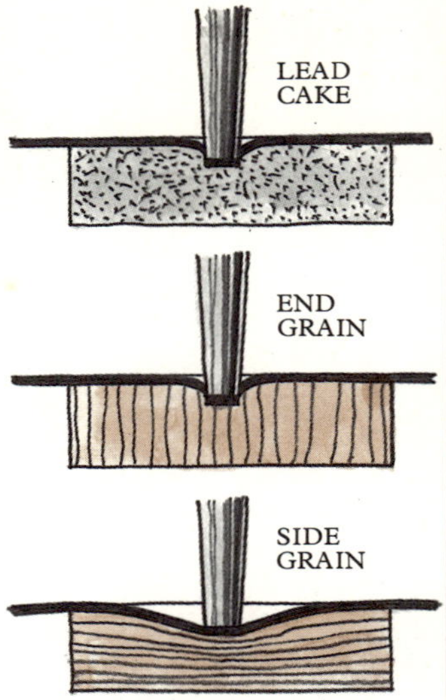

Incorrect backing
Do not use side grain timber to back up sheet metal as it distorts too easily.

Turn the sheet over and flatten the bulge with a mallet or hammer, using a block of wood to protect the work.

Lever Punch

OTHER NAME: Punch plier
SIZE: Hole diameter: *For metal:* 2 to 6.5mm; *For leather:* 2 to 4.5mm
MATERIAL: Various
USE: To punch small round holes in sheet metal or leather

Lever punches incorporate an interchangeable punch and a matching die or "anvil". The die backs up the material, prevents distortion and leaves a clean hole. This type of punch can only be used near the edge of the material because of the depth of the throat. The tool is operated by squeezing the handles together.

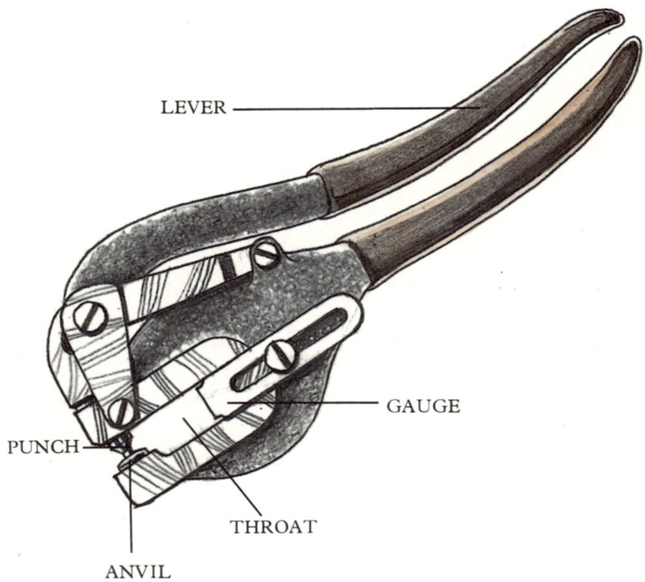

Crew Punch

OTHER NAME: Oblong punch
SIZE: Slot length: 6 to 28mm
MATERIAL: Steel
USE: To cut buckle slots in belts or straps

Crew punches are hollow punches which cut slots with rounded ends instead of round holes. The slots are made to accommodate buckle pins on belts or straps.

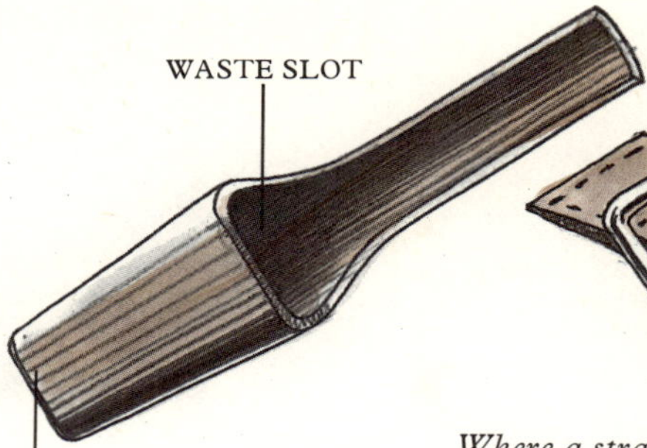

Where a strap is fitted with a buckle the slot allows the pin to move freely for easy adjustment.

Wad Punch

OTHER NAME: Arch punch
SIZE: Diameter 6 to 75mm
MATERIAL: Steel
USE: To punch large round holes in leather

The smaller wad punches can be used to cut holes in belts or straps but the larger ones may be used to cut discs of leather from the hide as well as larger holes. The name may derive from the fact that they were used to cut the "wad" or soft washer which is packed into guns along with the charge to make a gas-tight seal. Even today they are often included in the tool kit supplied for muzzle-loading sporting guns.

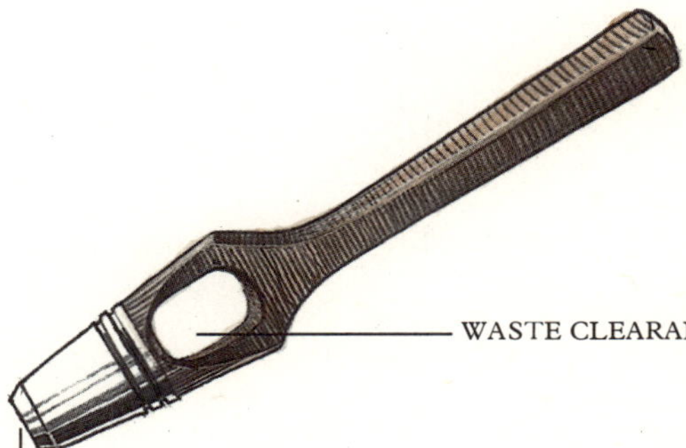

Saddler's Hollow Punch

OTHER NAME: Belt punch
SIZE: Hole diameter: up to 25mm (numbers 0 to 22)
MATERIAL: Steel
USE: To punch round holes in leather

The saddler's punch is used to punch holes in belts or straps. The punches are designated by numbers which refer to the diameter of the hole produced. Number 6 for example will punch a hole of 4.5mm while number 22 will be 25mm.

Using the punch
Position the punch on the work and strike the end with a mallet to cut the required hole.

Revolving Head Punch

OTHER NAME: Six way punch pliers
SIZE: *Length:* 200 and 225mm; *Hole diameter:* 2 to 4.5mm
MATERIAL: Various
USE: To punch small round holes in leather or other soft materials

The revolving head punch pliers incorporate the punches used in the standard lever punch. One of six sizes can be selected by revolving the head to line up with a soft metal anvil on the lower jaw.

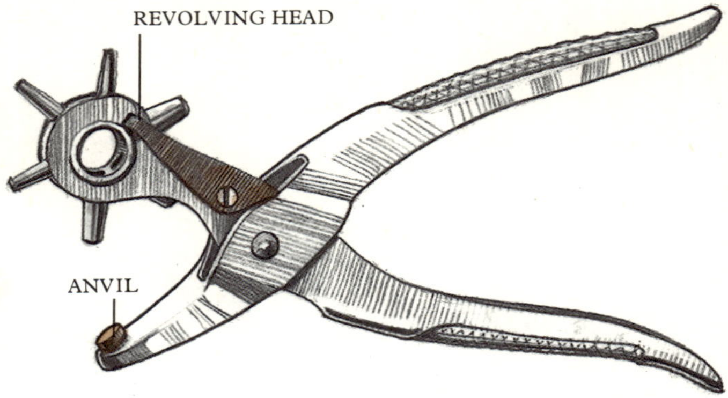

Wheel Pricker

OTHER NAME: Stitch marking wheel
SIZE: Measured in points per in.
MATERIAL: *Wheel:* stainless steel; *Handle:* hardwood
USE: To mark out a row of stitching

An evenly spaced row of stitching, although not essential for strength, makes leather work more attractive. Run the wheel pricker along a predetermined line to insure this even spacing. Then use an awl to pierce the marked holes in the leather.

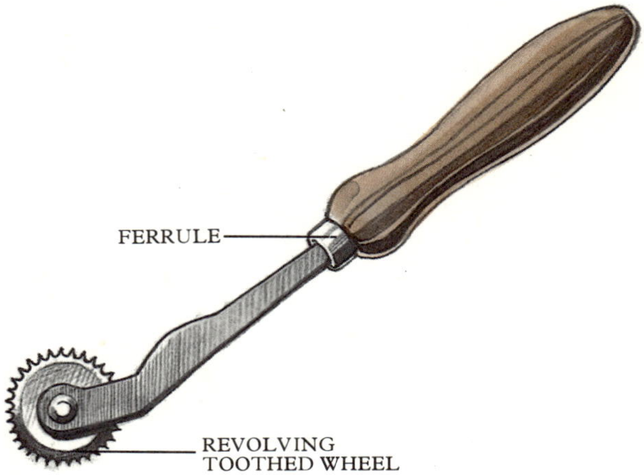

Pricking Iron

SIZE: Measured in teeth per in.
MATERIAL: Steel
USE: To mark out a row of stitching

The evenly spaced teeth of the pricking iron can mark out a row of stitch holes which are then pierced by an awl. Position the iron along the intended line of stitching and strike the end with a mallet. Continue the row by moving the iron and positioning the first two teeth in the last two marks to insure alignment and repeated even spacing. Keep striking and repositioning the iron until the row is complete. Thin leather can be pierced using the pricking iron alone.

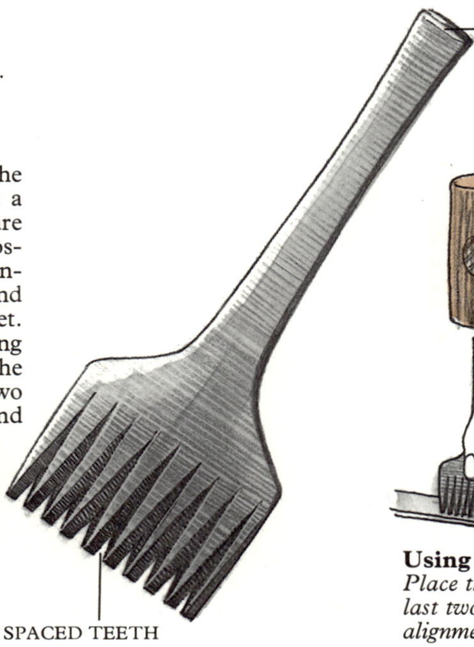

Using the iron
Place the first two teeth into the last two marks for accurate alignment. Strike with a mallet.

Awls

OTHER NAME: Bradawls
SIZE: Blade length: 37 to 87mm
MATERIAL: *Blade:* tempered steel; *Handle:* beech, boxwood, plastic
USE: To make starting holes for screws and nails in timber and to pierce holes in leather

Awls are made with blades of various section: round, square and diamond shaped. When pressure is applied all produce holes by pushing the fibres of the material apart. This works well with leather, but wood is apt to split along the grain unless a screwdriver type tip is used to make a starter hole. These tips are designed to overcome splitting by cutting the grain before the hole is made. When necessary repair awl tips with a smooth file and finish on an oilstone.

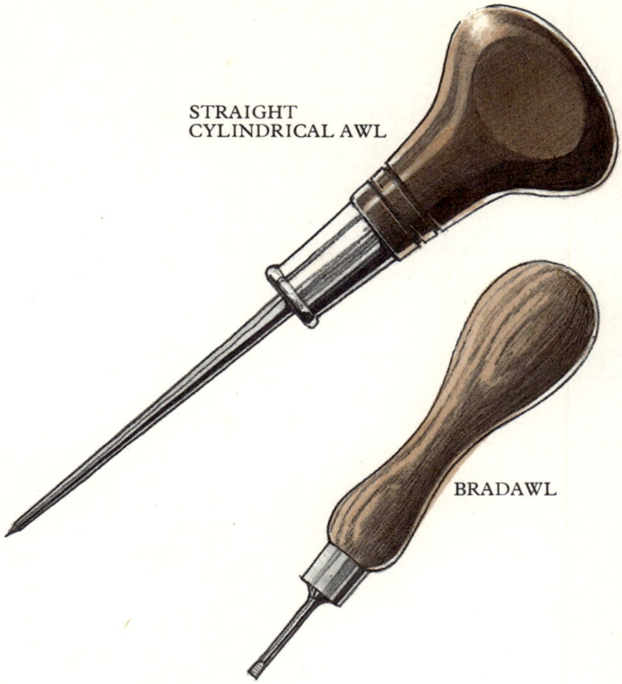

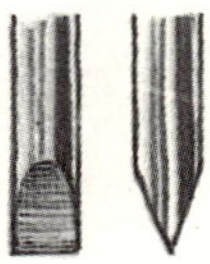

BRADAWL TIPS

BAYONET SECTION AWLS

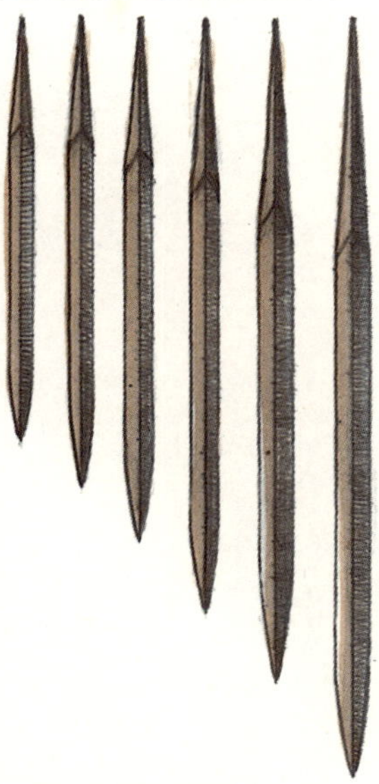

Bayonet awl blades
These are used for leatherwork and are made without handles. They terminate in a tang which fits into a holder.

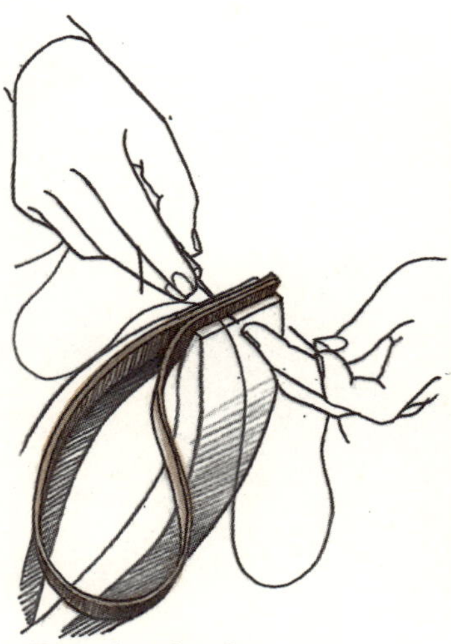

Piercing leather
Keep the awl handy to cut thread holes as necessary while working along the length of the leather.

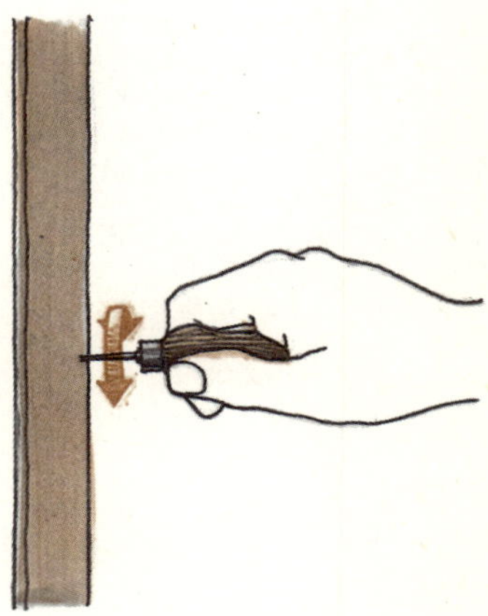

Piercing wood
Position the cutting edge across the grain and apply pressure, turning the tool to the right and left with a twist action only.

Jigs and Guides

From time immemorial woodworkers have made their own bench hooks, shooting boards and mitre boxes. Consequently they are rarely shown on illustrations or included in inventories, and have no official history. The profile gauge is a recent invention; one of the earliest examples occurs in a Swedish catalogue of 1957. Until the arrival of the power drill, dowelling jigs were also highly specialised; so much so, that one type which was used about a century ago for dowelling sash bars has only recently been identified. Although about a dozen were known, their use had been completely forgotten until now.

Mitre Box

OTHER NAME: Mitre machine
SIZE: 225 and 300mm
MATERIAL: Beech, cast iron
USE: To guide a saw to cut accurate mitre and right angle joints

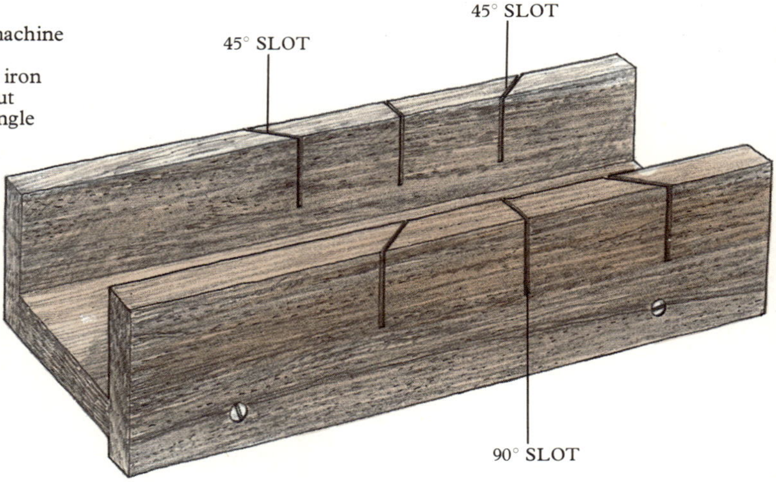

A mitre box is a jig which guides the blade of a back saw to cut 45° mitres and accurate squared ends.

The simplest versions are open wooden boxes with slots on two sides into which the saw blade fits. Brass guides are sometimes fitted on the top edge to reinforce the slots. The work is laid in the jig and pressed against the far sides by the free hand. To protect the wooden base, raise the work on a piece of scrap timber and align the mark indicating the cut with the edge of the appropriate slot. Make certain that you are cutting on the waste side of the line.

A simpler guide, known as a mitre block, is a one sided mitre box.

More sophisticated metal mitre boxes have tall guides which support the back saw and can be adjusted to cut angles for four, five, six, eight and twelve sided figures.

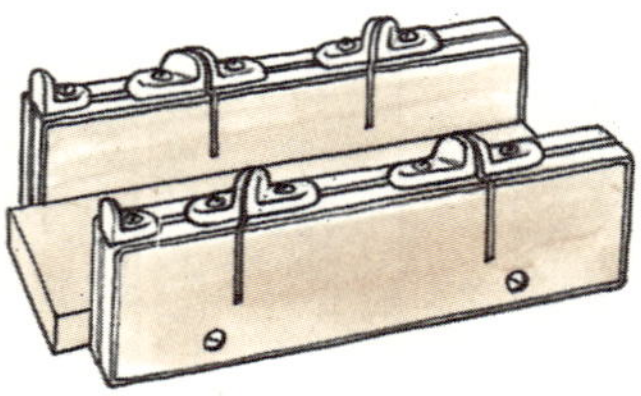

Mitre box with reinforcing

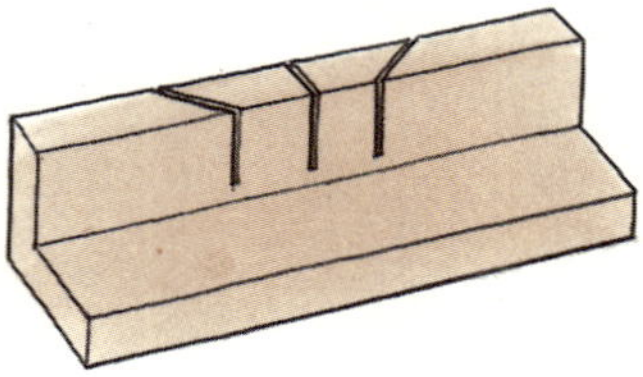

Mitre block

Using the mitre box

Make the first cuts with backward strokes, lowering the blade to horizontal as the cut progresses.

Metal mitre box

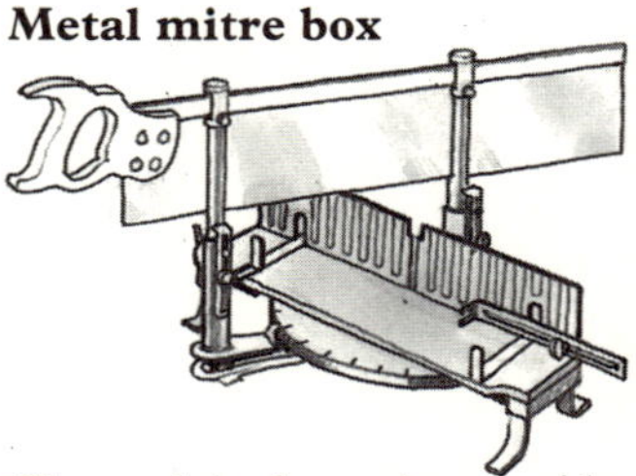

The work is clamped to a guide and an adjustable stop sets up work for repeated cutting.

Bench Hook

SIZE: 150 × 250mm
MATERIAL: Beech
USE: To support timber while it is sawn across the grain

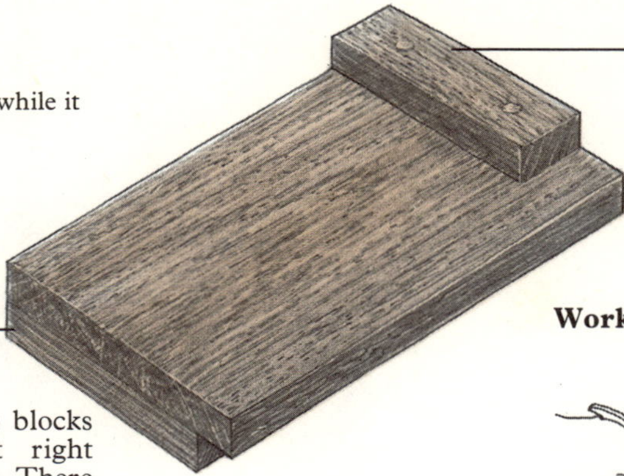

Bench hooks have two blocks accurately jointed at right angles to the long edges. There is one on each side. One block hooks over the front edge of the bench while the work is held against the other block. Either side can be used to support the work while it is sawn.

Working with bench hooks

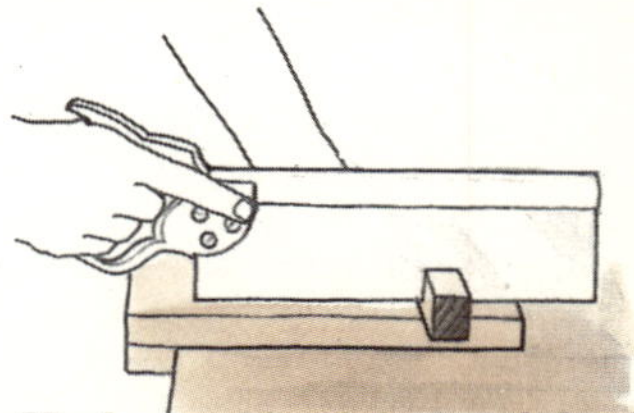

Hook one side of the bench hook on the front edge of the bench and hold the work against the other block.

Shooting Board

OTHER NAME: Mitre shooting board
SIZE: 750mm
MATERIAL: Beech
USE: To guide a plane to cut the end grain of timber to 90° or 45°

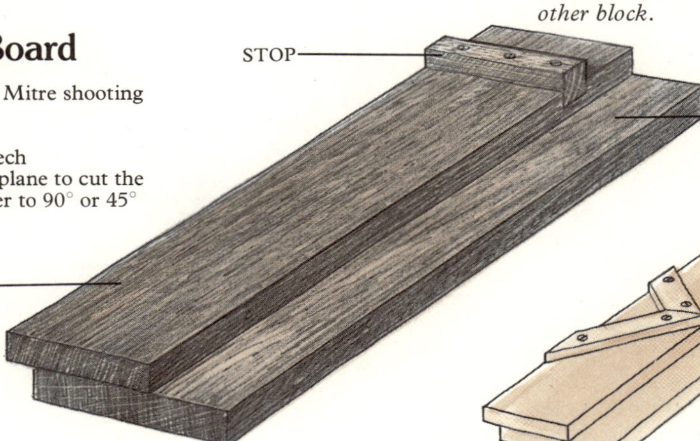

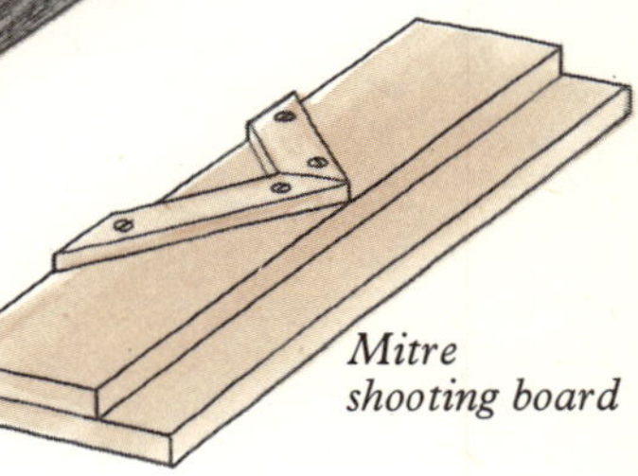

Mitre shooting board

The shooting board is a jig which guides a plane in relationship to the work so that the blade is square to the planed edge. It consists of two boards which are set parallel to each other to form a rebate. The upper board has a wooden stop let into the surface at right angles and secured with screws. The plane rests on its side on the lower board, the rebate acting as a guide for the sole of the plane. It is particularly useful when planing the end grain of solid timber.

A mitre shooting board has a 45° angle stop for planing the end grain of timber to make a 90° mitre joint.

Using the shooting board
Use a sharp, finely set plane. Set the blade accurately so that the cutting edge is parallel with the sole of the plane. Candle wax applied to the sole and side of the plane will help it to run smoothly.

Clamp the shooting board to the top of the bench between two bench stops. Hold the work firmly against the stop so that it projects to touch the sole of the plane. The stop prevents end grain splitting.

The long edges of thin panels can be accurately planed on a shooting board, as can a stack of veneers clamped to the board under a batten.

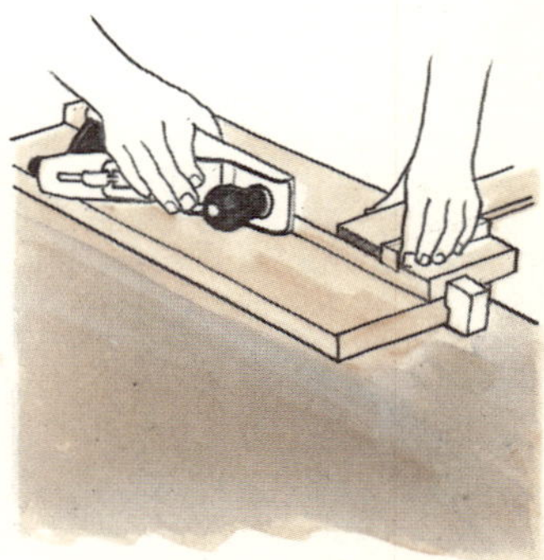

Planing with the board
With the work held against the stop, slide the plane up and down the board keeping it pressed into the rebate. Back up thick work with scrap wood.

Dowelling Jig

OTHER NAMES: Drill guide, dowel guide, dowel locator
SIZE: Various
MATERIAL: Aluminium alloy, steel
USE: To align matching holes for a dowel joint and to guide the drill bit square and true

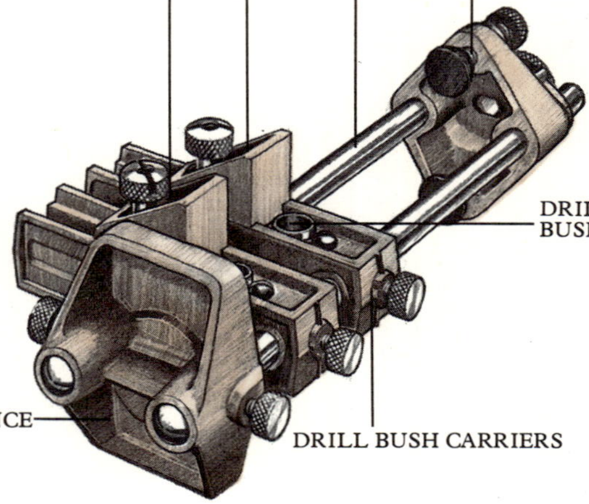

The simplest method of aligning holes for a dowel joint, and one that has been used traditionally for many years, is to mark both halves of the joint simultaneously with a doubled pointed nail or pin. This might be the heads of nails laid on their sides, or a nail driven into one half of the joint and the head cropped off to leave a sharp peg projecting.

Dowel locators are available which leave a clear mark and have a collar which prevents the pin being driven into the end grain of the timber before it has marked the side grain.

Mark out the hole centres on the work and press a locator into each centre. Position the second half of the joint, resting it lightly on the locators until it is accurately aligned, and press firmly on to the protruding points. Remove the locators and drill the holes.

Nails and locators still need to be drilled square and true into both halves of the joint. A dowelling jig will align the centre of the drill bit with the hole centre and guide the bit at the same time. Simple jigs clamp onto the work and align a steel bush with the hole centre. The bush (available in various sizes), matches the diameter of the bit and keeps it in a vertical position during the drilling.

A more versatile jig will guide the bit and will also align the holes in the two halves of the joint. It has two steel rods, which carry a fixed head or fence from which all measurements are taken, sliding bush carriers, which can be clamped in the required position according to a graduated scale, and a movable head or fence which clamps the tool on the work. Side fences on the bush carriers position the bushes relative to the work thickness.

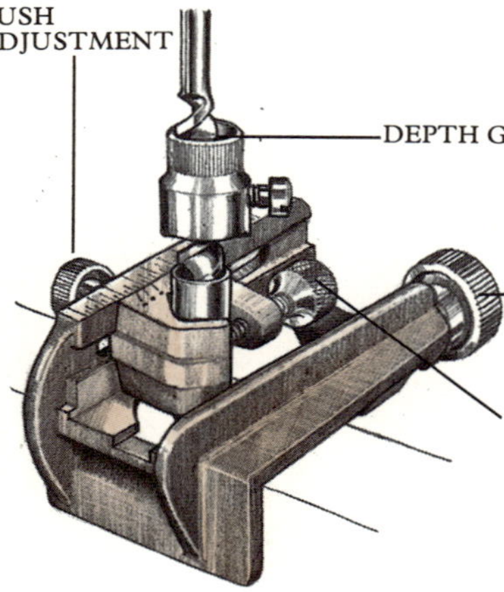

Making dowel joints
Position nails on one half of the joint. Align the other half and press on the nail to produce a matching mark.

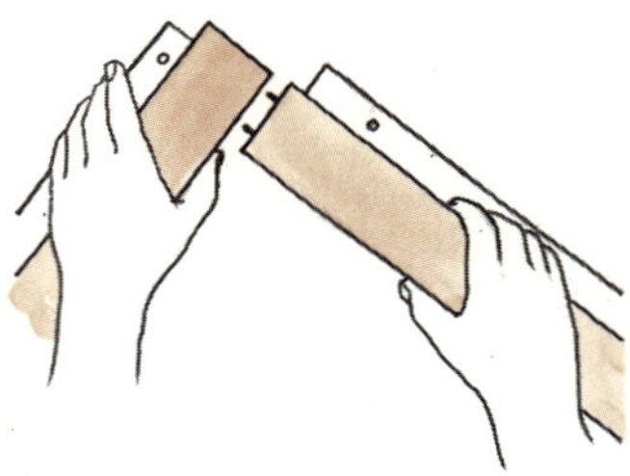

Simple marking jig
Make a simple jig from two short lengths of wood to accurately align the two halves of a dowel joint.

Screw the lengths of wood to the bench at right angles to each other. Holding the two halves of the joint against the wood pieces, push the cut off pins into the upright to mark the positions of the dowels.

Making a butt joint
A simple butt joint in softwood is jigged to drill the end grain first. Set up the jig components and clamp the adjustable head just clear of the wood width.

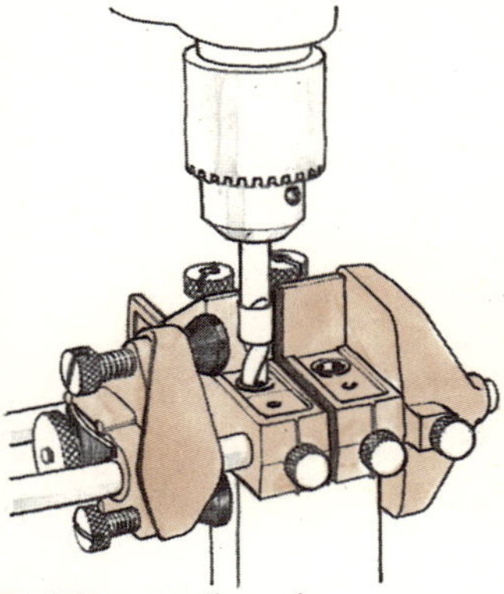

Drilling end grain
Position the jig on the work with fences and fixed head in contact with face side and edge, and clamp the tool in place with the clamping screw. Position the drill bit in the bushes and drill to the required depth. After you finish drilling the end grain it will be necessary to drill the side grain in order to complete the joint.

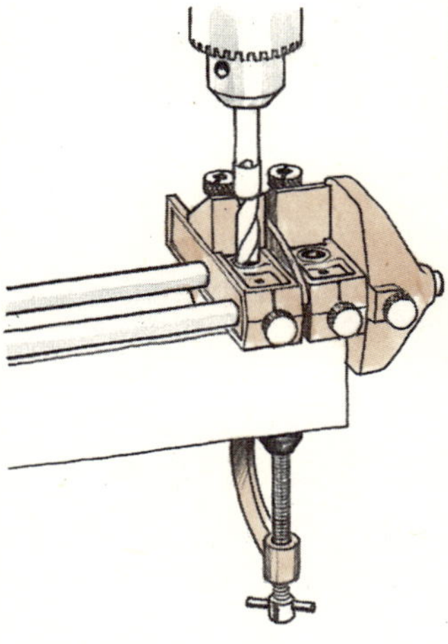

Drilling side grain
Remove the adjustable head and invert the jig before clamping it onto the other half of the joint. Leave a space between the bush carriers for the clamp when the tool is first set up. Drill as before and glue up the joint.

Drilling dowel joints

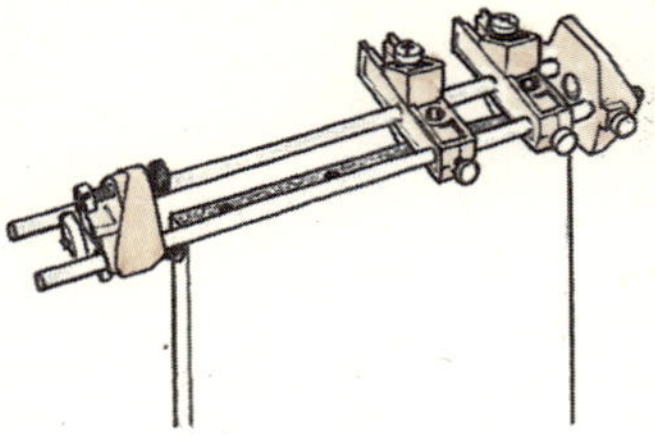

This type of jig is good for drilling dowel joints in composite boards. With the first board set up in a vice, adjust the jig as before and clamp it to the board. Drill first two holes.

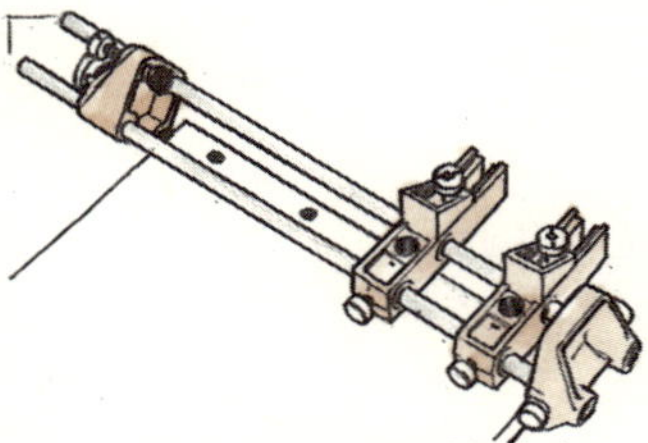

Position the second half of the joint in the jig, butting it against the fixed head and fences, and secure with the upper clamping screw. Release the bottom screw and invert the board to drill the holes in the second half. Repeat for other holes or fix additional carriers to the rods and drill all the holes at once.

Drilling longer boards

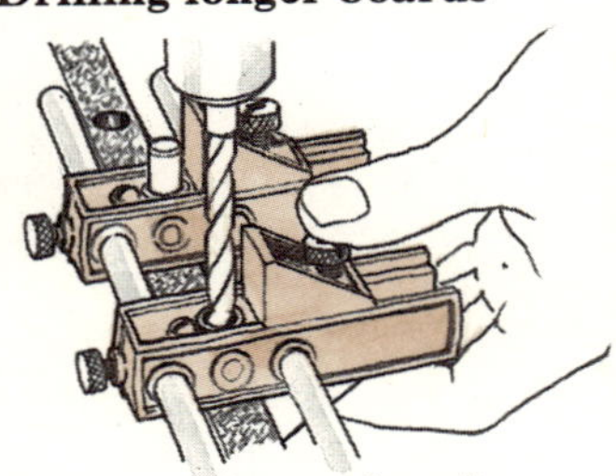

For boards longer than the rods, use the jig without either head, and hold it on the edge of the board with the fences pressed against the face side. Locate the first bush over a dowel fitted into the previously drilled hole to accurately space the holes along the board.

Using a similar set up, the jig can be used to drill various butt joints, mitre joints, and edge to edge joints.

Profile Gauge

OTHER NAME: Shape tracer
SIZE: 150mm
MATERIAL: Steel
USE: To reproduce a shape and act as a pattern for cutting to fit

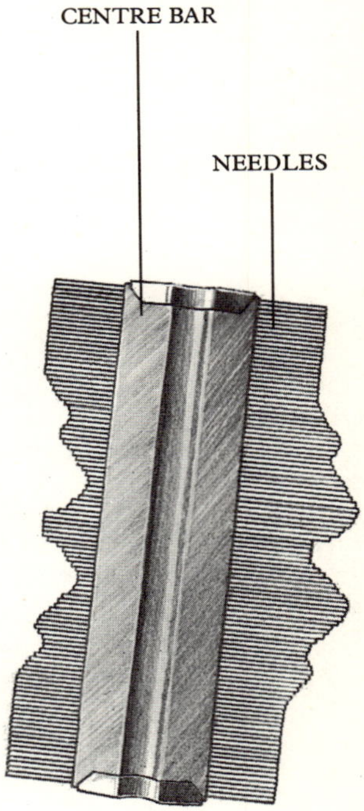

The profile gauge is a row of tightly packed steel needles. Pressed against an object, these slide backward to reproduce the shape. It is particularly useful where one material must be cut to fit another, such as vinyl floor tiles around pipework or door mouldings.

Before using the profile gauge, press it against a flat surface to align all the needles.

Benches and Vices

The first woodworking benches appeared in Greek and Roman times. The workpiece was held by pegs or holdfasts driven into holes bored in the top – a thick plank or split log supported on splayed legs. Further development depended on finding a way to hold a workpiece which was not lying flat on the bench. In the seventeenth century a hook shaped piece of wood, for holding boards, was nailed to the side of the bench top; a wooden screw was added later, making a prototype bench vice. By 1812, the screw was still near the righthand end of the cheek, the other end having a stiff runner to keep it parallel. Later the screw was moved to the middle with a runner on each side. Eighteenth-century wooden vises with a vertical cheek had a wooden screw threaded through the bench leg about halfway down. This was later brought nearer the top and worked in a nut under the bench, a style that was in general use until about fifty years ago.

Woodworking Bench

OTHER NAME: Cabinet maker's bench
SIZE: *Length:* 1.5 to 1.8m; *Width:* 600 to 700mm, *Height:* 840 to 920mm
MATERIAL: Hardwood
ACCESSORIES: Woodworker's vice, end vice, bench stops
USE: To provide a work surface

Apart from being the correct height, a woodworking bench must be rigid. A top or an underframe that flexes makes sawing or hammering difficult. A good woodworking bench is made of heavy sections of hardwood, usually beech, and is strongly morticed and tenoned and bolted together.

The top must be flat over most of its area, but some benches have a well at the back to hold tools in use without restricting the movement of a large sheet of material or a frame. A tool storage slot behind the well provides convenient temporary storage, but the projecting handles can sometimes be an obstruction.

An end vice fitted to the top will provide clamping force along the length of the bench. The jaws of the vice itself can be used for clamping, although those nearest the handle do not close completely, but the advantage of the end vice lies in its ability to clamp lengths of timber to the bench top so that they can be planed, drilled and so on. The timber is held between bench stops, sprung steel pegs, plugged into a series of square holes along the bench and in the end vice itself. Bench stops can provide tension if they are located on the inside of the frame and if the end vice is simultaneously opened.

A woodworker's vice should be fitted at one edge of the bench, near a leg to provide maximum support.

Protecting the metalwork bench

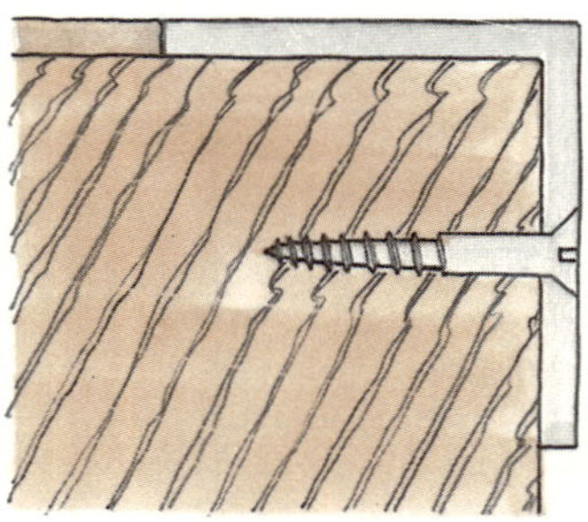

Protect the surface from oil stains and denting with a sheet of hardboard or plywood. A steel right angle will protect the front edge. Replace the edging and the surface as required.

METALWORKING BENCH

Traditionally, a metalworking bench is simpler than a woodworking bench, having no well, end vice, or tool rack. However, these features are just as convenient for metalwork especially as the work is generally smaller and consequently tools held in the rack will not be an inconvenience. You will need an engineer's vice rather than a woodworker's vice for this type of bench.

Workmate Bench

SIZE: *Folded:* 800 × 725 × 187mm; *Working height:* 612 and 812mm; *Jaw opening:* 100mm
MATERIAL: *Frame:* aluminium and steel; *Jaws:* plywood
ACCESSORIES: Vice pegs
USE: A portable work bench

The "workmate" is a small bench which can be folded for convenient storage and transported in the boot of a car.

Unfolded, it can be locked into position to provide work surfaces at two levels, a standard work bench height and a lower position which is a more convenient height for sawing timber and boards.

The entire work surface is formed by two long vice jaws. Using the adjusting handles, the jaws can be adjusted to hold parallel sided work or misaligned to hold a tapered workpiece. "V" slots are provided to hold pipework.

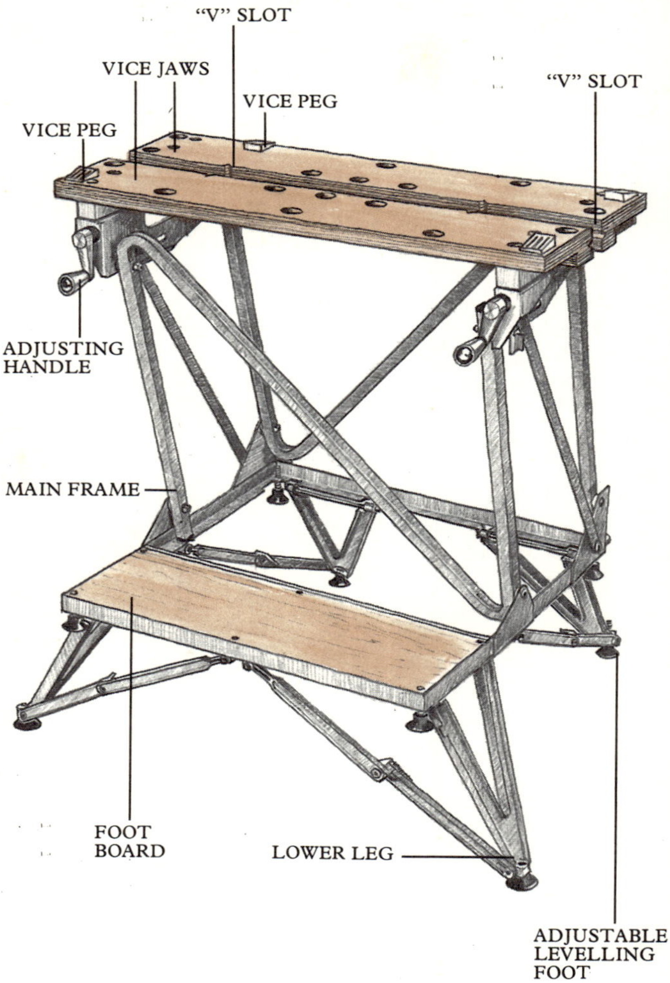

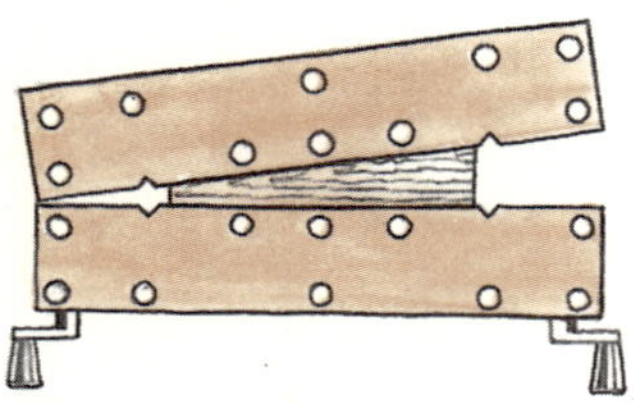

Plastic vice pegs locate in holes drilled in the work surface. They extend the jaw opening and also swivel to hold round and angular work.

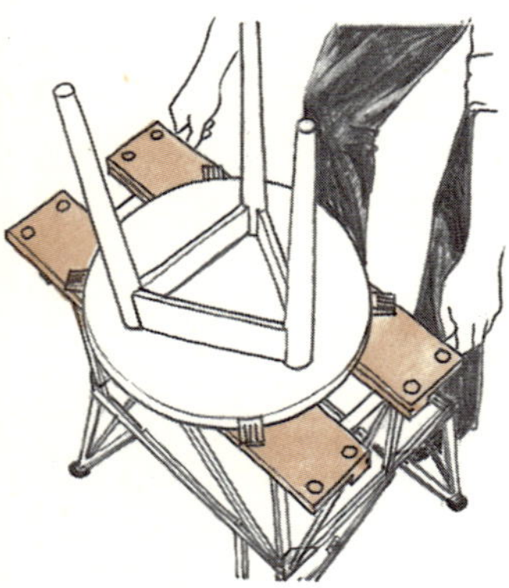

Adjusting the bench
Alter the position of the jaws and pegs in order to hold round and tapered workpieces.

Alternative work levels
Unfold the main frame for sawing wood. Add the lower leg frame to make a workbench.

Pasting Table

OTHER NAME: Paste table
SIZE: *Surface:* 1.8m × 550mm
Working height: 750 to 812mm
MATERIAL: *Top:* hardwood or plywood covered softwood; *Underframe:* softwood, tubular steel
USE: Portable surface for pasting wallpaper

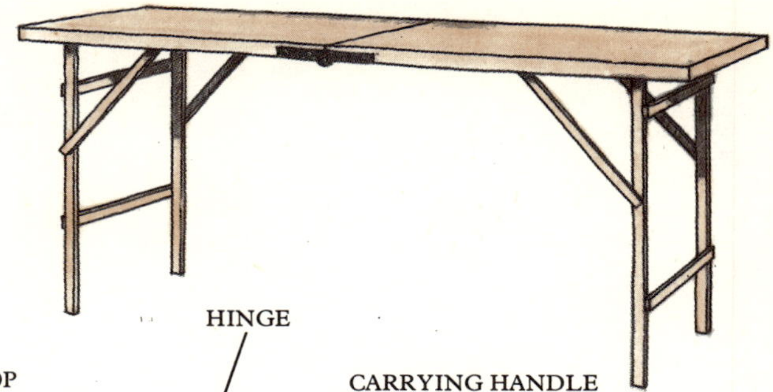

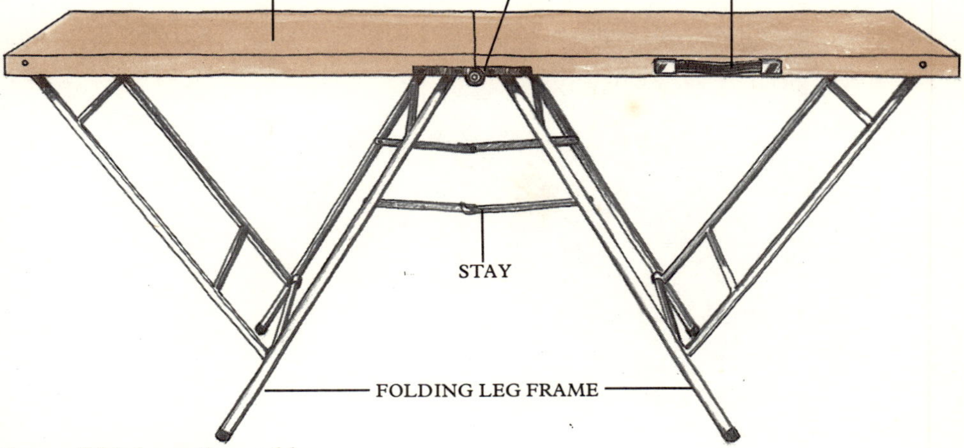

The unfolded pasting table provides a work surface at a convenient height for pasting wallpaper. The underframe folds flat under the top, which then hinges across the centre.

When wallpapering, position the table in the centre of the room to prevent the walls becoming covered in paste.

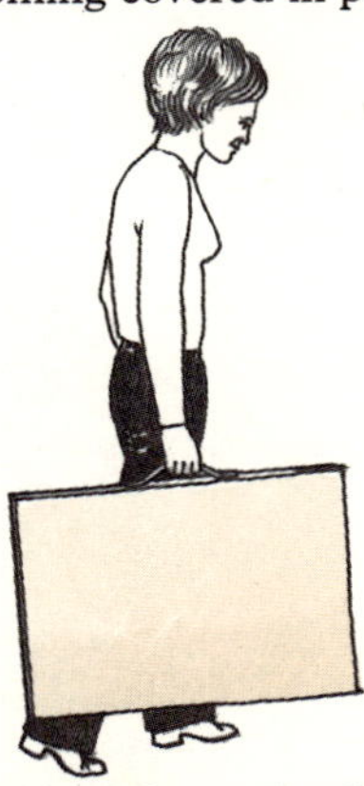

Lightweight underframe
The table's construction makes it easy for it to be carried to the worksite.

Pasting paper
Line up the paper with the far edge of the table. Apply the paste in sections, brushing out from the centre. Pull the paper toward you, line it up with the front edge and paste, brushing toward you. Slide the strip along the table, folding the completed section paste inward, and start again.

Woodworker's Vice

OTHER NAME: Woodworking vice
SIZE: *Jaw width:* 150, 175, 225, 262mm; *Opening capacity:* 112, 200, 325, 375mm
MATERIAL: *Jaws:* cast iron; *Slides/screw/handle:* steel
USE: To hold timber while it is worked

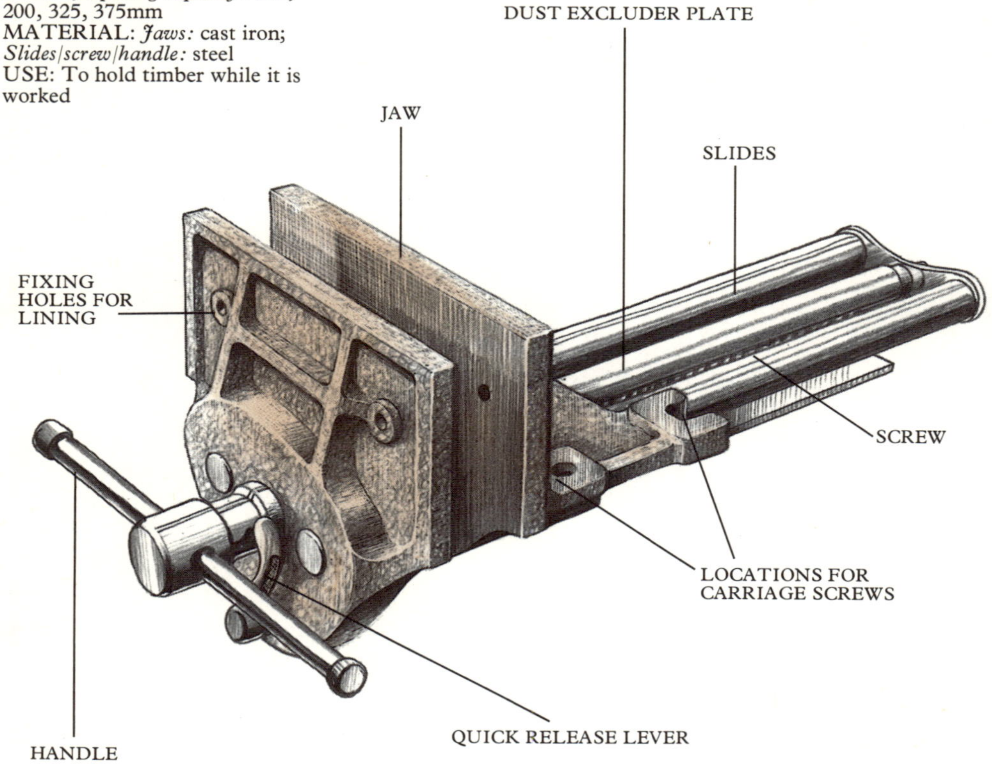

The woodworker's vice is designed to be attached to the underside of a bench top, on the front edge and close to a leg. The movable jaw is operated by the handle which revolves a screw running the length of the vice. Larger vices are fitted with a quick release mechanism which allows the jaw to be moved rapidly to accommodate a workpiece. The release lever is pressed inwards, lifting a half-nut clear of the screw allowing the jaw to move freely.

Line the jaws with hardwood about 18mm thick, to protect the work and prevent sharp tools being damaged. Allow the lining to project above the jaws and place an edging on the movable jaw lining to cover the top edge of the jaw itself.

Fixing a vice
Fix the body of the vice to the underside of the bench with four lag or carriage screws through the fixing holes provided. You may need a packing piece between the vice and the underside of the bench.

Screw the fixed jaw lining, through the jaw into the bench top, with countersunk screws. The movable jaw has two threaded holes for attaching the lining from the inside with countersunk machine screws, or screw the lining through the front of the jaw with countersunk wood screws.

When in use, do not strain the jaws by overtightening the vice. Clamp the work in the centre to prevent distortion or place a piece of wood of equal thickness in the opposite side.

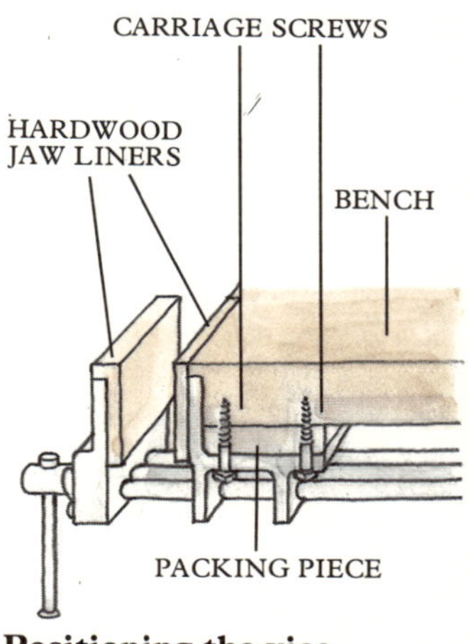

Positioning the vice
Fix the vice so that the fixed jaw lining is flush with the front edge and surface of the bench top.

Clamp-On Vice

OTHER NAME: Portable vice
SIZE: *Jaw width:* 125mm; *Opening capacity:* 87mm
MATERIAL: *Jaws:* aluminium; *Handle/slides/clamp:* steel
USE: To hold lightweight work

There are many small, portable vices for lightweight work, which clamp on to the edge of a table or bench. This version has two L-shaped jaws for holding the work both vertically and horizontally.

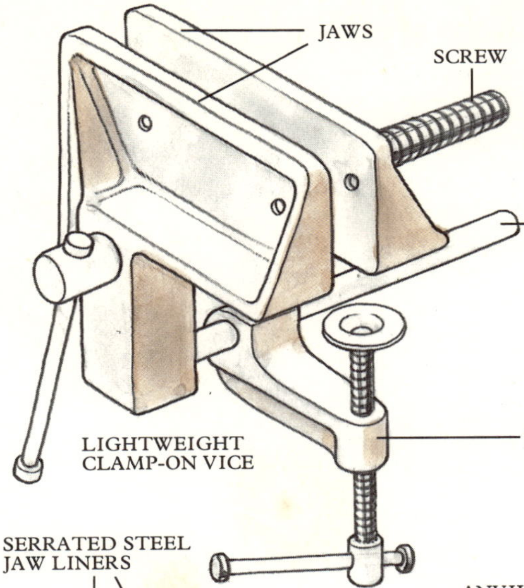

Machinist's Vice

OTHER NAMES: Engineer's vice, mechanic's vice, auto-garage vice, fitter's vice
SIZE: *Jaw width:* 62 to 200mm; *Opening capacity:* 62 to 231mm
MATERIAL: *Jaws:* cast iron; *Jaw linings/handle/screw:* steel
USE: To hold metal while it is being worked

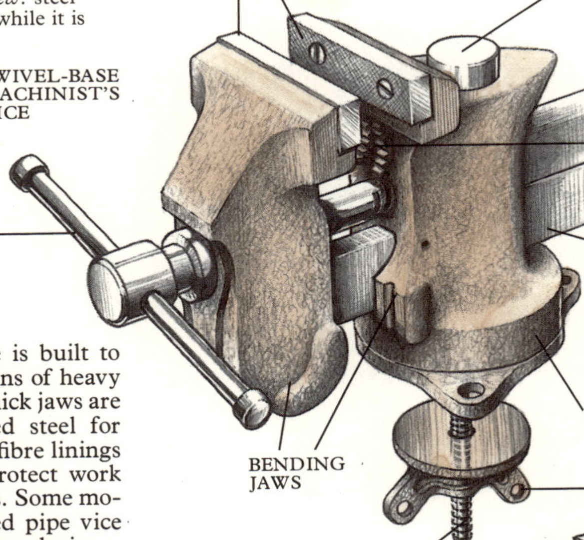

A machinist's vice is built to withstand the strains of heavy metal work. The thick jaws are lined with serrated steel for positive grip. Soft fibre linings can be fitted to protect work from the serrations. Some models have a toothed pipe vice for round stock below the jaws. Vices can be fixed-based or swivel-based, turning through 360° to accommodate different work. On a swivel-based model the base itself is bolted to the bench. A threaded rod on the underside of the vice passes through a hole in the centre of the base, through the bench, and is secured from the underside with a large wing nut and washer which is tightened to hold the vice in position. The joining faces of vice and base are studded and grooved to provide positive locations as the vice is swivelled.

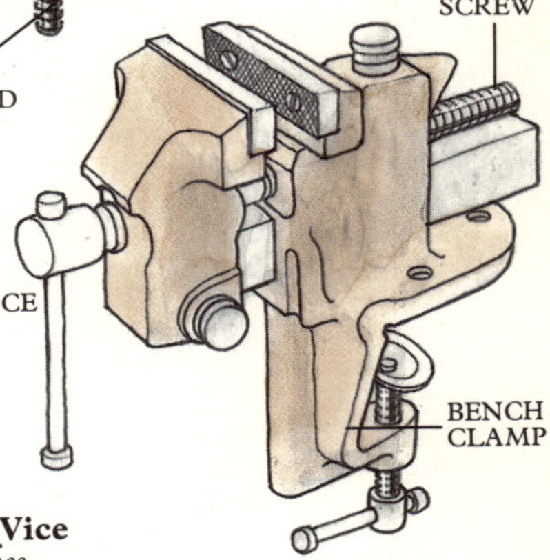

Clamp-on Machinist's Vice
Lightweight machinist's vices are clamped to the bench edge.

Drill Press Vice

OTHER NAME: Machine vice
SIZE: *Jaw width:* 56 to 100mm; *Opening capacity:* 37 to 75 mm
MATERIAL: *Base:* cast iron; *Jaws and screw:* steel
USE: To hold work being machined

The drill press vice is bolted to the worktable of a machine to hold small metal workpieces securely while they are drilled, tapped and so on. The jaws are grooved horizontally and vertically to hold round stock. On some models the jaws can be tilted and swiveled to present the work at an angle to the bit.

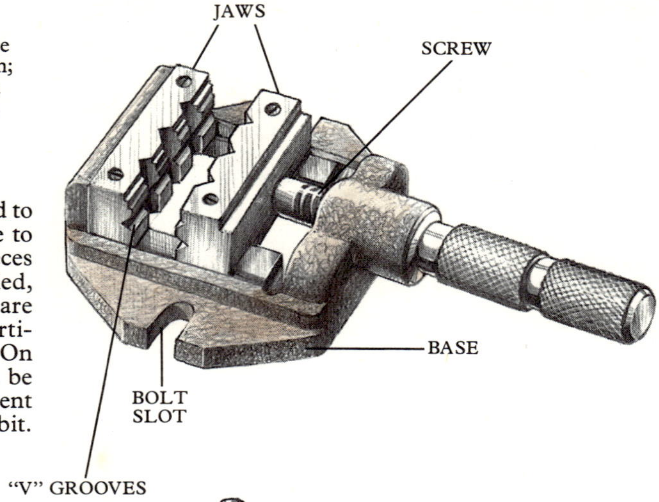

Holdfast

OTHER NAME: Hold down
SIZE: *Maximum reach:* 146, 176.5mm;
Maximum opening: 171, 190mm
MATERIAL: *Shaft/arm:* malleable iron; *Screw:* steel
USE: To hold material flat on a workbench while it is worked.

The lever arm of the holdfast is connected by a pivot to a notched shaft. As the screw and end of the lever arm bears on the end of the shaft, it forces the swivel shoe down on to the work. This wedges the shaft at an angle in its collar, tightening the whole assembly.

The metal collars reinforce the hole into which the shaft fits and should be housed just below the surface of the bench. Fit them so that the holdfast can reach timber being worked along the edge and one end of the bench. Two collars approximately 600mm apart, would enable you to hold large workpieces on the bench.

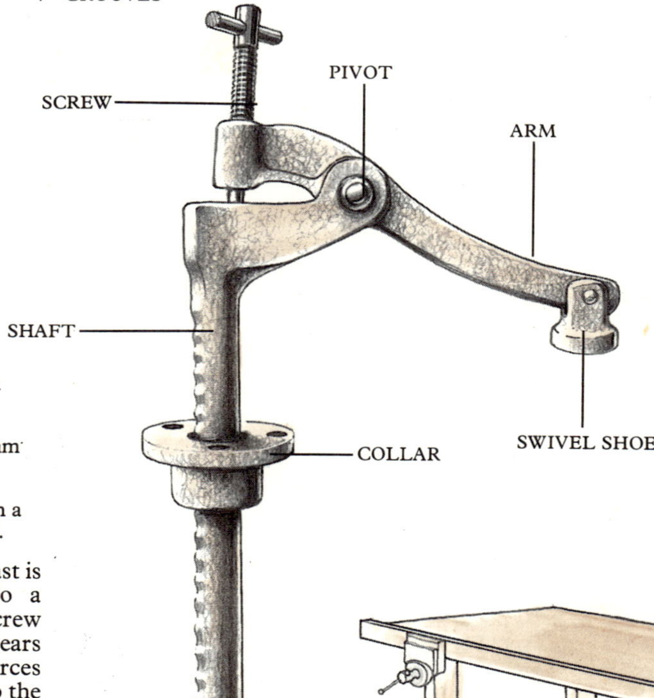

Holding timber
Fit the collar in one leg of the workbench to support long pieces of timber held in the vice at the other end of the bench.

Woodcarver's Screw

OTHER NAME: Carver's bench screw
SIZE: *Length:* 200 and 275mm; *Diameter:* 9 and 18mm
MATERIAL: *Screw:* steel; *Nut:* cast iron
USE: To hold wood being carved

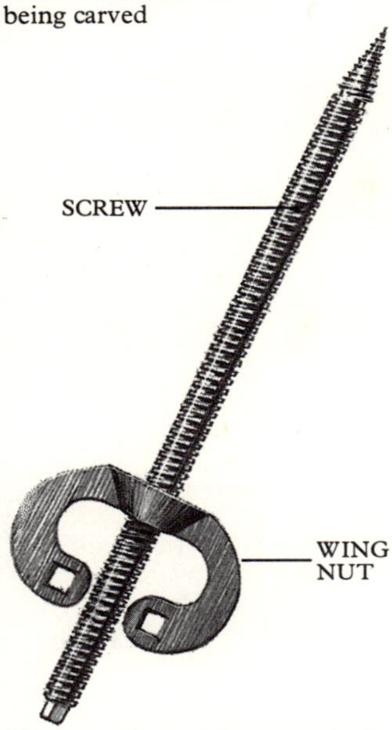

The woodcarver's screw is designed to hold a workpiece which is to be carved from all around. Drill a hole in the bench top and reinforce it with a steel tube. Insert the screw; drive it into a hole drilled in the base of the workpiece. Secure it by fitting the wing nut.

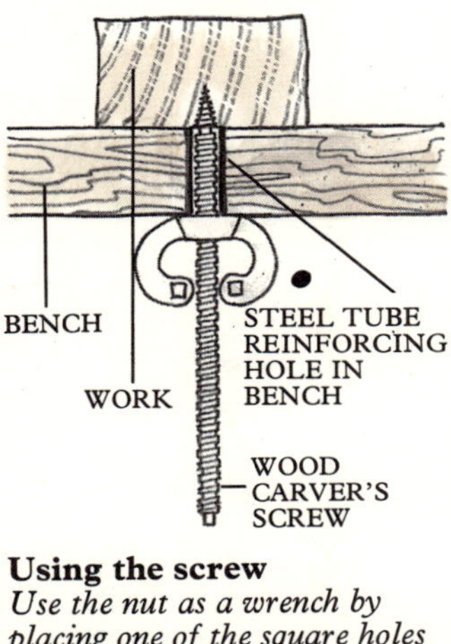

Using the screw
Use the nut as a wrench by placing one of the square holes onto the boss at the end of the screw. Turn to tighten and replace nut. Clamp under wood.

Saddler's Clam

OTHER NAME: Saddler's clamb
SIZE: 1.1m
MATERIAL: Beech
USE: To clamp pieces of leather being worked

The saddler's clam is a simple vice to hold leather parts while they are sewn together. The natural spring of each half of the tool is enough to clamp the leather, but some models have a strip which can be pulled with your foot to provide extra force.

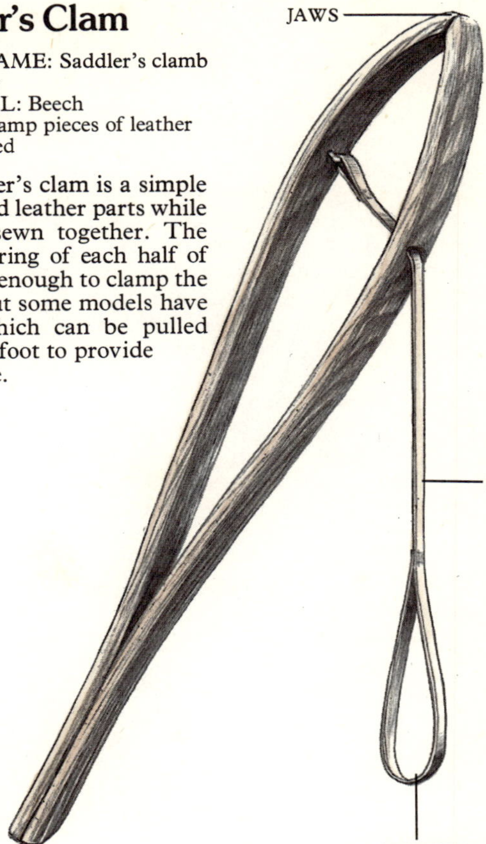

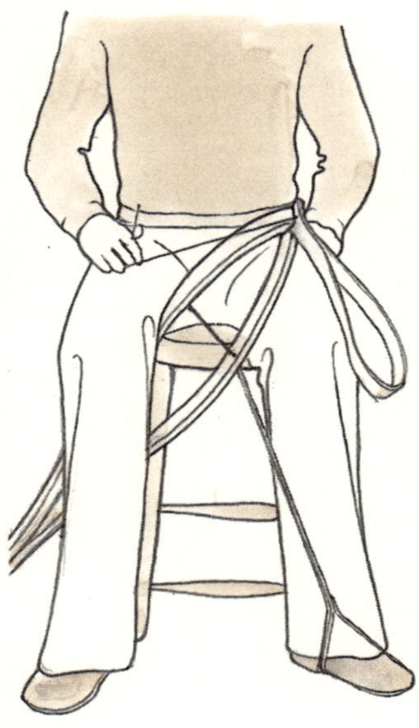

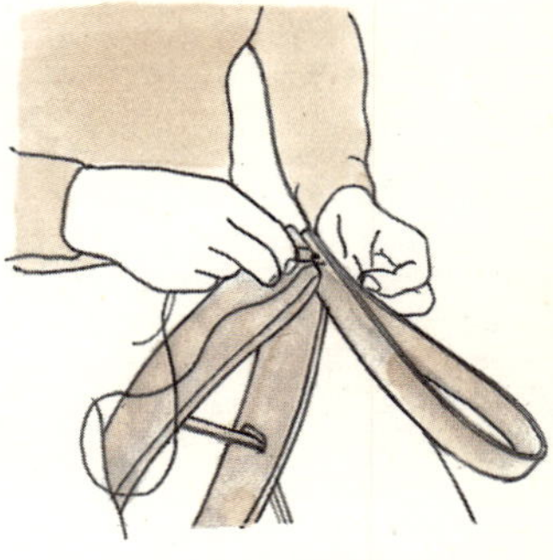

Using the saddler's clam
Use the tool sitting down, holding it at an angle between the knees.

Cramps

Metal devices using screws for holding or clamping small workpieces were first used by locksmiths in the late Middle Ages. When suitable taps and screw boxes became available in the seventeenth century, the metal cramps were taken over by woodworkers, especially carpenters, using their own material. An early "G" cramp in metal is shown in Bergeron (1816), but further development only became possible when machine-cut square threads replaced the "V" thread of the wooden screws.

Handscrews were a portable version of the double screw wooden bench vice with parallel jaws. The modern pattern seems to have been an English brainwave. It is rarely found in foreign workshops or tool lists, although one Russian textbook shows an example, describing it as "heavy and rather clumsy in use".

"G" Cramp

OTHER NAME: "C" cramp
SIZE: Open capacity: 20 to 300mm
MATERIAL: *Frame:* aluminium, malleable iron, pressed steel; *Screw:* steel
USE: To clamp wood and metal work

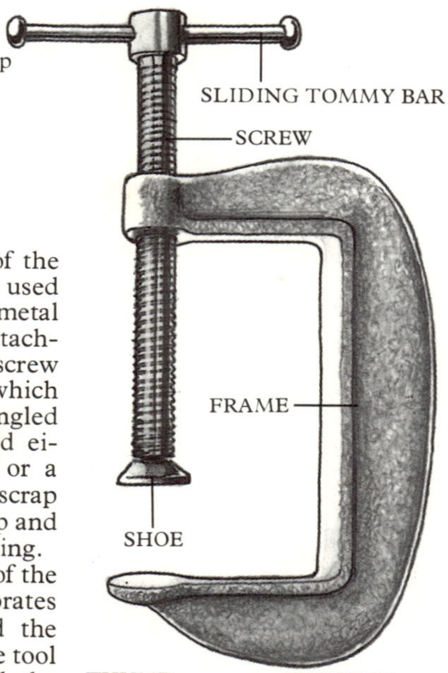

The "G" cramp is one of the most versatile and widely used cramps in both wood and metal workshops. The shoe is attached to the end of the screw thread by a ball joint which enables it to adapt to angled work. Pressure is applied either by a thumb screw or a tommy bar. Use blocks of scrap timber between the cramp and the work to prevent marking.

There is also a version of the "G" cramp which incorporates a knurled wheel around the screw thread, allowing the tool to be spun finger tight with the finger and thumb of one hand while the other hand holds the work. Final pressure is then applied in the normal way. Hand pressure should be sufficient to tighten any "G" cramp. Extra leverage can either damage the work or distort the frame of the cramp.

Small lightweight aluminium cramps are available for model work. Normally they need only be finger tight but extra pressure can be applied by a spanner or screwdriver.

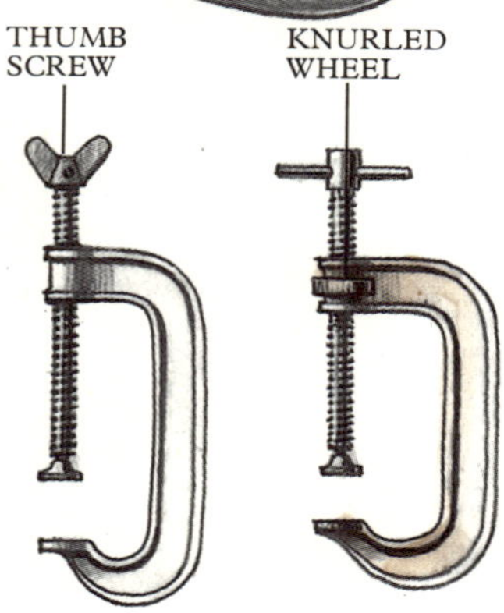

Long reach cramps
"Long reach" cramps are specifically designed to hold the workpiece some distance from the edge.

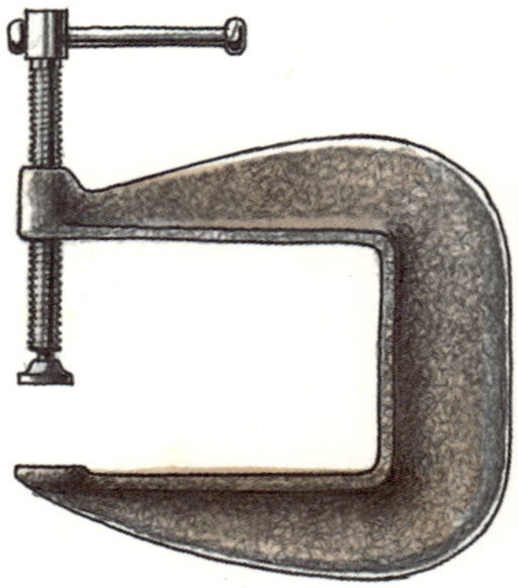

Edge cramps
Special "G" cramps are also available to hold edgings onto the end of a workpiece.

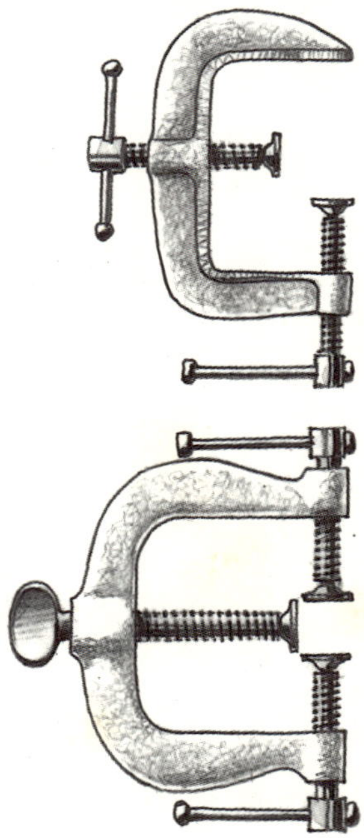

They are either regular "G" cramps with one additional screw thread at right angles to the first, or modified with three screw threads which give greater flexibility for positioning the centre screw accurately on the workpiece.

Handscrew

OTHER NAME: Parallel cramps
SIZE: Open capacity: 50 to 300mm
MATERIAL: *Jaws:* beech, maple, steel; *Screws:* hornbeam, steel
USE: To clamp angled work

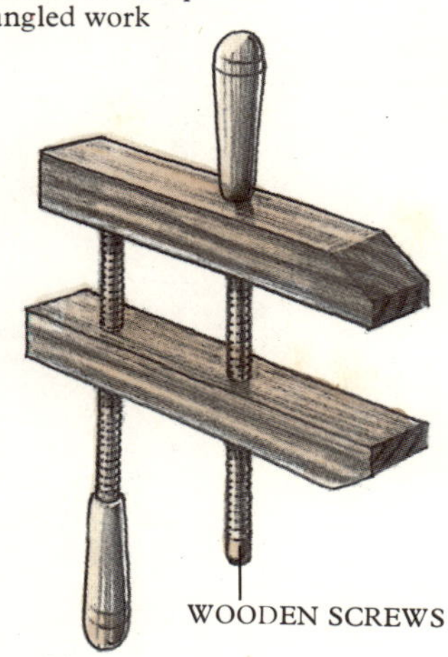

Wooden handscrews have been used for many years in woodworking shops. Earlier designs have two wooden screws to adjust the jaws. The handle end of the forward screw runs freely in a hole while the other end of the screw works in a threaded hole in the other jaw. The rear screw follows the same arrangement, but the other way around.

Modern handscrews are fitted with metal threaded spindles in place of a threaded hole in the jaw itself. These rotate freely in the jaw, to accommodate angled work. The screws are also metal and the direction of thread reverses halfway along the rod so that each jaw can be advanced or retracted at the same time.

Adjusting the handscrew
Grip each handle and rotate the tool either toward or away from you to close or open the jaws (right). Place the tool on the work and adjust the jaws to fit. Tighten them by adjusting the rear screw.

Protect the jaws from accidental gluing during use with a coating of wax, or place paper or plastic sheeting between the tool and the job.

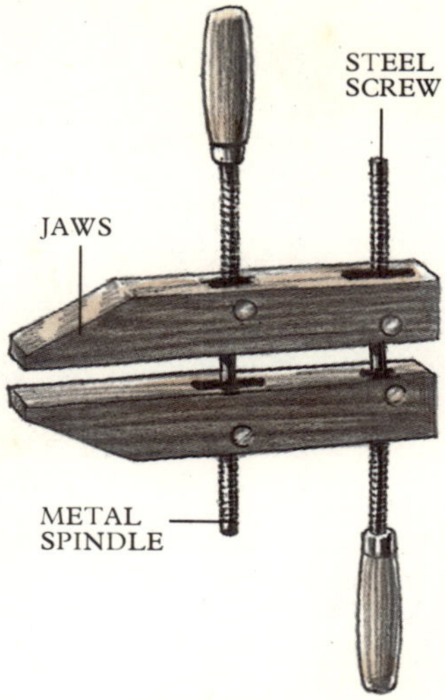

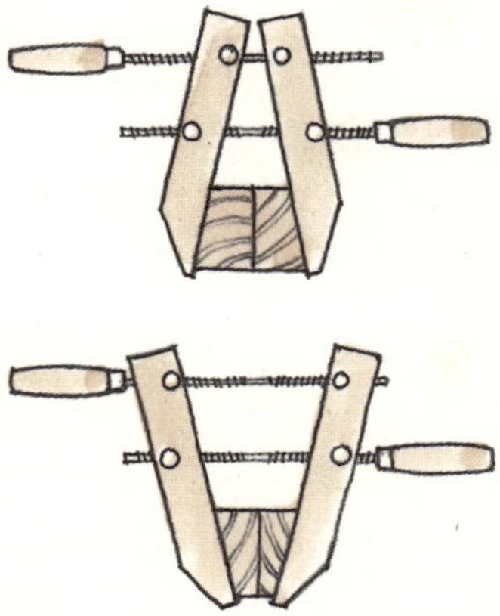

Handscrews adjust to any angle.

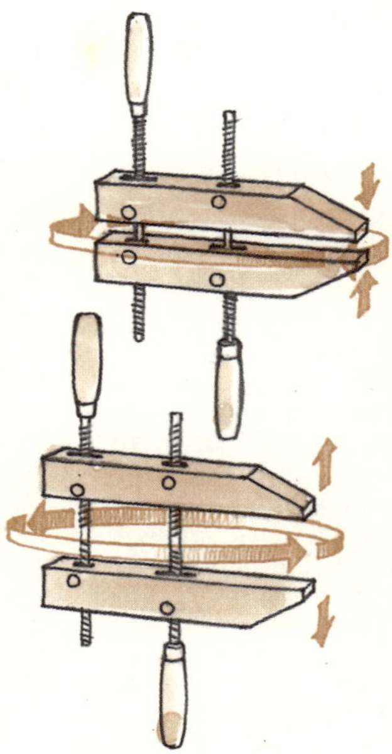

Spring Cramp

SIZE: Open capacity 25 to 75mm
MATERIAL: Steel
USE: To provide light pressure while gluing

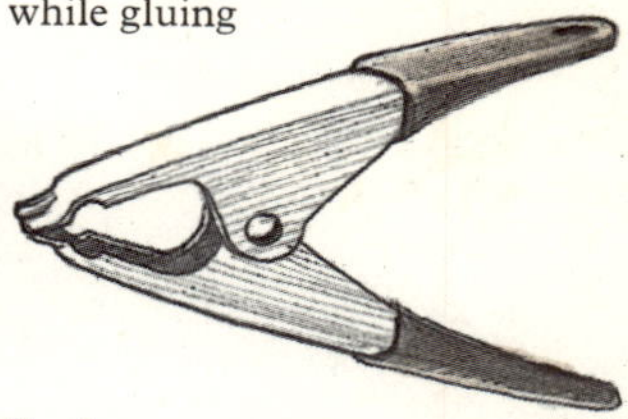

Spring cramps are entirely hand operated. The jaws are opened by squeezing the handles together. The cramp is positioned on the work and the handles released.

The jaws may be shaped to clamp on round stock as well as flat areas. On some models, the jaws are dipped in plastic to prevent them marking the work. If the surface is too delicate for such local pressure, spread the load by inserting scraps of hardboard between the cramp and the work.

Joiner's Dog

OTHER NAMES: Joint clamp, pinch dog
SIZE: 10 to 75mm
MATERIAL: Steel
USE: To hold boards together while gluing

The two tapered points of the joiner's dog straddle the joint between two boards being glued together. As the dog is driven into the end grain it automatically pulls the boards tightly together. For a tight glue line along the entire length of the board, make sure that the two halves of the joint are completely flat.

Fast Action Cramp

SIZE: Jaw: 100 to 1000mm
MATERIAL: *Jaws:* malleable cast iron; *Bar/screw:* steel; *Handle:* hardwood
USE: To clamp woodwork

The fast action cramp is used in similar circumstances to the "G" cramp.

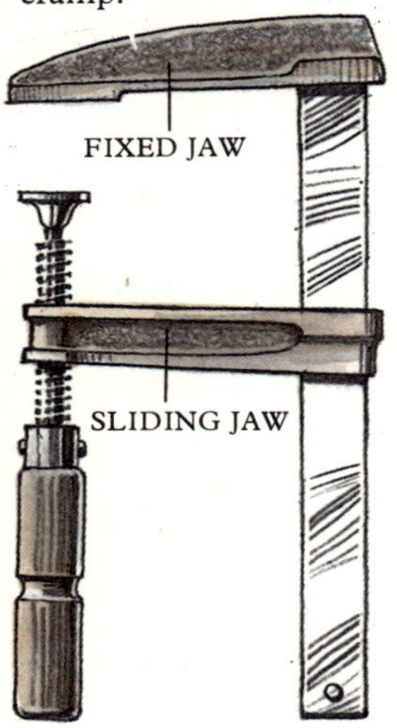

The jaw holding the adjusting screw is free to move on the normal rectangular sectioned steel bar. The fixed jaw is fastened to the work and the movable jaw is slid along the bar until the ball-jointed shoe also comes into contact with the work. The handle is then turned, automatically locking the movable jaw in place as pressure is applied.

Some fast action clamps are supplied with nylon jaw covers to protect the work. Alternatively, you can use softwood blocks in the normal way.

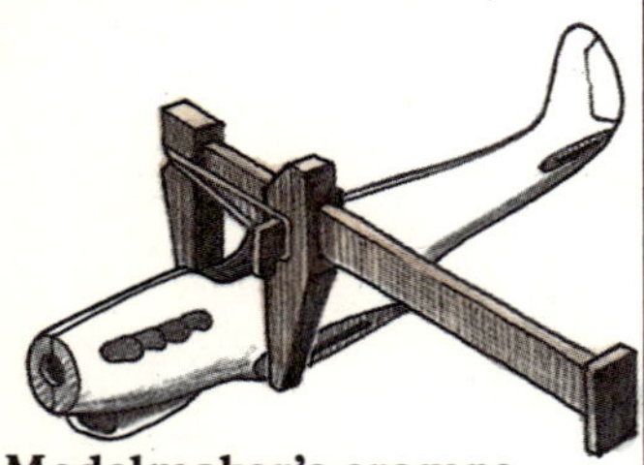

Modelmaker's cramps
These are small solid nylon cramps which work on the fast action principle. Rubber bands apply pressure to the jaws.

Bar Cramp

SIZE: *Length:* 600 to 1500mm; *Capacity:* 460 to 1370mm
MATERIAL: *Bar:* steel; *Cramp head:* malleable iron
USE: To hold large boards or frames together while gluing

The bar cramp is a simple rectangular sectioned steel bar, drilled at intervals to take the fixing peg of a cast iron tail slide. The retaining peg, a tapered steel pin attached to the tail slide by a stout length of chain, is inserted in the hole behind the slide to act as a stop. A nut and bolt is located in the last hole of the bar to prevent the tail slide falling off. At the other end of the bar is an adjustable jaw which takes up final adjustment by means of a steel screw.

Some bar cramps have tail slides with an integral spring-loaded catch operated by a push button. With the button depressed, the slide can be adjusted to a new position where the pin will automatically locate in the hole. Unlike the loose retaining pin this type of catch cannot fall out as the cramp is turned over.

There are also some models which have a bar with notches on the underside instead of holes. The tail slide has a fixed pin which locates in the notches and tightens under load.

An extra long cramp can be improvised by bolting two bars together side by side.

Cramp Heads

SIZE: To fit 25mm wooden rail
MATERIAL: Malleable iron
USE: To make up a bar cramp

Cramp heads are used to build a bar cramp to any length. One foot of the cramp is fixed and the other adjusts to locate over a wooden rail of the desired length, 25mm thick and a minimum of 38mm wide. The cramps are secured by steel pins, which pass through 10mm diameter holes drilled through the rail. As the length of the rail increases it may be necessary to increase the width in proportion to keep the cramp sufficiently rigid.

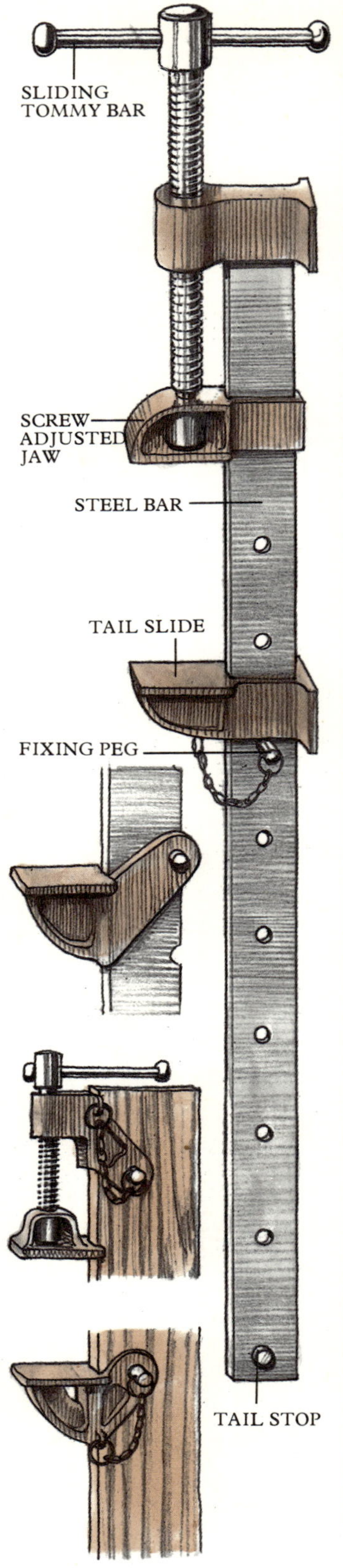

Pipe Cramp

SIZE: *Length:* as required; *Bar:* 12 and 19mm
MATERIAL: *Bar:* steel; *Cramp heads:* cast iron
USE: To hold large boards or frames together while gluing

The pipe cramp provides another way to make up a cramp of non-standard length. A black iron or mild steel pipe of convenient size is threaded at one end to take the frame of a screw adjusted jaw. The sliding jaw runs on the pipe to the required position. It is locked either by a lever-operated cam, or a one-way clutch mechanism which operates when the slide is under load.

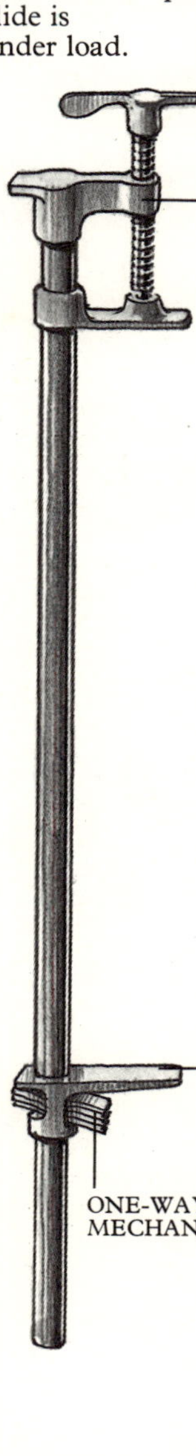

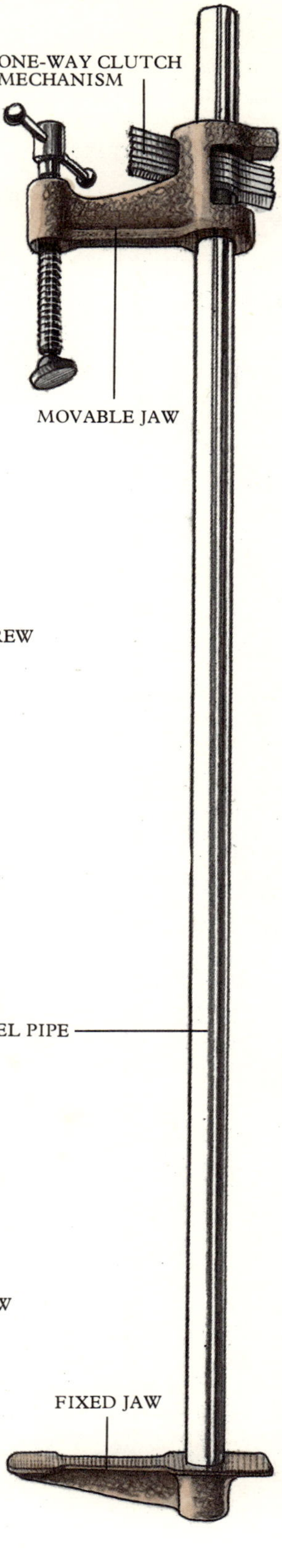

Cramping frames
Position each bar cramp in line with and centred on the joints. Use softwood blocks to protect the work and to spread the load. Position the tail slide to fit the work, leaving the adjustable shoe enough thread for final adjustment. Glue and assemble the frame. Increase the pressure on the cramps working from one to the other to even up the forces.

When the frame has been fully clamped excess glue may be gradually pressed out from the joints; the cramps may need slight adjustment after a few minutes.

Cramping planks
Bar cramps are used to hold glued planks together when making a wide board. Place the cramps alternately over and under the workpiece to prevent the boards from bowing in either direction.

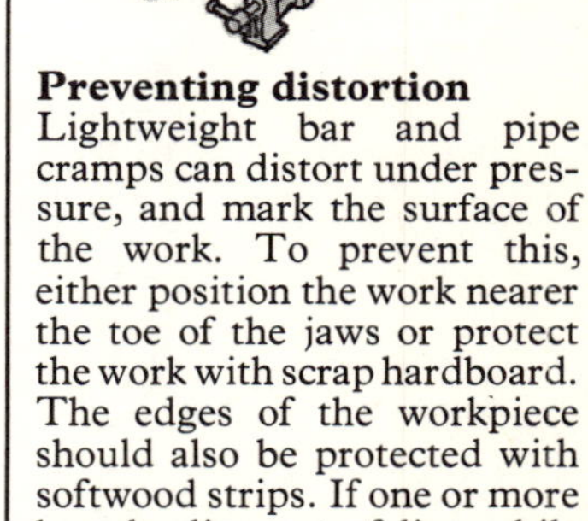

Preventing distortion
Lightweight bar and pipe cramps can distort under pressure, and mark the surface of the work. To prevent this, either position the work nearer the toe of the jaws or protect the work with scrap hardboard. The edges of the workpiece should also be protected with softwood strips. If one or more boards slips out of line while clamping, place a softwood block over the joint and knock it flush with a mallet.

"T" Bar Cramp

SIZE: *Length:* 900 to 2100mm; *Capacity:* 750 to 2000mm
MATERIAL: *Bar:* steel; *Cramp heads:* malleable iron
USE: Heavy duty cramping

The "T" bar cramp is a heavy duty version of the bar cramp. The "T" section of the bar is designed to resist bending when under pressure.

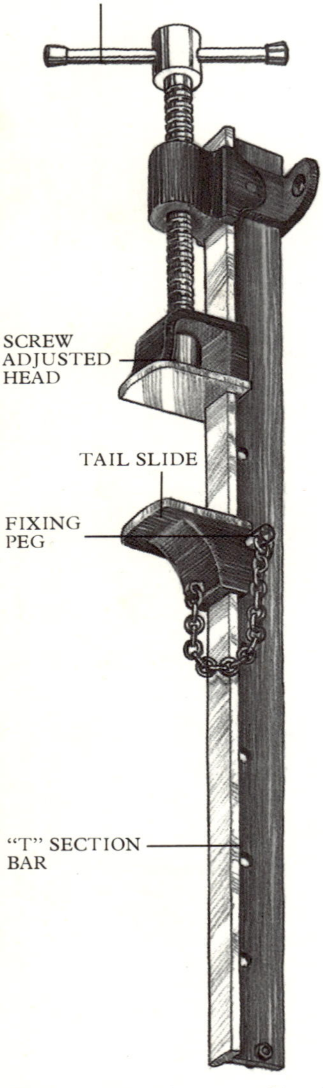

The cramp heads are machined to fit over the top piece of the section and are proportionally larger than those used on standard bar cramps.

Web Cramp

OTHER NAMES: Strap cramp, band cramp
SIZE: *Length:* 4.5m; *Width:* 25mm
MATERIAL: *Webbing:* nylon; *Mechanism:* steel
USE: To apply even pressure to frames while gluing

The web cramp is used to apply even pressure around square and tapered frames. It is especially useful for making or mending chairs. The loop formed by the webbing is extended to fit around the frame being glued.

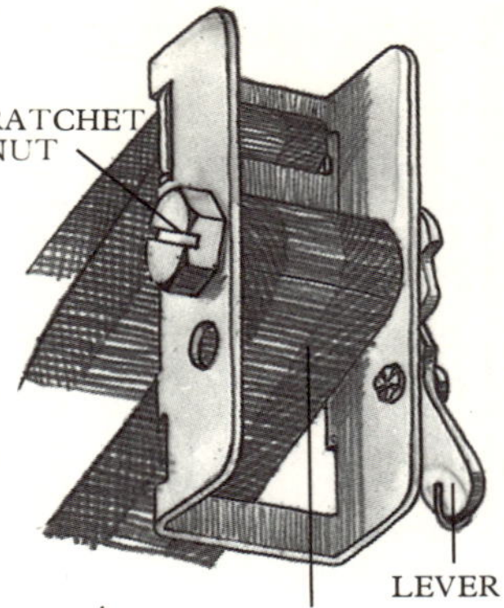

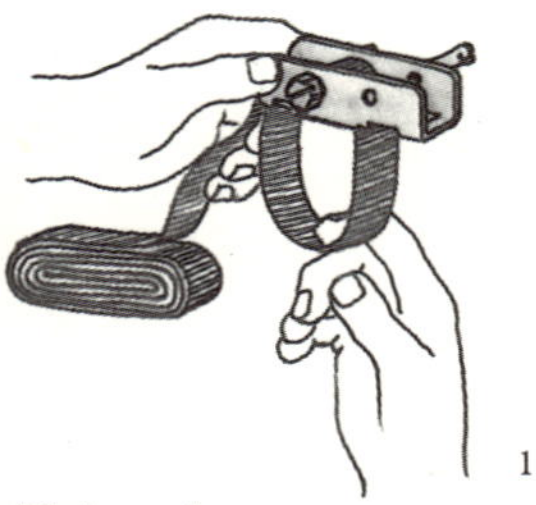

Using the cramp
The cramp is tightened by pulling on the free end of the webbing (1). Additional pressure is applied by tightening a ratchet nut on the mechanism with either a spanner or a screwdriver (2). To loosen the cramp, operate the lever which locks the rachet and pull on the webbing (3).

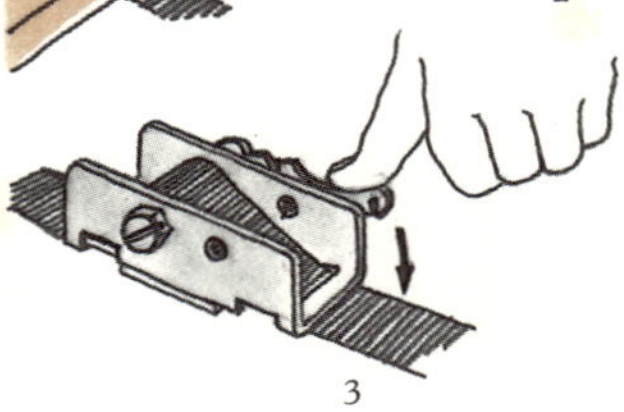

Jet Cramp

SIZE: Length: 300, 600, 900mm
MATERIAL: Steel
USE: To cramp wood and metal work

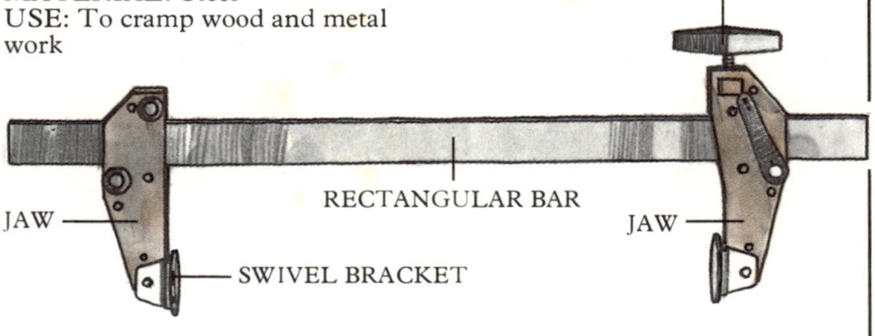

A jet cramp consists of two movable jaws which slide on a plain rectangular sectioned bar to any position to form a cramp of the required length. Both jaws are fitted with swivel brackets on which protective rubber, smooth metal, textured metal or L shaped pads can be fitted. When both jaws are in contact with the work, the slack can be taken up by turning the thumb screw on one of the jaws. Both the jaws are reversible so that outward pressure can be applied.

Frame Cramp

SIZE: Up to 900mm square
MATERIAL: *Corner blocks:* plastic, aluminium; *Tension device:* steel screws, plastic cord
USE: To cramp a mitred picture frame while gluing

Frame cramps are usually used in sets of four. Each corner block is held under tension in one of two ways. The simplest form consists of a cord passed around the frame and back through a cleat. The cord is pulled and held in tension by the cleat, so that equal pressure is applied to each joint.

In the alternative design, tension is provided by knurled nuts running on threaded rods which pass from block to block. Apply even pressure alternately to each joint.

Improvised frame cramp
Protect the corners of the frame with thick cardboard. Cut a length of strong twine twice the circumference of the frame. Double it and tie it around the frame. Insert a piece of dowel between the lengths of twine and turn it to apply tension. Tie off the dowel against the frame until the glue is set.

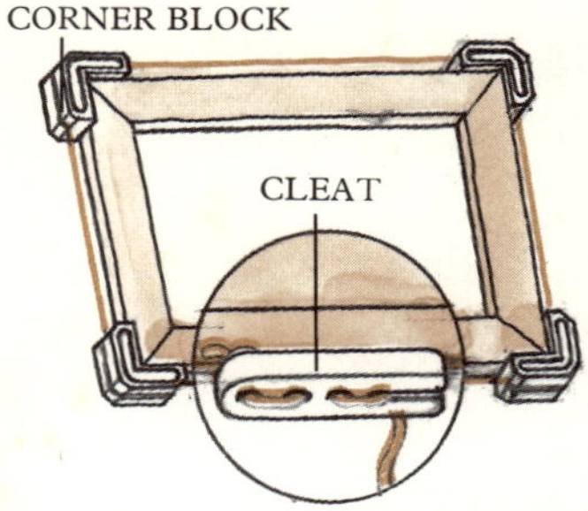

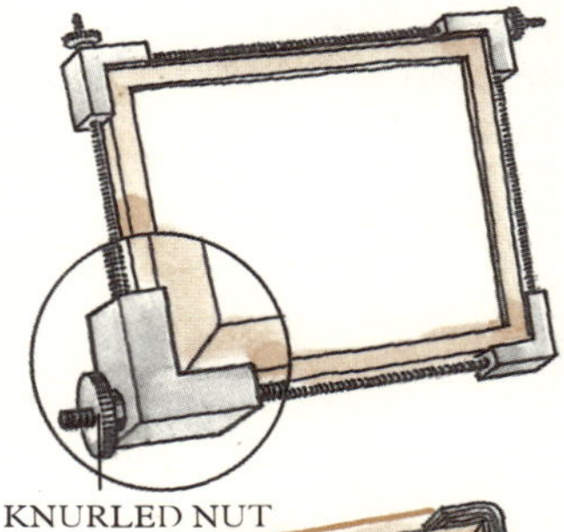

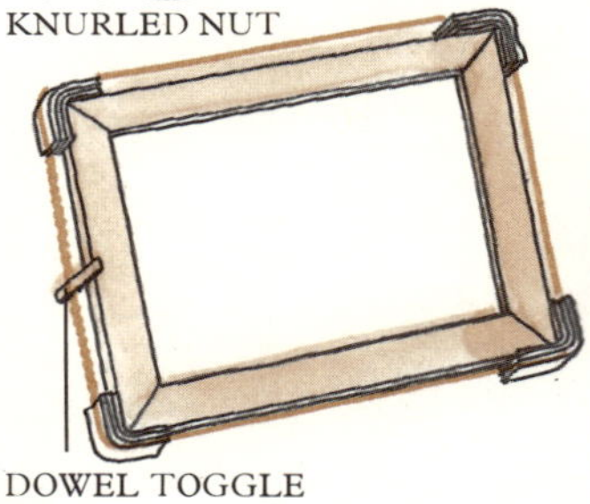

Mitre Cramp

OTHER NAME: Corner cramp
SIZE: Capacity 50 to 115mm
MATERIAL: Aluminium alloy, cast iron
USE: To cramp mitred joints

The mitre cramp has two screw adjusted "feet" set at right angles to each other, which will hold the two halves of a mitre joint against a right angled fence. Some cramps incorporate a slot, which bisects the angle; this guides the blade of a tenon saw to cut the parts of the joint accurately to 45°.

After gluing the two halves of the joint, locate them in the cramp together ensuring that they meet before pressure is applied to either screw. Gently adjust the pressure alternately to each half of the joint until it is firmly held in place. The joint can be further strengthened by nailing.

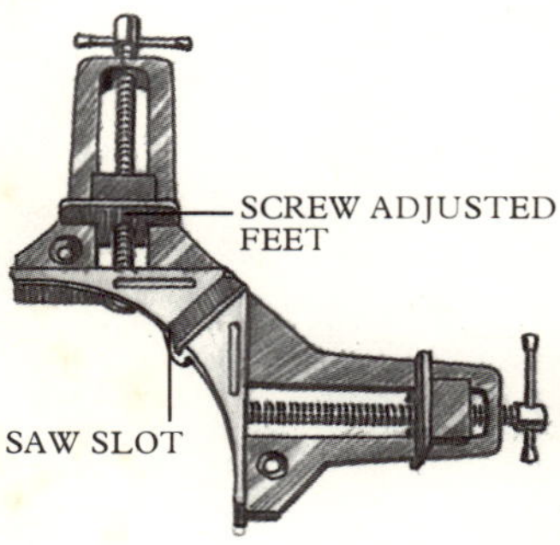

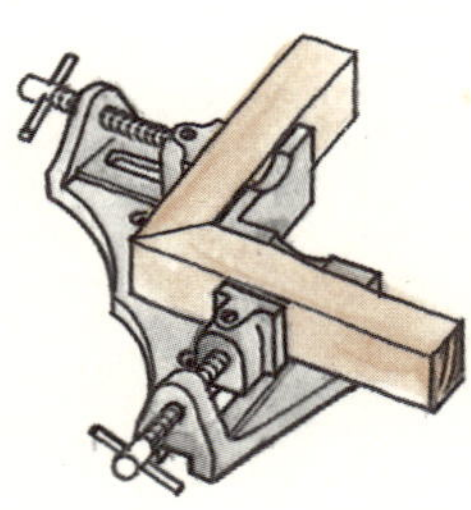

Mitre cramps in place.

Flooring Cramp

SIZE: To fit a 38 to 90mm wide joist
MATERIAL: Various
USE: To close up floorboards before nailing them to joists

Flooring cramps are used to make sure that floorboards fit together snugly.

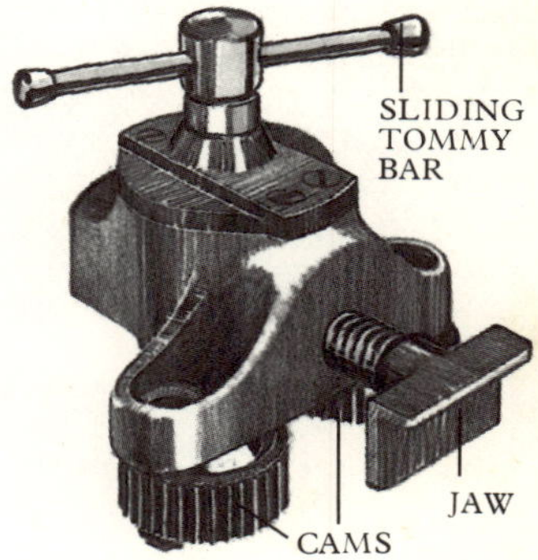

The cramp has spring-loaded cams on the underside which fit over the joist behind the floorboard. The jaw locates over the edge of the board and pressure is applied through beveled gears by turning the tommy bar. As the pressure increases the knurled cams tighten on the joists.

Improvised flooring cramp

Lay three pairs of wedges evenly along the length of the board. Nail scrap timber behind the wedges and drive them toward each other.

Sharpening Tools

For sharpening, natural stones such as Washita or Arkansas produce the keenest edge, but they are very expensive. Man-made stones are produced from vitrified aluminium oxide or silicon carbide grit. The resulting stone is harder than natural stone, but it does not normally have such fine grit or the close density which characterizes the very best of sharp edges. The grit is graded as coarse, medium and fine. Coarse grit stones would be used to regrind a damaged blade; medium and fine grit for sharpening.

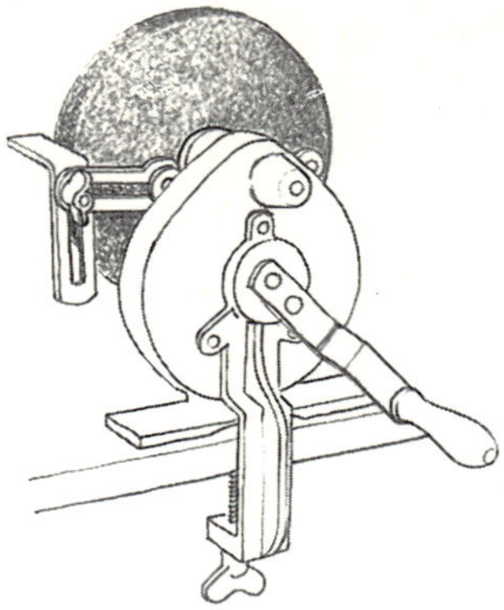

Hand grinder
Hand cranked grinding wheels are still available, but they are inconvenient to use with one hand only.

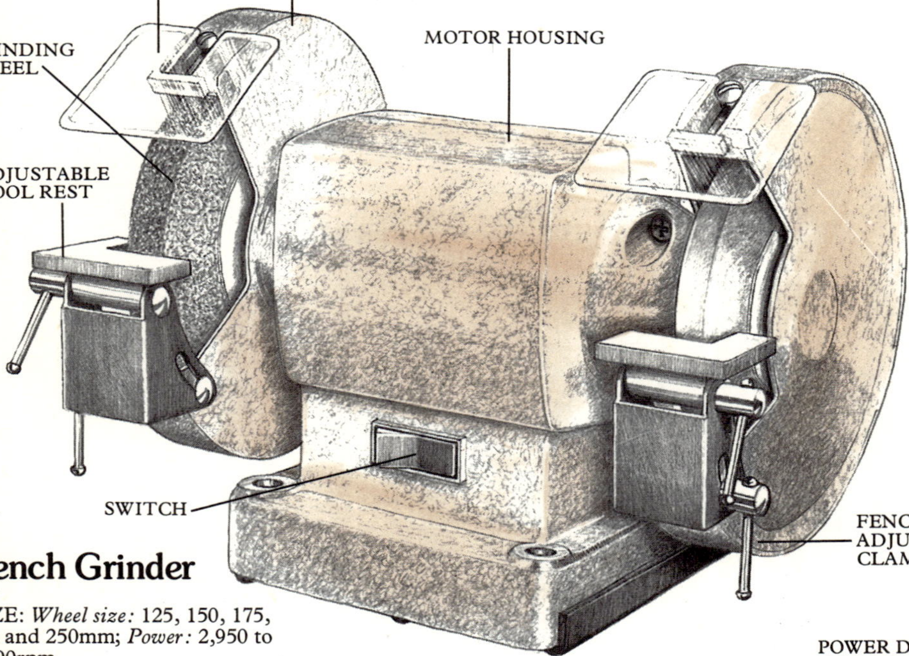

Bench Grinder

SIZE: *Wheel size:* 125, 150, 175, 200 and 250mm; *Power:* 2,950 to 3,600rpm
MATERIALS: Various
ACCESSORIES: Grinding wheels, wire wheels, buffing mops
USE: To sharpen tools and clean up metal

A bench grinder can grind the cutting edge of tools square and sharp, remove burrs from the anvil ends of cold chisels, repair screwdrivers, drill bits and the point of punches, sharpen scissors and polish metal work. Most bench grinders have an electric motor which drives two wheels simultaneously, so you can mount wheels of different abrasive or grain at each end, or couple a wire wheel or buffing mop with a medium grinding wheel.

The grinder must be bolted firmly to the bench top and must be fitted with wheel guards, eye shields and tool rests at all times.

Grinder size is specified by the maximum size of wheel it can take. Choose a 125 to 175mm grinder for use in the home workshop.

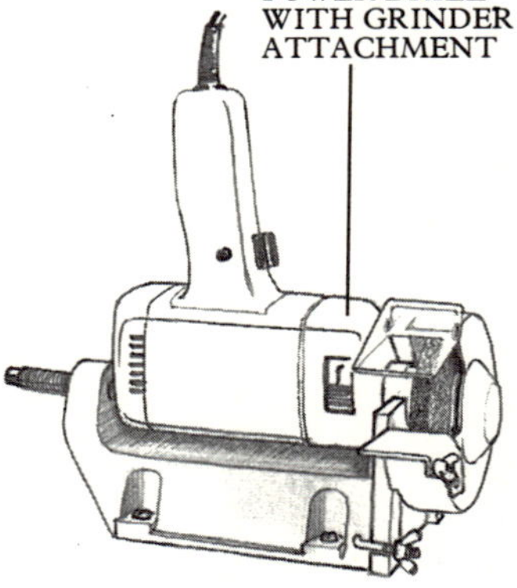

Grinding wheels

Bench grinder wheels are not natural stones, but grains of abrasive material bonded together at a high temperature. The abrasive material is either aluminium oxide, which is ideal for grinding steel tools, or silicon carbide, which is good for brass, aluminium or copper.

The *grain size* determines whether the wheel will be coarse, medium or fine. The *grade* of the wheel refers to the hardness of the bond. Soft grades let the abrasive fall away easily and are used to grind hard materials, whereas hard grade wheels are for grinding soft materials. The *structure* of the wheel depends on how closely the grains are packed together. Wheels can be close, medium or wide structured. Hard materials should be ground on close structured wheels, whereas wide structured wheels are less likely to clog with soft materials.

Testing the wheel

Make certain that a grinding wheel is in good condition before fitting it. To inspect for cracks, suspend the wheel on a rod through its centre hole and tap it with a piece of wood. A good wheel will ring; a dull sound indicates a crack and the wheel should not be used.

Never run a wheel faster than at the designated safe speed, which is indicated on the wheel.

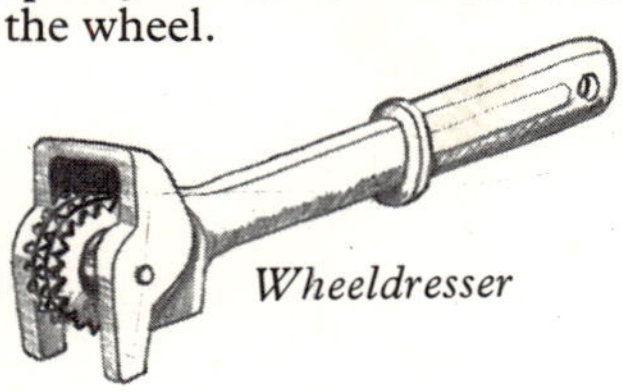

Wheeldresser

Dressing the wheel

The wheel needs "dressing" periodically. The abrasive grains wear in use, becoming dull and clogged with metal particles. The surface must be abraded with a dresser, which has revolving star wheels, to expose new grains.

To dress the wheel, place the dresser on the tool rest and move it from side to side across the edge of the wheel.

Mounting a wheel

Remove the wheel guard and slacken the clamp nut. Remove the wheel along with the washer. Fit a new wheel and replace the washer and lock nut. Replace the guard, switch on the machine and let it run at top speed for about one minute before using it.

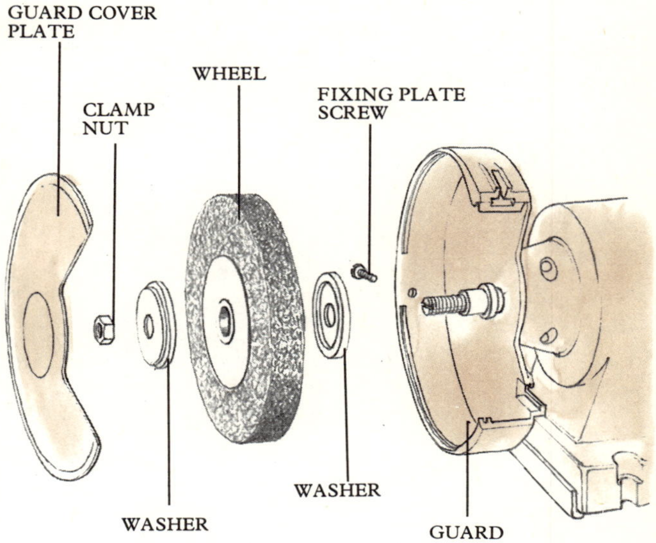

Grinding a chisel or plane blade

Chisel and plane blades are ground in the same way. Always wear protective goggles.

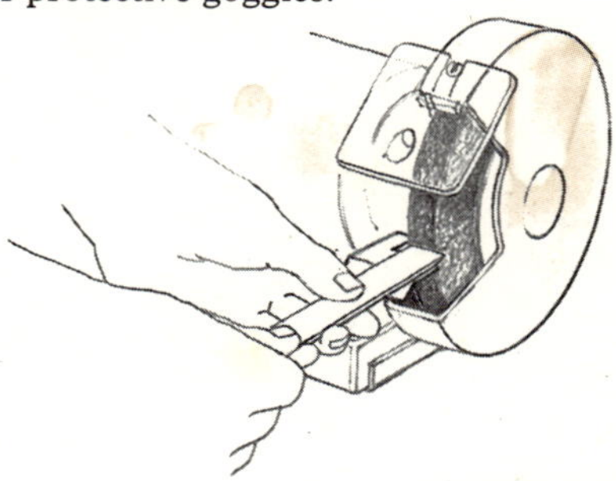

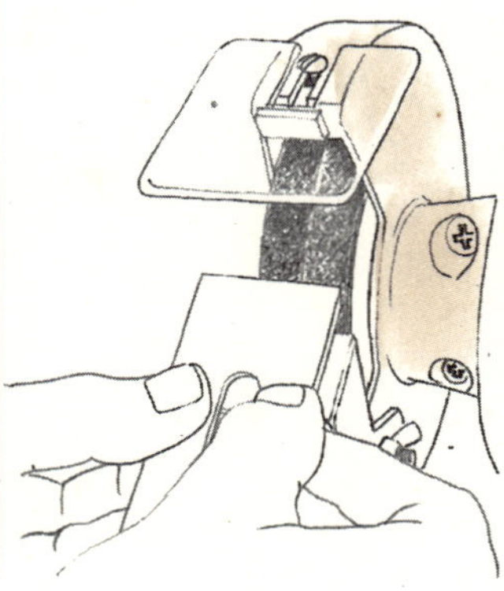

To repair a chipped or rounded cutting edge, set the tool rest 3mm from the wheel and grind the edge square, keeping the blade perpendicular to the wheel and moving it from side to side.

To grind the bevel, set the tool rest to present the blade at an angle of 25° to the wheel. Move the blade lightly from side to side across the wheel dipping the tool repeatedly in water to keep it cool. After grinding, hone the edge on an oilstone.

Grinding a screwdriver

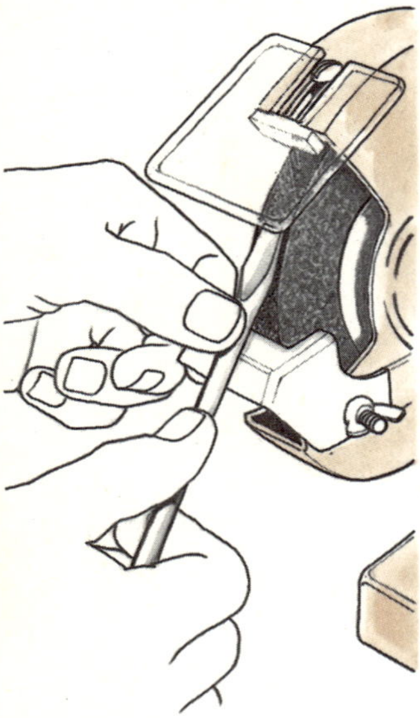

Repair a damaged screwdriver tip by hollow grinding each side and finally grinding the tip square.

Grinding drill bits

Hold the drill bit in one hand and the shank in the other. Press the bit lightly against the wheel, turning the drill in a clockwise direction while following the angle on the end of the bit. Repeat with the other cutting edge and check that the point is central. Do not allow the bit to overheat while grinding, but avoid using water as a coolant as it could cause hair cracks in the bit.

Holding the drill bit

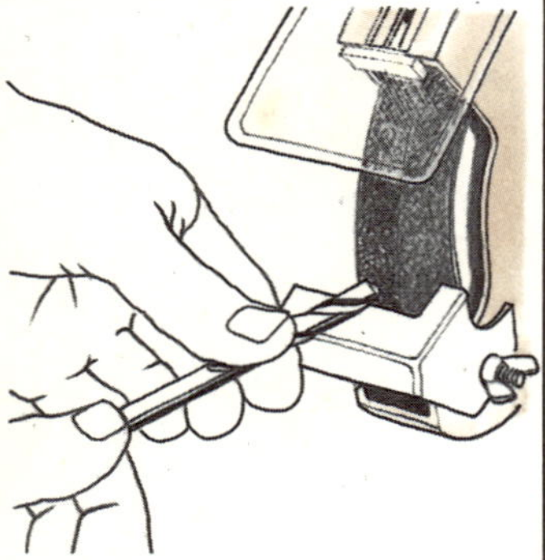

Align the one cutting edge with the edge of the wheel.

Grinding a punch

Grind the symmetrical point of a punch by holding the tool at the required angle to the wheel and turning it in the fingers.

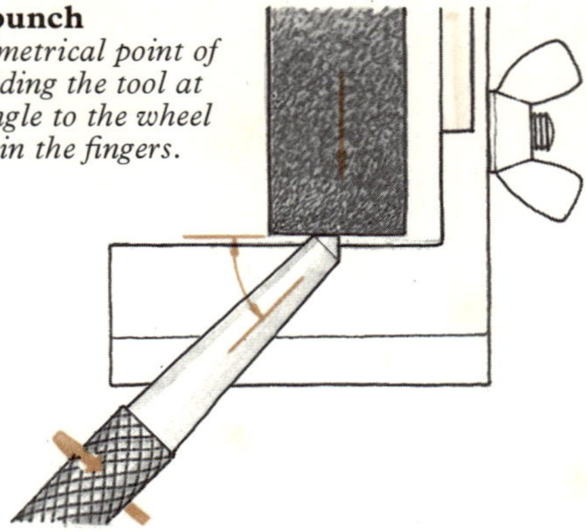

Grinding scissor blades

To sharpen scissors open the blades and support the tool on the rest, presenting the cutting angle to the wheel. Press the blade lightly against the wheel moving it from pivot to point. Grind both blades in the same way and finally hone the edges with a slipstone.

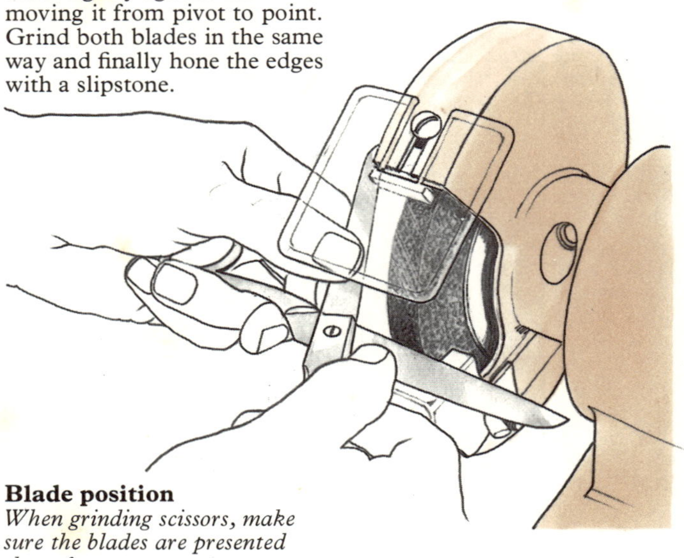

Blade position

When grinding scissors, make sure the blades are presented shear face uppermost.

Wire brushing and buffing

The wire brush removes rust and keys the surface of metal. The technique for using it is identical to that shown for brush drill attachments on page 297.

A buff is used with a polishing compound to polish metal objects. Set the machine running, apply the stick of compound to the buff and hold the workpiece firmly against it. Never hold a sharp edge directly against a buff or it will catch and throw the workpiece.

Holding the workpiece

Hold the workpiece so that the edge faces downward and press the object against the wheel just below the centre of the buff.

Drill Bit Sharpener

SIZE: Takes drill bits 3 to 9mm;
MATERIAL: Various
USE: To sharpen twist drill bits

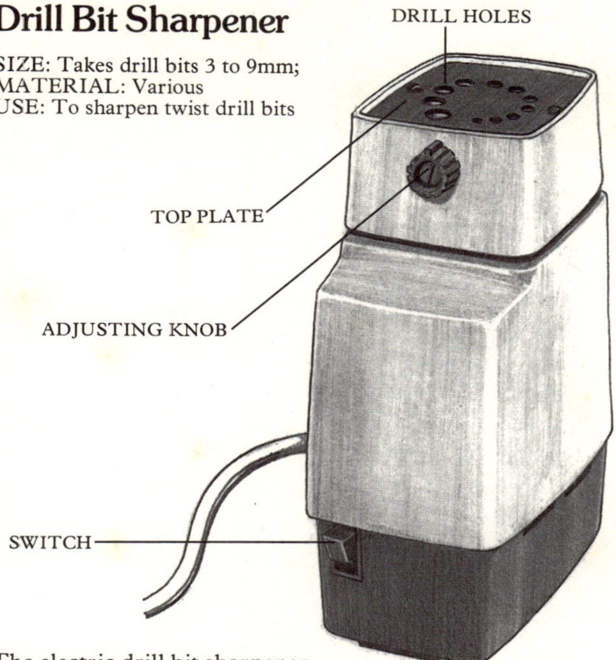

The electric drill bit sharpener makes the normally tricky job of regrinding drill bits easy.

Fit the bit in the appropriate hole in the top plate. Turn the bit clockwise until it stops. Holding it in this position, depress the starter switch and apply a light to medium pressure on the drill bit for 1 to 3 seconds. Do not revolve the bit during the grinding. Remove the bit, revolve it half a turn so that the sharpened side faces the centre of the top plate and replace it in the hole. Repeat the grinding sequence.

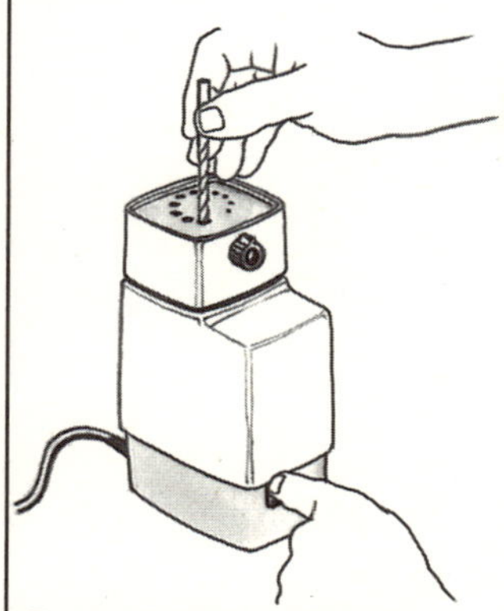

Inserting the drill bit
With the adjusting knob in the central position, insert the bit in the smallest hole that takes it.

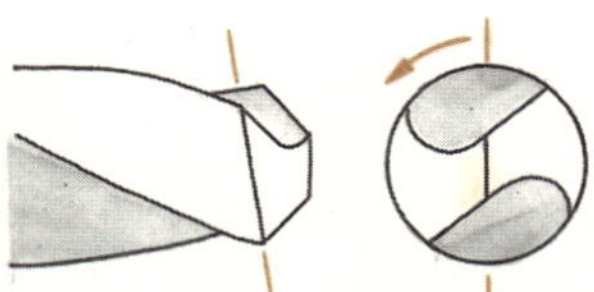

Correcting cutting relief
Check that the bit has been equally sharpened on both sides. If this is the case, the point should be centered.

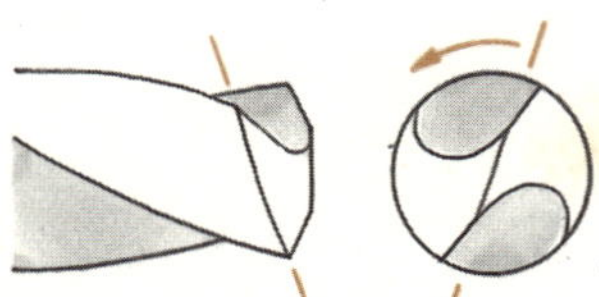

Oversharpening diminishes the point. To correct this fault, adjust the knob below the top plate and re-sharpen.

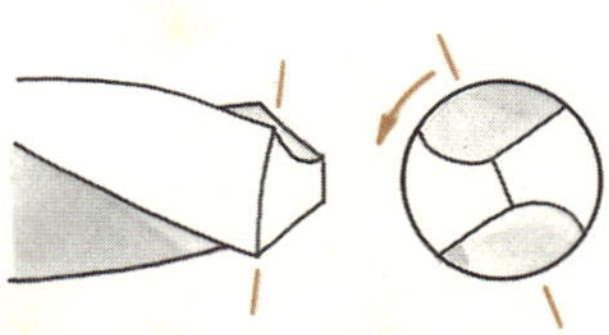

Inadequate sharpening produces a flattened point. To correct the relief, adjust the knob and try once again.

Points and Wheels

OTHER NAME: Miniature grindstones
SIZE: Various
MATERIAL: Aluminium oxide, silicon carbide
USE: To grind metal

These small grindstones are mounted on a steel shaft which fits directly into the chuck of a portable electric drill or into the flexible drive.

There are three kinds of shape: point, wheel and ball and they are used to open up holes and slots, round off edges, grind grooves and so on.

Oilstone

OTHER NAMES: Whetstone, bench stone
SIZE: 150 × 37 × 12mm; 200 × 50 × 25mm
MATERIAL: Natural stone, aluminium oxide, silicon carbide
USE: To sharpen tools

Oilstones are rectangular blocks of natural man-made stone, used to grind tool blades to a sharp edge. Stones are made with coarse, medium or fine grit, or with a different grit on each side. For the home workshop a combination stone, with medium grit on one side to remove the metal quickly and fine grit on the other to put the final edge on a blade, would be ideal.

When the surface of a stone wears, regrind it as shown below. The surface itself may become clogged with oil, dust and metal particles which prevent it cutting efficiently. scrub the surface with paraffin using a stiff bristle brush.

Grinding an oilstone
Sprinkle carborundum powder on a sheet of glass and, keeping the surface of the stone wet, rub it over the surface until it is ground flat.

Sharpening a chisel or plane blade
A new plane blade or chisel will already have an angle of 25° ground on the cutting edge. Before it can be used, a second bevel of 30° must be honed on the edge with an oilstone.

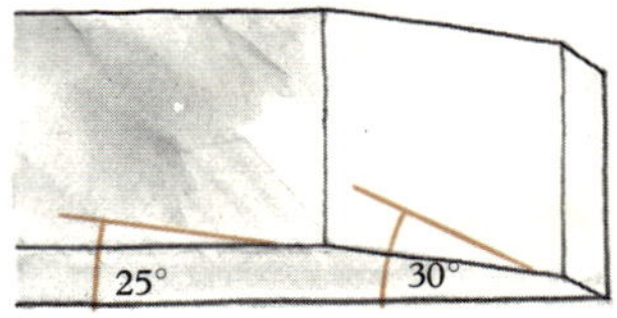

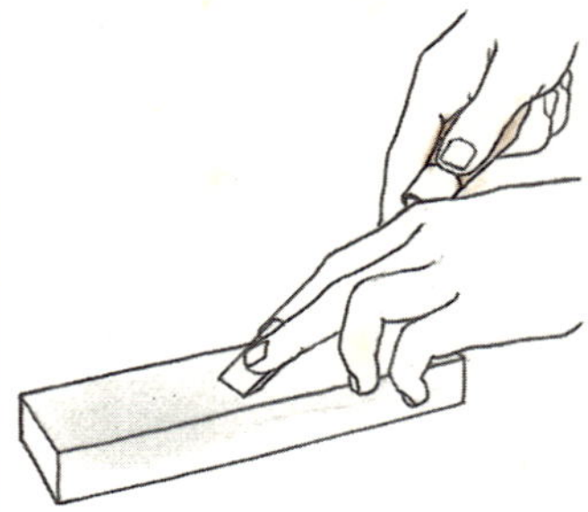

Put a little oil on the stone and rub the blade at the required angle up and down the stone in a figure of "X" pattern, using the whole surface to avoid uneven wear. Maintain a constant pressure behind the bevel with the tips of the fingers. When the plane blade is wider than the stone, angle it slightly until the blade fits.

Continue the rubbing action until a burr is raised on the flat side of the blade. Feel for the burr with your thumb and then return (remove) the burr on the oilstone.

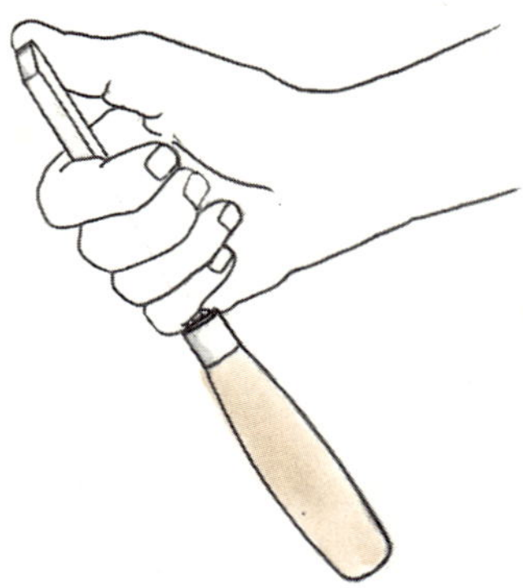

Feeling the burr
Rest your thumb on the flat of the blade and rub it across the back of the cutting edge to feel the burr.

Returning the burr
To return the burr, hold the flat of the blade on the stone and move it from side to side.

Making a sharp edge
The alternate raising and returning of the burr will eventually break it off, leaving a perfectly sharp edge.

Finally, strop the blade on a leather strap. Test the sharp edge by stroking the thumb across the blade at right angles to the edge.

With a sharp blade you will feel a marked increase in friction between your skin and the tool's blade.

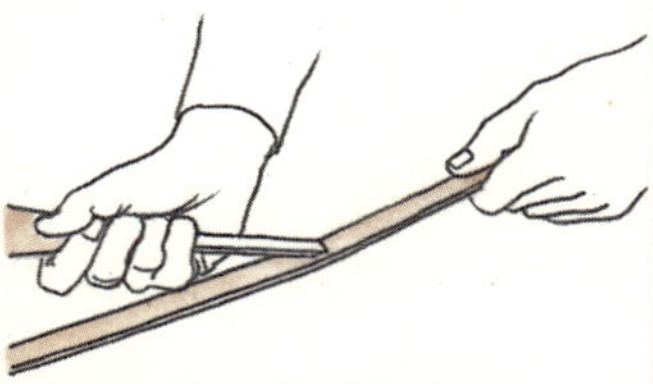

Stropping the blade
For a really sharp blade, strop it on a leather strap, and test for a sharp edge.

Razor sharp edge
A properly sharpened tool should be able to slice through a hanging sheet of paper.

Honing Guide

OTHER NAME: Sharpening jig
SIZE: To take blades 3 to 59mm wide
MATERIAL: *Body:* steel; *Angle gauge/rollers:* nylon
USE: To hold the blades at the correct sharpening angle

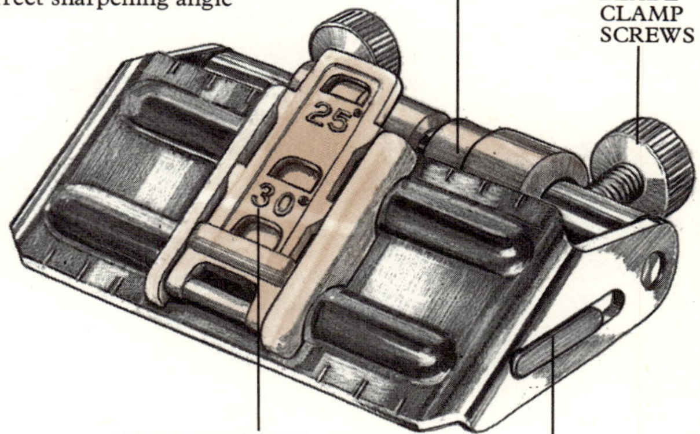

A blade should be sharpened at a constant angle to prevent it being ground with a rounded edge. Although with practice this can be done by hand, it is quite difficult when sharpening spokeshaves and small blades from plough and combination planes. The honing guide makes it easy.

Sharpening a mounted blade

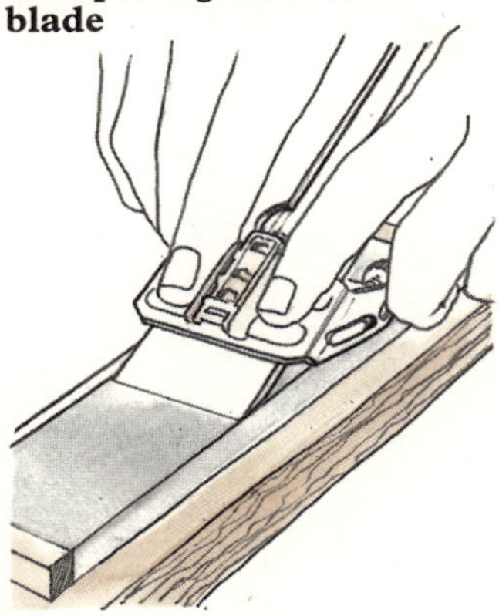

Sharpen the blade mounted in a honing guide on an oilstone, as you would free-hand.

Gauging the angle

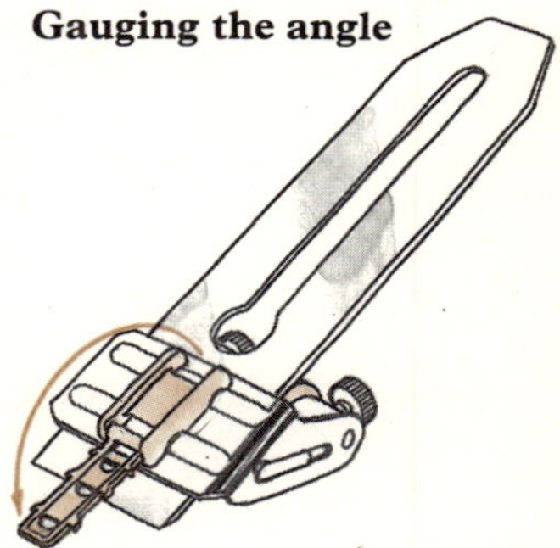

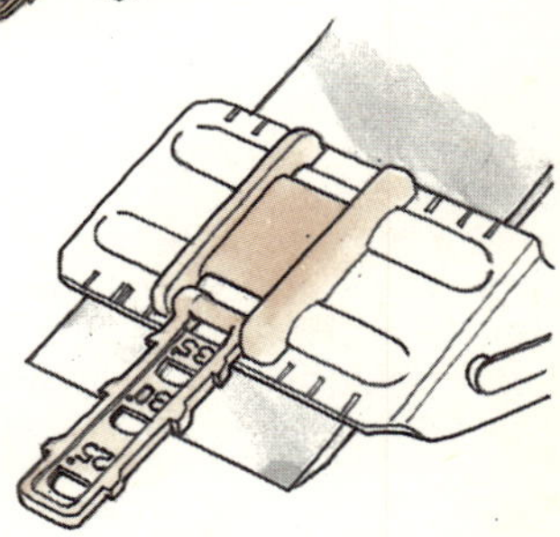

Insert the blade in the guide and adjust for the required angle: 30° for chisels, bench planes and spokeshaves, and 35° for plough planes. Square up the blade to the front edge of the honing guide and tighten the clamp.

Slipstones

SIZE: 100 to 150mm
MATERIAL: Natural stone, silicon carbide, aluminium oxide
USE: To sharpen irregular shaped tools such as gouges

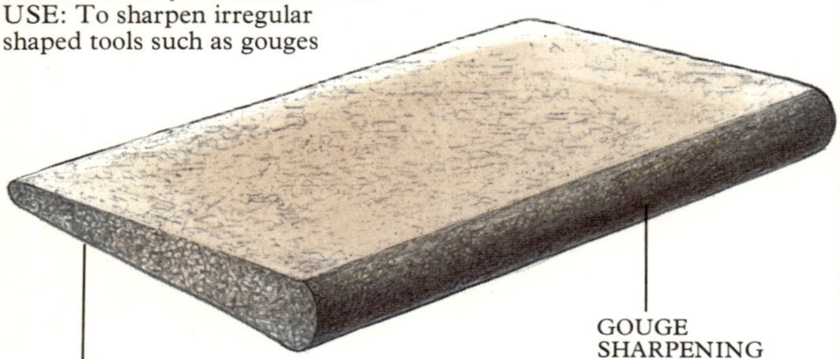

Slipstones, like oilstones, are used to put the final sharp edge on cutting tools, but in this case they are applied to the tool instead of the other way around. They are shaped to fit more irregular cutting edges such as various gouges, parting tools and machine cutters. The most common shapes are triangular, square, round, rectangular and tapered.

Keep slipstones or oilstones in a box or well wrapped in cloth or newspaper to protect them from dirt and damage.

Common shapes of stones
Slipstones are most commonly found in a rectangular, circular or triangular shape. Squares and tapered shapes are also available.

Sharpening gouges
Gouges have grinding angles of 25° and honing angles of 30°.

Outside bevel
To hone a gouge, hold the tool upright and move it from side to side, using the whole stone.

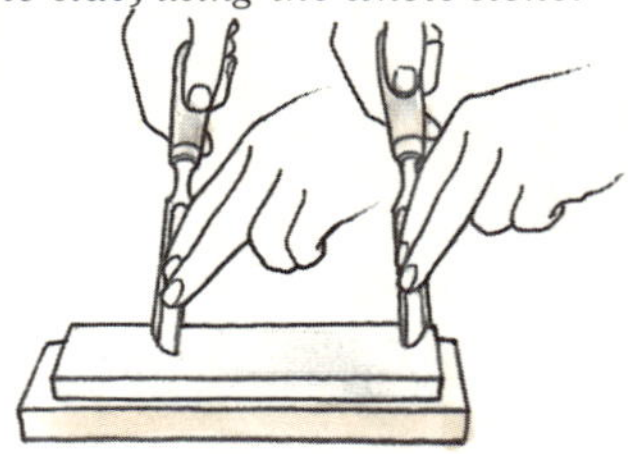

Rock the blade along the stone to produce an even cutting edge.

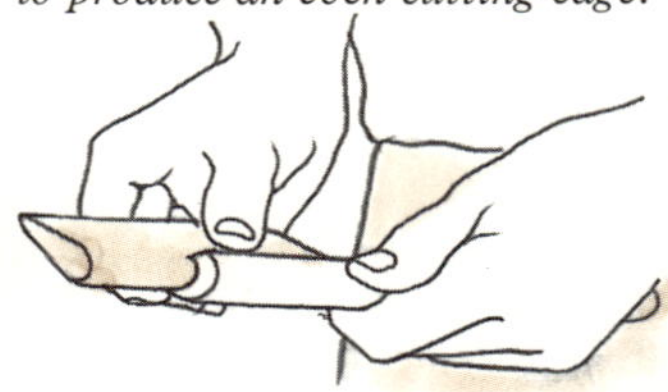

Return the burr by rubbing an oiled slipstone flat on the inside of the gouge.

Inside bevel

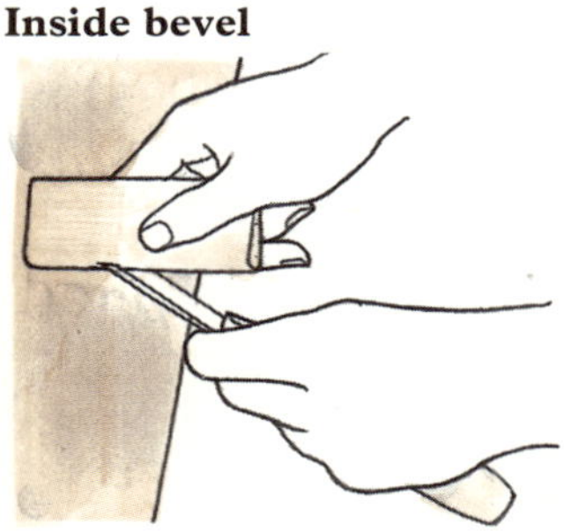

Use an oiled, tapered slipstone to raise the burr.

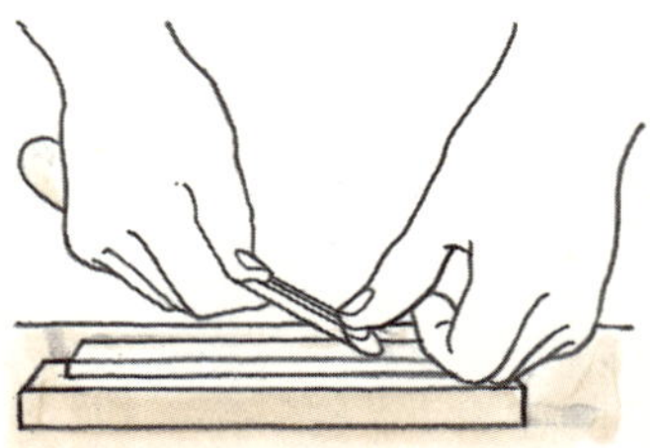

Return the burr by holding the gouge flat on an oilstone and moving it from side to side, simultaneously rocking it. Strop gouge with a leather-wrapped slipstone.

Scythe Stone

SIZE: 231 to 300mm;
MATERIAL: Natural stone, silicon carbide, aluminium oxide
USE: To sharpen scythes and sickles

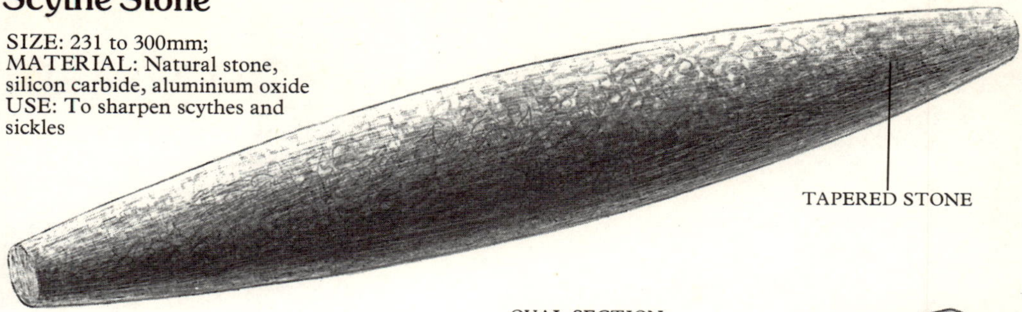

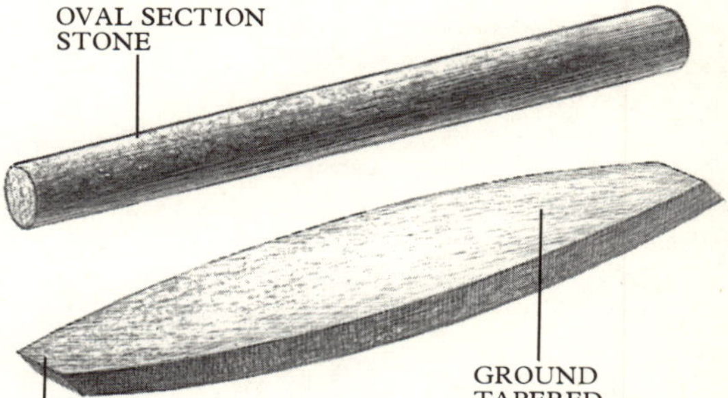

Scythes are sharpened with long, shaped stones which are either flat tapered, ground tapered or oval in section.

Stand the scythe on the point of its blade. Lubricate the scythe stone with oil or water and hone the scythe edge by stroking the blade from the end nearest the shaft. Sharpen both sides of the blade, finally holding the blade horizontally to hone the last few centimetres nearest the point. Keep the stone flat on the blade or the scythe's edge may become rounded over.

Hand Stone

SIZE: Diameter: 100mm
MATERIAL: Silicon carbide
USE: To sharpen axe blades

Once an axe has been ground on a grindstone, the edge is honed with a hand stone. Hold the stone in the palm of the hand with the fingers gripping the groove which protects them from the blade edge.

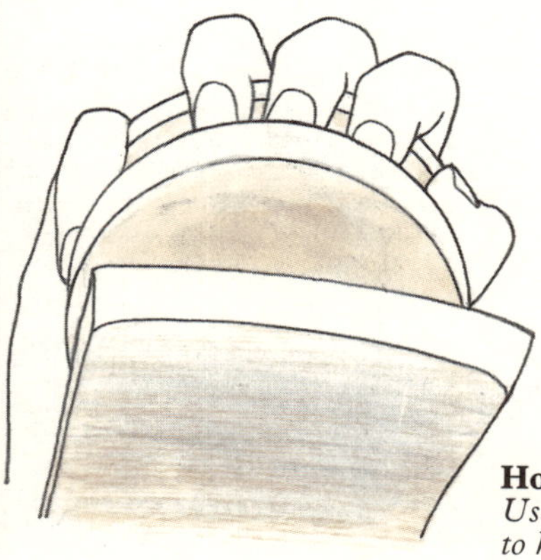

Honing an axe
Use a series of circular strokes to hone the axe blade.

Saws

The invention and development of the saw followed soon after the discovery of copper in the Near East about four thousand years ago. The early Egyptians used copper hand saws up to 500mm long, with a pistol-shaped handle lashed to the tang. Cretan carpenters about 1600 BC had large bronze saws for cross cutting and ripping.

The first iron saws were no stronger than the bronze ones they replaced; the only advantage was that the iron was more readily available. Later on, the Greeks and Romans made many important improvements to the iron hand saws, including various types of wooden frames for straining the blade and setting the teeth alternately so that the saw kerf could be cut slightly wider than the thickness of the saw. The cutting edge could then be made straight and the teeth shaped to cut on the push stroke, giving a more accurate and efficient action.

During the Middle Ages, improvements to the tools were confined to the design of the wooden frames and handles and various methods of cutting and setting the teeth.

About the middle of the seventeenth century the development of the process of rolling wide steel strip, mainly at Sheffield in England and in Holland, ushered in significant changes in the design of hand saws. The wider plates thus obtained were strong enough to dispense with wooden frames for straining the blades and the main problem became the shape and method of fixing the handles. The Dutch and Scandinavian sawmakers used a pistol-shaped handle with a ferrule fixed to a tang on the upper part of the blade. The English makers, however, preferred a handle nearly as wide as the heel of the saw, cut from a flat plank about 25mm thick, with an oval hand hole and angled grip, riveted or screwed to the blade. With further refinements in detail, this became the standard pattern for hand saws of all types almost everywhere. For accurate work on the bench, carpenters, cabinetmakers and the like in the early eighteenth century also used sash, tenon and dovetail saws with fine teeth on a thinner blade, which was strengthened by a steel or brass back. These "backed" saws were also fitted with the new type of handle.

Although the traditional framed saws with narrow blades are still widely used in Europe for all types of bench work, ripping and cross cutting, their use in English-speaking countries is confined to compassed or curved work. These "bow" saws or turning saws have changed very little since medieval times.

Saw teeth

The groove cut in a piece of wood by a saw is called the kerf. To prevent the saw blade continuously jamming in the kerf, the teeth are "set", that is, bent sideways alternately to the right and left, so that they cut a kerf slightly wider than the thickness of the blade.

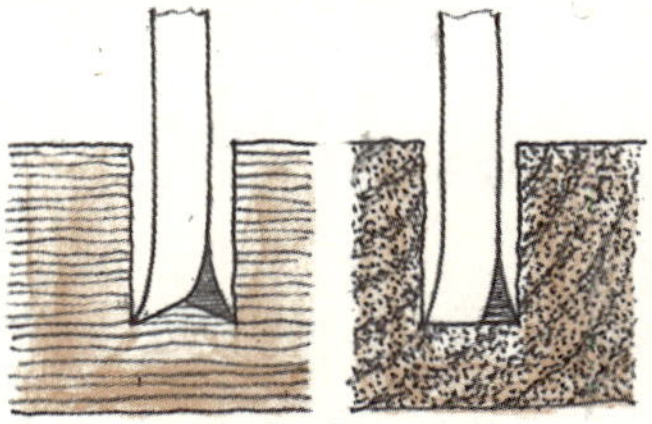

Saw teeth design

Cross cut saw teeth (left) act as knife points to sever the wood fibres while rip saw teeth (right) work like a chisel.

The design of the saw tooth also depends on the kind of timber to be cut. For cutting with the grain it is best to use a rip saw, which has teeth filed at 90° across the blade. These act like a series of tiny chisels, cutting along the grain. For crossgrain timber use a cross cut saw with teeth filed at an angle of 65° to 75° across the blade. These act like knife blades to score on each side of the cut.

The size of saw teeth varies enormously. Large teeth with deep spaces or "gullets" in between are best suited to cut softwood. They offer little resistance to the saw and so a lot of sawdust is produced, which is carried clear of the kerf by the large gullets. Hardwoods, on the other hand, are more difficult to cut and therefore require more and smaller teeth per inch. The nature of the work also determines the size of the tooth. Coarse ripping can be done with large teeth while fine joint cutting requires small, finely set teeth.

Teeth are specified in points per 25mm. This measurement includes the teeth at each end, therefore a measurement of 8 points per 25mm would actually mean 7 teeth within that space. Fine bow saws are measured in teeth per 25mm.

Sharpening a saw
There are several stages to sharpening a saw depending on its condition. Through persistent misuse a saw may have hollows worn in the row of teeth or it may have been badly sharpened to produce uneven sized teeth. In either case it will require leveling to begin the process of bringing it back to its original condition.

A file mounted in hardwood should be used to level the teeth along the entire length of the saw. The wood acts as a jig, running against the face of the saw blade to keep the file square and flat on the teeth.

Shaping the teeth
The teeth must now be shaped with a saw file to regulate their size and shape. The object is to maintain an even "pitch" to each tooth. Pitch is the angle at which the front of the tooth leans toward the toe of the saw. Try to keep to the original pitch of the saw, which may be up to 14° for a cross cut saw, moving back to upright for a rip saw.

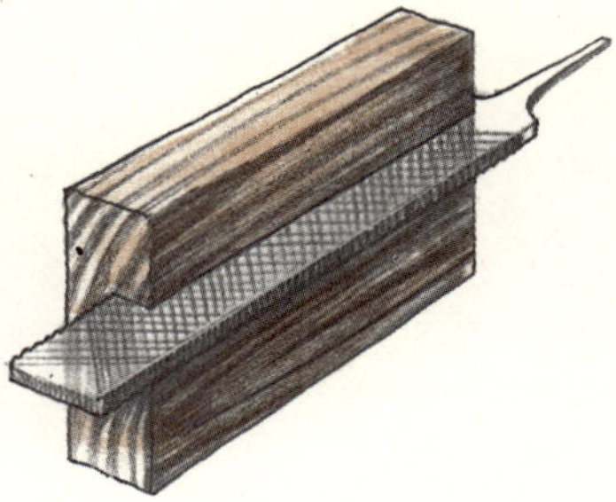

Mounting the file
Mount the smooth file in a block of hardwood.

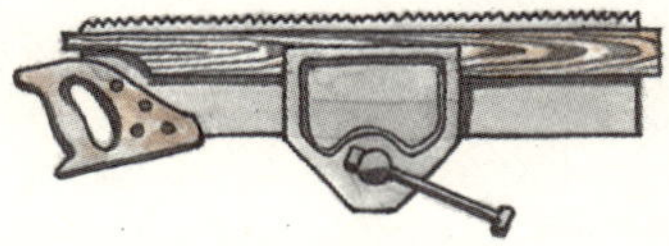

Positioning the saw
Hold the saw, teeth uppermost, between two softwood lengths and clamp it in a vice.

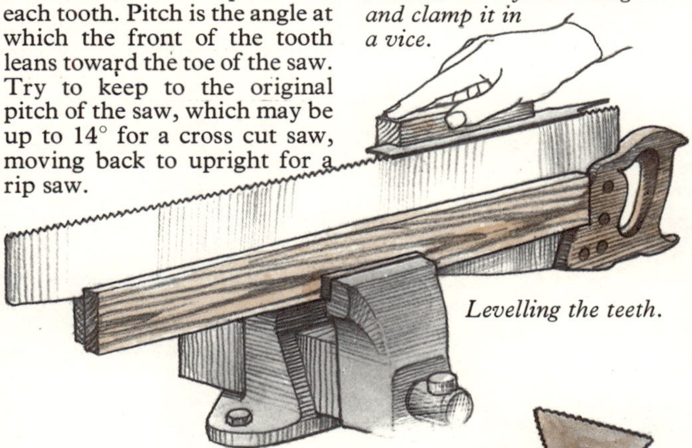

Levelling the teeth.

The angle between each tooth of any saw is a constant 60°. Lower the saw between two strips in the vice as near as possible to the teeth. Choose a saw file which is just over twice the depth of the tooth. Place the file in the first gullet, holding it horizontally and at right angles to the blade. Maintain the correct pitch while holding the file in one hand and the tip between thumb and finger of the other. File with even forward strokes. File each gullet in turn until all the flats are removed and the teeth are uniform in shape. Any burrs produced on one side of the blade can be removed by a light dressing with an oilstone.

Filing a gullet

A file which is twice the depth of the teeth will maintain its accuracy for longer.

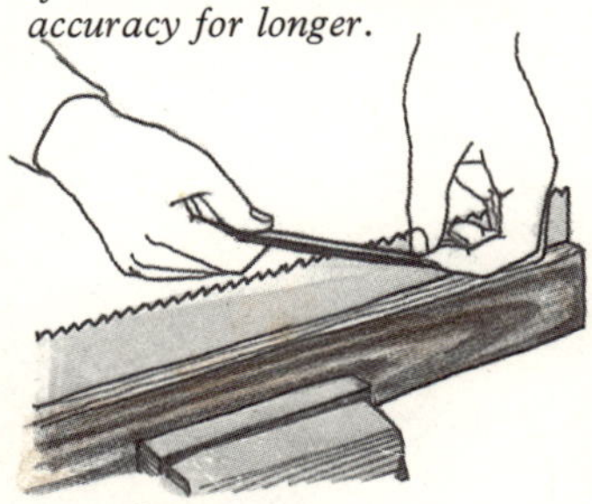

Saw file position
Hold the file at an approximate angle of 70° to the blade.

Setting the teeth
The teeth must now be set to produce the correct width of kerf. The easiest method is to use a saw set (see page 76) which automatically bends each alternate tooth exactly the right amount and to the correct depth. Adjust the saw set to correspond with the points per inch of the saw. Starting at one end of the saw, position the saw set over alternate teeth, lining them up with the plunger, and squeeze the handles to press the teeth against the anvil. Reverse the saw and repeat the sequence on the intermediate teeth. Before final sharpening, make sure the set is even. To do this, hold the saw horizontally at eye level and against the light. Any unevenness will show up clearly and the set can be adjusted.

Depth of set

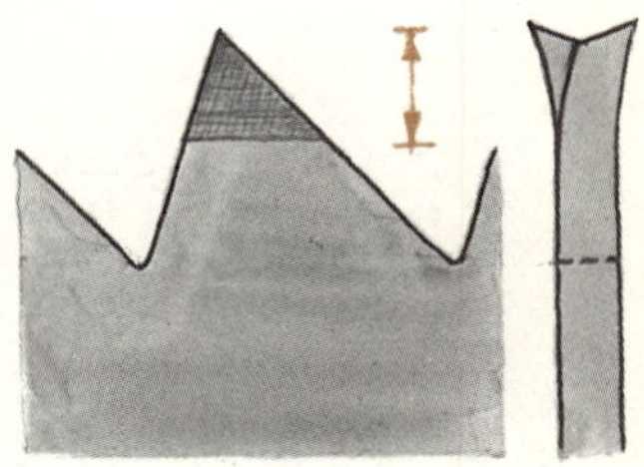

Only the top half of the tooth is bent when setting.

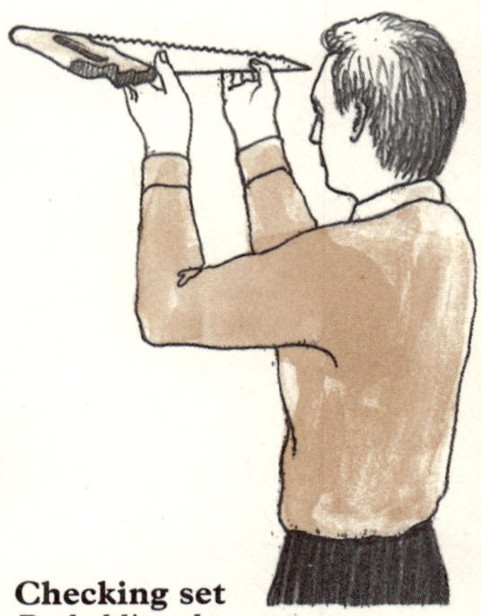

Checking set
By holding the saw horizontally at eye level, the correctness of the set can be easily confirmed.

Final sharpening
To complete the operation the front edge of each tooth must be filed to the correct angle. With the saw still held in the vise, position the saw handle to your right. Place the file on the front edge of the first tooth set toward you. Keeping the file horizontal, give the tooth two or three firm yet steady strokes. Move the file along the blade filing each alternate tooth in the same way. Reverse the saw and file the intermediate teeth.

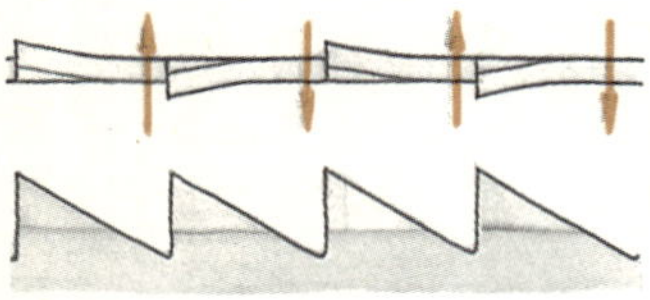

Rip saw teeth
Rip saw teeth are filed at right angles across the saw blade.

Cross cut teeth
Cross cut teeth are sharpened in the same way. The back edge of each tooth will be filed automatically as you file the front edge of the tooth from behind. When the saw is reversed make sure that the handle of the file is angled away from the saw handle again when filing the intermediate teeth.

Hardened teeth on some modern saws cannot be file sharpened; they must be maintained by the supplier.

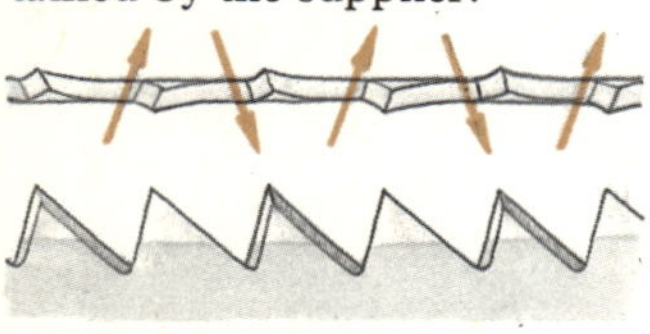

Cross cut teeth are filed at 70° across the blade.

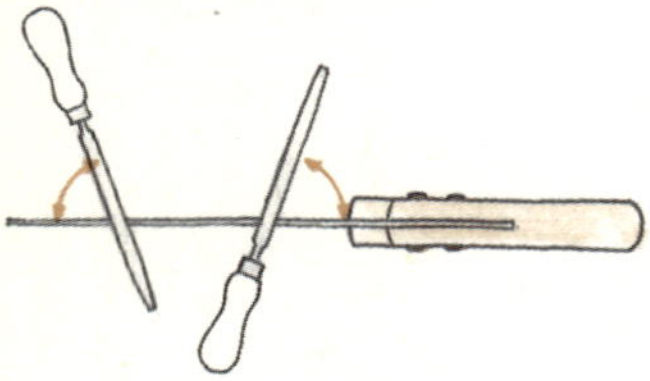

Hold the file at an approximate angle of 70° to the blade.

Saw Set

SIZE: To set saws from 4 to 16 points per 25mm
MATERIAL: Cast metal, reinforced nylon
USE: To set saw teeth to the correct angle

The saw set is designed to bend the teeth of a saw to exactly the right angle to produce the required cut or kerf. When the handles are squeezed together a plunger presses the tooth against an anvil (a wheel with a graduated angle on the face) which corresponds to the correct setting for saws with teeth from 4 to 16 points per 25mm. Saws that measure more than 16 points per 25mm should be reset by a saw repair specialist.

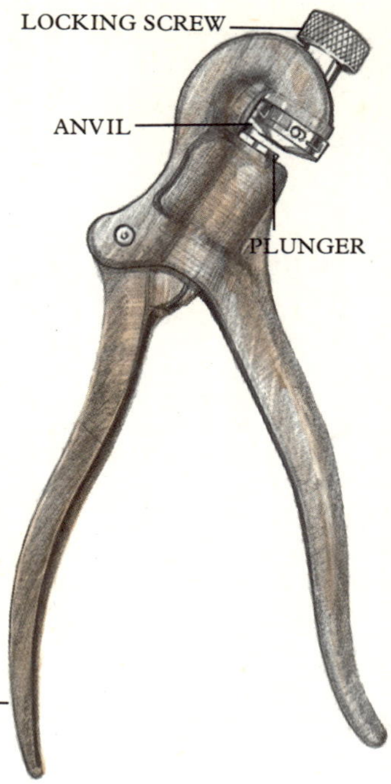

The plunger presses the saw teeth against the anvil to produce the required "set".

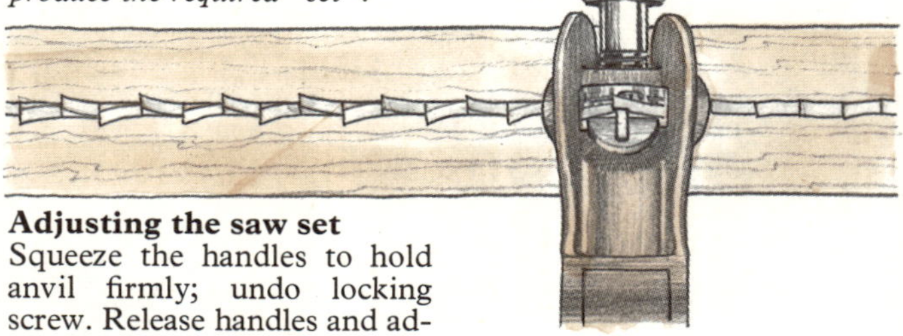

Adjusting the saw set
Squeeze the handles to hold anvil firmly; undo locking screw. Release handles and adjust anvil until relevant point number engraved in top edge lines up with plunger. Squeeze the handles again and tighten the locking screw. Set the teeth of the saw as on page 75.

Move the saw set along the blade locating it over alternate teeth. Reverse the saw and set the remaining teeth.

Two-Man Cross Cut Saw

SIZE: 1.2 to 2.1m
MATERIAL: *Blade:* steel;
Handle: hardwood
USE: To fell trees and cut logs

The two handed cross cut saw is one of the oldest style of saws surviving in modern catalogues. It consists of a long flat blade with cutting teeth on the underside and an upright handle at each end. The shape of the blade seems to have been originally determined by local tradition and does not affect the cut in any obvious way. The shape of the teeth on the other hand, is very important.

The simplest cross cut design, known as the "peg" tooth, is an evenly spaced row of V-shaped teeth. Each tooth is filed on both edges so that it cuts in both directions. Another shape has a deep gullet between each tooth. While the teeth do the cutting, the sawdust is carried out of the cut in the gullets. This prevents the saw jamming in the cut and is especially important for cutting unseasoned wood.

The other design for cross cut saws has rows of cutting teeth interspersed by unsharpened "raker" teeth, designed to rake the sawdust clear of the kerf. The "lance" tooth saw has a group of 4 cutting teeth and a pair of rakers separated by deep gullets.

PEG TOOTH

TOOTH AND GULLET COMBINATION

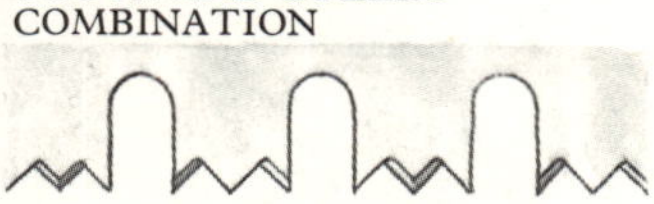

GREAT AMERICAN TOOTH

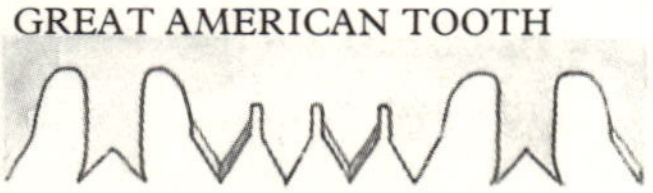

LANCE TOOTH

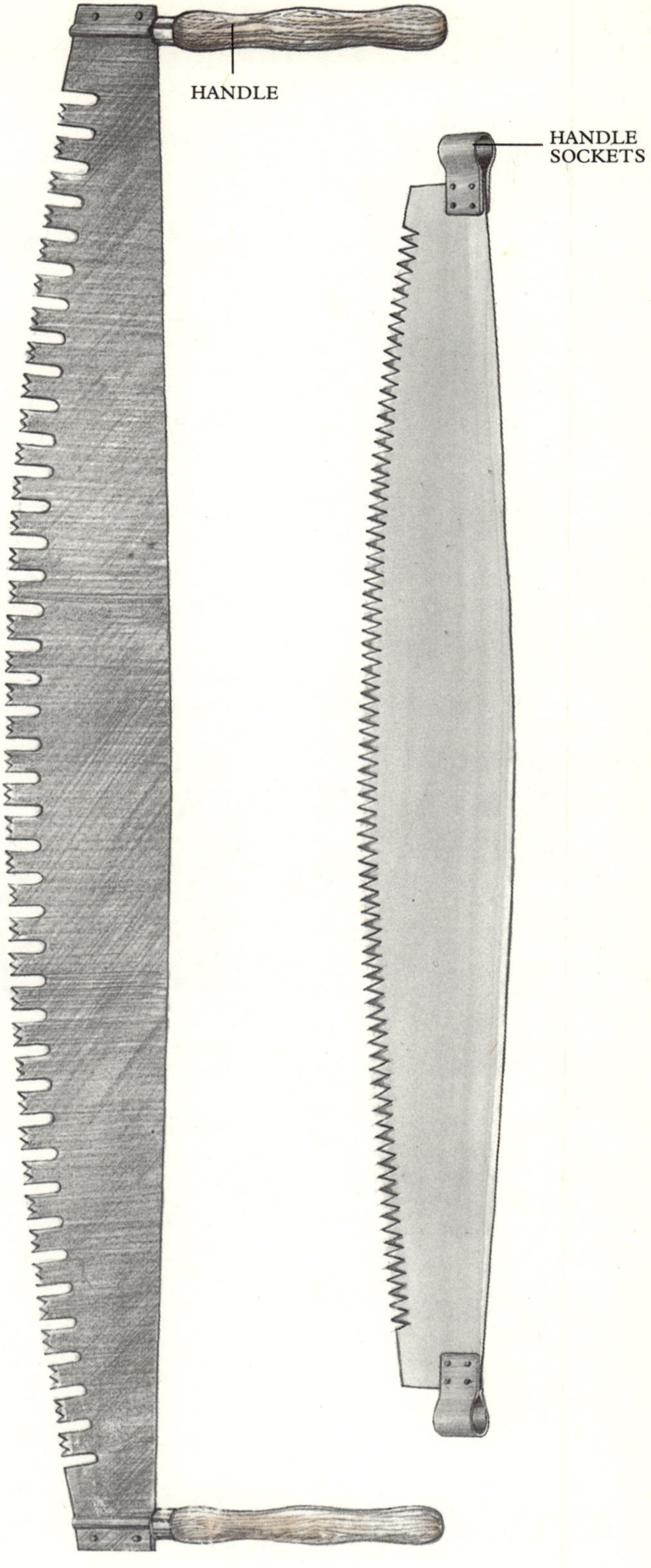

Felling trees
Felling large trees is a skilled operation and should not be attempted by an amateur without expert help and advice. The following is a description of the way a two-man cross cut saw is used in tree felling and should not be regarded as complete instructions.

The tree is "undercut" on the side facing the direction in which it is to fall. Above this cut a notch, angled to 45°, is chopped out with an axe. The cross cut is used once more to make the "backcut", another horizontal cut in the opposite side of the tree approximately 50mm above the bottom of the notch, stopping within 50mm of the notch. The wood between the cuts acts as a hinge for the falling tree. At this stage, the tree will usually fall under its own weight, and experienced workmen will stand aside, one of them removing the saw. If it does not fall naturally, drive wedges into the backcut.

Cutting down the tree

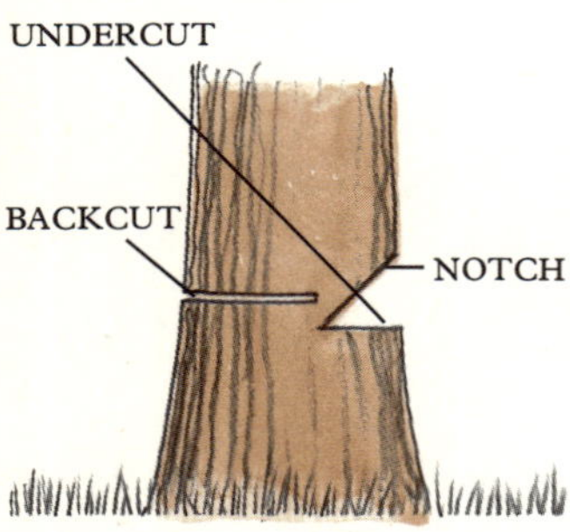

Make the undercut 300mm from the ground. Above the cut, chop out the angled notch with an axe. Make the backcut. Let the tree fall or encourage it with wedges.

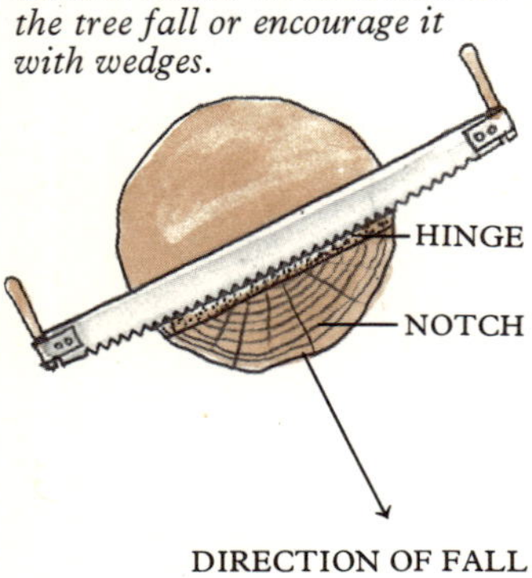

One-Man Cross Cut Saw

SIZE: 750mm to 1.5m
MATERIAL: *Blade:* steel; *Handle:* hardwood
USE: To fell trees and to cut logs to length

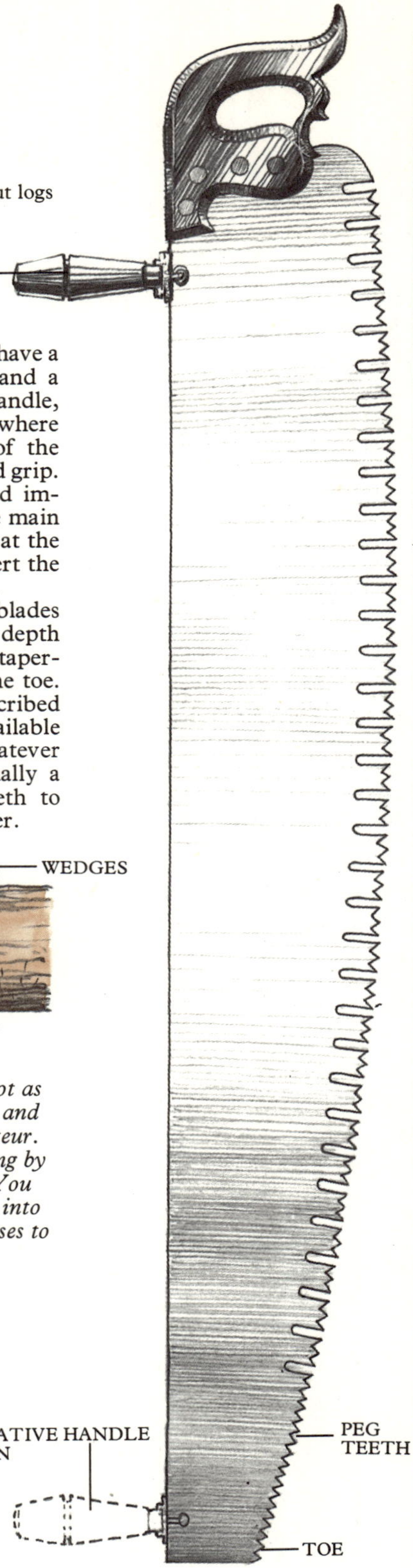

One-man cross cut saws have a hand saw style handle and a supplementary upright handle, which can be fitted anywhere along the upper edge of the blade as a secondary hand grip. It is normally positioned immediately in front of the main handle but can be fitted at the toe of the blade to convert the tool into a two-man saw.

One-man cross cut blades normally retain their full depth for most of their length, tapering rather abruptly at the toe. All the styles of teeth described for two-man saws are available for the one-man, but whatever the design there is usually a short length of peg teeth to correspond with the taper.

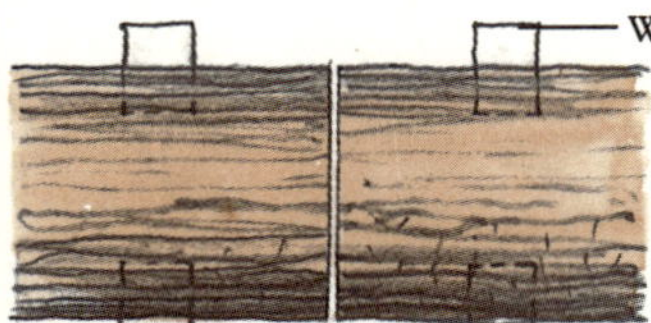

Cutting logs to length
Cutting logs to length is not as dangerous as felling trees, and can be tackled by an amateur. Prevent the log from rolling by wedging it on both sides. You may have to drive wedges into the kerf as the cut progresses to prevent the saw jamming.

Chain Saw

OTHER NAME: Buzz saw
SIZE: *Bar length:* 250 to 500mm
Power: electric: 1100 to 1200 watts; petrol engine: 3½ to 5½hp
MATERIAL: Various
USE: To fell trees and cut logs to length

A modern chain saw cuts fast and efficiently even through unseasoned timber. A petrol engine or electric motor drives a continuous toothed chain which is supported and guided by a metal blade which is known as the guide bar.

Safety features are incorporated to prevent accidental starting of the tool. Electric saws are fitted with a "lock-off" button and engine driven saws have a centrifugal clutch, which disengages when the engine is idling.

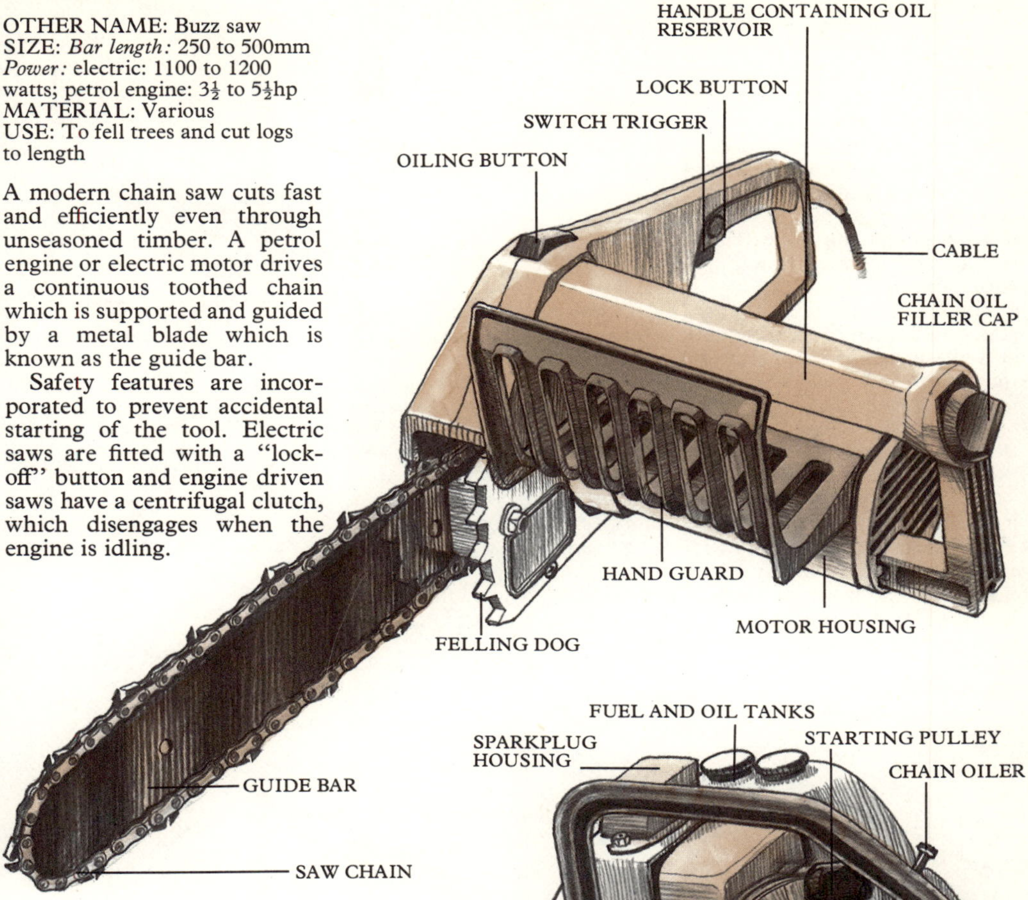

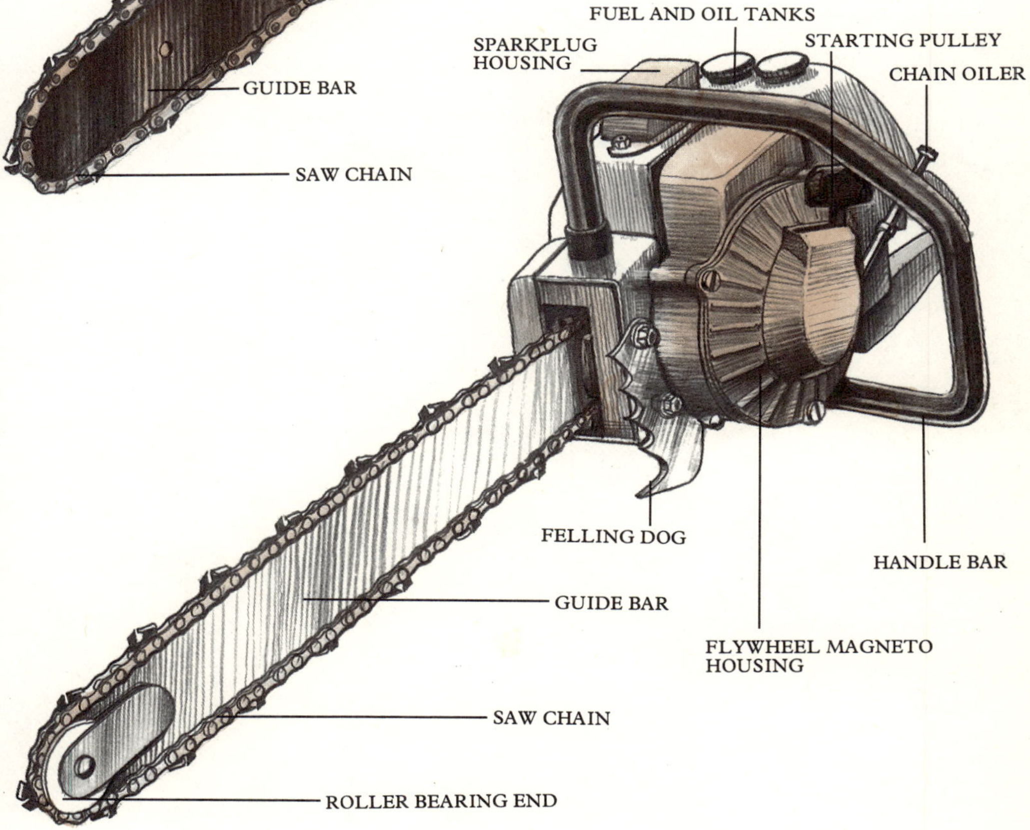

Felling with a chain saw

Felling large trees with a chain saw is just as hazardous as using a two-man cross cut saw, and the operation should only be undertaken with expert supervision. The chain saw makes undercutting very simple as it can be used to make both the initial horizontal cut and the angled notch. This dispenses with the axe needed to make the notch when felling with a two-man cross cut.

For a normal felling cut, start the backcut 50mm above and 50mm behind one end of the notch and swing the bar into the tree keeping it parallel to the bottom of the undercut. Be careful not to cut through the tree hinge.

To cut through a tree which is wider than the length of the guide bar, make successive cuts around the tree making sure that each cut is in the same plane as the previous one.

Normal felling cuts

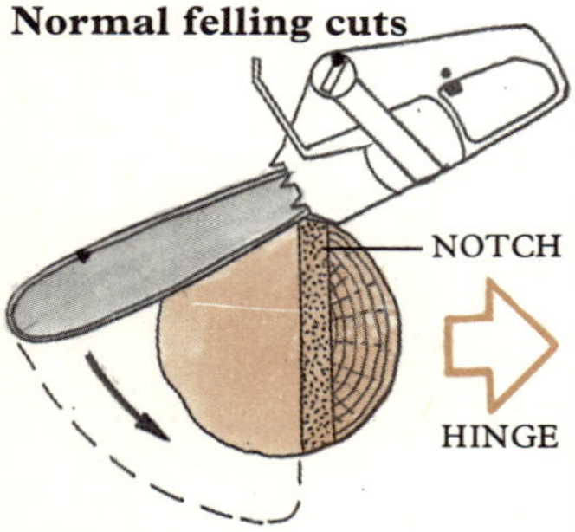

Swing the bar into the tree keeping it parallel to the bottom of the undercut.

Wider felling cuts

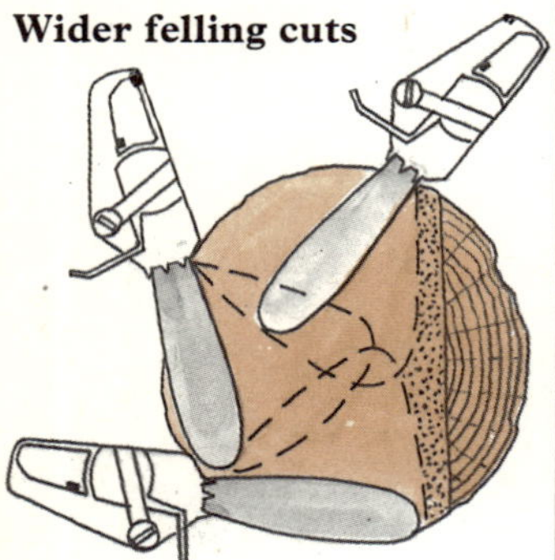

Make successive cuts around the tree keeping them in the same plane.

Folding Saw

OTHER NAMES: Flexible saw, chain saw
SIZE: 1.2m
MATERIAL: Steel
USE: To cut off branches

The folding saw is a length of flexible, toothed steel with a loop at either end.

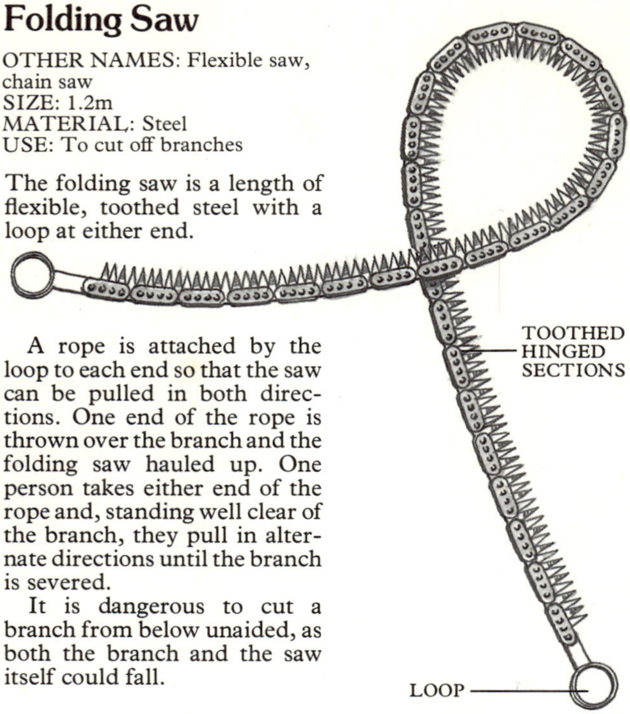

A rope is attached by the loop to each end so that the saw can be pulled in both directions. One end of the rope is thrown over the branch and the folding saw hauled up. One person takes either end of the rope and, standing well clear of the branch, they pull in alternate directions until the branch is severed.

It is dangerous to cut a branch from below unaided, as both the branch and the saw itself could fall.

Log Saw

SIZE: 600 to 900mm
MATERIAL: *Blade:* steel; *Frame:* tubular steel
USE: To cut logs to length and prune trees

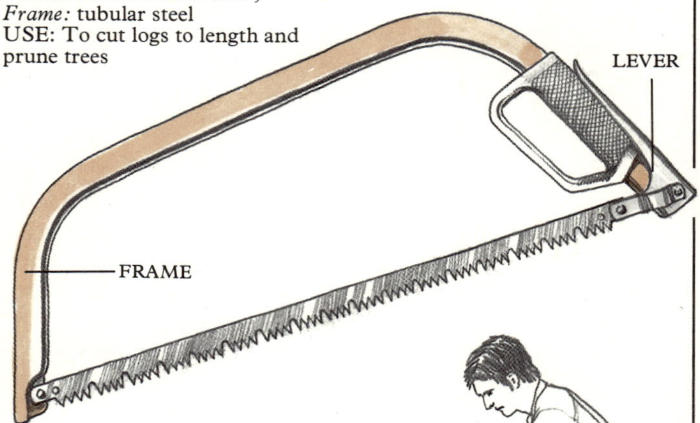

The blade is held under tension in a tubular steel frame. In modern versions tension is applied by a quick-release lever. The lever combined with an oval sectioned frame provides a comfortable hand grip. The blades, which are replaceable, are made up of pegged teeth or a combination of pegged teeth and gullets to provide cutting action in both directions.

Cutting with the log saw.

Hand Saw

OTHER NAMES: Rip saw, cross cut saw, panel saw
SIZE: **Rip saw:** *Length:* 650mm; *Points:* 5 per 25mm; **Cross cut:** *Length:* 600 to 650mm; *Points:* 6 to 8 per 25mm; **Panel:** *Length:* 500 to 550mm; *Points:* 10 per 25mm
MATERIAL: *Blade:* steel; *Handle:* beech, plastic
USE: To cut large planks or panels

Hand saws as a group have long, tapering, unsupported blades fitted with a closed handle. Although they vary in length, the main difference lies in the number and shape of the cutting teeth (see pages 74–76). The shape of the blade varies with the quality of the saw. A lot of modern saws, and some more cheaply produced traditional style saws, have a straight back and a blade of uniform thickness throughout. The better traditional saw has a pronounced dipping curved back, known as a "skew" back. This is to reduce the weight at the toe thus improving the balance of the tool. They are also "taper ground", that is, ground on both sides of the blade to taper from the handle to the toe on the back of the saw while remaining a constant thickness just above the teeth. This improves the clearance of the saw in the kerf, even with a minimum set, which makes the saw easier to drive and wastes less wood.

The traditional hand saw handle is cut from a close grain hardwood, usually beech. In some ways it is a curious design, for it is impossible to cut a handle from solid wood without leaving short grain somewhere, and it is puzzling that the cross grain strength of plywood was never used for saw handles. Modern saws are often fitted with moulded plastic handles of a less elaborate design. In either case a well designed handle should be set low on the back of the blade for correct balance and it should be angled to produce maximum thrust approximately halfway along the cutting edge.

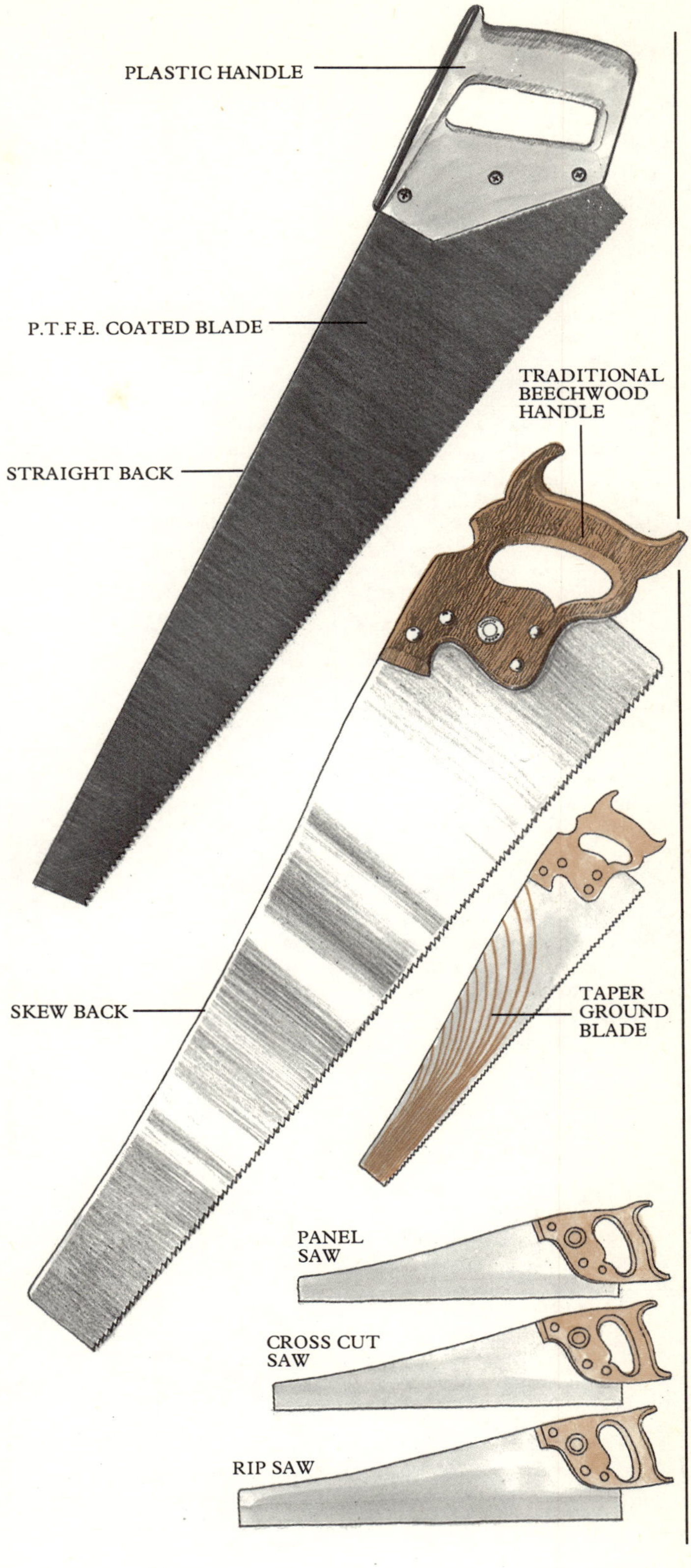

RIP SAWS

The rip saw with its chisel-like teeth is designed specifically for cutting timber along its length, that is, with the grain.

Using the rip saw

When cutting wood it is important for the board to be supported on saw horses. Make sure the board is high enough to prevent the toe of the saw from striking the ground and low enough to get your shoulder above the job. Rest one knee on the board to hold it in place and position the saw on the waste side of the marked line. Your saw arm should be free to move alongside your body, the forearm in line with the blade. Grip the handle naturally but extend the forefinger in line with the blade to prevent the tool twisting in the hand and making the cut wander off line.

Hold the saw at approximately 45° to the work and guide the blade with the thumb of the left hand until the cut is well-established. Make short backward strokes until the cut is under way and then take full strokes using almost the full length of the blade. A reasonably slow, even stroke will be far less tiring and if the saw is sharp and correctly set it will quickly cut through the board. Sometimes stress builds up in timber during the drying process, so that as you cut into the board, stress is released and the wood begins to move. This may close on the blade of the saw. To keep the cut open drive small hardwood wedges into it behind the saw blade.

Sawing at the board's end

As you approach the board's end it is often easier to finish the cut by reversing the board and making a second cut to meet the first.

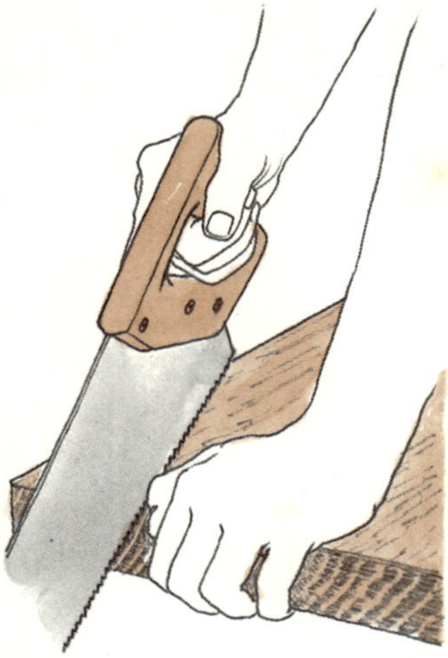

Holding the saw

Hold the saw at approximately 45° to the work. Use the thumb of the left hand as a guide.

Positioning the board

Rest your knee on the board to hold it on the saw horses.

Finishing the cut

It is often easier to reverse the board and make a second cut to meet the first.

CROSS CUT AND PANEL SAWS

Cross cut saws are designed to cut timber across the grain. The teeth are filed so that they score two lines and remove the waste between. The panel saw is a smaller version of the cross cut and is particularly useful for cutting panels of hardboard, plywood and particle board to size.

Using a cross cut saw

When using a cross cut saw, support the wood on saw horses as before, but stand to the inside with one knee resting on the work. Make sure that your own weight does not close up the cut, jamming the saw. Start and proceed with the cut as for a rip saw.

Ending the cut

Support the waste with the other hand and make slow careful strokes to prevent the waste breaking off.

Supporting a panel

Support a springy panel on either side of the cut; large panels can be supported by planks across the saw horses.

Back Saw

OTHER NAMES: Tenon saw, dovetail saw
SIZE: *Length:* 200 to 350mm; *Points:* 11 to 20 per 25mm
MATERIAL: *Blade:* steel; *Handle:* beech, plastic
USE: To cut joints

Back saws have a straight blade, parallel top and bottom, with a heavy strip of steel or brass wrapped along the back to provide rigidity.

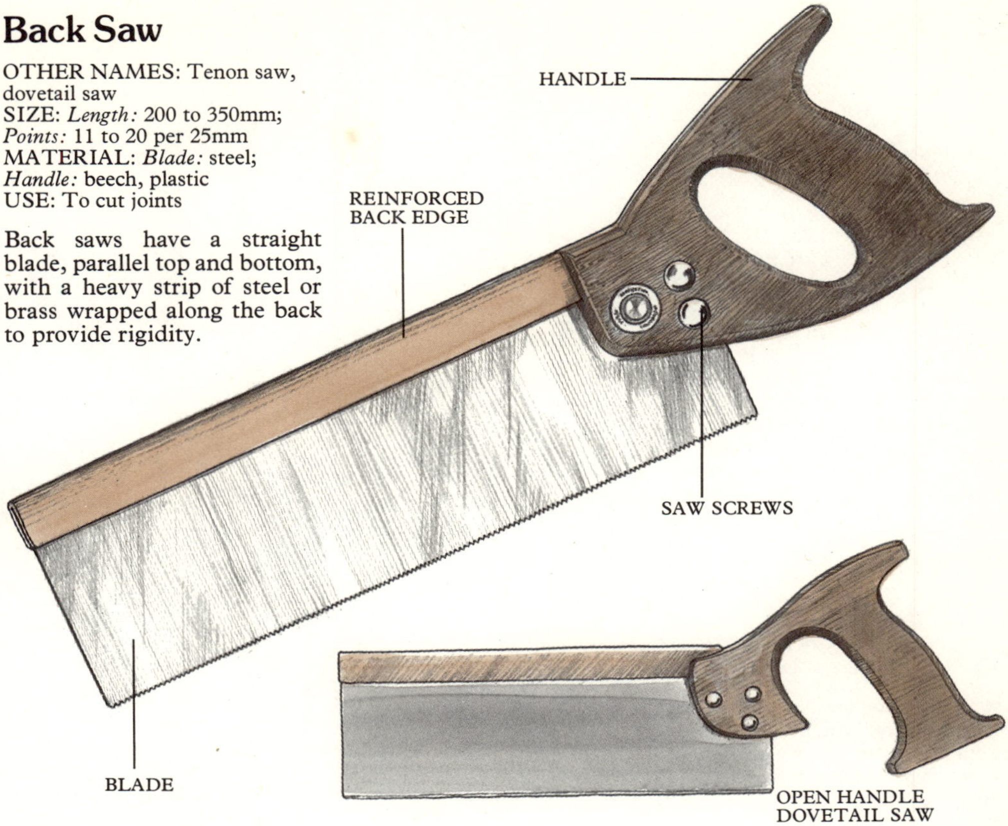

The handles are similar in shape to those on hand saws except that they are generally mounted higher. Smaller back saws are often fitted with an open handle. They are known as dovetail saws in Britain.

Back saws typically have cross cut teeth for general bench work, such as cutting smaller sections of timber to length. Smaller back saws, used to cut dovetails by working mainly in line with the grain, are sharpened with fine rip saw type teeth.

When starting the cut, back saws are presented to the work at an angle in a way similar to that described for cross cut and rip saws. Once the cut is established, these saws are used more square to the work than hand saws are.

Cutting a tenon
A tenon is cut entirely with a back saw, its size depending on the nature of the work.

1. *Hold the wood in a vice angled away from you and saw from one corner down to the shoulder line. Reverse the work and saw the opposite corner down to the other shoulder line.*

2. *Stand the work upright in the vice and join the two cuts, finishing parallel with the marked shoulder line.*

3. *To cut shoulder line place work on a bench hook. Keep blade parallel to tenon; do not cut into it at one end before the waste is removed.*

Gent's Saw

OTHER NAME: Dovetail saw
SIZE: *Length:* 100 to 250mm; *Points:* 15 to 21 per 25mm
MATERIAL: *Blade:* steel; *Handle:* beechwood
USE: To cut very fine joints

The gent's saw is a small back saw with a straight chisel-type handle. The small teeth are finely set to cut a very narrow kerf required for fine joints. The term "gent's" saw refers to the smaller, delicate tools given to "gentlemen" of an earlier date who enjoyed woodworking as a hobby.

Saws with very fine teeth and narrow blades are called "bead" and "jeweler's" saws.

Veneer Saw

SIZE: Blade length: 75mm
MATERIAL: *Blade:* steel; *Handle:* hardwood
USE: To cut thick veneers

The veneer saw has two curved serrated edges. One set of teeth is sharpened for cross cutting, the other for cutting veneers with the grain.

Pruning Saw

SIZE: 300mm to 500mm.
MATERIAL: *Blade:* steel; *Handle:* hardwood
USE: To prune trees

The simplest form of pruning saw, a descendant of one of the earliest forms of saw, is known in modern catalogues as the "Grecian" pattern. The curved, knife-like blade is serrated on the underside with regular teeth facing backward which cut on the pull stroke. The curve of the blade automatically progresses the cut.

The folding pruning saw has a handle the same length as or a little longer than the blade which folds into the handle for storage and safety.

A double edged pruning saw is also available. It normally has fine peg teeth on one side of the blade and a coarser peg tooth and gullet combination on the other side.

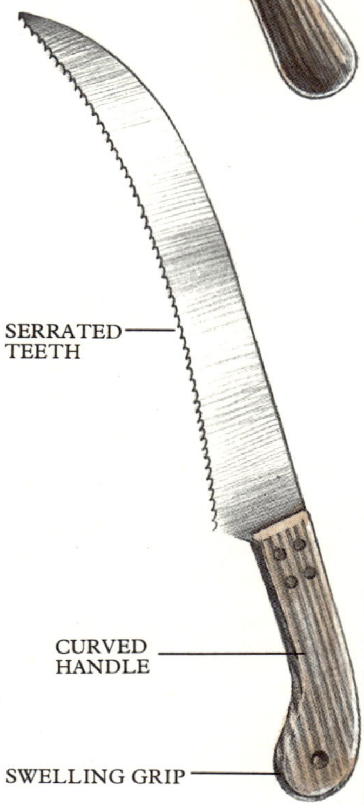

Flooring Saw

SIZE: *Length:* 312mm; *Points:* 8 per 25mm
MATERIAL: *Blade:* steel; *Handle:* beechwood
USE: To cut through floor boards

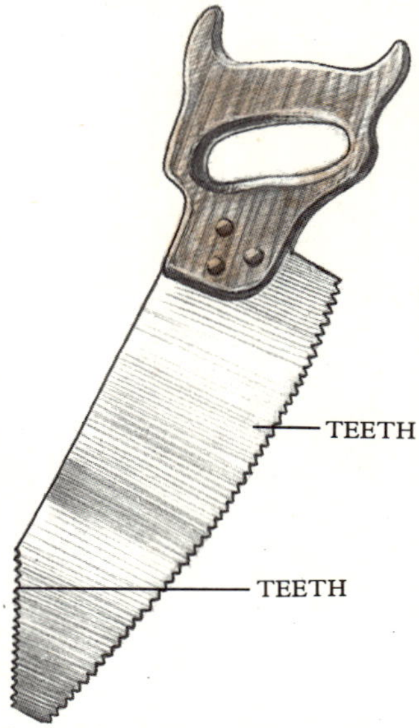

A flooring saw makes it easy to lift floor boards to check plumbing or electrical wiring. The saw has a curving blade with teeth on the underside and an angled section. The curved blade of the flooring saw lets you cut into a board without having to start with a drill or keyhole saw, and the curved cutting edge is less likely to damage boards either side. The teeth on the back edge let you cut up to a skirting board while keeping the handle clear of the wall.

Using the saw

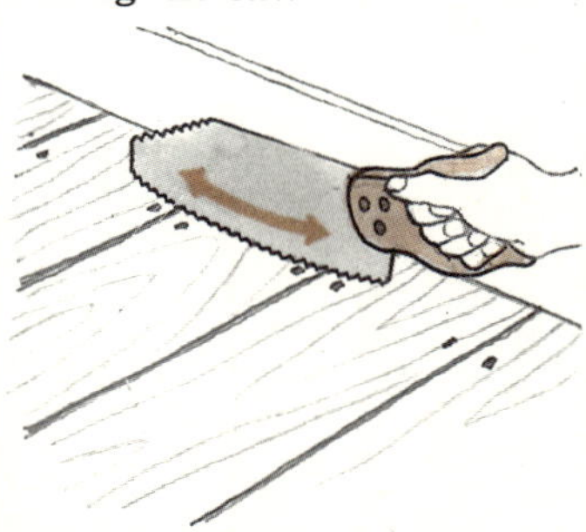

Pry up one end of the board and wedge it open with a piece of scrap wood. Cut across the board at or near the joist.

Portable Circular Saw

OTHER NAMES: Cut-off saw, utility saw, builder's saw, electric hand saw
SIZE: *Unloaded blade speed:* 3,000 to 5,500 rpm; *Weight:* 3.4 to 6.35kg
MATERIAL: Various
ACCESSORIES: Saw blades, guide fence, saw bench
USE: To cut solid timber and board to size

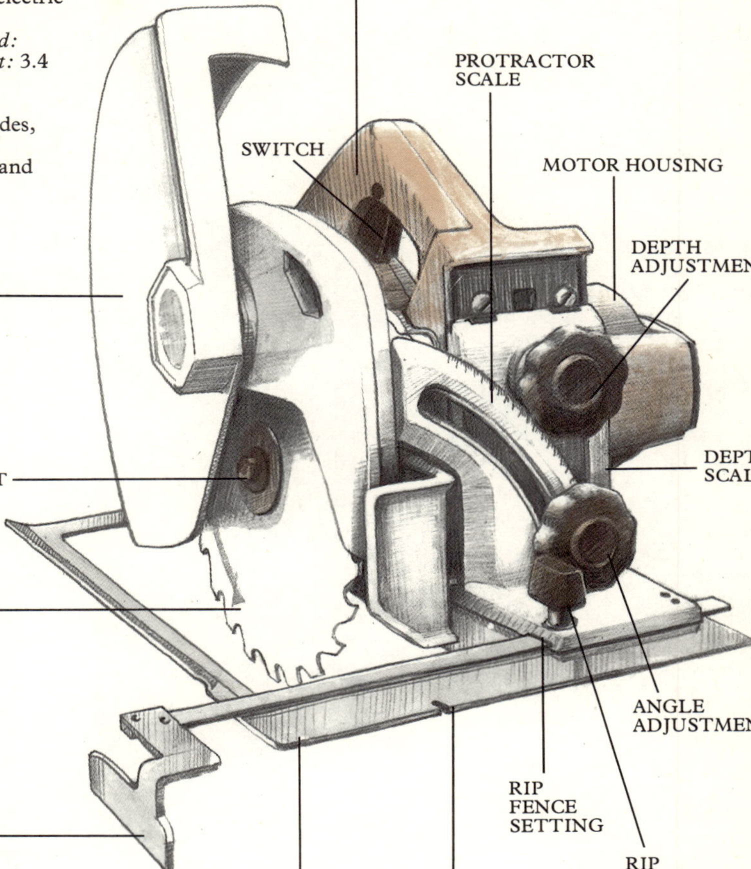

The portable circular saw is an invaluable power tool. It is primarily a woodworking tool, but with special blades fitted, it can cut a number of materials with equal ease. Saws are manufactured as a purpose made tool or as an attachment to a power drill; the latter may be underpowered for some jobs, but it is much cheaper. Larger industrial saws are available, but a saw which takes a 125mm or 187mm diameter blade is normally sufficient.

All portable circular saws should be fitted with a fixed upper blade guard and a lower blade guard which is pushed back as the saw passes through the work. The lower guard is spring-loaded to return automatically as the blade clears the work. Check that the guard is working efficiently before using the saw and never fix it in an open position when the saw is running. Choose the right blade for the job and disconnect the saw before fitting it.

Drill attachment
This is a cheaper though occasionally underpowered alternative to the circular saw.

SAW BLADES

Blades are specially designed to cut timber efficiently as well as a variety of other materials. Choose the right blade for the job. An unsuitable blade can ruin the work, wear the blade or strain the motor. Keep the blades sharp for quick clean cutting. Circular saw blades are best sharpened by a professional.

RIP BLADE

Used for cutting timber parallel with the grain.

CROSS CUT BLADE

This is designed to cut across the grain of solid timber.

COMBINATION BLADE

This is suitable for cutting timber in any direction, and for composite boards.

CARBIDE TIPPED BLADE

These hardened tipped teeth stay sharp longer, especially when cutting particle boards.

ABRASIVE DISC

Abrasive discs are flexible and shatterproof. A silicon carbide disc will cut marble, slate and building blocks. An aluminium oxide disc cuts thin gauge ferrous pipes, such as drain pipes and guttering.

METAL CUTTING BLADE

Suitable for aluminium, copper, lead and brass.

PLANER BLADE

Produces a fine finish on all timber and boards.

FLOORING BLADE

Should be used on secondhand timber, especially where there is the danger of cutting through nails. Also useful for high glue content materials, such as particle board.

FRICTION BLADE

These blades are for cutting through corrugated iron and thin sheet metal.

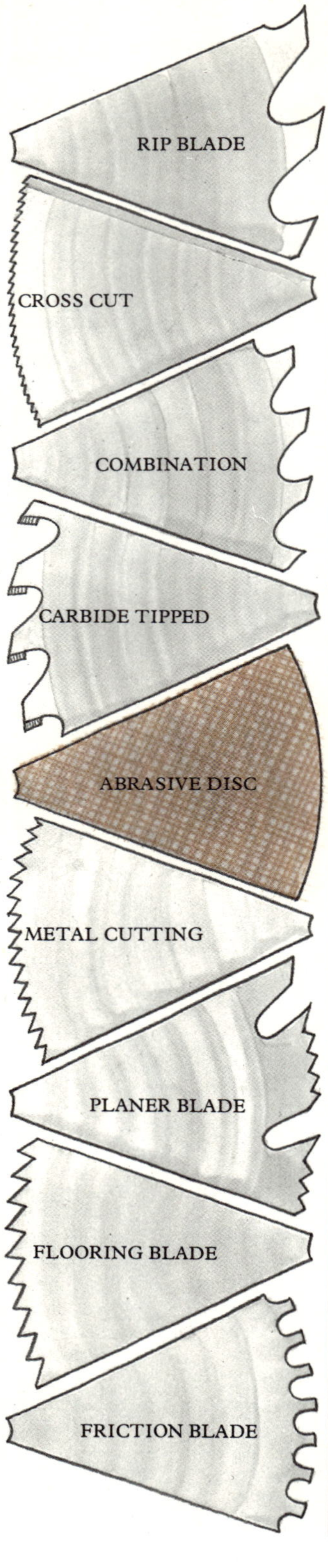

Changing a blade

Make sure that the saw is disconnected from the power supply. Check maker's instructions carefully for particular information regarding removal.

Rest the sole plate on the front of the bench with the teeth against the edge. Pull back the lower blade guard and fit a spanner on the blade bolt. Tap the spanner sharply with a mallet to free the bolt and unscrew it by hand. Remove the washer and blade. Looking at the machine from the blade side, the saw blade revolves in a counter clockwise direction; most blades will have an arrow printed on one side to show the direction of rotation. This should be facing you when the blade is fitted. Pass the blade through the slot in the sole plate and replace the bolt and washer to secure the blade to the motor drive shaft. Tighten the bolt with a spanner.

Removing the bolt
Tap spanner with mallet to loosen bolt. Unscrew by hand.

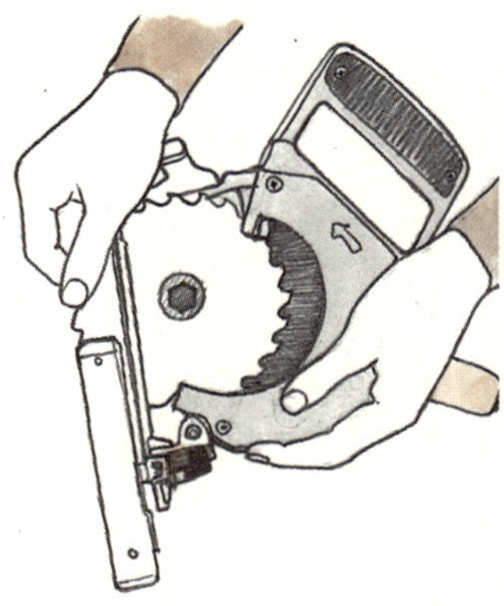

Fitting the blade
With the directional arrow facing you, pass the blade through the slot in the sole plate.

Setting the depth of cut
To cut right through the material with minimum splintering, the blade should be adjusted to project 3mm from the underside (*a*). Place the sole plate on the workpiece with the guard in the open position and the blade against the side edge. Release the depth adjustment knob and swing the body of the saw up, or down, keeping the sole plate flat on the work until the blade is at the required depth. Tighten the knob.

To set the blade to cut partially through the material mark the depth of cut on the edge of the work. Position the blade so that at the lowest point of its arc, the point of a tooth just touches the line *(b)*.

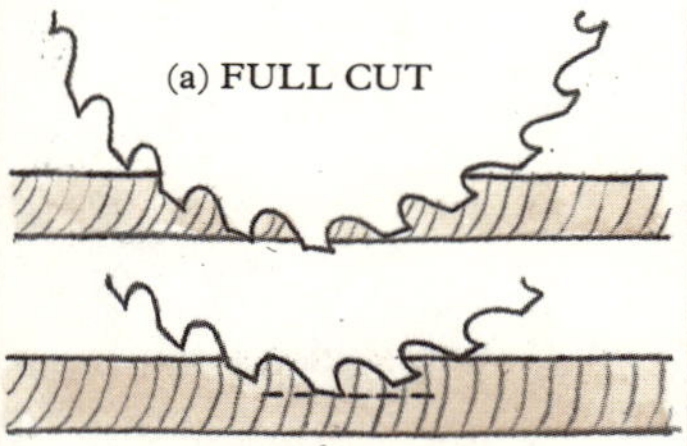

Setting for an angled cut
The sole plate can be adjusted to tilt the saw blade to any angle up to 45°. The bracket fitted to the sole plate is marked with a protractor scale to indicate the desired angle and can be locked in place by the angle adjustment knob. Try the cut on a piece of waste wood to check the accuracy of the angle with a sliding bevel.

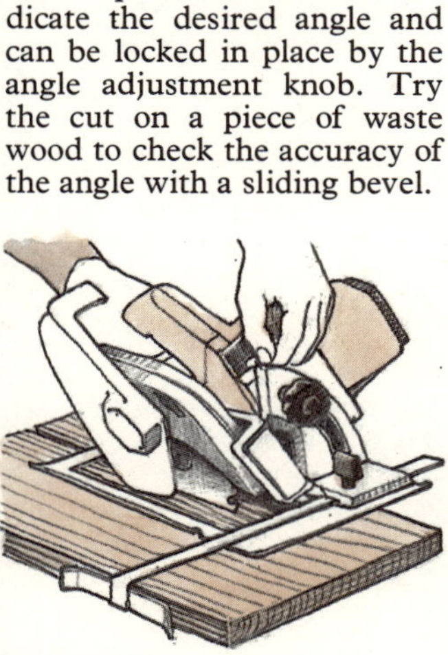

When the blade is set at an angle, the depth of the cut is decreased and should be reset.

Free-hand rip cuts
The saw can be used free-hand to make a rip cut by following a marked line. When positioning this line remember to allow for the thickness of the kerf, which may differ for different blades. Rest the front of the sole plate on the lumber so that the blade just clears the edge. Check position as shown, right. Switch on the saw and wait for it to reach top speed before starting the cut. Advance the saw through the work with a steady pressure, neither so fast that it strains the motor nor so slow that the blade overheats. The sound of the saw is your best guide. Keep your eye on the cutting guide to make sure that the cut does not wander. If the saw jams, or the motor is straining, back off a little to allow the saw to run up to speed again before continuing.

Using a fence guide
A rip fence acts as a guide for making repeated rip cuts quickly and accurately without marking out the work. The fence, which is adjustable, can be fitted to either side of the saw. Set the fence for the width of the cut by measuring from the inside of the fence to the blade. Allow for the set of the blade and position it.

Align free-hand cutting guide, usually marked on the sole plate, with the cutting line.

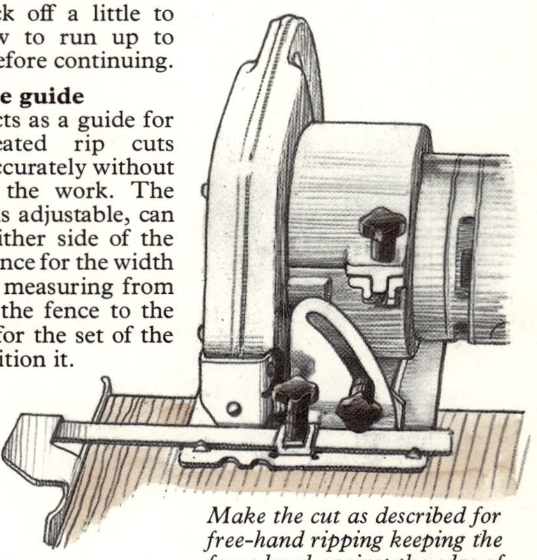

Make the cut as described for free-hand ripping keeping the fence hard against the edge of the work.

Using a guide batten
Clamp a batten to the work parallel to the cut line. Run the edge of the sole against it.

Making a cross cut
For an accurate cross cut, you need a guide against which the sole plate of the saw can run. Screw two battens together in the form of a "T" square. One batten rests against the far side of the work, while the other lies across the work to form an accurate right angle. Position the "T" square as shown. Run the saw through the work keeping the sole plate pressed against the leg of the "T" square. If the top piece of the "T" is left over length, the saw will cut through it as the cut is finished leaving the remaining piece the exact distance from the blade to the "T" square leg. On subsequent cuts, align the cut end of the "T" head with the cutting line marked on the work to automatically position the leg in the right place.

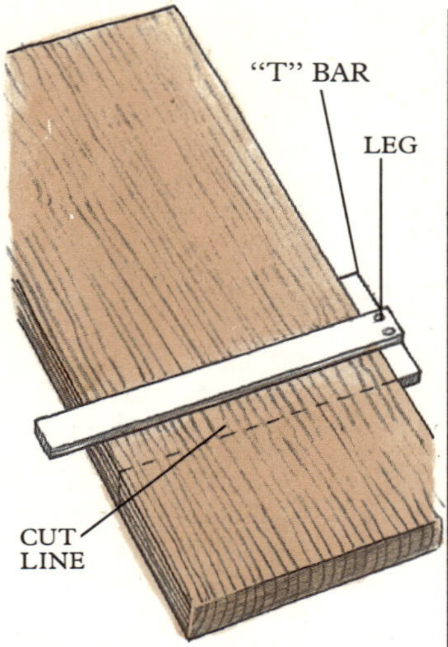

Positioning the "T" square
From the cut line, measure the distance from the blade to the edge of the sole plate and clamp the "T" square on this line.

Cutting panels
Before a large panel is cut, support it securely on saw horses with battens on each side of the cut. Place the board face side downward to achieve the cleanest cut on that side. Clamp a guide batten parallel with the required cutting line and operate the saw in the normal way. On a long saw cut the kerf may close up, pinching the blade. Stop the motor and place a small wedge in the cut behind the saw before continuing.

Cutting a groove
To cut a groove or housing with a circular saw set the blade to the required depth and the guide fence to make a cut for each edge of the groove. Reset the guide to make intermediate cuts and clear out the waste with a wood chisel.

Making a mitre cut
Clamp a guide batten to the work at the required angle for accurate results.

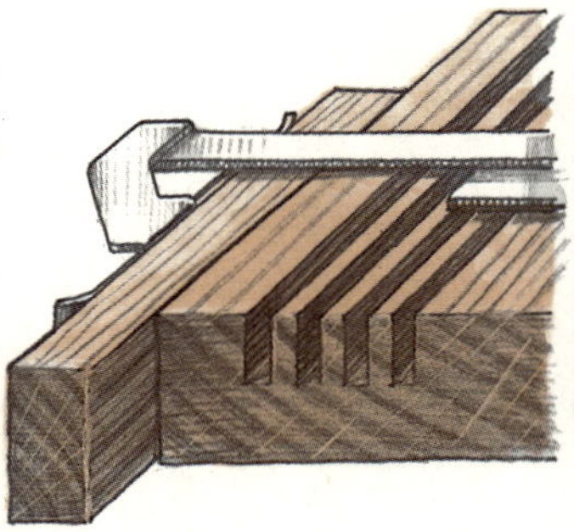

Extending the fence
Screw a hardwood strip to the bench to provide better control and protect the work edge.

Cutting boards to the same length
To cut several boards to the same length, screw a softwood batten to the bench and butt the squared ends of the boards against it. Clamp another batten across all the boards to act as a guide for the saw. Cut all the ends of the boards at once in one pass.

Safety factors
Support the work securely and make sure that the blade will not cut anything underneath the work. Do not force the cut or twist the blade. Take up a steady stance and where possible stand to one side of the cutting line. Keep the cable away from the blade and check it regularly for condition. Do not put the saw down while it is still running and never adjust the saw while it is connected to a power supply.

Saw Bench Attachment

SIZE: Table size: 368 × 250 to 500 × 400mm
MATERIAL: Steel
ACCESSORIES: Portable circular saw
USE: To convert a portable saw to a table saw

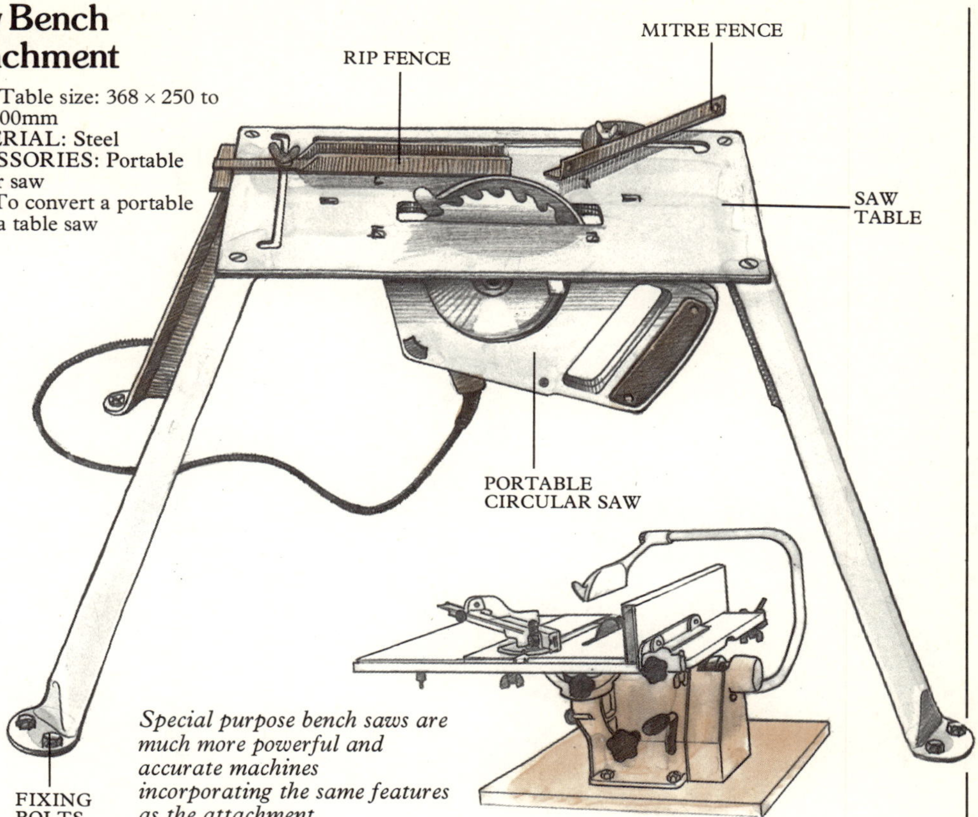

Special purpose bench saws are much more powerful and accurate machines incorporating the same features as the attachment.

Some manufacturers supply a saw bench attachment, designed to convert their portable circular saw into a saw table. These are small, lightweight tables and normally will not take other makes of saw. If you are thinking of using this attachment it may influence your choice of saw.

The saw is fitted upside down to the underside of the table with the blade and guard protruding above the surface. It must be fixed securely and accurately aligned with the bench guides. The saw bench has four legs, which must be securely bolted to a work bench. Alternatively it could be fixed to a composite board base, which could be clamped to a bench when required. This has the advantage of portability and clears the work surface when the saw bench is not required. The angle and depth of the blade is adjusted by the portable saw controls.

Rip sawing

The saw bench is ideal for ripping boards to width, as it leaves both hands free to guide the work. Raise the saw blade to just clear the thickness of the material to be sawn. Set the rip fence the required distance from the blade.

Run the saw until it is up to speed before feeding the work against the blade. Holding the work firmly against the fence push it steadily over the blade. Keep both hands well clear of the blade. Do not lean on the work as your own weight may force the cut to close and jam the saw.

Finishing the cut

To finish the cut, use a push stick, a length of softwood with a notch cut in one end, to feed the work over the blade.

Cross cutting

To cut the ends of rails square, set the mitre fence at right angles to the saw blade. Mark the cut on the front edge of the rail and align it carefully with the blade before switching on. Hold the rail against the fence and slide it in its groove to push the work into the saw.

The ends of the rails can be cut to any angle by setting the mitre fence accordingly and proceeding as for a normal cross cut.

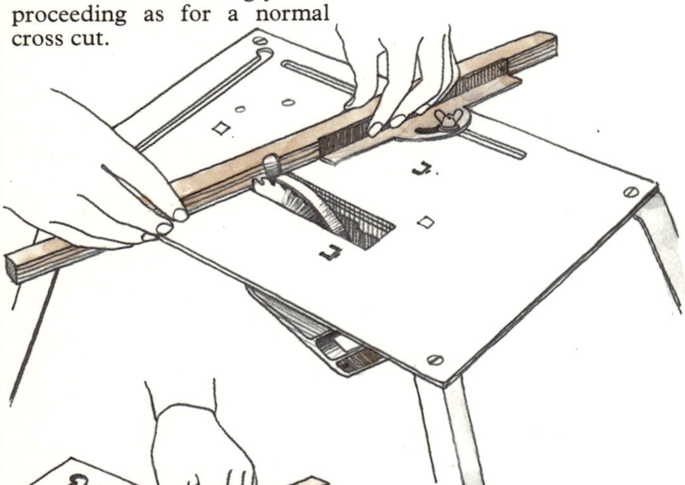

Cutting rail ends
Use both hands for large offcuts and one hand for dealing with smaller wood lengths.

Cutting a rebate

A rebate can be cut by using the rip fence with the blade set to cut the depth of the rebate. Cut one face of the rebate, reset the saw and cut the other face, removing the waste at the same time.

FIRST CUT FINISHING CUT

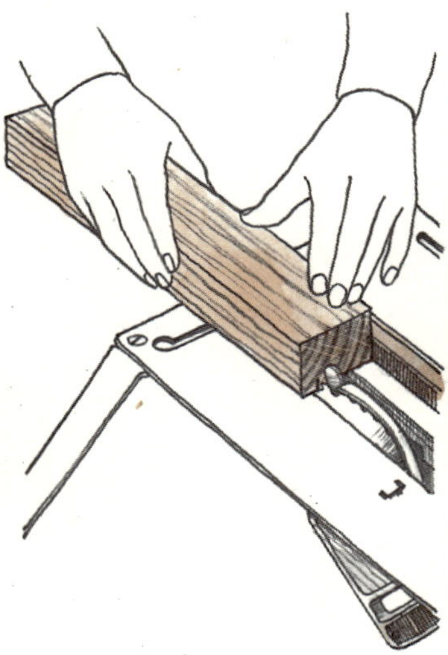

Cutting a housing

Set the rip fence to make one cut on each side of the groove and make the intermediate cuts to remove the waste. Bevelled or "wobble" washers can be fitted to the blade to increase the kerf width considerably when removing the waste. Bevelled washers set the blade at an angle so that as it revolves the teeth move from one side to the other.

Cutting a tenon

Cut an accurate tenon joint using the mitre fence set at 90° to the blade. Set the saw to match the depth of the shoulder. Make sure the depth is accurately matched, as otherwise the tenon may weaken. You can cut the length of the tenon with a cross cut hand saw, then cut the shoulder line with the saw bench for accuracy. Turn the work over and repeat the sequence. Mount blade with a bevelled washer to remove the waste quickly.

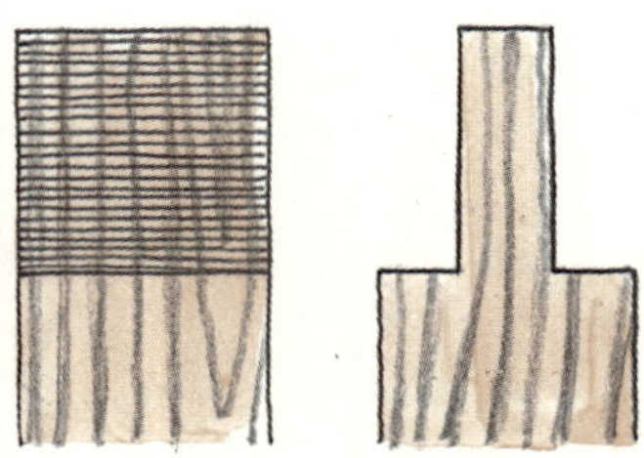

Make the first cut along the shoulder line and on the waste side. Make further cuts on the waste side one blade width at a time until the joint is complete.

Frame Saw

OTHER NAMES: Bow saw, sweep saw, turning saw
SIZE: *Length:* 200 to 700mm; *Width:* 3 to 87mm
MATERIAL: *Blade:* steel; *Frame:* beechwood
USE: To rip, cross cut and cut curves in timber

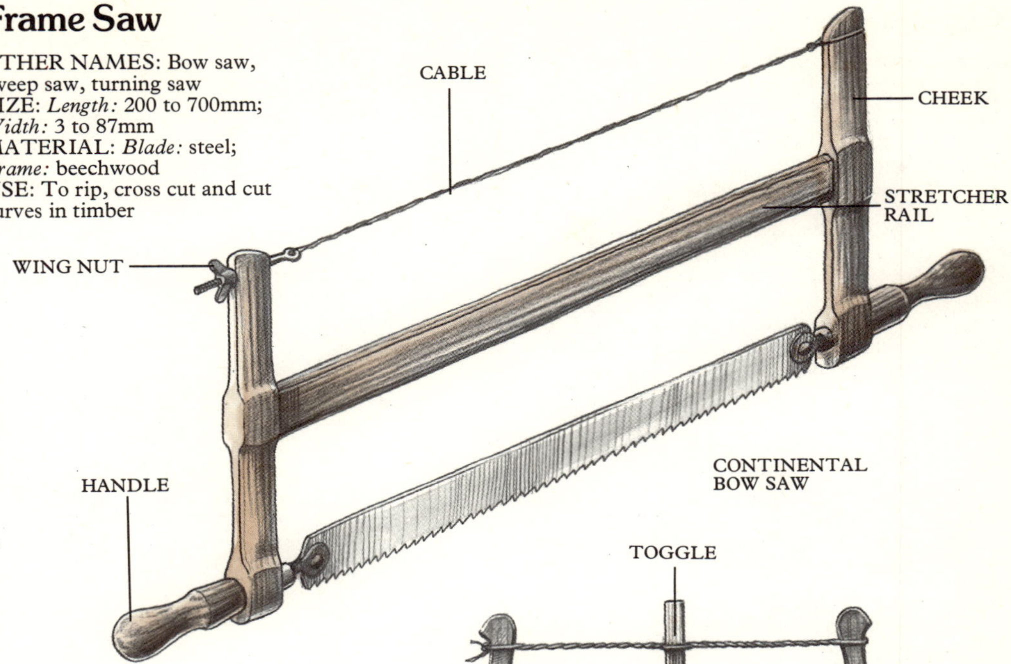

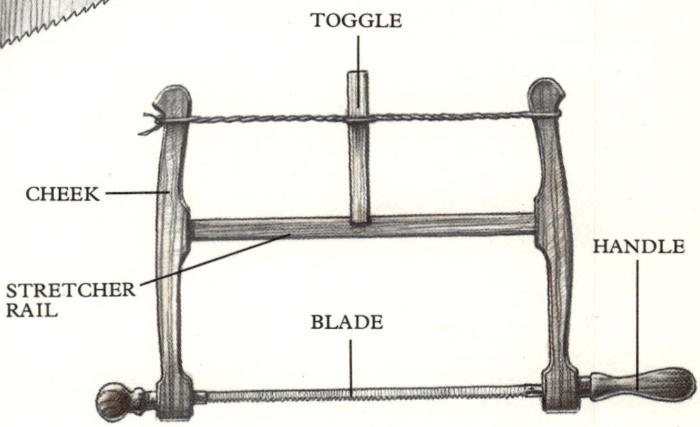

The modern frame saw is based on centuries-old construction. A relatively narrow blade is held in tension by the side pieces or "cheeks" of the frame, pivoting about their centres on the ends of a stretcher rail. The top ends of the cheeks are pulled toward each other either by a twisted cord and toggle stick, or by a threaded rod or a cable, tensioned by wing nuts. The stretcher rail and cheeks are either joined by a dry stub mortise and tenon or a bridle joint.

The traditional two-handed method of holding the frame saw controls the direction of the blade and supports the frame. Grip the handle with one hand, the index finger extended in the direction of the blade. Take the blade fixing between the index and second finger of the other hand, wrap the thumb around the cheek and clasp the other fingers around the other hand.

On some European models the blades are fixed in a vertical position for cross cutting, but with a swivel blade for ripping. The British type of frame saw, the bow saw, has a smaller frame and is used for curves.

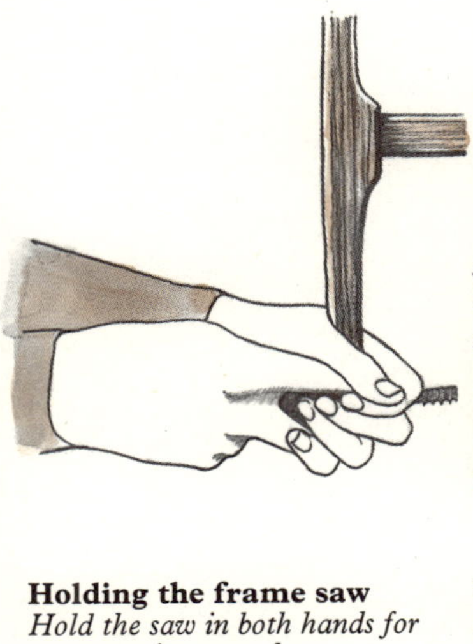

Holding the frame saw
Hold the saw in both hands for more precise control.

Using the swivel blade
Swing the frame aside to clear long boards when rip sawing.

Coping Saw

SIZE: *Length:* 159mm; *Bow depth:* 118 and 168mm
MATERIAL: *Blade/frame:* steel; *Handle:* hardwood
USE: To make curved cuts in wood or plastic

The blade of the coping saw is very narrow and has fine teeth grouped at 14 per 25mm. It is held under tension by the spring of the frame. It can be angled to cut in any direction, by twisting the pins extending from the blade holders.

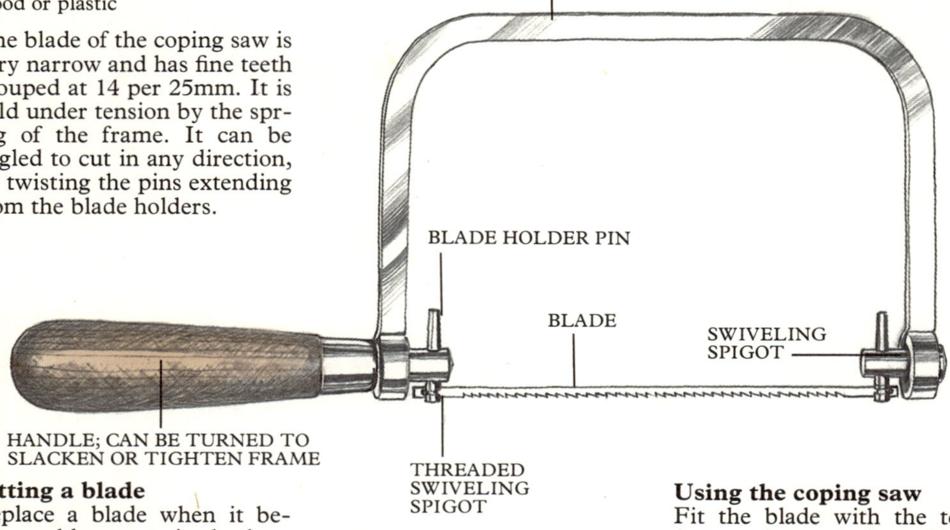

Fitting a blade
Replace a blade when it becomes blunt or is broken. Slacken the saw by turning the handle counter clockwise while restraining the blade holder. Place one end of the blade in the slot in the front blade holder, then insert the other end as shown below.

Tension the frame by turning the handle clockwise. To straighten the blade, line it up with the holder pins.

Securing the blade

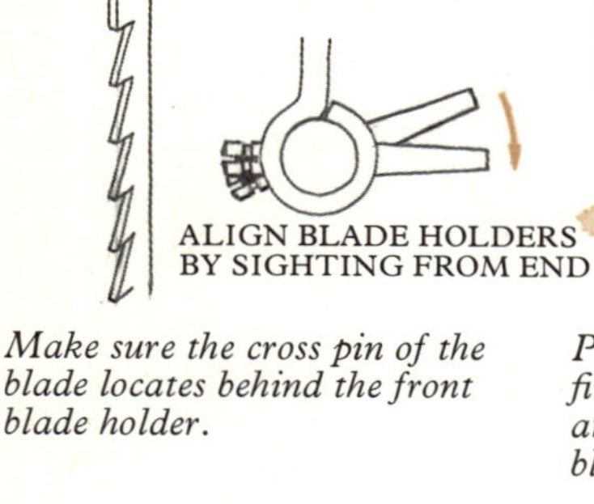

Make sure the cross pin of the blade locates behind the front blade holder.

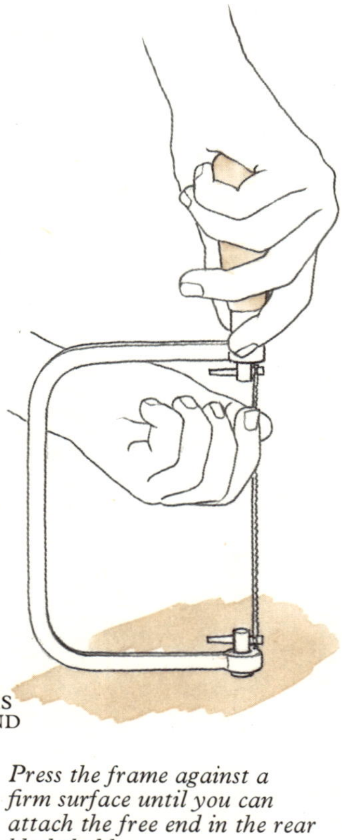

Press the frame against a firm surface until you can attach the free end in the rear blade holder.

Using the coping saw
Fit the blade with the teeth facing forward for thicker stock. For thin material, set the teeth to face backward and cut by holding the work flat on a bench as for a fret saw. Turn the blade when necessary to clear the work. This is particularly useful when cutting shapes in a panel. First drill a hole in one edge of the shape. Pass the blade through on its own, then connect it to each end of the frame.

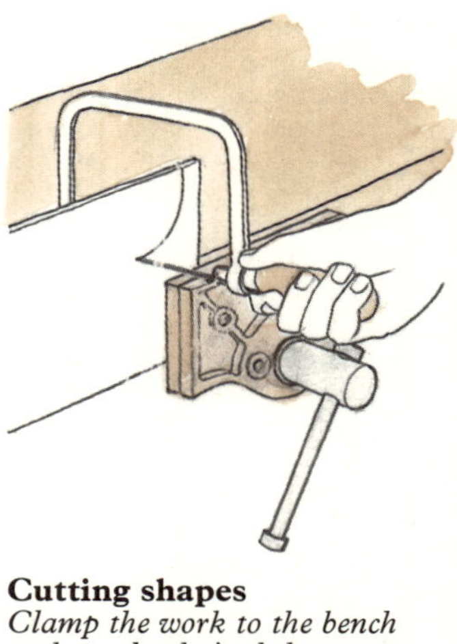

Cutting shapes
Clamp the work to the bench and cut the desired shape, angling the blades as necessary.

Fret Saw

OTHER NAMES: Scroll saw, deep-throat coping saw
SIZE: *Length:* 125mm; *Bow depth:* 287mm
MATERIAL: *Blade/frame:* steel; *Handle:* hardwood
USE: To cut tight curves in wood and plastic

The fret saw is used to work thin sheet materials. It is very similar to the coping saw, but has a much deeper bow to the frame and can, therefore, be used to cut shapes well inboard from the edge of a panel. The blade is so fine, up to 32 teeth per 25mm, that it can cut curves without being angled.

The blade is held at each end by a simple, thumb screw operated clamp. It is fitted like the blade of a coping saw, but the operation is much simpler as the spring of the frame itself is sufficient to tension the blade without further help.

To use the saw, hold the work flat on a bench overhanging the edge. With the saw teeth set to face the handle, saw from below using a pull stroke. The bench backs up the work as it is cut.

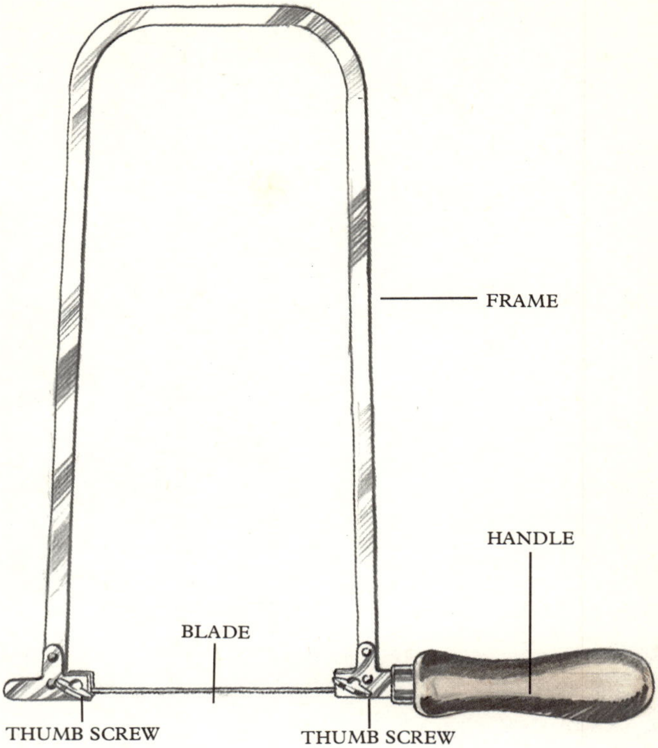

Piercing Saw

OTHER NAMES: Lightweight fret saw, jeweller's piercing saw
SIZE: *Length:* 125 to 150mm; *Bow depth:* 68 and 84mm
MATERIAL: *Blade/frame:* steel; *Handle:* hardwood
USE: To cut tight curves in thin sheet metal

The piercing saw is constructed in exactly the same way as a fret saw, but its extremely fine blade, up to 80 teeth per 25mm, is specifically designed for cutting thin sheet metals, such as steel, copper, brass and aluminium. Jewellers and silversmiths use the saw to cut gold and silver sheet.

The blade is fitted and used as for a fret saw. Some frames adjust to take blades of different lengths, which is a useful and economic way to re-use broken but otherwise functioning blades.

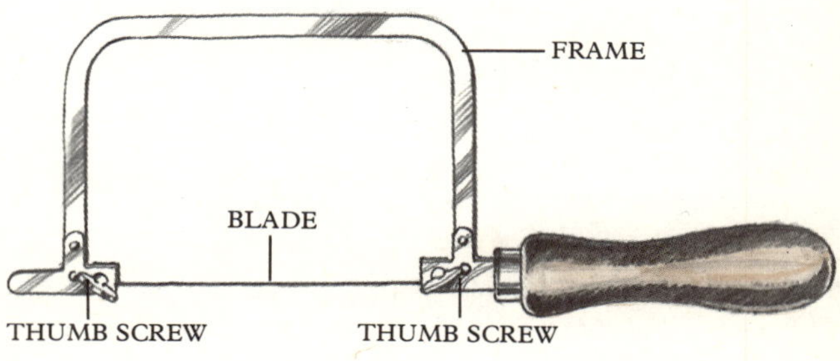

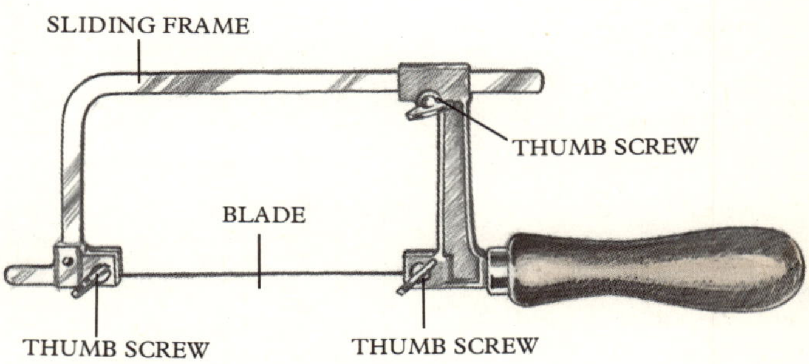

Sabre Saw

OTHER NAME: Powered jig saw
SIZE: *Unloaded speed:* 2,700 to 3,300 strokes per minute; *Weight:* 1.7 to 2.72kg
MATERIAL: Various
ACCESSORIES: Saw blade, guide fence
USE: To cut curves in various materials

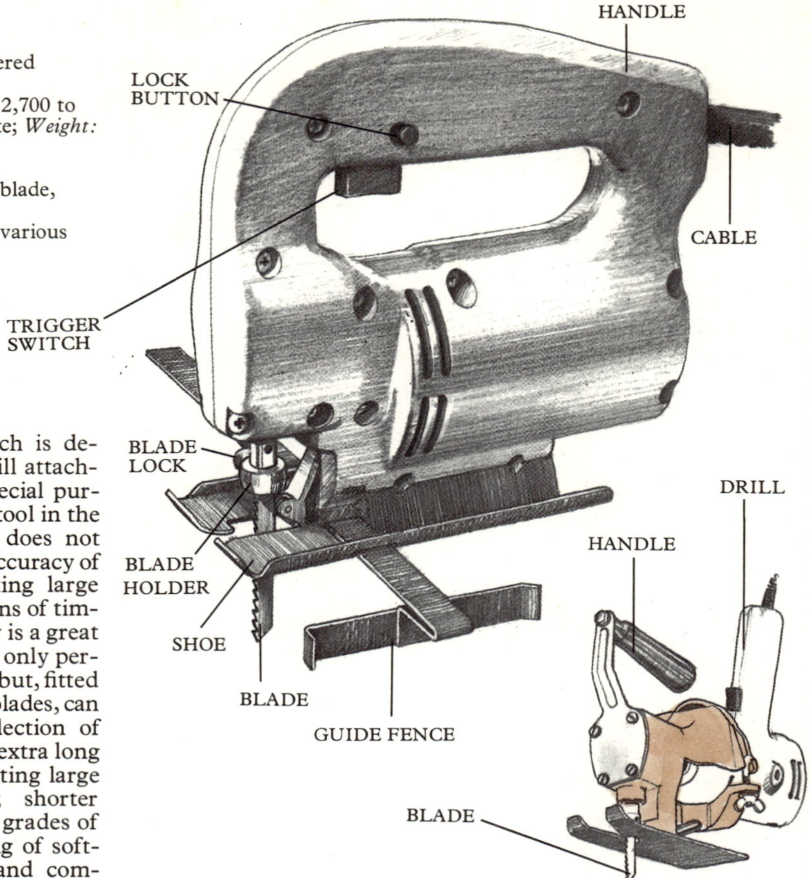

The sabre saw, which is designed as a power drill attachment as well as a special purpose saw, is a useful tool in the home workshop. It does not have the power and accuracy of larger saws for cutting large panels or thick sections of timber, but its versatility is a great advantage. It can not only perform a variety of cuts but, fitted with the appropriate blades, can also saw a large selection of materials. There are extra long coarse blades for cutting large sections of timber; shorter blades with different grades of teeth for finer cutting of softwoods, hardwoods and composite boards; hack saw-like blades for cutting metal; and special blades for cutting plastics, masonry, plasterboard, leather, rubber and cardboard. A superior blade is available with carbide tipped teeth and there are also blades edged with tungsten carbide chips of different grades. They cut slower than many blades and are a little more expensive, but last longer and produce a very clean cut with virtually no splintering. They will also tackle ceramics.

Blades should be fitted according to the maker's instructions. Make sure they are securely held and aligned as accurately as possible. Not all manufacturers produce the same range of blades, but some makes are interchangeable. Check that the fitting is identical by comparing a blade from your own machine with any prospective purchase.

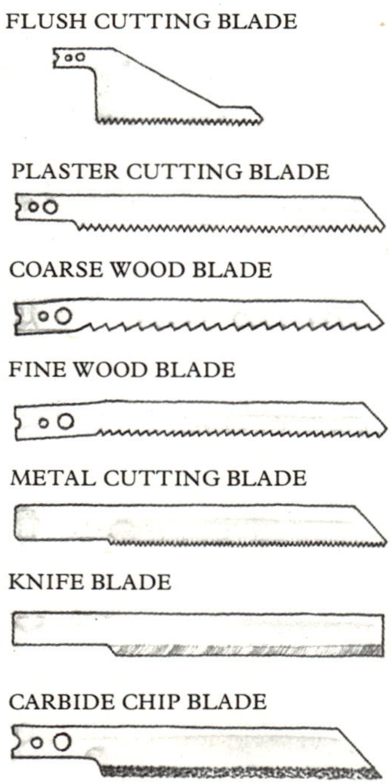

Using the saw
The saw is operated by squeezing the trigger. It switches off as soon as the trigger is released. Most models have a lock button which can be pressed to run the saw continuously. The button can be automatically released by squeezing the trigger again. Some types of saw have variable speeds. Use a slow speed for hard materials and a faster speed for soft materials.

Rest the front of the shoe on the work, with the blade just clear of the edge. Advance the saw through the cut keeping the sole on the work and providing just enough forward pressure to cut easily. Forcing the pace will blunt the blade, if not break it. If the cut is too slow, either the blade is blunt, or it is not the right type for the job. When the cut is complete switch off and hold the saw until the blade stops running.

Making a straight cut
Hold work firmly on a safe surface which allows enough clearance beneath the cut for the blade to work unimpeded. As the saw cuts on the up-stroke, any splintering is likely to occur on the top surface so lay the finished face of the material downward. The saw can be used free hand following a marked line.

Some saws have a rip fence accessory to fix to the shoe. The fence runs on the edge of the work to guide the blade in a line parallel to the edge. The sabre saw does not do this job as well as a circular saw: the blade must be perfectly lined up with the fence to cut a straight line without being distorted, and on most models this is difficult to achieve. A guide strip can be clamped to the work to prevent the saw wandering off line.

Angled cuts
The sole on many saws can be adjusted to swing the blade over to angles up to 45°.

Cutting holes in a panel
To cut an opening in the face of a board, mark and then drill a hole 9mm in diameter next to the marked line on the waste side. Insert the blade of the sabre saw and follow the line. Cut a circular hole in one operation.

Cut a square hole as shown right. Cut each corner until the waste drops out. Saw in the other direction to remove the remaining waste.

Plunge cutting
Cuts can be made inboard of a panel without drilling a starting hole. This method is known as "plunge" cutting, and needs practice to stop the saw jumping as the blade attempts to enter the work and to prevent the shoe slipping.

Tip the saw forward on the front edge of the shoe with the blade above the surface of the work. Switch on and pivot the saw about the front edge of the shoe until the blade begins to cut. Do not make a forward cut until the shoe is resting firmly on the work.

Starting the cut

Rest the front of the shoe on the work, line up the blade with the marked line and switch on.

Using a square as a guide

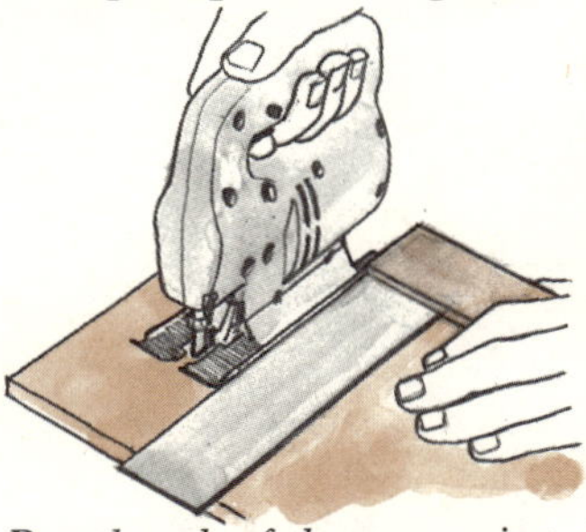

Run the sole of the saw against a square held across the work for an accurate square cross cut.

Cutting a square hole

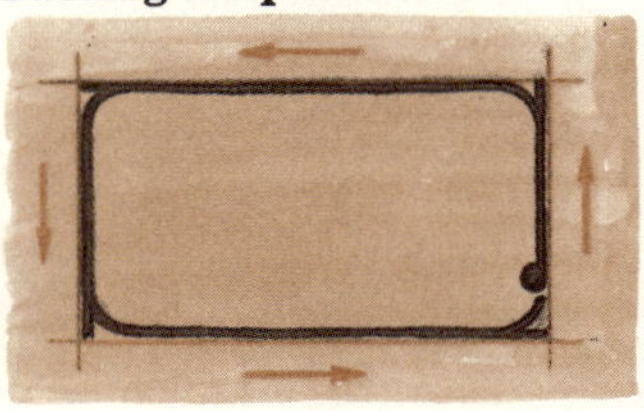

Run the blade into a corner, back off 25mm and cut a tight curve to the next side.

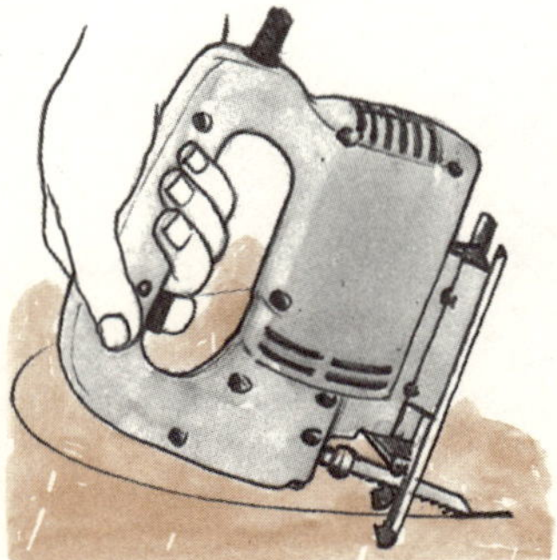

Saw position for plunge cutting.

Curved cuts
Most sabre saw blades are narrow enough to cut tight curves. Follow the line by eye, cutting on the waste side. Do not force the blade to cut a curve which is straining it. Either change to a narrower blade or remove some of the waste with straight cuts to give greater clearance for the blade.

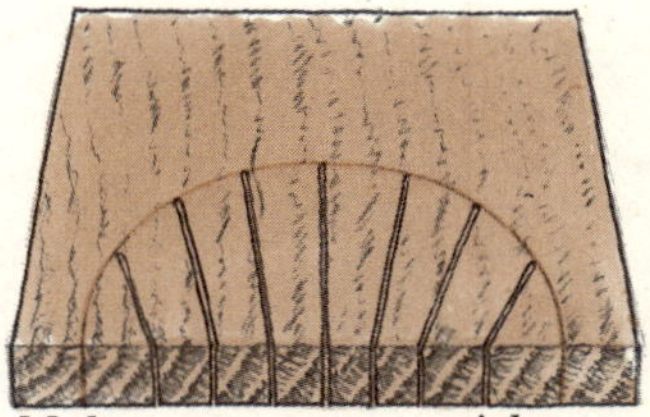

Make preparatory straight cuts to either a concave (above) or convex (below) curve.

Cutting metal
The sabre saw fitted with the appropriate blade will cut any metal which is normally worked by a hack saw. Back up thin sheet metal with a sheet of composite board, both being cut together to give a clean finish and avoid distorting the metal. Spread a thin film of oil along the cut line and proceed at a steady pace.

Cutting plastic laminates
Saw sheet laminate as for thin sheet metal, keeping it held down firmly onto the backing board. Lay the laminate face downward to avoid chipping on the face side. Always use the blade recommended for fine metal work.

Safety factors
Unplug the sabre saw before inserting a blade and make sure that the "lock on" button is not operative before plugging the saw in. Keep the cable away from the blade and take particular care that it does not pass under the work where it may be severed by the blade.

Hack Saw

SIZE: To take 200, 250, 300mm blades
MATERIAL: *Frame/blade:* steel; *Handle:* zinc, alloy, hardwood
USE: To cut metal

Hack saws are used to cut most metals. The bow frame is adjustable to take different lengths of blade, and may be fitted with a pistol grip handle or a straight hardwood grip. The pistol grip is much more comfortable to use and is less likely to twist in your hand.

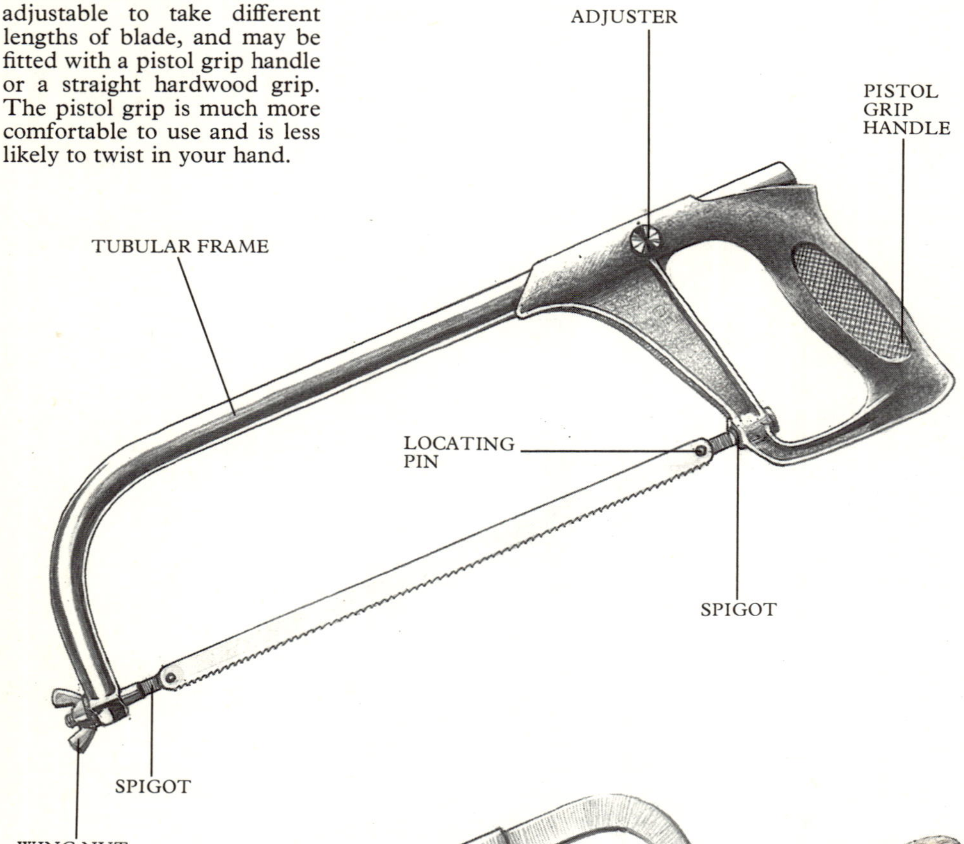

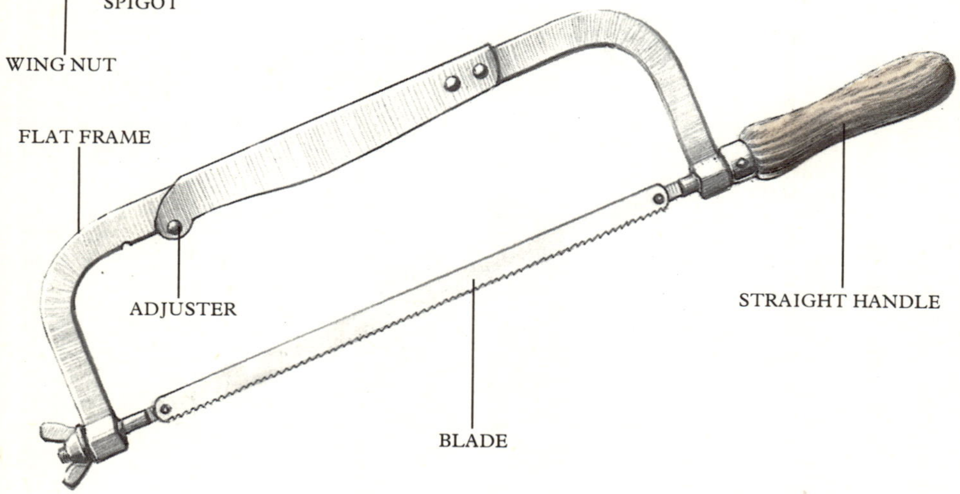

Using a hack saw

Secure the work firmly in a vice. Use your thumb to guide the blade when making short backward strokes to establish the cut, then use the hand to steady the frame. Proceed with full length strokes, establishing a steady rhythm.

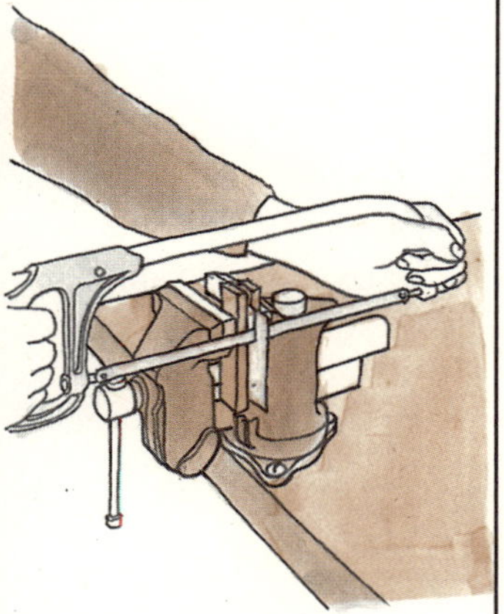

Use the hand to steady the frame. Cut on the forward stroke and release pressure on the return stroke.

Cutting thick sections

Saw on all sides working toward the centre to keep the cut square. Mark the metal all around and proceed with the cut using a light oil as a lubricant. Cut away the metal in the centre using the previous cuts as a guide.

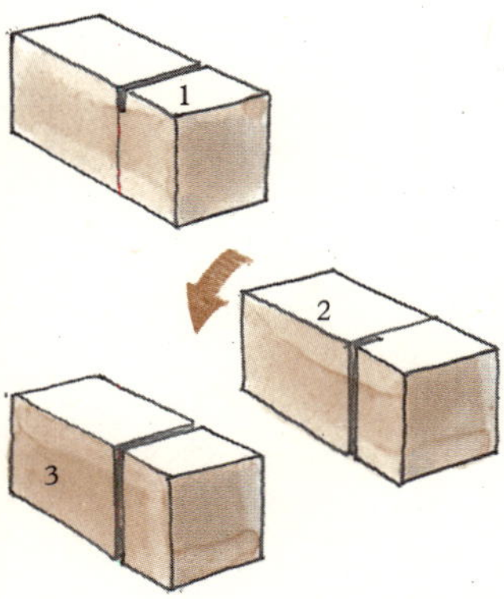

Saw to the depth of the blade, rotate the work away from you and continue all around until the cut is established.

Round stock

Hack saws will cut round stock and sheet metal if you adapt the sawing technique. Sandwich sheet metal between plywood.

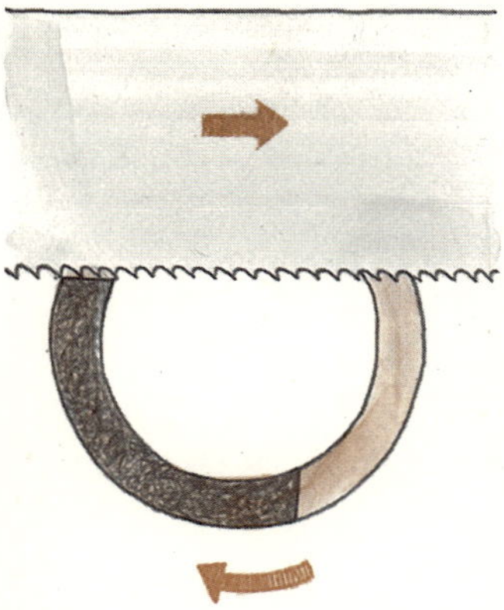

Rotate metal tube away from you during the cut to prevent the blade snatching and to keep the guide line in view.

If the saw wanders off line, you are probably twisting the frame out of line with the cut. If the blade snaps in the middle of a cut line, start with a new blade at the opposite end whenever possible. A new blade will be slightly thicker than a used one and is likely to jam in the old cut line.

Always use new blades to cut brass as a worn blade may slip.

Cutting sheet metal

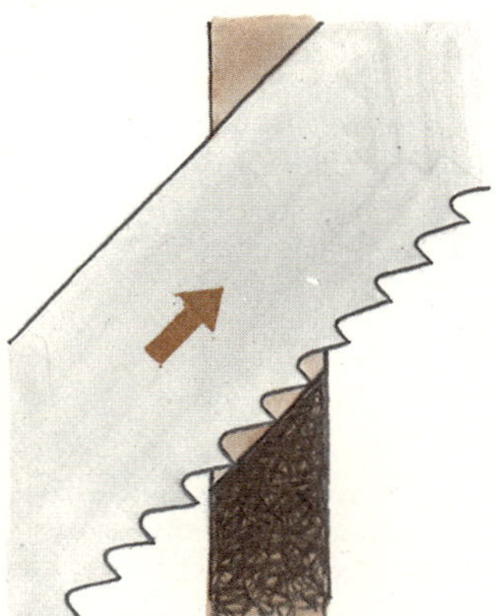

Cut thin sheet metal at an angle keeping as many teeth in contact with the work as you can.

Blades

Hack saw blades are made with different sizes of teeth to suit the material being cut. The normal range of sizes is 14, 18, 24, and 32 teeth per 25mm. As a guide, 3 teeth should fit the thickness of the material. Choose fine teeth for sawing thin sheet material or hard metal, and coarse teeth for soft metals like aluminium which would clog finer teeth. Coarse teeth are "raker" set for efficient chip clearance and are recommended for thick sections of soft metals. A wavy set is used for fine teeth.

Fully hardened blades are brittle, and likely to break easily in the hands of an amateur. They are also very expensive. For general purpose work, use a flexible steel blade with hardened teeth.

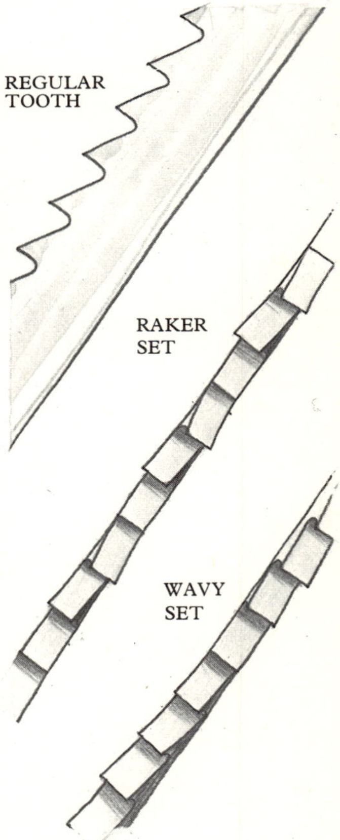

Hack saw blades have fine, regularly spaced teeth which can be raker set or wavy set.

Fitting a blade
Hack saw blades are held under tension by a wing nut on the end of the frame. To replace a blade, slacken the nut until the blade slips free of the frame. Hook the holes in each end of the new blade over the locating pins so that the teeth face away from the handle and apply tension. Experiment to get the right tension when fixing the blade. If it is too tight, it will arch up toward the frame, if too loose it will bend while in use and probably snap. The locating pins protrude from a spigot which has square shoulders to angle the blade in one of four positions at 90° to one another. This allows you to fit the blades sideways or even inverted.

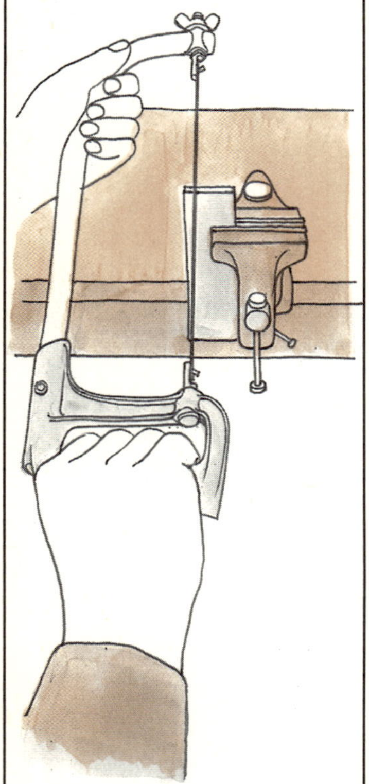

Hack saw blades can be fitted inverted or at an angle to make cuts longer than the frame normally permits, or where access space is limited.

Junior Hack Saw

SIZE: Blade length: 150mm
MATERIAL: *Frame:* steel; *Handle:* nylon, zinc or aluminium alloy
USE: Fine metal work

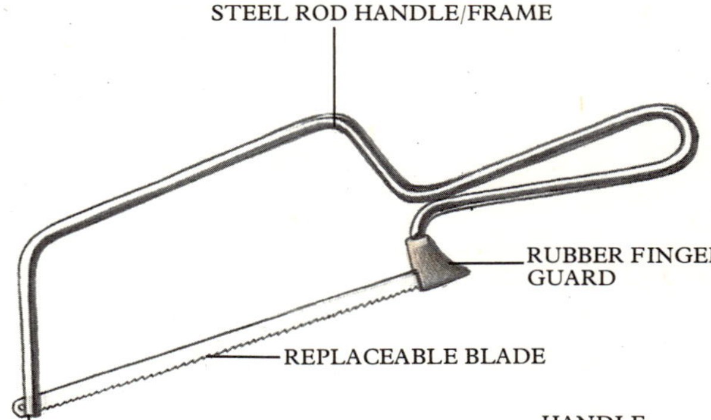

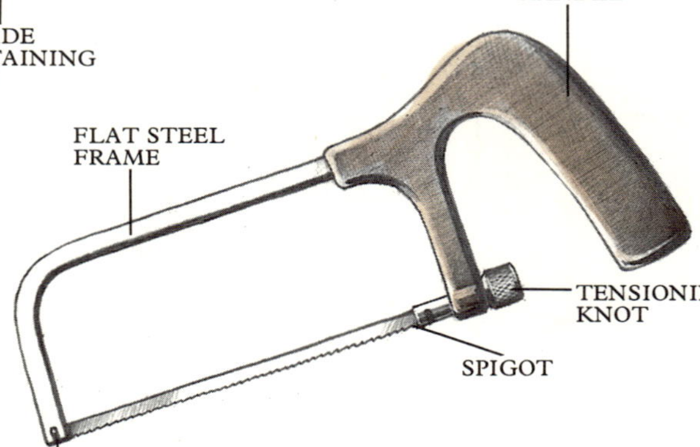

The junior hack saw is more convenient to use in confined spaces but must be used to make fine cuts only.

The frame and handle of the simplest junior hack saw is made in one piece from a bent steel rod. The blade, which has 32 teeth per 25mm, is held under tension by the natural spring of the frame and held in place by slots. The pins which project from each side of the blade hold it in position once it is inserted in the slots.

Another version of the saw has a pistol grip. The blade is located in a slot at the front end of the frame, but fits into a tensioning device at the rear.

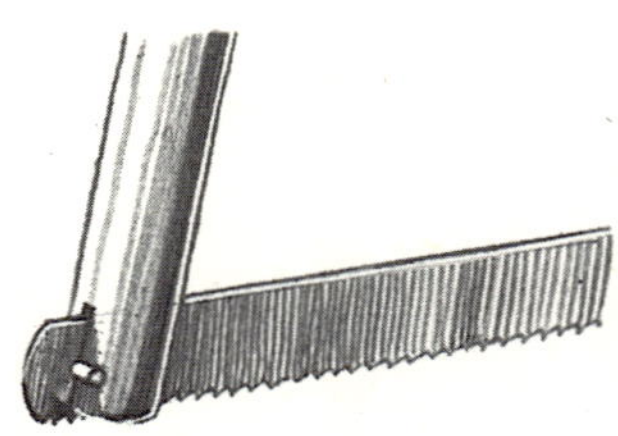

Replacing a blade
Fit the front end of the blade in to its slot; press the end of the frame firmly and locate the other end of the blade in its slot.

Mini Hack Saw

SIZE: Length: 200mm
MATERIAL: Plastic
ACCESSORY: Hack saw blade
USE: To use where a standard hack saw is unsuitable

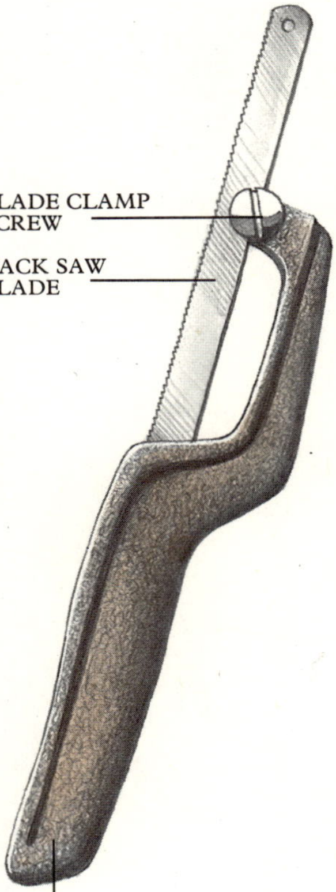

The mini hack saw is a one-piece handle and frame which accommodates a hack saw blade. It will hold broken blades as well as new ones. It is used to cut metal in confined spaces which would be inaccessible to a standard hack saw. The blade slides into the handle and is secured by a screw clamp at the front end.

Sheet Saw

SIZE: Length: 300 to 400mm
MATERIAL: *Blade:* steel; *Handle:* zinc alloy
USE: To cut sheet materials

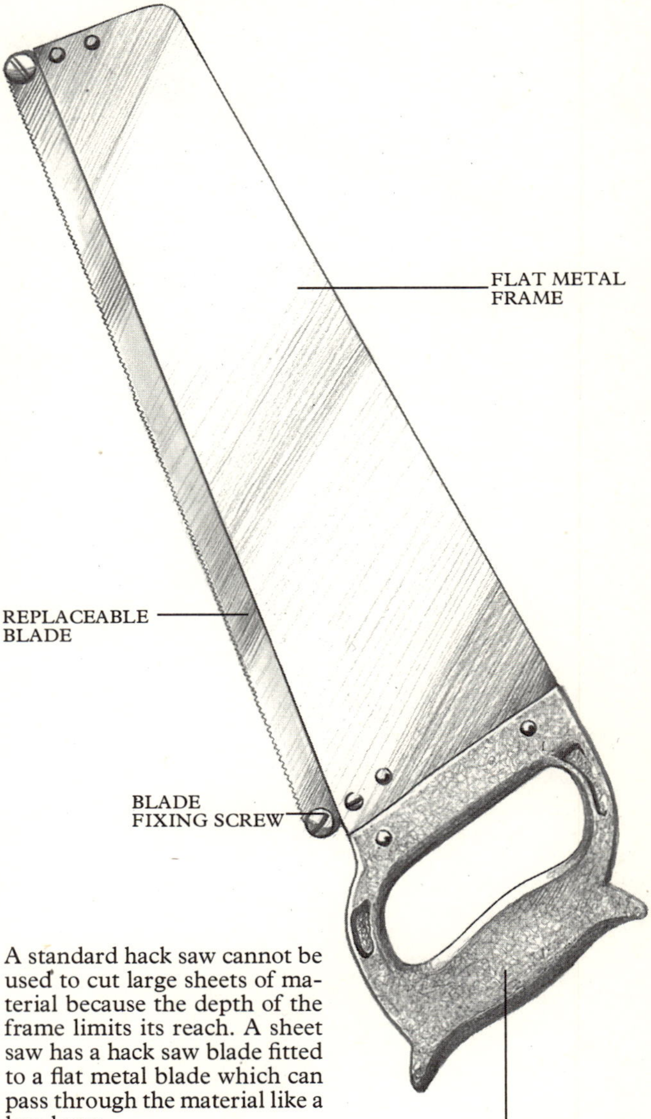

A standard hack saw cannot be used to cut large sheets of material because the depth of the frame limits its reach. A sheet saw has a hack saw blade fitted to a flat metal blade which can pass through the material like a hand saw.

The smaller version has a standard 300mm blade and is used to cut flat or corrugated steel, brass, copper and so on. It will also cut asbestos, plastic and slate. The larger saw takes a special 400mm blade with 6 or 10 teeth per 25mm. This saw will cut thicker sheet material, thermo-plastic bricks and metal covered plywood.

Saw File

OTHER NAME: Rod saw, tension file
SIZE: 150 to 200mm
MATERIAL: Steel
USE: To cut metal, ceramics and plastics

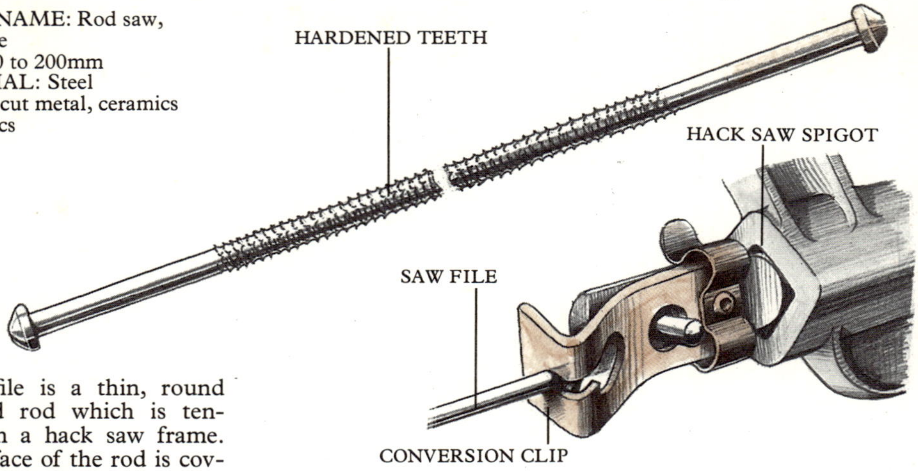

A saw file is a thin, round sectioned rod which is tensioned in a hack saw frame. The surface of the rod is covered either with tiny hardened teeth or by tungsten carbide particles. The file can cut in any direction and will turn in its own thickness. This makes it extremely useful for cutting very intricate curves in materials which are normally difficult to work, for example wall tiles can be cut to fit around shower fittings.

Some manufacturers provide special hack saw-like frames to tension the saw file, but with special clips, they can be used in standard hack saw frames. Files are also produced with wire handles at each end to be used without a frame at all. They are extremely useful in confined spaces where a standard frame saw would be unsuitable.

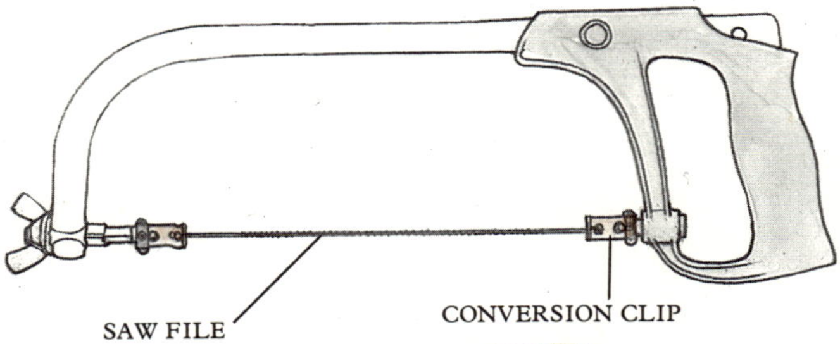

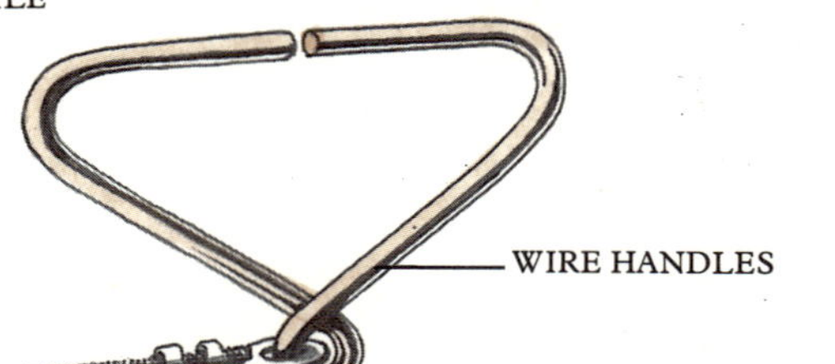

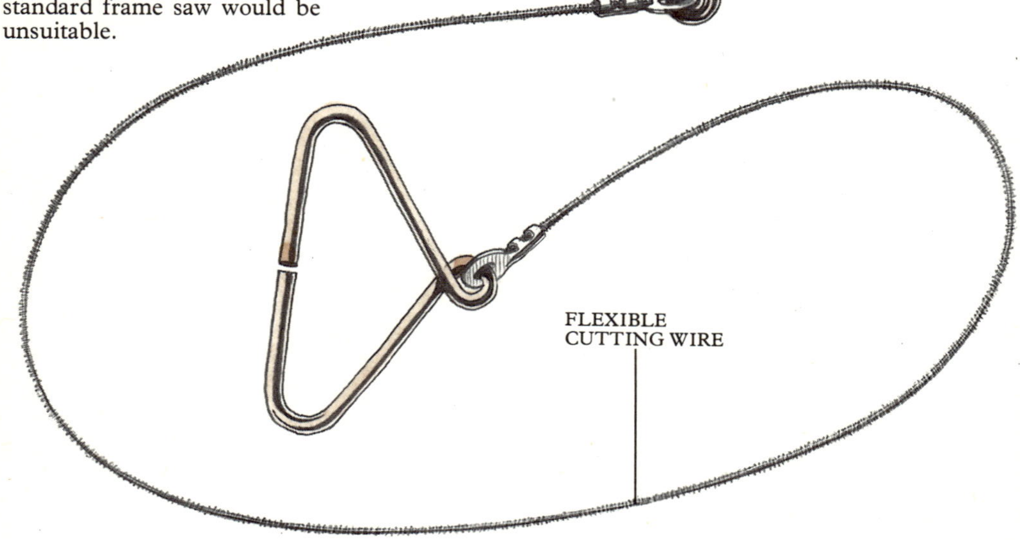

Band Saw

SIZE: *Depth of throat:* 237 to 362mm; *Table:* 175 × 175mm to 450 × 450mm
MATERIAL: Various
ACCESSORIES: Blades
USE: To convert large sections of lumber to size and to cut curves

A band saw is a power tool which is widely used in industry to cut timber to size, particularly where curves are involved. Smaller versions are available for the home workshop. The blade is a steel loop which is driven around two wheels inside the casing to give a continuous cutting edge. Depending on the model, home workshop band saws will cut wood up to 150mm thick.

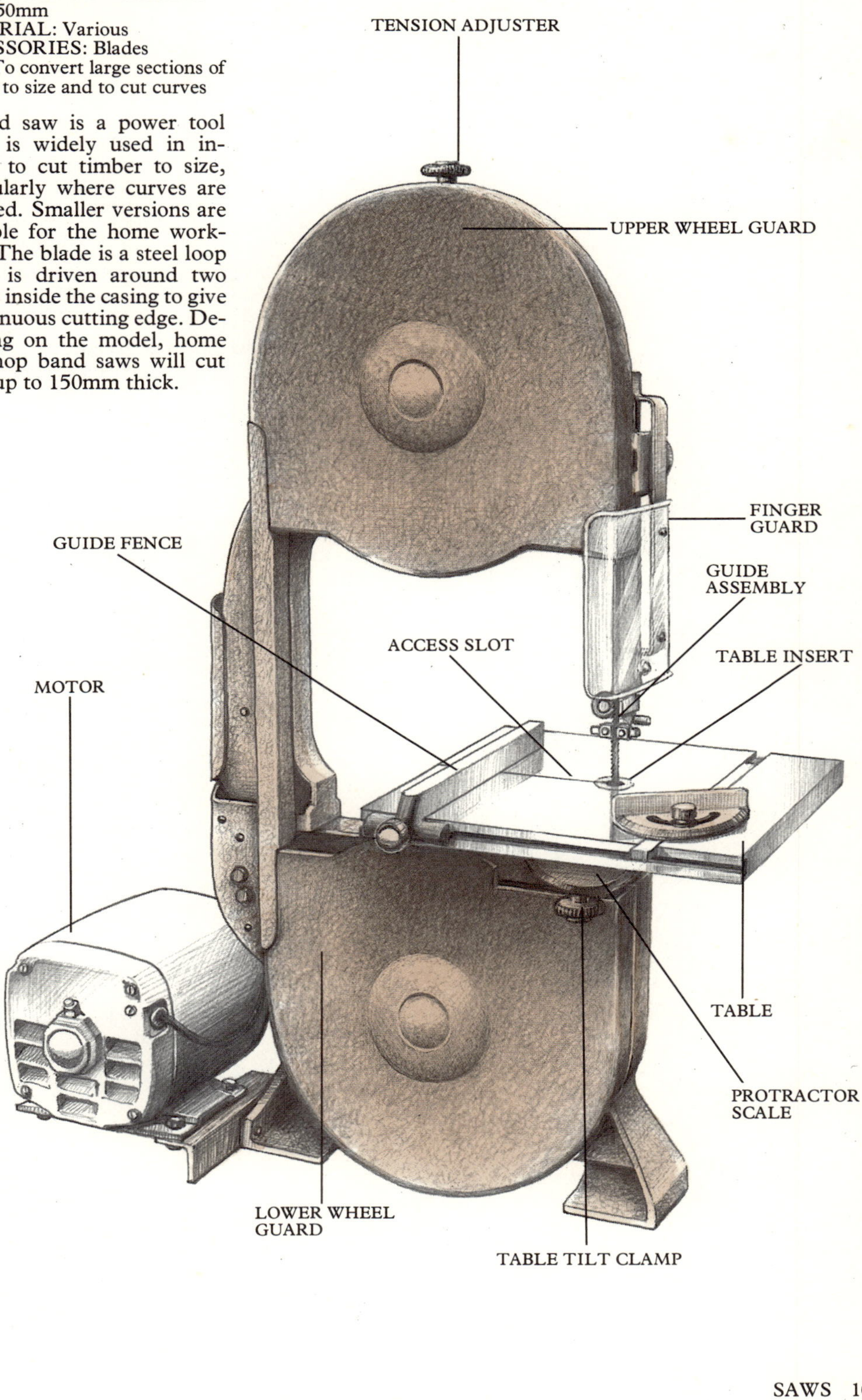

Blades
Band saw blades are toothed steel bands welded into a continuous loop. On the smaller domestic machines, they range from 3mm to 6mm wide. The narrow blades are used for cutting tight curves; wider blades make straighter cuts. The teeth are spaced at 6 to 24 teeth per 25mm. Coarse blades are for cutting through large sections of timber, while fine teeth are for cutting metal. The shape of the teeth also varies. Like the hack saw, the band saw has standard, skip tooth and hook tooth blades. The set of the teeth also varies from blade to blade. The common woodworking blade has teeth set alternately to the right and left like any hand saw. For coarse metal working, there is often a raker or unset tooth positioned between a pair of teeth to clear the waste quickly. Fine metal cutting teeth have a wavy set like a normal hack saw.

Toothless blades are available for cutting ceramics and plastics. The cutting edge is surfaced with tungsten carbide chips. This kind of blade will also cut timber and board; it produces a very smooth finish but is rather slow to work.

Blades are raker or wavy set like a hack saw or alternate set like a hand saw. Skip and hook teeth clear waste quickly.

Fitting blades
Open the wheel guards to get to the two wheels over which the blade runs. The lower wheel is driven by the motor. The idler wheel is adjustable for tensioning and sometimes tracking. Both wheels are covered with rubber to protect the set of the blade. Slacken the upper wheel tension adjuster (usually located at the top of the machine) so the blade will be able to fit easily over both wheels. Retract both blade guide assemblies as far as possible and remove the table insert. (The table has an access slot to allow the blade to pass through to the center.) With the teeth facing you fit the blade over the wheels. Take up the tension by the adjuster.

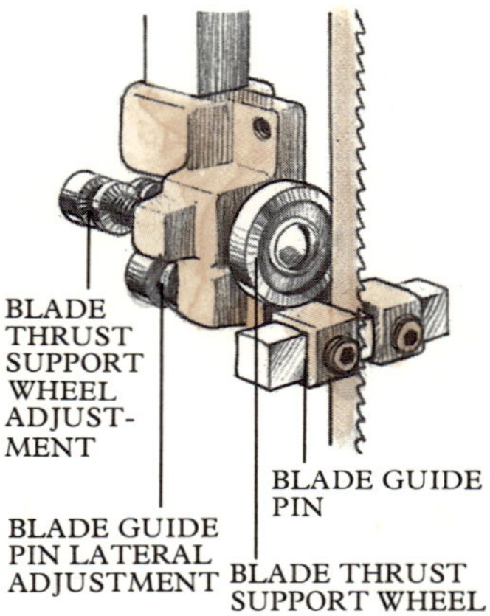

Some saws have a scale to indicate the correct tension for each blade; if yours does not, tension the blade until it flexes no more than 6mm sideways under finger pressure.

Tracking
On some machines the blade will automatically track in the centre of the wheels. Otherwise, a tracking adjustment mechanism will be provided. Check manufacturer's instructions for the exact procedure.

On machines without automatic tracking, set the support wheels about 0.35mm behind the blade. They should not be in contact with the blade until force is applied to it. Check the tracking by rotating the lower wheel by hand.

Setting the guide pins
Set the guide pins to clear each side of the blade by 0.010mm. Use a feeler gauge to measure the clearance or a piece of paper as a rough guide. They should also be adjusted to fit just behind the teeth. If they are positioned too far forward, they will spoil the set. Rotate the saw by hand once more to check the settings.

Close the wheel guards and replace the table insert. The upper blade guide assembly can be raised or lowered to accommodate the thickness of the work. Adjust the guide to just clear the work's surface.

Maintenance
Clean the band saw regularly to remove the accumulated dust. Replace rubber wheel linings if necessary. Hang the blades in a loop or fold them into a coil for convenient storage.

Folding a blade

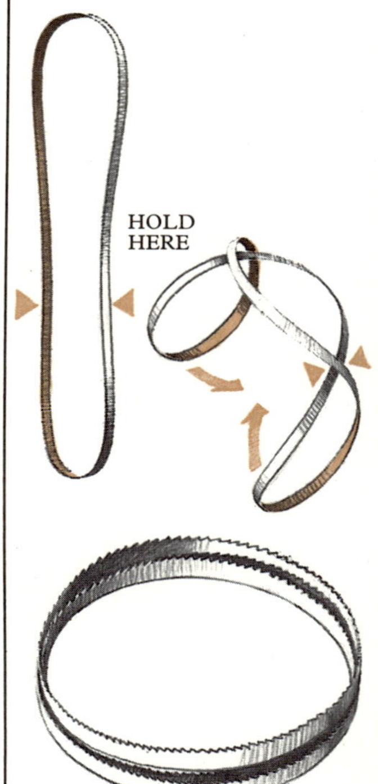

With the teeth facing away from you, hold the band about one third up from the bottom of the loop. Cross the band, left over right, to form three loops.

Straight cuts
Straight cuts are best made against a guide fence. Mark the width of the cut on the work and adjust the fence to line up the mark with the blade. If your machine does not incorporate a rip fence, clamp a temporary softwood fence to the table. Switch on the power and feed the work past the blade with steady pressure. Use a push stick to feed narrow work efficiently.

If the blade wanders off line, even with a guide fence, check the condition of the set and the adjustment of the blade guides.

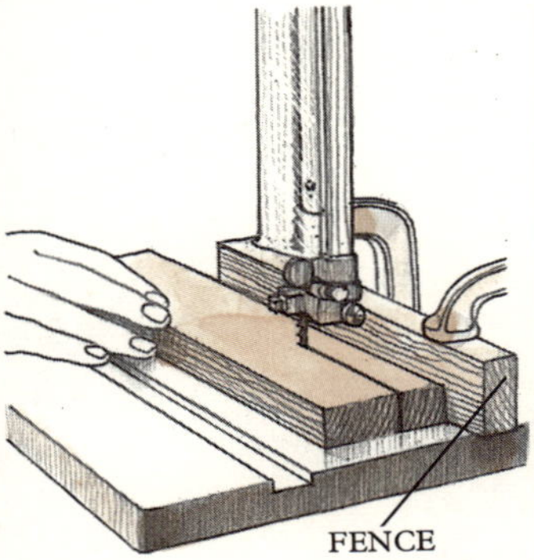

Cutting with a softwood fence.

Cross cuts
Set the mitre fence at right angles to the line of the blade to make a square cross cut. Make a trial cut on waste material and check with a try square.

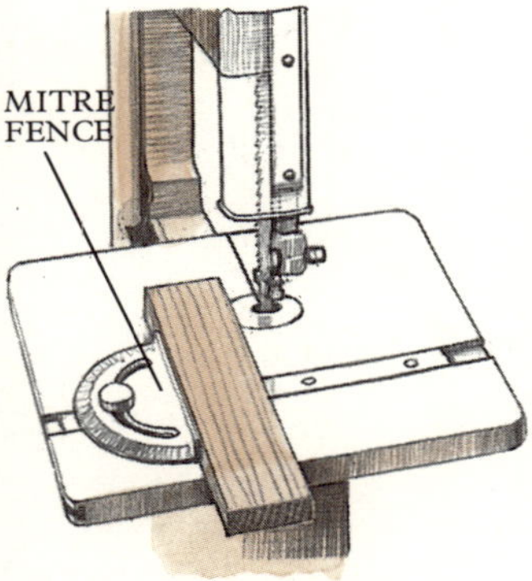

Making a cross cut
Hold the work firmly against the fence and feed the work past the blade.

Mitre cuts
The mitre fence can be set to any angle up to 45° to make mitre cuts. Proceed as for square cross cuts.

Make compound angled cross cuts by using the mitre fence while the table is tilted.

Beveled cuts
The table can be angled to cut beveled rip and cross cuts. Slacken the table tilt clamp and move the table by hand to the required angle indicated on the protractor scale. Relock the table tilt clamp.

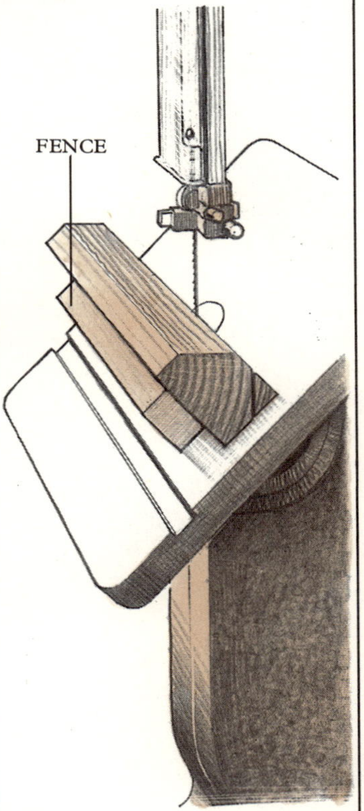

Making a bevelled cut
For bevelled rip cuts, position the fence below the blade so that the work is supported during the operation.

Free-hand bevelled cuts can be made by removing all fences and following by eye a marked line on the work.

Curved cuts
When cutting curves, take care not to twist the blade out of line. As soon as the curve becomes too tight for the blade to take easily, run the blade out of the work on a tangential cut.

If necessary, the blade can be backed out of a cut in order to correct the line or move in another direction. Bring the blade out slowly and avoid pulling or twisting it.

Cut several identical shapes in thin sheet material by pinning several pieces together through the waste. Follow the pattern on the top sheet to cut all the boards simultaneously. Thin sheet metal can be backed up by sandwiching it between sheets of scrap plywood.

Negotiating a curve
Make a tangential cut to get the blade out. Remove the waste, and start again, making tangential cuts as necessary until the curve is complete.

Masonry Saw

OTHER NAME: Stonemason's saw
SIZE: 300mm to 1m
MATERIAL: *Blade:* steel; *Handle:* hardwood
USE: To saw through masonry

Masonry saws have carbide tipped teeth for sawing through bricks, stone, cement and building blocks. The two-man wall saw will cut a whole section from a masonry wall to insert a door or window, or can be used to cut between brick courses to insert waterproofing in an older house.

The smallest version, known as a chasing saw, is used by electricians and plumbers to channel out masonry for the insertion of cable, conduit, or pipework.

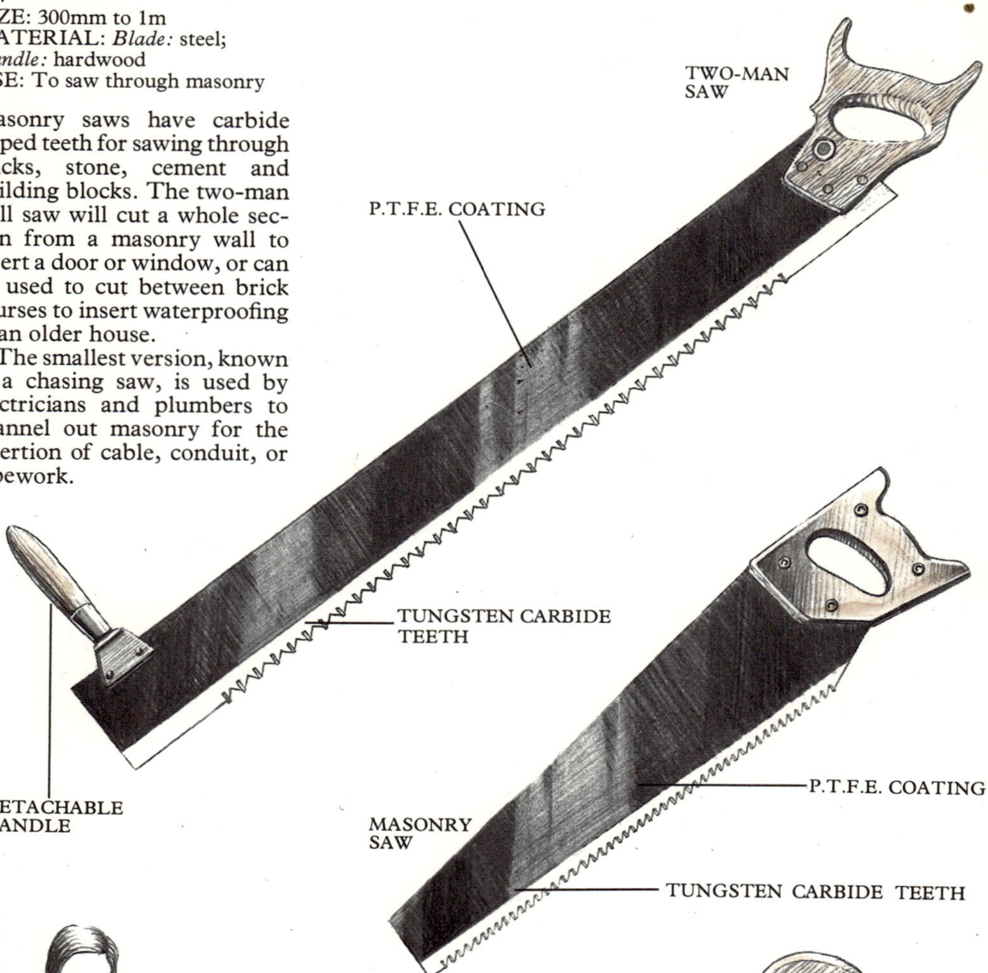

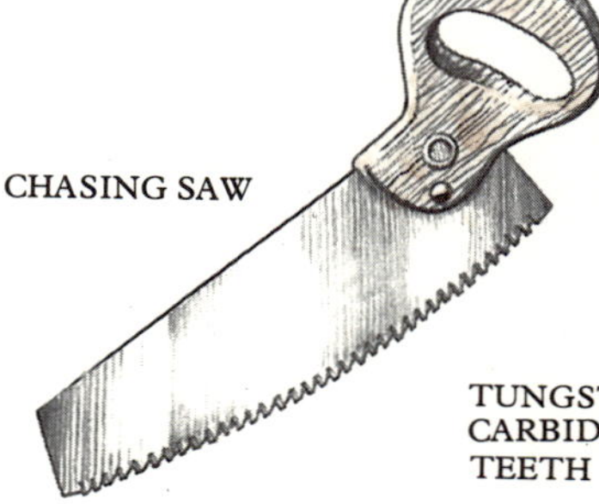

A general masonry saw is used like a hand saw to cut all types of masonry, roofing tiles, and earthenware pipes to size.

Hole Saw

OTHER NAME: Hole cutter
SIZE: Diameter: 12 to 100mm
MATERIAL: *Blade/drill bit:* steel; *Backing plate:* plastic, zinc or aluminium alloy
USE: To cut large holes in various materials

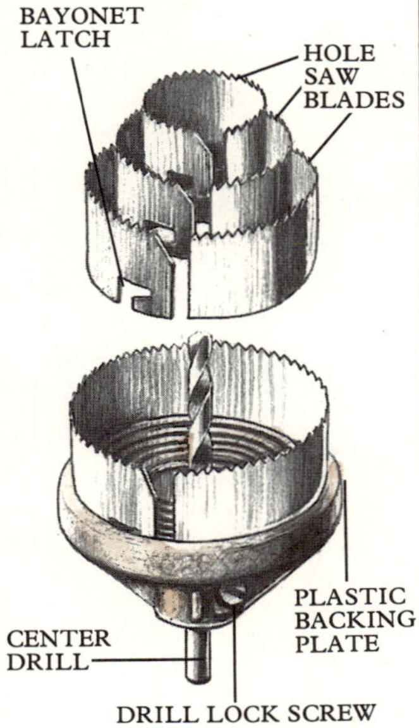

The hole saw has a drill bit centred on a cylindrical saw blade. The blade is either cup shaped, being pressed in one piece, or curved, and fits into a backing plate. Each set is sold with a range of sizes. Blades are made in various materials to cut wood, cast iron, sheet steel, stainless steel, aluminium, brass and plastics.

Secure the hole saw in the chuck of a portable electric drill or a drill press. Mark the centre of the hole with a centre punch, and locate the point of the drill bit. Select a slower speed than normal as the blade itself will be moving much faster than the central drill bit. Feed the saw into the work at a steady rate.

To cut a ring, set up the saw in a drill press and clamp the work to the table with a backing sheet. Drill out the centre of the ring, fit the larger blade of the set and cut the circumference of the ring without moving the clamped work.

Pad Saw

OTHER NAMES: Compass saw; keyhole saw; wallboard saw
SIZE: Blade length: 125 to 375mm; 8 to 10 points per 25mm
MATERIAL; *Blade:* steel; *Handle:* zinc alloy, hardwood
USE: To cut holes in a panel

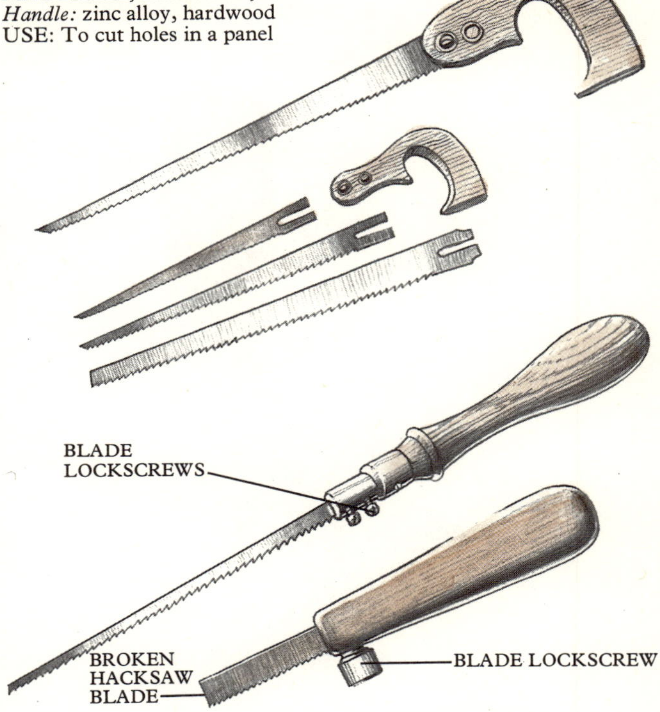

The pad saw has no frame, so it can be used in places where a coping saw, for instance, would be limited to the edge of a board or panel. The pad saw has a tapered narrow blade and can be used to cut a letterbox hole, keyhole, lock hole, or a hole for a switch plate or a socket box in plasterboard.

Some types take only one type and size of blade; others take a small range of interchangeable blades of different sizes, usually small, medium and large. There are also pad saws that will take whole or broken hack saw blades, which make them a useful general purpose short stroke saw.

For small diameter holes use a saw with a pointed blade; for cutting thin wood such as plywood or hardboard use a saw with fine teeth; for cutting through fairly thick panels of timber use the wider blades.

Fitting a blade
Blades are held in place either by a knob or a screw on the ferruled neck of the handle. Turn the knob or screw counter clockwise, withdraw the blade, slot in a replacement and then tighten.

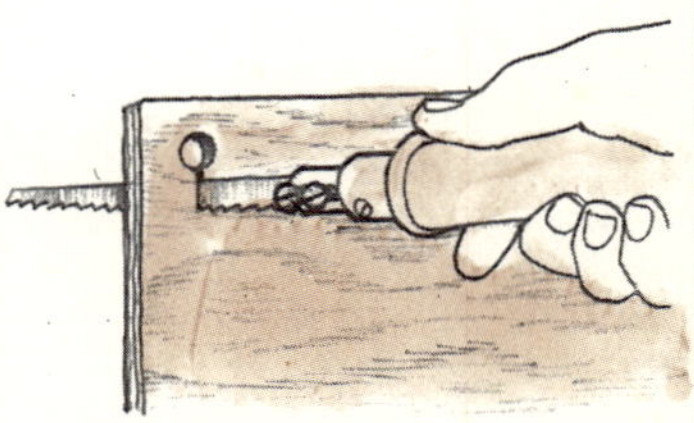

Using the saw
Drill a small hole in the wood to receive the tip of the blade and gradually cut into the wood using a series of careful short strokes.

The thin, high grade, tempered steel blades easily bend and can often jam if the cutting action is too rigorous.

Reciprocating Saw

OTHER NAMES: All purpose saw, sabre saw, heavy duty saw, bayonet saw
SIZE: *Unloaded speed:* 1,600 to 3,000 strokes per minute; *Weight:* 2.72 to 4kg
MATERIAL: Various
USE: To cut various materials

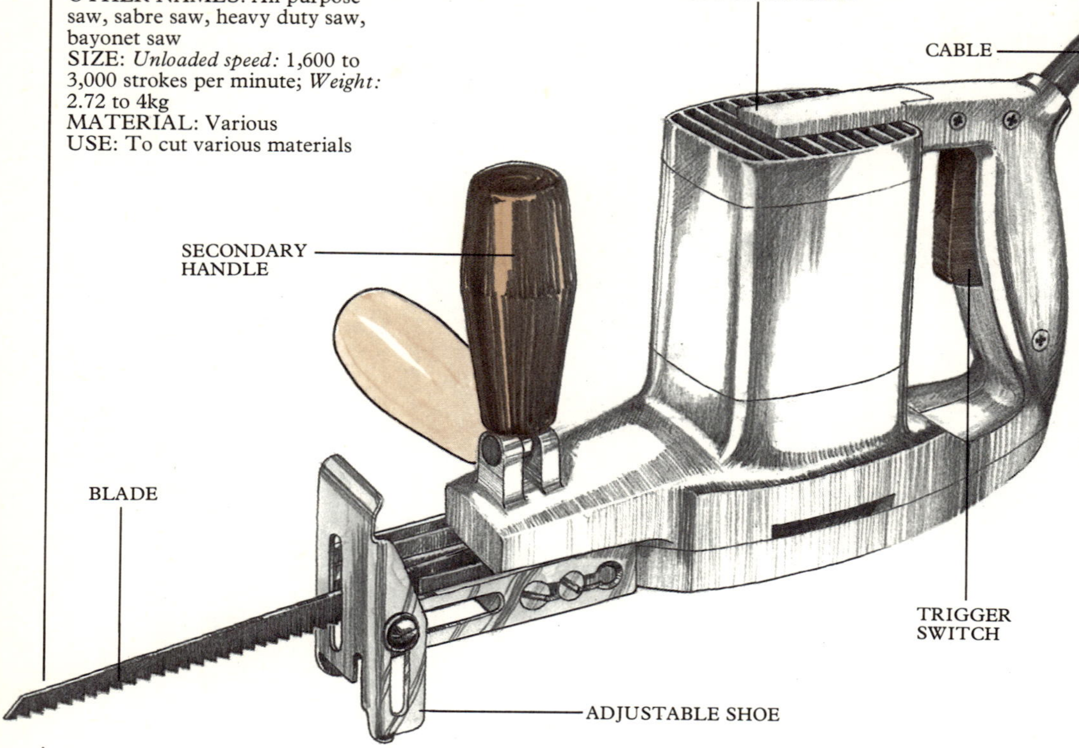

The reciprocating saw is a portable heavy duty version of the sabre saw except that the blade moves backward and forward rather than up and down. It is a two-handed tool with both a fixed and a secondary handle. The blades which can extend up to 300mm long can saw through large logs or through a wood wall to install windows or pipework. The blades can also be turned to cut in different directions and fitted to cut flush with the surface.

With the appropriate blade the reciprocating saw will cut equally well through wood, metal, plastic and composite boards. Some versions incorporate variable speeds to work all the different materials efficiently.

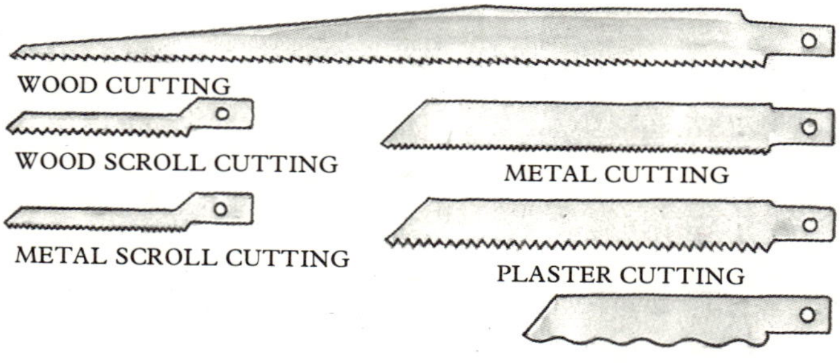

Using a reciprocating saw

A fixed handle incorporates the trigger switch and speed control, while a secondary handle can be turned to control the saw in a variety of positions.

Bench Jigsaw

OTHER NAME: Scroll saw
SIZE: Depth of throat: 400 to 625mm
MATERIAL: Various
ACCESSORIES: Jeweller's blade, sabre saw blades
ATTACHMENTS: Files, sanding attachment
USE: To cut scroll work

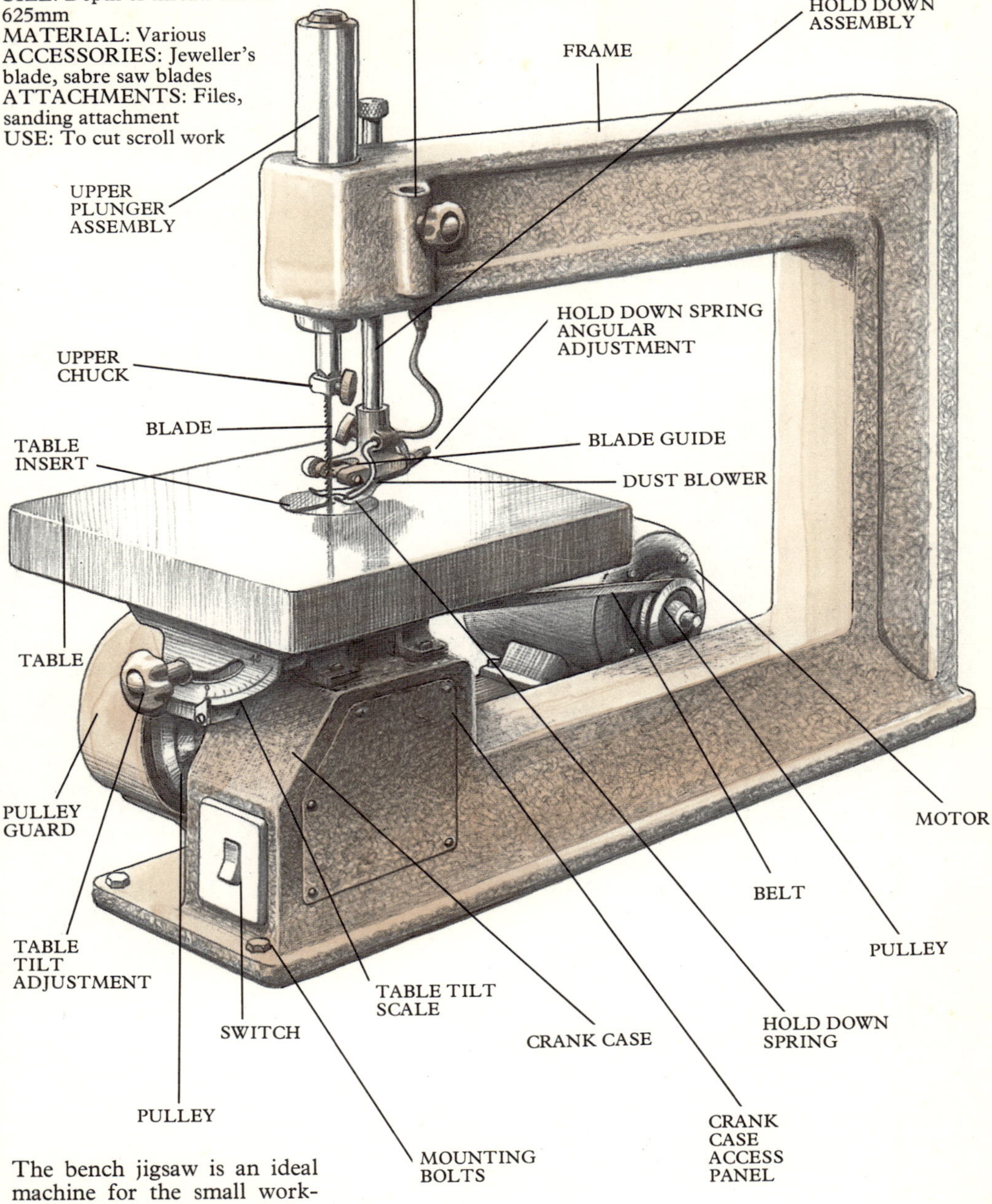

The bench jigsaw is an ideal machine for the small workshop, its main advantage being the ability to make even, tight curved cuts while leaving both hands free to guide the work. Fitted with the correct blade it can handle straight cuts in work up to approximately 50mm thick. It will also cut a variety of materials.

Blades
The blades used in a sabre saw can be fitted in a jigsaw (in the lower chuck only), but the jeweller's blade is specifically designed for it.

JEWELLER'S BLADES

Jeweller's blades, available for cutting wood, composites, metal and plastic, are about 150mm long and range from 0.5 to 6mm wide, with between 7 and 32 teeth per 25mm.

Fitting the blade

Raise the hold down assembly and remove the table insert. Move the drive belt until the bottom assembly is at the top of its travel. Place the bottom end of the blade in the chuck, teeth facing forward and downward, and secure it with the locking screw. Check that the blade is

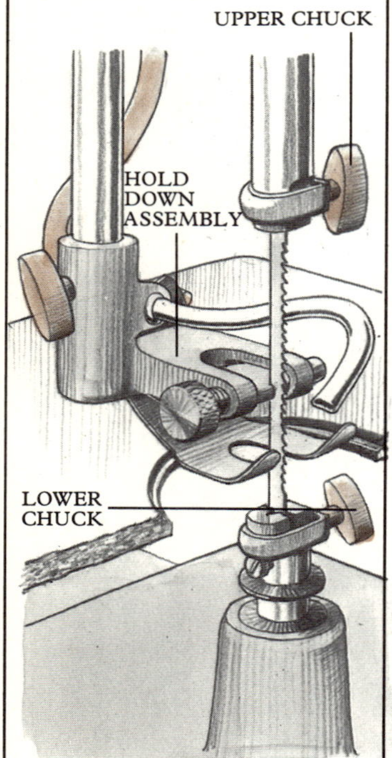

vertical in all directions with a try square before pulling down the upper chuck assembly and fitting the top end of the blade.

Blades can be fitted parallel or at right angles to the arm, whichever gives best clearance. The blade must be correctly tensioned to cut accurately and avoid constant breakage. All machines have a tensioning device as part of the top blade fixing assembly. Generally, thinner blades require more tension than wider ones.

Blade guide

The blade guide prevents the blade twisting and bending. While the device may differ

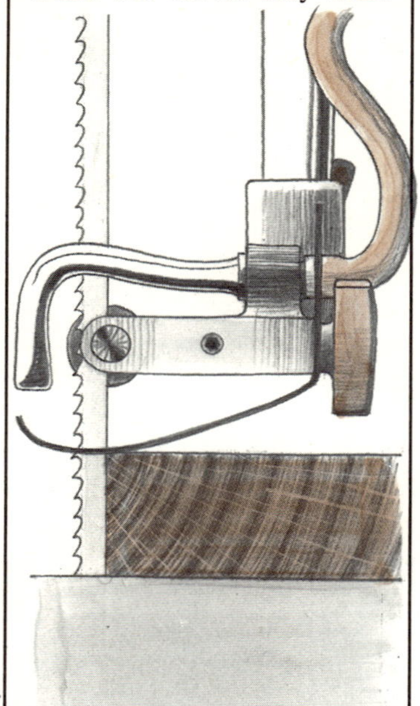

depending on the individual saw, it is usually a slot in a disc or tube which can be adjusted to encompass the blade. A "back-up" lightly supports the back edge of the blade. Ensure that the blade is free to move and runs in the guides.

Using the saw

The work must be held down during the cutting operation. All machines have a sprung foot, adjustable vertically to take work of different thickness. Adjust it to just touch the work. Too much pressure can mark the surface and even make it difficult to feed the work. Orientate the air blower nozzle to the most convenient position.

Select the right speed for the job. Each manufacturer will supply recommendations for their individual machine. As a guide, the heavier the blade the slower the speed; the faster the speed the better the finish.

Before switching on the power it is a good idea to move the machine by hand through one complete revolution to make certain that all adjustments are correct.

Correcting faults

If the blades are breaking too frequently, check the tension and guide alignment or adjust the speed. If the cut wanders or is out of square, the guides are probably out of line or the tension insufficient. If the work vibrates excessively, check that the hold down is adjusted properly or slow down the speed.

Making curved cuts

For very tight intricate curves, use a narrow blade. Use wider blades for shallow curves.

You can make interior cuts in a sheet of material. Drill a hole in the waste through which the blade can pass. With a sabre saw blade fitted, pass the blade through the hole and operate the saw. With a jeweller's blade disconnect it from the top assembly, pass the work over the blade and reconnect. See sabre saw, pages 94–95 for cutting internal square corners.

On some jigsaws the entire frame and upper assembly can be removed so that large boards can be cut unrestricted with a sabre saw blade. Cut thin sheet material, sandwiched between sheets of plywood to prevent distortion and reduce burring.

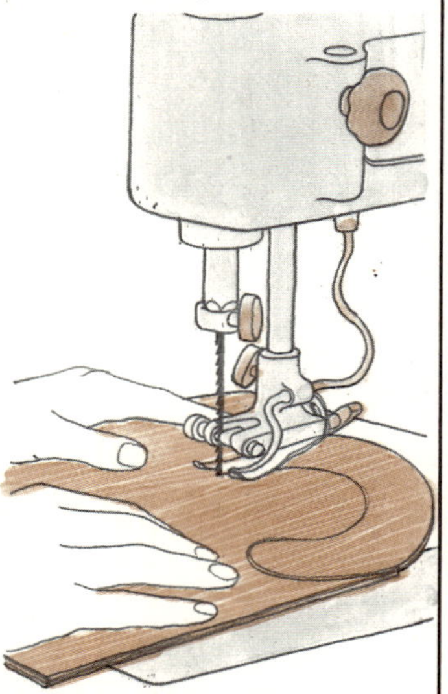

Cutting tight curves
Keep up a steady pressure on the work as you feed it in. Take tight curves slowly without twisting the blade.

Making straight cuts

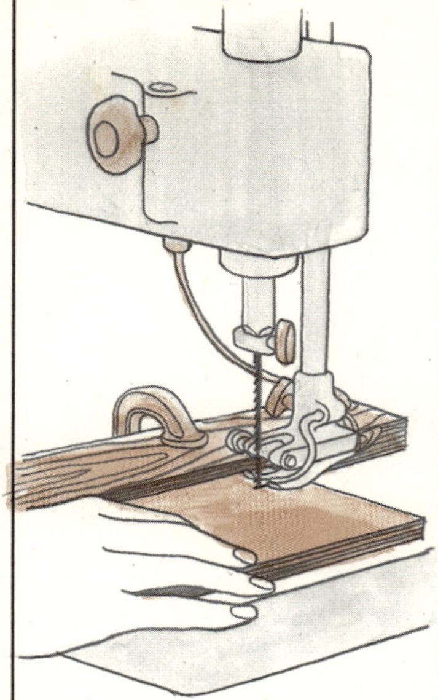

Fit a wide blade and clamp a temporary fence to the table. Feed the work steadily against the fence. Use a push stick for narrow work.

Bevel cuts

Bevelled cuts can be made by tilting the whole table. Tighten the clamp before using the saw. Readjust the hold down assembly to suit. The hold down foot on some saws can be angled to align with the work.

Angling the table

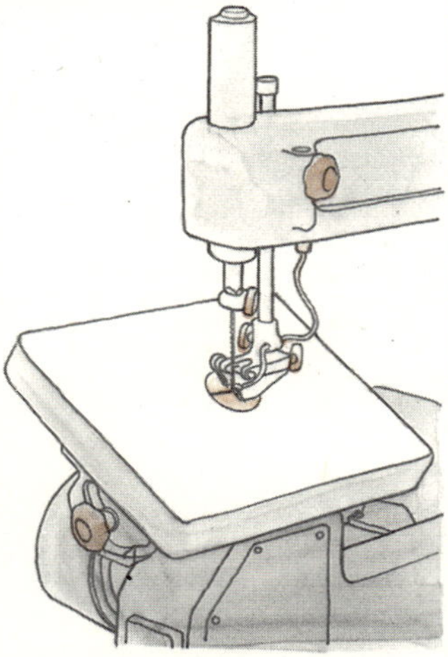

Raise the hold down assembly, slacken the tilt clamp and move the table by hand to the angle indicated on the protractor.

Filling

Files are specially made for use with the bench jigsaw. They have 3mm or 6mm diameter shanks, which fit into the "V" block in the lower chuck only. A variety of shapes are available in different grades.

Lift the hold down assembly out of the way and remove the standard table insert. Replace it with a special insert with a 6mm diameter hole drilled in the centre. Check the vertical alignment of the file with a try square.

Use a slow speed for filing. Simply run the work against the file to achieve the required finish, but avoid excessive pressure. Clean the teeth of the file periodically with a file card or wire brush.

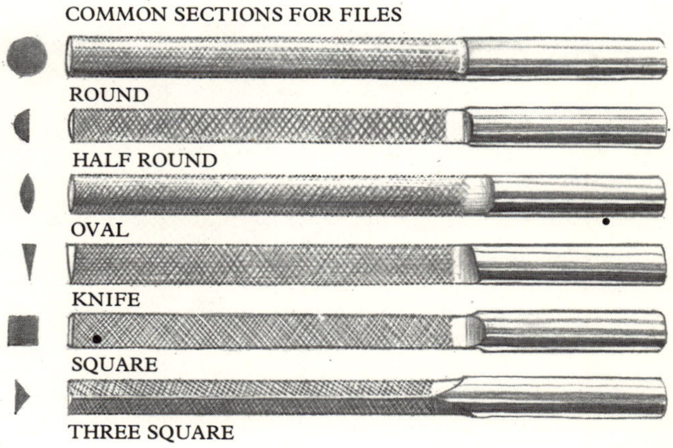

Sanding

Commercial sanding attachments are available for the jigsaw, but it is easy to make your own. Glue a 6mm diameter metal rod into the end of a length of wooden dowel. Stick adhesive paper to the outside of the dowel and fit the rod in the lower chuck as you would a file.

Use a slow speed when operating the machine for sanding for best results.

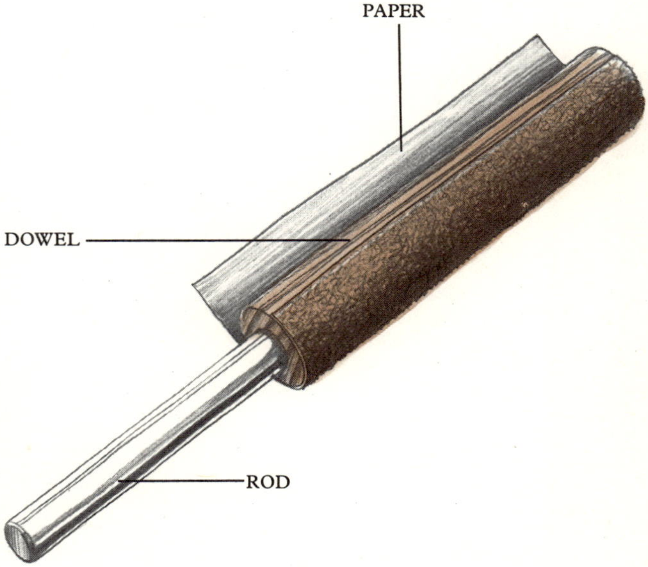

Radial Arm Saw

SIZE: *Cross cut capacity:* 350 to 400mm; *Rip cut capacity:* 325 to 662mm; *Horsepower:* 1.35 to 4.5
MATERIAL: Various
ACCESSORIES: Saw blades
ATTACHMENTS: Dado head, shaping and jointing head, drum sander, disc sander, drill chuck, router chuck, tool guard
USE: Multi-purpose bench saw

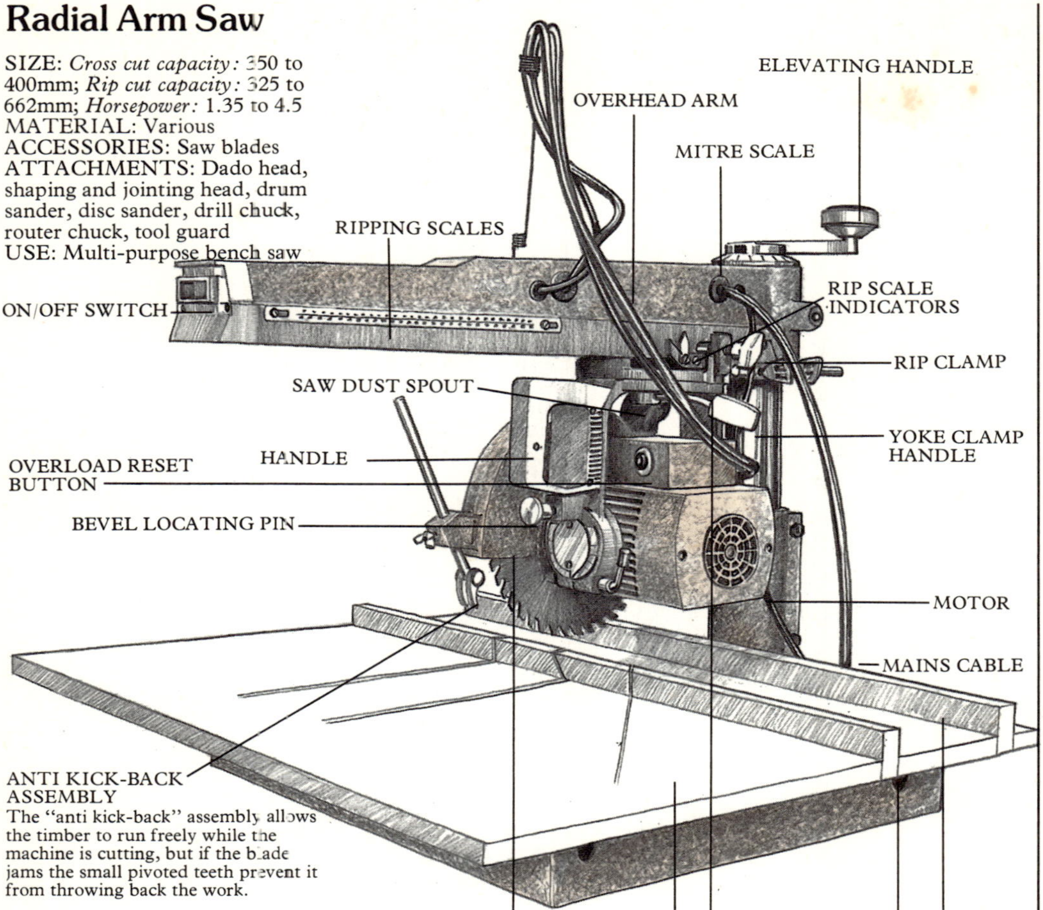

ANTI KICK-BACK ASSEMBLY
The "anti kick-back" assembly allows the timber to run freely while the machine is cutting, but if the blade jams the small pivoted teeth prevent it from throwing back the work.

BLADE GUARD
The blade guard can be adjusted to cover the maximum amount of teeth for each cut. Position the guard carefully before switching on the power.

YOKE
The yoke runs on an overhead arm, which can be pivoted through 180° and locked at any angle in between. It can also be raised or lowered along with the column mounted to the rear of the machine.

WORKTABLE
The fixed worktable is fitted with two fences, the forward fence for cross cutting and the rear fence for rip sawing. Always sweep sawdust away from either fence before using the machine.

The radial arm saw is one of the most versatile power tools available for the home workshop. It not only provides a variety of saw cuts, in metal, timber and composite boards but fitted with various attachments, it will cut housings, grooves, rebates, joints and mouldings. It can also be converted to a drilling machine and a drum or disc sander.

All radial arm saws share certain features. The motor and blade are hung in a yoke which allows the blade to be pivoted and tilted to any angle in both the vertical and the horizontal planes.

The blade actually cuts into the work table itself when in use, consequently it is advisable to cover surface of the table with a sheet of thin, easily replaceable plywood.

Blades and discs

There are several blades or discs available for use on the radial arm saw. The most obvious are the cross cut and rip saw blades but these are really only suitable for a long run of work. A better blade for the home workshop is the combination blade, which can make rip or cross cuts as well as bevel cuts of various kinds. The combination blade has groups of cutting teeth separated by a raker. There is also a planer combination blade that will leave a perfectly clean finish after the cut. To produce the same kind of finish on plywood, use a plywood combination blade which does not splinter the surface veneer. If you use a standard blade to cut high glue content, composite boards such as chip board, it will blunt very quickly. A blade with tungsten carbide tipped teeth will last up to ten times longer and will cut solid lumber as well as all the composite boards equally well.

There are various blades and abrasive disks for cutting all kinds of metals, bricks and ceramic tiles.

Combination blade
This blade is the most versatile for the home workshop.

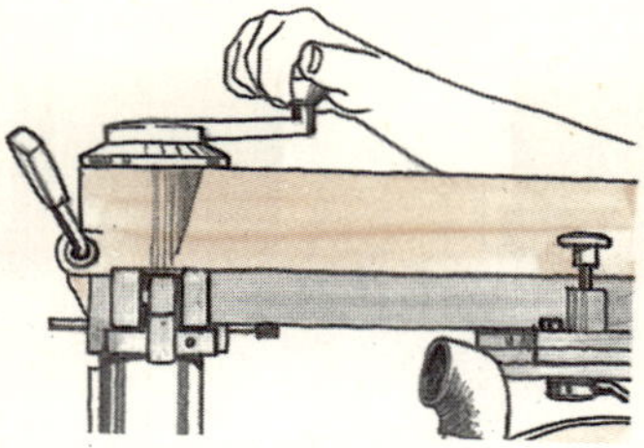

Adjusting the arm
The arm can be raised or lowered by turning the elevating handle. Switch on the machine and lower the arm until the blade cuts about 1.5mm into the table.

Pivoting the arm
The arm rotates right or left for angled cross cuts. Release the mitre clamp and lift the latch to position the arm at 90° or 45°. Pivot the arm to the required angle indicated on the miter scale. Tighten clamp.

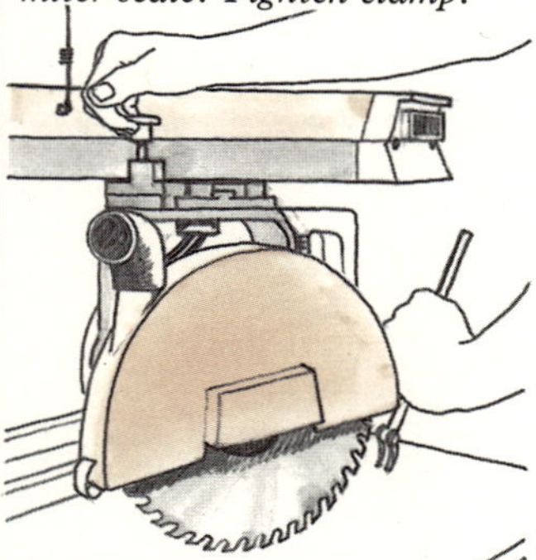

Rotating the yoke
The yoke rotates to position the blade for cross or rip cutting. Release the yoke clamp and lift the locating pin to allow the yoke to swivel. The pin will automatically position the yoke in one of four positions at 90° to one another. Tighten the clamp before using the saw.

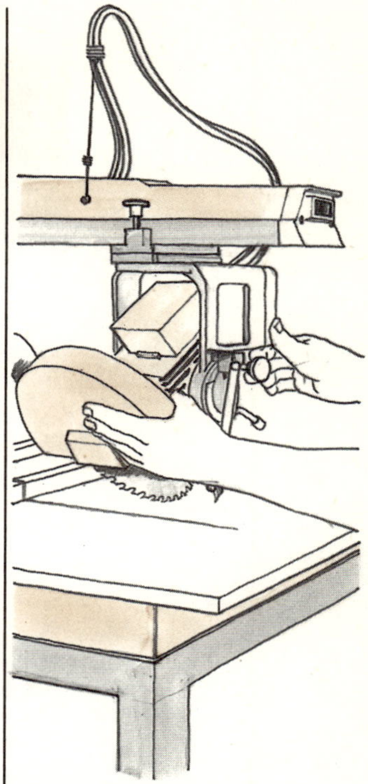

Tilting the saw
Elevate the arm to clear the saw blade from the table. Release the bevel clamp and pull the locating pin to allow the saw to tilt in the yoke. Read the required angle on the bevel scale and relock the clamp. The locating pin automatically locates the blade at angles of 90° and 45° and in the horizontal position.

Safety factors

Always switch off the power supply before fitting any type of new blade.

Make sure that any blade or cutter is securely fitted before switching on the saw and that all clamps are tightened.

Adjust the blade and anti kick-back assembly to suit each different cut.

Keep the machine free from dust, particularly the arm tracks and bearing surfaces.

Keep your hands well away from the blade whenever the saw is running.

Cross cuts

Set the yoke so that the blade is at 90° to the work and make certain that the mitre scale on the arm reads zero. Check that all clamps are secure except the rip clamp, which must be loosened to allow the yoke to run freely along the arm. Slide the carriage to the rear of the table and set up the cross cut fence. Lower the arm. Mark the work with a try square and position it against the fence, face side up. Position the marks so that the blade cuts on the waste side. Hold the work securely against the fence, switch on and pull the blade steadily toward you. When the cut is complete, return the blade to the rear of the machine and switch off.

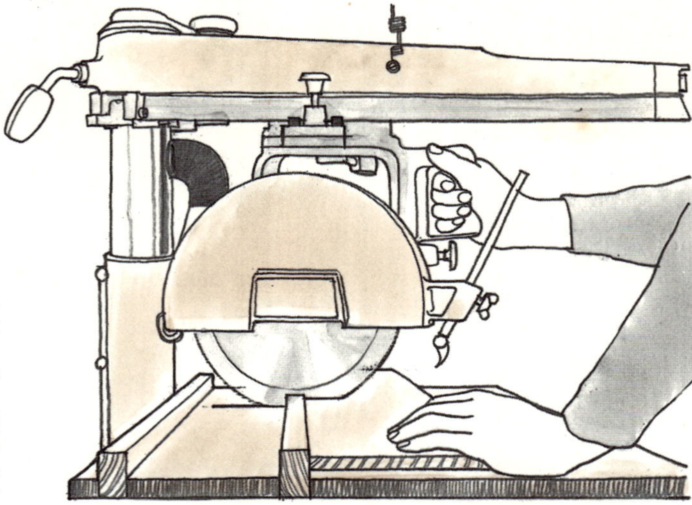

Cutting wide work

If the work is wider than the full travel of the saw, there are two things you can do to cut the work. If it is important to preserve the top surface, remove the normal cross cut fence and use the rip fence. Reposition the blade in the kerf and continue with the cut.

The second method for dealing with a workpiece which is wider than the saw's travel is to turn the work over and make a second cut to meet the first. It is important to set up a stop on the fence so as to position the second cut accurately.

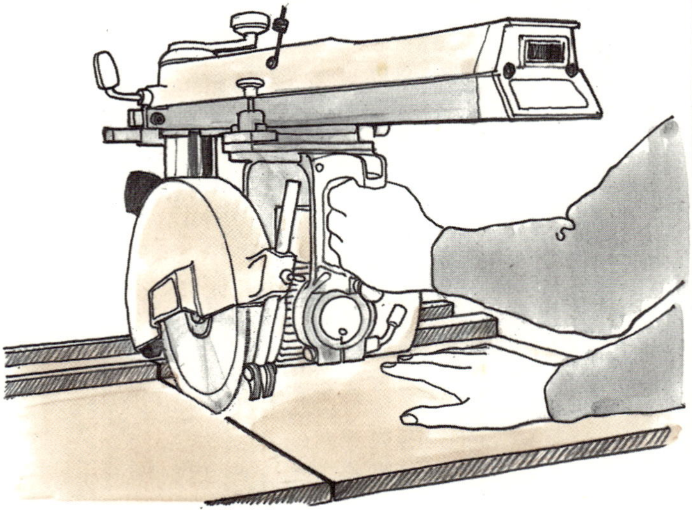

Cutting multiples

If you want to cut several pieces of timber to the same length, clamp a block of wood to the fence or across the table to act as a stop. Position the first piece against the blade, butt the block against the end and clamp it in position

An alternative method is to lay several pieces together on the work table against the clamped stop and cut them all in one pass.

Rip cuts
To make a rip cut cut down the length of a board, rotate the yoke to position the blade parallel with the guide fence.

The blade can be in two positions, for narrow and wide ripping depending on the distance of the cut from the fence. Remove the cross cut fence to set the necessary width of cut. Position the blade accurately by moving the yoke on the arm, check the width of cut on the rip scale and tighten the rip clamp. For absolute accuracy, check with a rule by measuring from the fence to the blade, or make a trial cut in scrap timber and measure the cut itself.

Feed the work into the blade from the side opposite the anti kick-back assembly, known as the "infeed" side. Position the work, or a scrap piece of the same thickness, against the infeed side of the blade and adjust the guard until it almost touches the surface. Position the work on the other side of the blade and adjust the anti kick-back assembly so that the teeth are approximately 3mm below the surface of the board when hanging free. Position the teeth on the work and test them by pushing the work toward the saw: they should bite into the work to prevent its movement. If they do not, lower the assembly further.

With the work pressed against the fence, switch on the saw and feed the work steadily into the blade. For very narrow pieces of work, use a notched stick to push the last part of the work through the blade.

Wide ripping
For very wide boards it is a good idea to have someone help support the work as you feed it into the blade.

Bevel cuts
By tilting the saw, bevels can be cut as easily as a square shoulder. With the saw set up for rip cutting, any angle can be cut along the entire work edge.

Chamfers

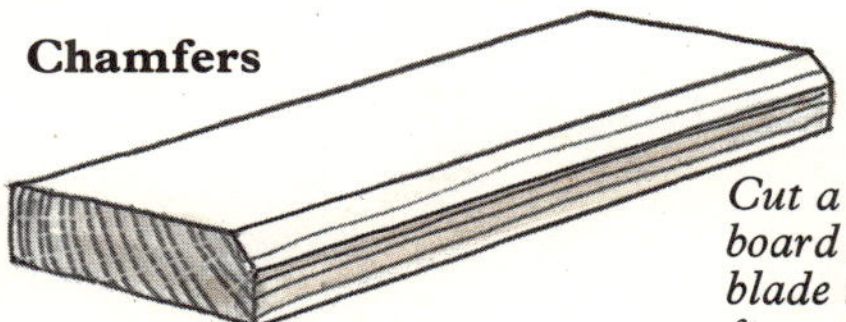

Cut a chamfer on the edge of a board as for a bevel. Tilt the blade to 45° and set up the fence so that the blade will remove the top corner only.

"V" cuts

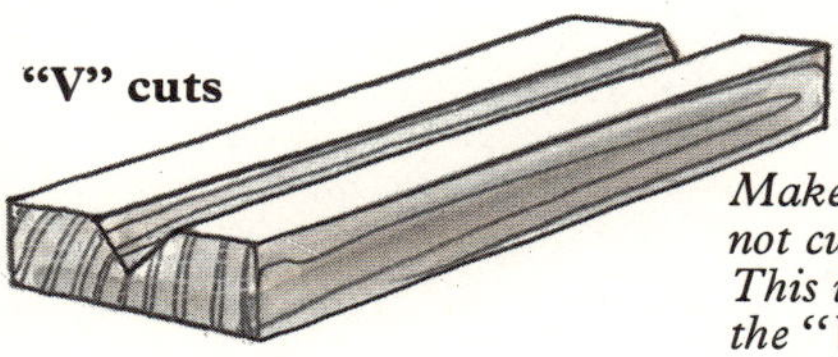

Make two bevel cuts which do not cut right through the work. This is an easy way to make the "V" blocks used to hold round stock for drilling.

Cross bevel cuts

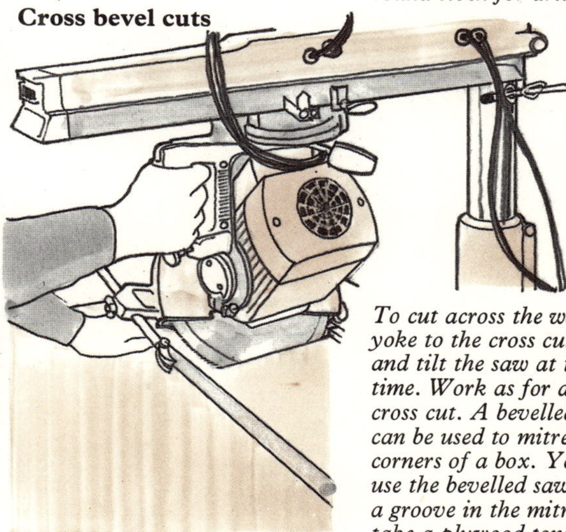

To cut across the work turn the yoke to the cross cut position and tilt the saw at the same time. Work as for a standard cross cut. A bevelled cross cut can be used to mitre joint the corners of a box. You can also use the bevelled saw blade to cut a groove in the mitred face to take a plywood tongue.

Mitre cuts

To mitre joint a frame, keep the saw blade in the vertical plane, but swing the saw arm over to 45°. Cross cut in the normal way to produce a mitred joint which will meet at 90°. The two halves of the joint can be cut with the saw at the same angle if the timber is square or round, but for a moulded frame, the blade must be swung in the opposite direction to cut the second half of the joint.

Compound angled cuts
By combining the swivel arm and tilting blade, the saw can cut a wide variety of compound angles.

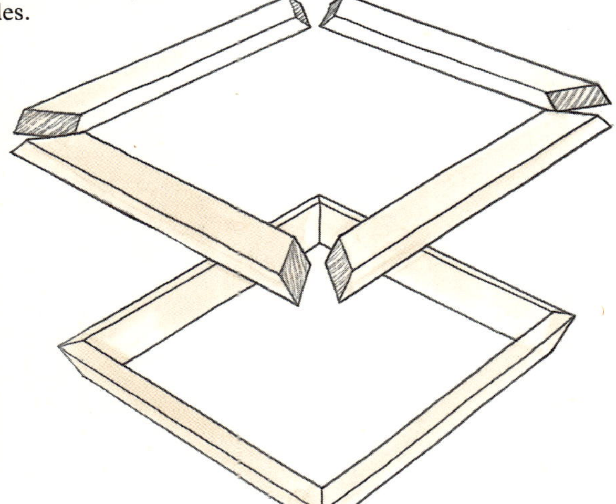

Housings and grooves
A housing is a channel cut across a piece of timber, while the groove is a channel running with the grain. Both housings and grooves can be cut with a radial arm saw by setting up the controls to make a rip or cross cut.

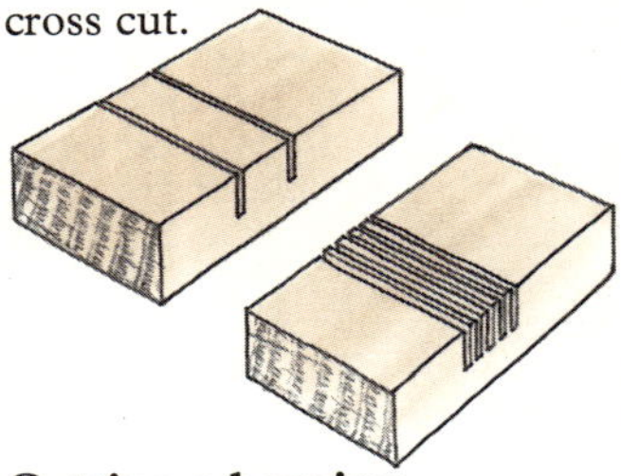

Cutting a housing
Lower the saw until it will cut the depth of the dado. Position the work so that the blade will make a cut for each side of the dado on the waste side of the line. Remove the waste between with successive cuts.

Cutting a groove
Move the yoke along the arm for each cut and lock it in place with the rip clamp.

Dado head
A dado head allows you to cut the entire width of a housing in one pass. The most common version has two combination blades to cut the edges of the housing simultaneously.

"Chipper" blades, with large teeth, are sandwiched between the combination blades to remove the waste. Paper washers separate the blades and allow them to be put together in various combinations to cut housings up to 20mm.

The dado head will cut housings and grooves by setting the saw up for cross cutting or ripping. Feed the work steadily through the cutter assembly.

Cutting a rebate

In addition to cutting housings and grooves, a dado head can also be used to cut a rebate. It should be used on the edge of the workpiece. Lower the dado head to the depth of the rebate. Operate the machine for normal rip cutting, but feed the work a little more slowly. To cut a rebate wider than 24mm, make a second cut by moving the yoke along the arm the required amount while leaving the depth adjustment unchanged.

Cutting a lap joint

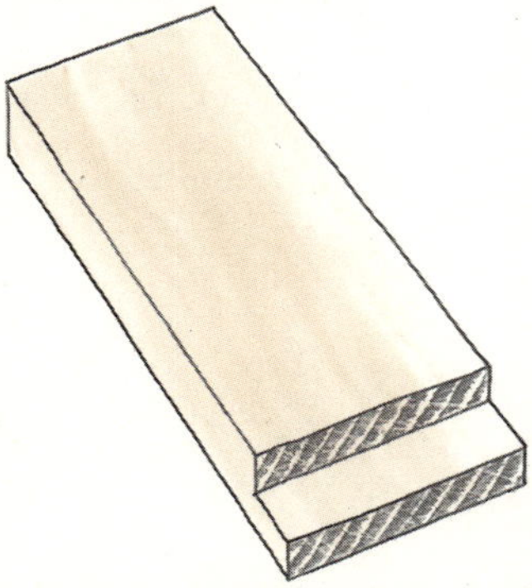

Make lap joints quickly and accurately by setting up a dado head to cut a rebate in the cross cut position. Cut several joints at one go by positioning an end stop across the table.

Cutting a tenon

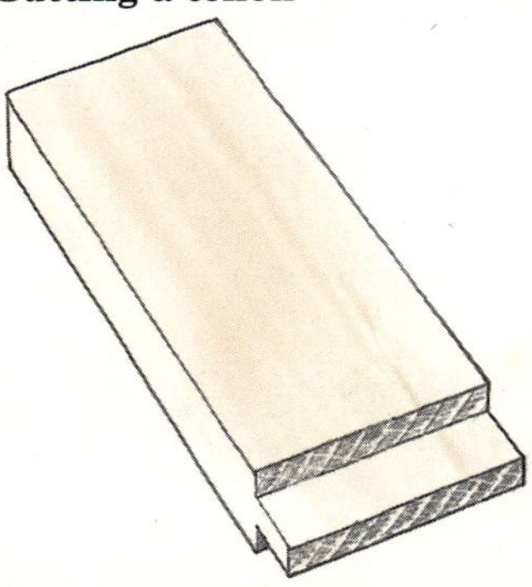

Cut a tenon in the same way as a lap joint by turning the workpiece over between cuts.

Shaping and moulding

The saw blade can be replaced by a cutter head which takes two or three shaped knives. A three knived head will make a cleaner cut. The cutter head fits on to the saw arbor, usually with some kind of bushing, and is secured by the arbor nut.

The knives of the cutter head locate in slots in the edge of the head and are secured by Allen screws. The assembly must be protected by a special tool guard. Revolve the cutters by hand to check the clearance before connecting the saw to the power supply.

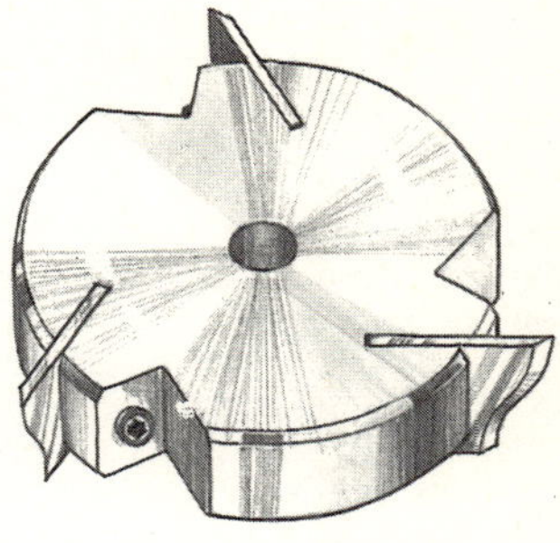

CUTTER HEAD

Setting up for moulding

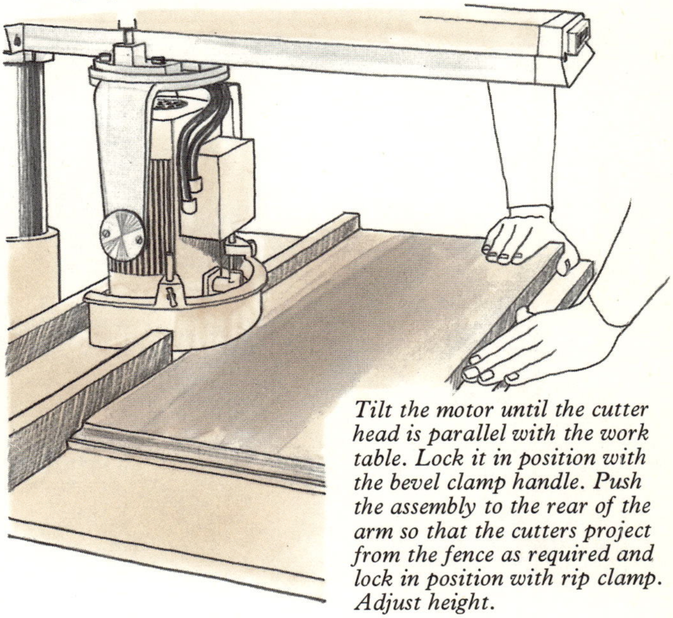

Tilt the motor until the cutter head is parallel with the work table. Lock it in position with the bevel clamp handle. Push the assembly to the rear of the arm so that the cutters project from the fence as required and lock in position with rip clamp. Adjust height.

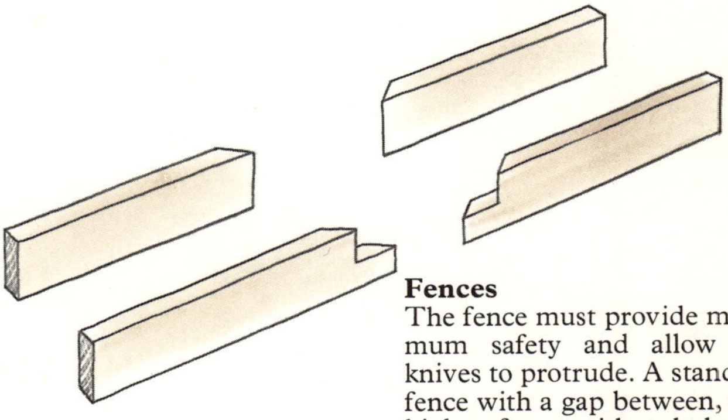

Fences

The fence must provide maximum safety and allow the knives to protrude. A standard fence with a gap between, or a higher fence with a hole cut through it will do. (The tool guard must also be in position before the machine is used.)

Cutter head knives

There are many shaped knives for use with the cutter head. They can be used to cut edge joints, such as a tongue and groove or rebate joint, or various mouldings. As illustrated, some of the cutters can be used to achieve more than one finish.

Position the work in relation to the cutters by placing it against the fence so that one blade is resting against the end of the work. Adjust the depth of cut by moving the yoke and lock it in position. Adjust the guard so that it just clears the workpiece.

Feed the work against the direction of cutter rotation by pressing it against the fence on the infeed side and passing it through the cutter at a steady rate. Where possible cut with the grain for the cleanest cut.

Some cutters remove a considerable amount of wood, so with some hardwoods it may be necessary to remove the waste in two passes, adjusting the depth of cut between each pass.

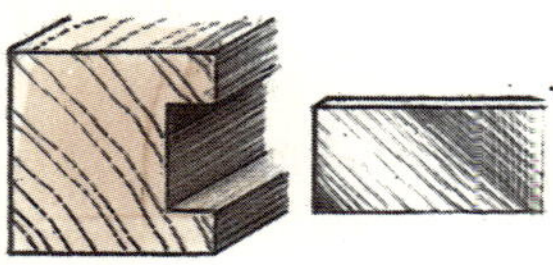

PLANE

FLUTE

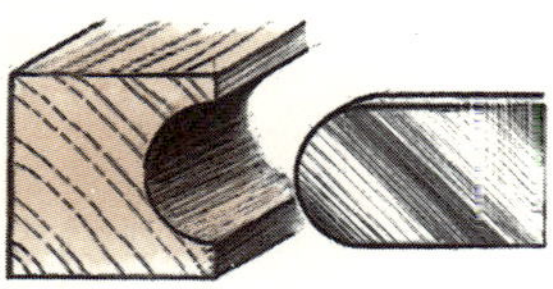

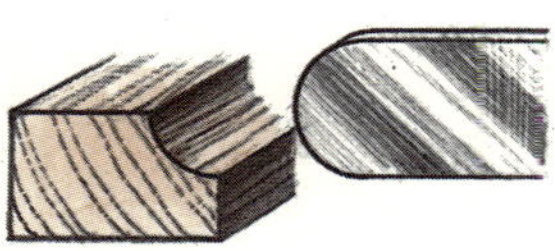

OGEE

BEAD

QUARTER ROUND

DIAMOND FLUTE

LIP

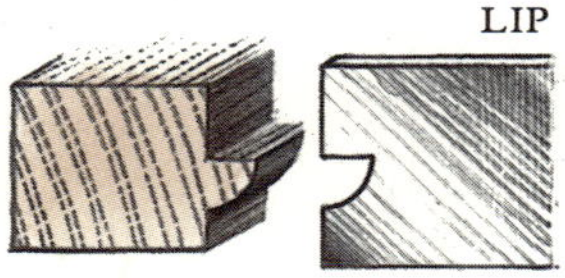

GLUE JOINT

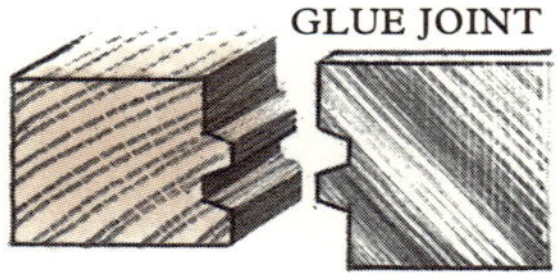

3 BEAD

TONGUE AND GROOVE

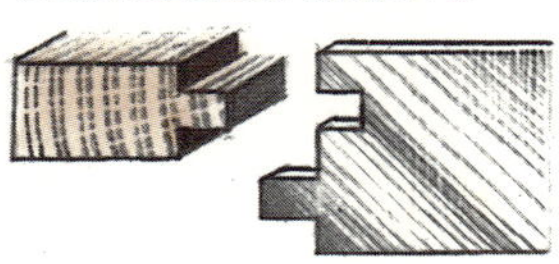

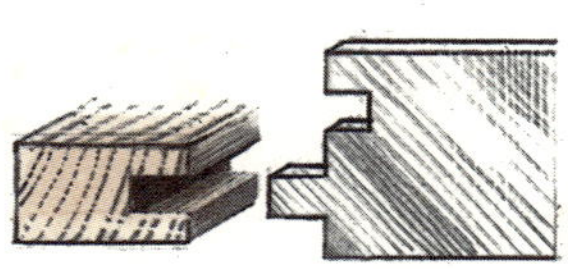

Cutting mouldings

To cut a moulding on the end grain, back up the work with scrap timber of the same thickness to avoid breaking out at the end of the cut. When cutting a moulding all around a panel, cut the end grain first so that the final cut along the grain will remove all damage from splitting out.

It is often better to produce a narrow strip moulding by cutting the shape on a large board and then rip cutting it down afterward.

Where only part of the edge of the workpiece is removed, as with a rebate for instance, the two halves of the fence should be in line. For this kind of work use a straight fence.

A different technique is necessary when the entire edge is being cut away.

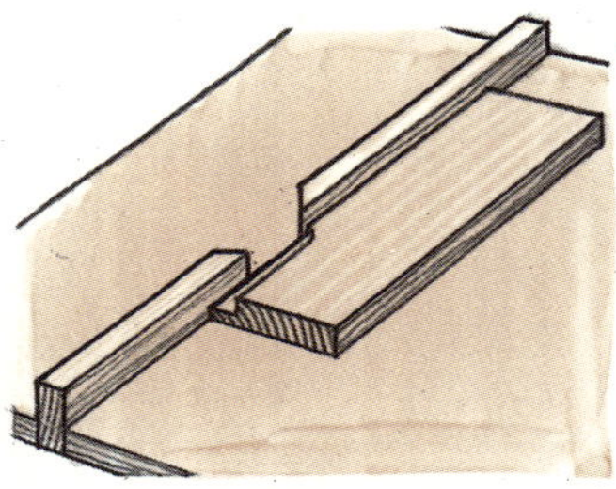

Removing the entire edge

The outfeed side of the fence must be out of line with the infeed side to support the work after the cut.

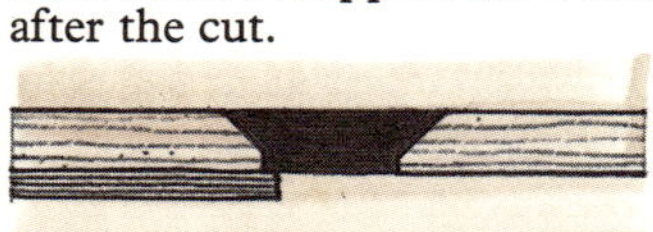

Method one

Pin a strip of timber to the outfeed fence which matches exactly the amount being cut away from the work.

Method two

Sandwich spacers between the fences and the edge of the work table to position the fences out of line. On the infeed side the spacers will be in front of the fence, and on the outfeed side, behind. They should be flush with the surface of the table.

Drilling
Most radial arm saws can be converted to a drilling machine by fitting a chuck on the opposite end of the arbor from the saw blades.

The motor, with chuck fitted, should be adjusted to the wide ripping position so that the drill bit faces the column to the rear of the machine. Make a special fence to back up the work and to raise it to the level of the drill bit.

Method of drilling
Adjust the position of the bit in relation to the work by using the elevating handle. To position the bit to the right or left, move the work itself. Clamp a depth gauge to the bit to act as a depth stop. Move the yoke toward and away from the work on the arm as for cross cutting. Lock the yoke with the rip clamp between operations. Drill holes at an angle by pivoting the arm.

Special drilling fence
Screw a 37mm thick support to a wide upstand. The lower portion of the upstand should be clamped in the work table.

Mortice drilling
To drill into end grain while mortising, adjust the yoke so that the drill bit faces to one side of the machine. Make a box to lift the work to the required height, and fit a secondary fence on the box parallel to the regular fence. Clamp the back of the box to the regular fence and carefully feed the work into the drill against the secondary fence.

Cut a mortise by drilling a series of holes in the waste and removing the remainder with a chisel afterward.

A special box-like attachment to lift the work to the proper height and a secondary fence are needed when drilling end grain wood.

Disc sanding
The abrasive paper itself is glued to the metal disc. Paper discs are available from coarse to fine grades. Make a box to raise the work to just below the centre of the wheel, and clamp it securely to worktable or fence. Angle the fence to sand mitres. Remove the fence for free-hand sanding, but use the down side of the disc as much as possible.

Sanding end grain
Screw a fence to the top of the box so that the work is fed against the down side of the disk. Move the motor assembly along the arm to avoid sanding too long on one part of the disc.

Drum sanding
Either fit a worktable with a hole cut into it so that the end of the sander can be lowered below the surface, or construct a box to raise the work.

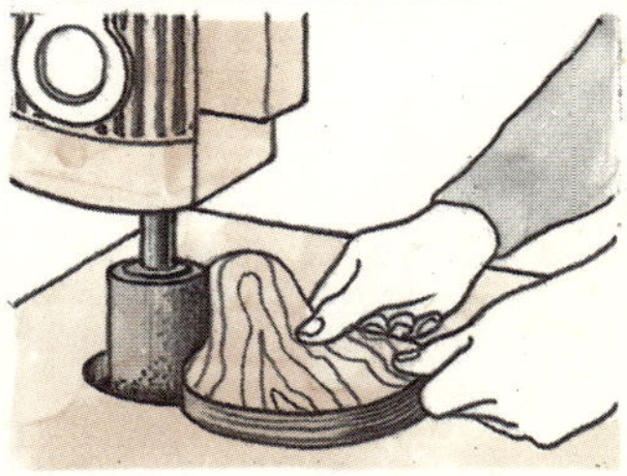

Curved shapes can be sanded free-hand against the drum which attaches to the arbor.

Sanding straight edges
Set up the drum sander in relation to the fence so that the work passes over the sander having the fence as a guide.

Other uses
The radial arm saw has several other attachments which further increase its versatility. It can be converted for routing, spindle moulding, jigsawing, turning and grinding as well as for polishing.

Chisels and Gouges

Tools with narrow cutting edges were used for making mortices in the Late Stone, the Bronze and Early Iron Ages. Medieval carpenters also used the "former", a chisel with a wide, flared blade, for rough shaping. From the sixteenth century onward, general purpose chisels were made which were stouter and had parallel sides. These were called "firmer chisels", as they could also be used with the mallet. Carpenters also had longer, thinner tools called "paring chisels", for hand use only. Special types such as the "bevelled edge" and "lock-mortice" chisels and the "bolting iron" were developed later by cabinetmakers and other craftsmen for particular purposes. For turning work on pole lathes, a wide range of chisels and gouges has been available since the Iron Age.

Modern chisels are fitted with smoothly curved bulbous handles, usually round in section and domed at the end for a comfortable grip. These are made from boxwood or impact-resistant plastic, although traditional shaped handles such as the "London Pattern" are still available made in ash.

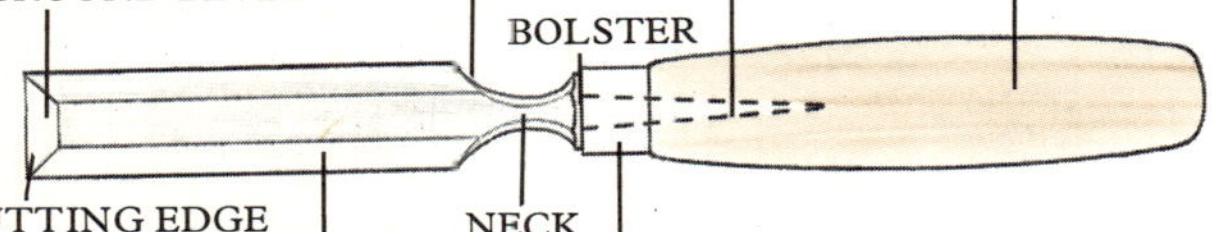

MODERN HANDLE IMPACT-RESISTANT PLASTIC

CARVING PATTERN BOXWOOD

TRADITIONAL ROUND LONDON PATTERN

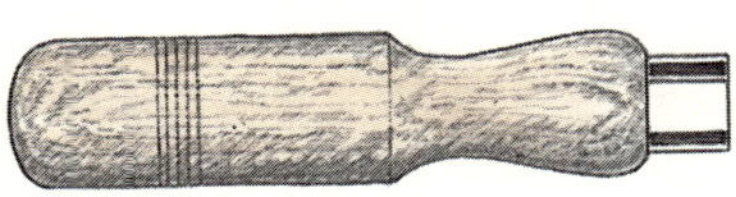

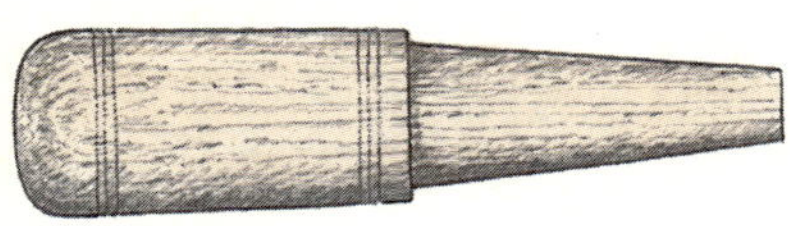

BEECH SOCKET

Firmer Chisel

OTHER NAME: Wood chisel
SIZE: Blade width: 3 to 50mm
MATERIAL: *Blade:* steel; *Handle:* ash, beech, boxwood, plastic
USE: To trim and chop wood

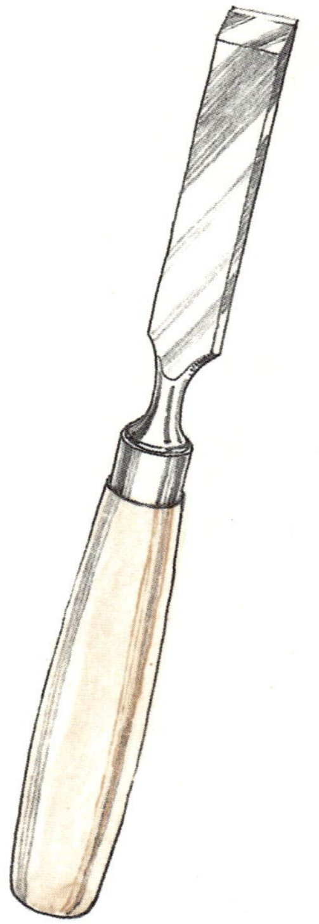

The firmer chisel is a general purpose wood-cutting tool with a blade approximately 100mm long and rectangular in section. The blade has parallel sides and tapers slightly from the bolster to the cutting edge. Common widths of blade range from 3mm to 18mm increasing in 3mm steps; and 25mm to 37mm increasing in 6mm steps. Chisels up to 50mm wide are also available. For most domestic uses, a selection including 6mm, 12mm, 18mm and 50mm widths should be sufficient.

Because the firmer chisel has a stout blade it can be driven with a mallet. Use only wooden or soft faced mallets on wooden handles; a hammer may be used on the plastic ones.

Bevelled Edge Firmer Chisel

OTHER NAME: Butt chisel
SIZE: Blade width: 3 to 50mm
MATERIAL: *Blade:* alloy steel; *Handle:* ash, beech, boxwood, plastic
USE: Light general woodworking

The bevelled edge chisel is identical to the firmer chisel in all respects except that the blade is bevelled on the top face of the two long sides. This reduces the rigidity of the blade, making it suitable only for lighter woodworking. It is not intended for use with a mallet, but light tapping is tolerated. Because of the bevelled edge, the chisel can be used to work undercuts such as in dovetail housing.

Paring Chisel

SIZE: Blade width: 6 to 37mm
MATERIAL: *Blade:* alloy steel; *Handle:* boxwood
USE: To pare long housings

The paring chisel has a comparatively long blade, about 175mm, and can be either of the firmer or the bevelled edge type. It is used to trim long grooves such as those in stair or shelf construction.

All-Steel Wood Chisel

SIZE: Blade width: 12mm, 18mm, 25mm, 31mm
MATERIAL: Steel
USE: Carpentry work

The all-steel chisel has a short, bevelled edge blade and a hexagonal handle. The end of the handle is formed into a slightly domed mushroom shape so it can be easily driven with a hammer. This is a very strong chisel, suitable for heavy carpentry work.

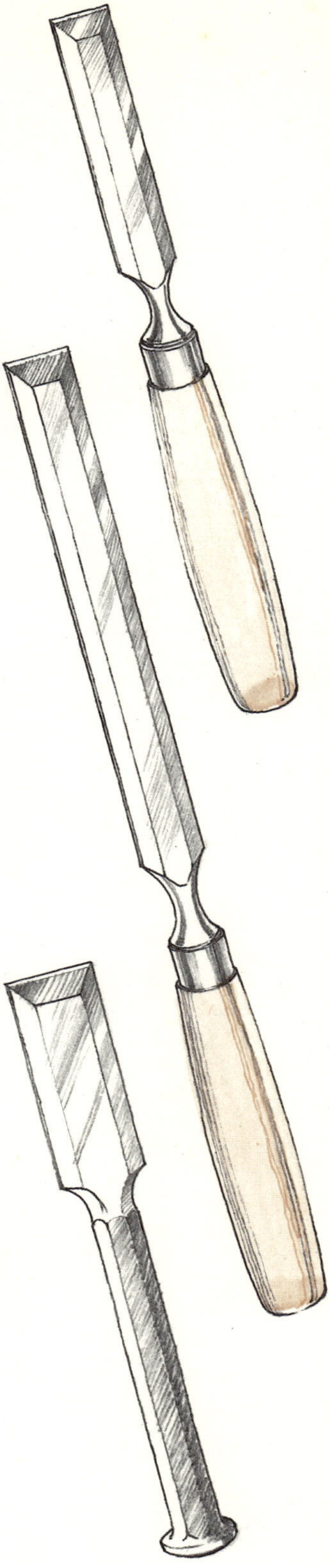

Using wood chisels
Wood chisels are designed to trim wood and clear the waste from joints. Start within the waste area and work toward the previously marked line – if the first cut is made *on* the line, the bevel can force the cutting edge beyond. Make the last cut on the line with the cutting bevel facing away.

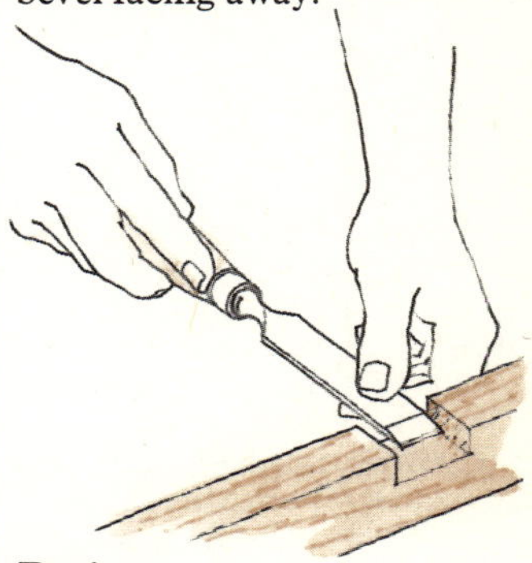

Paring
When paring (removing the waste in thin layers) hold the blade between the thumb and forefinger, resting the hand on the bench or against the work piece to steady it. This allows you to align the cutting edge accurately and control the speed at which the chisel is driven. With the other hand, apply pressure to the handle, striking the end with the heel of your hand for extra force.

Many jobs only need hand pressure, but when considerable force is needed to drive the chisel, use a mallet.

Getting more power
If you need more force use the shoulder to assist the hand.

Firmer Gouge

SIZE: Blade width: 6mm, 9mm, 12mm, 15mm, 18mm, 25mm
MATERIAL: *Blade:* steel;
Handle: boxwood, ash
USE: To cut hollow or curved shoulders

The firmer gouge is similar to the firmer chisel, but it has a blade which is curved in cross section. The blade is usually about 100mm long and has parallel sides like its chisel counterpart. The common sizes are 6mm to 25mm, although larger sizes are made with standard curves.

There are two types of blade: those with the cutting bevel ground on the outside, known as out-cannel, and those ground on the inside, known as in-cannel. Both have square cutting edges, though the out-cannel is sometimes rounded for deep hollow cutting.

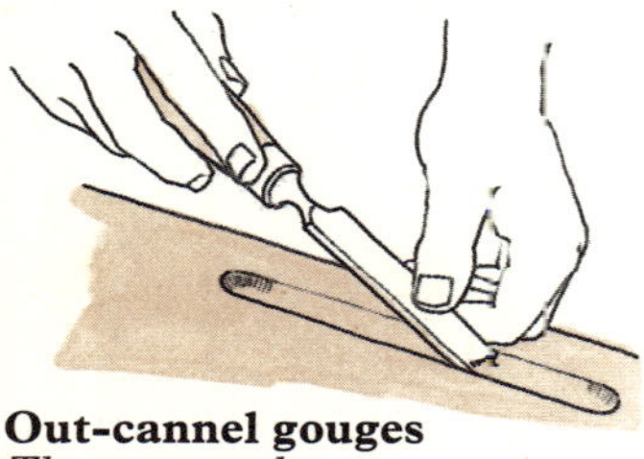

Out-cannel gouges
These are used to cut concave shapes such as finger pulls for a drawer or flaps for a leaf-table. The blade is used as a lever on the ground bevel when making a scalloped cut.

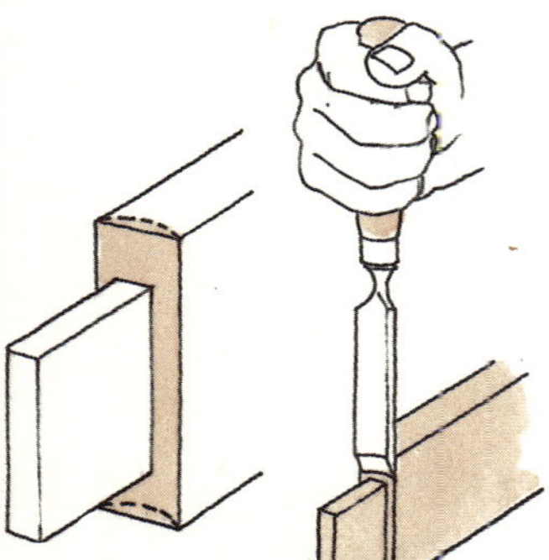

In-cannel gauges
The in-cannel gouge is used to make straight cuts which are curved in section, such as when scribing the shoulder of a tenon to meet a mortice in a round leg.

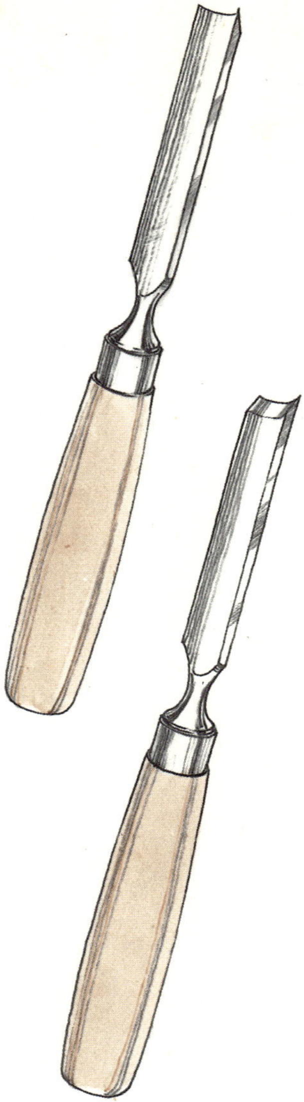

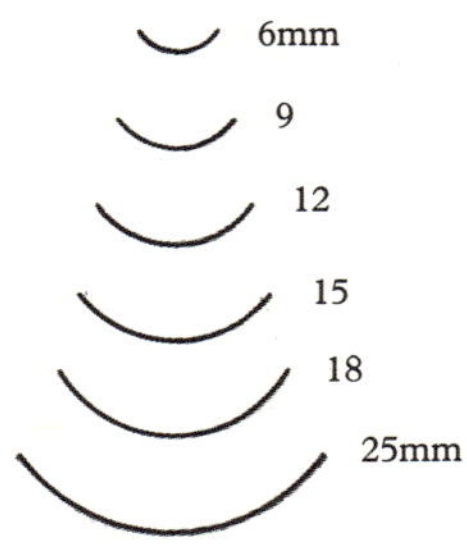

Blade sizes and curves

Paring Gouge

OTHER NAME: Scribing gouge
SIZE: Blade width: 6 to 31mm
MATERIAL: *Blade:* steel;
Handle: boxwood
USE: To shape work

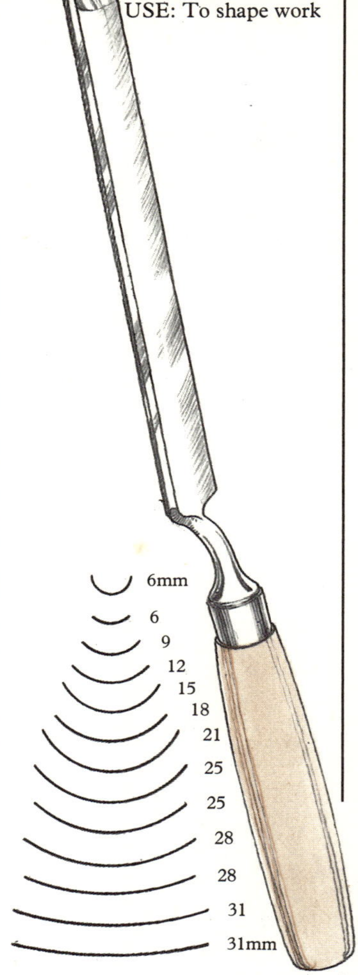

The paring gouge is a lighter, elongated version of the in-cannel firmer gouge. The 175mm blade, which has parallel sides, is usually fitted with a carving pattern handle. The neck may be straight, or cranked to raise the handle to let the hand clear the work surface.

The gouge is generally used for hand paring without the aid of a mallet, unlike the in-cannel firmer gouge. Its range of different curved sections for a given width gives it greater flexibility for cutting curved shapes of all kinds.

Mortice Chisel

OTHER NAME: Joiner's mortice chisel
SIZE: Blade width: 12, 15, 18mm
MATERIAL: *Blade:* steel; *Handle:* beech
USE: To cut large mortices

The mortice chisel has a thick, stiff blade for clearing out waste and wide side edges that help to keep the chisel square in the mortice. The bolster is oval as is the handle: a leather shock-absorbing washer is often fitted between them. The handle has a wide curved end specially designed to be hit with a mallet.

Sash Mortice Chisel

SIZE: Blade width: 6mm, 7.5mm, 9mm, 12mm
MATERIAL: *Blade:* steel; *Handle:* boxwood, ash, beech
USE: Light carpentry work in softwood

The sash mortice chisel is similar in use to the mortice chisel, but is intended for lighter work. It is usually fitted with a carved turning pattern handle with a single ferrule and a leather shock-absorbing washer between it and the bolster.

Registered Mortise Chisel

SIZE: Blade width: 18 to 37mm
MATERIAL: *Blade:* steel; *Handle:* ash
USE: To work hardwood

The registered mortice chisel is distinguished from the firmer type by its handle. This is made of hardwood with a traditional shape but it has two ferrules, one against the bolster, the other at the striking end. It is meant to be used with a mallet, and the end ferrule prevents the wood from splitting. A shock-absorbent leather washer is fitted between the bolster and the handle.

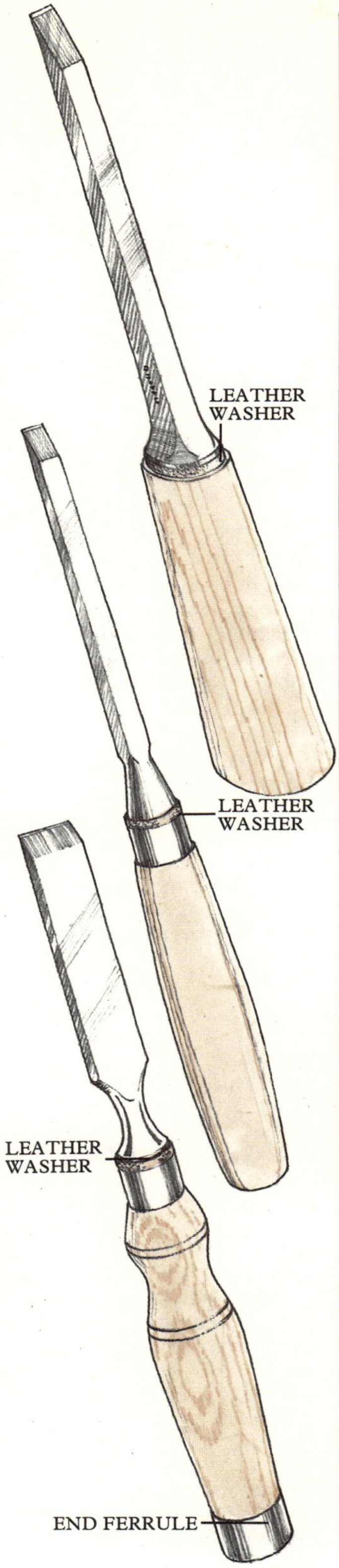

Lock Mortise Chisel

OTHER NAME: Swan neck mortice chisel
SIZE: Blade width: 11 to 15mm
MATERIAL: *Blade:* steel; *Handle:* beech
USE: To remove waste from deep mortices

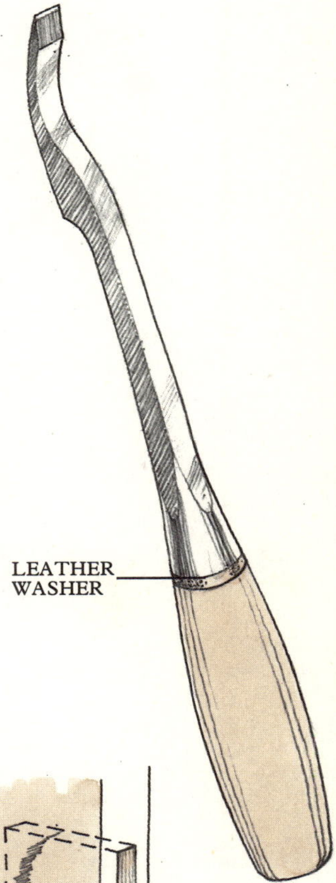

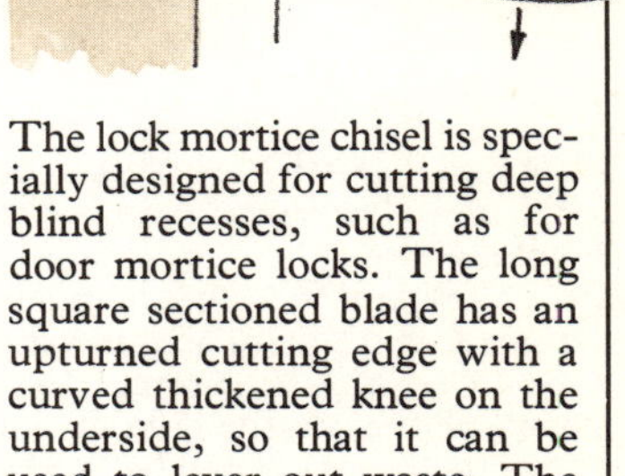

The lock mortice chisel is specially designed for cutting deep blind recesses, such as for door mortice locks. The long square sectioned blade has an upturned cutting edge with a curved thickened knee on the underside, so that it can be used to lever out waste. The chisel is fitted with a socket type handle.

Drawer Lock Chisel

OTHER NAMES: Bolt chisel, bolting iron, lock bolt chisel
SIZE: 150mm
MATERIAL: Steel
USE: To cut lock recesses

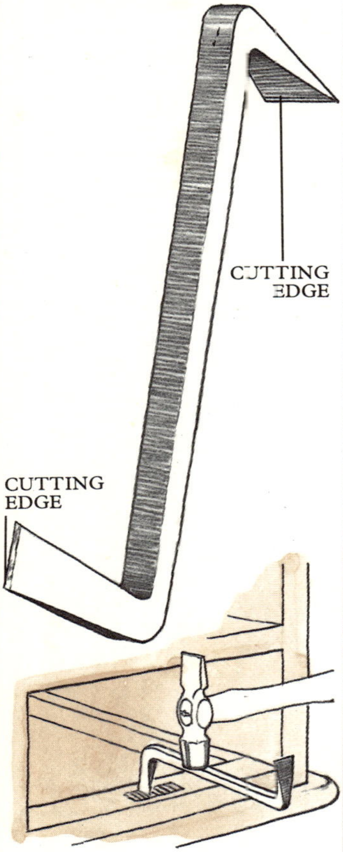

The drawer lock chisel is used for cutting housings or mortices for locks where there is not enough room to use a conventional chisel. It is a square sectioned steel bar, cranked at right angles at both ends. Each end is tapered and ground to a sharp edge. One cutting edge is set parallel with the long axis of the tool, the other is set at right angles to it.

The cutting edge is positioned on the work and its back is struck with a hammer. In a confined space the side of the hammer may have to be used.

Cutting a mortice
Mark out the width of the mortice with a mortice gauge set to the width of the chisel. Use a chisel that is one third the width of the rail or leg, whichever is smaller. Do not try to drive the chisel too deep at one stroke: the wood could split or the chisel could get stuck in the workpiece.

1. *Hold the chisel upright in the centre of the marked mortice, the bevel facing away from you. Strike the end with a mallet to cut across the grain.*

2. *Gradually work back toward one end of the mortice stopping 3mm from the line.*

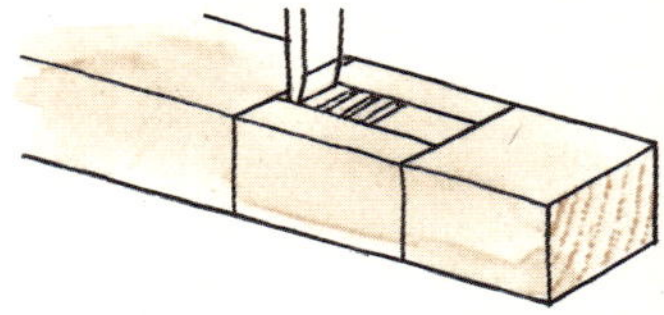

3. *Start at the centre again and work back toward the other end of the mortice.*

4. *Clean out the waste and repeat until the required depth is reached.*

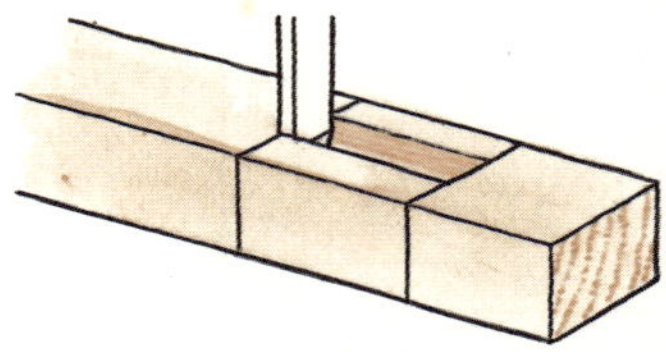

5. *Finally chop the remaining 3mm of waste from both ends of the mortice. Cut a through mortice from both sides. Pare away any waste from the sides of mortice with the widest chisel you have.*

Maintenance
Keep chisels sharp. A blunt edge will not leave a clean cut and unnecessary force will be needed to drive it. This could limit the amount of control and be dangerous to the user.

Store chisels in racks so the cutting edges do not become dulled or chipped by knocking against other tools. If the chisels are not to be used frequently, give the blades a light oiling to prevent rust.

Never use a metal hammer to drive a chisel unless it has been specially designed to take the force, otherwise you will damage the handle. Damaged chisel handles can be reshaped with a file.

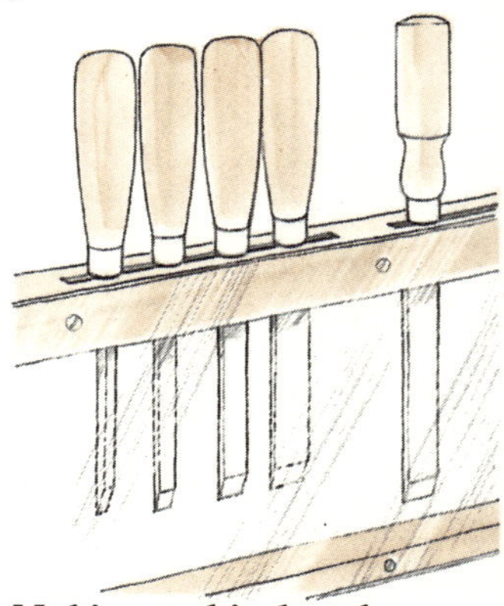

Making a chisel rack
Nail two wood strips together, leaving a slit wide enough for the chisel blade, and mount a plastic shield on the rack.

Ripping Chisel

SIZE: *Blade width:* 37 to 50mm; *Length:* 450mm
MATERIAL: Steel
USE: To split boards

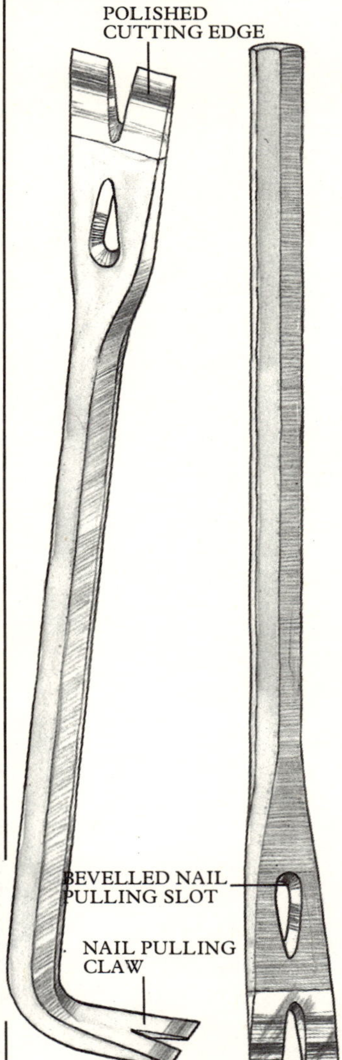

The ripping chisel is like a ripping bar, but it has a wider and sharper chisel end. It is made from a hexagonal sectioned steel bar, and is either straight with a single cutting edge or goose necked and notched at one end for nail-pulling. It is used for rough work, such as splitting boards along the grain or levering nailed boards apart. To split a board, drive the chisel into the end following the grain.

Floor Board Chisel

OTHER NAME: Electrician's chisel
SIZE: *Blade width:* 62 to 68mm; *Length:* 200 to 300mm
MATERIAL: Alloy steel
USE: To cut and lift floor boards

The floor board chisel has a wide spade-shaped blade and an integral octagonal handle.

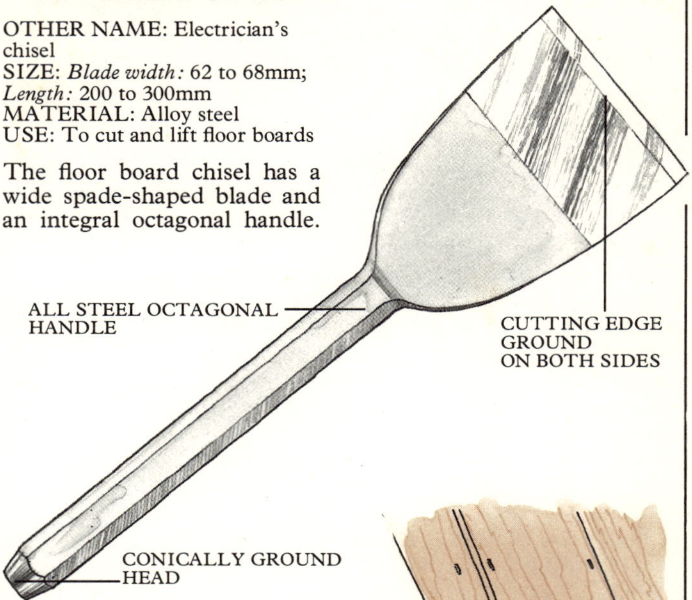

The end of the handle is either tapered, or mushroom-shaped so it can be driven efficiently with a hammer.

This chisel is used by professionals to cut through the tongues in tongue and groove flooring and for levering up boards. The wide blade spreads the load to prevent damage to adjacent boards.

Glazier's Chisel

SIZE: Blade width: 50mm
MATERIAL: *Blade:* alloy steel; *Handle:* plastic
USE: To remove old putty from window frames

The glazier's chisel is a strong firmer type chisel with a wide blade. Sometimes a steel cap is fitted into the plastic handle so it can be driven with a hammer.

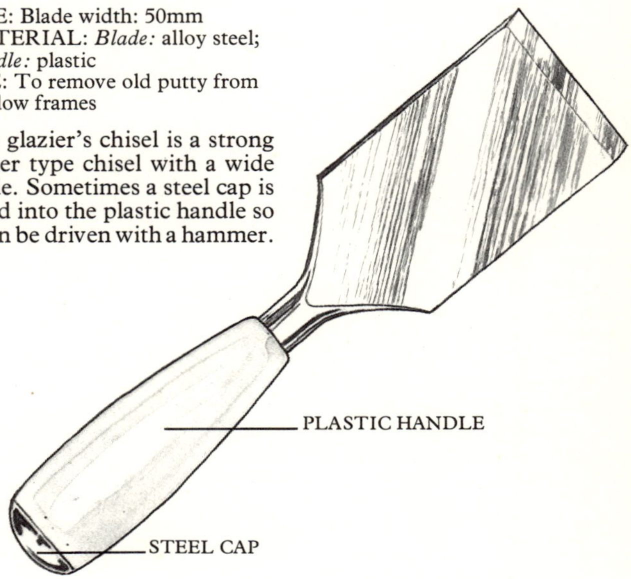

Wood Turning Tools

Wood turning chisels and gouges are specifically made for lathe work, where the force is applied across the blade rather than along its length. A wood turning tool is extra long, and has a thick blade and long tang without a bolster. It is fitted with a long turned hardwood handle with a bulbous section behind the brass ferrule which tapers and then flares slightly toward the end. This long handle provides the necessary leverage for delicate control. Tools for heavy work may have extra long handles which can be tucked under the arm to give maximum leverage and control.

Turning tools are held in both hands, with the blade resting on the part of the lathe known as a tool rest. One hand, knuckles uppermost, grips the blade close to the cutting edge and controls the speed and direction of the tool along the rest. The other hand grips the handle and steadies the tool against the turning work.

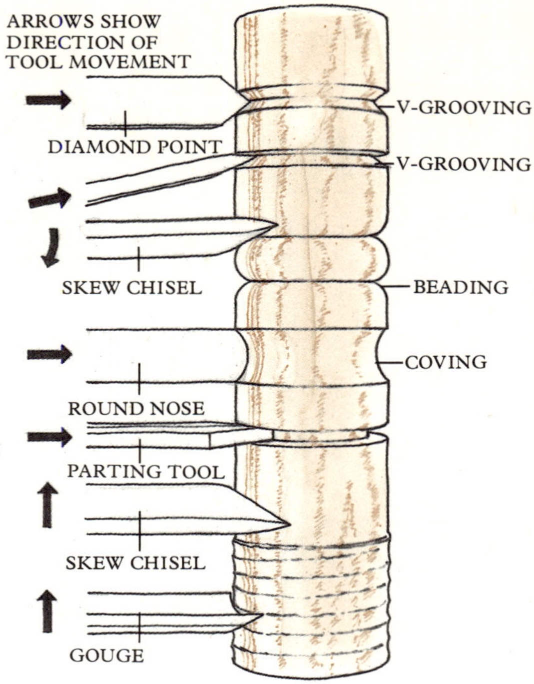

Wood Turning Gouge

SIZE: *Blade:* 9, 12, 16, 18, 25mm; *Length:* 412mm (standard), 337mm (small)
MATERIAL: *Blade:* steel;
Handle: ash
USE: To size turned work roughly

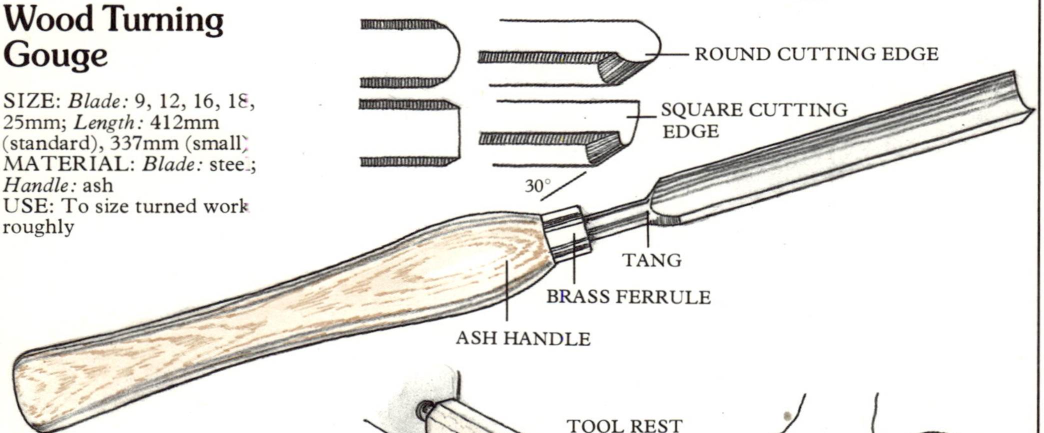

The standard wood turning gouge is ground on the outside and has a square or round cutting edge. Gouges are generally used for roughing or quickly sizing the work. The square type is normally used for turning down work between lathe centres. The 25mm gauge is recommended for first cut. It moves along the tool rest with the bottom part of the cutting edge doing the work. The resulting finish is usually a ribbed cut, which needs to be cleaned up afterward with a turning chisel.

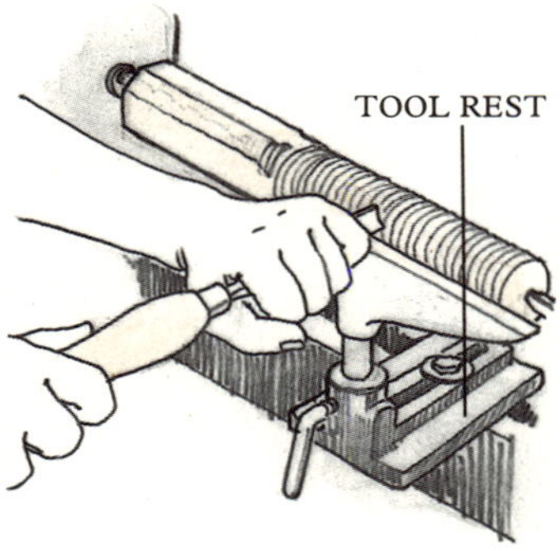

Using the square nosed gouge
Place the blade on the tool rest. Holding the tool at right angles to the work, turn it partly on edge in the direction of the cut.

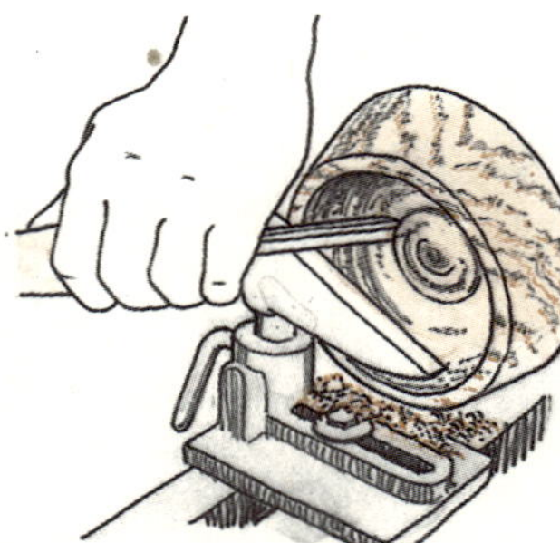

Using the round nosed gouge
This is generally used for turning hollow work, such as bowls or shaped spindles. The absence of corners prevents the cutting edge from digging in and damaging the work.

Wood Turning Chisel

SIZE: *Blade:* 12, 18, 25mm;
Length: 412mm (standard), 337mm (small)
MATERIAL: *Blade:* steel;
Handle: ash
USE: To smooth work after rough sizing

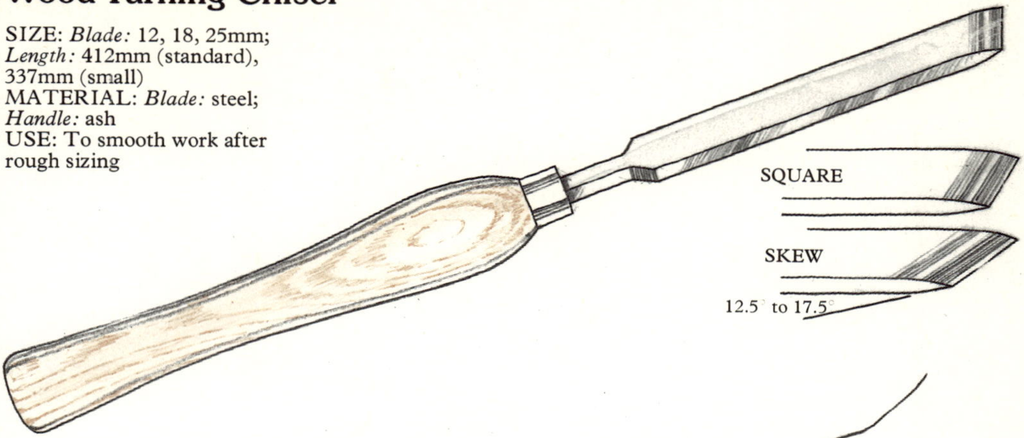

The wood turning chisel has a flat blade with a square or angled cutting edge. It is ground on both sides, so it can cut with a slicing action and move in either direction along the work. These chisels are used to make smooth finishing cuts, cutting the shoulders of square sinkings and forming beads.

Using the chisel
Hold the blade flat on the rest, or slightly tilted in the direction of the cut. With the tool rest set correctly, the cut should be near the work's top.

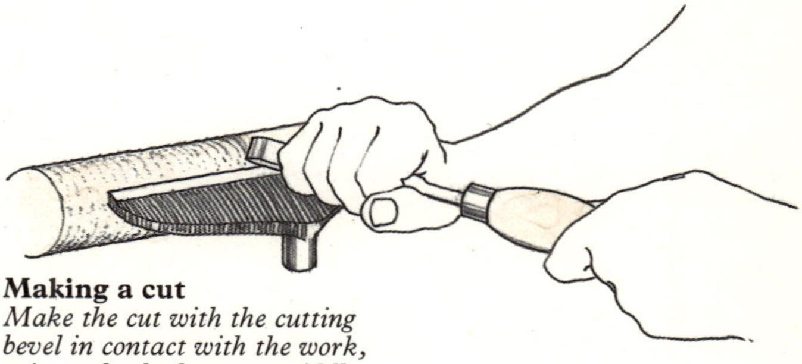

Making a cut
Make the cut with the cutting bevel in contact with the work, using only the lower to middle portion of the cutting edge. The point of the chisel must always be clear of the work, otherwise the tool might grab and damage the work.

Round Nosed Chisel

SIZE: *Blade:* 12, 18, 25mm;
Length: 412mm (standard), 337mm (small)
MATERIAL: *Blade:* steel;
Handle: ash
USES: To cut coves and shape work

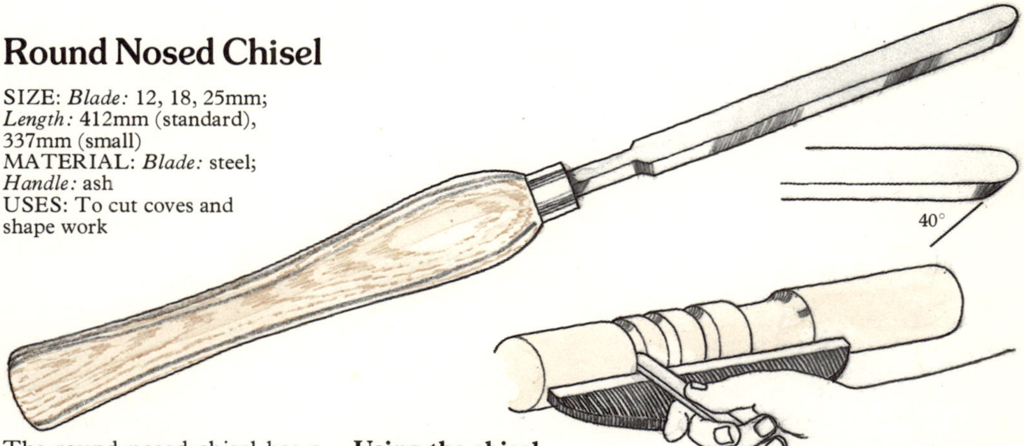

The round nosed chisel has a flat rectangular blade and is ground into a round cutting edge with a single bevel. It cuts with a scraping action and it is one of the simplest tools you can use for cutting concave shapes for decorative work, or a variety of mouldings.

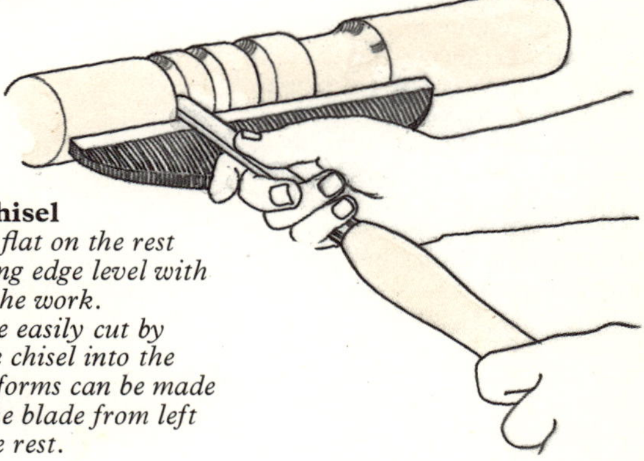

Using the chisel
Hold the tool flat on the rest with the cutting edge level with the centre of the work. Mouldings are easily cut by advancing the chisel into the work. Wider forms can be made by pivoting the blade from left to right on the rest.

Diamond Point Chisel

OTHER NAME: Spear point chisel
SIZE: *Blade width:* 12, 18, 25mm; *Length:* 412mm (standard), 337mm (small)
MATERIAL: *Blade:* Steel; *Handle:* ash
USE: To cut "V" grooves and square shoulders

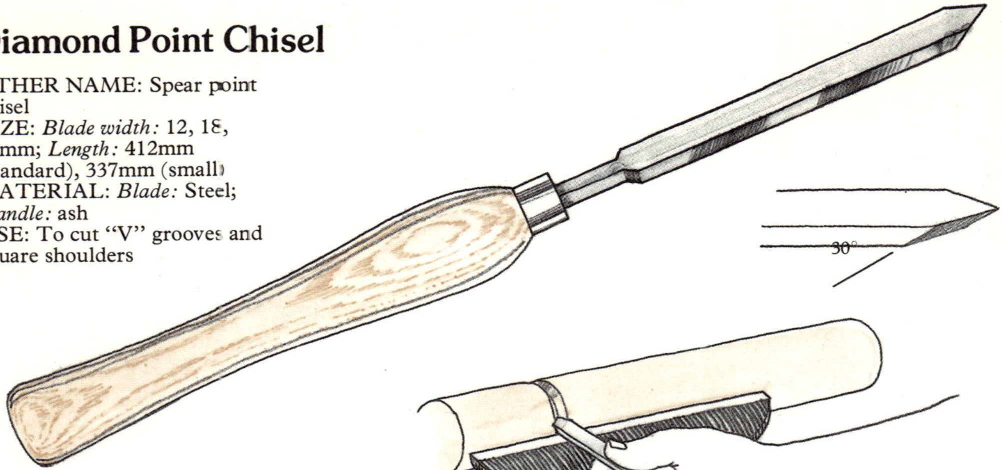

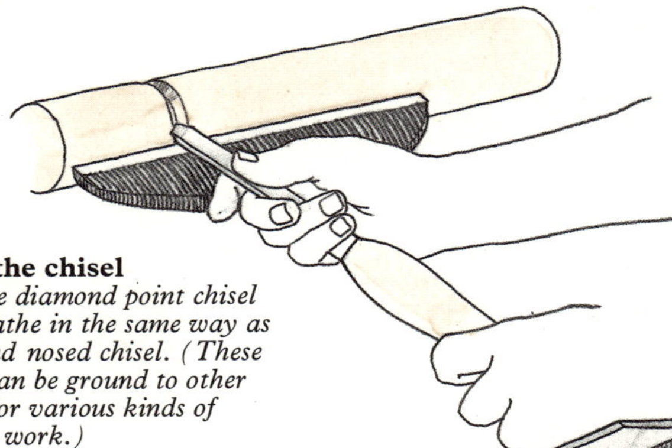

Like the round nosed chisel, the diamond point has a flat rectangular blade ground on one side. It cuts with a scraping action, but the cutting edge is V-shaped. The point is usually ground to an included angle of 90°, which makes it useful for cleaning up squared shoulders.

Using the chisel
Hold the diamond point chisel on the lathe in the same way as the round nosed chisel. (These chisels can be ground to other shapes for various kinds of molding work.)

Parting Tool

SIZE: *Blade width:* 4mm; *Length:* 412mm (standard), 337mm (small)
MATERIAL: *Blade:* steel; *Handle:* ash
USE: To cut to length

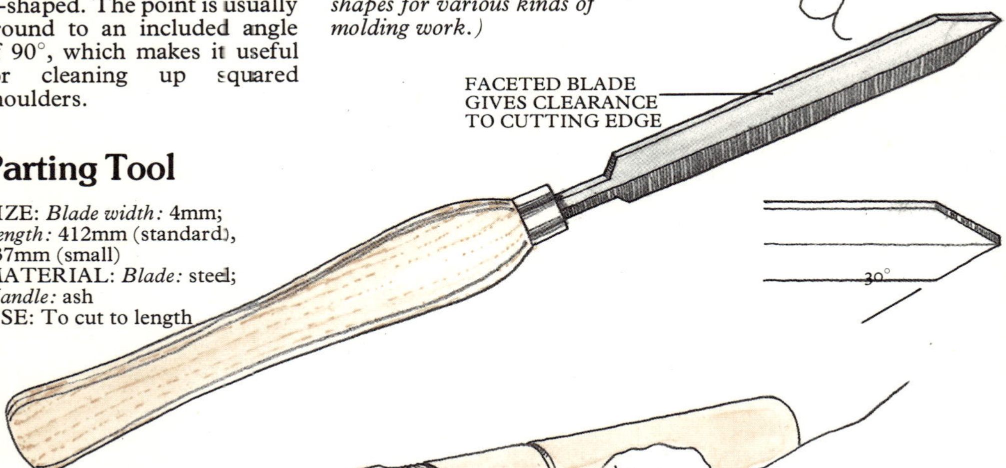

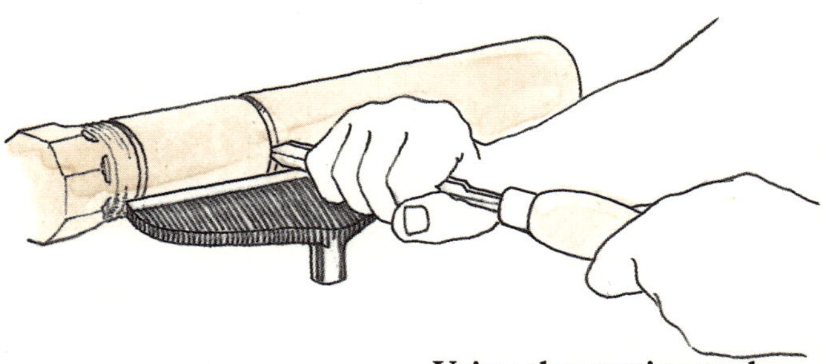

The parting tool is made in only one blade width. It is usually rectangular in section, but some are faceted on the two side faces. The blade is square ground to make a long point and it is used on edge as a narrow chisel. The parting tool is primarily used for parting or cutting the finished work from the waste and for squaring off the work end.

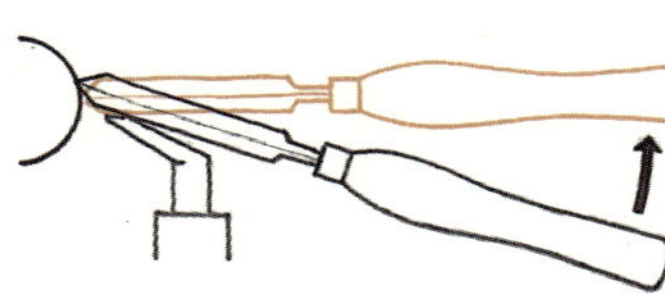

Parting tool position

Using the parting tool
Hold the tool at right angles to the work with the handle lowered. Lift the handle to allow the edge to make the cut; the depth of cut will depend on the diameter of the work. Finish with a fine saw using the groove cut by the chisel as a guide. Trim the sawn end with a wood chisel.

Carving Gouge

SIZE: *Blade width:* 3 to 25mm; *Length:* 237mm, 200mm, 162mm
MATERIAL: *Blade:* steel; *Handle:* beech, ash, rosewood, plastic
USE: Preliminary shaping

The carving gouge is similar to the firmer gouge, but it is lighter and available in a wide range of curved sections. All carving gouges are out-canneled, that is ground on the outside face. The carving gouge has a blade about 100mm long with a slim round or square neck and a neat bolster. The blade may have parallel sides or taper toward the bolster, which gives greater clearance for working wood carvings.

Handles are usually of the carving pattern, turned from hardwood, with a single brass ferrule. Earlier types were often octagonal in section.

Using a mallet
Carving gouges may be lightly driven with a beechwood carver's mallet.

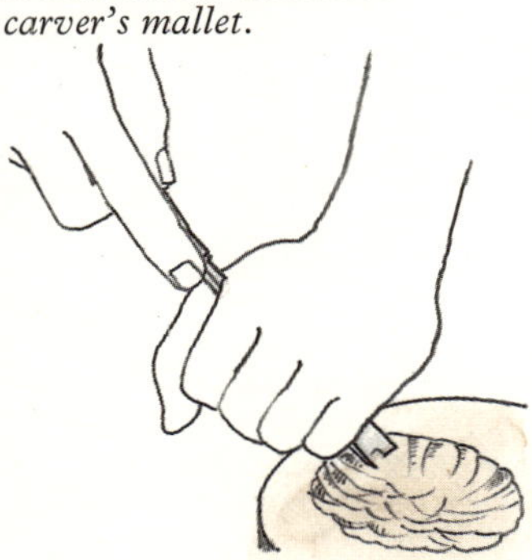

Unaided carving
Like most wood carving tools, carving gouges are worked with hand pressure only.

STRAIGHT GOUGE
This type of gouge has a straight blade in line with the handle. Do not use it on concave surfaces.

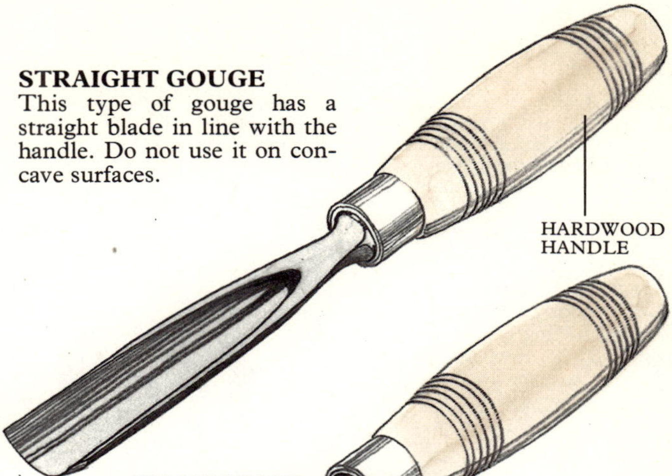

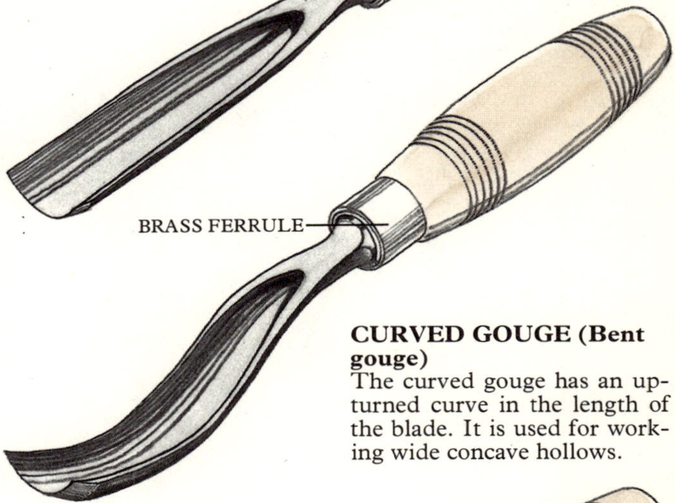

CURVED GOUGE (Bent gouge)
The curved gouge has an upturned curve in the length of the blade. It is used for working wide concave hollows.

SPOON BIT GOUGE (Front bent gouge)
This is similar to the curved gouge, but it has a very sharply defined curve on the front section of the blade only. It is used to work small, deep recesses.

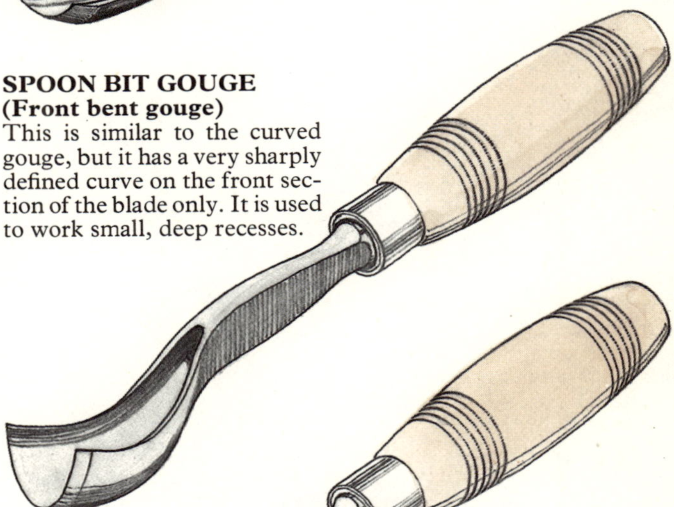

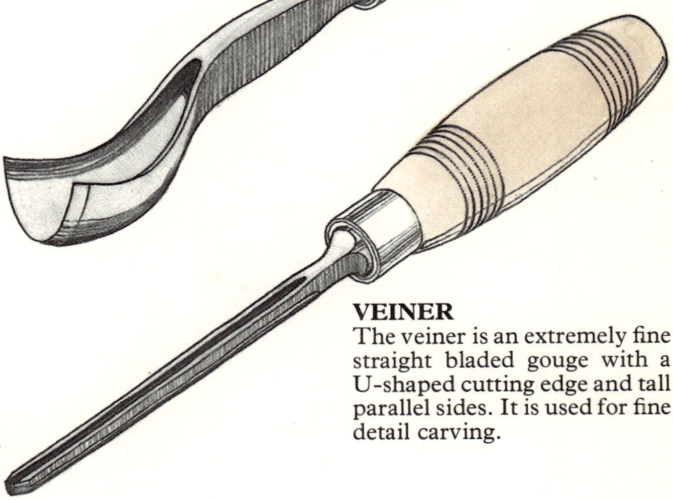

VEINER
The veiner is an extremely fine straight bladed gouge with a U-shaped cutting edge and tall parallel sides. It is used for fine detail carving.

Carving Chisel

SIZE: *Blade width:* 6 to 12mm; *Length:* 237mm (large), 200mm (medium), 162mm (small)
MATERIAL: *Blade:* steel; *Handle:* beech, ash, rosewood, plastic
USE: To shape and finish

STRAIGHT CHISEL
The straight carving chisel has a flat, rectangular blade ground on both faces and either a square or skewed cutting edge. The honing and grinding angles are run together to form a curved cutting bevel. The cutting edge rides on the curved bevel, which helps prevent it digging in too deeply. The skew type is used for undercuts or detail that is inaccessible to the square chisel.

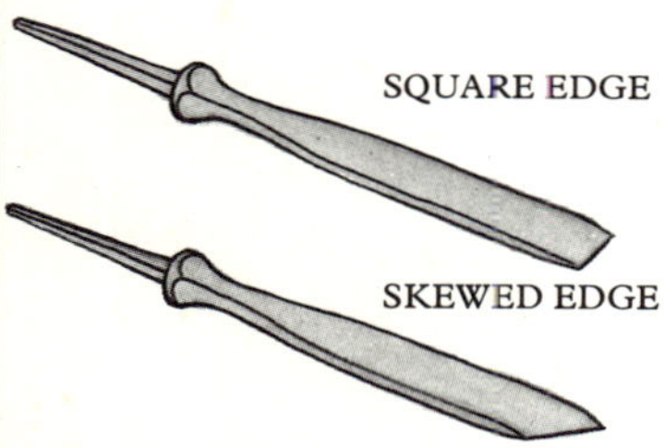

CURVED CHISEL (Bent chisel)
This chisel is about the same size as the curved gouge and is used to finish the scalloped surface produced by the gouge. A curved chisel is ground on the underside only.

SPOON BIT CHISEL
This is used to finish work after preliminary shaping by the spoon bit gouge.

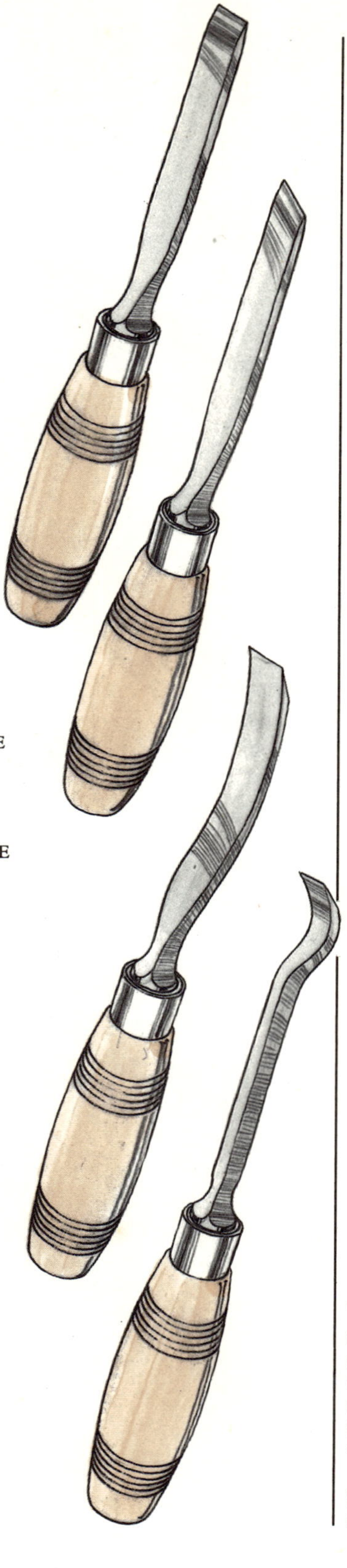

Parting Tool

OTHER NAME: "V" tool
SIZE: *Blade width:* 6 to 12mm; *Length:* 237mm (large), 200mm (medium), 162mm; (small)
MATERIAL: *Blade:* steel; *Handle:* beech, ash, rosewood, plastic
USE: To make grooves

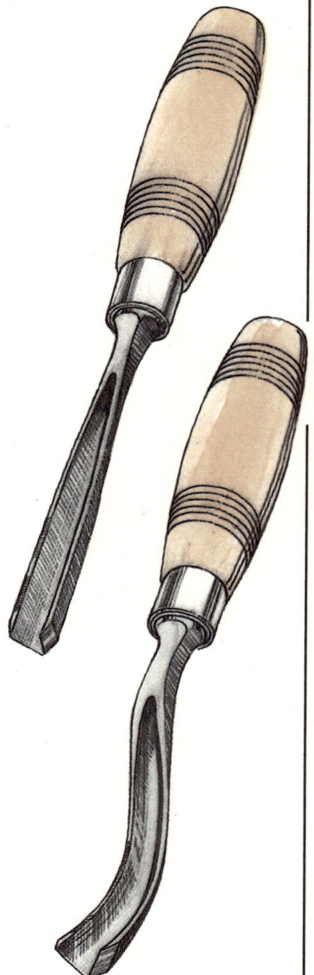

The parting tool has a V-shaped cutting edge and is available with different included angles. Like the sharp cornered gouge it is ground on the outside faces, and is made with straight or curved blades.

It is used for grooving and for making square cornered cutouts.

Cold Chisel

OTHER NAME: Flat chisel
SIZE: *Length:* 125 to 206mm; *Long pattern:* 300 to 450mm; *Bit width:* 6 to 25mm
MATERIAL: Steel
USE: To cut metal

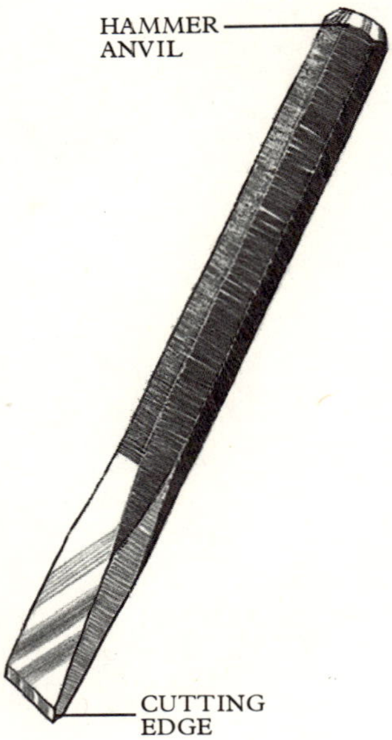

The cold chisel is used in various trades for rough cutting cold metal, where other tools such as snips or hacksaws are unsuitable. It can be used in a number of ways: to chip away waste material from solid stock prior to filing; cutting through round stock such as chain links; cutting sheet metal; and cutting off rivet or bolt heads.

The chisel is made from hexagonal sectioned steel, and has a flat, wedge shaped bit that is slightly wider than the shank. The cutting edge is ground on both sides to an included angle of 60° and is slightly curved across its width. The head is chamfered to reduce burring from continuous hammering. Maintain the chamfer to prevent chips of metal flying off as it is struck with a hammer.

The tool is held in the same way for all types of work. The forefingers grip the stock with the thumb either tucked under or covering the index finger.

Using the cold chisel

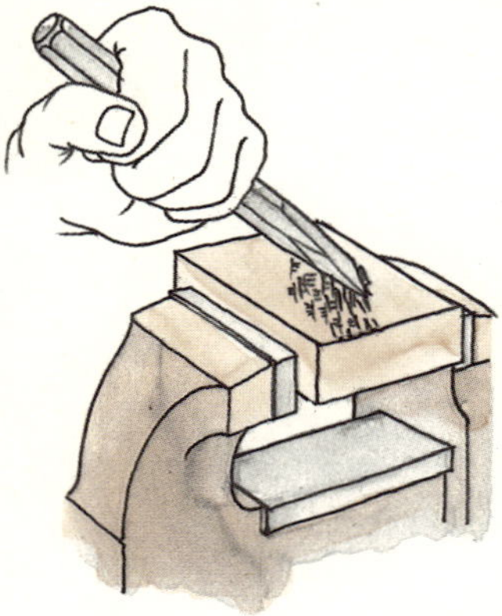

To chip
When chipping, present the cutting edge to the face of the workpiece at an angle. This will determine the depth of cut. Use a ball pein hammer to drive the tool.

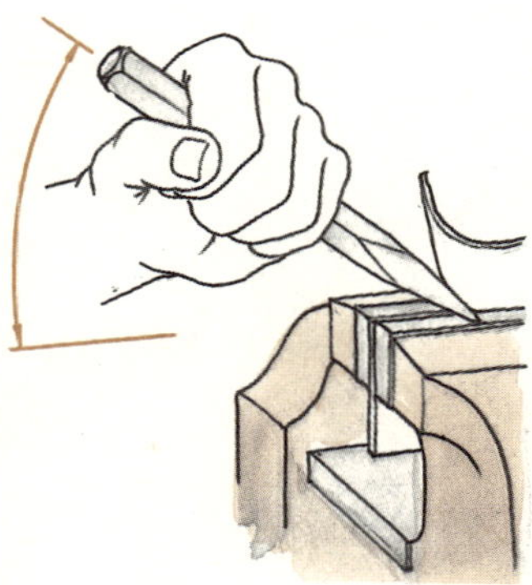

To cut sheet or plate metal
Fix it in a vice with the marked cutting line level with the jaws. Hold the chisel at approximately 45° to the face of the plate and 30° from horizontal, with the lower ground bevel resting on the top of the vice against the edge of the workpiece. Drive the chisel along the vice with even hammer blows, slicing through the plate as you go. For larger sheet cutting rest the metal on a flat work surface with the marked line level with the edge.

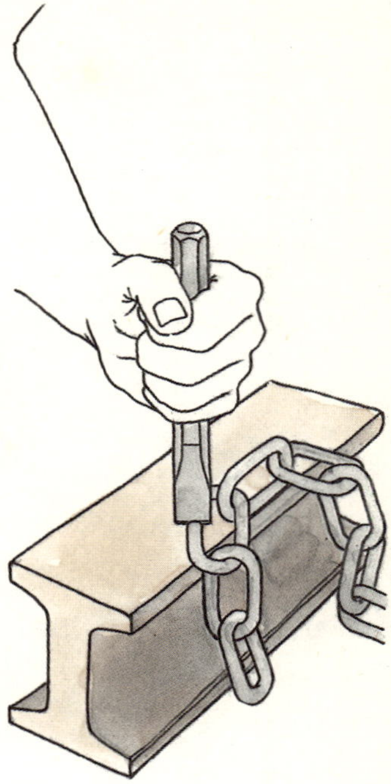

To cut round stock
Place the workpiece on a firm support, such as an anvil, and hold the chisel upright on the marked cutting line. Strike the chisel with a heavy hammer to chop through. Cut halfway through then reverse the workpiece and finish from the other side.

To cut rivets
Position the chisel against the side of the rivet head, with the bottom ground bevel level with the surface and drive the chisel with a ball pein hammer. Cut bolt heads in the same way, or first cut down from the top, then hit from the side. Split nuts by cutting down on one or both sides.

Cape Chisel

OTHER NAME: Cross cut chisel
SIZE: *Length:* 168 to 206mm;
Bit width: 6 to 12mm
MATERIAL: Steel
USE: To cut grooves in metal or masonry

The cape chisel is used for making narrow cuts or grooves in metal or masonry. It has a deep wedge shaped bit, which is narrower than the hexagonal sectioned stock. When new, the blade is parallel sided with a slight flair at the tip and is ground on the upper and lower faces to 60°. The extra depth stiffens the narrow cutting edge of the tool.

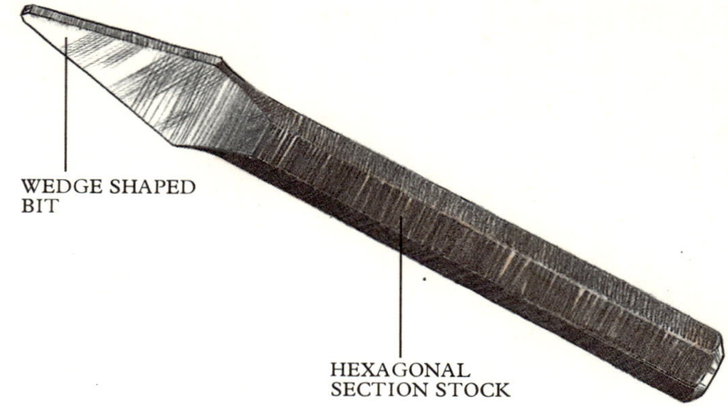

Round Nosed Chisel

OTHER NAME: Half round chisel
SIZE: *Length:* 168 to 206mm;
Bit width: 6 to 12mm
MATERIAL: Steel
USE: To cut grooves and to reposition a misaligned hole centre

The round nosed chisel is similar to the cape chisel, but has a semi-circular cutting edge with a single cutting bevel ground on the top face.

Rivet Buster

SIZE: *Length:* 300mm
Bit width: 15mm
MATERIAL: Steel
USE: To cut rivets

This is a heavy chisel, similar to the diamond point in overall shape but with a wider, single ground flat cutting edge. It is used specifically for cutting through rivet heads.

Diamond Point Chisel

SIZE: *Length:* 168 to 206mm;
Bit width: 6 to 12mm
MATERIAL: Steel
USE: To cut "V" grooves and clean corners in metal

The hexagonal sectioned stock of the diamond point chisel is formed into a four sided taper, which is single ground across a diagonal to make a diamond shaped cutting face.

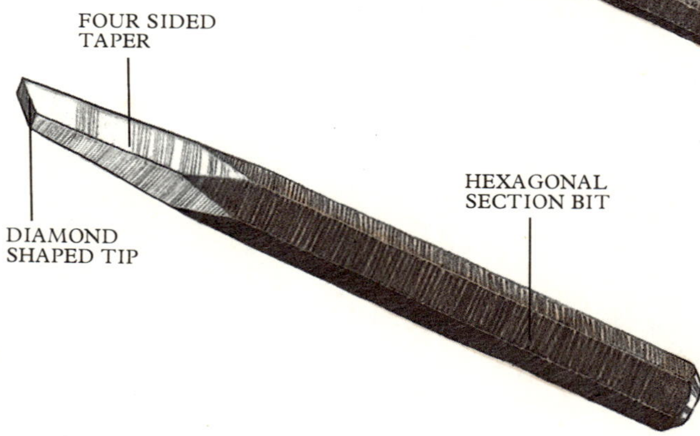

Brick Bolster

OTHER NAMES: Brick chisel, bricklayer's cold chisel
SIZE: *Length:* 175 to 187mm; *Cutting edge width:* 75 to 100mm
MATERIAL: Steel
USE: To cut bricks

The brick bolster has a very wide spade shaped bit, an integral hexagonal sectioned handle and a cutting edge ground on both sides. It is held in the same way as the metal cutting cold chisel and is used with a club hammer to cut bricks.

Cutting a brick
Position the cutting edge of the bolster on one face of the brick, holding the chisel at right angles. Strike the bolster with a hammer hard enough to leave a cut line. Repeat on the other brick faces so that the cut lines meet all around. On wider bricks or blocks make a series of cuts to form a line, then realign the bolster on the cut line and drive it with heavier blows.

Plugging Chisel

OTHER NAME: Seam drill
SIZE: *Length:* 250mm; *Point width:* 6mm
MATERIAL: Steel
USE: To cut grooves and plug holes in masonry

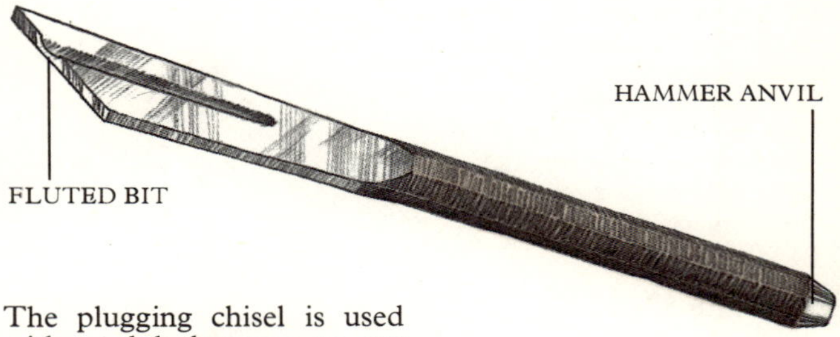

The plugging chisel is used with a club hammer to cut away the mortar between brickwork to allow for fixing wooden plugs. These are wide, flat wedges set in the brickwork to receive fixings for door frame linings, window frames and so on. It is an all-steel chisel with an octagonal stock and a long flat bit, which is rectangular in section. The bit is skewed and is available plain or fluted.

Chisels for Masonry Work

Mason's chisels are of an all-steel construction and generally have an hexagonal sectioned stock. The stock may have parallel sides or taper toward the head. Like cold chisels, mason's chisels are available with conically ground heads for striking with a hammer or slightly domed, mushroom shaped heads for use with a wooden mallet. Generally, the hammer pattern is used for initial rough cutting and the mallet pattern for lighter finishing work.

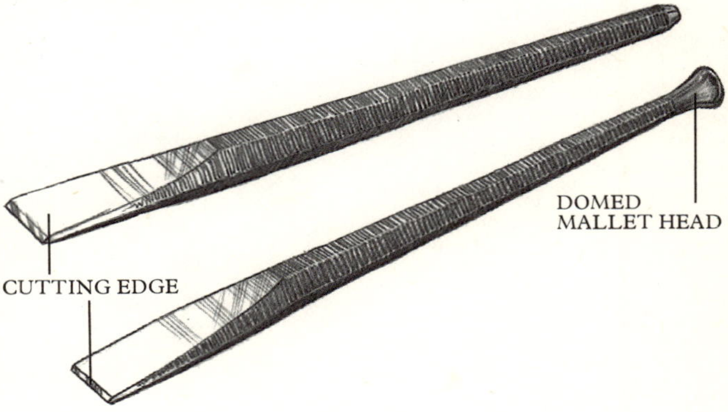

Point

OTHER NAME: Punch
SIZE: 200 to 250mm
MATERIAL: Steel
USE: To rough finish stone

The point and the punch are basically the same tool. The punch is a heavier version of the point. Both are used in the preliminary stages of smoothing rough stone by concentrating the hammering force to shatter the stone locally. The stock of the tool is hexagonal in section and ground to a four sided blunt point.

Mason's Bolster

SIZE: Bit width 50 to 75mm
MATERIAL: Steel
USE: To chisel wide surfaces

The mason's bolster is a wide chisel with a short bit and a cutting bevel ground on both sides. It can be used to smooth wide flat surfaces or to split blocks like a brick chisel.

Tooler

SIZE: Blade width: 75mm or over
MATERIAL: Steel
USE: To chisel wide surfaces

The tooler is the same as the mason's bolster, but has a wider bit and a heavier stock.

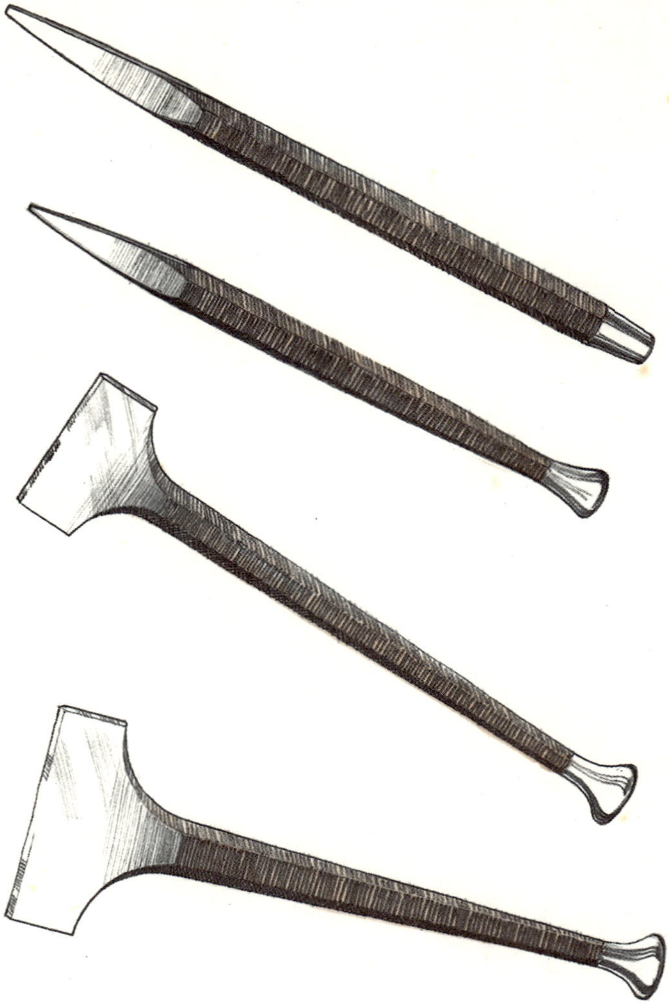

Mason's Carving Chisels and Gouges

SIZE: Bit width: 6, 9, 12mm
MATERIAL: Steel
USE: To finely shape and finish stone

Mason's carving chisels and gouges are craftsmen's tools for the final dressing and decoration of stone. They have slim hexagonal sectioned stocks, which taper down to the short bit and to the head. This shape makes the tool comfortable to hold, while its slim form allows it to reach into restricted spaces. Both tools are made with the hammer or mallet type head.

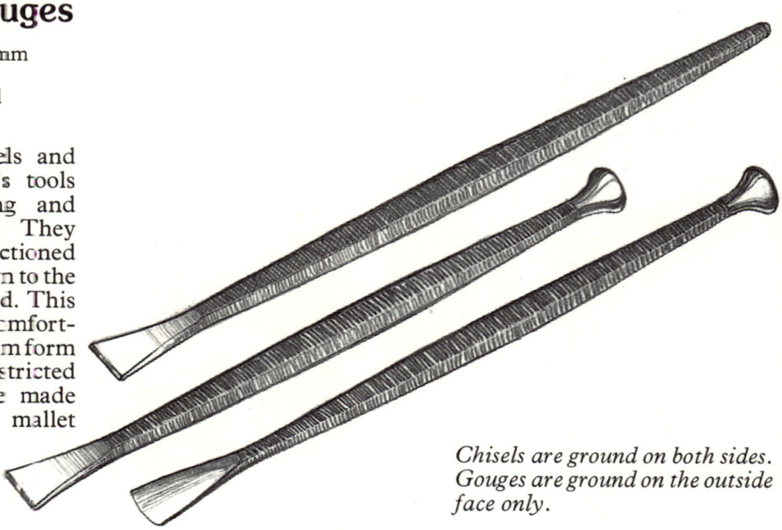

Chisels are ground on both sides. Gouges are ground on the outside face only.

Mason's Scutch Holder

OTHER NAME: Claw
SIZE: Scutch width: 25mm, 37mm, 50mm
MATERIAL: Steel
USE: To finish stone

The mason's scutch holder is a special chisel type tool, which looks similar to the mason's bolster but is made to hold a replaceable cutting edge called a scutch.

The holder has an hexagonal stock and a mallet pattern head. The double sided scutch can be plain or toothed.

The scutch tool is used to prepare flat surfaces. It follows the point chisel to reduce the uneven surface into a series of shallow furrows for further finishing with a plain chisel. Work diagonally across the surface, away from the edge.

Hold the scutch at 45° and drive with a wooden mallet. Slightly overlap the cuts.

Mason's Chisel

SIZE: Bit width: 12 to 50mm
MATERIAL: Steel
USE: To shape and smooth stone

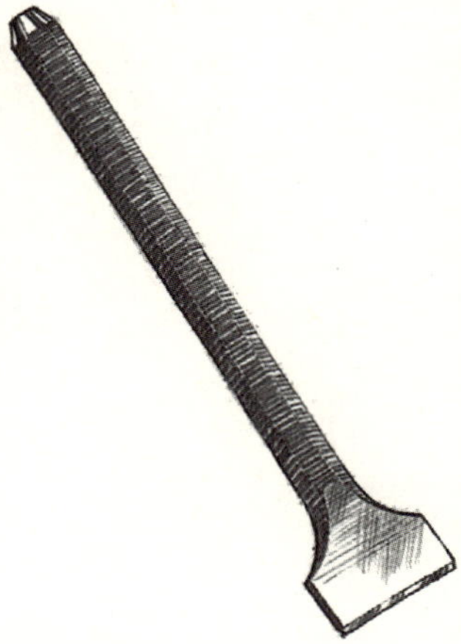

This chisel is used to smooth the rippled surface left by the scutching tool prior to rubbing with a carborundum stone. The narrow chisel is sometimes known as an "edging-in" chisel. It gets the name from the process used to split blocks of stone.

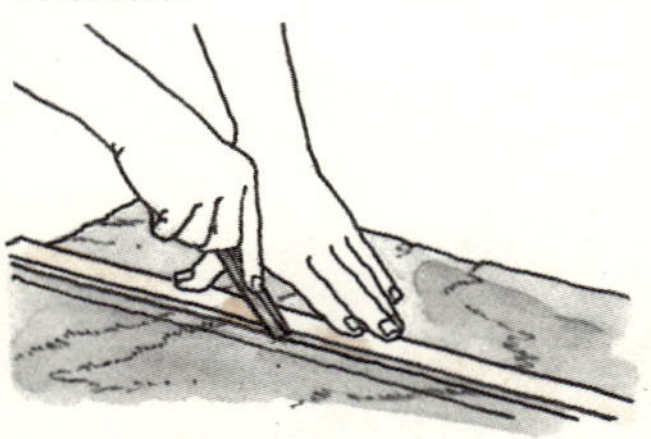

Using the chisel
With the aid of a straight edge, use the chisel to score two parallel lines, 12mm apart, all around the block.

Cut a deep "V" groove between the marked lines to weaken the block. Split the block by holding a brick chisel or bolster in the groove and striking it hard as you move it along to cut around the whole block.

Pitching Tool

SIZE: Bit width: 37mm
MATERIAL: Steel
USE: To trim soft stone

The pitching tool is like the bolster, but the bit is single ground at a steep angle. It is used to remove excess material from slabs of sandstone.

With the finished cut line established with the edging chisel, the waste is cut away in layers using the pitching tool. A layer 25mm thick can be removed from limestone and up to 37mm from sandstone.

Using the pitching tool
Hold the chisel against the stone with the cutting edge parallel to the line, at an angle slightly less than 90° to the face of the stone. Strike the chisel with a club hammer to remove the stone in strips.

Planes

Greek carpenters probably had both bench and moulding planes, but the earliest known tools of this type are Roman, dating from the first century. The bench planes, about the size of a small jack, have iron soles and side plates riveted to a wooden stock, with the sloping iron wedged against a bar across the mouth.

During the Middle Ages most carpenters' planes had wooden stocks, but small metal smoothers were also used, mainly by instrument makers and the like. Down to the eighteenth century all craftsmen made their own planes, but from about 1710 some of them began to specialize in making these tools for others. Close co-operation between the skilled tradesmen and the specialist tool makers brought many improvements, including the standardization of the length of moulding planes at 9½in. Dating from about 1760–70 bench planes were first provided with double irons. In 1840, bench planes were made with steel or gunmetal soles and ingenious screw devices were introduced to regulate the cut of the iron and the size of the mouth. About twenty years later the Stanley-Bailey metal planes were first marketed.

German wooden plane with screw adjusted rather than hand adjusted blades.

Jack Plane

OTHER NAME: Fore plane
SIZE: **Metal:** *Length:* 355 to 380mm; *Cutting iron width:* 60mm; **Wooden:** *Length:* 355 to 455mm; *Cutting iron width:* 50mm
MATERIAL: **Metal:** *Body:* cast iron; *Cutting iron:* steel; *Handle/knob:* wood; **Wooden:** *Body:* beech or boxwood; *Cutting iron:* steel
USE: To dimension timber

Most surviving wooden jack planes have a simple rectangular section body or stock, and are fitted with an open, shaped handle also known as the toat. The later patterns are fitted with a cap iron screwed to the cutting iron, like a modern metal bench plane. The cutting iron is held in place by a wooden wedge. The usual angle or "pitch" of the cutting iron is 45° and the cutting bevel faces downward.

The modern metal jack plane works like a wooden plane, but has the added advantage of a hard-wearing sole and a method of fine adjustment so it can be used as a general bench plane.

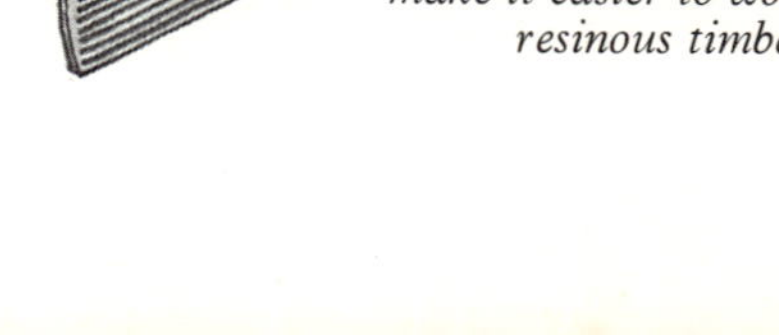

Corrugated soles make it easier to work resinous timber.

Smoothing Plane

OTHER NAMES: Smooth plane, coffin plane (wooden)
SIZE: **Metal:** *Length* 230 to 260mm; *Cutting iron width:* 45 to 60mm; **Wooden:** *Length:* 165 to 230mm; *Cuting iron width:* 40 to 65mm
MATERIAL: **Metal:** *Body:* cast iron; *Cutting iron:* steel; *Handle/knob:* wood; **Wooden:** *Body:* beech or boxwood; *Sole:* part or whole hardwood; *Cutting iron:* steel
USE: To smooth plane timber

Wooden smoothing planes have no handle, but are tapered at the front and back to provide a comfortable grip. The resulting shape accounts for the name "coffin" plane. The cutting iron is mounted in the same way as the jack plane. A finely set smoothing plane is used for the final cleaning up and surfacing of timber.

Like all bench planes, the modern smoothing plane was developed in America, and now follows the one basic design, differing only in size.

Jointer Plane

OTHER NAMES: Trying plane, try plane, long plane
SIZE: **Metal:** *Length:* 560 to 610mm; *Cutting iron width:* 60 to 65mm; **Wooden:** *Length:* 510 to 760mm; *Cutting iron width:* 55 to 70mm
MATERIAL: **Metal:** *Body:* cast iron; *Cutting iron:* steel; *Handle/knob:* wood; **Wooden:** *Body:* beech or boxwood; *Cutting iron:* steel
USE: To square long edges of timber usually for jointing

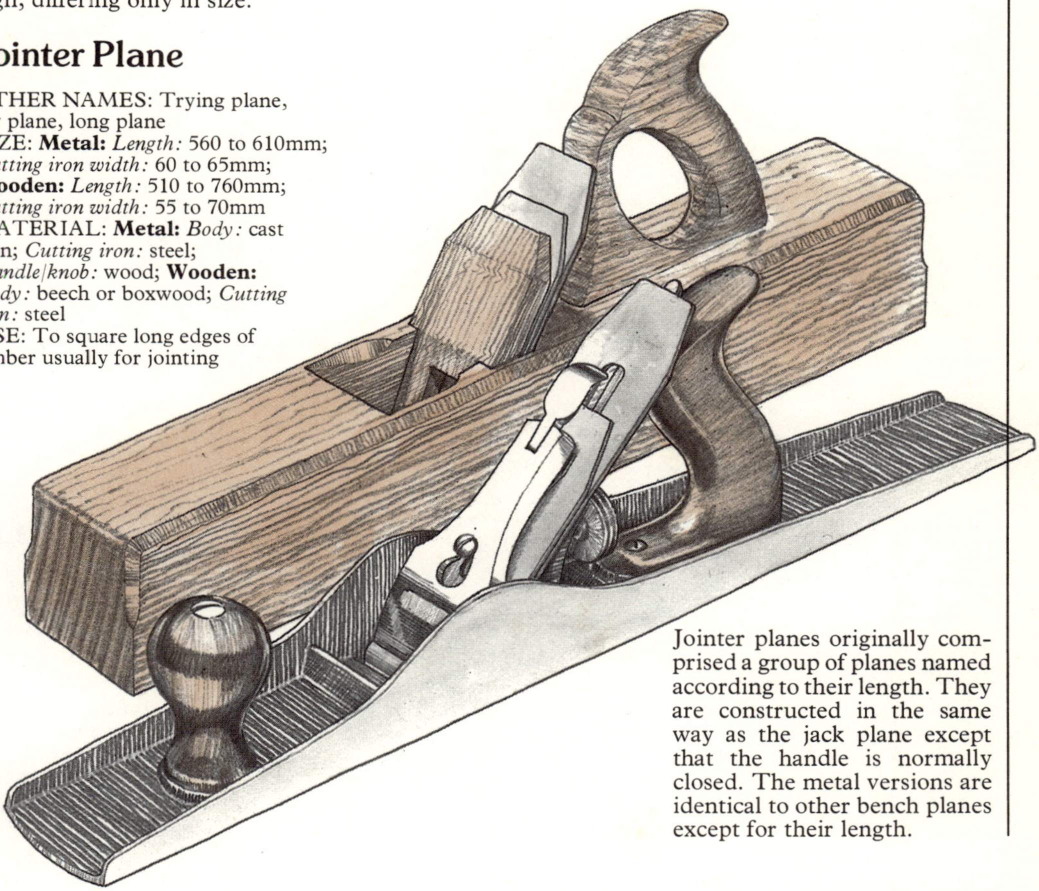

Jointer planes originally comprised a group of planes named according to their length. They are constructed in the same way as the jack plane except that the handle is normally closed. The metal versions are identical to other bench planes except for their length.

Adjusting bench planes

Smoothing planes, jack planes and jointers are bench planes. They are dismantled in the same way, although the method of adjusting wooden planes differs from that of adjusting metal ones.

The cutting iron assembly in a wooden plane is held firmly in place by a wooden wedge. The wedge and cutting iron assembly can be removed and dismantled for sharpening. The wedge of a jack plane is "shocked" to loosen it by striking the top of the toe end with a mallet or by striking the plane itself on a bench. A hardwood "striking button" is sometimes set into the stock to protect it from damage. A smoothing plane wedge is loosened by striking the rear end of the body.

After sharpening, the plane is reassembled in the reverse order and the wedge tapped in to secure the cutting iron.

The cutting iron is removed by releasing the lever on the lever cap, sliding it from under the screw head and lifting out the cutting iron assembly. Undo the locking screw to separate the cap iron from the cutting iron.

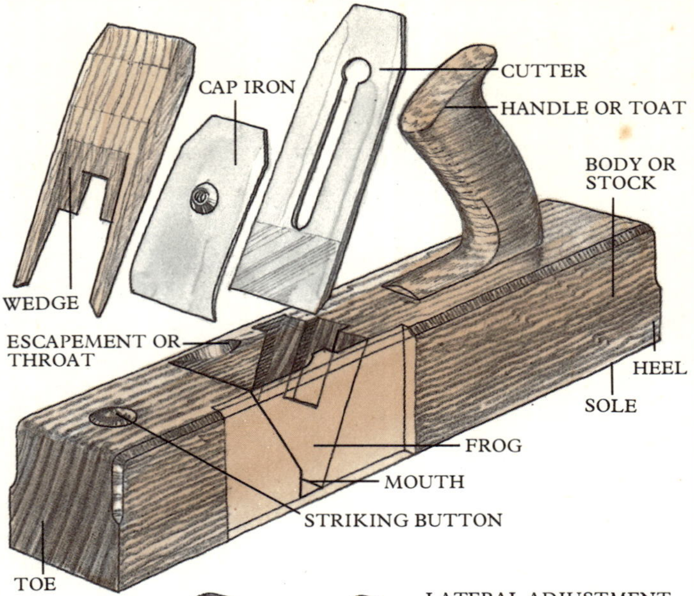

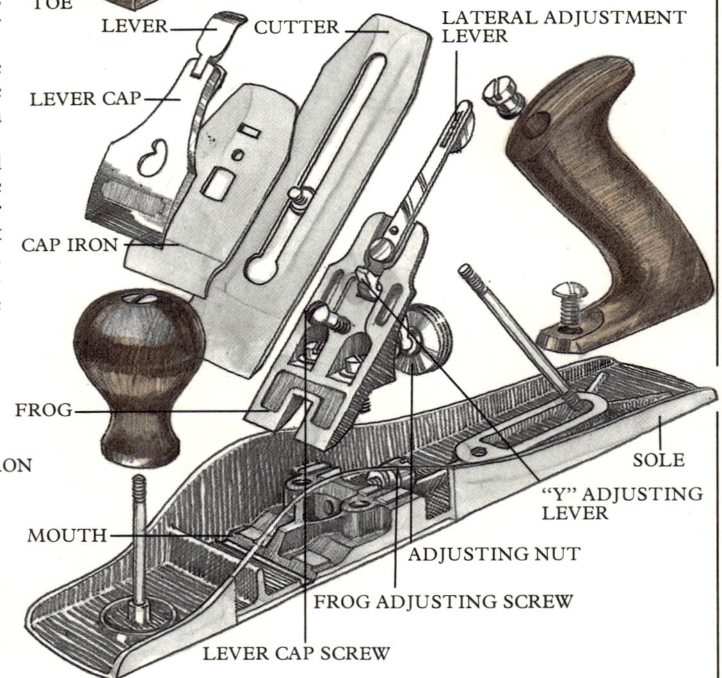

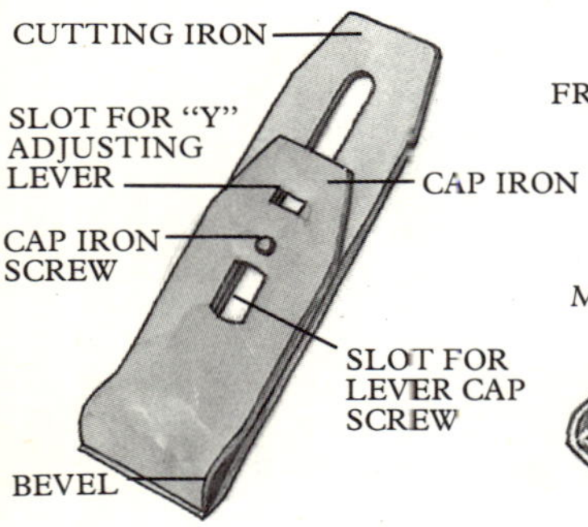

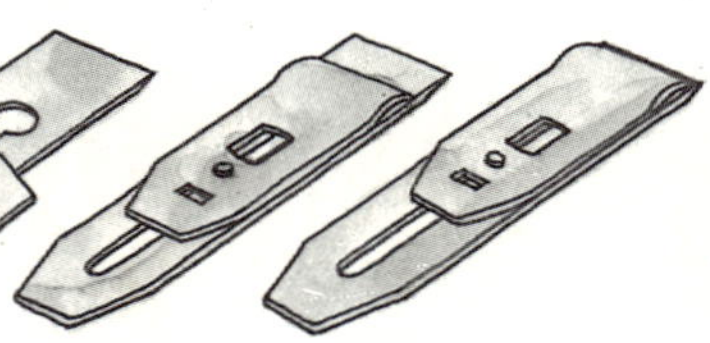

Replacing the cap iron
With the cap iron at right angles to the cutting iron, locate the screw head with the hole in the blade with the bevel facing away from you. Slide the cap iron away from the edge.

Locking the cap iron
Turn it until both irons are parallel. Tighten the locking screw when the edge of the cap iron is 1.5mm from the edge of the blade. This gap can be reduced to 0.5mm for very fine work.

Testing the assembly
Make sure that the edge of the cap iron lies flat on the cutting iron to prevent shavings jamming. A properly adjusted cap iron will break the shaving curling from out of the throat.

Replacing the cutting iron

Replace the cutting iron assembly in the plane, bevel downward, locating the slots in the cutting iron on the lateral adjustment lever and the adjusting screw, and replace the lever cap. Adjust the lever cap screw to get the exact tension.

Fine adjustment is made by sighting down the sole of the plane from the toe, and turning the adjusting screw until the

edge of the blade protrudes. The blade will show up clearly as a dark line against the shine of the sole. Use the lateral adjustment lever to level the edge with the mouth of the plane, and back off the adjustment screw until the blade protrudes just enough to achieve the required depth of cut.

The mouth of the plane can also be adjusted by loosening the frog fixing screws and turning the adjusting screws. For a coarse cut, open the mouth; for a fine cut close it. The settings of the mouth and cutting iron should be related: a finely set mouth used with a coarsely set iron would soon become clogged with shavings.

Maintenance

Store planes on their side with the cutting iron withdrawn into the mouth. If the tool is to be stored for a long time, dismantle the parts and clean off any dust or resin. Lightly grease any bright metal parts to prevent rusting. Except for the sole, wooden planes will benefit from an occasional coat of clear varnish.

Using bench planes

Make sure that the plane is sharp and properly adjusted before using. Wood must be held securely during all operations. Use vice or bench stops.

Planing an edge

Use the longest plane available to true up a long edge. A short, smoothing plane could just follow the contours of the workpiece, whereas a jointer will bridge any gaps.

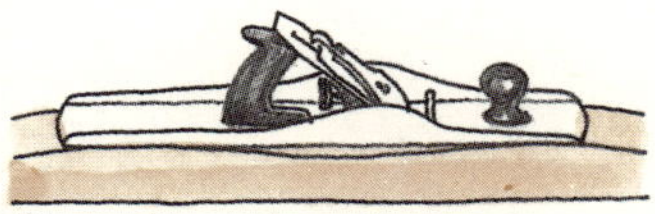

Use a long plane for accurate results on a long edge.

A short plane reinforces existing contours.

"Dipping", where the workpiece is rounded off at either end, is a common fault. It is caused by allowing the plane to rock backward and forward at each end of the cut.

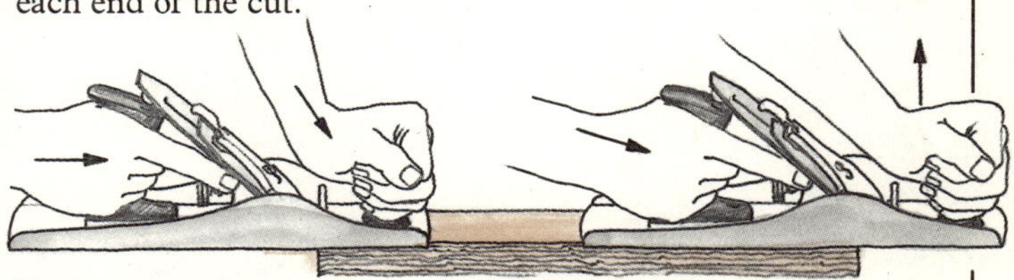

Preventing dipping
Maintain pressure on the plane with the forward hand at the beginning of the cut, and with the rear hand at the end.

Levelling a flat surface

Where boards have been glued together, perhaps to make a table top, they will have to be levelled. Using a sharp, finely set jack plane, or a jointer if the workpiece is very large, plane directly across the grain for hardwoods and diagonally across the grain in two directions for softwoods. Holding the plane at an angle to the direction of the cut will help to produce a smooth slicing action. Having levelled the surface, finally plane in the direction of the grain to produce a finished surface.

Before using any plane, check the work for nails and screws which will chip the cutting edge. To help the plane move easily across the work, wax the sole with a candle.

Keeping a narrow edge square
Prevent the plane from rocking by holding the edge of the plane with the forward hand, using the fingers as a guide.

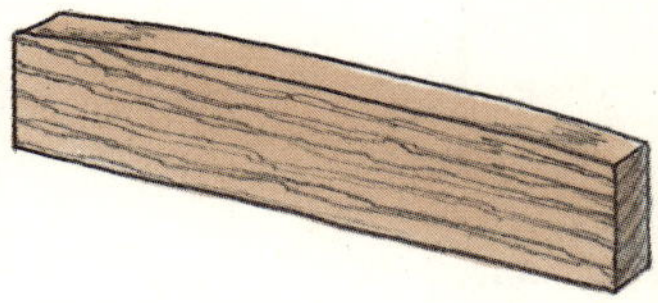

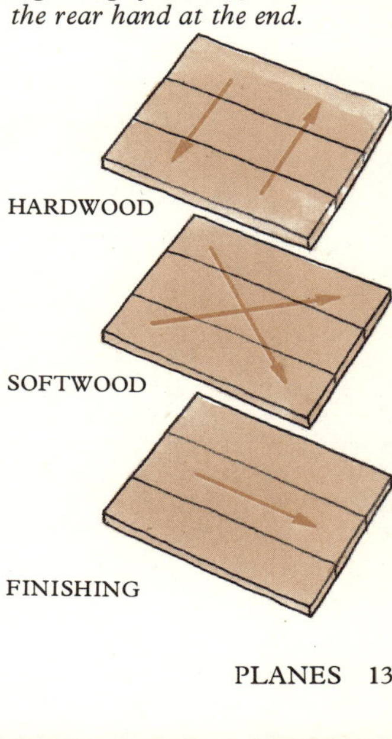

Bull Nose Plane

SIZE: *Length:* 75 to 115mm;
Cutting iron width: 10 to 29mm
MATERIAL: *Body:* cast iron;
Cutting iron: steel
USE: To plane up to a right angle such as a stopped rebate

Bull nose planes are constructed and adjusted in the same way as shoulder planes. There are fixed and multi-adjustable versions. The simplest and smallest version has a hardwood wedge to hold the blade in position.

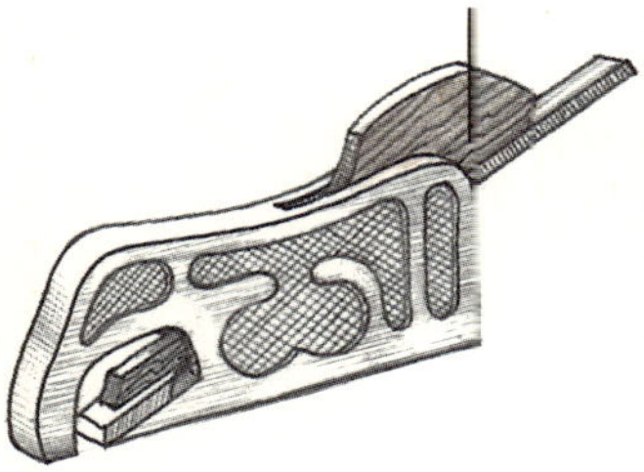

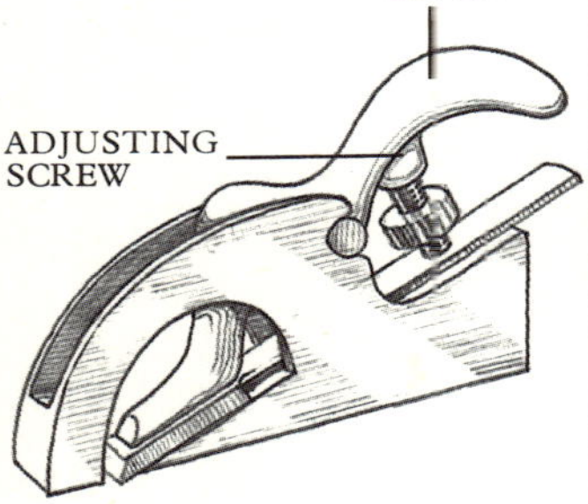

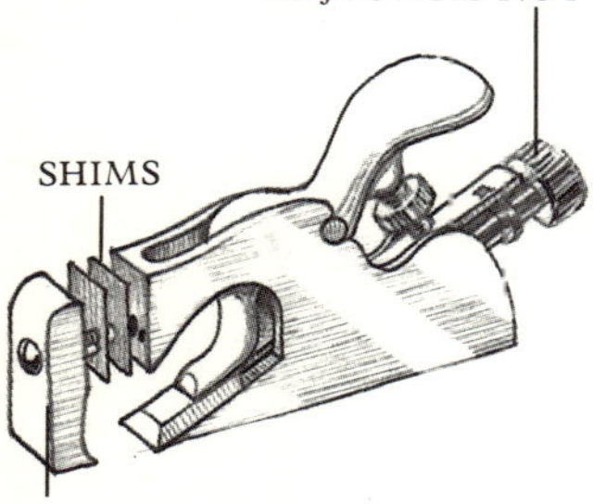

The most versatile models have an adjustable front end to allow for mouth adjustment and to convert the tool into a chisel plane.

Bench Rebate Plane

OTHER NAMES: Bench rabbet plane, coachmaker's rebate plane, carriagemaker's rebate plane
SIZE: *Length:* 230 to 330mm;
Cutting iron width: 55mm
MATERIAL: *Body:* cast iron;
cutting iron: steel;
Handle/knob: wood
USE: To cut wide rebates

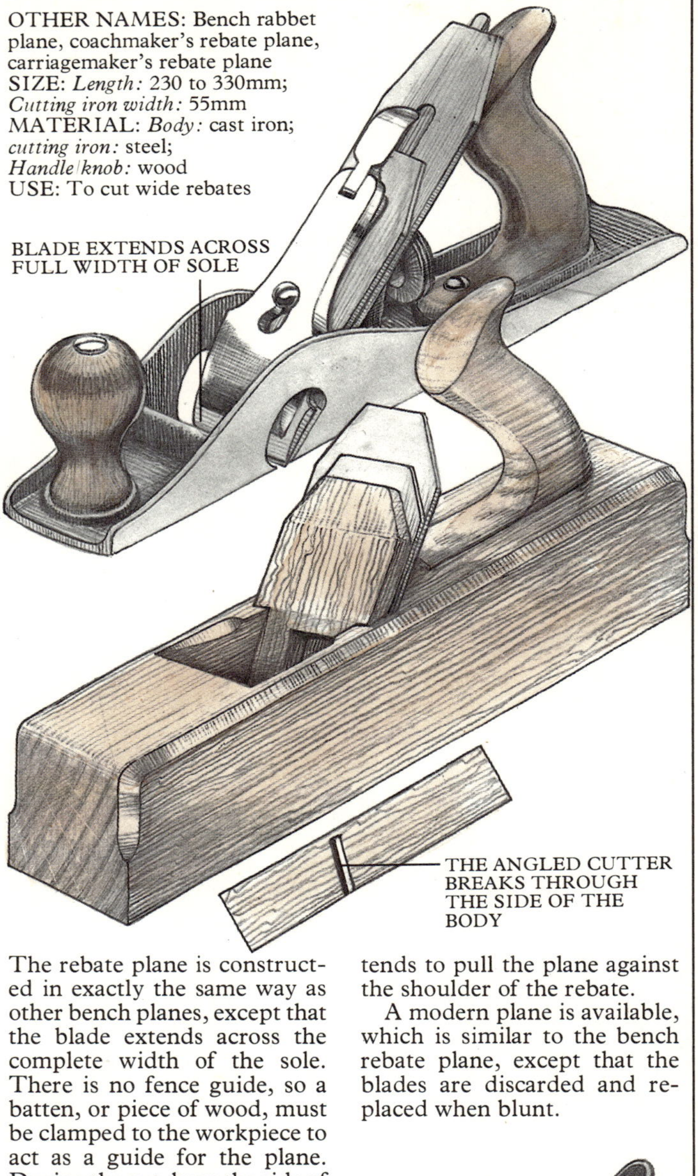

The rebate plane is constructed in exactly the same way as other bench planes, except that the blade extends across the complete width of the sole. There is no fence guide, so a batten, or piece of wood, must be clamped to the workpiece to act as a guide for the plane. During the cut, keep the side of the plane firmly pressed against the batten, working down to a depth line drawn on the edge of the workpiece. Check the rebate with a square at frequent intervals as work progresses.

Wooden planes of the jack plane type exist where the cutting iron breaks through the body on one side enabling the tool to plane a rebate. The blade is set at an angle which tends to pull the plane against the shoulder of the rebate.

A modern plane is available, which is similar to the bench rebate plane, except that the blades are discarded and replaced when blunt.

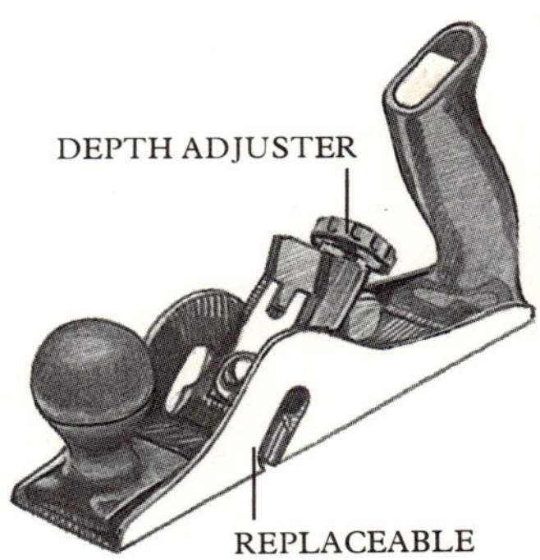

Rebate and Filister Plane

OTHER NAME: Rabbet and filister plane
SIZE: *Length:* 250mm; *Cutting iron width:* 40mm
MATERIAL: *Body:* cast iron; *Cutting iron:* steel
ACCESSORIES: Guide fence; depth gauge; spur
USE: To cut rebates and timber

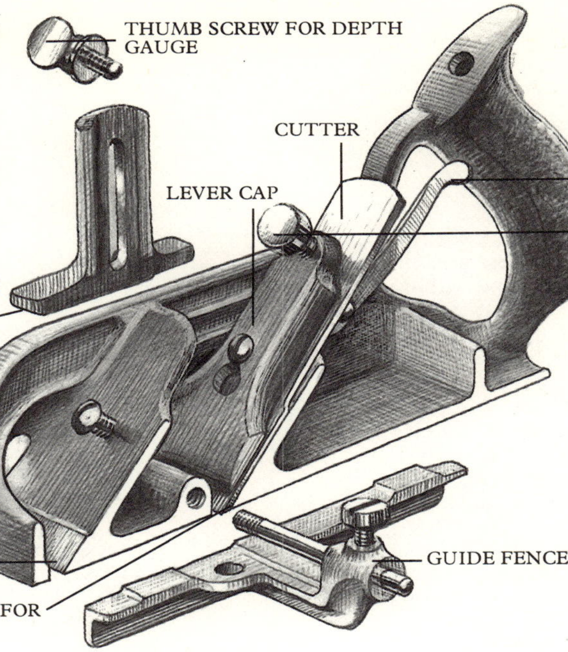

The plane can be used as a standard rebate plane without the guide accessories, using a guide batten clamped to the work as for a bench rebate plane. Rebates wider than the cutting iron can be cut by making more than one pass, moving the guide batten back to the finished line between passes. Once the cut has been established the guide batten can be removed and the wall of the rebate used as a guide.

Adjustment
The cutting iron, which has no back iron, is mounted bevel downward and is secured by a lever cap tightened by a locking screw. Corrugations on the underside of the blade locate on a spigot on the fine adjustment lever. With the lever cap in position but not fully tightened, the lever is operated to the required setting and the locking screw is finally tightened. The cutting iron can be mounted in the center of the plane for normal work, or at the forward end for bull nose work. No fine adjustment is provided at the forward position and the cutting iron must be accurately positioned by hand before the lever cap can be tightened.

Accessories
With the guide accessories fitted, the rebate plane becomes a filister plane, which can cut identical rebates without constant rechecking. The guide fence is attached to the tool by one or two threaded arm rods. It slides on these rods to the required setting and is clamped in position by locking screws.

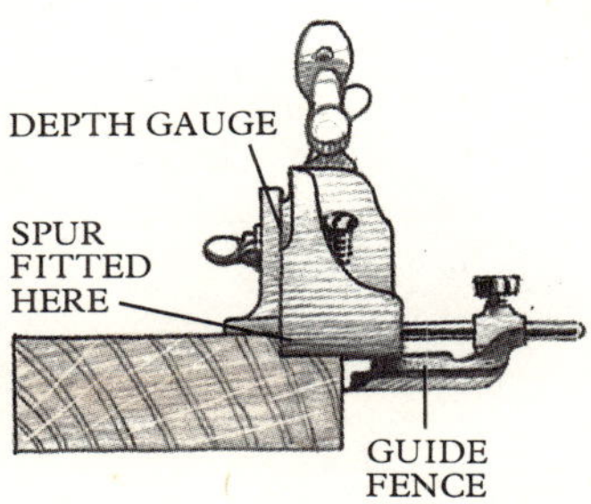

The filister plane with depth gauge and guide fence in place. The guide fence can be fitted on either side of the plane.

The depth gauge, which is fitted on one side only, is fixed at a measurement from the cutting edge equivalent to the depth of the rebate. A spur is provided on the right hand side of the stock to scribe a line in advance of the cutter.

Using the plane
For a standard rebate, set the accessories as required, and mount the blade in the central position. With the workpiece fixed securely in a vice or between bench stops, rest the tool on the forward end maintaining pressure against the fence with the left hand. Make short strokes with the plane, gradually moving backward as the rebate becomes established. Continue with the operation until the depth stop comes into contact with the work and no further shavings can be produced from the work.

Chisel out the front end of a stopped rebate. Change the cutting iron to the forward position, and proceed as above.

Block Plane

SIZE: *Length:* 90 to 205mm; *Cutting iron width:* 25 to 40mm
MATERIAL: *Body:* cast iron; *Cutting iron:* steel; *Knob:* wood or metal
USE: To trim end grain and other fine work

Block planes exist in a variety of patterns but they are all designed to cut end grain. They were originally developed to level butcher's and possibly engraver's blocks, both made of endgrain timber.

Block planes have their blades mounted at a low angle. The normal pitch is 20° but it can be as low as 12° on some planes. They can be used single handed with the lever cap resting in the palm of the hand, and the thumb and fingers located in recesses on either side of the body. A knob is provided at the toe of the plane where pressure can be applied with the fingers.

Varieties of block plane

SIMPLE NON-ADJUSTABLE PLANE

The shallow pitch of the block plane cutting iron means that it is mounted bevel side up. Consequently a back iron is not required, the bevel doing the job itself. The simplest form of block plane has the cutting iron held in place by a knurled wheel operating on a screw. Adjust the blade before the wheel is tightened.

DOUBLE ENDED BLOCK PLANE

Like the simple non-adjustable plane, this tool has no screw adjustment for the blade, but it has two positions allowing it to be used as a bull nose plane.

FULLY ADJUSTABLE BLOCK PLANE

Block planes are made with partial and full adjustment. The lever cap is often secured by a laterally moving lever which operates a cam. The depth of the cutting iron can be adjusted by a variety of screws, and lateral movement controlled by means of a lever. Some planes have an adjustable mouth operated by a lever attached to the guide knob.

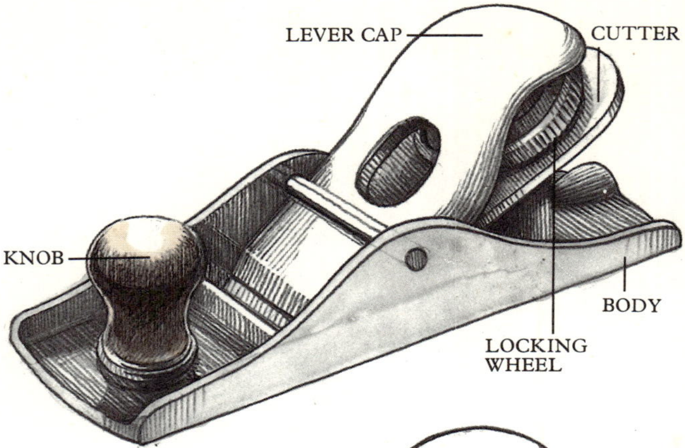

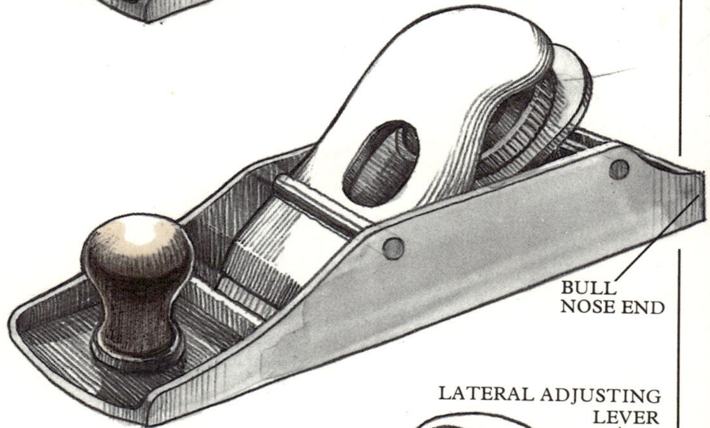

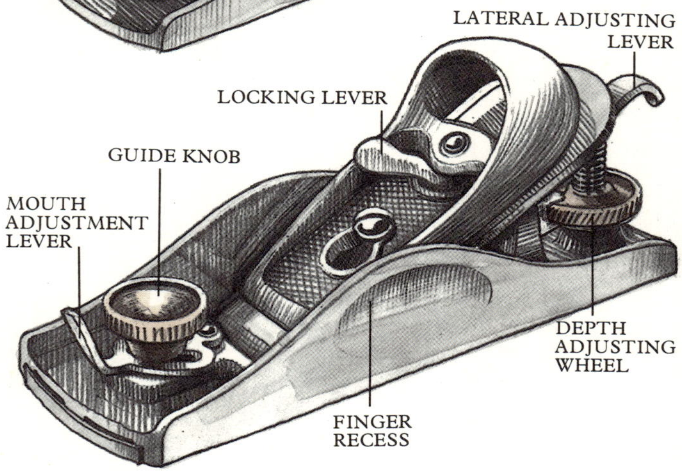

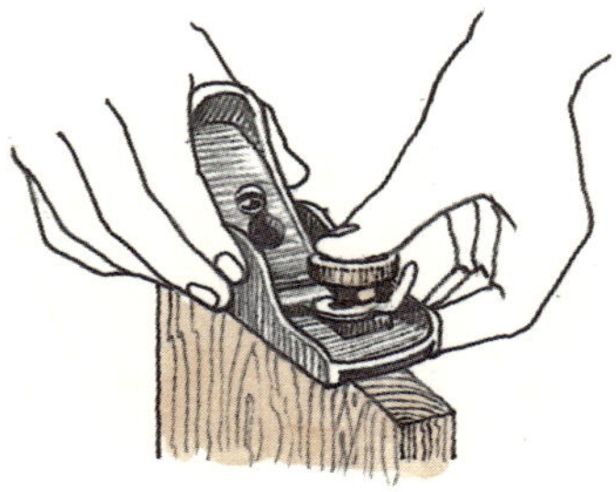

Using a block plane

The main purpose of the block plane is to cut end grain. Keep it extremely sharp and set to produce a fine cut. Plane from either end to prevent the grain splitting or plane a chamfer on the far end first.

Shoulder Plane

OTHER NAME: Rebate plane
SIZE: *Length:* 115 to 205mm; *Cutting iron width:* 15 to 31mm
MATERIAL: *Body:* cast iron; *Cutting iron:* steel
USE: To trim shoulders of large joints and to cut rebates

Shoulder planes are accurately machined so that the sole and each side of the body are perfect right angles. Together with a blade which extends right across the sole of the tool, this enables the plane to trim shoulders and rebates. As with the block plane, the cutting iron is mounted bevel uppermost and at a low angle to trim end grain.

Varieties of shoulder plane
Some shoulder planes have a lever cap which holds the cutting iron in position and is secured by a locking screw. With this slackened the blade can be removed for sharpening. To replace, carefully locate the slot at one end of the cutting iron over the adjustment screw. Replace the cap, adjust depth of cut and lock in place. The mouth can be adjusted by a screw in the nose of the plane.

The mouths of other shoulder planes are adjusted by moving the greater part of the body and nose in one piece. It can be removed altogether by loosening the locking screw on the top and sliding it forward. With the top section of the body removed, the tool can be used as a chisel plane which can work right up into a corner or finish a stopped rebate.

The cap which clamps the cutting iron in place is slackened by the screw to the rear. The cutting iron can then be dislocated from the adjusting screw and withdrawn forward. Reassemble in the reverse order and adjust the cutting iron to the required depth before finally tightening the lever screw.

Combination planes have detachable noses, one to make a conventional shoulder plane, another a bull nose plane. It can be used as a chisel plane.

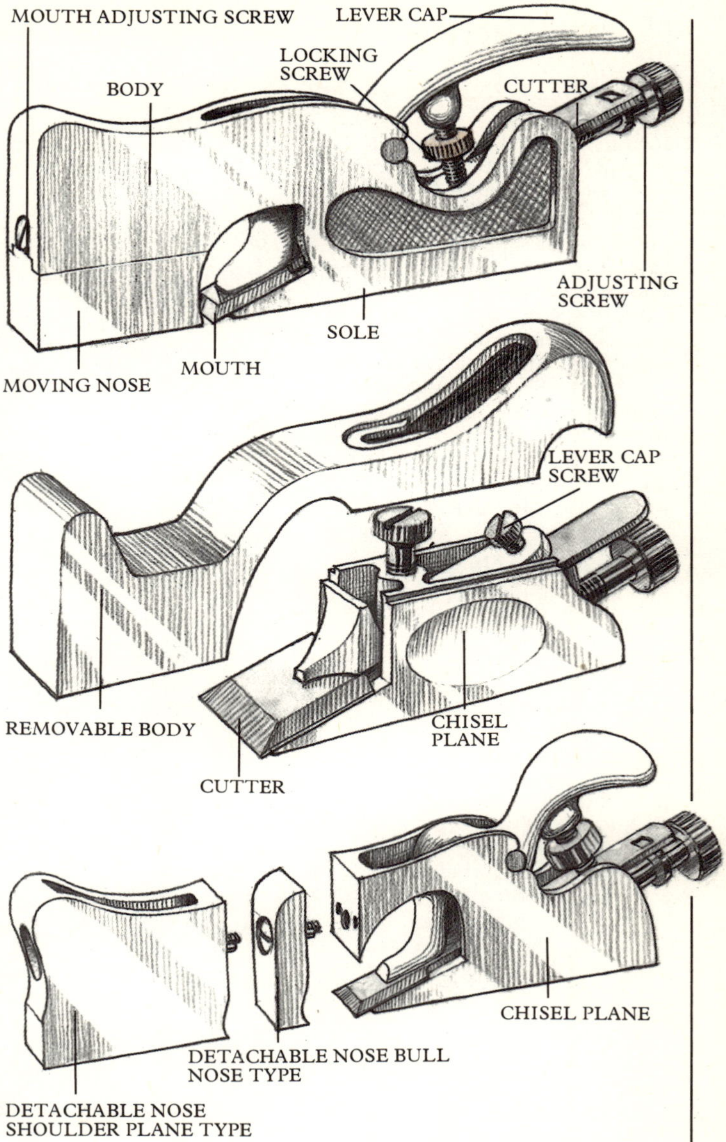

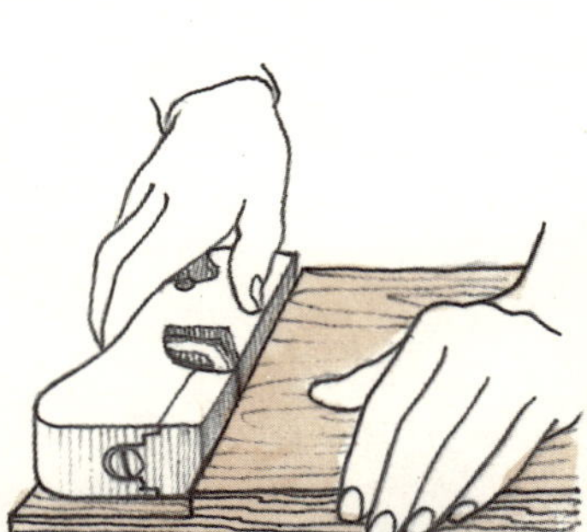

Using a shoulder plane
To run on a tenon, lay a finely set shoulder plane on its side. Clamp the work in a vice to use the shoulder plane two handed. Cut rebates as with a bench rebate plane.

Compass Plane

OTHER NAME: Circular plane
SIZE: *Length:* 250mm; *Cutting iron width:* 45mm
MATERIAL: *Stock:* cast iron; *Sole:* steel; *Cutting iron:* steel
USE: To cut concave and convex wooden sections

Metal compass planes have an adjustable, flexible sole that can be used on both concave and convex surfaces to any radius between limits. Either a handle is provided or the stock is shaped to fit the hands at either end of the plane. Older wooden compass planes were made to a pre-determined radius, and separate planes were needed to work concave and convex sections.

Adjusting the plane
Two basic patterns are common today. Both take the standard bench plane assembly of cutting iron, back iron and lever cap, all of which are mounted and adjusted as for bench planes. In the first model, the sole is fitted to either end of a fixed stock while the centre, fixed to the frog of the tool, is moved up or down by means of an adjusting screw. In the second model, the centre of the sole is fixed to the frog while both ends of the sole move up or down simultaneously operated by levers connected to an adjustment screw.

To adjust the tool, rest it on the roughly cut workpiece and adjust the sole until it corresponds with the required radius of the work.

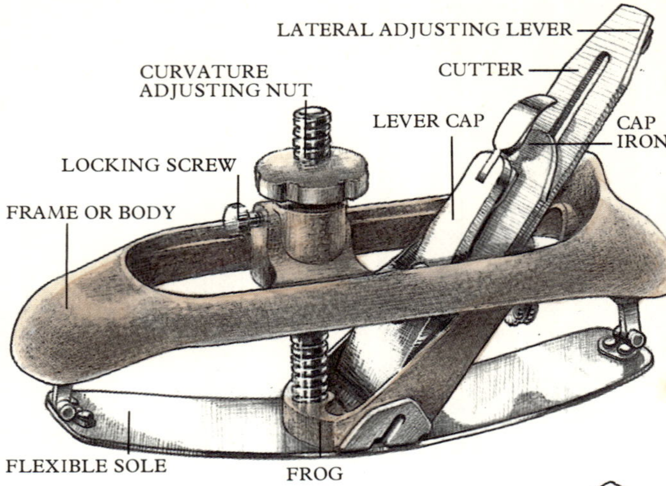

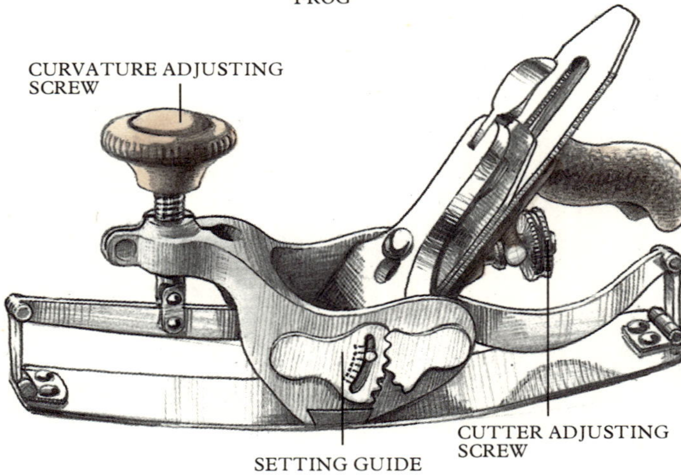

Using the plane
The compass plane is used in the same way as any bench plane but the tool must be kept square to the direction of the curve to maintain an accurate radius. As when working any curved section, the direction of cut must be changed to suit the direction of the grain.

Rasp Plane

OTHER NAME: Surform plane
SIZE: *Blade length:* 140mm and 250mm; *Blade width:* 40mm
MATERIAL: *Blade:* hardened steel; *Stock:* zinc alloy; *Handle:* plastic
USE: To shape wood, plastic and soft metals

With a rasp plane, unlike a conventional rasp, the waste does not clog the teeth, but is easily cleared through holes in the blade during the cut. This blade, used throughout the entire range of Surform tools, is made up of a series of small teeth pressed out of a steel sheet, ground and set to one cutting angle.

Standard size blades are fitted into a series of holders, two of which resemble more conventional planes. The smaller pattern is designed to be used one handed while the two handed version is sometimes adapted to a file type tool by reversing the handle.

Fitting the blades
Blades are never sharpened, but replaced when blunt. One end hooks over the rear of the stock, while the other locates on a screw adjustable tension bar. The teeth face forward.

Using the rasp plane
The tool is handled as a conventional plane, but the design of the blade enables it to be used against the grain of timber without tearing it. It is used for preliminary shaping only and the surface may require further finishing.

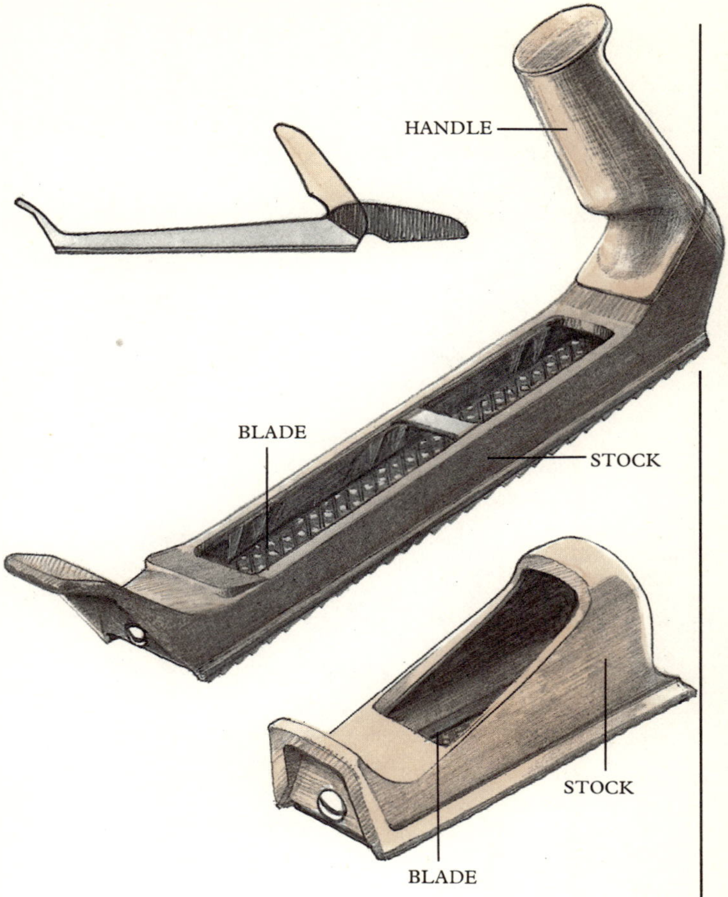

Toothing Plane

SIZE: *Length:* 165 to 230mm; *Cutting iron width:* 50mm
MATERIAL: *Body:* beech; *Cutting iron:* steel
USE: To score a wooden surface prior to gluing or veneering

Made and adjusted like a smoothing plane, the traditional toothing plane is a toothed scraper held almost vertically in a jig. The serrated edge scores the surface to provide escape for excess air and glue which would otherwise leave bubbles under the veneer.

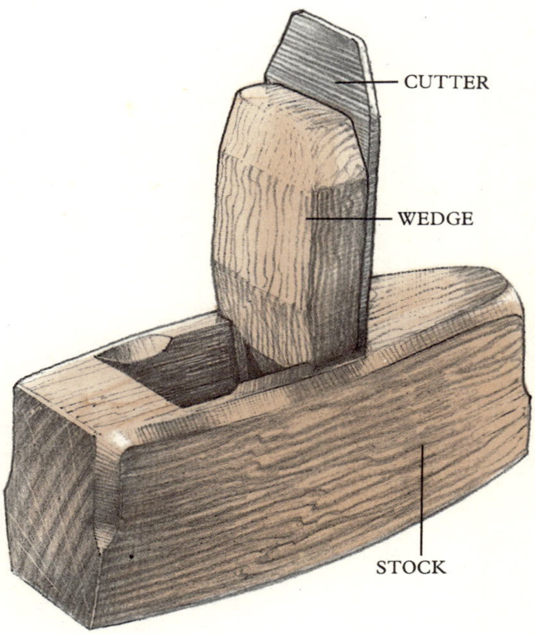

Side Rebate Plane

OTHER NAME: Side rabbet plane
SIZE: *Length:* 137mm; *Cutting iron width:* 6 and 12mm
MATERIAL: *Body:* zinc; *Cutting iron:* steel; *Handle:* rosewood
ACCESSORIES: Depth gauge
USE: To relieve the side walls of rebates and grooves

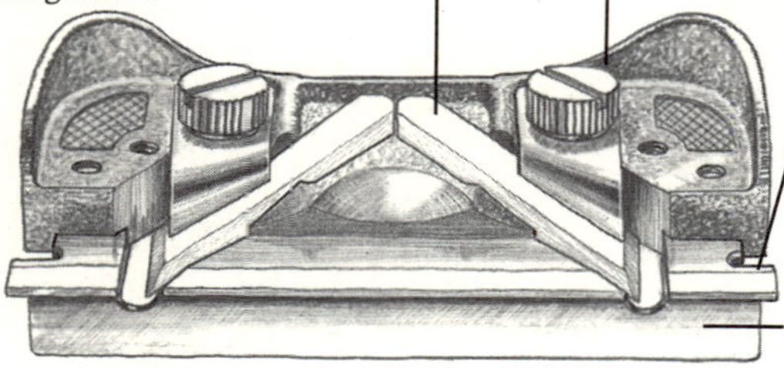

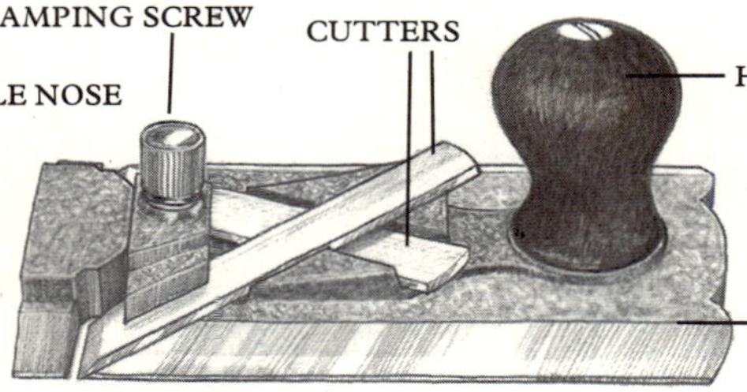

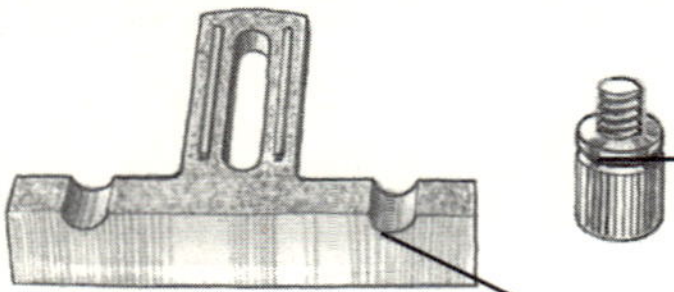

Side rebate planes are fitted with two blades so the tool can be used from right to left or vice versa. This is important when trimming both sides of a groove where you can only work from one end to accommodate the direction of the grain. The nose pieces are removable up to the end of a stopped groove.

Be sure to set the blades to the required depth of cut before finally securing them with the clamp.

Depth gauge

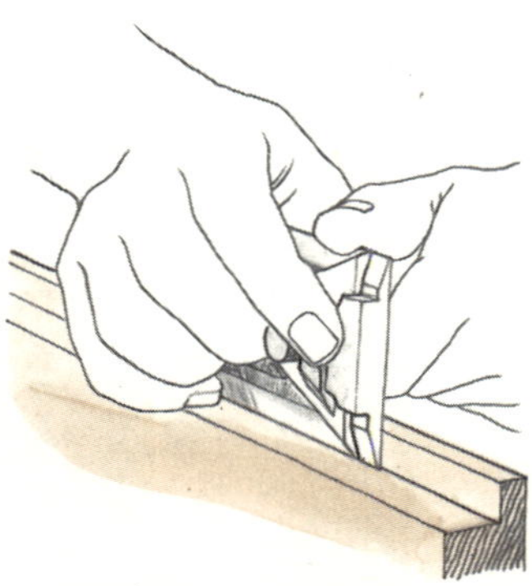

Use the gauge to prevent the blade from catching the work. Adjust the gauge so the point just touches the bottom of the rebate. The gauge also helps to keep the flat base square against the groove wall.

Molding Plane

SIZE: *Length:* 237mm; *Width:* 9, 12, 15mm
MATERIAL: *Blade:* steel; *Stock/wedge:* beech, hornbeam
USE: To cut mouldings in wood

Older craftsmen had many varied wooden moulding planes to produce windows, door frames and furniture mouldings.

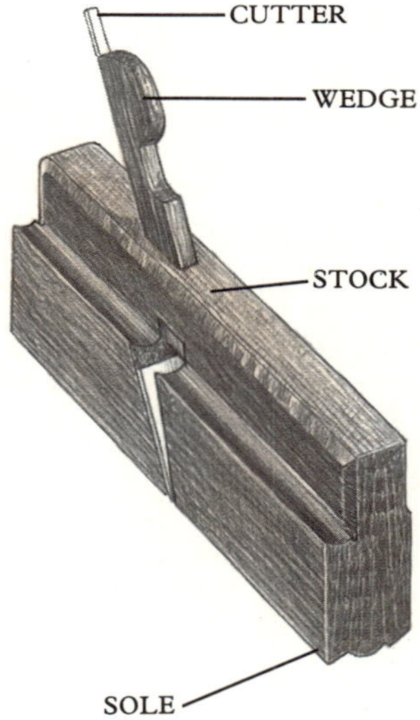

Today a much reduced range of moulding planes is still available from some modern tool catalogues and suppliers.

Moulding plane blades are ground to form the reverse of the moulding they are intended to produce. The sole of the plane is shaped to match the edge of the blade, and there is a depth stop and side fence in the form of small rebates.

To release the wedge and remove the blade for sharpening, cup the iron and wedge in one hand and tap the notch in the wedge with the cheek of a hammer. Sharpen the blade with shaped stones. Replace the cutter and push in the wedge just enough to hold it. Adjust the setting by tapping either the iron (if you want a deep cut) or the heel of the stock (for a shallow cut). Drive the wedge home tight.

Tongue and Groove Planes

SIZE: *Length:* 237mm
Width: 15, 37mm
MATERIAL: *Cutting iron:* steel;
Stock: beech
USE: To cut a tongue and groove joint on the edge of boards

Tongue and groove planes are sold in pairs to cut the tongue on the edge of one board and a matching groove in the edge of another board. The tongue and groove will then slot together to make a perfect joint.

The tongue plane has a shaped cutter to plane away timber on both sides of the tongue which is left protruding from the edge of the board. The groove plane should be set to cut a groove slightly deeper than the height of the tongue.

Hollowing and Rounding Planes

SIZE: *Length:* 237mm; *Width:* 6 to 18mm
MATERIAL: *Cutting iron:* steel;
Stock: beech
USE: To cut moulding

Like the tongue and groove planes, hollowing and rounding planes are sold in pairs. They cut matching concave and convex curves, which can be used in combination to form various mouldings. At one time, the full set of planes would have run to 18 pairs, but modern catalogues offer a more limited range.

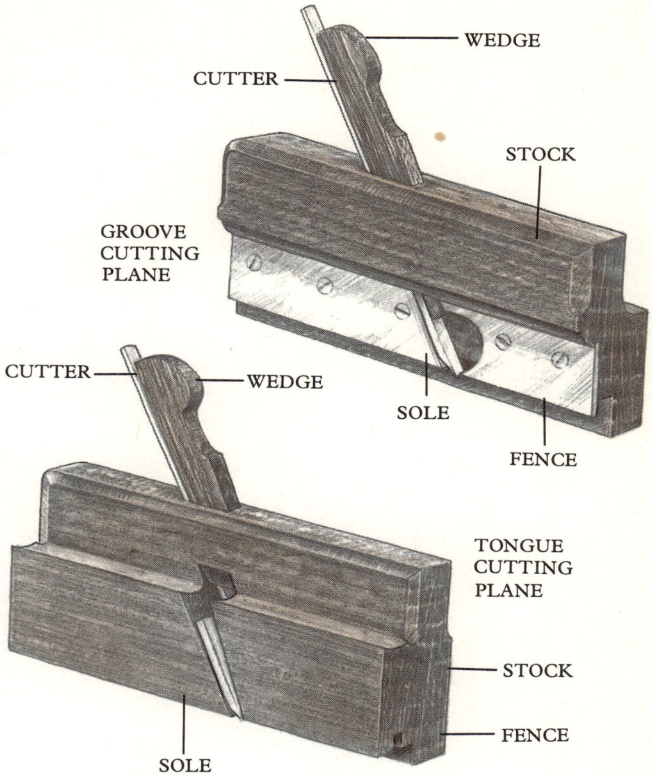

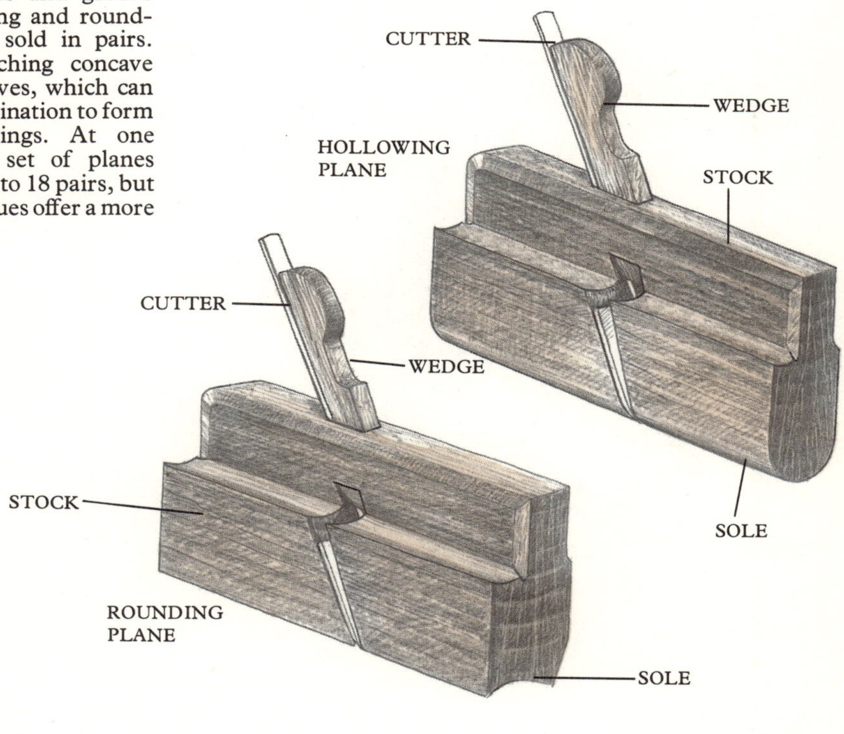

Plough Plane

SIZE: Cuts grooves and rebates from 3 to 12mm wide
MATERIAL: *Body:* cast iron; *Cutting iron:* steel; *Handle:* plastic, iron
USE: To cut grooves and rebates

The plough plane is built to make specific cuts while being guided by fences and depth gauges. It is designed primarily to cut grooves but will also cut rebates up to 12mm wide in one pass.

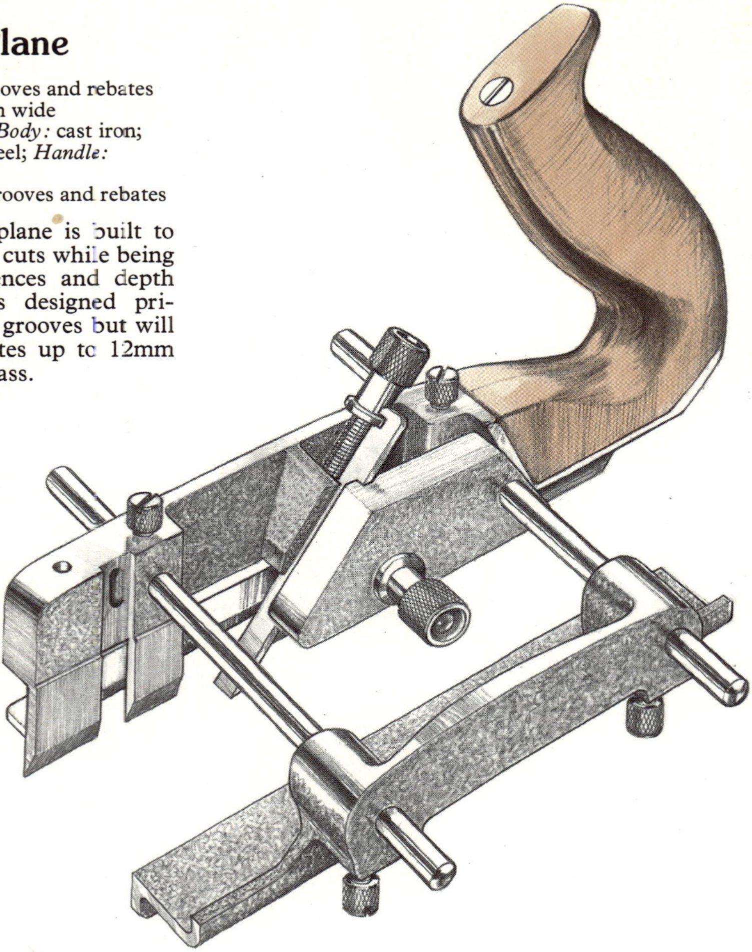

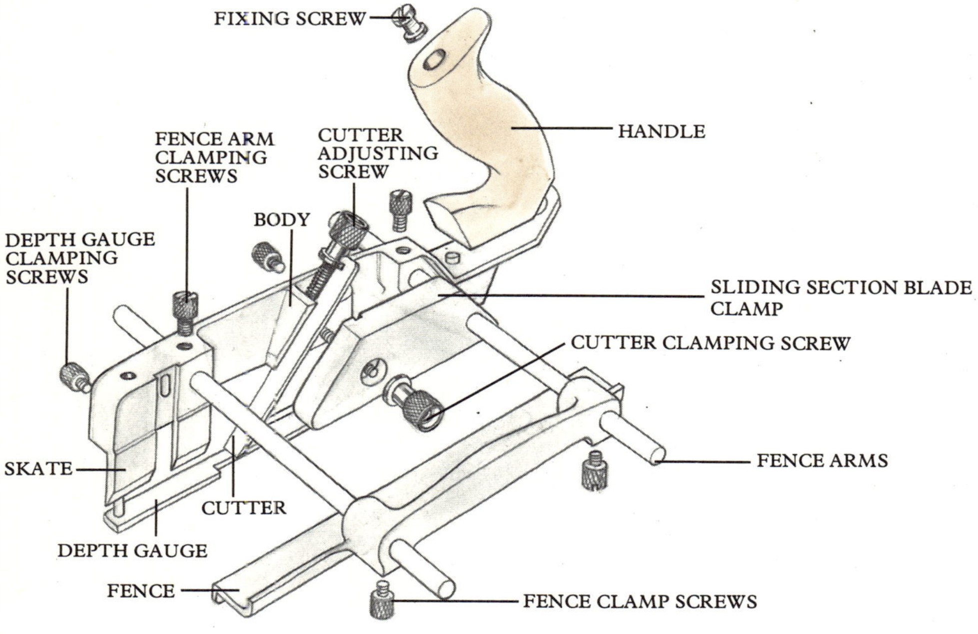

Fitting the blade
Specific models of plough planes differ slightly in detail, but the principles are the same. A clamp and screw hold the blades in the body of the plane. Slacken the clamp and insert the cutter from the top, with the bevel on the underside. A slot on one side of the cutter locates on the shoulder of an adjusting screw. Tighten the clamp slightly and adjust the blade to the required depth before finally securing the screw and clamp.

Very narrow blades do not have a slot to fit the adjusting screw and must be set by hand.

Plough plane cutters are available with only a grinding angle, not a honing angle.

Setting the depth gauge
The depth gauge is a horizontal fence fitted on one side of the body. Use a rule to set the gauge to the required depth from the bottom of the skate and finger tighten the locking screw. Long gauges should be checked at both ends to ensure that they are parallel with the bottom of the skate. Tighten the screw when you are satisfied with the setting.

Setting the guide fence
A fence is provided to guide the cutter the required distance from the edge of the work. It is clamped to the metal guide rods on either side of the plane. Use a rule to set the fence the required distance from the blade and tighten the clamping screws to hold it in place.

Maintenance
Lightly oil machine threads on the adjusting screws, and rub candle wax on the fences to provide a smooth action.

Blades are ground to an angle of 35° and should be sharpened on an oilstone, preferably with a honing gauge.

Combination Plane

SIZE: Cuts grooves along or across the grain and rebates up to 21mm wide; beads 3 to 12mm wide; tongues 6mm wide
MATERIAL: *Body:* cast iron; *Cutting iron:* steel; *Handle:* plastic, cast iron
USE: To cut grooves, rebates beads and tongue and groove

The combination plane is like the plough plane but boasts additional features. The blade assembly, depth gauge and guide fence are identical, but spurs are provided so that cuts can be made across the grain. Spurs have knife edges to cut the grain ahead of the blade. One spur is fixed to the body and another to the sliding section.

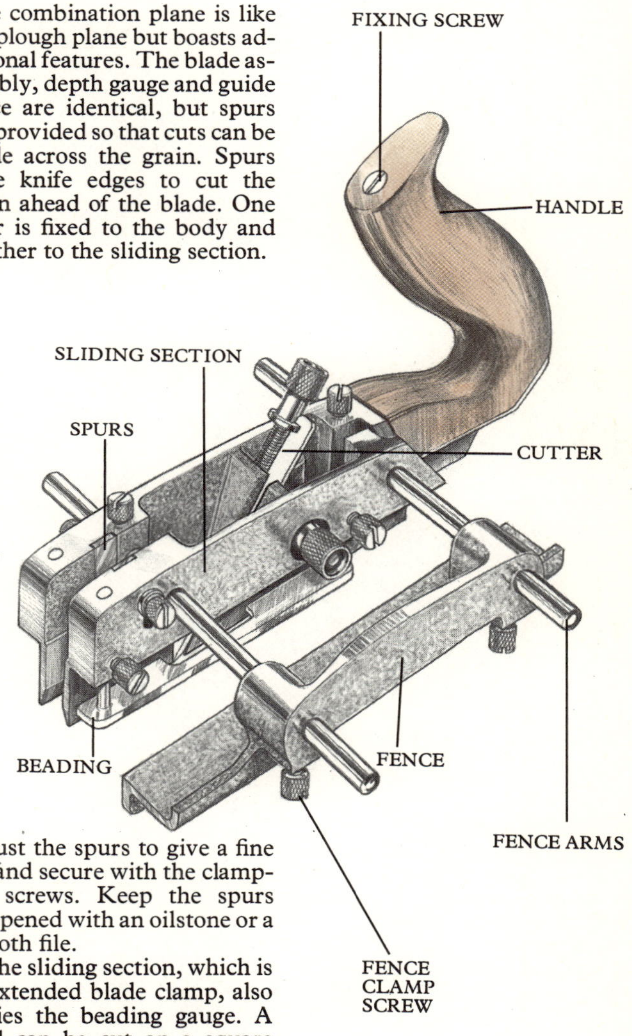

Adjust the spurs to give a fine cut and secure with the clamping screws. Keep the spurs sharpened with an oilstone or a smooth file.

The sliding section, which is an extended blade clamp, also carries the beading gauge. A bead can be cut on a square edge of a board using the standard fence as a guide, but on a tongued edge the beading gauge acts as a fence. It is adjusted in exactly the same way as the depth gauge.

Sharpen the beading cutters as you would the plough cutters, but use a slipstone to hone the curved edge.

Multi-Plane

SIZE: Cuts grooves, rebates and housings 3 to 12mm wide; beads 3 to 12mm wide; tongues 4.5 and 6mm wide; ovolos 6 and 9mm wide; sash mouldings 37 and 43mm; grouped reeds 3 and 6mm wide; hollows and rounds 12 to 25mm wide; stair nosings 41.5mm

MATERIAL: *Body:* cast iron; *Cutting iron:* steel; *Handle* fence: hardwood

USE: To cut grooves, rebates, housings, beads, tongue and groove joints and mouldings

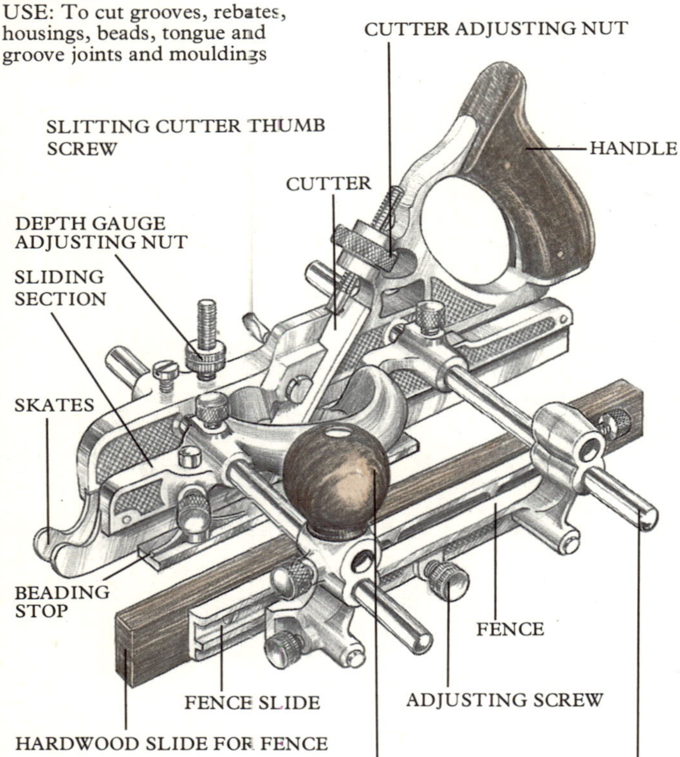

The multi-plane combines the features of the plough and combination planes, but is made even more versatile by the addition of extra cutters. The blades are fitted and the depth gauge and guide fence adjusted like those on the plough and combination planes. A slitting knife can be fitted instead of a blade which can cut a strip from the edge of a board.

The multi-plane can be converted by substituting special bases in place of the sliding section. Bases to make hollow and rounding planes are also easy to obtain.

Another shaped base and cutter will plane stair nosings.

Using the plane
Move the plane backward along the work, gradually cutting the groove. Continue until the depth gauge comes into contact with the work.

Cutting a groove
A plough, combination or multi-plane can cut a groove. Fit the required cutter, and set the depth gauge and fence. Try where possible to work with the grain for a smoother cut, starting at the far end of the work with the plane held upright and the fence hard against the edge.

To cut a groove in end grain, use a saw and chisel to cut out the first half of the groove to prevent splitting.

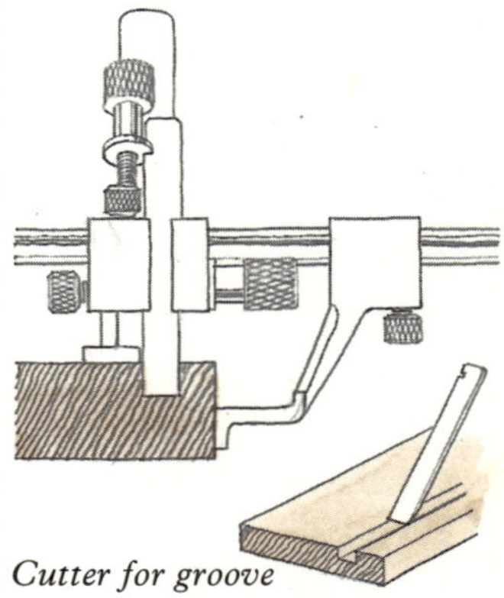

Cutter for groove

Cutting a rebate
Choose a blade just wider than the rebate itself, and set the depth gauge and guide fence. The fence will pass under the blade when cutting a rebate. Use the plane as described for the groove. Any of the planes will cut a rebate with the grain. To cut a rebate across the grain, fit a spur to a combination or a multi-plane to score ahead of the blade.

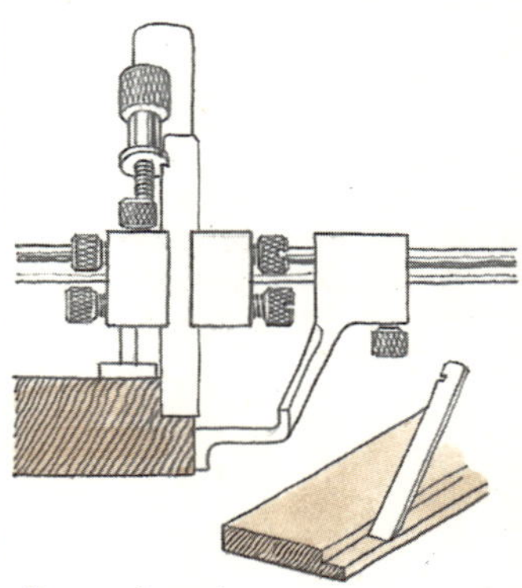

Cutter for rebate

Cutting a housing

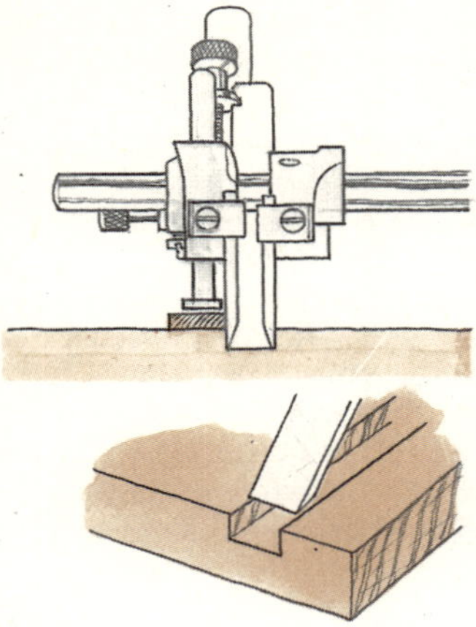

As with the cross grain rebate, a housing can only be cut with the combination or multi-plane. Select the appropriate blade and adjust the sliding section so that both spurs line up with the edges of the cutter. Nail a straight edge batten across the work against which you can run the body of the combination or multi-plane.

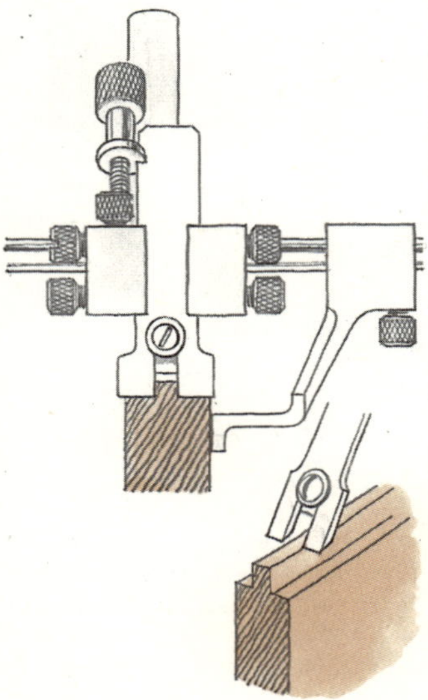

Cutting a tongue and groove joint

Combination and multi-planes are supplied with special tongue cutting blades. There is an adjustable stop on the blade itself to regulate the tongue.

Cutting a bead

Combination and multi-planes both have beading cutters. If you do not require a shoulder on the outside edge, set the guide fence under the cutter to move it out the required amount. Tongued and grooved boards are often beaded in this way to mask the join. Use the beading gauge as a fence, but continue to use the depth gauge throughout.

A centre bead, that is one set away from the edge of a board, can be cut with plough or combination planes. The multi-plane has a foot attached to the forward arm which supports the plane when the bead is a long way from the edge.

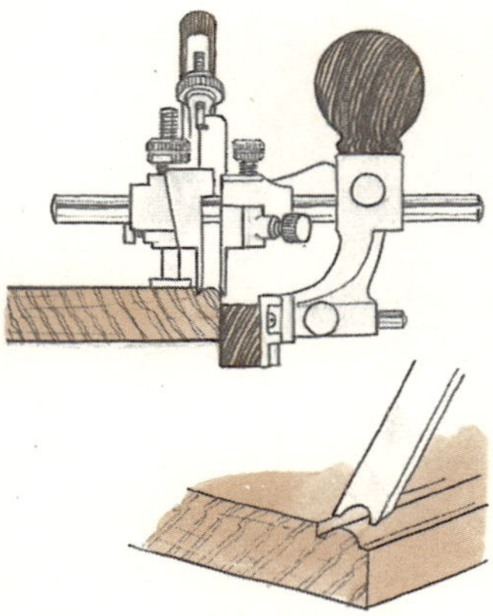

Bead with a shoulder

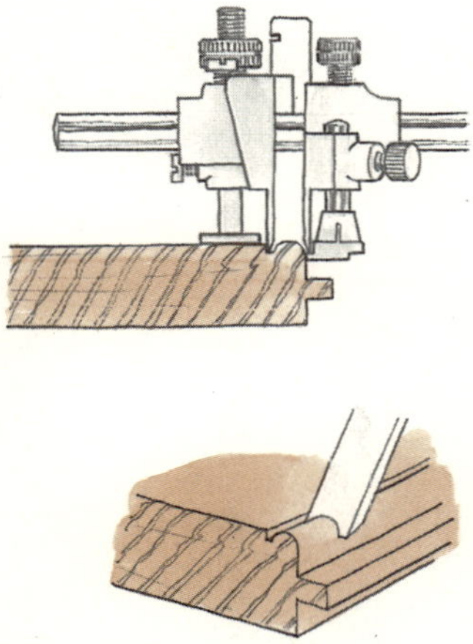

Bead without a shoulder

Cutting reeds

A series of beads grouped together is known as reeding. Special cutters are available for the multi-plane to cut up to five reeds in one pass. Set up the plane as for beading.

Cutting a flute

With the appropriate cutter fitted set up the multi-plane to cut a flute as for a centre bead.

Cutting an ovolo moulding

Fit an ovolo cutter and use a depth gauge and guide fence to cut the moulding on the edge of a board. Clamp wood to the work to prevent end grain splitting.

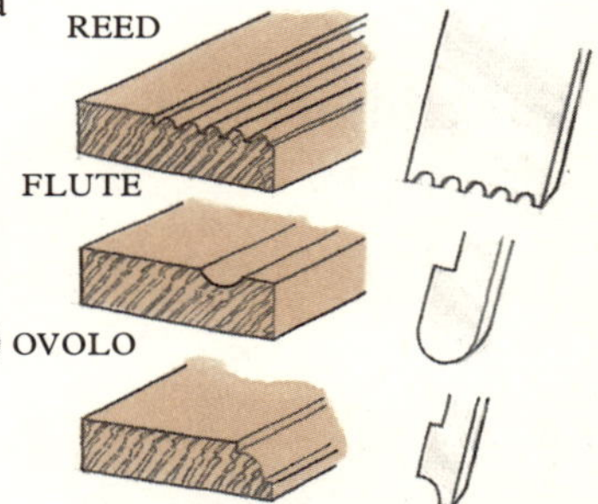

Cutting a sash moulding

The sash moulding cutter makes the window glass rebate and moulding in one pass. It has a depth stop on the blade.

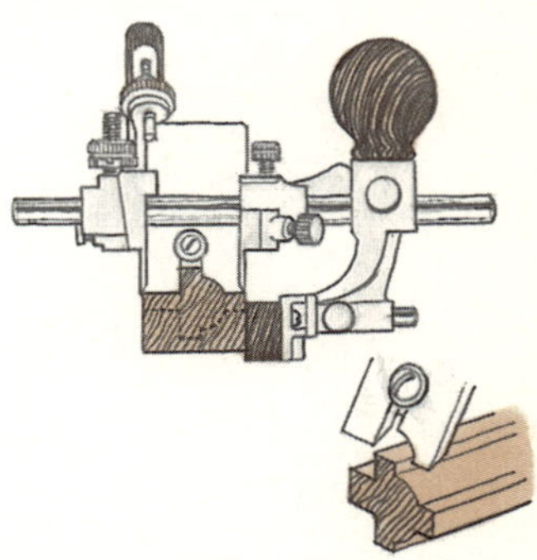

Align the cutter sliding section with its outside edge, and set the guide fence as required. Plane one half of the moulding, reverse the work and plane the other half. Plane the mouldings on the edge of a large board, cutting it off afterward.

Slitting a board

Cut narrow strips from the edge of a board by fitting the slitting knife just in front of the multi-plane handle.

Routers

The term router has come to be applied to a number of tools which differ from one another in purpose, operation, and appearance. The name is applied most appropriately to the router plane which is in fact used for "routing out" a depression in the surface of the work. But there is another group of tools known as routers which resemble spokeshaves in outward appearance though they differ in most other respects, including their narrow, frequently profiled cutters. Many of these were used by coachbuilders, but a larger version, the sash router, has large profiled cutters bedded like a plane and was used for making bow windows. Towards the end of the nineteenth century a number of metal routers were developed which aimed at replacing the older wooden routers and were used by carpenters, cabinet makers, and others for circular work on sashes, doors, hand rails, and furniture. Metal routers were seldom used by coachbuilders: they clung to the wooden version until the end. The forerunner of the portable electric router was the Sheffield cutlers' "parser", a kind of small bow drill with a bifurcated bit. It was used to cut recesses for ornamental plates in pocket knives and other tools.

Hand Router

OTHER NAMES: Router plane, depthing router
SIZE: *Width:* 212mm
MATERIAL: *Body:* cast metal; *Handles:* wood
ATTACHMENTS: Various cutters, guide fence, shoe
USE: To cut grooves and dados, to level, to remove wood waste

The router is most commonly used for cutting dados or grooves in a wooden surface. The router can also remove waste material from rougher cuttings and accurately level recesses in cabinet work or low relief carvings.

The standard cast metal router is most commonly made with an open throat, which gives a clearer view of the work and allows the shavings to be cleared from the housing. The bridge joining the two sides of the throat strengthens the stock and carries a clamp which holds an adjustable rod. An optional shoe for closing the throat is fitted to this rod. This shoe is necessary when working across narrow sections of wood to support the router on the edge of the work, and it must be set flush with the sole of the stock.

Routers are usually supplied with three cutters: 6 and 12mm wide chisels, and a V-shaped smoothing cutter. They are cranked to set the cutting edge at a shallow angle to produce a paring action.

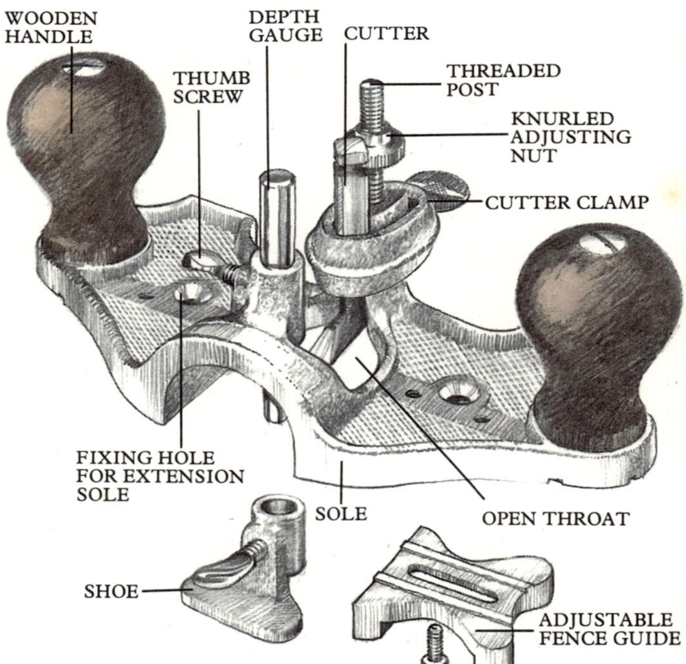

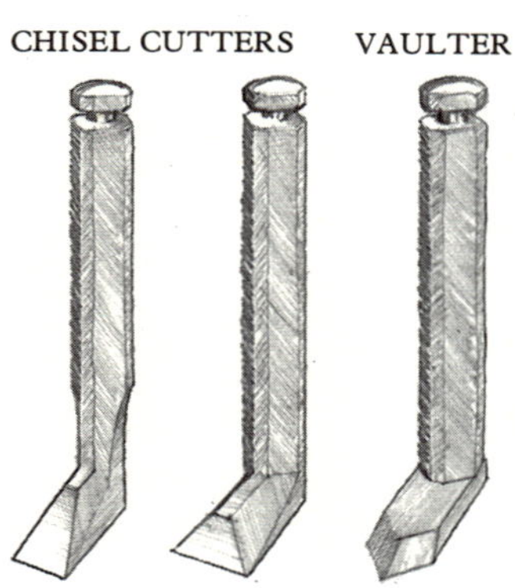

Using the cutters
To trim any wide housings, it may be necessary to make more than one pass across the width. The slicing action of the V-shaped cutter gives a smoother finish and can be used to undercut the bottom of a dovetail housing, or to clear out the corners of fine inlay work.

Sharpening cutters
Sharpen cutters like chisels but rub the cutting edge along an oilstone. Set the stone so cutter's edge clears the bench.

Setting the cutters

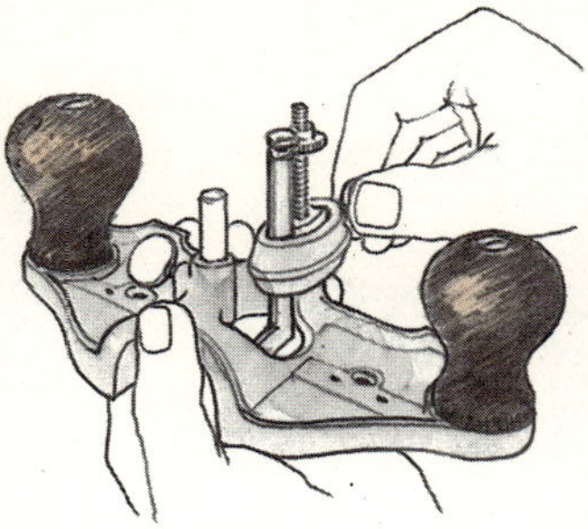

Cutters have square sectioned shafts set at 45° to the direction of the cut which are cradled in a "V" groove in the stock. The top section of the shaft is shaped to locate on the knurled adjusting nut which runs on a threaded rod fixed in the stock.

For through housings, insert the cutter in the cutter clamp from the underside, and locate the adjusting nut. Adjust the cutter against the depth gauge and tighten the thumb screw clamp, or mark the depth on the work edge and align the cutting edge with the marked line. Mark the depth of the housing on the edge of the work. Remove the bulk of the waste beforehand with a saw and chisel or set the cutter in stages to remove all the waste after making two saw cuts on the waste side.

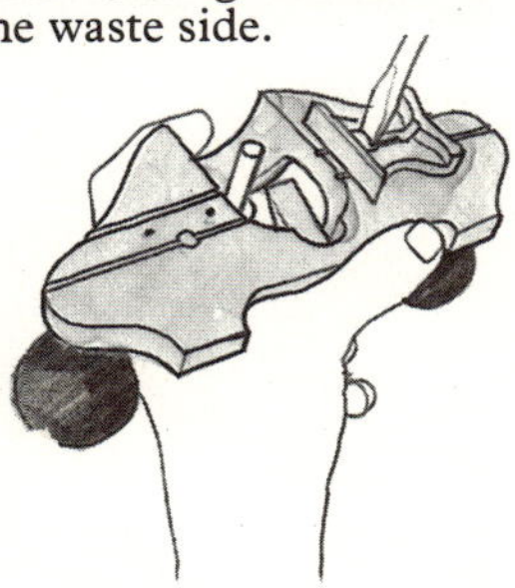

Adjustable fence
This positions the cutter the required distance from straight, concave or convex edges. It is located in grooves machined in the sole of the stock and locked in place with a slotted screw.

Curved grooves
When cutting curves work from two directions to prevent tearing the grain.

Stopped dados

Fit the cutter facing backward to align the cutting edge with the edge of the stock. You may have to reverse the cutter clamp to prevent the thumb screw hitting the work.

Through dados

Push the tool forward. To prevent breakout of the grain at the back edge, reverse tool and work back the other way.

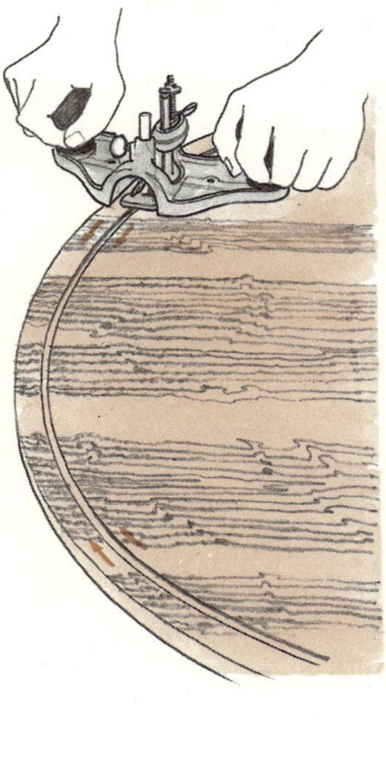

Miniature Router

SIZE: Width: 75mm
MATERIAL: Metal
ATTACHMENT: 6mm cutter
USE: To use as router plane but for fine, delicate work.

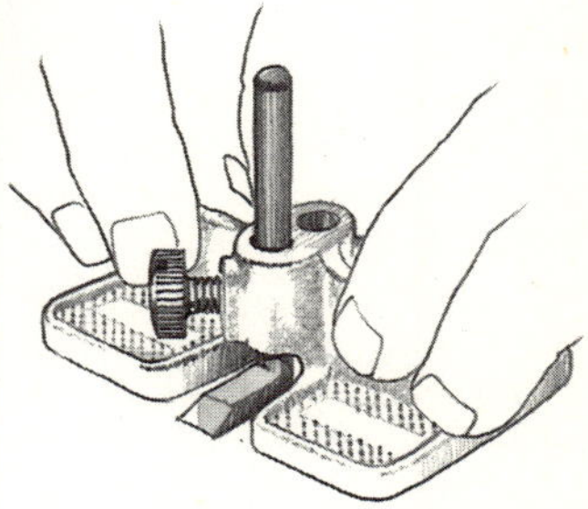

The cutter of the miniature router can be set for stopped or through housings. The depth must be set against a marked line on the work and the cutter secured by a knurled screw.

Granny's Tooth

OTHER NAME: Old woman's tooth
SIZE: *Width:* 100 to 150mm
MATERIAL: Hardwood
ATTACHMENT: Steel cutter
USE: To work as for router plane

This is a wooden bodied router with the cutter set at a steep angle and held by a wooden wedge. The blade is adjusted by tapping with a hammer as for wooden planes. The front edge of some models is notched back to the mouth for checking the work and to allow the shavings to clear the slot.

Portable Electric Router

OTHER NAME: Power router
SIZE: **Light duty:** *Motor:* $\frac{1}{4}$ to $\frac{1}{2}$hp; *Power:* 18,000 to 22,000 rpm; *Weight:* 1.7 to 2.7kg; **Heavy duty:** *Motor:* $\frac{3}{4}$ to $1\frac{1}{2}$hp; *Power:* 23,000 to 27,000 rpm; *Weight:* 3.3 to 4kg
MATERIAL: Die cast aluminium alloy
ACCESSORIES: Fence guide; template guide; laminate trimming guide
ATTACHMENT: Dovetail jig
USE: To cut grooves, housings, rebates and mouldings; to trim

The electric router, in use for about twenty years, is a versatile power tool which superseded the hand router and moulding planes. It is used to cut grooves or mouldings quickly and cleanly. The motor is fitted with a chuck and is held in a vertical position by a sleeve fitted with two integral handles. It stands on a flat circular base which slides on the work. A bit or "cutter" is fitted into the chuck and protrudes through the base plate. The bit can be finely adjusted and locked at the required setting.

Because the router runs at extremely high speeds it produces a very smooth cut which requires little sanding. While the lighter machines are suitable for the average domestic user, more than one cut may be necessary to produce a successful groove or moulding.

Operating the router
The router has a tendency to twist when starting, so keep a firm grip on the machine when switching on. The motor must reach maximum speed before a cut is made and the machine should never be switched on or off while it is in contact with the work. The router is fed into the work against the clockwise rotation of the bit so that the cutting edge pulls itself into the work making a vibration-free, accurate cut.

Move the cutter at a steady rate: too much speed may strain the motor; too little speed may cause friction resulting in damaged work or cutters. With a little experience, the sound of the motor will be your best guide.

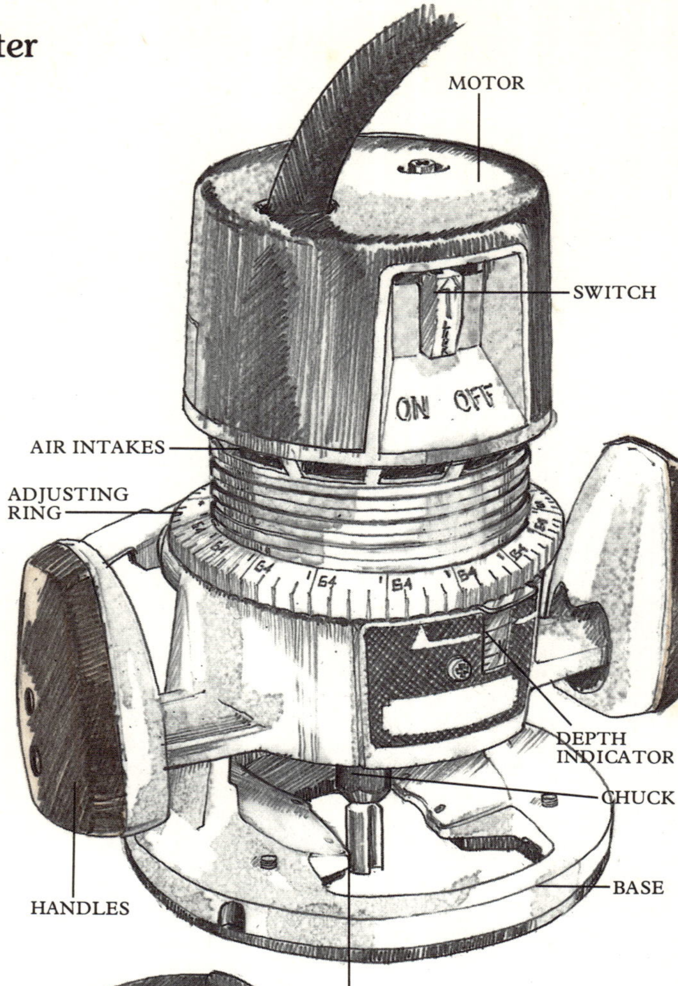

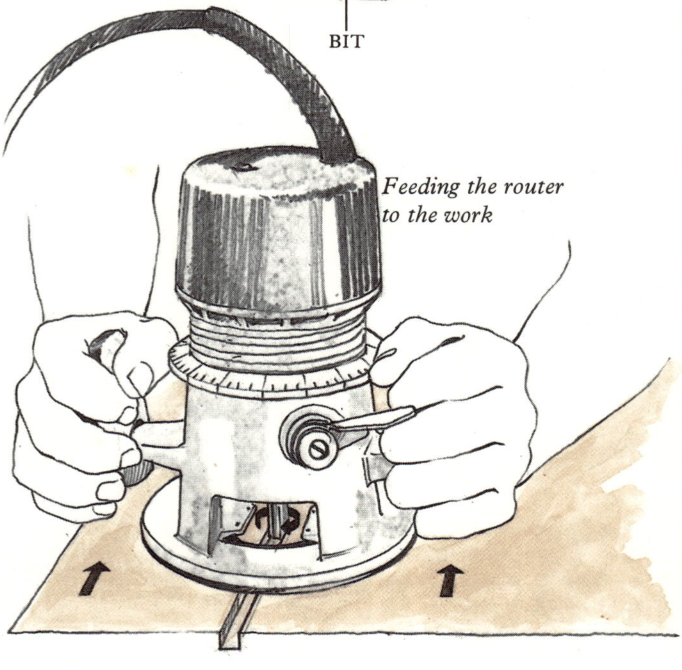

Feeding the router to the work

BITS

Bits are available in shank sizes ranging from 6mm to 12mm and are made of high speed steel or tungsten carbide.

Carbide bits can either be solid or tipped; a tungsten carbide cutting edge is brazed onto the shank. While the high speed steel bits perform well on most woods, plastics and soft metals and are available in the widest range of shapes, both types of carbide bits are longer lasting. They have a greater resistance to heat and therefore do not blunt as quickly, particularly when cutting more abrasive materials such as laminates, plywood, particle board and so forth.

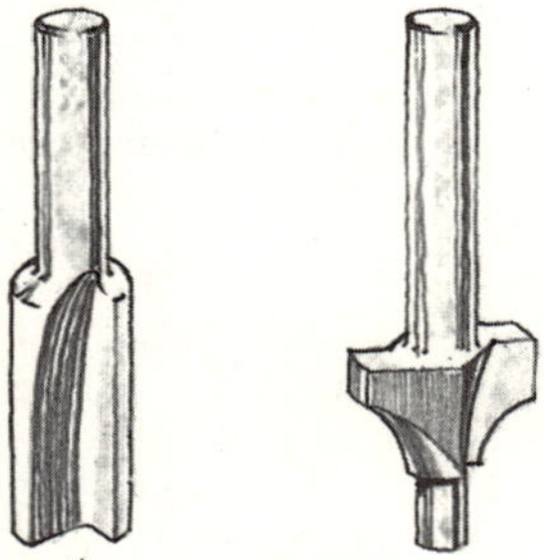

Cutting edge design
Double fluted bits (left) cut simple grooves quickly and unguided. More elaborate bits (right) have a pilot tip.

Solid carbide bits are the strongest but are the most expensive and are the best suited to heavy duty machines.

The cutting edge on a bit may be either single or double fluted, or spiral shaped. Single fluted bits cut faster as there is more clearance for the waste, but they tend to leave a rippled cut. Double fluted bits make two cuts for each revolution and give a much smoother finish. The spiral bit has a slicing action which produces a very smooth cut but is slower to use.

Most shaped bits have a pilot tip which rides along the edges of the work. These bits can have straight or bevelled cutting edges. Pilot tips eliminate the need for other guide accessories but the edge of the work should be clean and true or the bit will copy any irregularities.

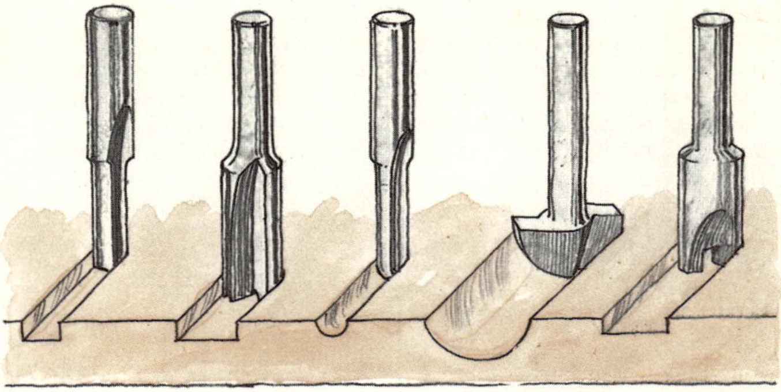

SINGLE FLUTE — DOUBLE FLUTE — VEINING BIT — CORE BOX BIT — HINGE MORTICE BIT

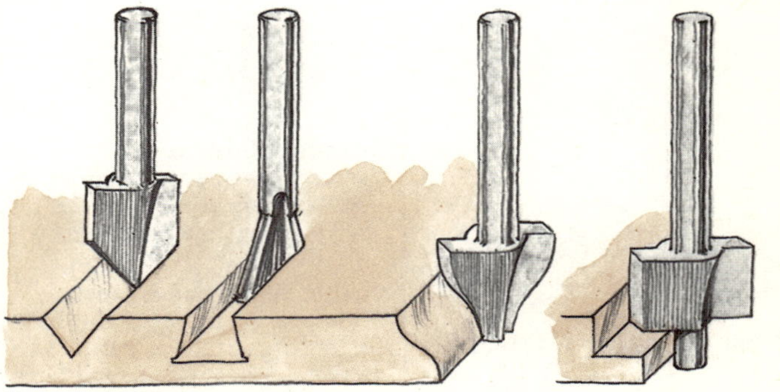

"V" GROOVE BIT — DOVETAIL BIT — OGEE BIT — REBATE BIT

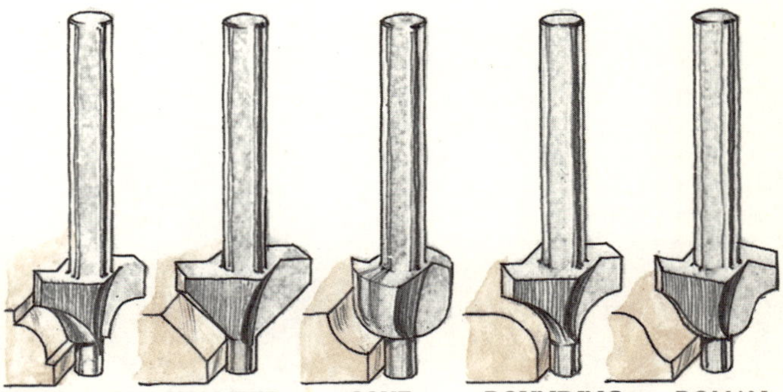

BEADING BIT — CHAMFER BIT — COVE BIT — ROUNDING OVER BIT — ROMAN OGEE BIT

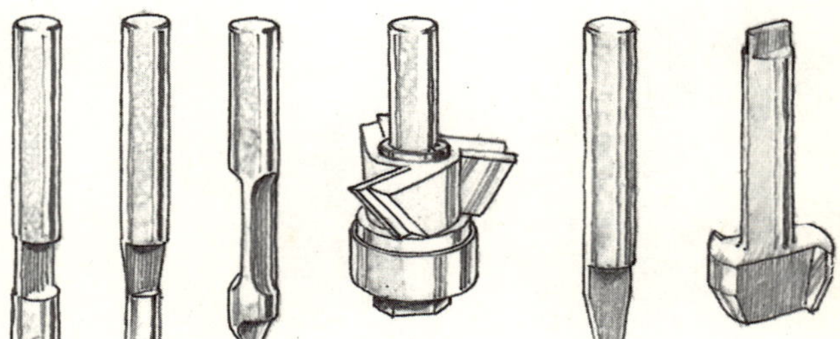

PILOTED LAMINATE TRIM BITS — LAMINATE TRIM BIT — COMBINATION BITS

Fitting and setting bits

Before attempting to fit any bits, disconnect the machine from the power supply. Insert 6 to 18mm of the shank into the chuck before tightening.

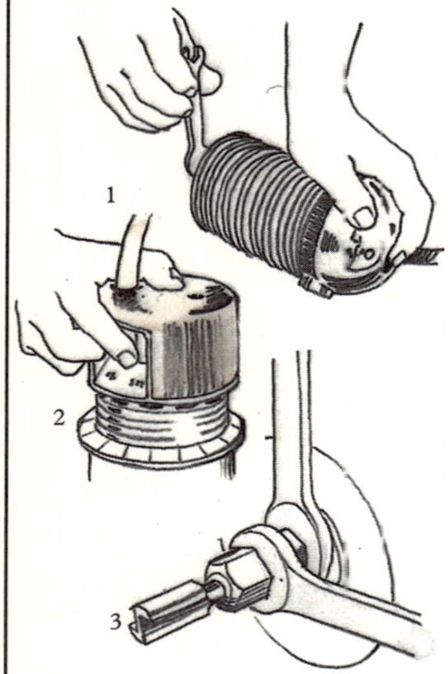

While the method of fitting bits varies according to the machine, the motor must always be locked so that the chuck can be loosened with a spanner. Some models have a built-in locking device incorporated in the on-off switch. In the off position the switch is pushed upward to lock the motor shaft (1). Other types have a separate push button (2). A third type (3) uses two spanners. One fits the shaft while the other turns the chuck.

Setting the cut depth

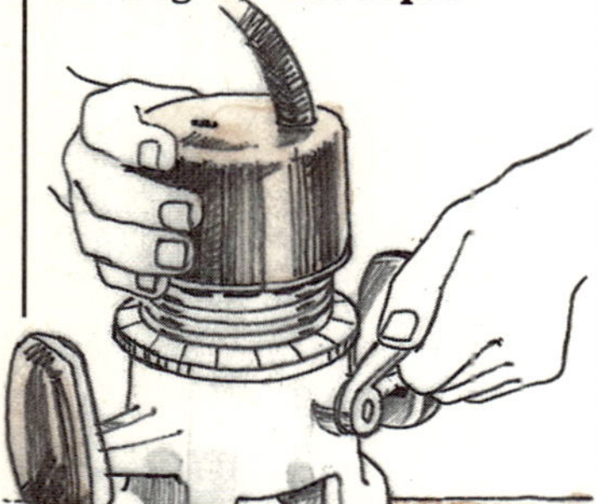

Loosen the base clamp. Move the motor body back up or down as required and lock into place. Most routers have calibrated dials for fine setting.

Making through cuts

Steady the forward half of the base on the surface of the wood and carefully feed the cutter into the work against the clockwise rotation of the bit.

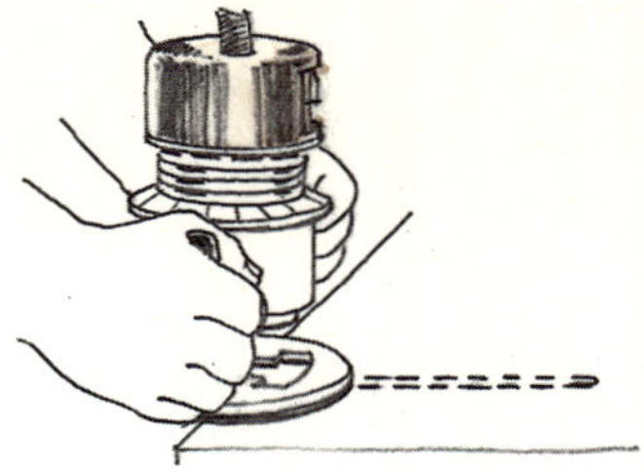

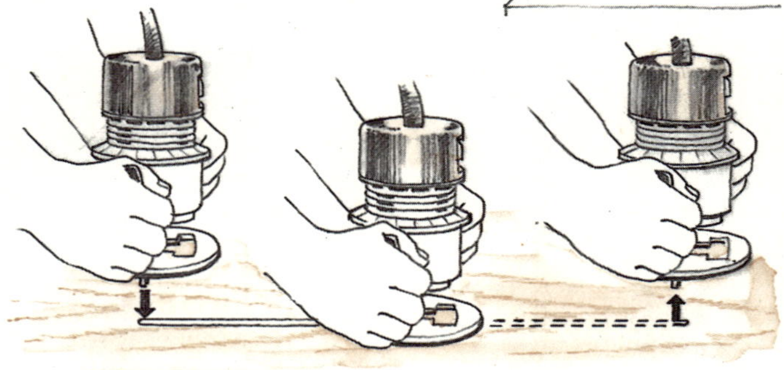

Stopped housings

Lower the tool perpendicularly down into the work allowing the bit to drill into the surface.

Make the cut in the normal way and lift the machine clear before switching off.

Guide fence accessory

This can be fitted to the base for cutting grooves parallel to an edge. The guide usually has two rods which plug into the router base and can be locked in place with two thumb screws. Some types have an additional Vernier adjustment for fine setting and a trammel point for cutting curves or circles. For better support, the fence can be extended with a length of wood screwed to it.

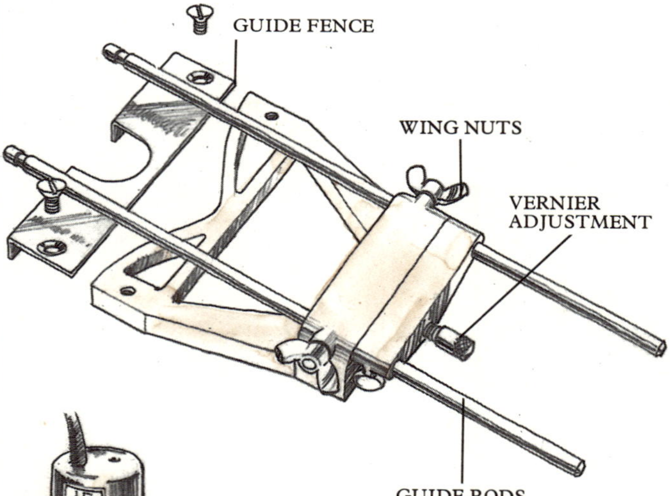

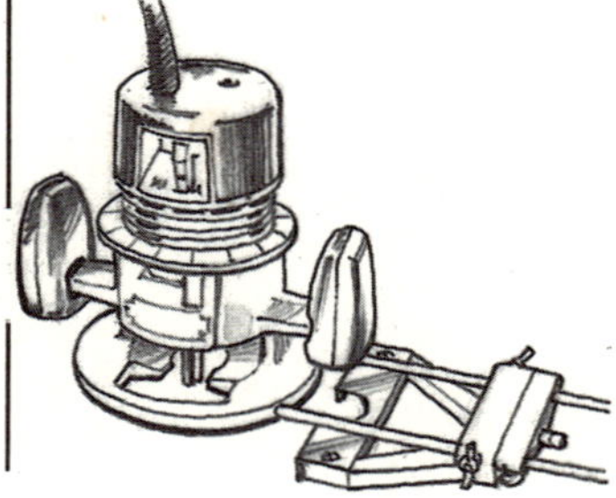

Attaching a guide fence

Plug the guide rods into the router base. Adjust the fence along the rods and lock with the two wing nuts.

Using the router

Cutting housings and grooves

Routers can cut housings or grooves to any angle. Clamped lengths of wood can be used as guides if necessary.

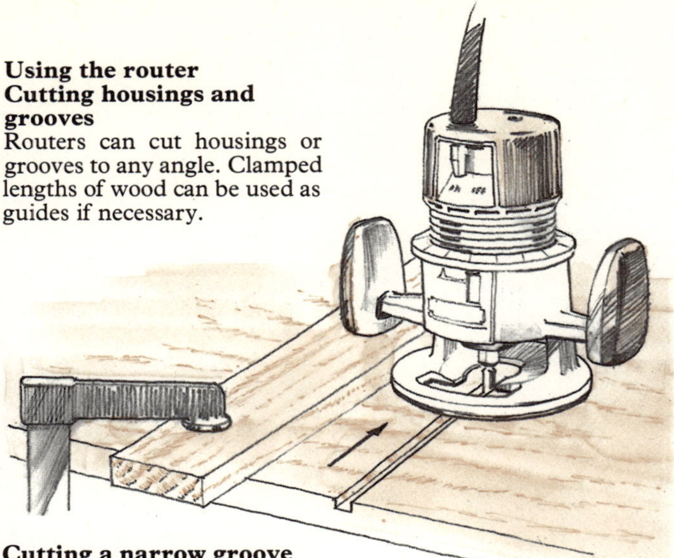

Cutting a narrow groove
Use a single length of wood as a guide for the router base.

Cutting a wide groove
Clamp two parallel lengths of wood across the work, run the router against each length in turn before using it free-hand to remove the central portion.

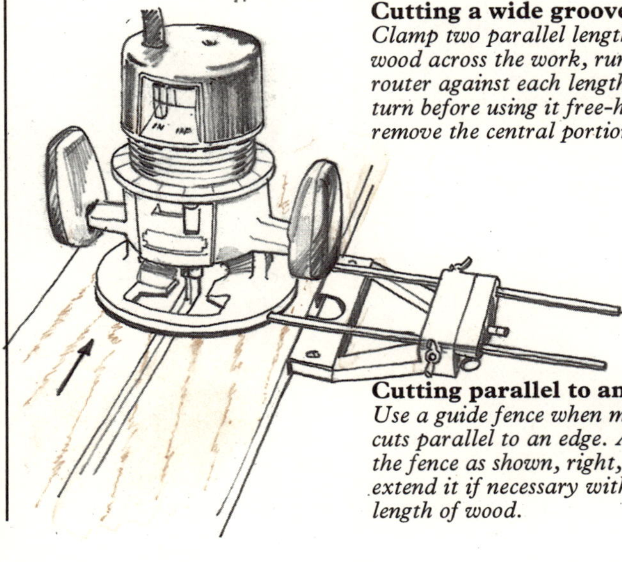

Cutting parallel to an edge
Use a guide fence when making cuts parallel to an edge. Attach the fence as shown, right, and extend it if necessary with a length of wood.

Mouldings and rebates

You can cut a whole range of shapes commonly used in furniture construction by using the wide variety of shaped, piloted router bits.

Molding an outside edge
For table tops or panels, first cut the end grain and then the side edges. This will prevent the grain splitting out. If the mouldings are to be cut across the end grain only, work from either end toward the middle.

Cutting a rebate
To cut a rebate on the inside of an assembled frame, fix a right angle block to the guide fence. The block must be centred on the guide so that both sides of the cut are even.

Cutting circles or discs
Use an adjustable trammel guide for this. Some guide fences come already equipped with these guides. For thicker beads you may have to adjust the cutter between passes.

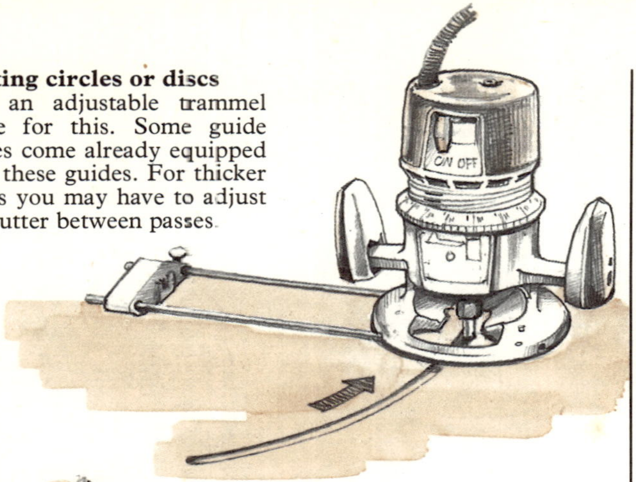

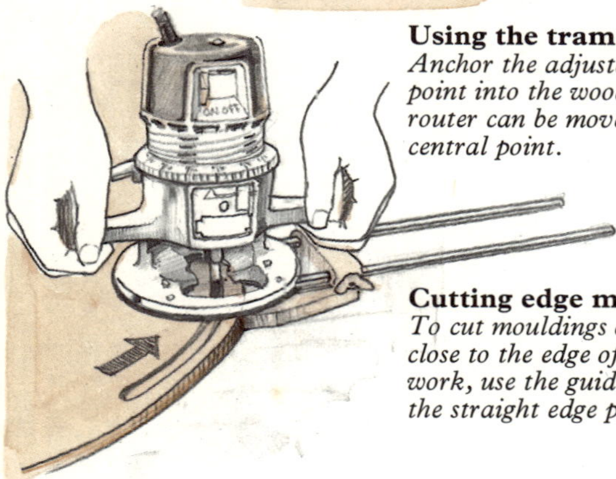

Using the trammel guide
Anchor the adjustable trammel point into the wood so that the router can be moved around the central point.

Cutting edge mouldings
To cut mouldings or grooves close to the edge of curved work, use the guide fence with the straight edge plate removed.

Template routing
You can accurately duplicate compass curves or free form shapes by running the edge of the router base against 12mm thick plywood templates clamped or tacked to the wood. Bear in mind that the work being cut will vary in size from that of the template's by the distance between the bit and the router's edge. Therefore, when cutting large shapes remember to compensate for this difference.

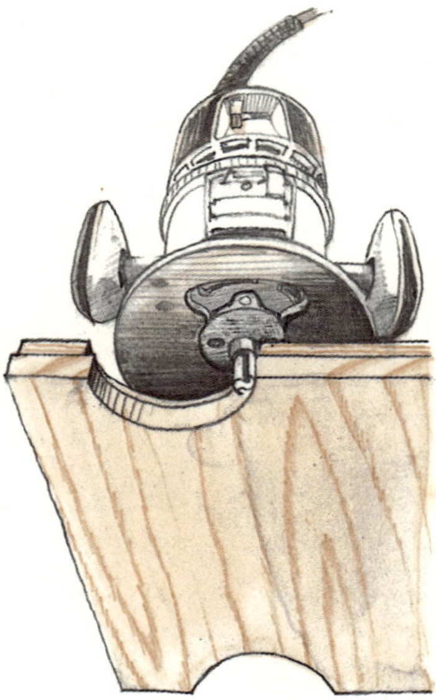

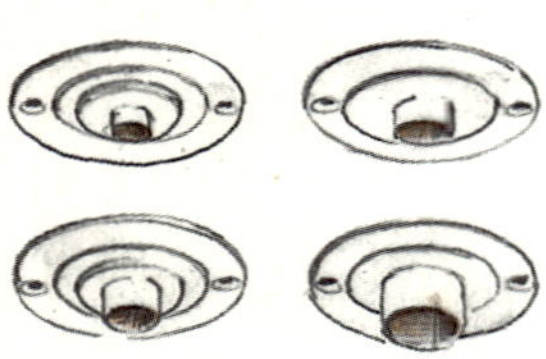

Copying delicate work
For finer work you can fit an appropriately sized template guide into the base plate. This is a metal disc with a tubular collar which projects below the router base. The collar rides against the template while the bit passes through the tube to make the cut. Compensate on the template for the distance between the cutting edge and the outside face of the collar.

CUTTING JOINTS
By setting the depth of cut and guide fence in different ways, you can use the router to quickly and accurately produce a wide variety of joints.

Cutting a mortice
Fit a straight bit which has a diameter slightly less than the width of the desired mortice. Make the first cut. Turn the tool around resting the guide fence on the other side of the rail and make a second cut. This ensures that the mortice is centred on the rail. Square off curved ends with a chisel.

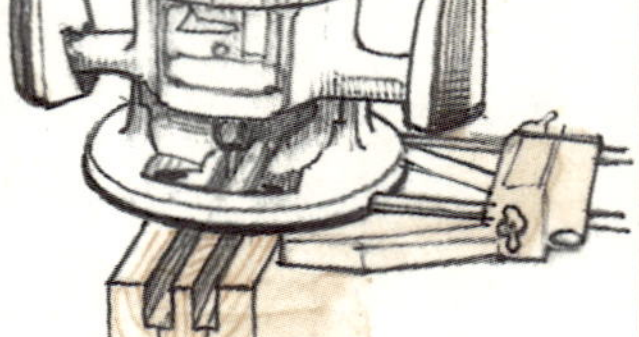

Cutting a short tenon
Hold the work vertically between two battens. Make sure that the ends of the rails are flush. Set the fence to produce a tenon to fit the cut mortice. Make a pass from each side.

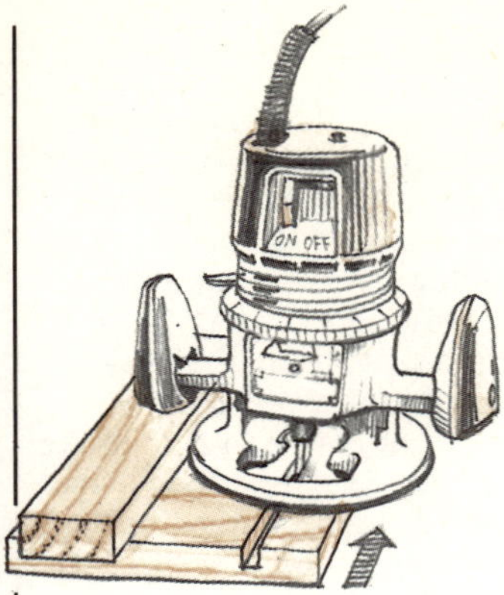

Cutting a long tenon
Set depth of the bit to equal distance between mortice and edge of rail. Cut first shoulder against the guide. Remove waste and repeat on other side of rails.

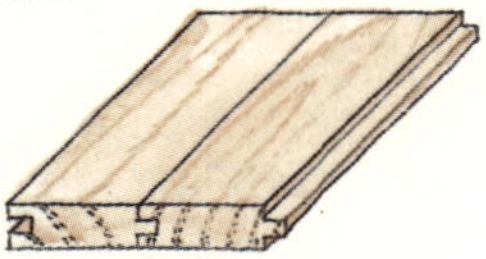

Tongue and groove
To cut a tongue and groove joint in the edge of the work, clamp the board between two wide pieces of wood to provide a flush surface for the base of the router to ride on. Adjust the fence to cut the groove first.

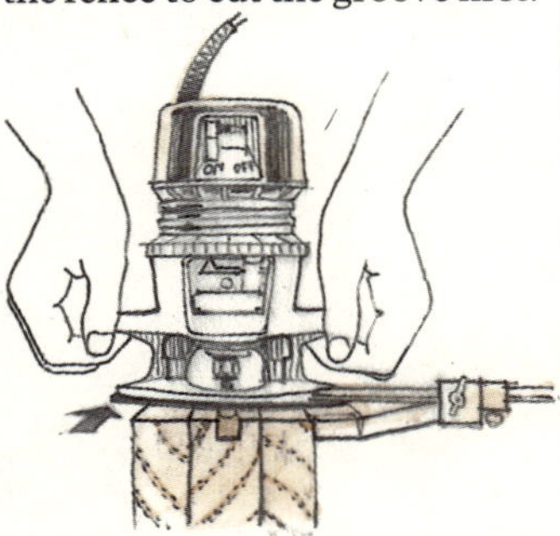

Cutting the groove
Set the fence to cut the groove down the centre of the work.

To make the tongue, re-set the fence and make two cuts, one on each side of the work, cutting partly into the support pieces. Make sure they are the same depth. The tongue should push into the groove.

While a standard tongue and groove joint can be made using a straight bit, a dovetail shaped bit makes a stronger joint.

Dovetail joints
This form of joint, normally used in drawer construction, requires a high degree of skill if cut by hand. However, if a dovetail jig and a router fitted with the matching bit are used, both halves of the joint can be cut simultaneously resulting in a perfect fit.

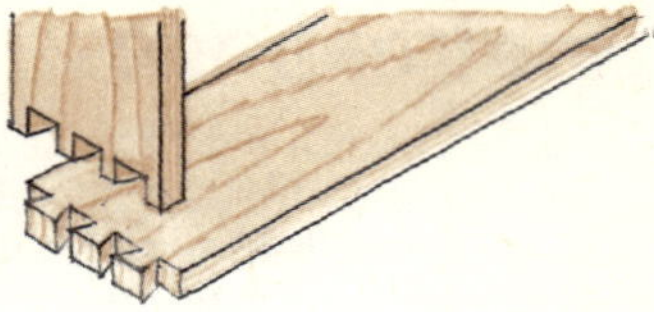

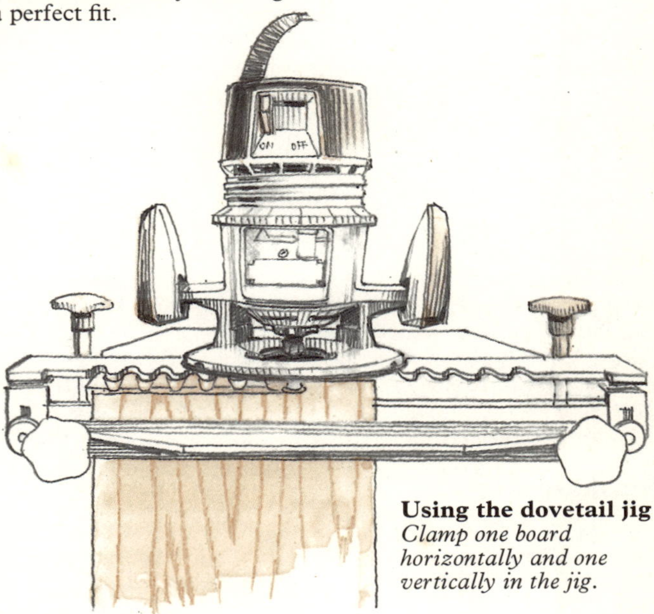

Using the dovetail jig
Clamp one board horizontally and one vertically in the jig.

Simultaneous dovetailing
The dovetail bit follows the fingers of the guide, cutting into both boards to remove waste. It leaves the pins in the horizontal board and the tails in the vertical board.

Methods of fitting and adjusting the dovetail jig, and therefore positioning the boards, differ with each manufacturer. Check with the maker's instructions before you start.

Cutting a dovetail tongue and groove

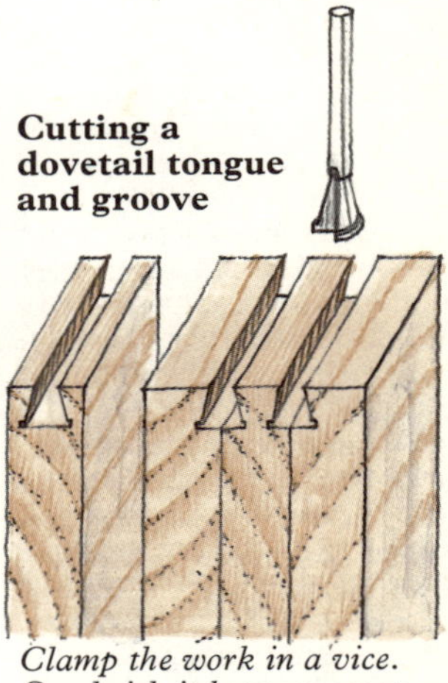

Clamp the work in a vice. Sandwich it between scrap wood if it is thin or you are cutting the tongue. For the groove, centre the bit on the board. For the tongue, make two cuts of equal depth, leaving the tongue projecting centrally.

Spokeshaves

In its original form the wooden spokeshave is unique; no other woodworking tool has its cutter fixed in such a simple but highly effective manner. It is also rather odd that most of the spokeshaves mentioned in the records from the early sixteenth century onward occur in lists of coopers' tools, rather than the more obvious wheelwrights. The earliest known illustration of the wooden spokeshave is in Smith's *Key to the Manufactories of Sheffield* (1816), again among the cooper's tools.

There is reason to think that the cooper's "spokeshave" of the late medieval references was a kind of drawing knife for cleaning up wooden hoops. Tools of this type used on a shaving-horse are usually pulled, hence the general term "draw knife"; although a spokeshave can be used in this way, for best results it is more usual to work away from the body with a pushing action.

In many other European languages the name of this tool is the same as that for "scraper". The nearest to the English "spokeshave" is the Dutch *spookschaaf*, but *spook* in Dutch means the same as it does in English. However, it may be significant that in Norwich in 1558 and again in 1589 a cooper's apprentice was promised at the end of his term a "spooke shave" by the master. It seems likely that the Dutch borrowed the tool and the East Anglian way of spelling it at that time. It must therefore be regretfully confessed that the genius who invented the spokeshave, and where and when he did it, is not definitely known, but he may have been an East Anglian cooper of the late sixteenth century.

The modern metal spokeshave was a spin-off from the development of metal bench planes in the 1860s and 1870s, the main difference being that the cutters are now fixed and adjusted like plane irons.

Spokeshave

SIZE: **Metal:** *Length:* 225 to 250mm; *Cutter width:* 43 to 53mm
Wooden: *Length:* 200 to 400mm; *Cutter width:* 50 to 100mm
MATERIAL: *Stock:* beech, boxwood, cast iron; *Cutter:* steel
USE: To smooth curved wood

The spokeshave produces the same result as a smoothing plane, but it is specifically designed to finish narrow curved sections of timber. The face is curved for concave shapes or flat for convex curves.

Wooden spokeshaves are not common today. Although they are efficient in use, their narrow section wears very quickly, which makes it difficult to set the cutter finely. Some of the more expensive wooden spokeshaves are reinforced at the critical points with brass, but they are rare. The cutters have a tapered tang at either end turned up at right angles. These tangs are tapped into the matching holes in the stock holding the cutter at the required setting by friction alone. Modern catalogues have largely dropped the wooden spokeshave, replacing it with the metal version.

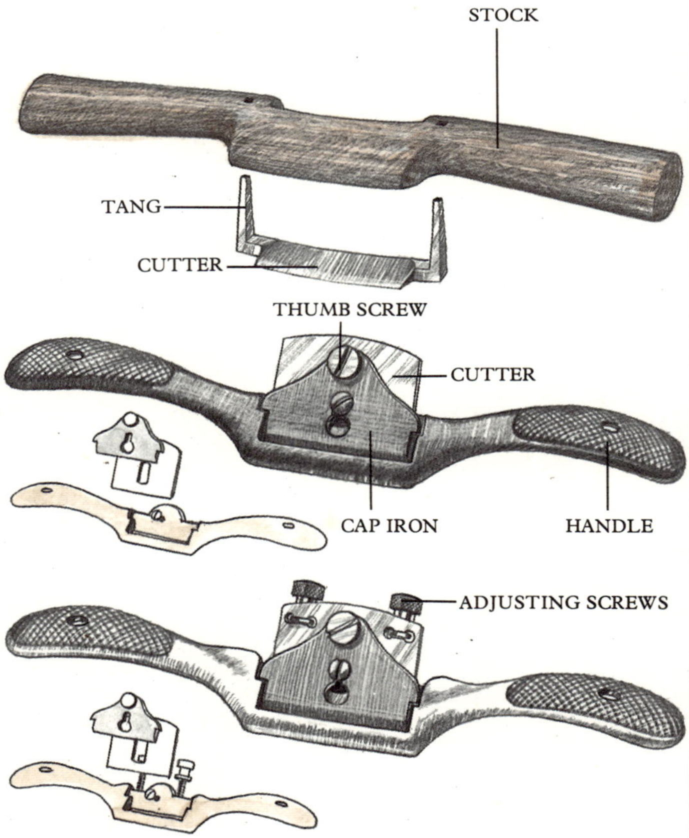

Adjusting spokeshaves

All-metal spokeshaves have straight or slightly curved winglike handles on either side of the stock. The main difference between the various types of spokeshave lies in the method of securing and adjusting the cutter of the tool.

The cutter, in all versions, is essentially a small plane iron. On the simplest type the cutter is positioned by hand before being clamped by a cap iron, which is then secured by a thumb screw. Fine adjustment can only be achieved by slightly slackening the thumb screw and lightly tapping the top edge of the cutter with a hammer. If the setting is too coarse, the cutter must be retracted by hand and fine adjustment begun again.

There is a superior version of the spokeshave which has a cutter adjusted by means of two screws, one on either side, located near the top edge. The cap iron is secured with a thumb screw as on the humbler types of spokeshave, but the cutter can be finely set up or down as well as accurately aligned with the face before being finally clamped in place.

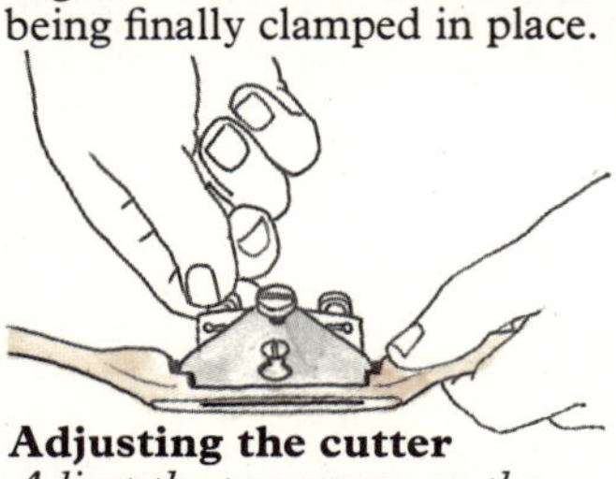

Adjusting the cutter

Adjust the two screws on the top edge to set the cutter accurately before clamping into place with the thumb screw.

Round and flat face spokeshaves

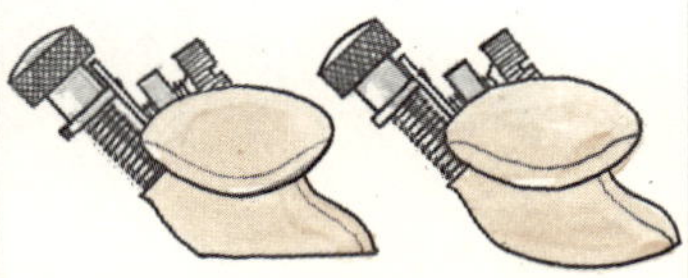

A round shaped spokeshave has a curved underside to accommodate concave curves, while a flat face spokeshave is designed to cut convex shapes.

Sharpening a cutter

The metal spokeshave blade is sharpened like a plane blade (see pages 70–71). A honing guide is useful for keeping the short blade at the correct angle. To remove the cutter from a wooden spokeshave tap the ends of the tangs with a hammer. Remove the burr from the flat face of the cutter on a flat oilstone. Refit the blade and adjust the depth of cut with light hammer taps.

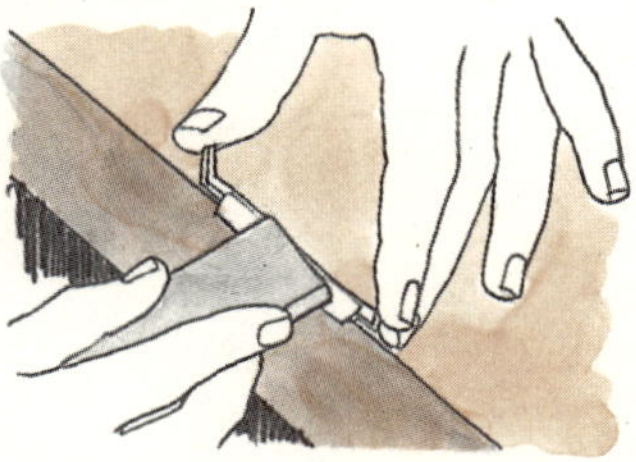

Hold the cutter flat on a bench overhanging the edge and hone the cutting edge with an oiled slipstone. Remove the burr with the same slipstone.

Stand an oilstone on edge while holding the cutter, bevel face down, at an angle across it. Apply oil to the stone and sharpen the entire edge as you would a chisel or plane iron.

Using the spokeshave

Hold one handle in each hand with the thumbs placed on the back edges to control the angle of the tool. Push the spokeshave away from you as you would a plane. To prevent tearing, work from both ends of a curve in the direction of the grain. (This applies equally to convex or concave curves.) For finished work set the blade finely, as you would for a plane.

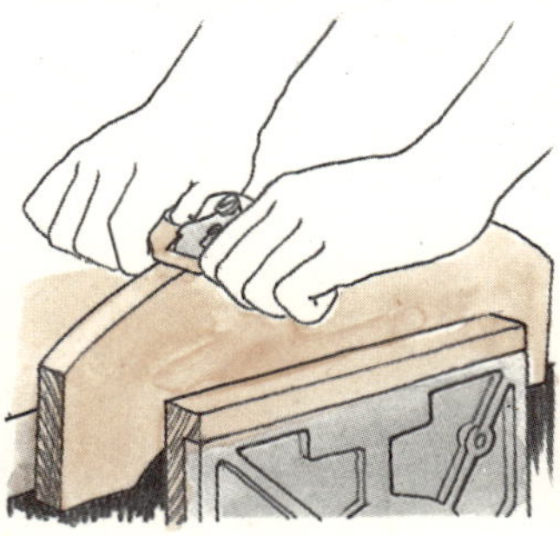

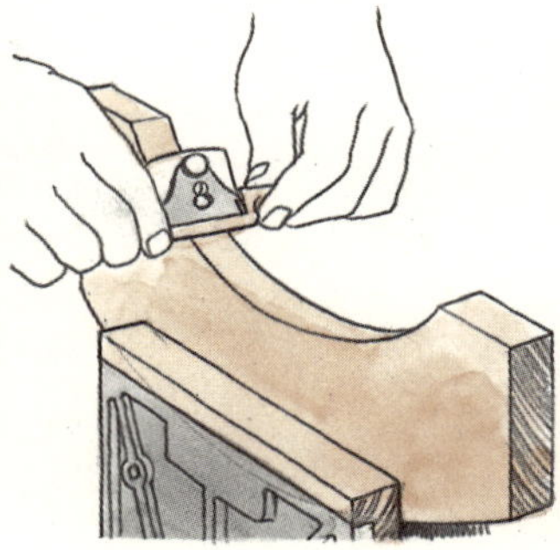

Convex curves

Push the spokeshave down each side from the centre.

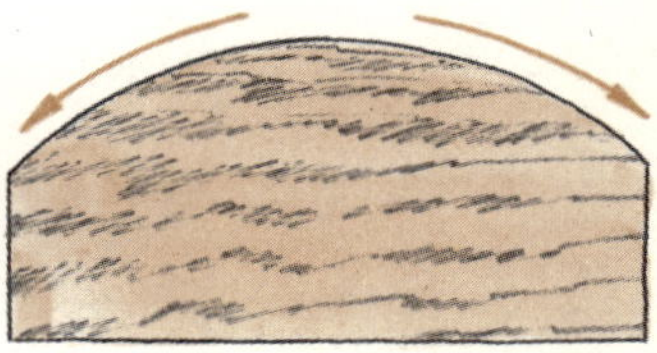

Concave curves

Push the spokeshave down toward the centre from each side of the curve.

Half Round Spokeshave

OTHER NAME: Hollow spokeshave
SIZE: *Length:* 250mm; *Cutter width:* 51.5mm
MATERIAL: *Stock:* cast iron; *Cutter:* steel
USE: To smooth sections of wood which are curved in two directions

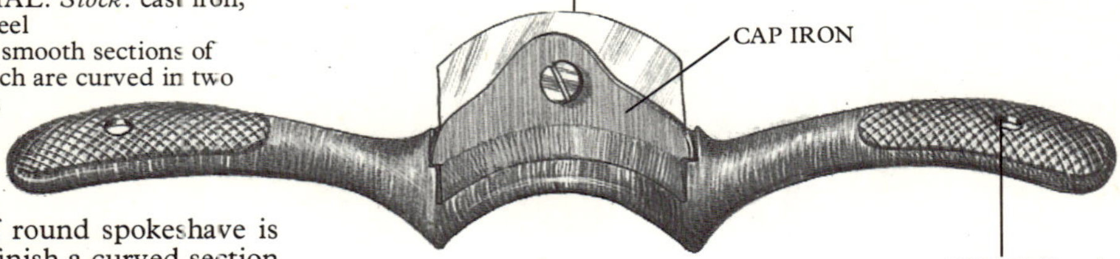

The half round spokeshave is used to finish a curved section of wood which is also rounded off on the top edge, such as a curved seat rail. It is similar to a standard spokeshave, but has a concave face and matching blade. The blade must be adjusted by hand as it is simply clamped by a back iron. Hone the cutter with a slipstone.

Combination Spokeshave

SIZE: *Length:* 250mm; *Cutter width:* **curved:** 34mm; **flat:** 40mm
MATERIAL: *Stock:* cast iron; *Cutters:* steel
USE: To do the work of a flat face and hollow face spokeshave

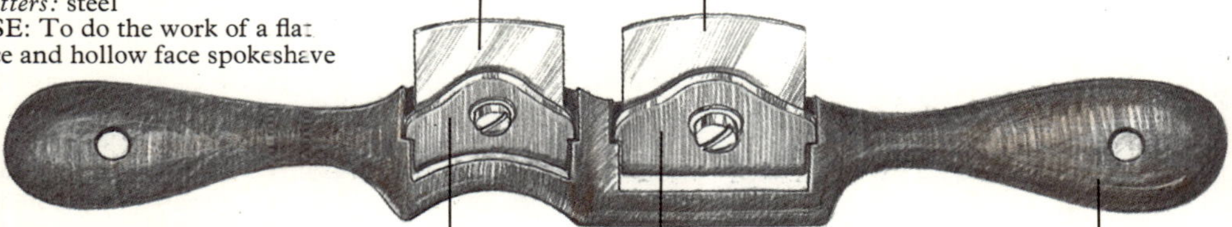

The combination spokeshave is a dual-purpose tool, having a hollow edged cutter mounted alongside a flat edged cutter. It has the advantage of costing little more than the single spokeshave of either variety.

Chamfer Spokeshave

SIZE: 262mm
MATERIAL: *Stock:* cast iron; *Cutter:* alloy steel
USE: To accurately cut chamfers to size

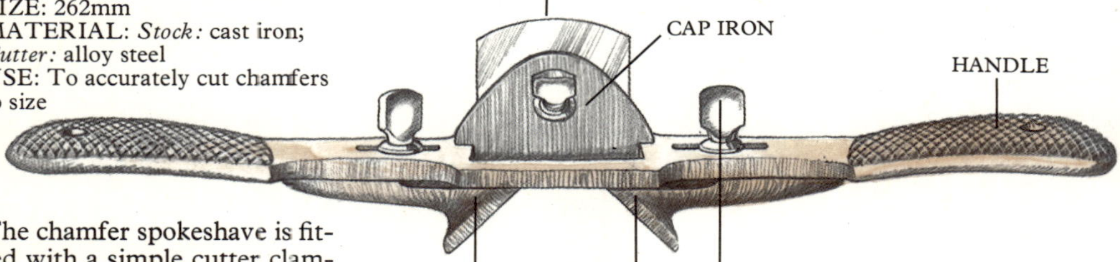

The chamfer spokeshave is fitted with a simple cutter clamped by a back iron. It has two angled fences on the underside which can be adjusted to cut chamfers up to 37mm wide. The fences are secured by a thumb screw on each side.

Double Handed Scraper

OTHER NAMES: Cabinet scraper, scraper plane
SIZE: *Length:* 287mm; *Cutter width:* 68mm
MATERIAL: *Stock:* cast iron; *Cutter:* steel
USE: To scrape wood prior to polishing

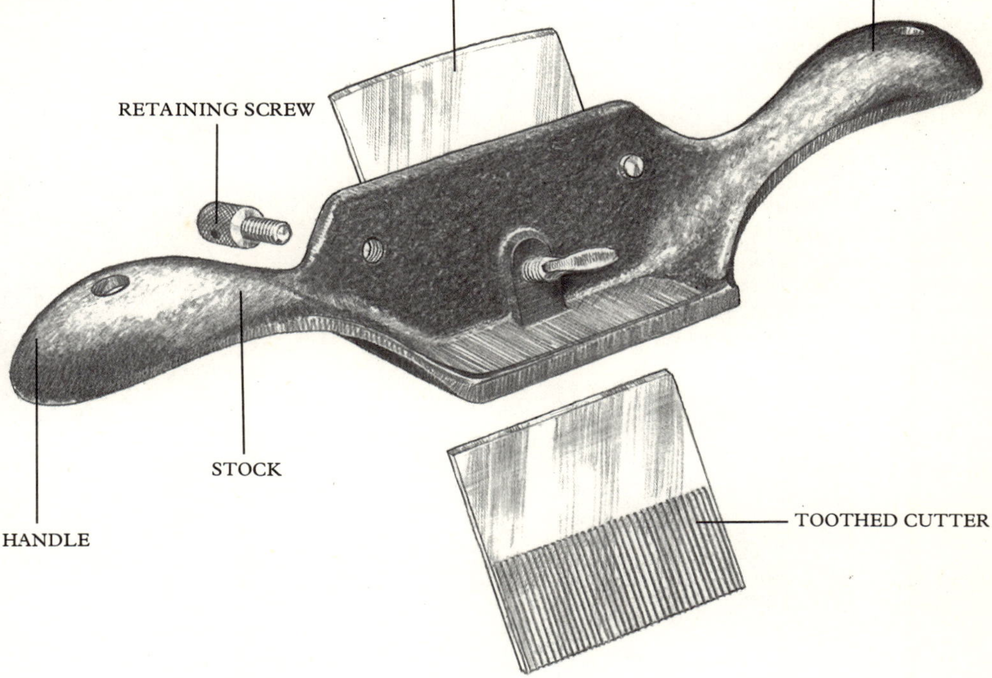

The double handed scraper provides a method of jigging a scraper blade at a constant angle while curving it to produce the required shaving. It takes all the hard work out of using a standard cabinet scraper by providing comfortable handles which relieve the strain on the thumbs. The stock and handles are shaped very much like a spokeshave, and the tool is used in a similar way, but the blade, while in use, is angled away from the worker. It is held between a clamp and the stock by two retaining screws. The curve on the blade is adjusted by means of a thumb screw fitted in the center of the stock.

The standard double edged blade can be replaced by a toothed cutter to convert the scraper into a toothing plane.

Sharpening the blade
Remove the blade from the holder and file off any remaining burr from the flat sides of the blade.

If necessary grind each cutting edge to an angle of 45°. Hone this angle on an oilstone. Do not hone a second angle on the bevel as you would on a plane iron.

Raise a burr on each cutting edge with the method described for cabinet scrapers.

Place the stock of the tool on the bench and insert the blade, bevel side away from the retaining screws.

Tighten the screws while leaving the curve adjustment thumb screw slack. Test the tool and adjust the thumb screw to produce the required depth of shaving.

Using the scraper
With the blade angled away from you, push the tool away from you keeping the base of the stock flat on the work.

Scrapers

The Romans, if not the Greeks, had a word for it. They used a *radula*, or scraper, something like our modern shave hook to scrape paint or tar. The cabinet scraper did not appear until the seventeenth century, with the development of thin steel plate for hand saws and the increasing use of hardwoods for furniture making early in the following century. They are first mentioned in New England cabinetmakers' inventories from about 1720. The earliest known illustration, however, occurs in Roubo's *Joinery*, and shows a steel plate 65 to 75mm wide set in a wooden handle. The Bailey catalogue of 1888 has a "Veneer Scraper" with a blade held in a small metal plane stock with cross handles, the angle of the iron being adjustable. Improved models were introduced, but many cabinetmakers preferred the simpler, more flexible oblong steel plate. Hook scrapers appeared about 1930.

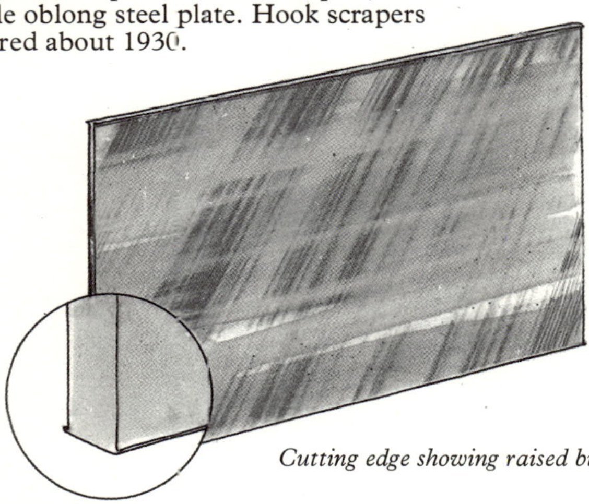

Cutting edge showing raised burr.

Cabinet Scraper

SIZE: 75 × 115 × 0.8mm
MATERIAL: Steel
USE: To finish wooden surfaces

The cabinet scraper is simply a rectangular piece of steel with two cutting edges for working flat areas. Curved scrapers are used for shaped work.

A properly sharpened scraper produces minute shavings and consequently leaves a cleaner finish than sand paper which tends to clog the grain with dust. Hardwoods benefit particularly well from this finish. Scrapers are very useful for removing patches of "wild" grain without disturbing the surrounding grain.

Curved scraper
Shaped scrapers for curved work have an all around cutting edge.

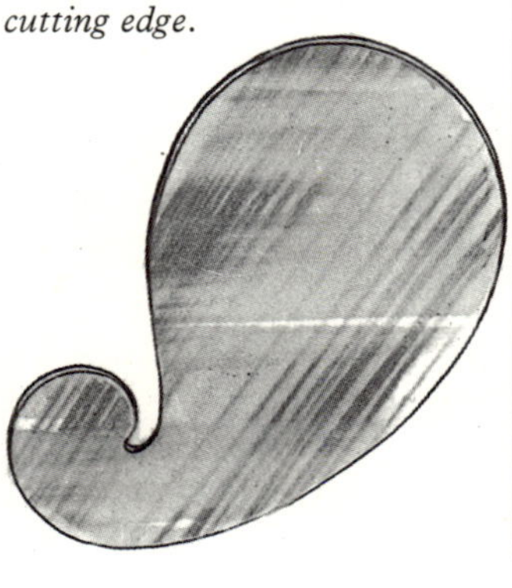

Sharpening a scraper
A cabinet scraper cuts with a burr raised on the cutting edge. Once it starts to produce dust instead of shavings it needs to be made square by draw filing, and sharpened.

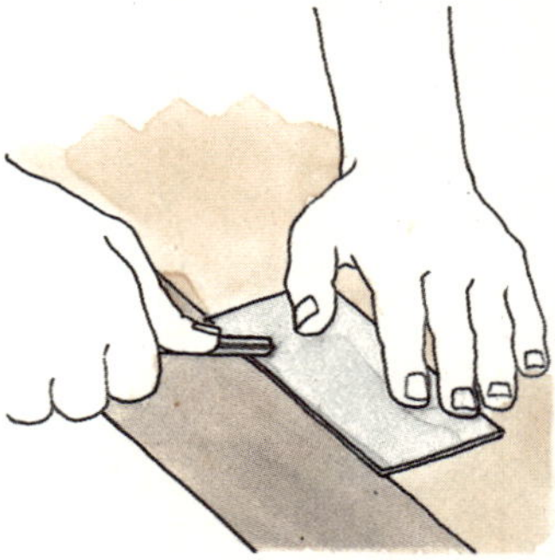

To produce a burr place the scraper flat on a bench and "draw" the burr with a round piece of steel, such as the back of a gouge. Hold the scraper against the bench with the fingers and stroke the cutting edge firmly towards you, keeping the gouge flat on the scraper. This will raise a burr perpendicular to the edge of the scraper which must then be turned over to form a sharp cutting edge.

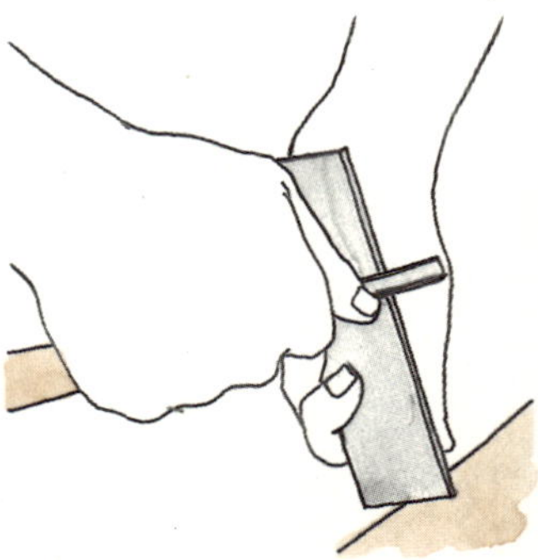

Up end the scraper on the bench and holding the gouge at a slight angle to the cutting edge, make firm vertical strokes to turn over the burr at the correct angle. If it is turned over too much, the tool will not cut well.

A shaped scraper is sharpened in the same way, but a little more practice is required to keep an even pressure on the cutting edge as you work with the back of the gouge.

Using the scraper
The amount of pressure applied by the thumbs will produce a varying curve in the cutting edge to localize the cut. Work away from you, holding the tool at a slight angle to the work. Experiment to find the most efficient angle. If a scraper is used too much in one spot, a hollow will be produced, which will show up when the surface is polished. Avoid this by working across a wider area diagonally in two directions and finishing in line with the grain.

Skarsten Scraper

OTHER NAME: Hook scraper
SIZE: *Length:* 120 to 380mm;
Blade width: 40 to 65mm
MATERIAL: *Blade:* steel;
Handle: hardwood, aluminium
ACCESSORIES: Shaped and serrated blades
USE: To smooth the surface of timber or to remove paint

The Skarsten scraper does the same job as a cabinet scraper. As well as a standard straight blade, concave, convex, serrated and double ended blades are available. The serrated blade is specially made to break up a layer of old paint, which can then be removed with the standard blade. Blades are replaced by sliding in a new one, which automatically ejects the worn blade. Double ended blades are reversed by undoing a locking screw to remove a clamp. Two kinds of handle are made, so that the tool can be used with one or two hands. For best results, work by pulling the tool toward you.

Longer handles provide extra leverage for heavy duty work such as scraping floors.

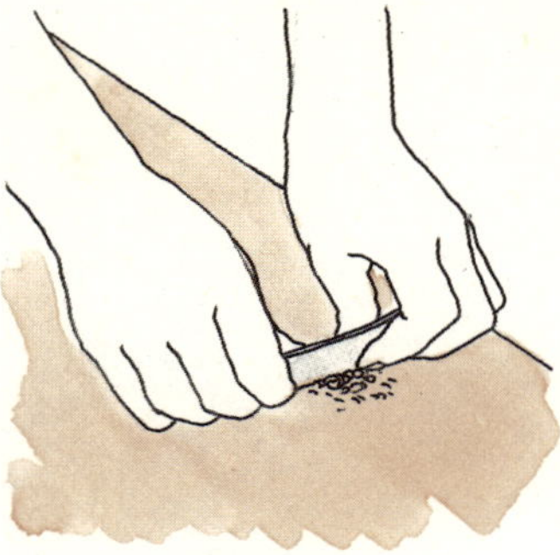

Holding the scraper
Hold the scraper in two hands with both thumbs pressed firmly into the back face close to the bottom edge.

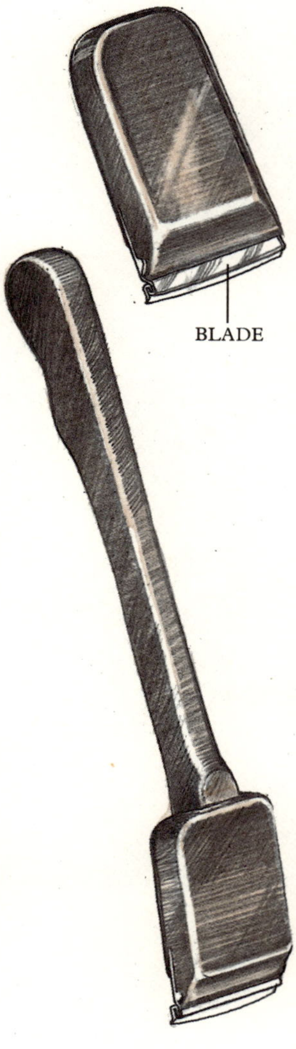

Shave Hook

SIZE: 175mm
MATERIAL: *Blade:* steel;
Handle: beech
USE: To remove old paint from mouldings

Shave hooks are made with a choice of three differently shaped blades; triangular, pear shaped and a combination blade. They are used to scrape softened paint from mouldings around windows and doors.

Paint Scraper

OTHER NAMES: Stripping knife, wallpaper scraper, chisel knife
SIZE: Blade width: 25 to 125mm
MATERIAL: *Blade:* steel;
Handle: rosewood
USE: To remove old paint and wallpaper

Paint scrapers remove softened paint or wallpaper which is unsuitable for repainting or covering. They are stronger versions of the filling knife, made in exactly the same way. The wider blades are used on wallpaper or large flat areas of paint, and the narrow blades on window frames. The narrow ones double as putty knives.

Electric Paint Stripper

SIZE: Power: 600 to 700 watts
MATERIAL: Various
USE: To soften old paintwork for stripping

Electric paint strippers contain an element which is heated and held a controlled distance from the painted surface to soften the paint. Various designs are available. They are used either in conjunction with a paint scraper or may have an integral scraper.

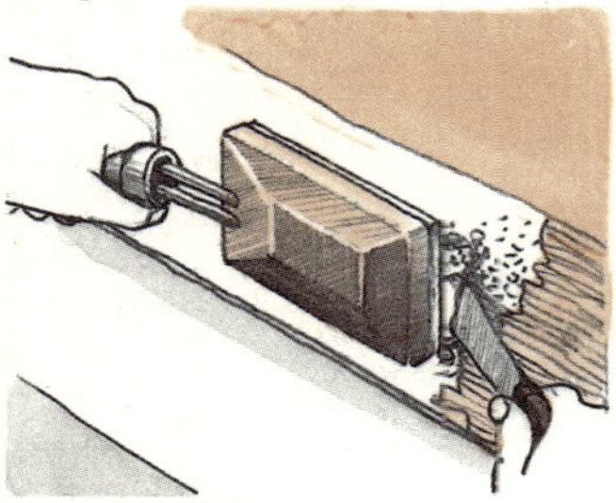

Using a paint stripper
The heating element softens the paint which is removed with a paint scraper.

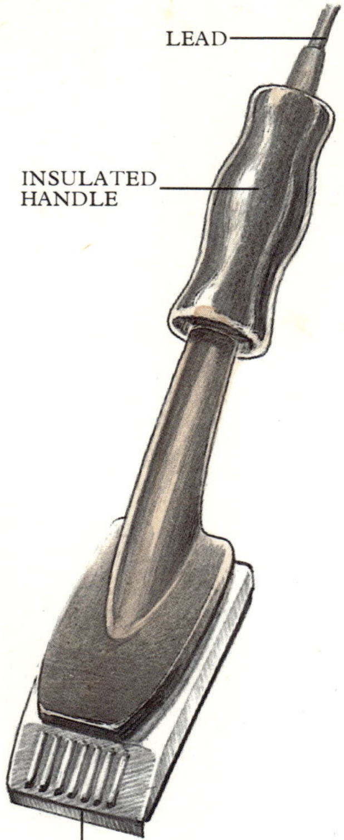

Window Scraper

SIZE: 150mm
MATERIAL: *Blade:* steel; *Holder:* plastic, hardwood and metal
ACCESSORIES: Razor blade, trimming knife blade
USE: To scrape excess paint from window panes

Any razor blade or sharp trimming knife blade can be used to remove dried paint from a window pane. The advantage of a window scraper is the holder, which keeps the blade fixed safely at the correct angle.

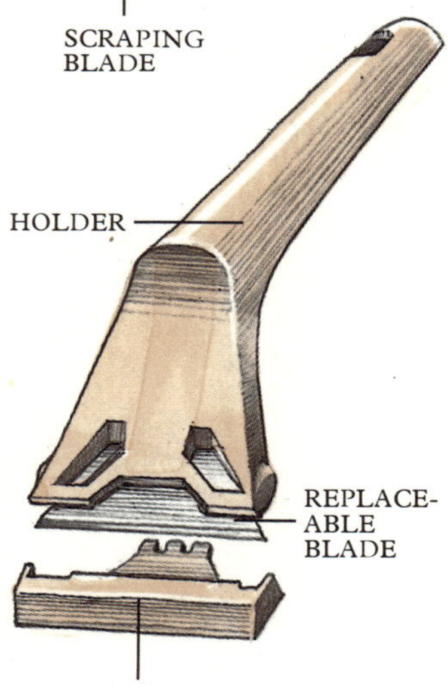

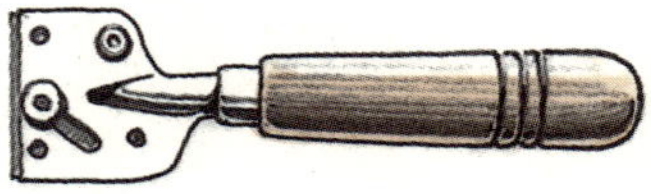

Starting flush with the frame scrape downward to remove dried paint.

Stripping old paint
Brand name chemical strippers are very effective against stubborn layers of old paint. Protect your eyes and skin, wear rubber gloves and spread newspapers on the floor.

Use an old paint brush to apply a liberal coat of stripper to the work and leave for the specified time until the paint softens.

Scrape off the paint with a shave hook or paint scraper. Apply more stripper if needed.

When all traces of paint have been removed, wash down the surface with paint thinner or cold water to neutralize the chemicals in the stripper.

Removing old wallpaper

Soak the old wallpaper with warm water or proprietary stripping solution.

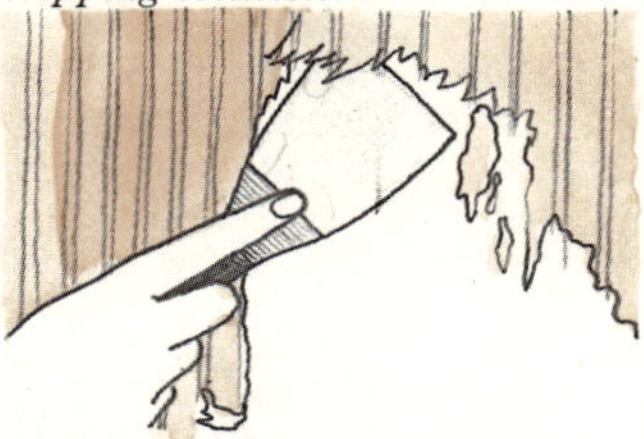

Leave for a few minutes to allow it to penetrate. Then strip the paper with a wide bladed paint scraper. Avoid digging the corners of the blade into the plaster. Re-soak any stubborn patches of paper before scraping again.

With textured, washable or painted wallpaper, first lightly scour the surface with a wire brush. This helps the solution to soak in.

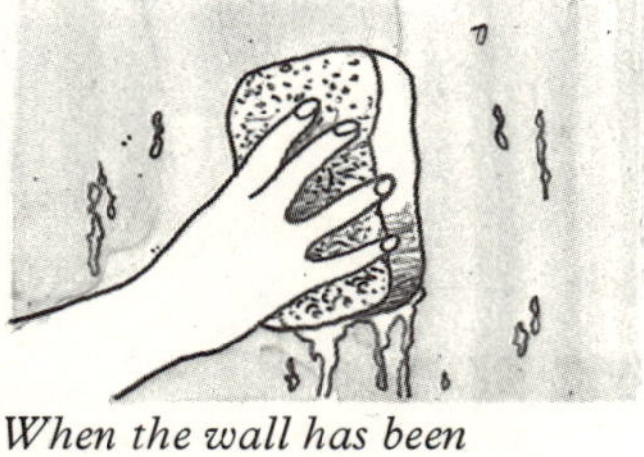

When the wall has been stripped wash the wall surface with clean hot water to remove any residue.

Blow Lamp

OTHER NAMES: Blow torch; propane lamp
SIZE: Fuel capacity: 250ml to 1l paraffin, 150 to 300g gas
MATERIALS: Various
ACCESSORIES: Flame spreader
USE: To soften old paint for stripping, to braze and solder metal

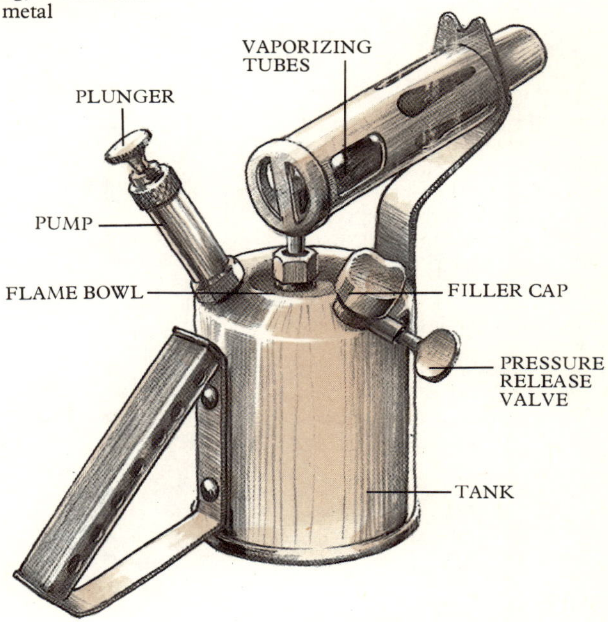

Modern blow lamps are fitted with canisters of liquefied gas which vaporizes at normal temperatures as pressure is released by operating the valve.

The more old-fashioned blow lamp uses paraffin as a fuel, which is vaporized as it is pumped through heated tubes to the jet where it is ignited. (See Propane Lamp page 275.)

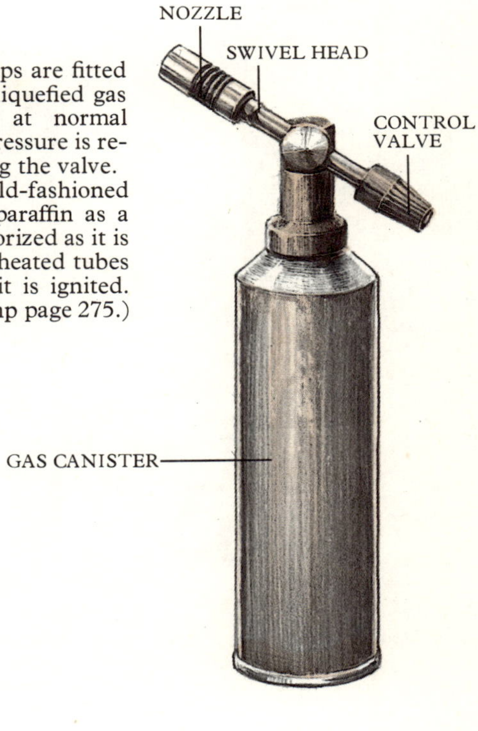

Lighting the gas lamp
The method of attaching the gas canister and operating the valve differs from model to model and the manufacturer's instructions should be carefully followed. Usually, the canister is screwed into its mounting, which automatically punctures the top of the canister or opens a valve in the canister itself.

To ignite the flame, hold a lighted match at the nozzle and regulate the flow of gas by operating the control knob. The flame can be adjusted from a small "pencil point" to a full frame spread. A flame spreader can be fitted to the nozzle to fan out the flames for efficient paint stripping.

Lighting the paraffin blow lamp
1. Fill tank three quarters full with paraffin using a funnel filter to exclude debris which might block jet.

2. Turn the pressure release knob to open the air valve.

3. Carefully fill the flame bowl with methylated spirit.

4. Guard the lamp against draughts and ignite the spirit. This will preheat the tubes to vaporize the paraffin.

5. When the flame dies down close the air valve.

6. Pump the plunger a few times. The lamp should ignite automatically.

7. If the flame does not ignite apply a lighted match to jet.

8. Increase the flame by pumping the plunger. Reduce it by opening air valve momentarily. Extinguish it by opening air valve completely.

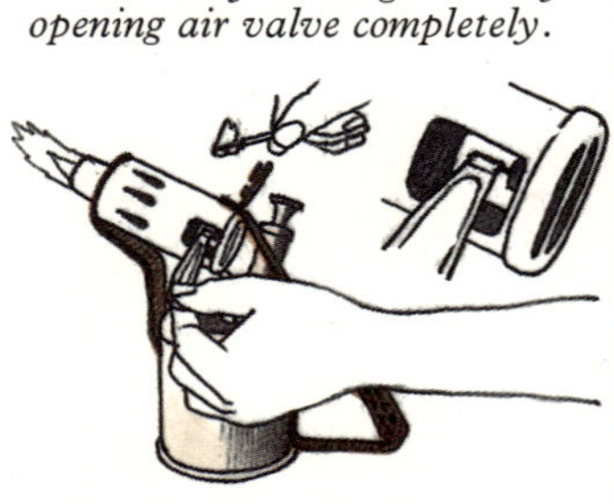

9. If the flame splutters or becomes smoky, clean out the jet with the "pricker" provided. Relight immediately.

Removing old paint with a blow lamp
Badly damaged paint will have to be completely stripped back to the wood. Radical stripping may also be necessary where successive coats of paint have obscured fine moulding.

Remove any inflammable materials from the vicinity. Make sure any burning paint falling to the ground is extinguished immediately. Work from the bottom upward to avoid scorching the stripped wood. Never hold the flame in one place for too long or the wood may char. Slight scorching can be rubbed down before repainting. When the stripping is complete rub down with sandpaper.

Mouldings
Apply heat by moving the flame across the paintwork until it softens and blisters.

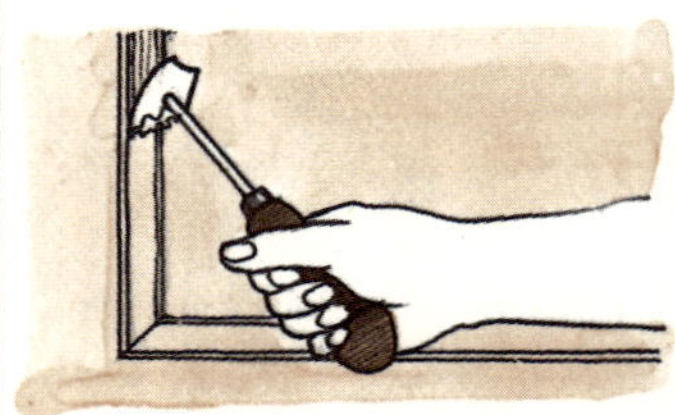

Remove the flame and scrape away the softened paint with a shave hook.

Flat paintwork
Treat in the same way, scraping off the softened paintwork with the help of a paint scraper.

Knives

The knife is one of the earliest tools of all and has played an important part in the tool kit of man, either as hunter or craftsman, from the Old Stone Age to the present day. Most Finns have two knives: "a small one for eating and a large one for working", identical in all respects except for size. Most of the rest of us have a different one for almost anything that requires cutting or shaping; the shape and size of the blade and handle and the relation between them depending on the material to be cut and the control needed to do the job properly. Some "knives" such as the putty knife, do not, in fact, cut anything; they just happen to resemble those which do.

Although in modern times various types of draw knife have been used all over western Europe by many tradesmen, particularly coopers and wheelwrights, the tool appears to have been unknown to the early civilizations of the Mediterranean area. One of the earliest known forms is the Russian *skobel*, with a curved blade from 100 to 137mm wide with a tang at each end to take wooden handles. These were found at Novgorod and date from the twelfth to the sixteenth century, the larger tools being the later. Plumbers' shaves of a similar type are shown in Felibien, but the first straight bladed draw knife occurs in Moxon's carpenter's kit (London, 1685).

Trimming Knife

OTHER NAME: Shop knife
SIZE: Various
MATERIAL: Various
ACCESSORIES: Special purpose blades for cutting linoleum, plastic laminates, wood and metal
USE: To trim various materials

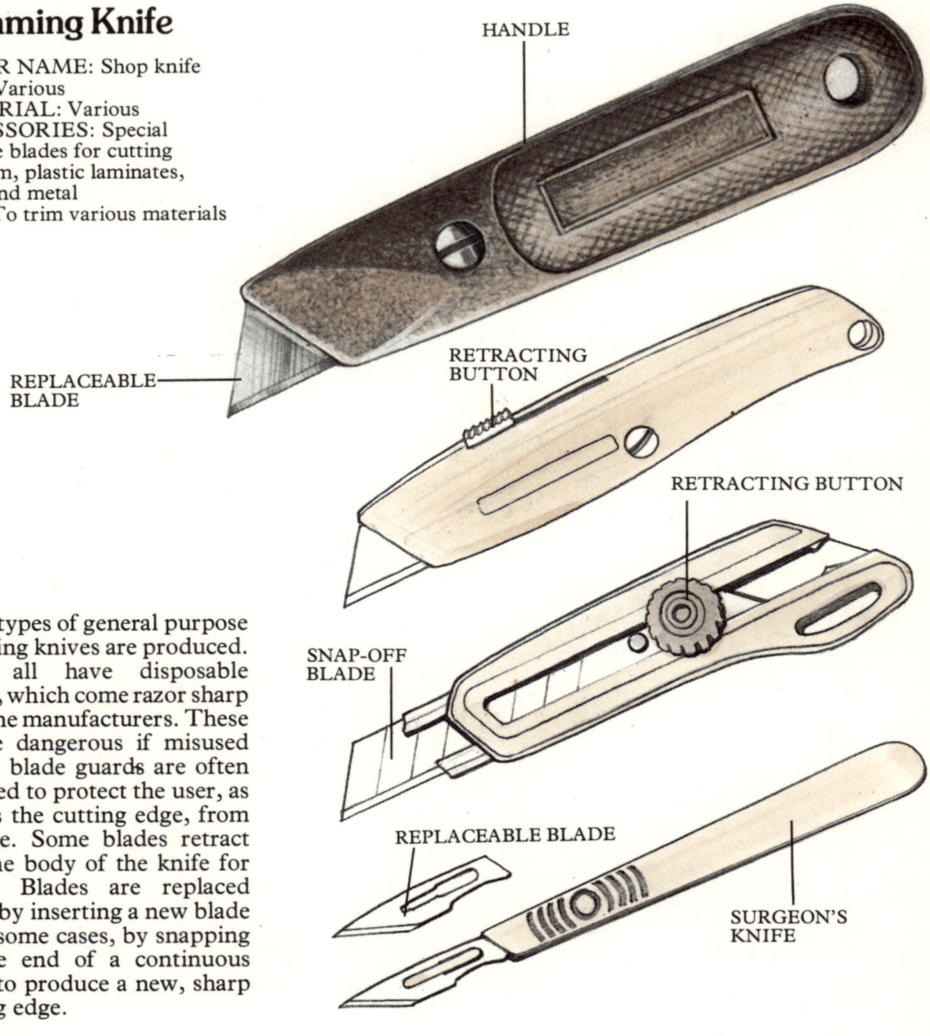

Many types of general purpose trimming knives are produced. They all have disposable blades, which come razor sharp from the manufacturers. These can be dangerous if misused and so blade guards are often supplied to protect the user, as well as the cutting edge, from damage. Some blades retract into the body of the knife for safety. Blades are replaced either by inserting a new blade or, in some cases, by snapping off the end of a continuous blade to produce a new, sharp cutting edge.

Types of blade
Special purpose blades are supplied for cutting specific materials or for better control.

STRAIGHT GENERAL PURPOSE BLADE
Used for trimming leather, paper, cardboard, plastic sheets and ceiling tiles. It can also be used to mark out wood.

HOOKED BLADES
Ideal for trimming linoleum or vinyl floor coverings. The hook, which is sharpened on the inside of the curve only, is less likely to slip out of the cut when working this kind of material. An exaggerated hook with a blunted point can be used to trim sheeting without damaging the surface beneath.

CURVED BLADES
Can be used for general trimming but are particularly useful when working materials at different angles.

PLASTIC LAMINATE BLADES
Special blades made to score this material. As the blade is pulled across the laminate the cutting edge works like a tiny "V" chisel, scoring a line in the hard surface. Use a straight edge to keep the blade true.

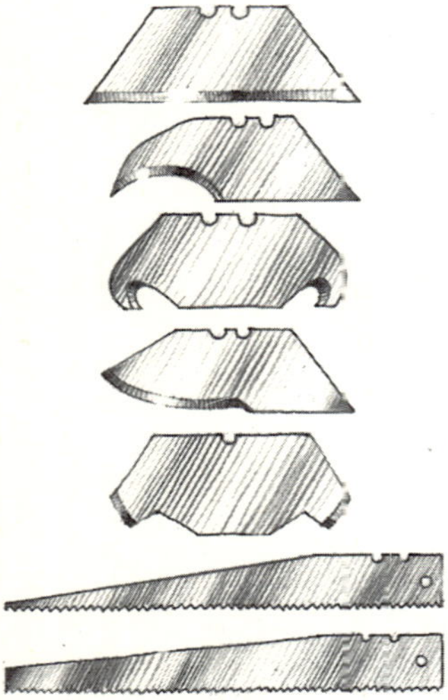

SERRATED BLADES
These convert the knife into a saw for metal and wood.

Modeller's Knives

SIZE: Handle length: 125mm
MATERIAL: *Blades:* steel; *Handle:* aluminium alloy, plastic
USE: To trim wood, plastic or cardboard for the construction of models or other fine work

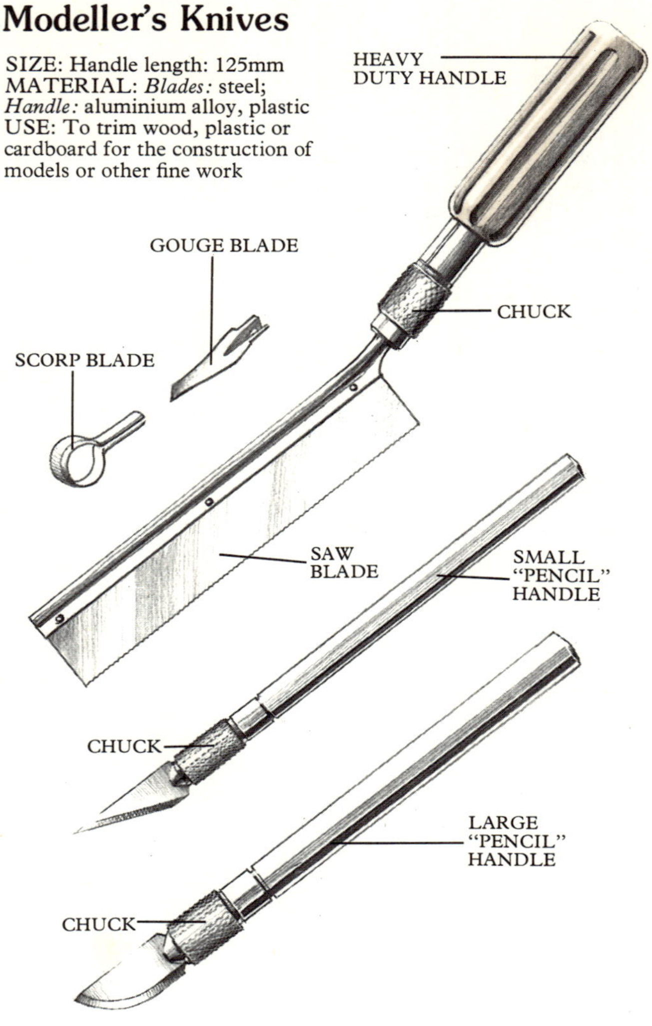

A set of modeller's knives comprises a group of handles of varying size made for different purposes, and a selection of blades to fit them.

In addition to the slimmer handles, the set also contains a handle for heavy duty work. It takes the larger knife blade, a series of gouge blades and miniature saw blades. The same handle will take miniature "scorp" blades, which cut by scooping material with a pull stroke.

The blades are held in the holder by a clamp type chuck which is tightened by turning the knurled collar.

Cutting irregular shapes

Use the slim pencil handle, which turns easily in the fingers, for cutting odd shapes free-hand or around a template.

Sheath Knife

SIZE: Various
MATERIAL: *Blade:* steel; *Handle:* hardwood, plastic, leather, steel
USE: General purpose knife

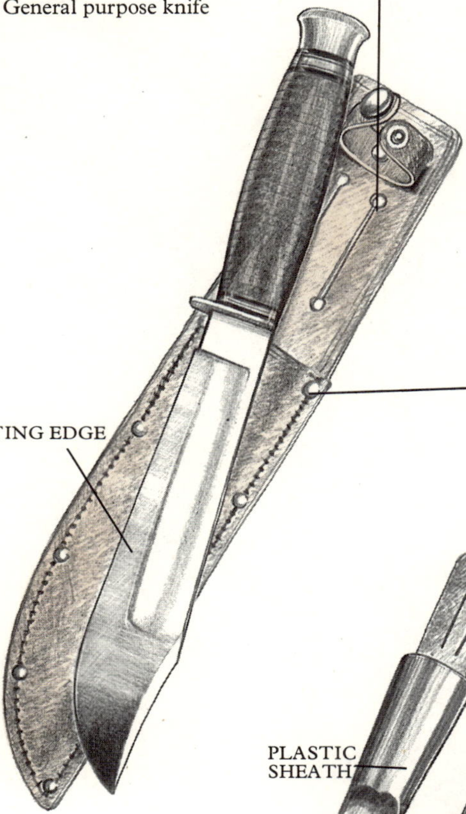

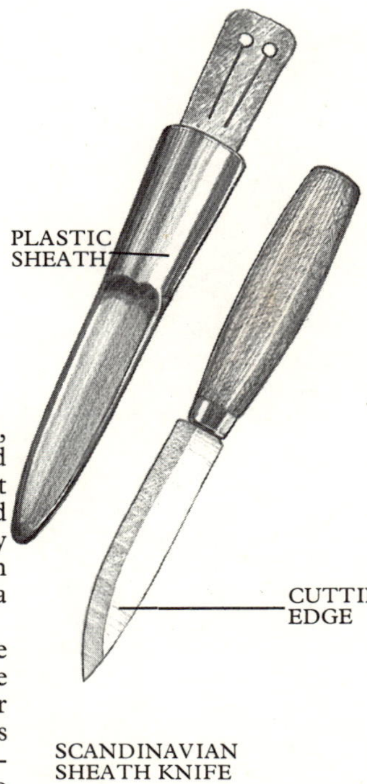

SCANDINAVIAN SHEATH KNIFE

All sheath knives have a fixed, wedge shaped blade sharpened on one edge. The blades must be as sharp as possible, and consequently are protected by a leather or plastic sheath which is normally hung on a belt around the waist.

Sheath knives are versatile tools which can carve, shape and trim wood. The larger knives have strong blades which can chop and split timber, and are indispensable to the woodsman or hunter.

Keep the blade sharp by stroking both sides of the cutting edge on or with an oilstone or slipstone. Use a circular motion. Finally, strop the blade on a leather strap.

Folding Knife

OTHER NAME: Army knife
SIZE: Various
MATERIAL: *Blades:* steel; *Handle:* various
USE: To pare and slice

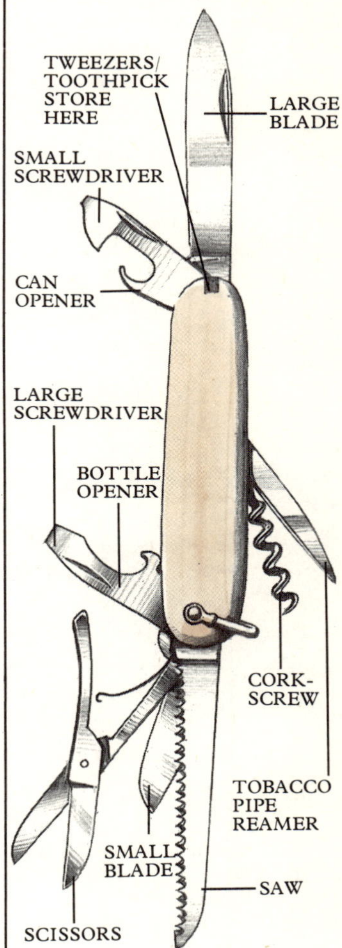

There are many versions of the folding knife, sometimes called the army knife, all of which provide a safe means of carrying a bladed tool. Some folding knives incorporate additional tools such as screwdrivers, cap lifters, bottle and can openers, reamers, files, scissors, saws, tweezers, corkscrews, and even toothpicks.

Putty Knife

OTHER NAMES: Stopping knife, glazing knife
SIZES: *Blade length:* 100 to 125mm; *Blade width:* 37 to 50mm
MATERIAL: *Blade:* steel; *Handle:* rosewood
USE: To apply putty when glazing windows

A putty knife is used to shape and smooth putty once the window glass is in place. The knives are available with straight, spearpoint or clipped point blades. The shape of the blade is a matter of choice, depending on the preference of the user. Some older knives have notches cut in the edges of the blade to "nibble" off small pieces of glass, but this feature is now obsolete.

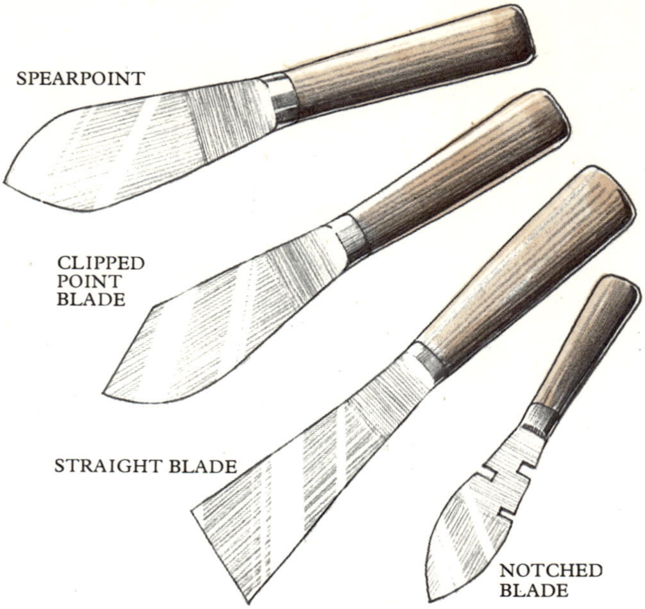

Replacing a broken window

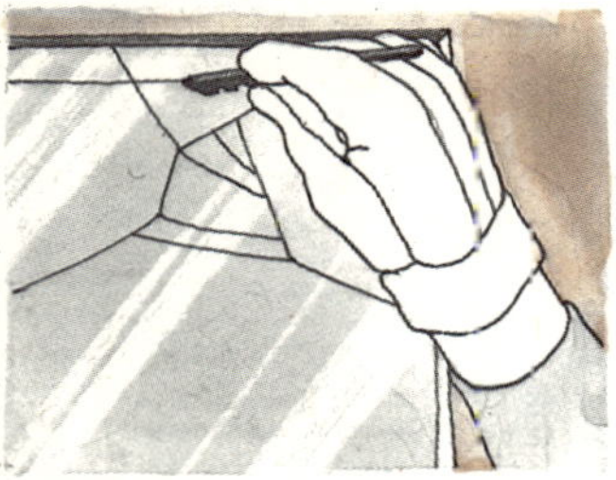

1. *Wear gloves to protect your hands. If the glass is only cracked score a line with a glass cutter approximately 25mm away from the frame and carefully remove the window in sections.*

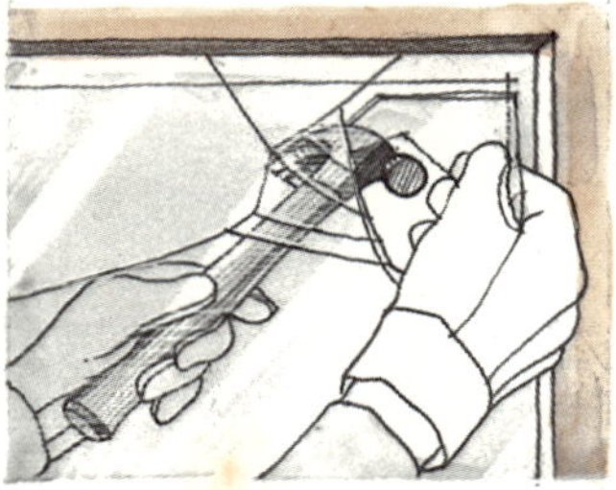

2. *Still wearing the gloves, remove any remaining broken glass from the frame by gently tapping it out from behind with a hammer.*

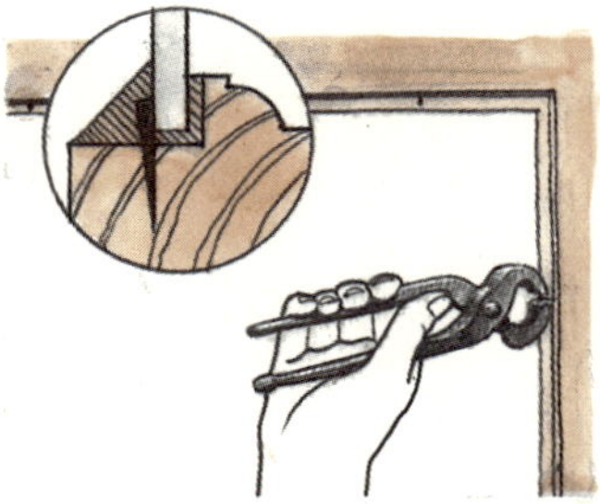

3. *Using a hacking knife or an old chisel, chip out any old putty from the frame and remove all glazing sprigs. Apply a thin layer of putty to the frame rebate and press the new sheet of glass in to it.*

4. *Secure the glass with glazing sprigs and remove excess putty with the putty knife. Roll more putty into a rope and press it into the frame with your fingers and the knife.*

5. *Occasionally dip the putty knife in water and shape the putty into an angle sloping from the glass down to the edge of the rebate.*

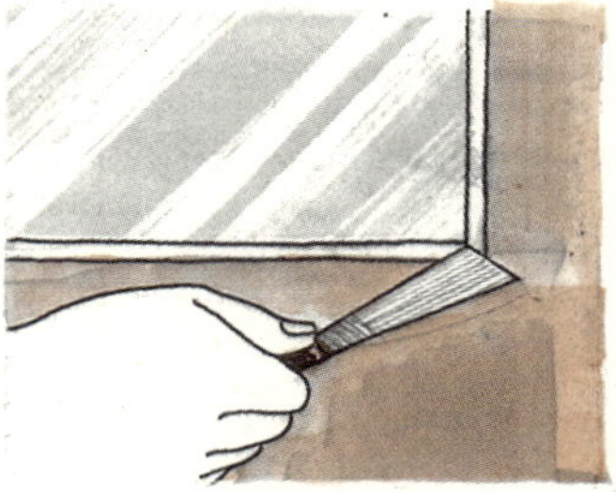

6. *Mitre the putty at the corners; an angled or "clipped" blade putty knife is particularly useful at this point. Allow the putty to dry as manufacturer recommends before painting.*

Hacking Knife

OTHER NAME: Chipping knife
SIZE: Blade length: 100 to 112mm
MATERIAL: *Blade:* steel;
Handle: leather
USE: To chop out old putty from a window frame

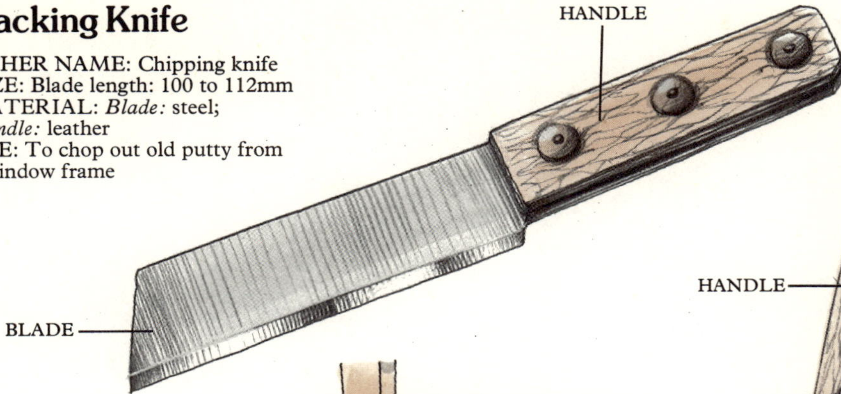

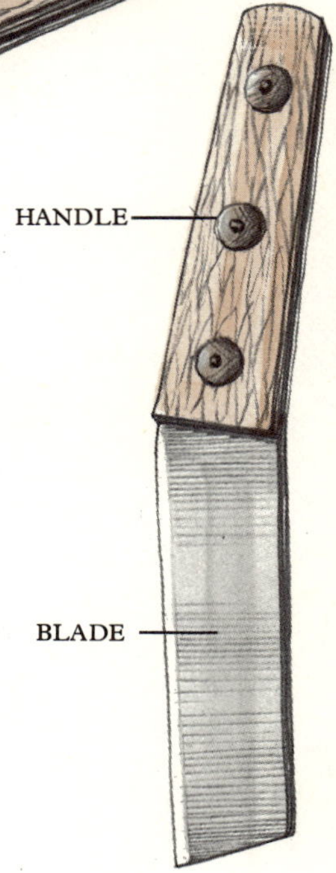

The hacking knife has a heavy blade, sharpened along the bottom edge and thickened along the top edge to withstand hammer blows. The blade has an extended point to get right into the corner of the window frame. The handle is leather and rivetted to the tang with brass rivets.

The only difference between a hacking knife and a chipping knife is the angle between the handle and the blade.

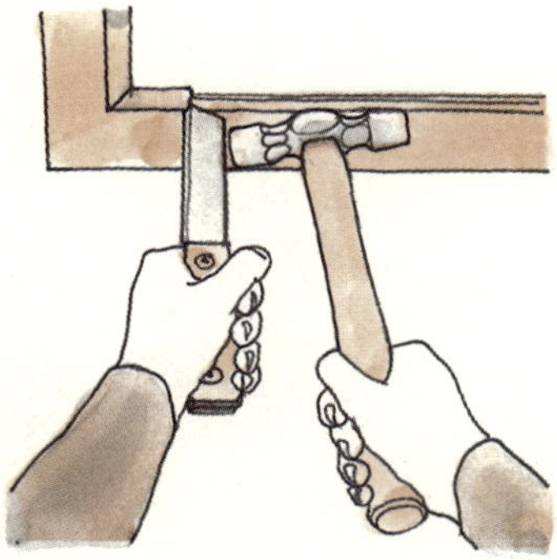

Using the knife
Hold the knife in one hand against the putty and tap the back with a hammer to move it along the frame rebate. Wear goggles to protect your eyes.

Filling Knife

SIZE: Width: 25 to 100mm
MATERIAL: *Blade:* steel:
Handle: rosewood
USE: To spread fillers in wood or plaster

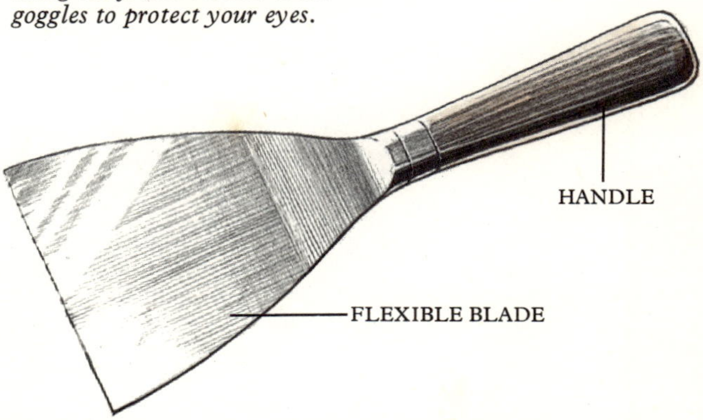

A filling knife has a flexible blade to enable it to push the filler down into the cracks or hole. Even new plaster cracks due to shrinkage and should be filled before decoration. Damp down the crack with water, if you are going to use a plaster base filler.

Filler applied in this way will often protrude slightly from the surface. This should be left, as it often contracts when drying and any irregularities can easily be sanded down afterward using fine sandpaper wrapped round a block of wood. Larger holes should be filled in stages to allow the filler to dry out thoroughly between applications.

Removing loose material
Use the corner of the knife to scrape out any loose material from the crack.

Applying filler
Scoop the filler on to the square end of the knife and run it down the crack.

Palette Knife

SIZE: Length: 100 to 300mm
MATERIAL: *Blade:* steel;
Handle: rosewood
USE: To mix paints

The palette knife has a long flexible blade used to mix and fold pigments on a board.

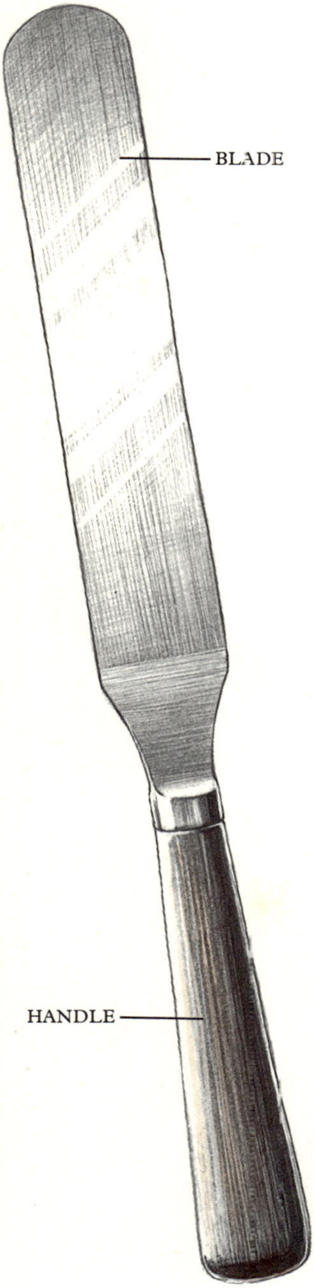

Wallpaper Trimmer

SIZES: *Cutter diameter:* 50mm;
Straight edge length: 1.8m
MATERIAL: *Housing:* zinc alloy; *Blade:* steel; *Straight edge:* aluminium
ACCESSORIES: Zinc backing strip
USE: To trim the edge from wallpaper

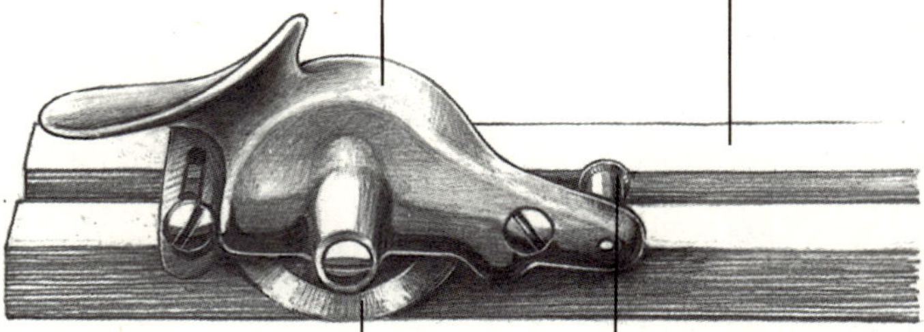

Although most modern wallpapers are ready trimmed to width, more exclusive papers still need to have the selvedge trimmed from their long edges before they can be butted together. This can be done with scissors or a straight edge and a knife, but as these wallpapers are so expensive professional paper hangers sometimes use a special purpose trimmer. This is a circular blade fitted in a cast housing which runs along a straight edge track. A zinc strip is placed under the paper which protects the table top while being soft enough to maintain the sharp edge of the cutter. The paper can be trimmed dry or pasted. The trimmer should face the near side edge of the table running from left to right.

The wallpaper trimmer is a relatively expensive tool and should be maintained. Clean any paste from the track or trimmer immediately after use and dry them thoroughly. Oil the moving parts and lightly grease the track.

Using the trimmer
With the zinc strip under the paper, align the straight edge along the cut line. Locate the rollers at the extreme lefthand end of the straight edge just before the end of the paper. Hold the straight edge in place and gently depress the thumb piece, moving the trimmer forward at the same time. Excessive pressure will damage the zinc strip and dull the cutting edge. Move the strip every few strokes. Use both sides of the strip regularly.

Paper Hanger's Knife

SIZE: Approximately 150mm;
MATERIAL: *Blade:* steel;
Handle: hardwood
USE: To trim the edge from wallpaper

Another method of trimming selvedge from wallpaper is to use a paper hanger's knife and a long straight edge. It is not a common tool today as most wallpapers are sold ready cut to width, and it is more convenient to use a trimming knife with a suitable blade than to buy a special purpose knife.

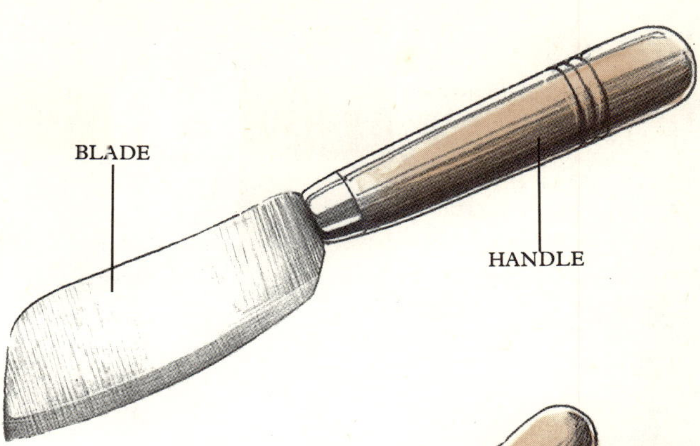

Casing Blade

OTHER NAME: Casing wheel
SIZE: Wheel diameter: 37mm;
MATERIAL: *Blade:* tool steel;
Handle: hardwood
USE: To trim excess wallpaper

Once the wallpaper has been hung, any excess can be removed by the casing blade, a sharpened steel wheel which revolves between a pair of forks. It is fitted with a handle so that it can be run along a junction of the skirting board and the wall, around light switches, light fittings and door and window frames to remove unwanted wallpaper.

A toothed wheel is available which is more suitable for delicate wallpapers.

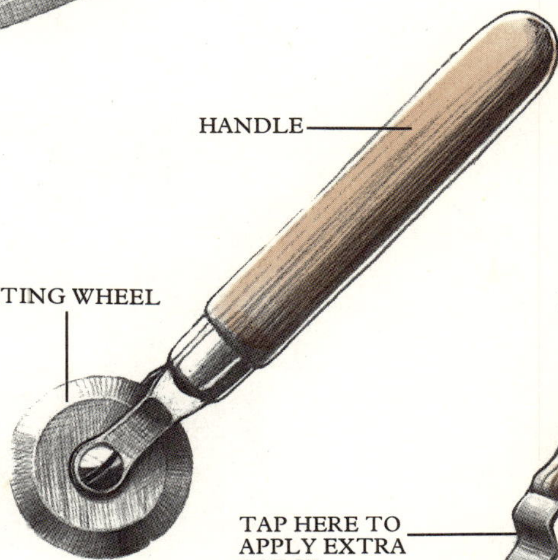

Slater's Ripper

OTHER NAME: Shingle nail remover
SIZE: 275 to 375mm;
MATERIAL: Steel
USE: To cut through the nails holding shingles or slates to the roof timbers.

Removing a single slate for repair is a difficult job as each row of roof slates overlaps the previous one, at the same time covering up the nails that fix them to the roof timbers. The ripper makes the job easier. It has a long, thin blade terminating in a sharpened hook on either side.

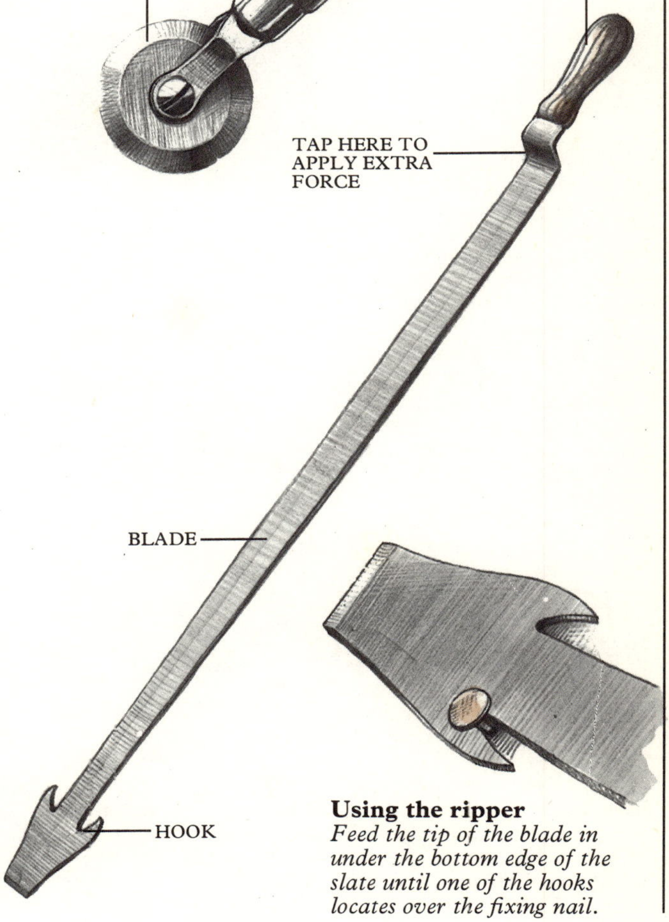

Using the ripper
Feed the tip of the blade in under the bottom edge of the slate until one of the hooks locates over the fixing nail.

Draw Knife

OTHER NAME: Drawing knife
SIZE: Blade length: 125 to 325mm
MATERIAL: *Blade:* steel;
Handles: hardwood
USE: To rough shape straight and curved lumber sections

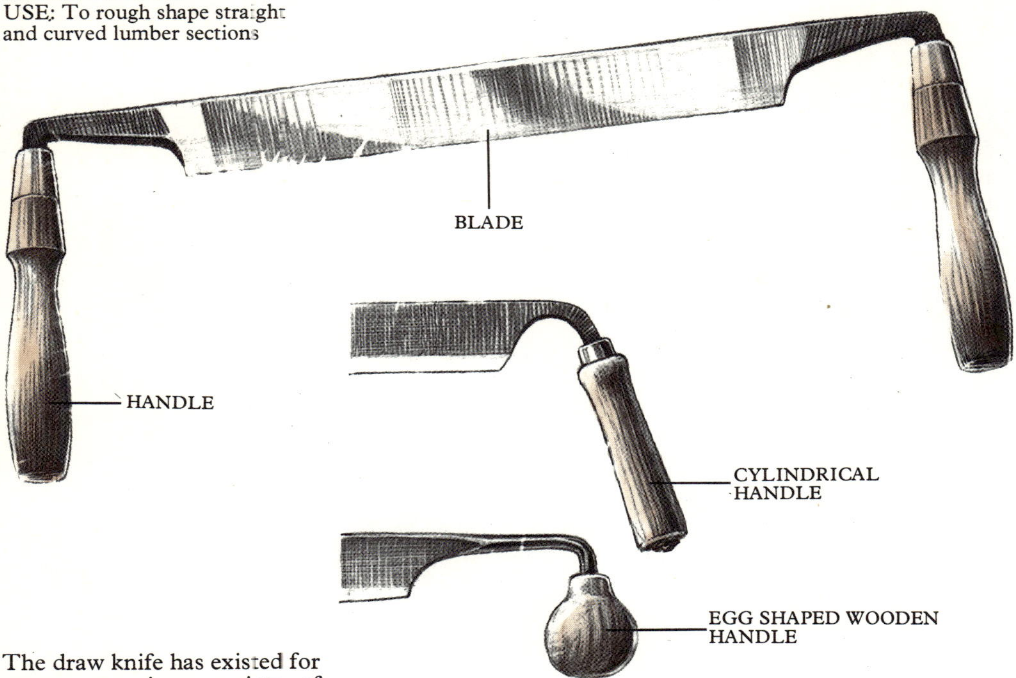

The draw knife has existed for many years in a variety of forms to suit various trades, but its main task is to shape timber sections roughly to size before applying a plane or spokeshave to the work.

The common form of draw knife has a flat blade, beveled on the top front edge only. The blade may have parallel back and cutting edges, or one curved blade, or only the cutting edge may be curved for slicing. This kind of knife is sometimes known as the English draw knife. However shaped, the blade is formed with a tang at each end which is bent round in the direction of the cutting edge, either at right angles or flared slightly outwards. Fitted to these tangs are hardwood handles which may be roughly cylindrical or spherical and egg shaped. The choice is a matter of personal preference. The knife must be kept as sharp as a chisel to work efficiently. Rest one handle on a bench and hone the cutting edge with an oilstone.

Convex and concave curves

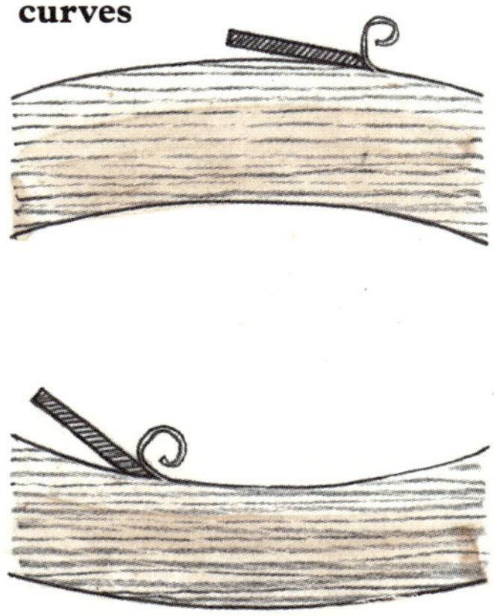

For convex curves use the tool bevel uppermost, but for concave work turn the knife over, so the bevel faces downward. This will prevent it cutting too deeply into the wood.

The cutting action

Always pull the knife toward you controlling the depth of the cut by the angle at which the blade is presented to the work. Cut with the grain to avoid tearing the work.

Scorp

OTHER NAME: Round shave
SIZE: Blade diameter: 50 to 100mm
MATERIAL: *Blade:* steel;
Handle: hardwood
USE: To cut deep hollows in lumber

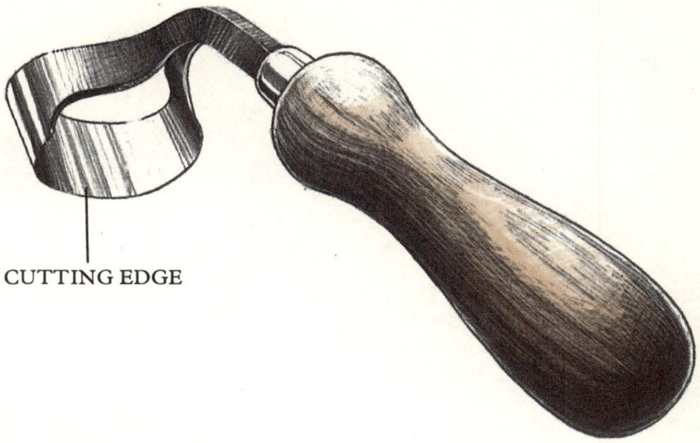

The scorp is a draw knife that has been bent completely into a circle with both tangs fitted into one handle. It is used to hollow out objects such as wooden bowls, and is operated one handed, being pulled toward the worker like a regular draw knife.

Inshave

OTHER NAME: Round shave
SIZE: Blade diameter 50 to 100mm
MATERIAL: *Blade:* steel;
Handle: hardwood
USE: To cut deep concave shapes in lumber

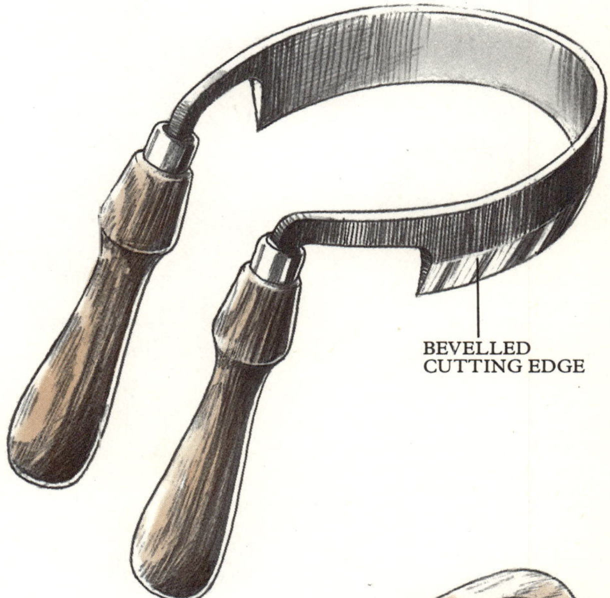

The inshave is like a regular draw knife bent into a tight curve. It is bevelled on the outside face to enable it to cut deep hollows for bowls and chair seats. It is used two handed, pulled toward the worker like a draw knife.

Wood Carver's Hook

SIZE: Overall length: 200mm
MATERIAL: *Blade:* steel;
Handle: hardwood
USE: Multi-purpose carving knife

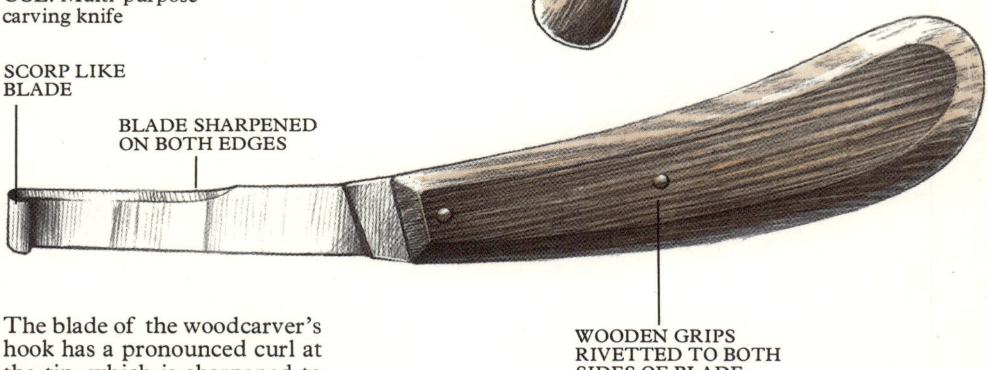

The blade of the woodcarver's hook has a pronounced curl at the tip, which is sharpened to form a scoop to rough out hollows in timber. The blade is also sharpened on both long edges. The hook is pulled toward the worker, like a scorp.

Chip Carving Knives

SIZE: Overall length 125 to 162mm
MATERIAL: *Blade:* steel; *Handles:* hardwood
USE: To carve low relief decoration in wood

Chip carving knives are made in various forms to produce the low relief carving popularly known as "chip" carving, usually a series of geometrical shapes. Some blades are sharpened on both edges for cutting toward and away from the carver; there are also chisel-like cutters, usually with an angled end, which are suitable for chip carving.

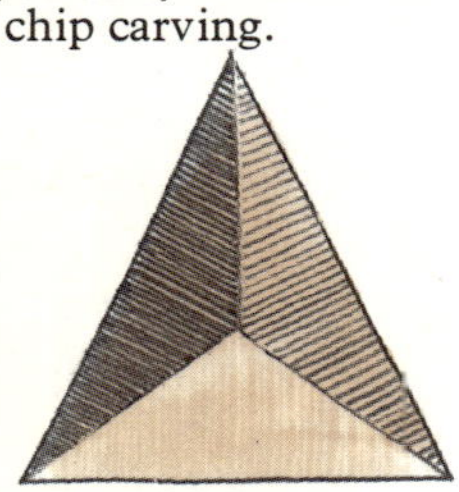

Producing a cut
A typical motif used in chip carving is the reverse three-sided pyramid. A chisel type knife with an angled end is ideal for this type of cut. The first cuts are always the vertical cuts along the lines A–D, B–D, C–D. These must meet in the center at the required depth and should run out to the surface at the points of the triangle. The sloping pyramid sides are then sliced out to produce a clean face.

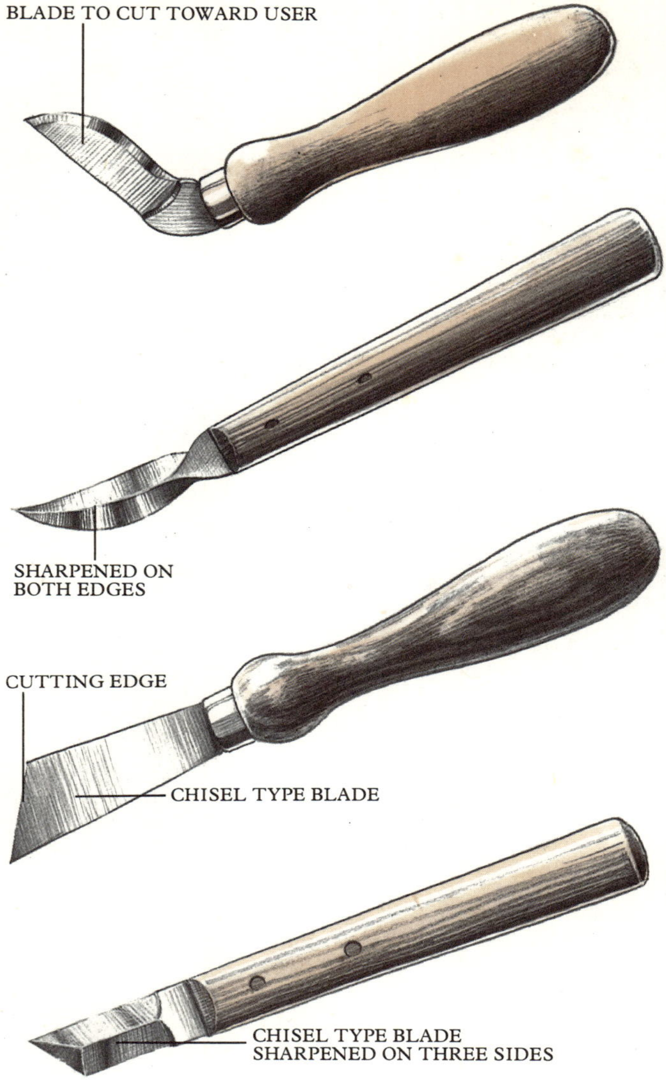

Marking Knife

SIZE: 150mm
MATERIAL: *Blade:* steel; *Handle:* hardwood
USE: To mark timber for cutting

Most marking knives are ground on one side of blade only so that the flat face can run against a try square when marking across the work. Hold the knife as you would a pencil and make firm strokes. The cut is square on the finished side of the line and bevelled on the waste side which results in a square shoulder, but leaves a clear line for the saw to follow.

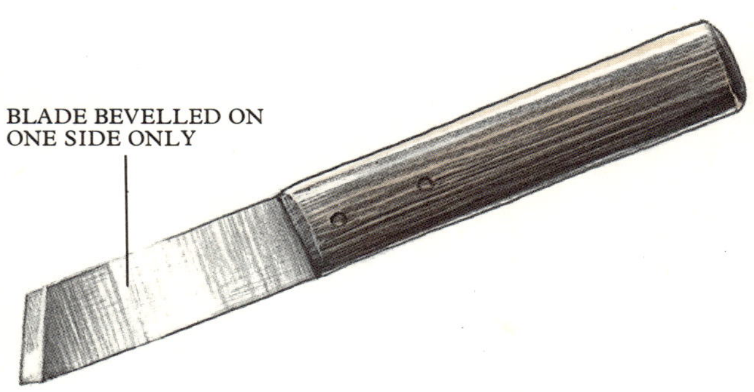

Round Knife

OTHER NAMES: Half round knife, head knife, half moon knife
SIZE: Diameter: up to 150mm
MATERIAL: *Blade:* steel; *Handle:* hardwood
USE: To cut leather

The round knife is a versatile tool used to work thick leather. Its curved blade, sharpened along the entire edge, produces an ideal slicing action. Small trimming jobs can easily be executed by simply rocking the blade across the leather.

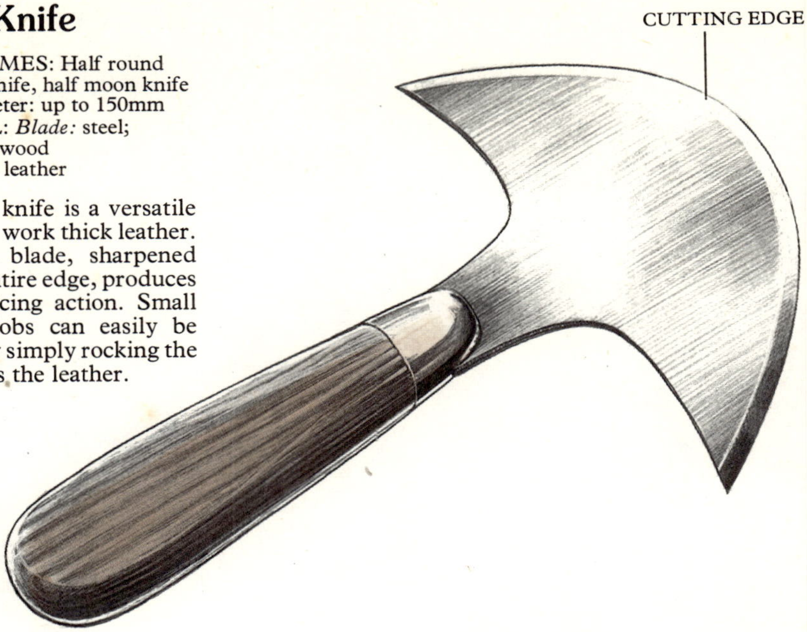

Using the round knife

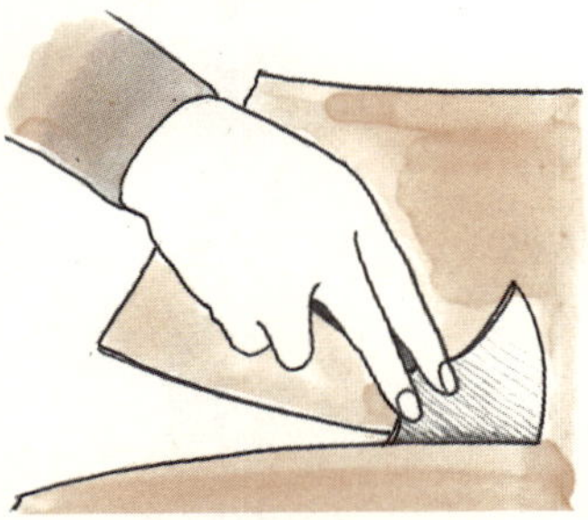

1. *Lift the edge of the leather and push the round knife along the cut line keeping the centre of the curved blade in line with the edge of the leather.*

2. *Or pull the knife through the leather holding it the other way around and standing to one side of the work. This is useful for long cuts.*

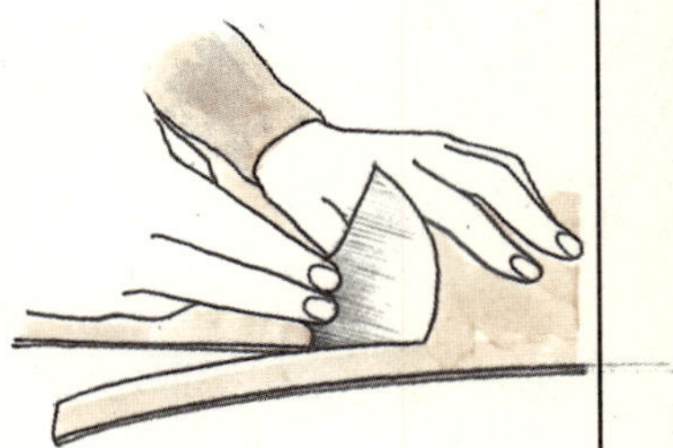

3. *Use the edge of the bench as a straight edge guide to cut a narrow strip. Keep the bottom half of the blade pressed against the front bench edge.*

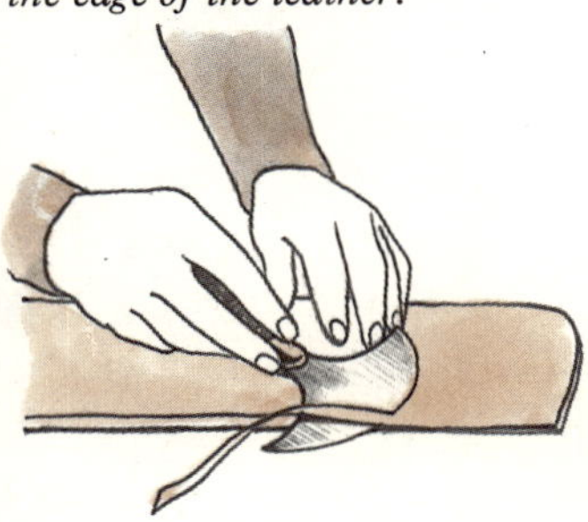

4. *Reducing the thickness of a hide is called "skiving". Reverse the leather and line up its edge with the bench edge. Hold the knife at the angle of the required bevel and push.*

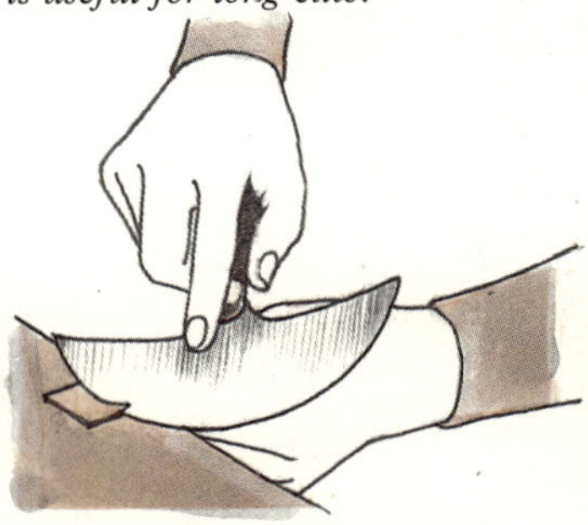

5. *Skive the ends of straps by supporting the strap on the bench and pushing the knife away from you, resisting the pull on the strap with your other hand.*

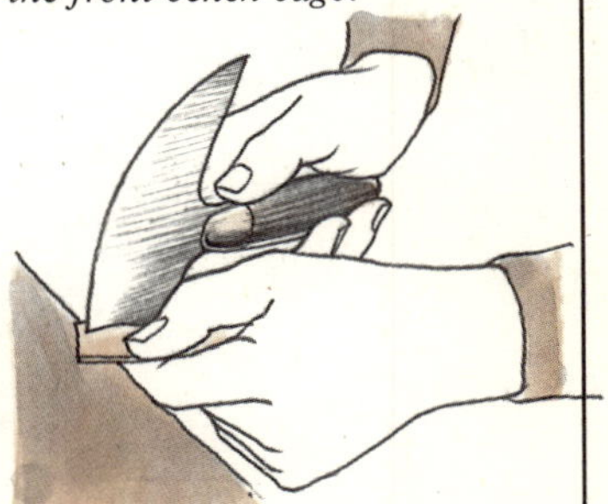

6. *Shape the ends with a similar action. Turn the knife on its edge and rest the lower end of the blade against the edge of the bench. Guide and pull the leather against it.*

Plough Gauge

OTHER NAMES: Strap cutter, saddler's plough knife, draw gauge
SIZE: To cut straps up to 125mm wide
MATERIAL: Steel; sometimes fitted with hardwood handle
USE: To cut straps from thick leather

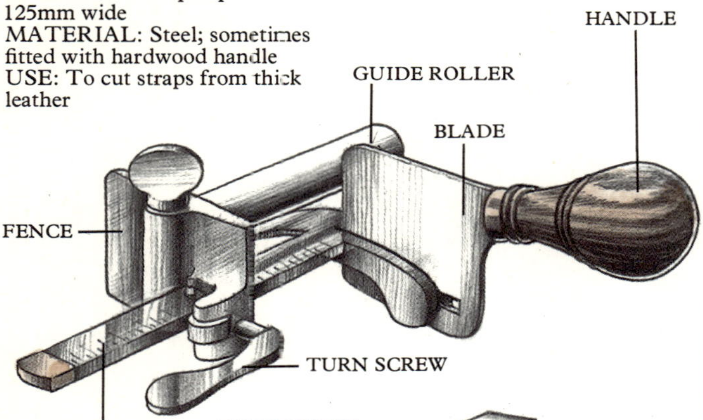

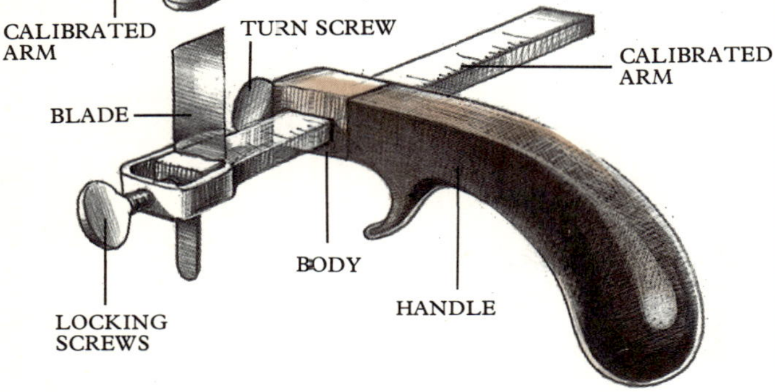

The plough gauge jigs a knife and fence to cut parallel slips of leather from a hide to make straps. Some models are designed to be pushed through the leather, while others, known as draw gauges, are pulled toward the worker. In either case the blade is held firmly by a locking screw. The fence slides on a calibrated arm and can be locked in place by a turn screw. The arm on a draw gauge passes through the body of the tool and is locked by a turn screw in the nose.

Using the plough gauge

Cut one edge of the leather straight. Set the fence to the required width.

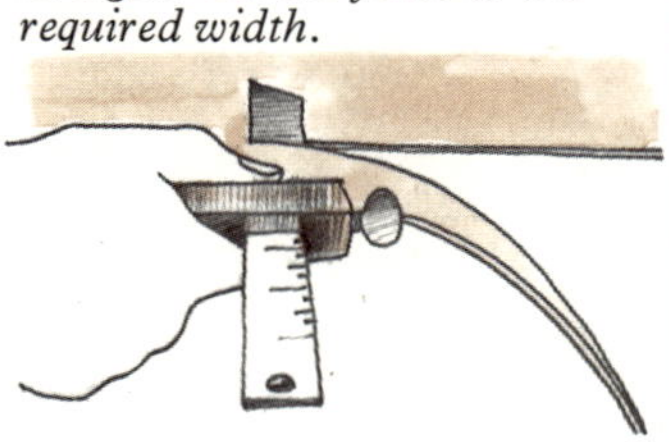

Push or pull the blade through the hide insuring that the fence runs against the straight edge.

Shoe Knife

OTHER NAME: Bevel point knife
SIZE: 112mm
MATERIAL: *Blade:* steel; *Handle:* rosewood, beech
USE: To trim leather

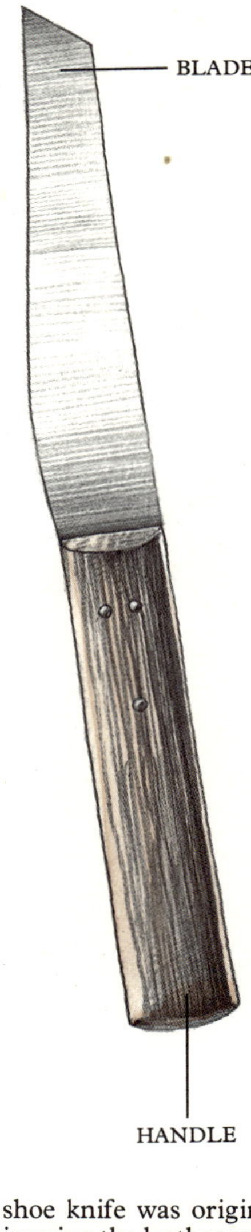

The shoe knife was originally for trimming the leather sole of a shoe, but has remained in modern catalogues as a general purpose knife. It can be used with a straight edge to cut leather to shape and makes a reasonable skiving knife with the edge of the leather supported, flesh side up, on the edge of the bench.

Edge Shave

OTHER NAME: Edge beveller
SIZE: Width of cut: 6 to 31mm
MATERIAL: *Blade:* steel;
Handle: hardwood
USE: To bevel the edge of leather

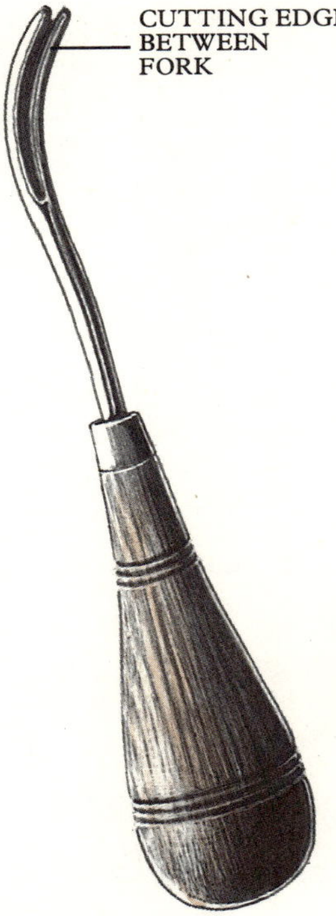

The working end of the edge shave is like a blunt two-pronged fork which is sharpened in between. It is used to finish the straight edges of leather work by cutting a bevel. This finishing bevel can be cut on both flesh and the grain side of the leather.

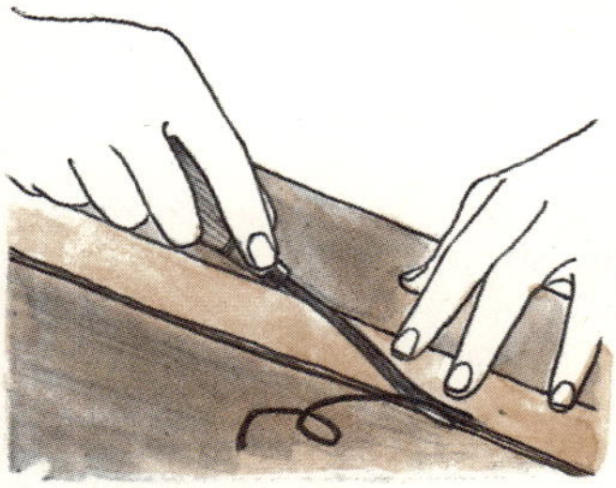

Using the shave
Hold the tool at the angle of the required bevel and push it away from you along a straight edge.

Lawn Edging Knife

SIZE: Length: 900 to 950mm
MATERIAL: *Blade:* steel;
Handle: hardwood, tubular steel, aluminum
USE: To cut back the edge of a lawn

Untidy or overgrown lawn edges can be cut back with a spade, but a better tool is the edging knife. The curved cutting edge will slice through the turf leaving a crisp edge.

Using the edging knife
Set up a straight line with two stakes and a length of string and cut along this line by pressing down on the tool.

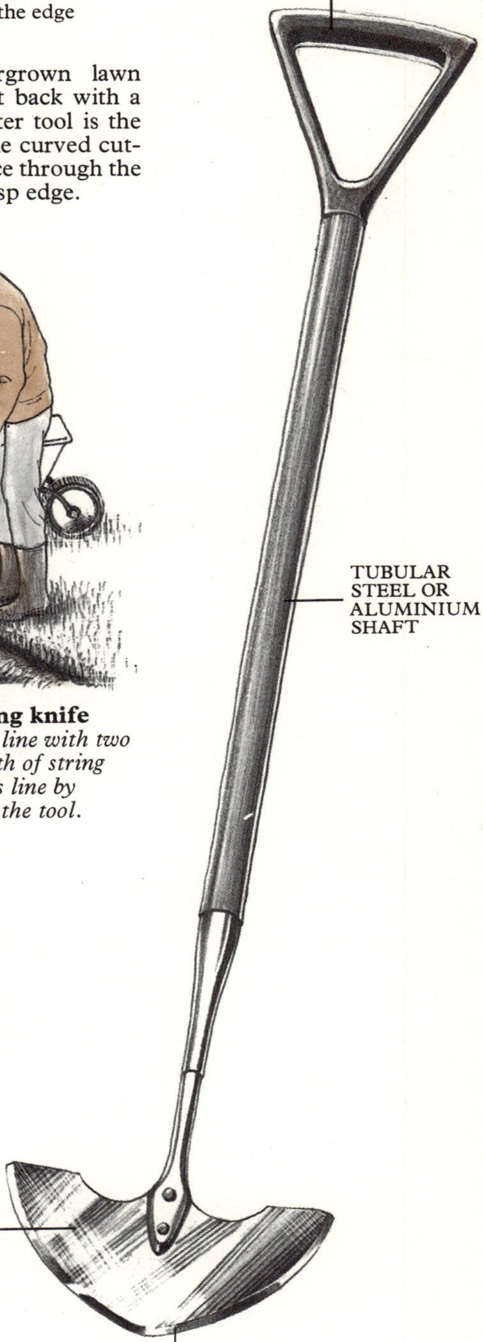

Staple Gun

OTHER NAME: Tacker gun
SIZE: Takes 6 to 15mm staples
MATERIAL: Various
USE: To drive staples

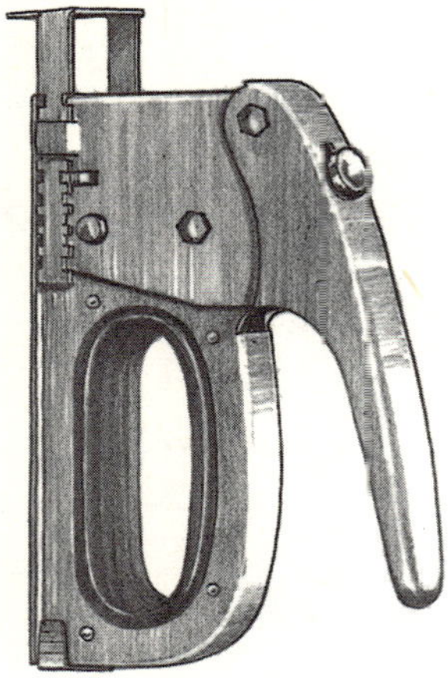

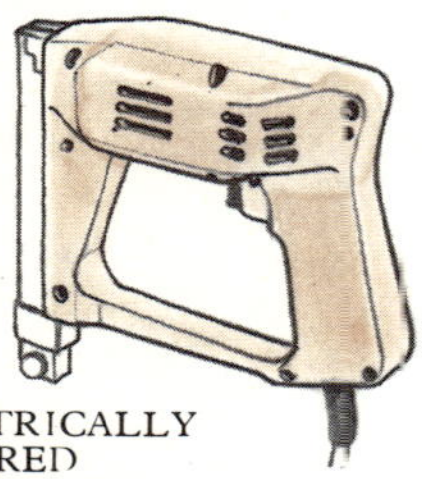

ELECTRICALLY POWERED STAPLE GUN

A staple gun drives staples for attaching a variety of materials. It is particularly useful when upholstering, as you can pull the fabric tight with one hand while operating the stapler with the other. It is also used for fitting carpets, wire netting, ceiling tiles, insulation and many other materials previously fixed by hand nailing.

The simple, hand operated gun has a magazine which is loaded with a strip of steel staples. The trigger lever is depressed, releasing a spring loaded striker which drives one staple at a time into the material. A dial regulates the force on the striker. On the nose of some tools is a reversible fence which can be extended to act as a guide for stapling in straight lines. It can be pressed against an upright surface, or when reversed, can be hooked over an edge.

Electrically powered staple guns drive heavy duty staples.

Hammers and Mallets

The original hammer was a stone held in the hand. Vase paintings show that Greek bronzesmiths were still using them in this way down to fourth century BC. Hammers with handles and metal heads followed the same sequence as axes. They were made of bronze, iron and finally steel and were fitted at first into a bent wooden handle and later provided with a shaft-hole or eye.

The medieval carpenter's hammer had an iron head of square section with a wedge shaped pein. This type is still widely used in Europe, but in England the striking head was made with a circular face and was known as the "Exeter" or "London" pattern. Modern carpenter's and engineer's hammers bring the cross pein up to the centre line of the head, with a neck on either side of the eye. This pattern was introduced early in the nineteenth century and is known as the "Warrington".

The claw hammer was used by carpenters even in Roman days and often occurs in medieval pictures; it is still the general purpose hammer for many trades. This is because most carpentry and allied crafts are mainly woodwork, built around or held together with nails and the claw is handy for pulling them out if necessary. Unfortunately this tends to loosen or strain the handle. Some types, especially those with slender handles, are fitted with straps fixed with screws or rivets, to spread the leverage. The modern solution, introduced about a century ago, was to deepen the eye to make it like an adze.

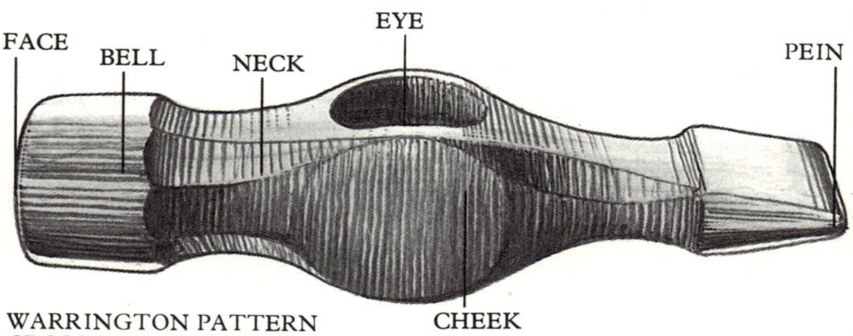

WARRINGTON PATTERN CROSS-PEIN HAMMER HEAD

MALLETS

The earliest mallets were a kind of club or cudgel, taken from a tree. The Egyptians used short lengths of hardwood shaped like a carver's or mason's mallet. The Roman mallet, round in section and slightly curved, with the handle fixed in a hole in the head became the standard in Europe; the English version, with a square section head and only the top curved, dates from the Middle Ages.

Replacing the handle

Cut off a damaged or broken handle near the head of the hammer and drive out the remaining portion.

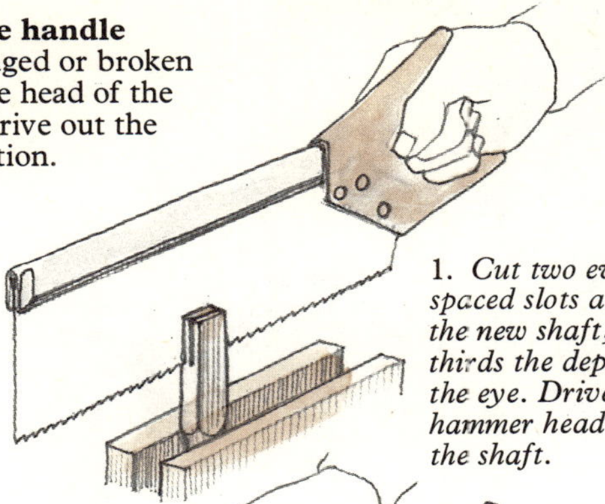

1. *Cut two evenly spaced slots across the new shaft, two thirds the depth of the eye. Drive the hammer head on to the shaft.*

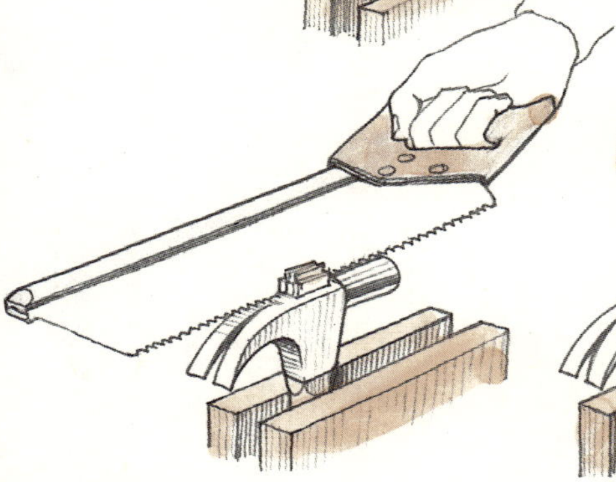

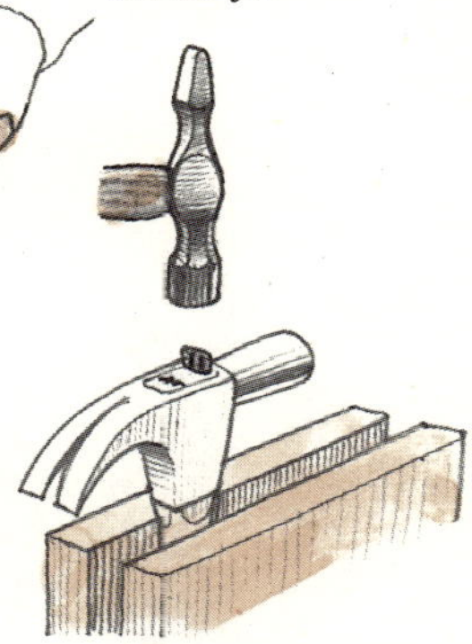

2. *Cut the shaft flush. Place the hammer in a warm oven for about one hour to dry the shaft thoroughly.*

3. *Drive in the metal wedges, tapping them alternately to spread the shaft evenly in the head. Grind or file the wedges flush and varnish exposed wood.*

Setting a nail

If working in hardwood, first drill a pilot hole to prevent splitting. Hold the hammer toward the end of the shaft, where it will feel balanced and you can apply greatest force.

If the nail is small, use the cross pein to start it off. When the nail is firm and upright drive home with full strokes. If you are using a very small nail, push it through a piece of thin cardboard or stiff paper. This makes it easier to hold while setting. Pull the paper clear of the pin before driving below the surface.

On display work finish with light taps taking care not to mark the work. Drive the nail flush with a nail set. If the work does become dented, immediately soak the local area with warm water. This will raise the grain and hopefully the dent with it. Sand the surface when dry.

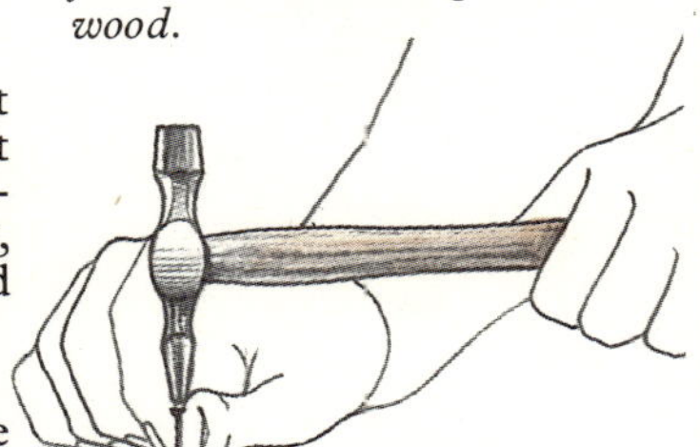

Hold the nail on the work between thumb and fingers and lightly tap it into the wood.

Support small nails in cardboard and drive with a hammer until just above the surface.

METHODS OF NAILING

Dovetail nailing

To insure a firm fixing, angle alternative nails in different directions and drive them home in the normal way.

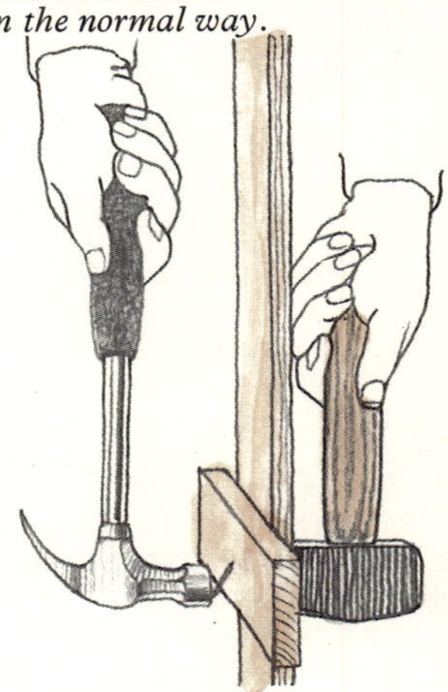

Clinching a nail

When a nail is long enough to pass through both halves of the work it can be bent over to clamp the fixing. Drive the nail flush with the surface, rest a heavy hammer against the head and bend the pointed end over to lie parallel with the grain with sideways blows from a second hammer. Place the work on a firm surface and drive the bent nail flush with the surface of the wood.

Blind nailing

Chisel up a sliver of wood, drive the nail below the surface with a nail set and glue back the sliver to cover the head.

Straightening a bent nail

Revolve a bent nail on a vice and straighten with light taps from a hammer.

Claw Hammer

SIZE: Head weight: up to 570g
MATERIAL: *Head:* steel;
Shaft: hickory, steel, fibre glass
USE: General carpentry work
and nail pulling

The claw hammer derives its name from the curved split pein which is used to pull nails, either when dismantling work or when replacing a bent nail. A good claw should be tapered on the underside as well as toward the eye in order to grip all sizes of nail heads.

The general purpose hammer is known as the "curved claw" and is probably the most widely used. A "straight claw" is available for levering up boards or laps. The claw is driven between the boards which are then levered up by the handle. This hammer is also known as a "ripping claw" or "framing hammer".

To withstand the force of levering boards or even pulling nails it is essential that the head be firmly attached to the shaft and to this end the "adze eye hammer" was developed. The adze eye, which is almost twice as deep as that of a standard hammer, is tapered to allow the hickory shaft to be spread by wedges. Modern steel or fibre glass shafted hammers are even stronger, the head being permanently fitted to the shaft. A rubber sleeve is fitted to the shaft to provide a comfortable shock-absorbing grip. Grease from the hand can cause the rubber grip to become slippery, but this is easily remedied by lightly scrubbing the grip with a nail brush using a mild detergent solution.

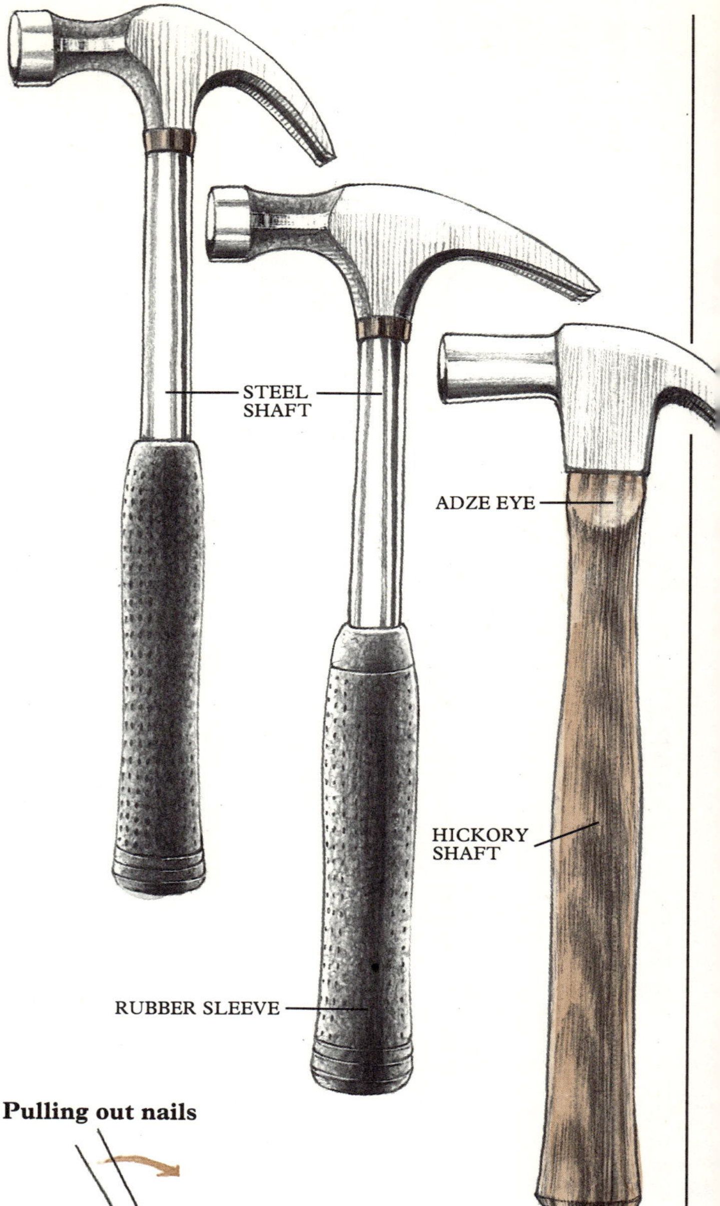

Nail pulling
A claw hammer by itself can only draw a partially driven nail. Slide the claw under the head and withdraw the nail by pulling on the handle.

In rough work, pull a driven nail through the workpiece by jamming the claw on to the shaft of the nail until it bites into the metal. Lever on the handle pulling the nail right through the workpiece.

Pulling out nails

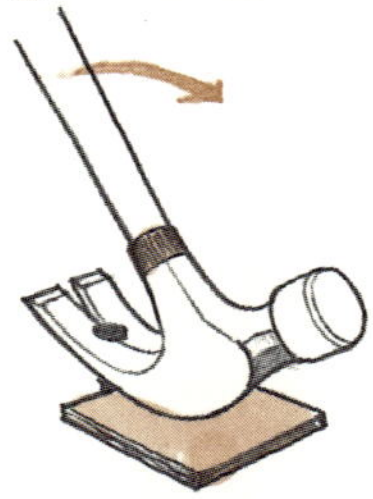

Protect the surface of the work by placing a piece of hardboard under the head of the hammer.

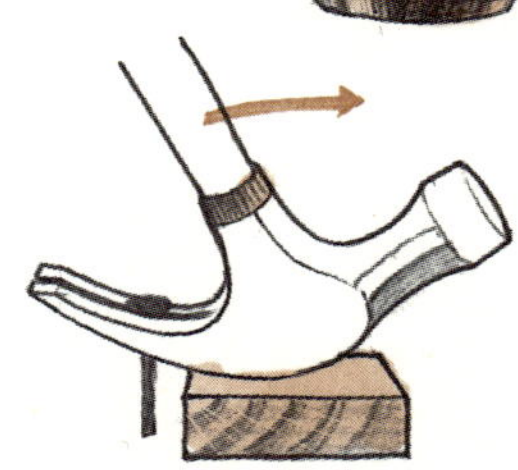

To withdraw a long nail, proceed in stages, using a block of wood to raise the hammer head to provide leverage.

Pin Hammer

OTHER NAME: Telephone hammer
SIZE: Head weight: up to 110g
MATERIAL: *Head:* alloy steel; *Shaft:* ash, hickory
USE: To drive pins or tacks

The pin hammer is a lightweight hammer ideally suited for driving small pins or tacks. Cross pein or ball patterns are available.

Its alternative name derives from the fact that telephone linesmen use it to fix cable.

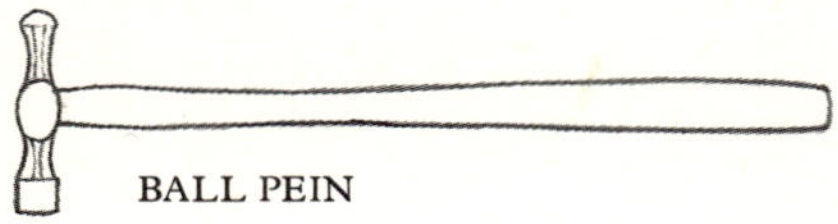

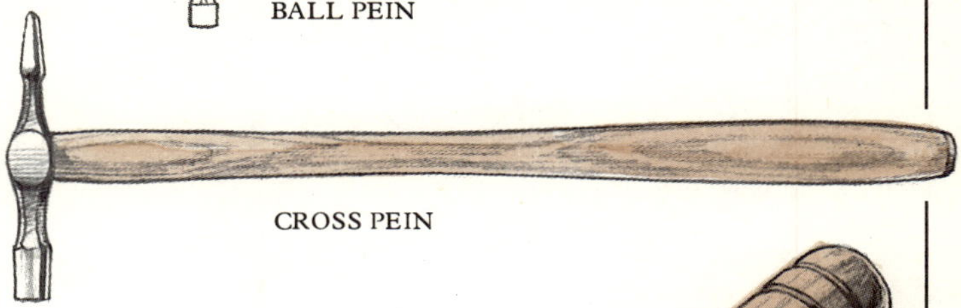

Sprig Hammer

OTHER NAME: Picture framer's hammer
SIZE: Head weight: 230g
MATERIAL: *Head/shaft:* steel; *Handle:* hardwood
USE: To drive sprigs or brads or glazing points, for picture or window framing

The sprig hammer has a square sectioned head, one face of which will slide on the glass or picture backing to drive the retaining sprig. The shaft is set at an angle to keep the knuckles of the hand clear while the head is flat on the surface.

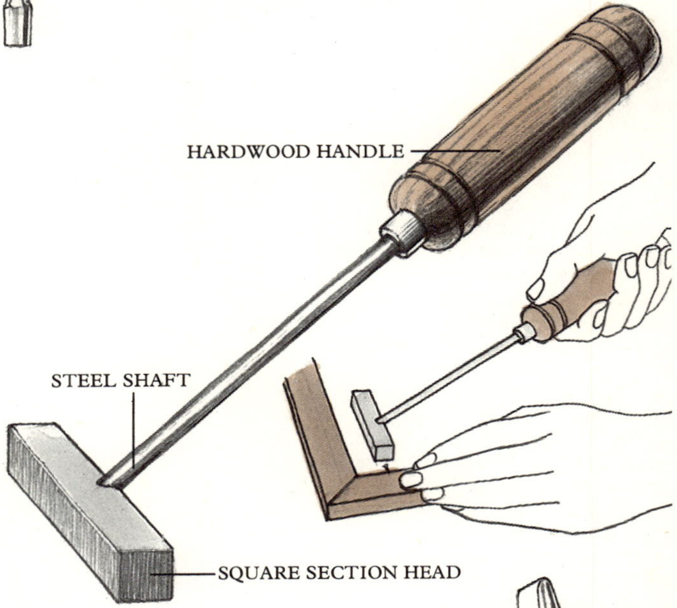

Cross Pein Hammer

SIZE: Head weight: up to 455g
MATERIAL: *Head:* steel; *Shaft:* ash, hickory
USE: General carpentry work

Cross pein hammers have a tapered pein which can start nails held between the fingers.

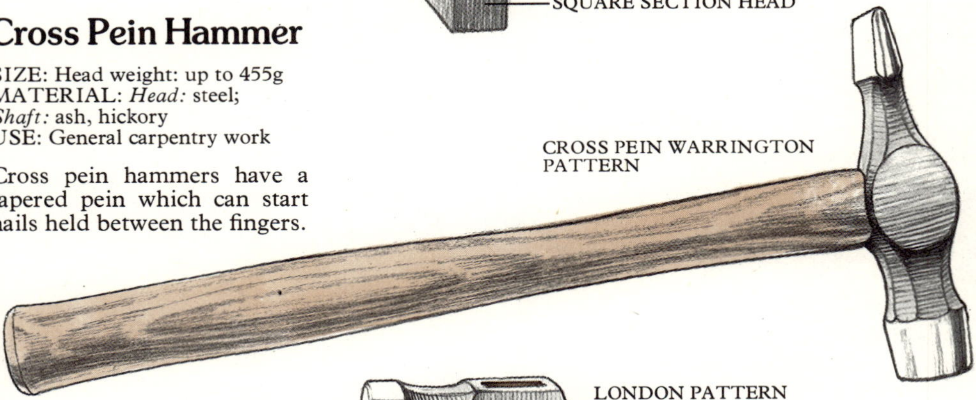

They are used in various parts of the world under different names and in a variety of shapes and sizes.

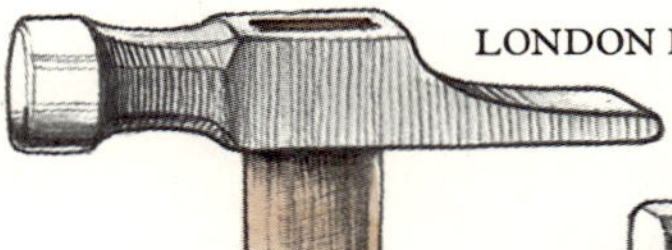

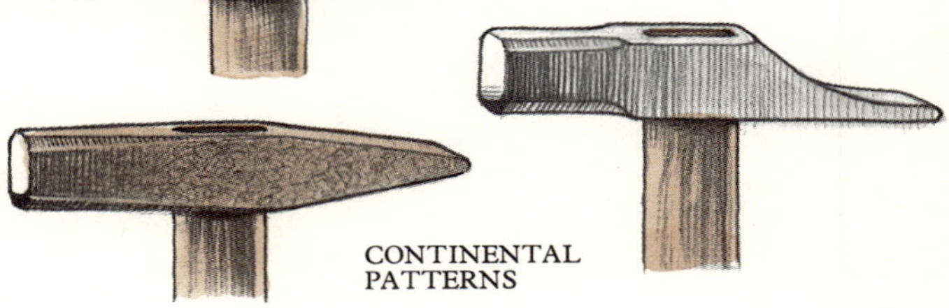

Upholsterer's Hammer

SIZE: Head weight: up to 200g
MATERIAL: *Head:* steel;
Shaft: hickory
USE: To drive tacks and chair nails used in upholstery

All upholstery hammers have a small circular face to drive tacks, which must often be done in confined spaces without damaging the surrounding woodwork. They are either double ended or fitted with a claw for pulling tacks. Alternatively a double ended hammer may have a side claw. Hammers with a larger face are often known as "tack hammers" in the USA.

One or sometimes both ends of the head are usually magnetized. This allows a tack to be attracted to the striking face and tapped in place before being driven home. The heads are either eyed to take a shaft or fitted by means of metal straps on either side of the shaft. The straps form a more positive fixing for the small head of the upholsterer's hammer.

Modern upholsterer's hammers have a shaft similar to the more common hammer. The more traditional shaft is a very elegant, balanced design with a pronounced swelling at the gripping end.

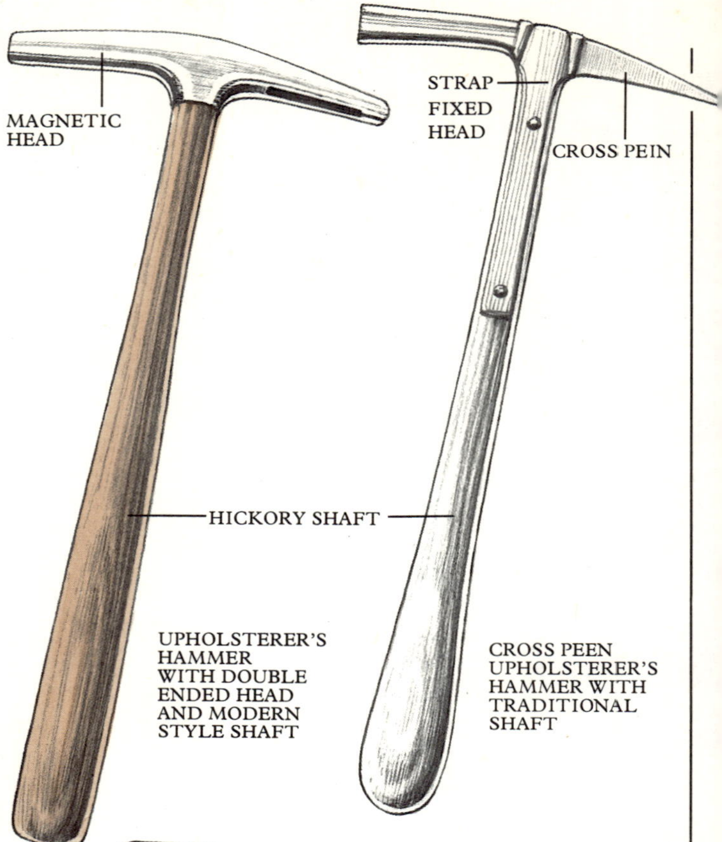

Saddler's Hammer

SIZE: Head weight: up to 570g
MATERIAL: *Head:* steel;
Shaft: hickory
USE: To drive nails or tacks into leather work

The saddler's hammer is very similar to an upholsterers hammer with a cross pein for starting tacks between the fingers. It sometimes has a side claw. In addition to driving tacks it is also used for shaping small leather items.

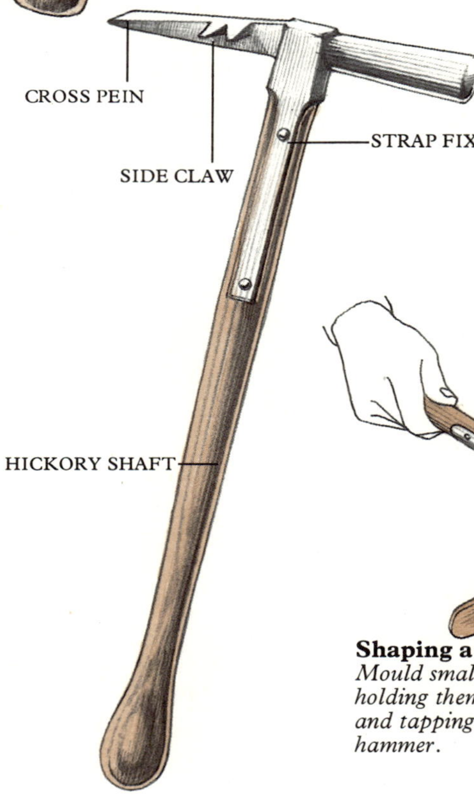

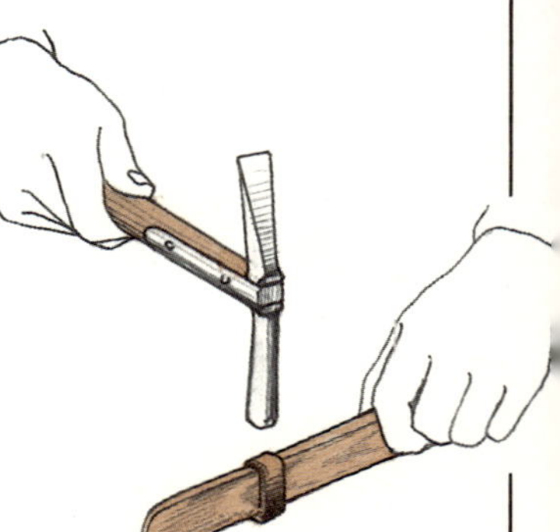

Shaping a leather loop
Mould small belt loops by holding them on a suitable stick and tapping with a saddler's hammer.

Engineer's Hammer

SIZE: Head weight: up to 1.3kg
MATERIAL: *Head:* steel;
Shaft: ash, hickory
USE: To drive punches and cold chisels and to form metal

The engineer's hammer is used in the metal workshop as a general purpose hammer in the same way that a carpenter uses a claw or cross pein hammer. Its flat face can be used to drive cold chisels and punches while various peins are used to shape metal. Cross pein and straight pein hammers are available but by far the most common is the ball pein hammer. This is primarily used in conjunction with the rivet set to rivet plates of metal together.

Forming a rivet
The rivet set is a combined tool with a deep narrow hole and a shallow depression, which is used to form a domed rivet.

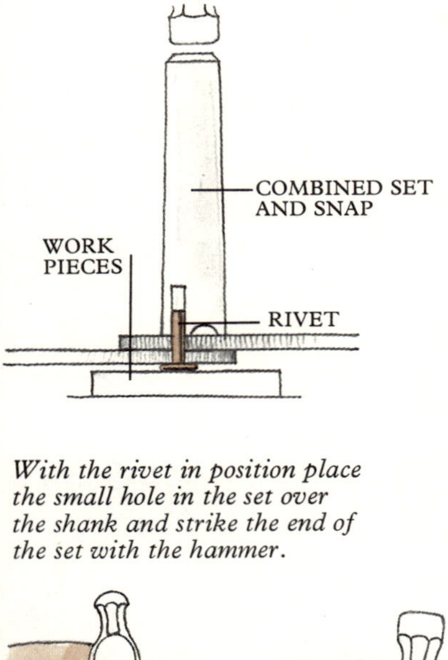

With the rivet in position place the small hole in the set over the shank and strike the end of the set with the hammer.

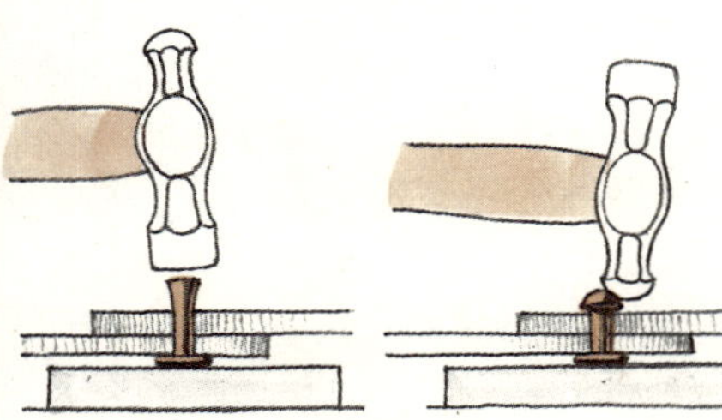

Seat both plates over rivet. Spread rivet shank with flat face of hammer.

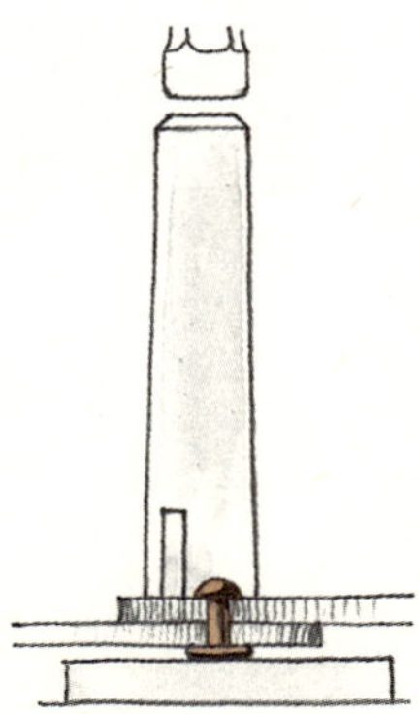

Shape it into a rough dome with ball pein. Fit depression in set over rivet and strike end with hammer.

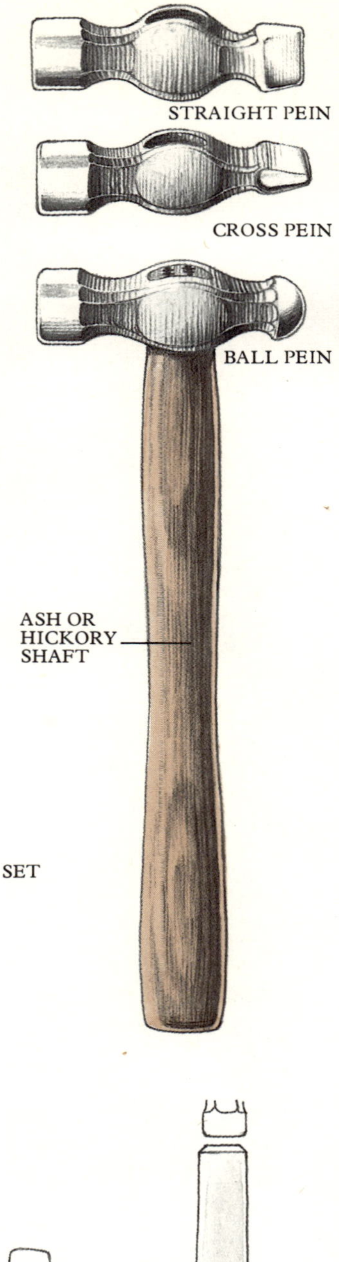

Club Hammer

OTHER NAMES: Lump hammer, hand drilling hammer
SIZE: Head weight: up to 1.8kg
MATERIAL: *Head:* steel;
Shaft: hickory, ash
USE: Heavy duty work

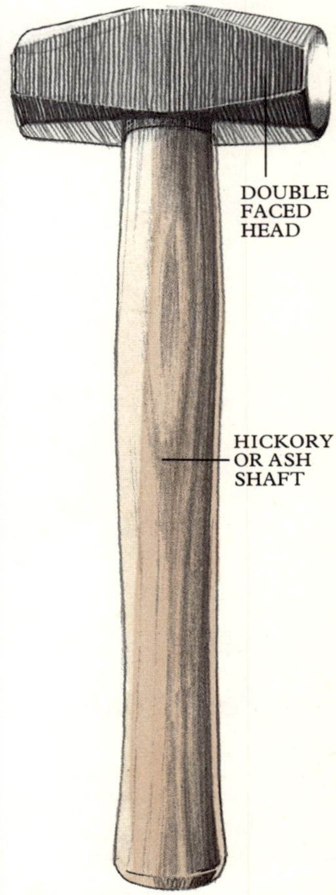

The double faced club hammer is used single handed to demolish masonry and drive steel chisels and masonry drills. It is wise to wear gloves and goggles while performing all these operations.

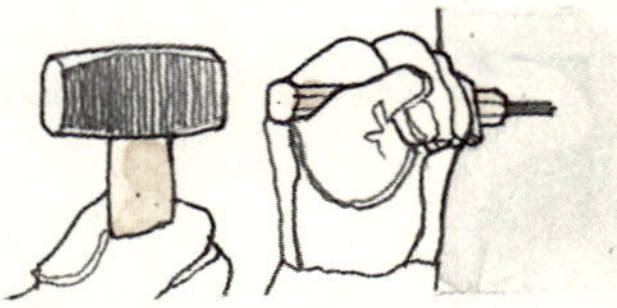

Using the hammer
With one hand hold the hand drill, rotating it between strokes of the club hammer.

Carver's Mallet

SIZE: Head diameter: 87 to 175mm
MATERIAL: *Head:* beech, lignum vitae; *Handle:* ash
USE: To drive carver's chisels and gouges

The carver's mallet is heavy to allow the craftsman to drive the chisel with short controlled strokes, rather than heavy blows. The round head enables him to work from a variety of angles without changing his grip on the tool.

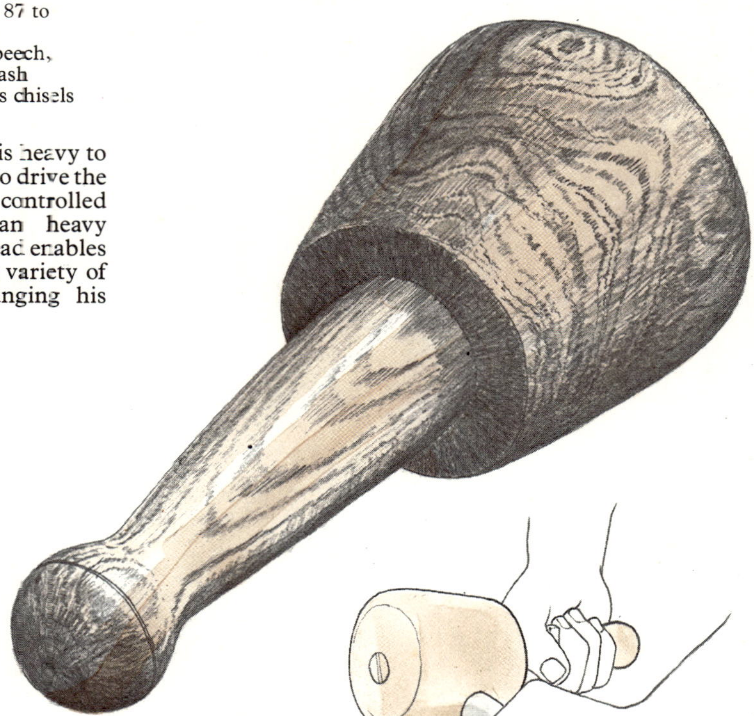

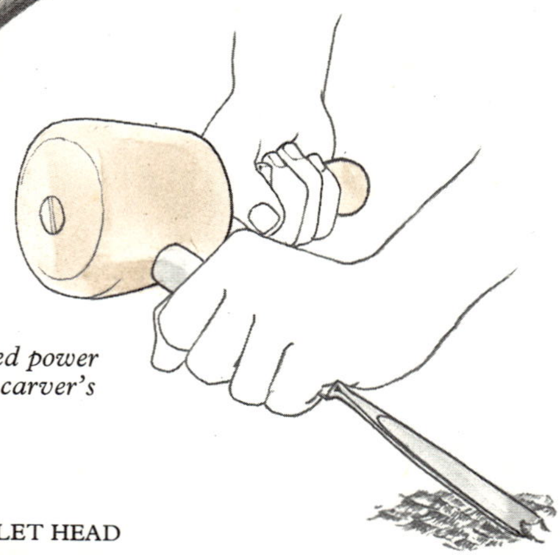

Controlled power from the carver's mallet

Soft Faced Mallet

SIZE: Head weight: Up to 1kg
MATERIAL: *Head:* rubber, rawhide; *Handle:* hickory
USE: To drive or shape material which would be damaged by standard hammers or mallets

Soft faced mallets have heads made of solid rubber or rawhide glued into a coil and sometimes loaded with lead.

RUBBER MALLET HEAD

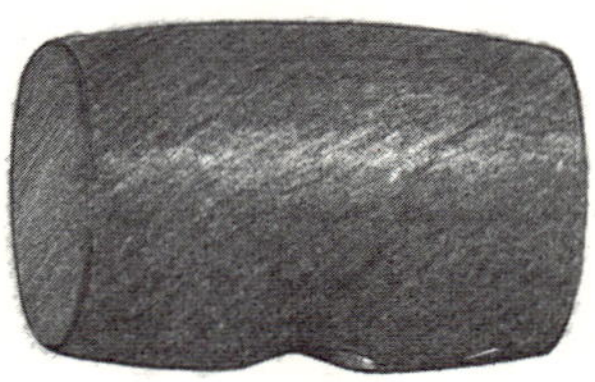

COILED RAWHIDE HEAD

They are used to shape metal parts, as in automobile repair work, where conventional hammers and mallets would damage the work.

Soft Faced Hammer

SIZE: Head weight: Up to 3.2kg
MATERIAL: *Head:* cast iron, metal alloy; *Handle:* hickory, ash, plastic; *Faces:* rawhide, copper, plastic, lead, rubber, aluminium
USE: To drive or shape material which would be damaged by standard hammers

Soft faced hammers normally have a socketed head into which soft bases are screwed. They are often fitted with a different material at each end for work on a variety of materials. Special shaped faces can be inserted for shaping work. It is not advisable to use a soft faced hammer to drive nails and it would be damaged if used to strike a sharp edge or a corner.

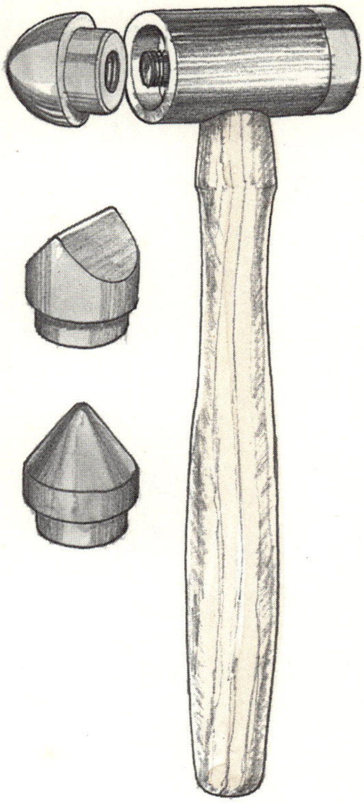

Veneer Hammer

SIZE: Blade width: 75 to 112mm
MATERIAL: Wooden *Head:* ash or beech: *Handle:* ash;
Metal *Head:* steel;
Handle: ash
USE: To press down wood veneer to a glued surface

The traditional veneer hammer, often made by the craftsman himself, has a flat or slightly tapered wooden head. A groove cut in the bottom edge takes a thin steel blade. The straight shaft passes through a hole in the head and is wedged in the normal way. The metal version has a flat hammer face and a wide cross pein opposite.

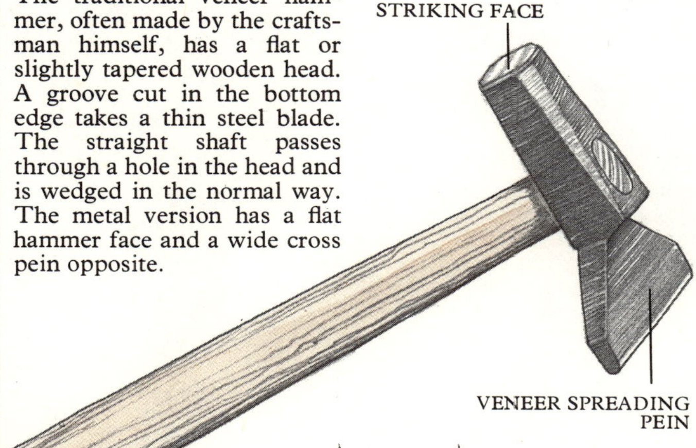

Using the veneer hammer
The veneer hammer is used to press a glued veneer flat on to its ground work by squeezing out excess glue and air. While maintaining pressure on the head of the hammer pull from the centre outward using a zig-zag action.

Pin Push

OTHER NAME: Brad driver
SIZE: Pin capacity: 14 and 16 gauge
MATERIAL: Metal and plastic
USE: To drive small nails without a hammer

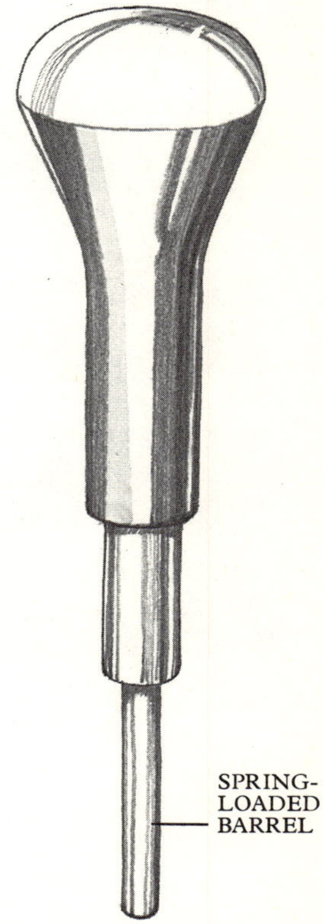

The pin or nail is held magnetically in the barrel. To drive the pin apply pressure to the handle, which automatically returns to repeat the action.

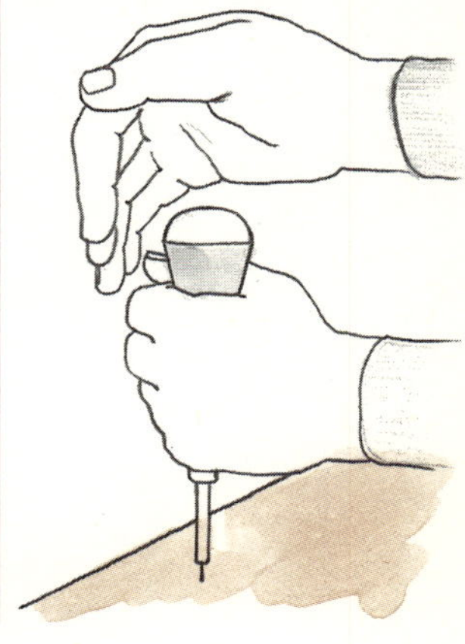

Sledge Hammer

SIZE: *Head weight:* up to 9kg;
Shaft length: 400 to 900mm
MATERIAL: *Head:* steel;
Shaft: hickory
USE: Very heavy duty work

Sledge hammers are used to drive stakes or to split stone. They are available double faced or with ball or straight peins.

Light blows can be applied by using the weight of the head only. For heavy work swing the tool as you would a felling axe (see page 324).

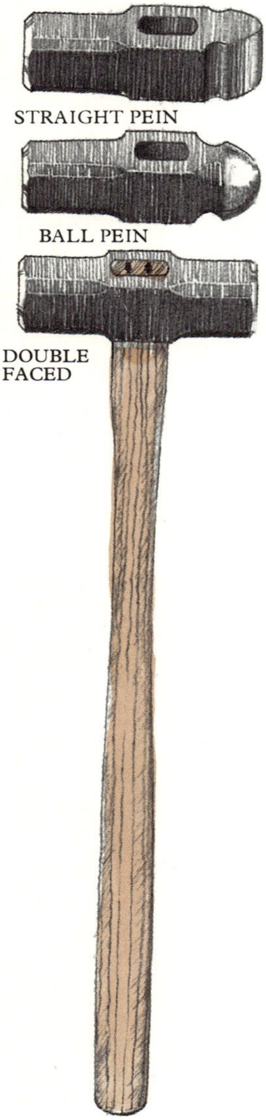

Brick Hammer

OTHER NAME: Bricklayer's hammer
SIZE: Head weight: up to 680g
MATERIAL: *Head:* steel; *Shaft:* hickory, steel
USE: To drive cold chisels and trim masonry

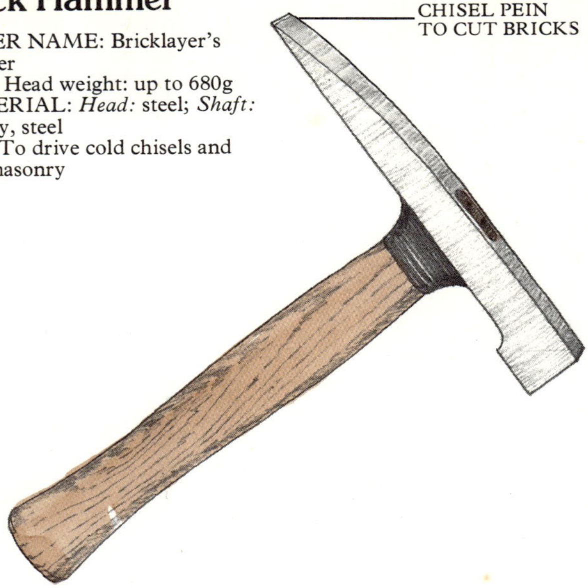

The brick hammer is used to strike a bolster or brick cutting chisel when splitting bricks. The curved chisel end of the hammer is used to trim the cut brick to shape.

Joiner's Mallet

OTHER NAME: Carpenter's mallet
SIZE: Head size: 62 to 175mm
MATERIAL: Beech
USE: General carpentry work

The joiner's mallet is used where a metal hammer would either damage the work or the tool being struck. As well as driving wood cutting chisels, it is often used to tap joints together or apart. The head is tapered toward the user so that it will strike the work squarely. The eye and handle are tapered so that the action of swinging the mallet automatically tightens the head on the handle.

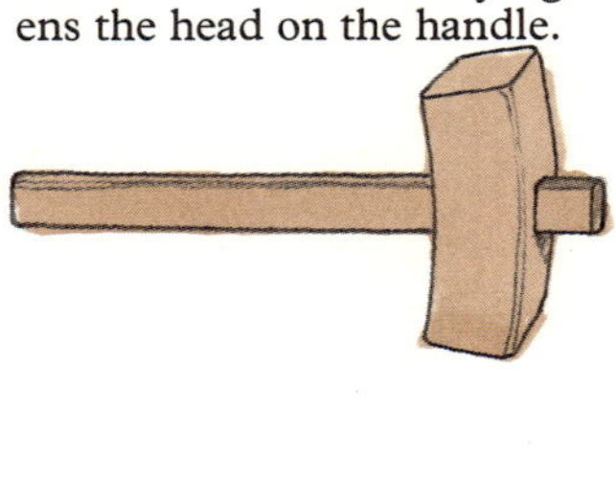

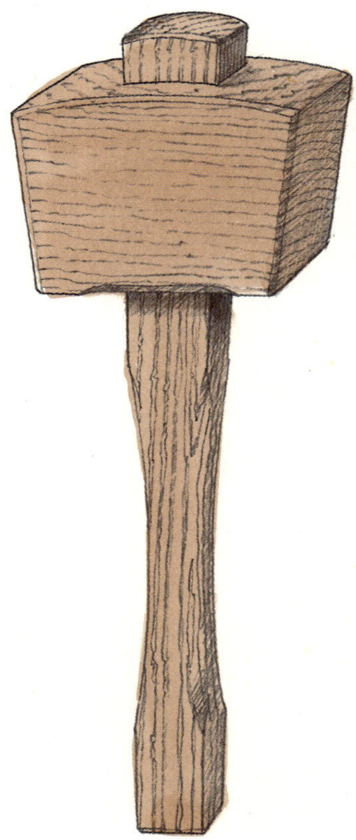

Glue Gun

SIZE: Length: 200mm
MATERIAL: Various
USE: To apply hot, liquid glue

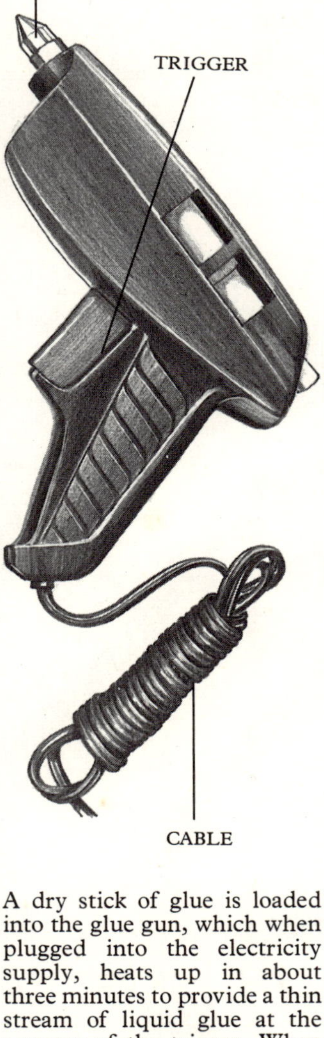

A dry stick of glue is loaded into the glue gun, which when plugged into the electricity supply, heats up in about three minutes to provide a thin stream of liquid glue at the squeeze of the trigger. When the trigger is released, the supply of glue is cut off preventing excess glue from dripping onto the work or bench. The glue dries in 60 seconds under hand pressure, which together with the control of application, makes it an ideal tool for the model maker.

The gun also makes an effective caulking tool when loaded with special caulking sticks instead of glue.

Miniature Power Tool

SIZE: *Length:* 200mm; *Speed:* 5,000 to 25,000 rpm
MATERIAL: Various
ACCESSORIES: Cutters, stones, brushes
ATTACHMENTS: Drill press stand, bench stand, router attachment, speed control unit
USE: To cut, grind, sand, abrade and polish on a small scale

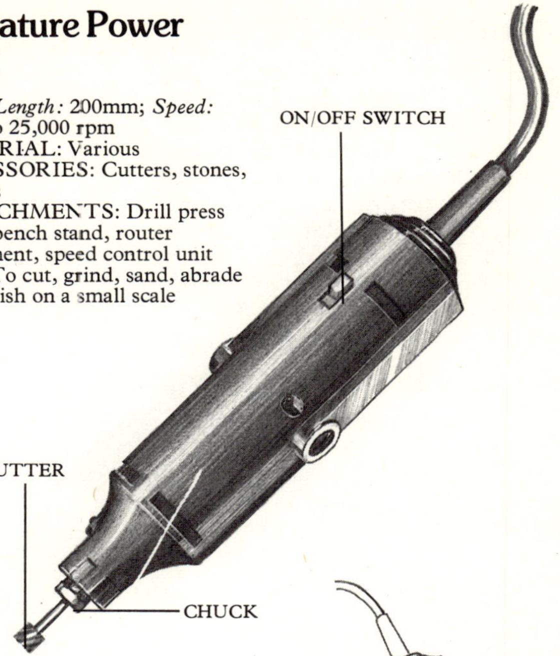

The miniature power tool provides most of the features incorporated in large scale power tools, but its size makes it particularly suitable for model makers. It is equally useful for work on small detail of any kind. Miniature grindstones, cutting wheels, wire brushes, files and drum sanders can all be fitted into the chuck of the miniature power tool.

The tool can be applied to the work free-hand or held in an adjustable bench stand, leaving both hands free to hold the work against the cutters. It can also be clamped in a drill press stand, which provides accurate vertical alignment. Both stands should be firmly attached to the bench. The router attachment jigs the depth of cut to provide surface routing, and can be used free-hand or with a fence, for straight cuts.

The finish of the cut is determined by the speed of the cutter. A variable speed model is preferable as it can be adjusted to suit the circumstances.

Be careful not to apply too much pressure to the tool, or you could damage the motor or bend the shaft of the cutter. Wear goggles when grinding any kind of metal.

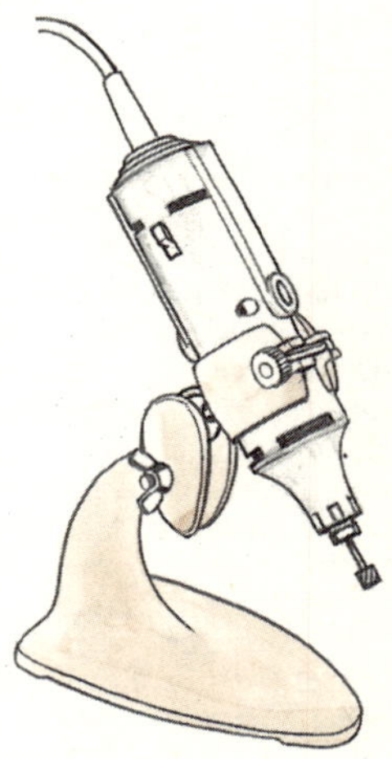

Tool in bench stand

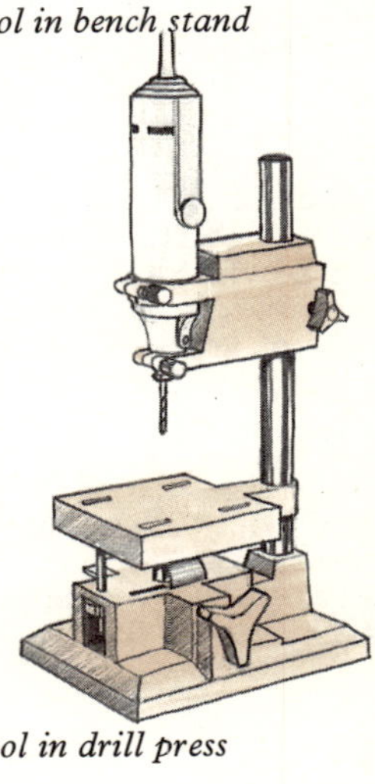

Tool in drill press

Pincers and Pliers

Although Roman blacksmiths made and used tongs of various kinds, the carpenters in those days seem to have relied mainly on their claw hammers for dealing with recalcitrant nails. Joseph Moxon made this point as late as 1685, speaking of the carpenter's claw hammer: "Its chief Use is for driving Nails into Work and drawing Nails out of work", and makes no mention of pincers. These appear occasionally in medieval pictures, but only when the carpenter is using an ordinary flat-peined hammer.

Pliers were special tools for cutting and manipulating wire which, apart from jewelry, was not in general use until comparatively modern times. Felibien in 1676 illustrates a pair of what we call "Glazier's pliers", but calls them *tenailles* (pincers). The French word for pliers is, of course, *pinces*, which is confusing.

Engineer's Pliers

OTHER NAMES: Combination pliers, linesmen's pliers
SIZE: 125 to 250mm
MATERIAL: Steel
USE: To grip and bend sheet metal and crop wire

Engineer's pliers are the standard type of pliers. The larger kinds are versatile, and incorporate a variety of functions. The various facilities of the engineer's pliers are operated by the simple action of opening and closing the handles.

The flat serrated jaw is used to grip and bend thin sheet metal. The sides or ends of the jaws are carefully aligned with the marked line to produce an accurate bend. To prevent the serrations marking the metal, wrap the jaws in insulation tape. Keep the metal clear of the side cutters to avoid accidental cutting. Some pliers include a curved section in the serrated jaws for gripping round section metal rod.

Immediately in front of the pivot, where great force can be applied, is a pair of side cutters for cropping wire. The cutting edges are situated to one side of the jaws so that they can cut close to a surface. Even greater cutting force can be exerted by the pair of croppers situated above the pivot. When the handles of the pliers are open, the two sections of the cropper are aligned so that a length of wire can be laid across them. Squeezing the handles together closes the croppers and shears the metal.

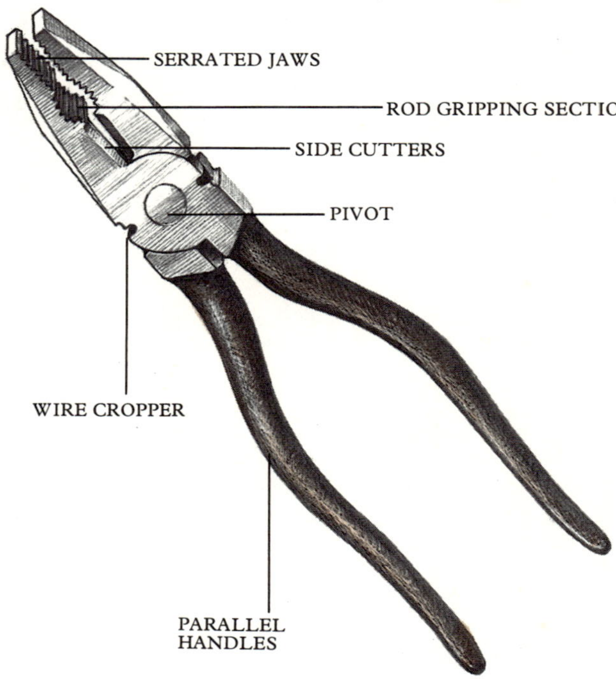

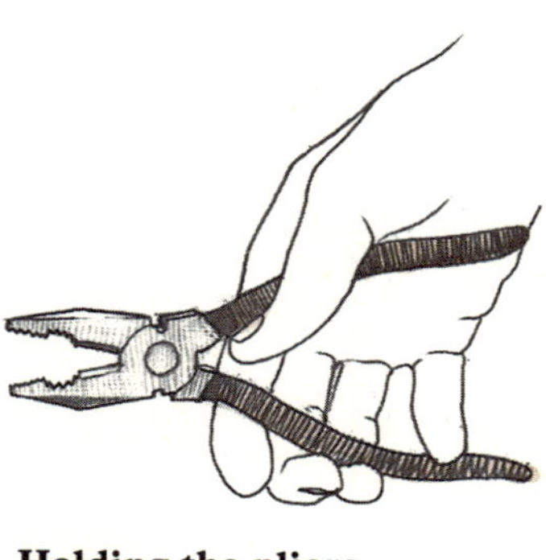

Holding the pliers
To control the pliers with one hand, hook the little finger on the inside of the handle to provide the opening force.

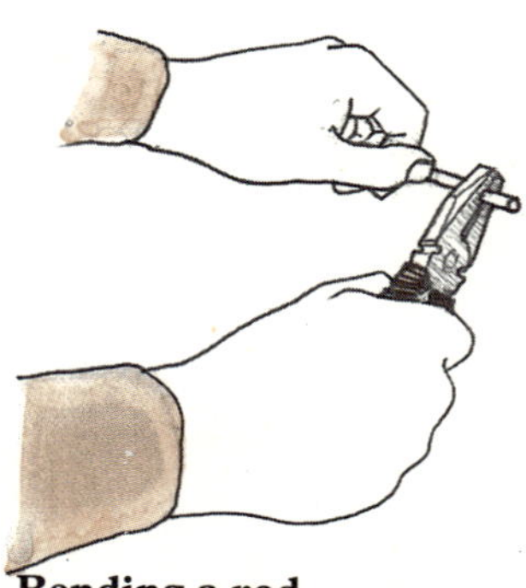

Bending a rod
Hold a long rod in your hand and bend it against a pair of pliers. For shorter lengths you will need two pairs of pliers.

Parallel Action Pliers

SIZE: 125 to 162mm
MATERIAL: Steel
USE: To grip metal with the jaws flat on the work

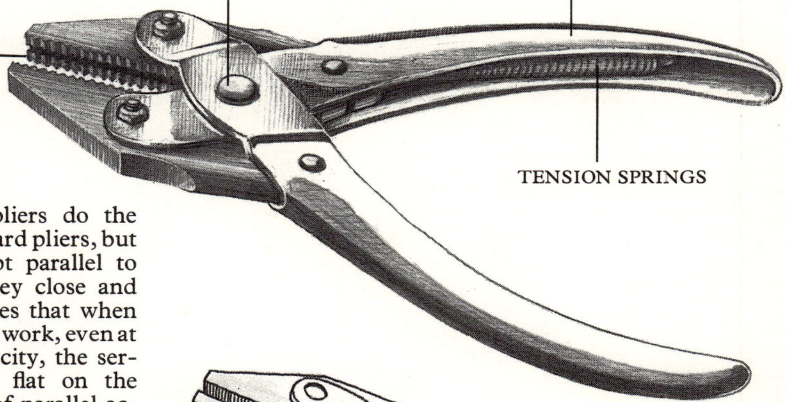

Parallel action pliers do the same job as standard pliers, but the jaws are kept parallel to each other as they close and open. This insures that when the pliers grip the work, even at their widest capacity, the serrated surface is flat on the work. The jaws of parallel action pliers are opened automatically by tension springs in the handles.

Although pliers are not a good substitute for a spanner, in an emergency the parallel action pliers will at least grip the flats of a nut securely.

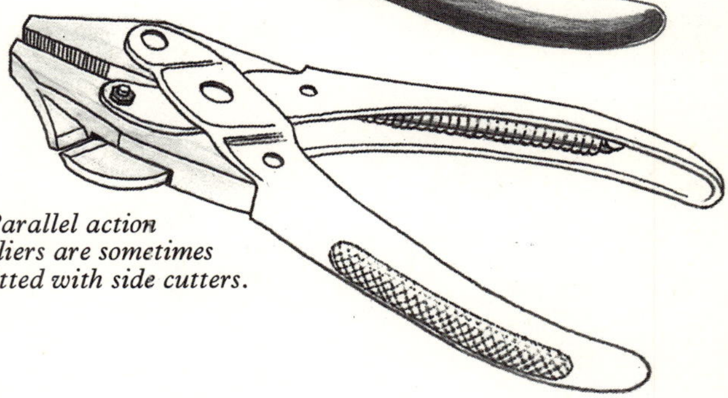

Parallel action pliers are sometimes fitted with side cutters.

Flat Nosed Pliers

OTHER NAMES: Square nosed pliers, duckbill pliers, pendulum pliers
SIZE: 100 to 187mm
MATERIAL: Steel
USE: To grip and bend sheet metal or wire

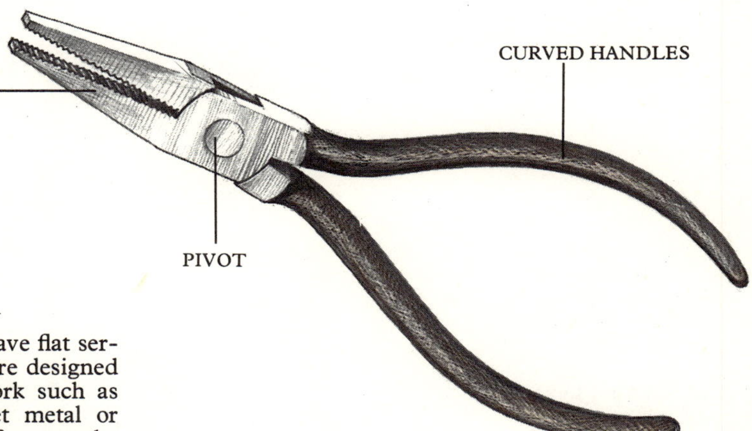

Flat nosed pliers have flat serrated jaws. They are designed for lightweight work such as bending thin sheet metal or wire. The greatest force can be applied immediately in front of the jaws.

Electrician's Pliers

OTHER NAME: Linesmen's pliers
SIZE: 150 to 200mm
MATERIAL: Steel; plastic handle covers
USE: To grip, bend and crop electrical cable

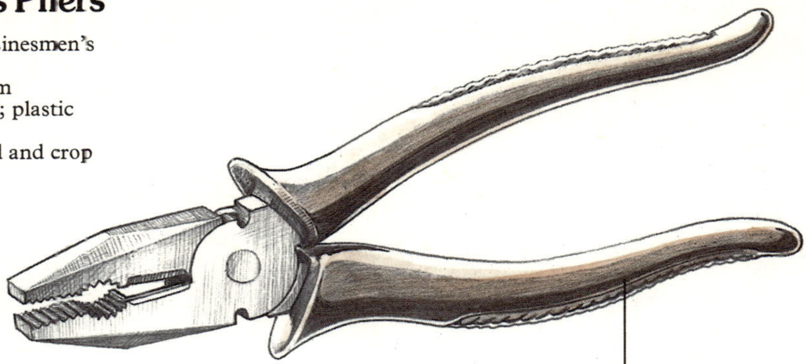

Electrician's pliers are basically the same tool as engineer's pliers, but they are fitted with two insulated handles. As a precaution, switch off the power before working on any equipment connected to the electrical supply. A large pair of pliers are needed to crop the thicker sections of cable and twist them together to make connections.

Snipe Nosed Pliers

OTHER NAMES: Needle nosed pliers, long nosed pliers, long chain pliers, radio pliers
SIZE: 112 to 200mm
MATERIAL: Steel
USE: To grip small objects in confined spaces

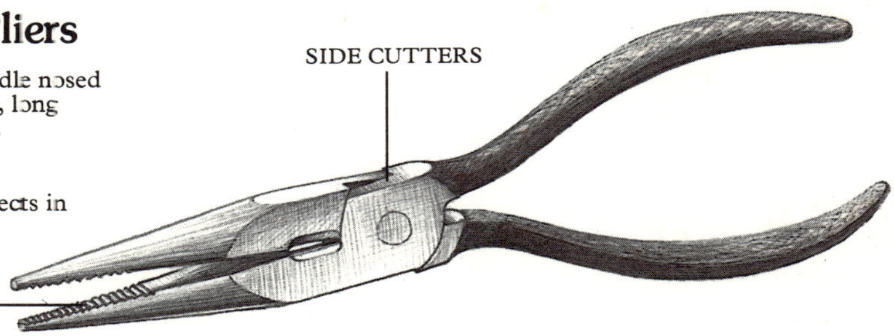

Snipe nosed pliers are manufactured in a variety of shapes and proportions but they all have serrated tapering jaws to work in confined spaces. Some models have side cutters to crop soft wire.

Needle nosed pliers are a variety of snipe nosed pliers with extra thin tapering jaws. The ends of bent snipe nosed pliers are bent to an angle of 45° or 90° to give better access in a confined space which is very useful for certain jobs.

Do not apply too much force when using snipe nosed pliers, as it is very easy to strain the jaws out of line.

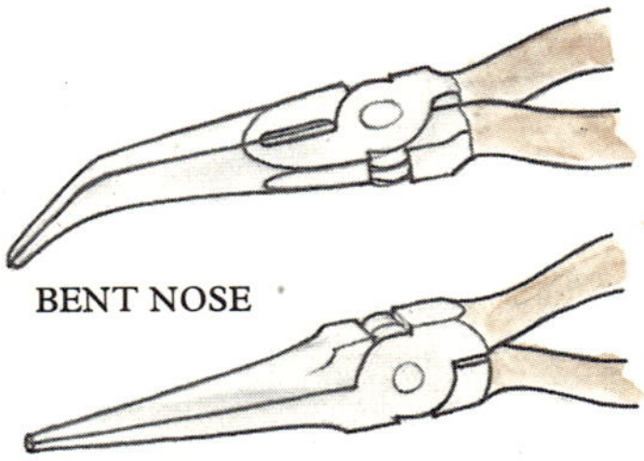

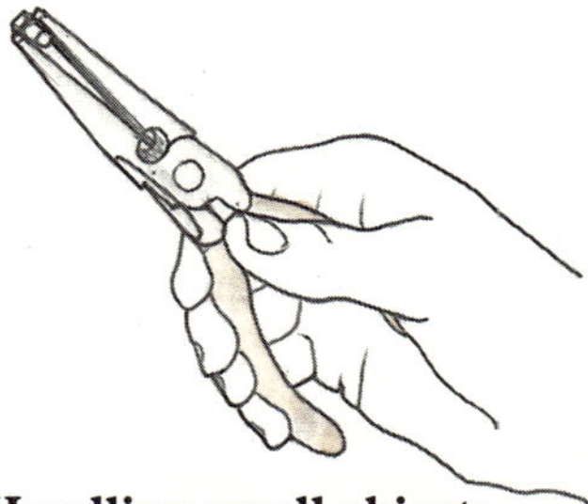

Handling small objects
Snipe nosed pliers are invaluable for placing small washers or nuts on to fittings and assembling delicate wiring.

Round Nosed Pliers

SIZE: 100 to 162mm
MATERIAL: Steel
USE: To bend wire into loops

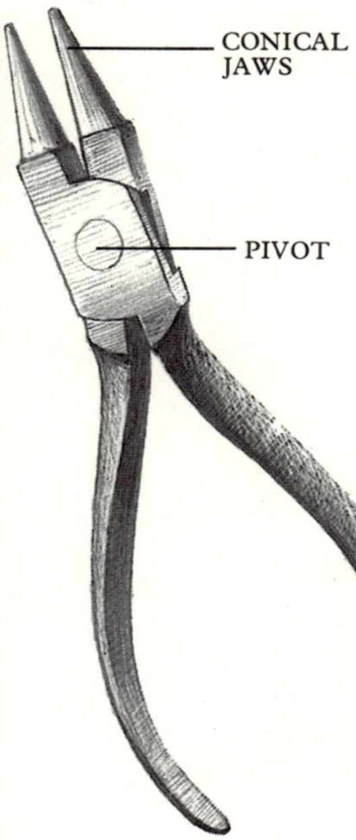

Round nosed pliers have a pair of smooth conical jaws, which are used to form loops in wire or thin strips of sheet metal. They are used by jewelers, and by electricians to make a loop in a cable to fit an electrical fitting. The tapered jaw allows for loops of different sizes.

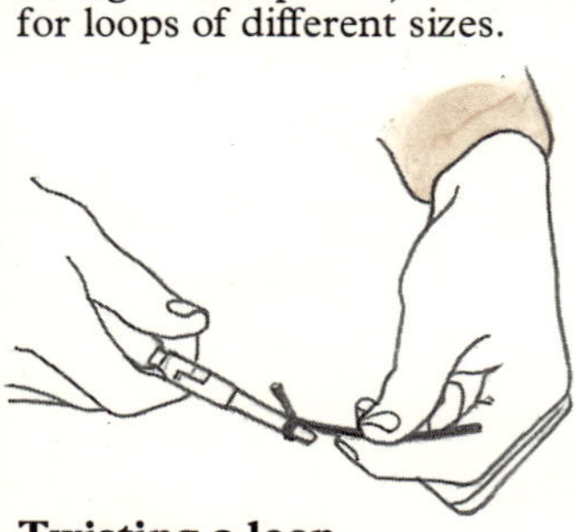

Twisting a loop
To form a loop grip the end of the wire between the jaws and twist the pliers, keeping the tension on the wire with the other hand.

Slip Joint Pliers

SIZE: 125 to 250mm
MATERIAL: Steel
USE: To work as standard pliers with a wider jaw capacity

The functions of the slip joint pliers are identical to those of standard pliers but their unique feature is the pivot point, which provides for two widths of jaw opening. Like standard pliers they have a flat section on the jaws incised with fine serrations and a curved section with coarser serrations.

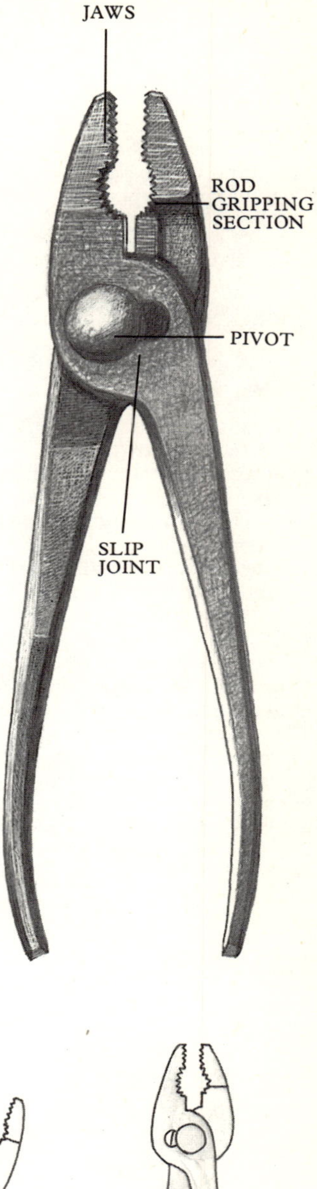

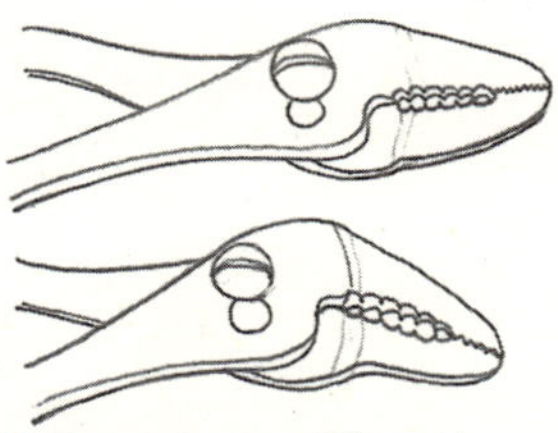

Other types of head
Slip joint pliers are also available with bent jaws or as narrow nosed pliers.

How slip joint pliers work

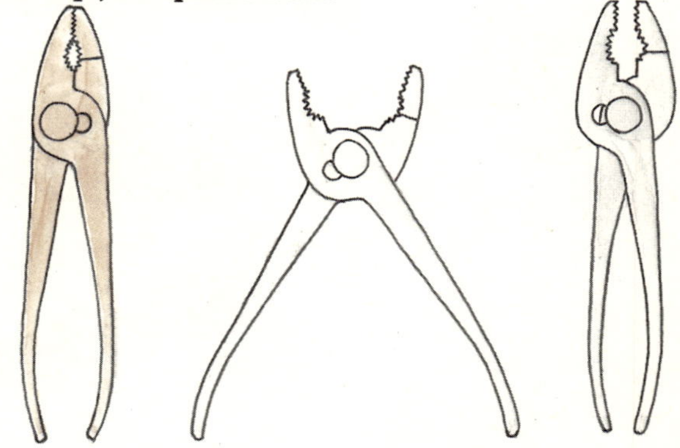

Open the handles and slide the joints sideways. The pivot will engage in a second position to give a wider jaw opening.

Waterpump Pliers

SIZE: 100 to 250mm
MATERIAL: Steel
USE: To grip pipework

Waterpump pliers were originally developed to work on plumbing fittings and are designed to grip pipework.

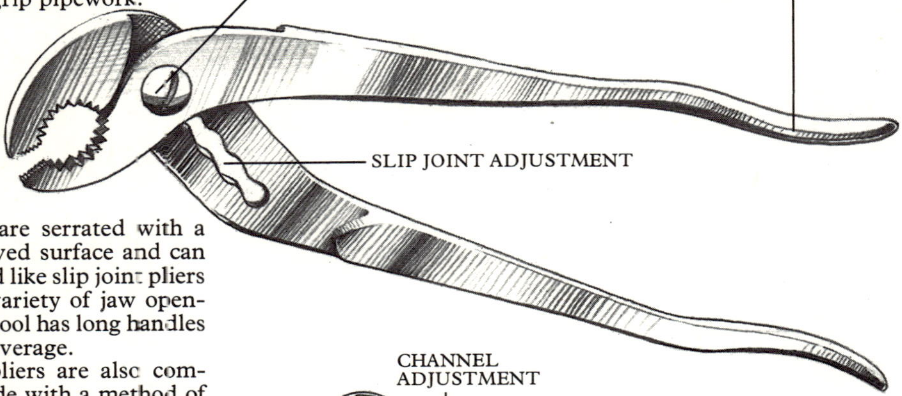

The jaws are serrated with a flat or curved surface and can be adjusted like slip joint pliers to give a variety of jaw openings. The tool has long handles for good leverage.

These pliers are also commonly made with a method of adjustment known as "channel" joints or "groove grip". Each jaw position depends on tongues in one half of the tool locating in grooves in the other half of the tool.

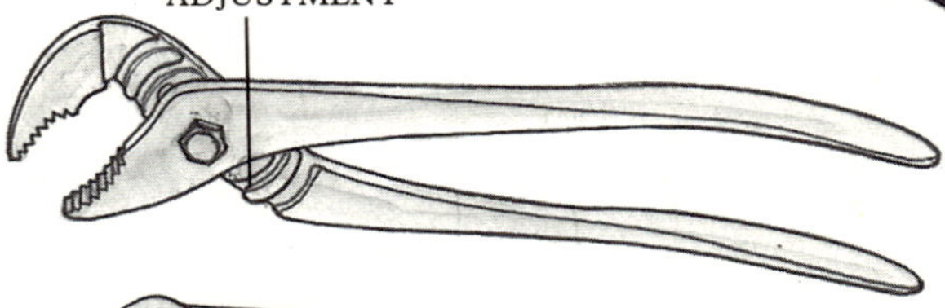

Another less common variety adjusts by locating the pivot in hooks in the other half of the tool. This strong form of location cannot slip even when very heavy loads are applied to the pliers.

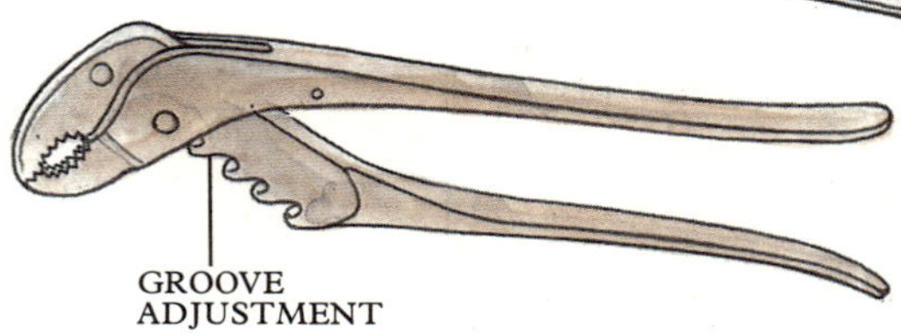

Gas Pliers

OTHER NAME: Scotch gas pliers
SIZE: 175 to 250mm
MATERIAL: Steel
USE: To grip pipework

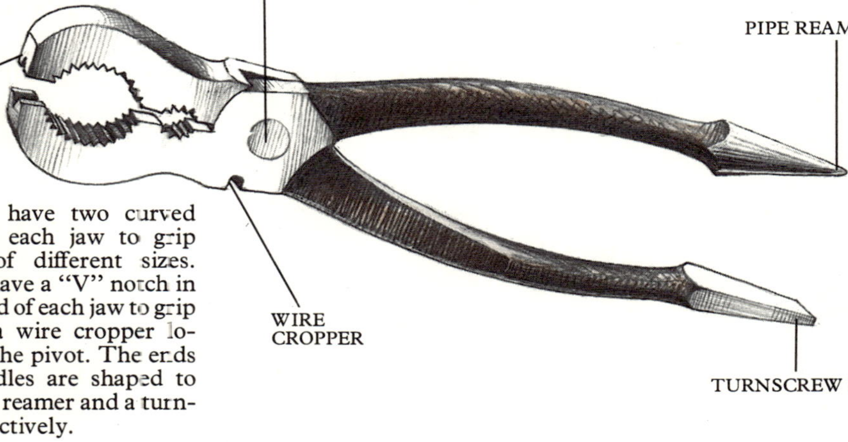

Gas pliers have two curved sections in each jaw to grip pipework of different sizes. They also have a "V" notch in the front end of each jaw to grip wire, and a wire cropper located near the pivot. The ends of the handles are shaped to form a pipe reamer and a turnscrew respectively.

Mole Grips

OTHER NAMES: Plier wrench, vice grip wrench, self-grip wrench
SIZE: 125 to 300mm
MATERIAL: Steel
USE: To grip sheet and round sectioned metal strongly

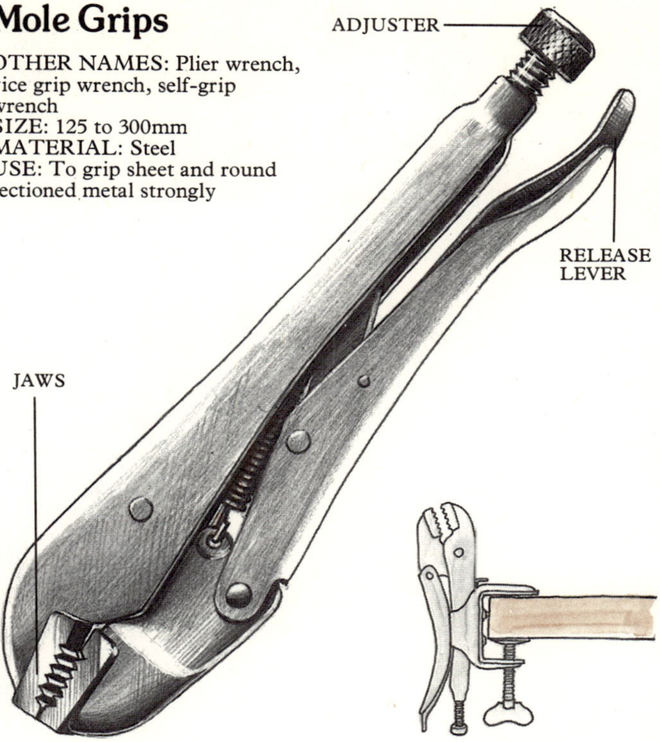

Mole grip jaws are controlled by turning an adjuster, so that when the handles are closed, considerable force is applied to the work. Furthermore, the grips will remain locked onto the work until the release lever is operated. This converts the tool into a mini-vice freeing the hands for other purposes. In fact you can improvise a vice by mounting the mole grips securely to the edge of the work bench with a table clamp.

Mole grips are manufactured with different jaws for specific work. The standard jaws are the straight serrated type; another version has curved serrated jaws. There is also a version with curved jaws which are smooth on the inside and one with wide, flat jaws which are perfectly smooth on the inside, for gripping sheets of metal without marking the surface. Yet another type has "G" cramp type jaws. Mole grips are also manufactured with jaws for more specific tasks such as holding work for welding.

TABLE CLAMP

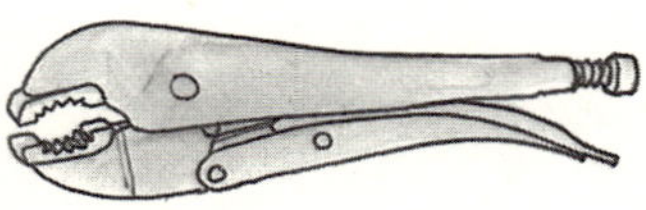

CURVED SERRATED JAW MOLE GRIPS

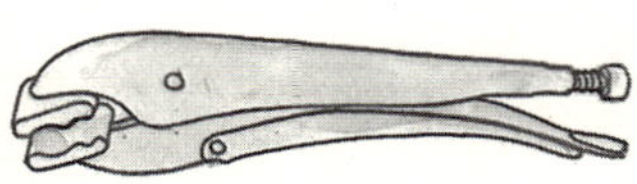

CURVED SMOOTH JAW MOLE GRIPS

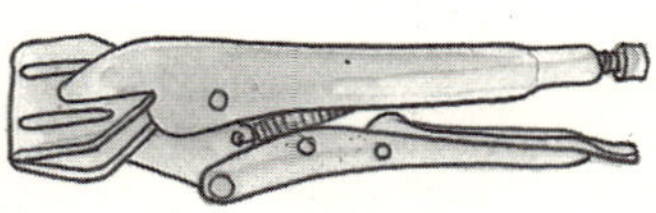

FLAT JAW MOLE GRIPS

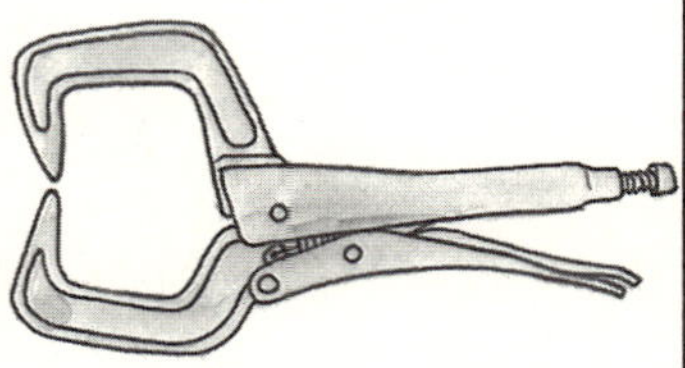

"G" CRAMP MOLE GRIPS

Adjusting the mole grips

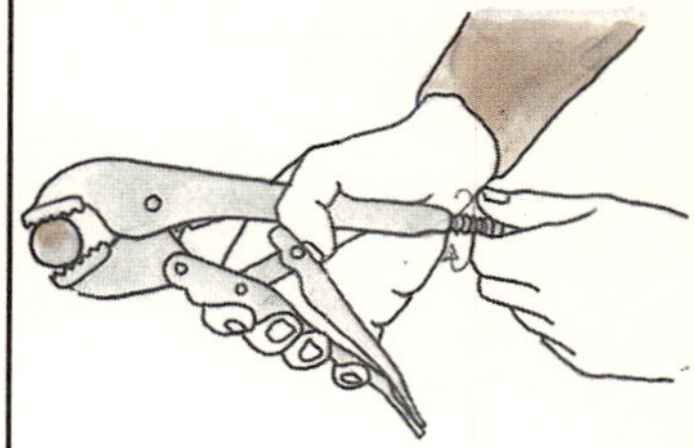

Close the grips onto the work by squeezing the handles. Turn the adjuster counter clockwise until the handles close. Be careful as the closing force could easily damage the work.

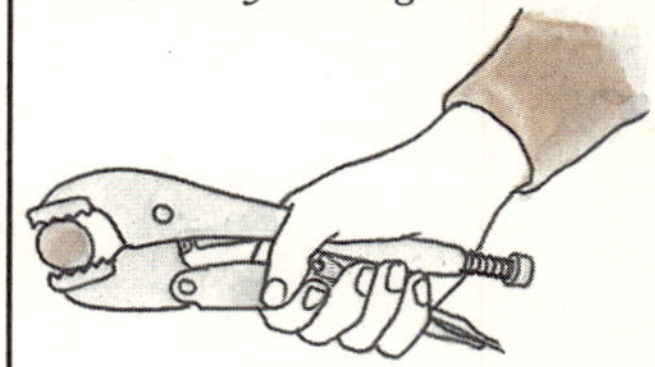

If the work is too wide to allow the tool to lock on, keep the pressure on the handles. Turn the adjuster counter clockwise again if necessary.

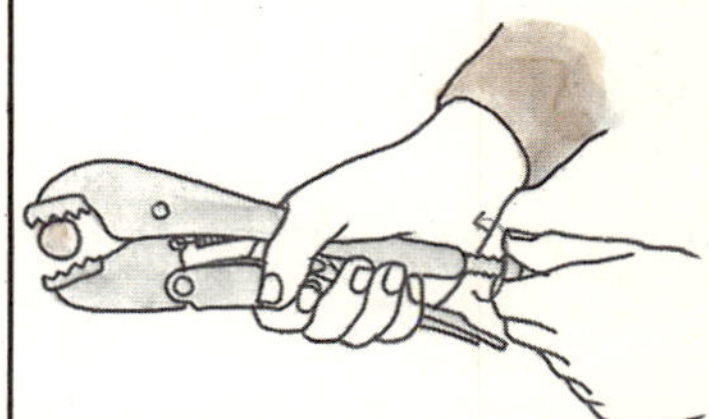

If the work is too narrow for the jaws when the handles are closed, turn the adjuster clockwise until the jaws touch the work and operate the release lever. Screw in the adjuster a little more and squeeze the handles to lock the tool onto the work.

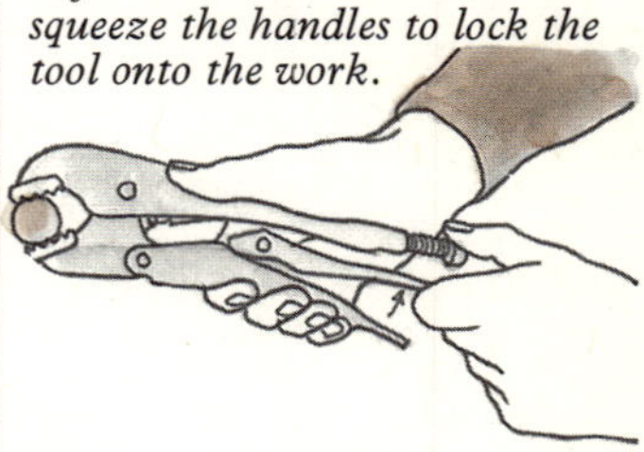

Release the mole grips by holding the handles firmly in one hand while pulling the release lever with the other.

Glazier's Pliers

OTHER NAME: Glass pliers
SIZE: 150 to 250mm
USE: To snap off strips of glass cut from a large sheet

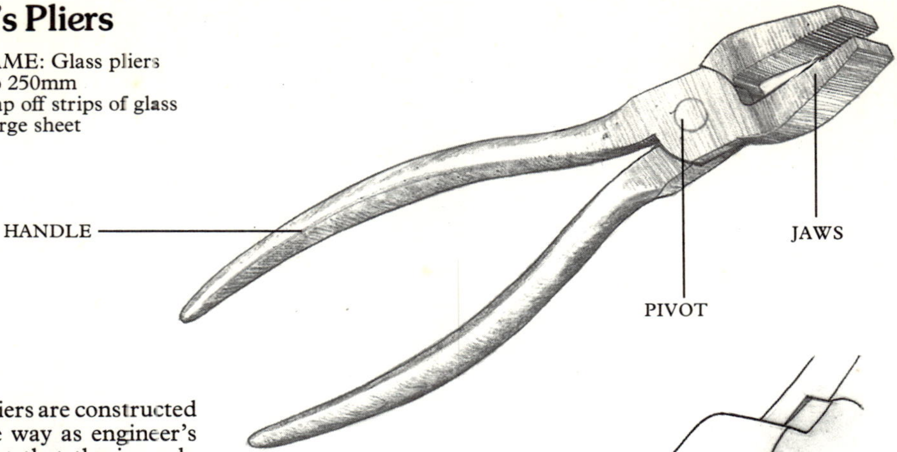

Glazier's pliers are constructed in the same way as engineer's pliers except that the jaws do not meet immediately in front of the pivot. This insures that the jaws can grip the glass up to the cut line instead of at the extreme edge only.

After the glass has been scored with a glass cutter, the glazier's pliers are used to snap off a narrow strip. They are also used to "nibble" off pieces of glass back to a line or around a curve.

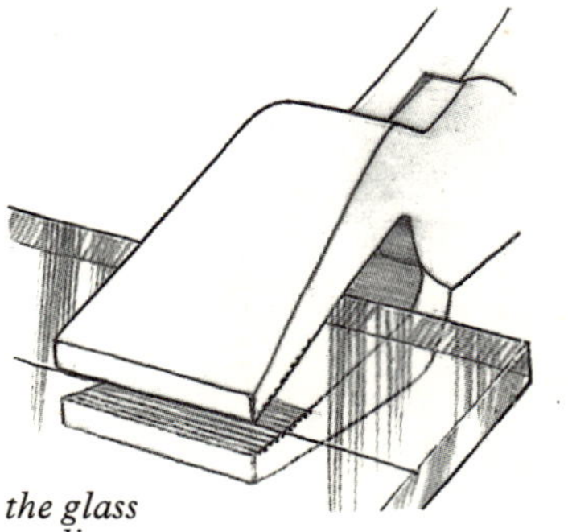

Gripping the glass up to the cut line.

Diagonal Cutting Pliers

OTHER NAMES: Diagonal cutting nippers, side cutting nippers
SIZE: 100 to 187mm
MATERIAL: Steel
USE: To crop metal wire close to a surface

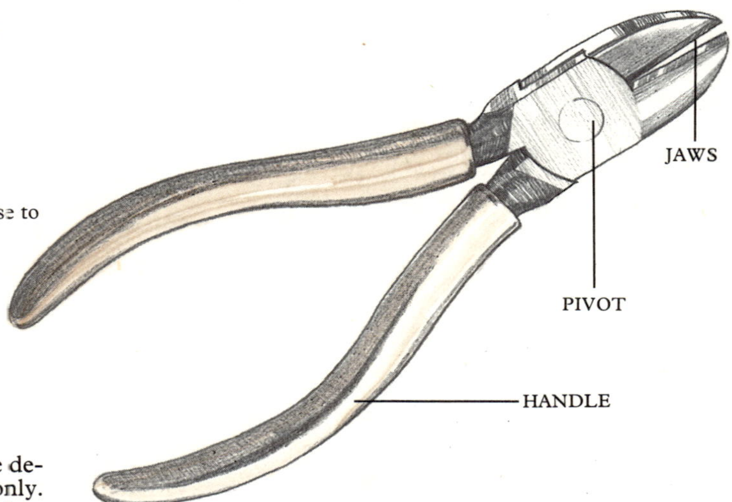

Diagonal cutting pliers are designed for cropping metal only. They should not be used as standard pliers to grip work because this can damage the cutting edges or the work itself. The jaws of the pliers are shaped so that the handles will give knuckle clearance while the side cutting face is flat on the surface. The handles are often automatically opened by a coil spring.

Angled jaws
The flat section of the blade cuts close to the work, but the shape of the jaws allows knuckle clearance for the user.

End Cutting Pliers

OTHER NAMES: Top cutting nippers, end cutting nippers
SIZE: 112 to 225mm
MATERIAL: Steel
USE: To crop wire close to a surface

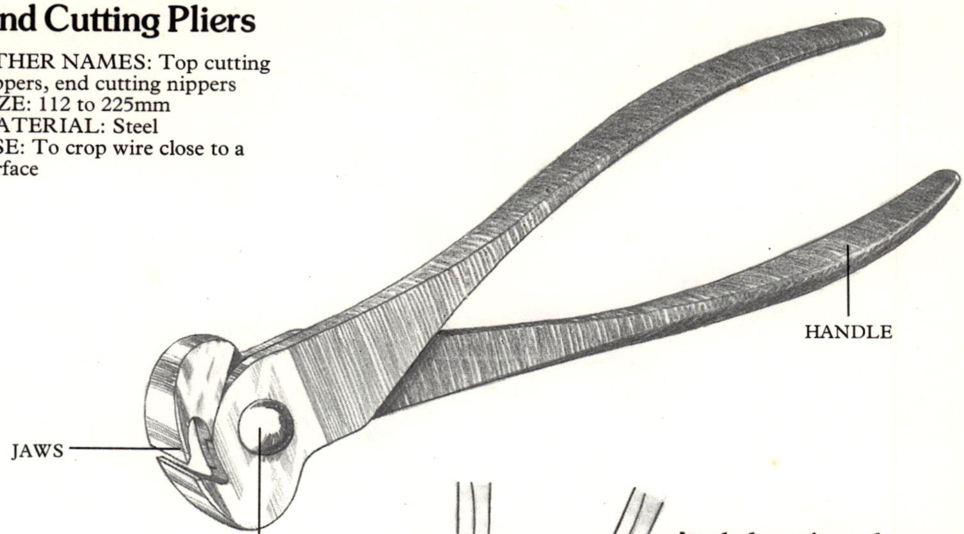

End cutting pliers also crop wire flush to the surface while keeping the knuckles clear of the work. The cutting edges are sometimes set at an angle to the handles.

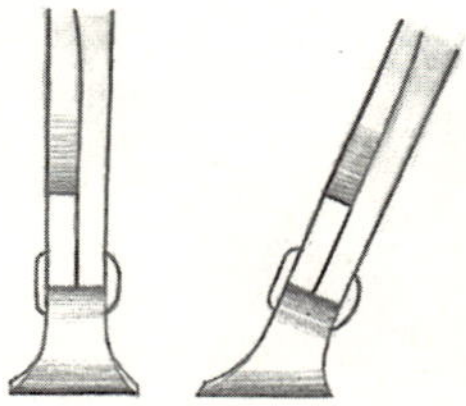

Angled cutting edges
End cutting pliers are usually positioned perpendicularly over the work, but some have angled cutting edges for work in confined spaces.

Fencing Pliers

SIZE: 250mm
MATERIAL: Steel
USE: To help erect wire fencing

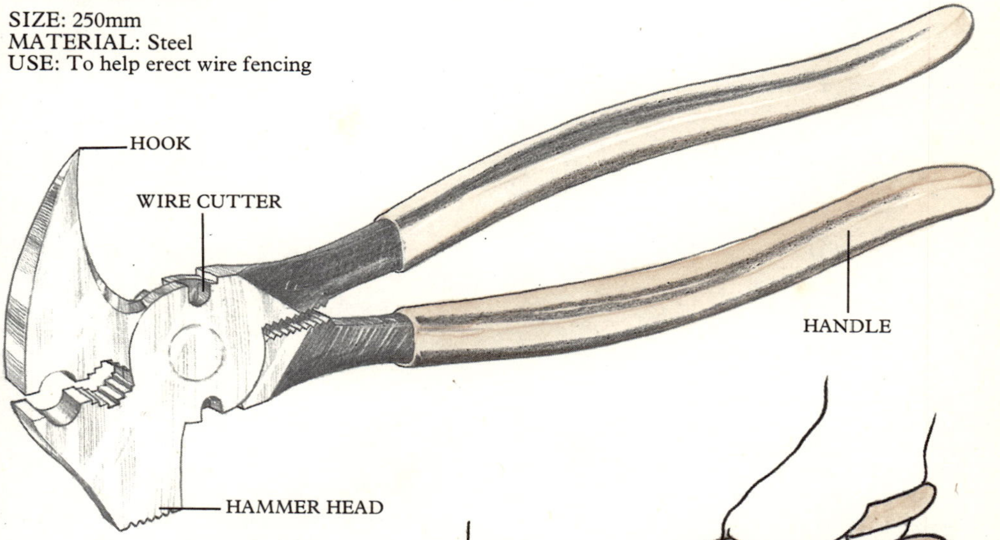

Fencing pliers incorporate several functions in one tool. They can be used to hammer staples as well as to extract them with the hook provided and also crop and tension the wire itself.

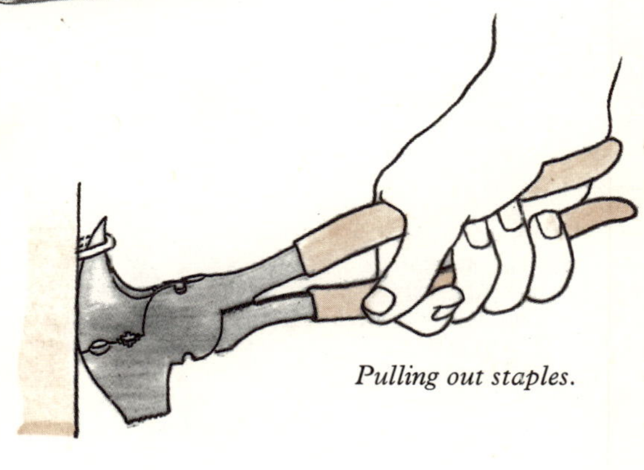

Pulling out staples.

Carpenter's Pincers

SIZE: 150 to 250mm
MATERIAL: Steel
USE: To extract nails and tacks

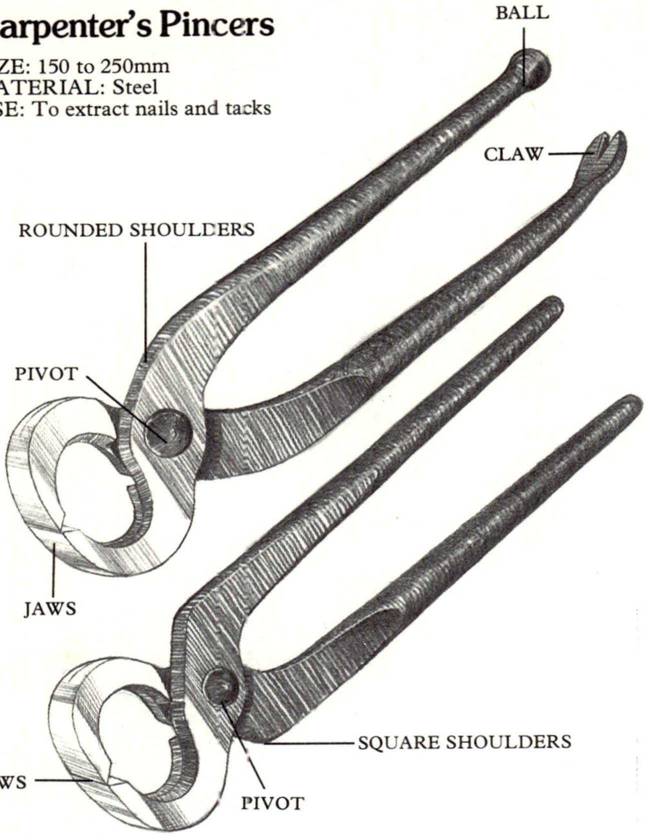

Carpenter's pincers are primarily designed to remove nails from timber. They are not as sharp as end cutting pliers, being designed to bite into the nail rather than cut through it. There are two common varieties. The "shouldered" variety has straight tapering handles with square shoulders just behind the pivot. The jaws which meet at a beveled cutting edge are somewhat flattened at the ends. The other version, sometimes known as "Tower" pincers, has rounded jaws and rounded shoulders, and the handles have a ball and claw at each end. The claw is for removing tacks, but the function of the ball is undetermined. Possibly it was for swaging pipe ends.

When using the pincers, position the tool vertically over the nail. If necessary place a piece of hardboard between the jaws and the wood to prevent marking the surface.

Using the pincers

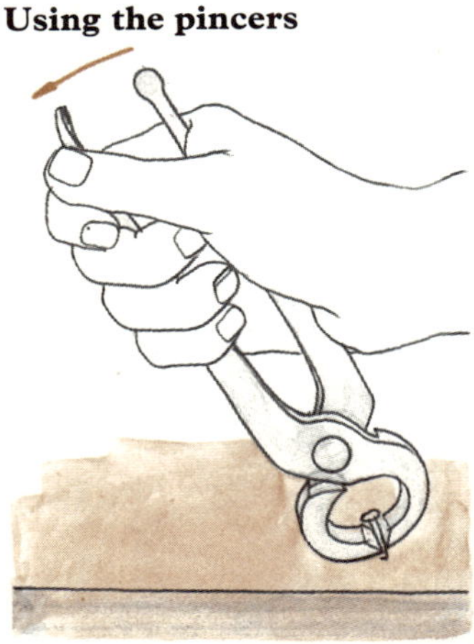

Grip the nail as near as possible to the surface. Squeeze the handles and rock the tool on the curved jaws, levering the nail out of the wood. If the nail does not come out of the wood entirely, grip it a second time further down the shaft and repeat the process.

Wrecking Bar

OTHER NAMES: Case opener, crowbar
SIZE: 350 to 900mm
MATERIAL: Steel
USE: To remove nails and lever structures apart

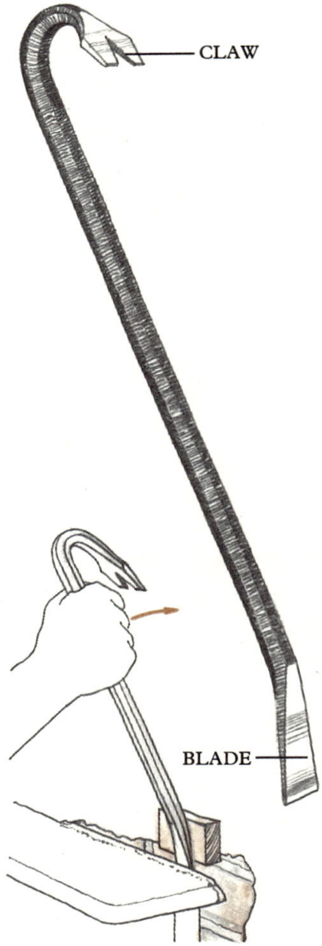

The wrecking bar is made from an octagonal section length of steel. One end is bent into a tight curve and terminates in a claw for removing nails. The other end is flattened to provide a blade for levering structures apart for demolition work. The length of bar provides considerable leverage for either job.

Wire Strippers

OTHER NAME: Wire stripping pliers
SIZE: 150 to 200mm
MATERIAL: Steel
USE: To strip insulation from electrical cable

Simple wire strippers have the tips of the jaws turned inward at right angles, the pronged tips being sharpened on the inside. They pass one inside the other to perform a shearing action. The jaws are fitted with an adjustable stop to close over a cable so that only the insulation is cut and the core remains undamaged. The jaws are closed by squeezing the handles which are usually sprung to open automatically.

Another version of wire strippers combines other functions to form a multi-purpose tool. The very tip of the jaws is sharpened to form a wire cutter, while immediately behind the cutter, the jaws are hollowed out for crimping terminals. Behind the pivot the handles are drilled out to take small bolts of various sizes. The bolt is passed through the hole and is cropped by the other half of the tool as the handles are closed. The handles are further incised to form wire strippers of various sizes to suit different weights of electrical cable.

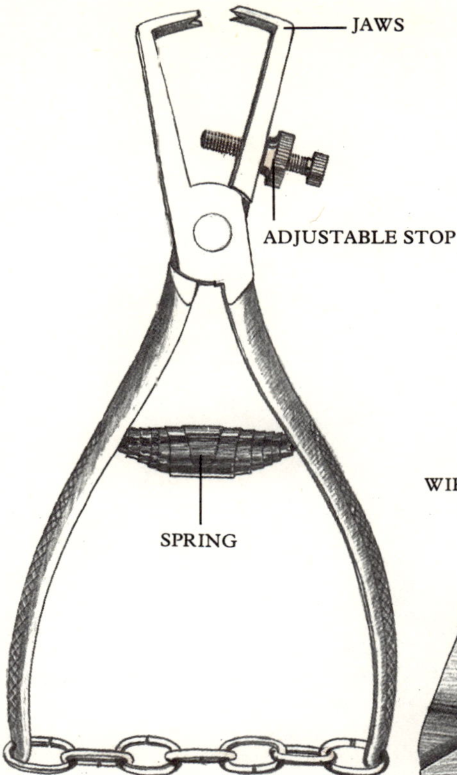

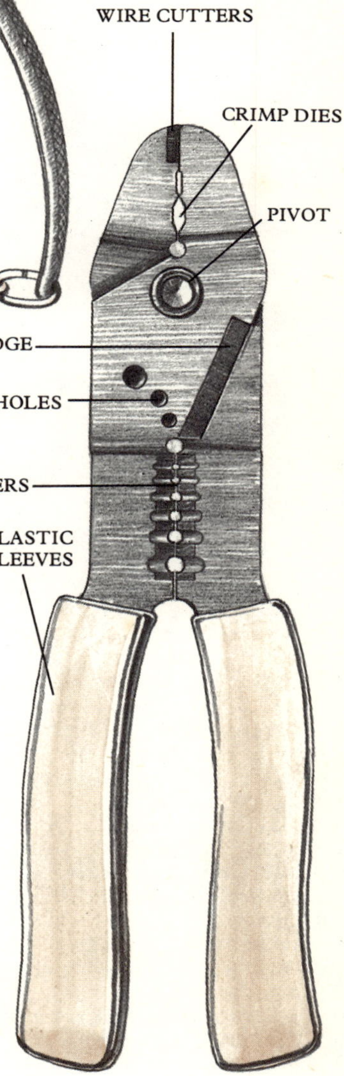

Stripping wires

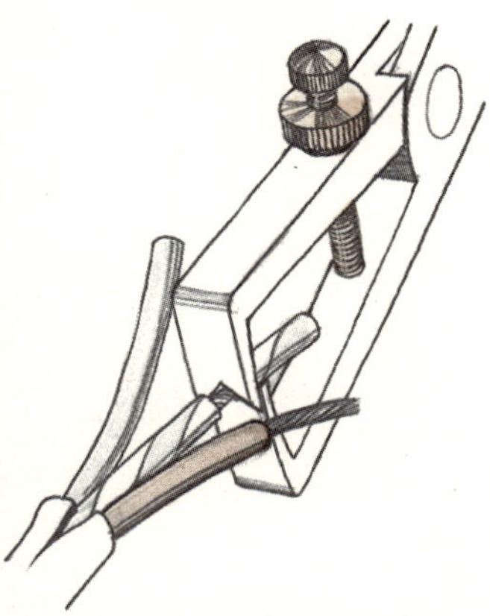

Peel back the outer sheathing. Separate the internal wires and place the ends in the wire stripper.

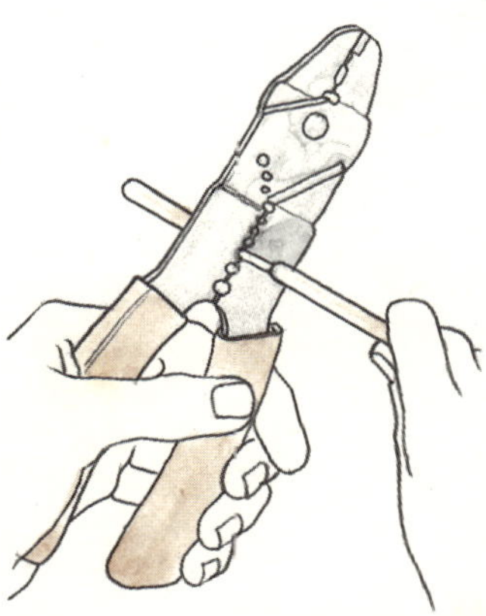

Twist the tool to insure that the insulation is cut right through and pull the wire through to strip it off.

Circlip Pliers

SIZE: 156 to 312mm
MATERIAL: Steel
USE: To insert or remove circlips

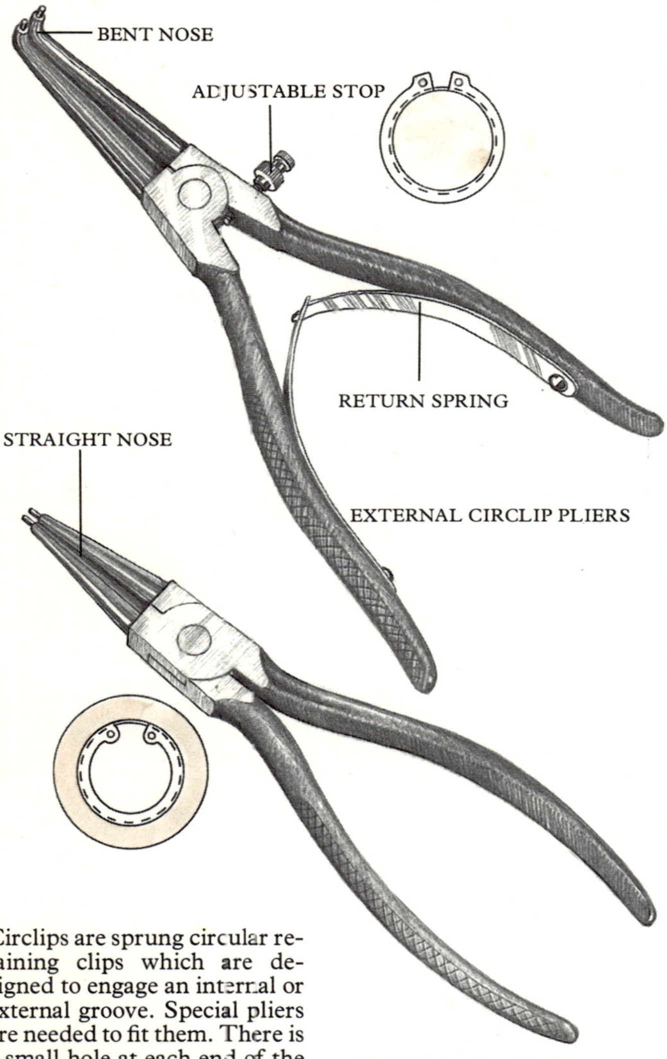

Circlips are sprung circular retaining clips which are designed to engage an internal or external groove. Special pliers are needed to fit them. There is a small hole at each end of the circlip. Circlip pliers have very narrow cylindrical tips to fit these holes. One version of circlip pliers is designed to fit internal clips while another spreads external clips. External circlip pliers are usually spring-loaded and some are fitted with a stop to prevent them distorting the clip by opening it too far. Both types of pliers are available with either bent or straight noses.

Upholsterer's Pliers

OTHER NAMES: Web pincers, upholsterer's pincers
SIZE: 200 to 212mm
MATERIAL: Steel
USE: To stretch webbing used in upholstery

The upholsterer's pliers have wide serrated jaws for gripping a length of upholsterer's woven webbing to tension it over a seat frame.

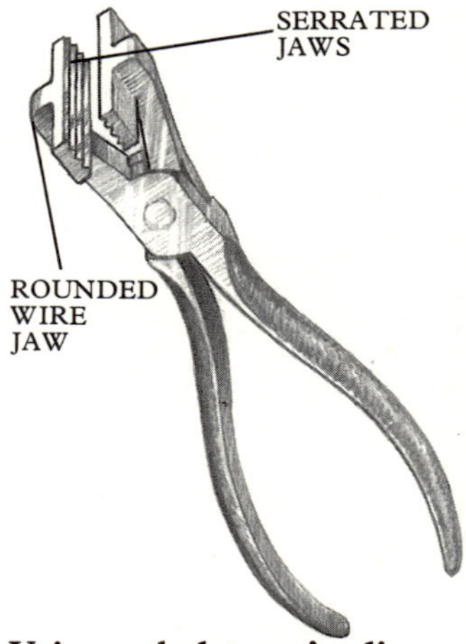

Using upholsterer's pliers

Fold over end of webbing, 37mm from the end; nail it to side of frame 12mm from the edge.

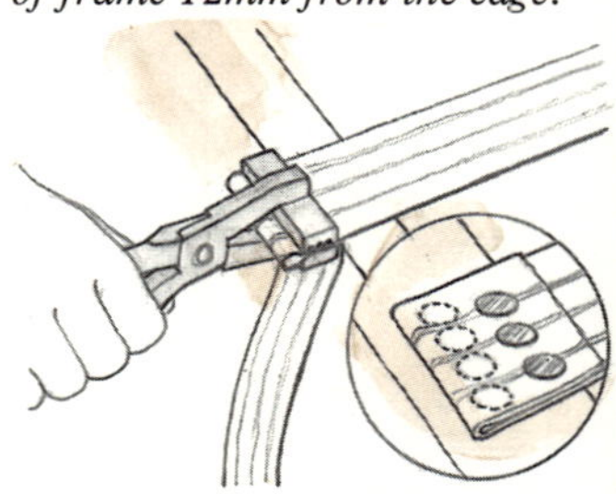

Stretch webbing across frame; grip folded end with pliers so lower jaw touches frame. Lever tool on curved lower jaw stretching webbing. Tack webbing to frame and cut off 37mm behind tacks. Fold loose end over and tack to frame.

Webbing Stretcher

SIZE: To take webbing up to 62mm wide
MATERIAL: Hardwood
USE: To stretch webbing across a seat frame

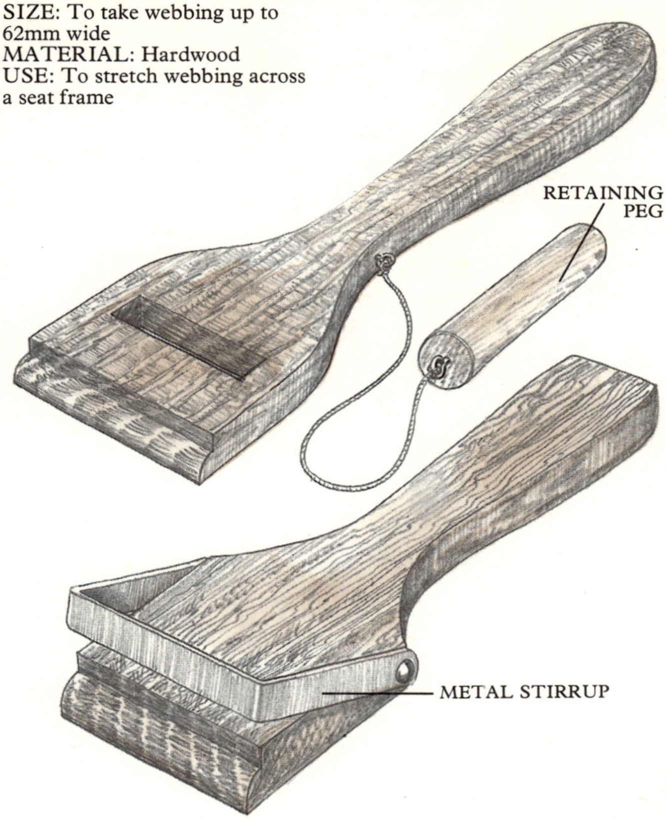

Webbing stretchers put the correct amount of tension on to woven seat webbing. There are other varieties, but two common types are cut from hardwood to form a paddle-like shape with a handle. The method for providing the tension differs. One uses a wooden peg while the other is fitted with a metal strip bent to form a stirrup.

Using a webbing stretcher
Nail off webbing as on previous page and loop free end, passing it through slot in peg type stretcher and pass peg through loop. Pull webbing tight and trap free end between stretcher and frame. Lever stretcher to tension webbing and nail off.

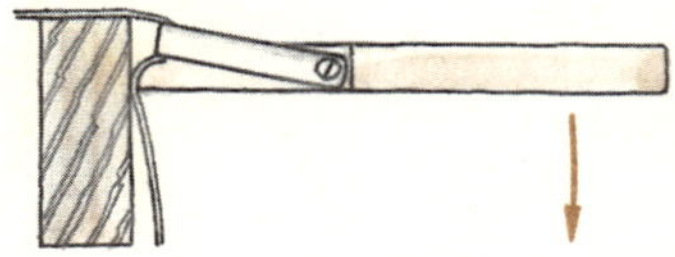

The stirrup variety is used in a similar way by passing the loose end of the webbing behind the stirrup and over the front edge of the stretcher which traps it against the frame.

Tack Lifter

SIZE: 162 to 200mm
MATERIAL: *Blade:* steel; *Handle:* beech, plastic
USE: To remove tacks used in upholstery

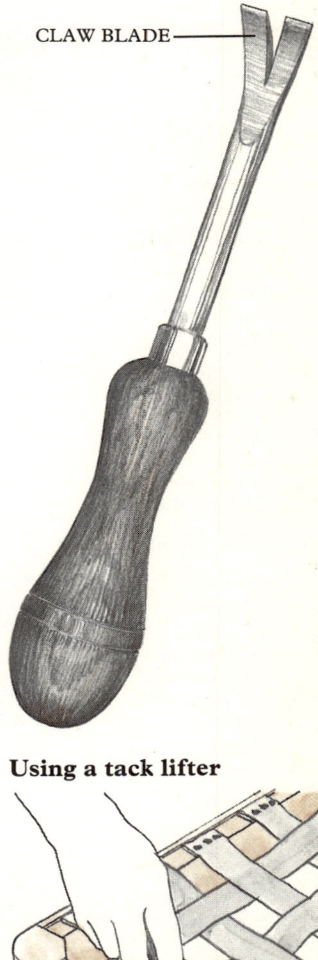

Using a tack lifter

Work the claw under the head of a tack and lever with the tool until the tack is removed. Where the head is deeply buried in the wood, you can cut access for the tack lifter with a chisel and mallet.

Auger and Gimlet

Some time after Caesar's conquest of Gaul the writer Pliny mentions a "Celtic drill" (*gallica terebra*). This was probably the auger, as used by the Celts of Central and Northern Europe, who were much admired by the Romans for their skill as carpenters and wheelwrights.

The early augers were spoon-shaped at the business end and up to 450mm long, with flat tangs or an eye to take the cross-handle. Later the spoon was twisted and drawn down to a point, as in the gimlet. The first true spiral or twist augers were invented late in the eighteenth century, but took some time to develop owing to manufacturing difficulties. The "Jennings pattern" with spurs or nickers was patented by Russell Jennings in 1855 and the solid-centre or "Irwin pattern" followed in 1884.

Auger

SIZE: Diameter: 6 to 31mm
MATERIAL: Steel
USE: To drill holes in wood

Augers are used to drill fairly large holes in timber. The boring end has a lead screw and twisted flutes like a drill bit to clear the waste. The common varieties are the "Jennings" pattern and solid centre augers. The shaft is about 600mm long with a collar at one end to take a removable handle.

Special end grain boring augers, up to 750mm long, are available. The thin, round-sectioned shaft is squared and tapered at one end to fit a handle. The other end has a shell bit fitted.

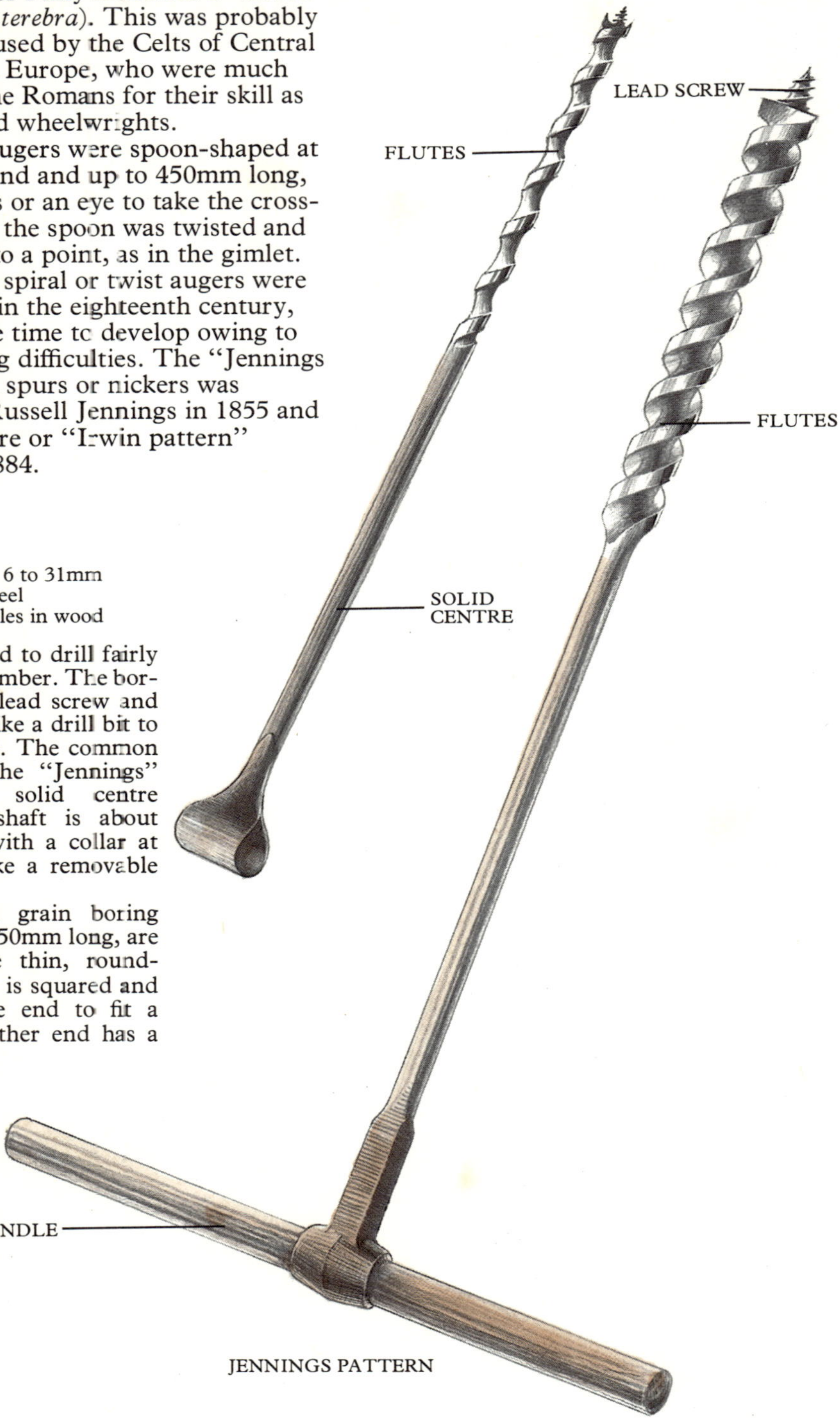

JENNINGS PATTERN

Gimlet

SIZE: 3 to 9mm
MATERIAL: *Body:* steel;
Handle: hardwood
USE: To bore holes in wood

The gimlet is used to bore shallow holes in timber, often to take a screw. The shaft terminates in a spiral lead screw followed by a "shell" or spiral fluted section for cutting and removing the waste. The remaining shaft, running to the handle, is either narrower than the cutting end, or tapers to reduce the friction in the hole. The cross handle is formed by the shaft itself being twisted to the required shape or it is squared and tapered to fit into a turned hardwood handle. The end of the shaft is rivetted over to fix it securely in the handle. The handle is held in the palm of the hand with the shaft projecting between the index and middle fingers.

To sharpen a gimlet, bore a 25mm hole with it in a piece of hardwood. Withdraw the tool and fill the hole with a mixture of oil and fine emery. Insert the gimlet to the depth of 12mm and turn it backward and forward until the cutting edge is honed. For a blunt gimlet you may need to top up the holes.

Using the gimlet

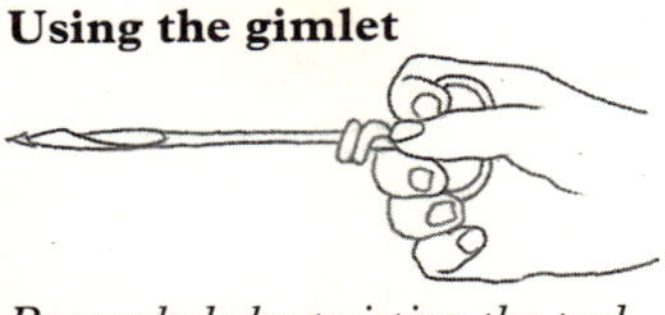

Bore a hole by twisting the tool until the lead screw pulls it into the wood. Twist in one direction only, not backward and forward as you would with a bradawl.

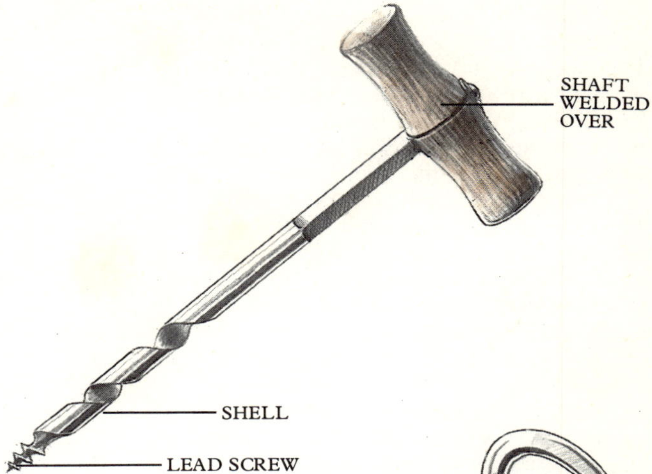

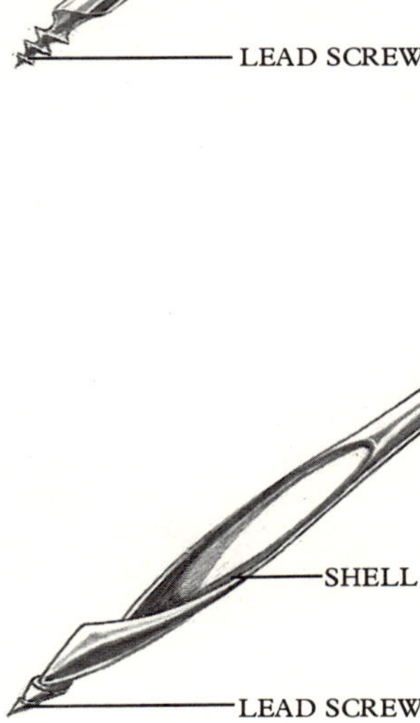

Taper Reamer

SIZE: 137mm
MATERIAL: *Body:* steel;
Handle: hardwood
USE: To ream a drilled hole

The taper reamer cannot drill a hole itself, but is used instead to enlarge and clean up a hole. Used from one side only, it will produce a tapered hole.

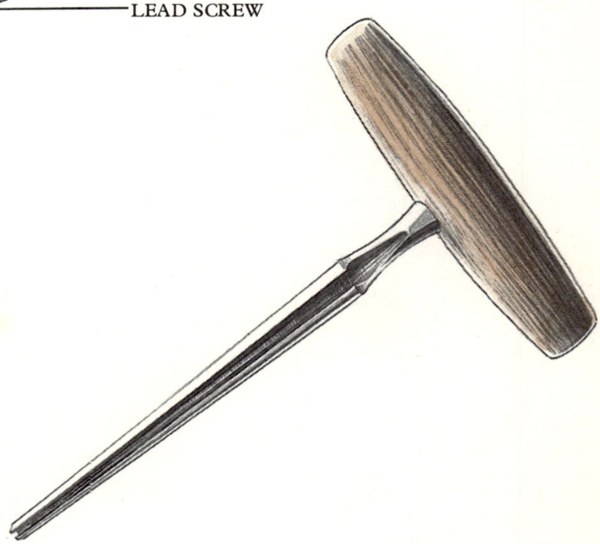

Braces and Drills

The carpenter's brace appeared in early fifteenth century Europe. Its main advantage for boring holes was that it gave a continuous and positive turning movement to the bit, instead of the intermittent action of gimlets, augers or bow and strap drills used previously.

The first braces all had fixed bits. By the sixteenth century each bit fitted into a wooden holder or "pad", which could then be held in a tapered hole in the stock with pins, wedges or screws. After the eighteenth century, the pads were dispensed with and a V-shaped notch was filed in the tangs of the bits which engaged with a springed pawl in the chuck. Wooden braces of this type were in common use until about 1900.

The Spofford split chuck brace of 1859 with a metal sweep did away with the need to notch the bits. In 1864 it was superseded by the "Barber" screwed shell chuck with springed jaws. This was soon fitted with a ratchet and is the standard type in present use.

Most early braces were fitted with shell or spoon bits similar in shape to the contemporary augers and gimlets. The first twist or screw augers appeared before 1800, but auger bits for use in braces came later; the Jennings pattern in 1855 and the solid core Irwin bits in 1884. Early forms of centre bit were used in the eighteenth century; the present form was finalized about 1800. The French call them "English three-point bits", indicating their probable origin. The expanding forms of centre bit date from Clarke's patent of about 1890.

The hand drill seems to have been first developed in France or Germany; one of the earliest was shown by Bergeron in 1816. The bevel gear wheels, with a ratio of 1:1, were carried in a U-shaped forging and driven by a small crank. In 1846 a side handle had been fitted and the gear ratio raised to about 3:1. The first American hand drills, introduced about 1870, carried the gears on an open-work iron frame and had a long, turned handle.

Brace

SIZE: Sweep: 125, 200, 250, 300, 350mm
MATERIAL: *Frame:* steel; *Head/handle:* hardwood, plastic
ACCESSORIES: Drill bits, screwdriver bit, countersink bit
USE: To bore holes in wood

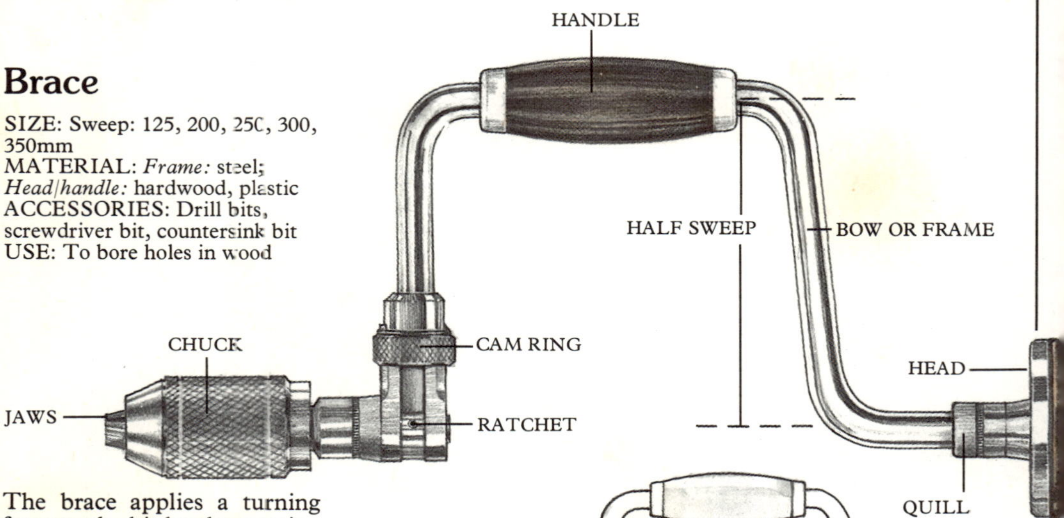

The brace applies a turning force to the bit by the rotation of the frame in a clockwise direction. The amount of space taken up by this action is known as "the sweep", and the size of the brace is given in terms of this measurement. Many braces have a ratchet fitted to the chuck, which allows the tool to be used in confined spaces where a complete sweep is impossible.

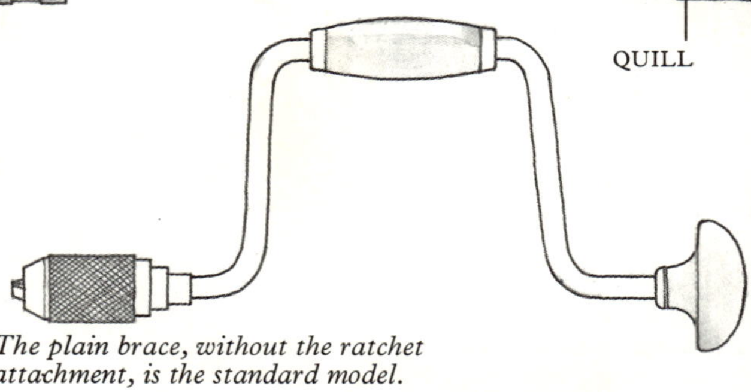

The plain brace, without the ratchet attachment, is the standard model.

Fitting the bits
Most bits used with the brace have a square tang at the end of the shank, which is gripped by "V" grooves in the jaws. Some braces have universal jaws, which will also take round shank bits. All brace bits have their diameter size stamped into the tang.

Engaging the ratchet
To engage the ratchet on a ratchet brace turn the cam ring clockwise against the stop. This will provide torque in a clockwise direction only, leaving the frame to move freely in the anti-clockwise direction. For the reverse effect, turn the cam ring in an anti-clockwise direction.

Using the brace
For easy location of the bit, you can either mark the centre of the hole with a bradawl or, if working in hardwood, drill a 2mm pilot hole.

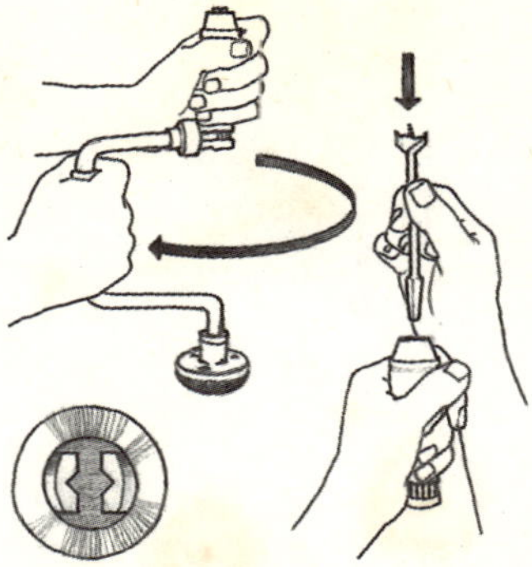

Fitting a bit to a ratchet
Locate the cam ring in its central position. Turn the frame clockwise until the jaws open to take the bit. Locate the tang in the "V" grooves. Check that the bit is square in the jaws before turning the frame anti-clockwise to tighten the chuck.

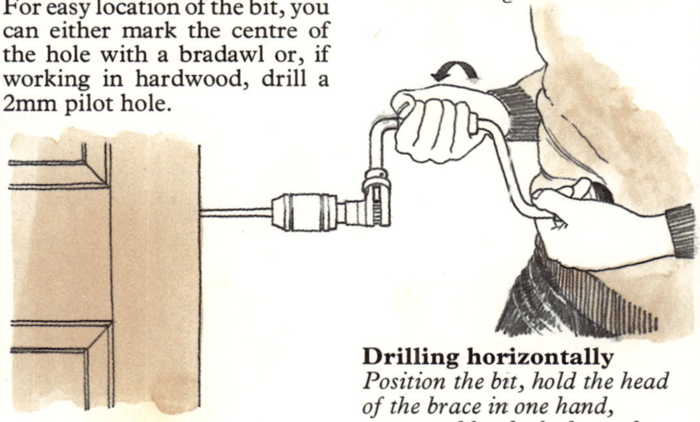

Drilling horizontally
Position the bit, hold the head of the brace in one hand, supported by the body, and place the other hand on the handle. Move the head to square up the brace with the work and turn the frame clockwise while applying pressure to the head.

Drilling vertically

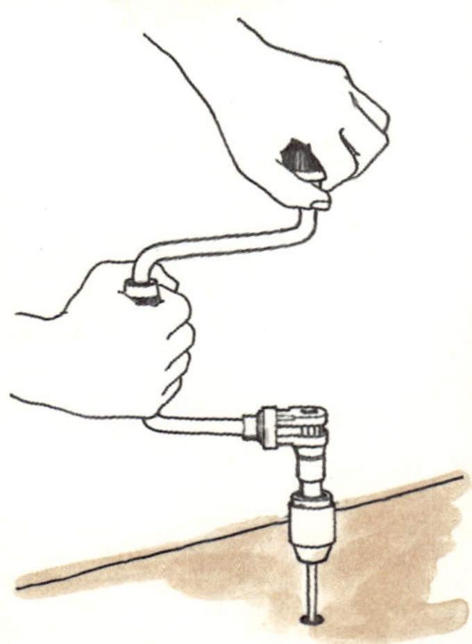

Apply pressure to the head with one hand. A square placed close to the brace will help as a guide to alignment.

Clearing waste
The waste from a deep hole must be cleared periodically. To extract the bit, reverse the action on a couple of turns releasing the lead screw, then turn the frame clockwise while pulling on the tool.

Avoid splitting out the back of the work by either clamping a block of waste timber to the back or removing the tool as soon as the lead screw appears. Then pick up the exit hole and drill out the remaining waste from the back.

Joist Brace

SIZE: Handle: 288mm
MATERIAL: *Lever/chuck:* steel; *Head/handle:* plastic
ACCESSORIES: Drill bits, screwdriver bit, countersink bit
USE: To drill in restricted space, such as between joists

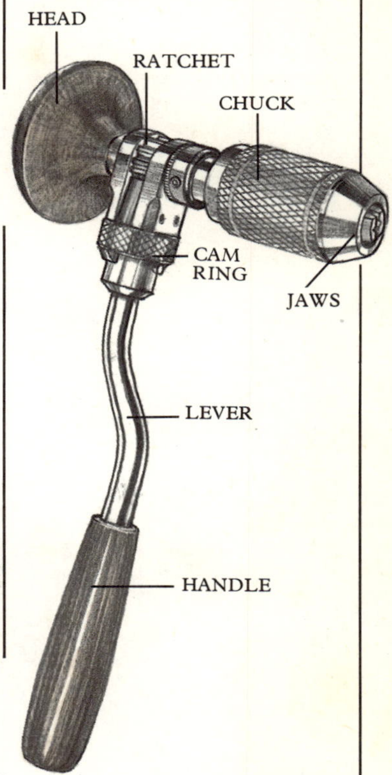

The chuck and ratchet of the joist brace is constructed in the same way as a standard brace, but instead of the conventional frame there is a lever at right angles to the line of the drill bit. With the ratchet set correctly, the lever is worked back and forth to turn the bit, while force is applied to the head mounted directly behind the chuck. This makes it a useful tool for work in a confined space where the handle of the conventional brace could not be fully rotated.

Maintenance
A modern brace requires very little maintenance other than an occasional oiling of the chuck mechanism, head and handle. Keep the bits sharp to produce clean accurate work.

Corner Brace

OTHER NAME: Gear frame brace
SIZE: Sweep: 200 and 250mm
MATERIAL: *Frame:* steel; *Head/handle:* hardwood, plastic
ACCESSORIES: Drill bits, screwdriver bit, countersink bit
USE: To drill in a restricted space such as into a skirting board

On a corner brace the conventional brace frame is fitted at an angle to a gear housing. This allows the chuck to be turned even when it is operating against a surface which would prevent a normal sweep.

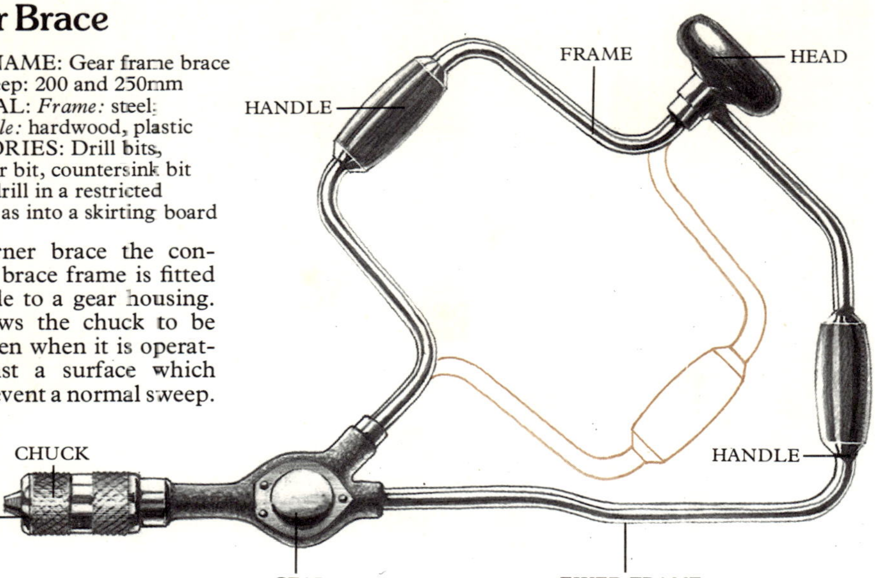

Pressure is applied on a handle mounted at the back of the tool.

Centre Bit

OTHER NAME: Screw point bit
SIZE: *Length:* 100 to 150mm; *Diameter:* 6 to 56mm
MATERIAL: Steel
USE: To drill holes in wood

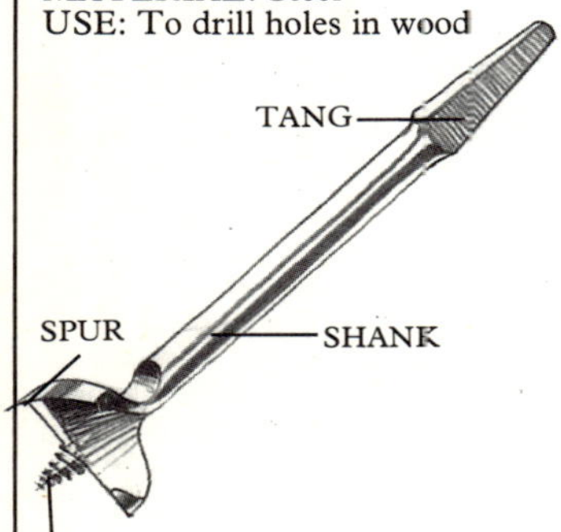

The centre bit has a solid, cylindrical shank with a square section tang which fits into the chuck of a brace. The cutting end of the bit has a helical twist which gives two cutting edges, a lead screw in the centre, and a single spur on one side to score the surface grain of the wood before the bit enters.

Once the lead screw has "taken" in the work, it will draw the bit after it with the minimum of pressure.

Auger Bit

OTHER NAME: Twist bit
SIZE: *Jennings pattern:* Length: 200 to 250mm; Diameter: 6 to 38mm; *Solid centre:* Length: 200 to 250mm; Diameter: 6 to 38mm; Length: 300 to 450mm; Diameter: 6 to 25mm
MATERIAL: Steel
USE: To drill holes in wood

There are two patterns of auger bit: the Jennings, or double twist, and the solid centre.

The Jennings pattern has a double helical twist which clears the waste from the hole as it progresses into the work. The solid centre has a single helical twist around a solid shank, which runs the whole length of the bit. This is the stronger version and is favoured for very long bits.

The main advantage of the auger bit, apart from efficient waste clearance, is that it is easier to keep centred in a deep hole.

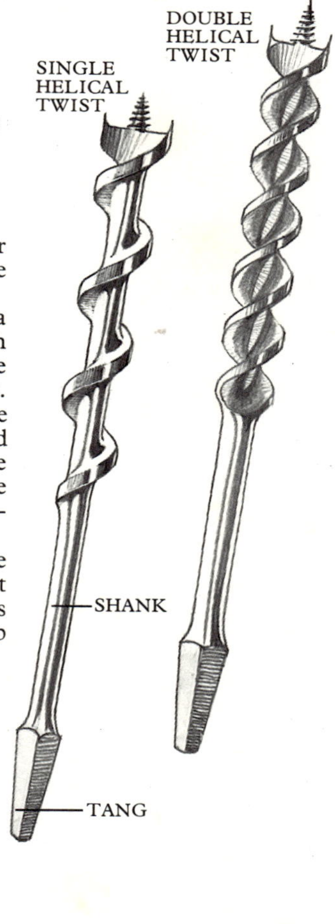

Expansive Bit

SIZE: *Small:* 13 to 38mm; *Large:* 22 to 75mm
MATERIAL: Steel
USE: To drill holes of various size in wood

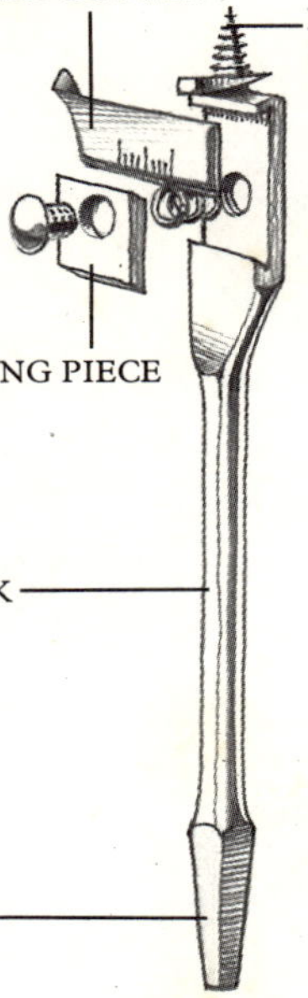

The expansive bit is similar in form to a solid centre bit, but has an additional, adjustable spurred cutter which moves out from the centre to enlarge the cutting diameter of the bit.

Adjusting the bit
The cutter is calibrated to show the diameter it will cut at any one setting. It is held by a screw fixed packing piece which releases for resetting, or a toothed, calibrated dial, which is turned for resetting.

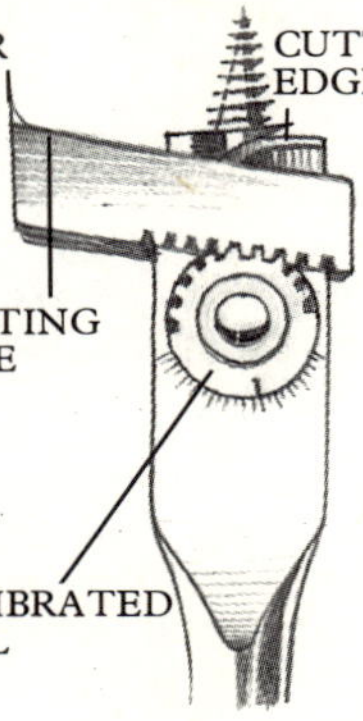

Forstner Bit

SIZE: 9 to 50mm
MATERIAL: Steel
USE: To drill holes in wood

Unlike the bits with a lead screw at the centre, the Forstner bit must be used under pressure in order to cut into the work. The cutting end has a deep rim and a small pointed centre, which means that it cuts a clean hole with a flat bottom and will not wander off centre by following the grain.

Its accuracy makes it very useful for veneer work and pattern making.

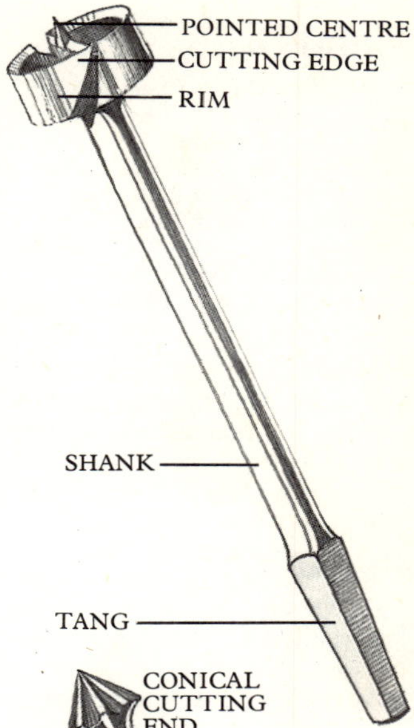

Countersink Bit

SIZE: 9, 13, 16mm
MATERIAL: Steel
USE: To recess a hole to accept a countersunk head screw

The cone shaped cutting end of the countersink bit matches the countersunk head of a wood screw. The bit is fitted into a brace and held vertically in the centre of a clearance hole already drilled in the work. Then it is rotated until it cuts a recess that will allow the screw head to lie flush with the wooden surface.

The "rosehead" type shown here is the commonest, but there is a flathead countersink bit, with two cutting edges and a flattened, V-shaped head, which is used to countersink hinges.

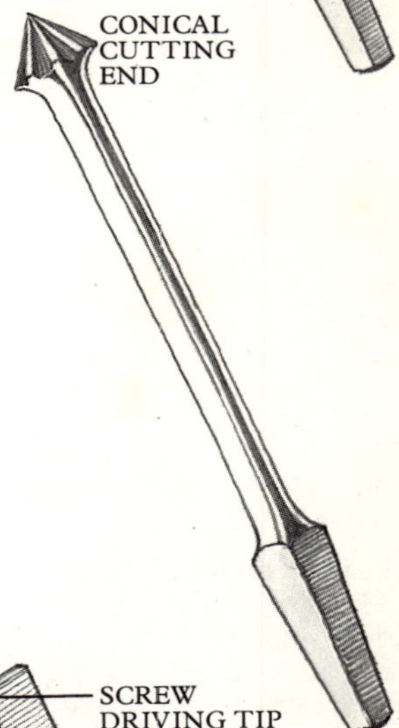

Turn Screw Bit

OTHER NAME: Screwdriver bit
SIZE: *Length:* 100 to 150mm; *Blade width:* 9, 13, 19mm
MATERIAL: Steel
USE: To drive screws with the aid of a brace

The turn screw bit is useful for driving large screws. It has a flat, screwdriver blade and a square tang which fits into the chuck of a brace. The pressure and extra torque provided by the brace make a very powerful screwdriver.

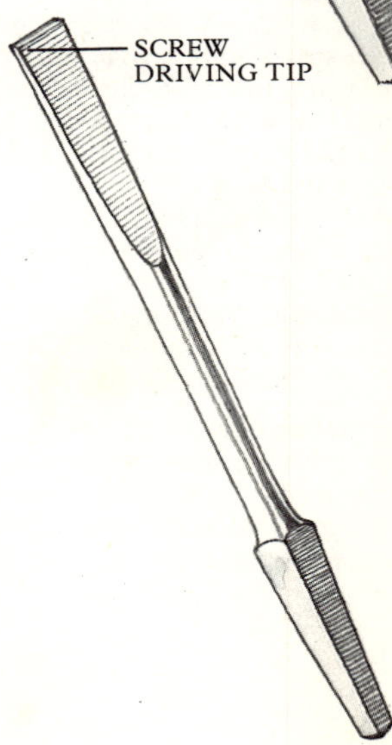

Hand Drill

OTHER NAME: Wheel brace
SIZE: *Length:* 225 to 325mm; *Capacity:* up to 8mm
MATERIAL: *Frame/body:* cast iron, aluminium or zinc; *Gear wheels:* cast iron; *Handles/knobs:* hardwood, plastic
ACCESSORIES: Twist drills
USE: To drill holes in wood and metal

The hand drill combines hand drive and gear ratio to provide a range of convenient speeds for different materials and types of work. The large gear wheel drives one or two pinions which apply torque to the chuck. On some models, the drive crank can be lengthened to provide greater torque. More modern drills have their gears completely enclosed in a cast body to protect them from dust.

The chuck usually has three self-centring jaws.

Fitting the bits
Holding the large gear wheel, turn the chuck shell anticlockwise to open the jaws. Centre the drill bit in the jaws and tighten them by turning the chuck clockwise. Check the accurate alignment of the bit before you finally tighten the jaws.

Using the hand drill
The hand drill is often used to drill pilot holes for screws or larger holes. With softwood and a small hole, it may not be necessary to mark the centre, but if the work is important or is in hardwood, start the hole with a bradawl.

For drilling in metal you will need a centre punch to mark the hole and prevent the drill wandering. Most metals need some sort of lubricant when they are being drilled.

Maintenance
Occasionally clean away dust from around the gear wheel and pinions and oil them lightly if necessary.

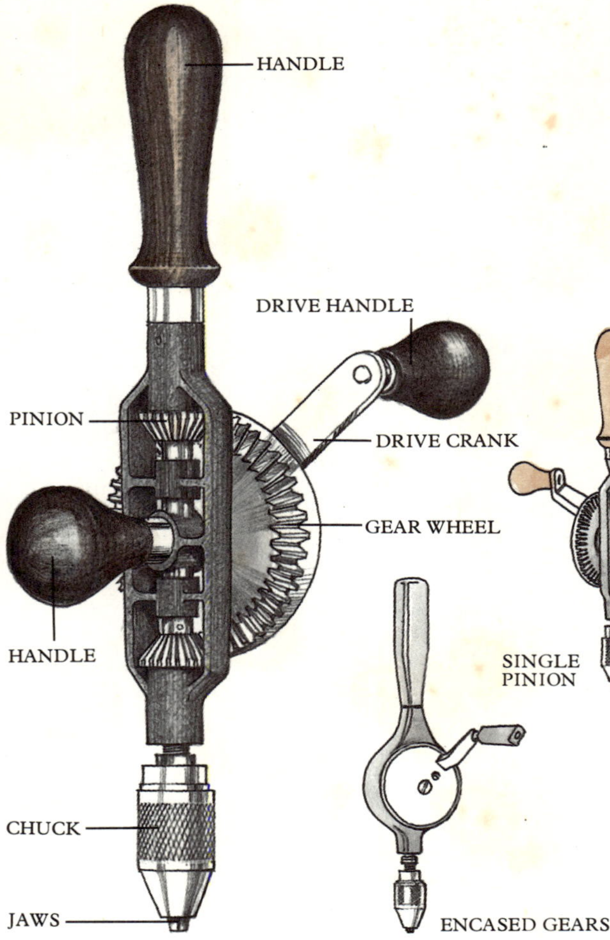

DOUBLE PINION

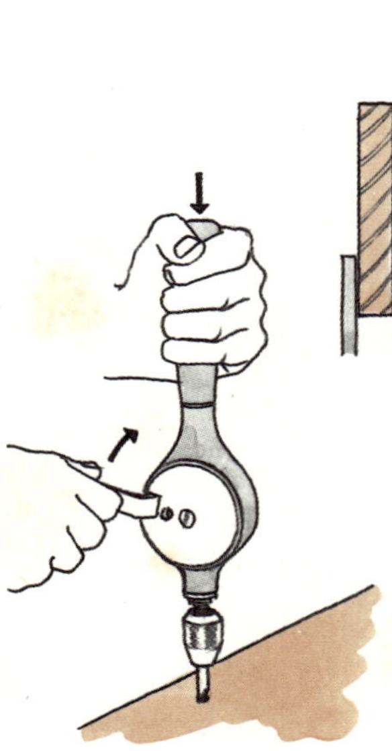

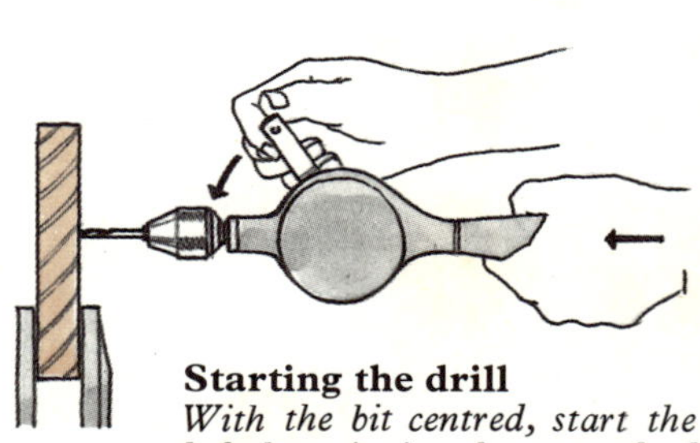

Starting the drill
With the bit centred, start the hole by gripping the gear wheel between thumb and fingers. Rotate the bit backward and forward to establish it then, grasping the gear wheel handle, use the tool at the required speed. A high speed with light feed will be necessary if you are drilling with small bits, to prevent them catching and possibly breaking as they enter the work.

Breast Drill

SIZE: *Capacity:* up to 13mm; *Length:* 275 to 450mm
MATERIAL: *Frame/body:* cast iron, steel, aluminium or zinc; *Gear wheels:* cast iron; *Handles:* hardwood, plastic; *Breastplate:* cast iron
ACCESSORIES: Twist drills, masonry bit
USE: To drill holes in wood, metal and masonry

The breast drill is a larger version of the hand drill, with the addition of a curved, saddle-shaped plate fitted to the top of the frame. You can lean on this to apply pressure. They are also fitted with a side handle with which you can steady the tool.

Most breast drills have two speeds. These are selected by engaging different size gear wheels either by fitting the drive crank onto the appropriate drive spigot, or by fitting the whole drive gear wheel in one of two positions, which automatically engages the required gear.

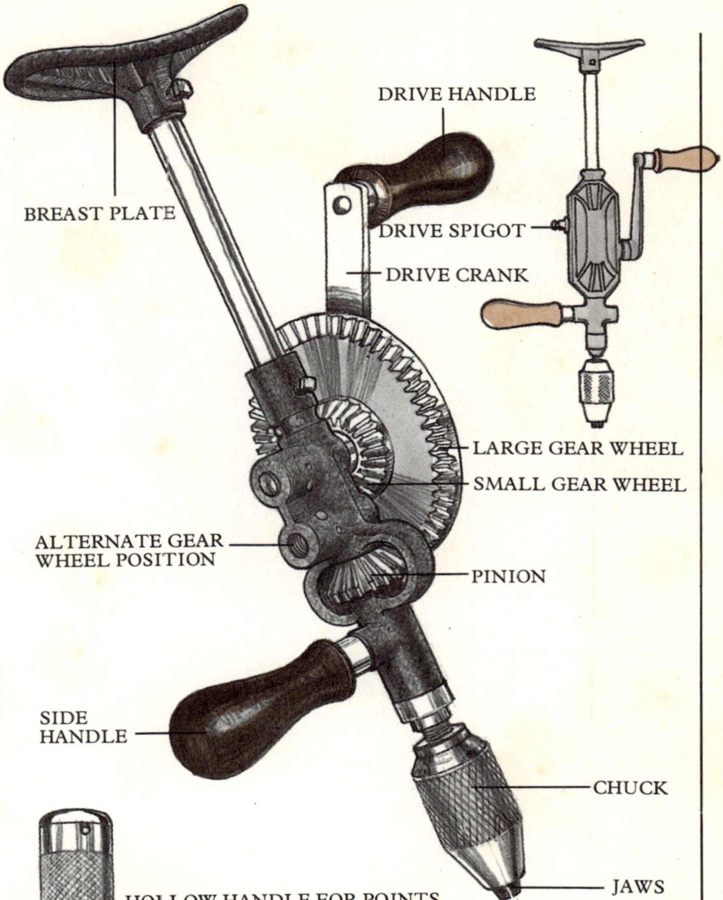

Push Drill

SIZE: Length: 263 to 288mm
MATERIAL: Combination of steel, plastic and aluminium
ACCESSORIES: Drill points
USE: To drill small holes in wood and plastic

The push drill takes special bits known as drill points, which are single, straight fluted bits ranging in size from 2 to 17mm. The bits are stored in the handle of the tool.

Torque is applied to the drill point by applying pressure to the handle of the drill.

Fitting the drill point
The drill point is fitted in the same way that bits are fitted to the hand drill. Take care to seat the point carefully before tightening the chuck.

Using the drill
To prevent the point wandering, start the hole with an awl. The drill point cuts on the forward stroke. When pressure is released, the handle returns, ready to repeat the action.

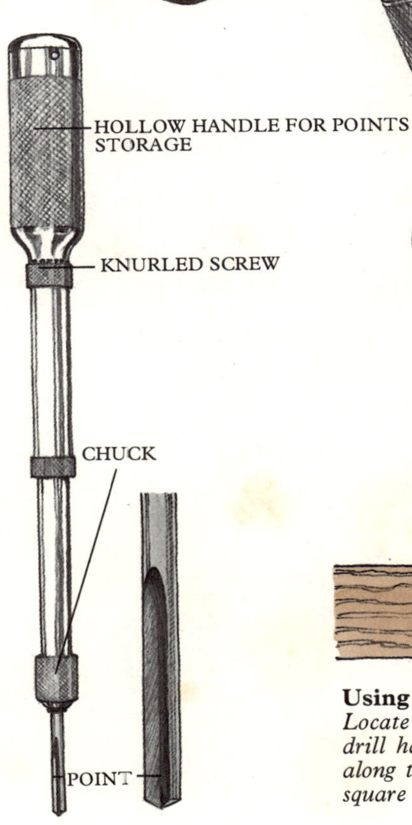

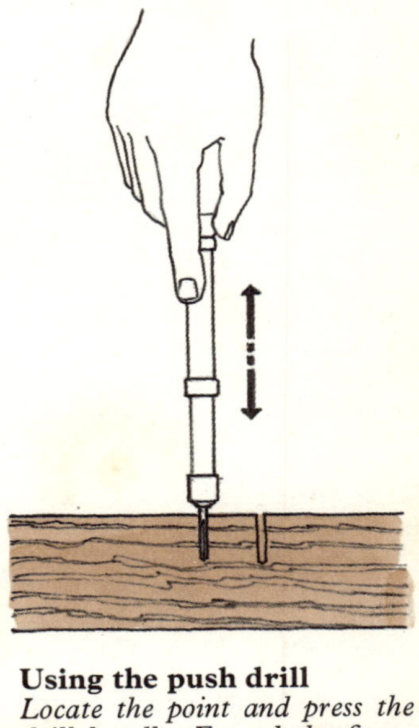

Using the push drill
Locate the point and press the drill handle. Extend the finger along the shaft to keep the tool square to the work.

Power Drill

SIZE: *Chuck capacity:* 6, 7.5, 12, 18, 25, 31mm; *Speed:* 2,750 to 3,500 rpm
MATERIAL: Various
ACCESSORIES: Drill bits, countersink bit, screw driver bit, plug cutter, bit extension, depth gauge, flexible drive, angled drive
ATTACHMENTS: Circular saw, jig saw, hole saw, saw bench, horizontal drill stand, vertical drill stand, sanding discs, sanding drums, finishing sander, buffs, wire brushes, grindstones and discs, rasps and files, lathe, hedge trimmer, paint spraying compressor, paint stirrer, pump
USE: To drill holes in various materials and coupled with attachments to perform a multitude of tasks

The power drill together with its many attachments and accessories, is probably the most versatile power tool available. It is also manufactured in many forms and sizes, which makes choosing the tool to suit your needs a complex task. In most cases it is advisable to choose the most versatile tool, unless you have to perform one task repeatedly, which is normal only in an industrial situation. Generally speaking, the attachments will not perform any one task as well as a specially made machine. For domestic use you must weigh versatility against efficiency.

Sizes and speeds
There are many different types of drill manufactured around the world, and the specifications given must be regarded as a guide only. Drills are specified by their chuck capacity and fall into three categories for domestic use: 6, 9 and 12mm; 18mm and over are available for industrial use. Smaller capacity drills can be used to drill larger holes by fitting them with spade bits, power bore bits or hole saws, which have narrow shanks compared with their heads.

Normally, the bigger the chuck capacity the larger the motor. As the power increases, the speed will reduce to give the extra torque needed when drilling large holes in masonry or steel.

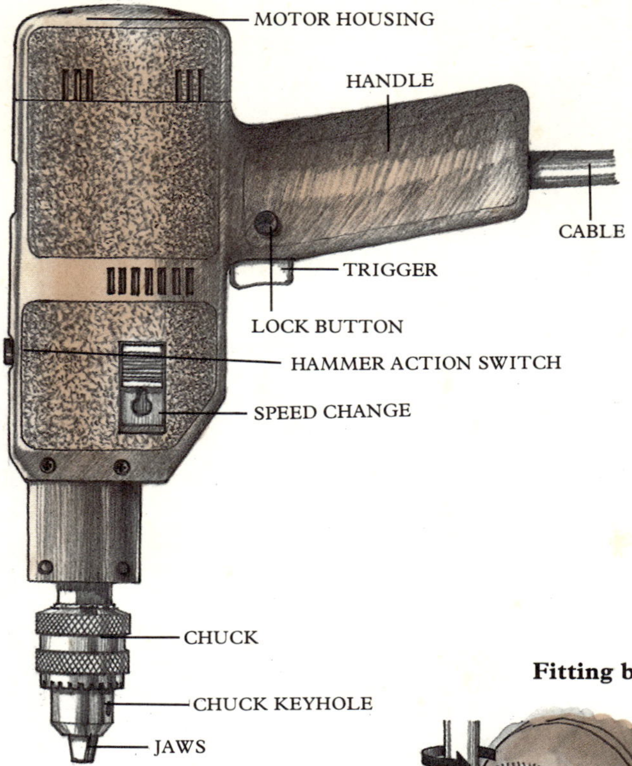

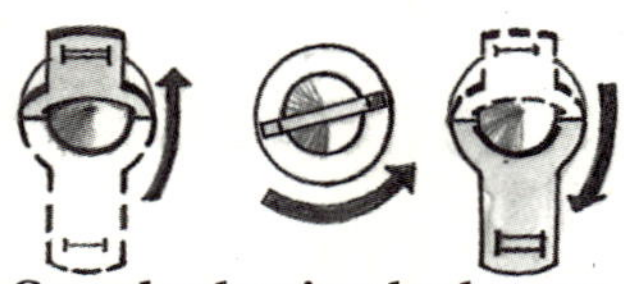

Speed selection by button

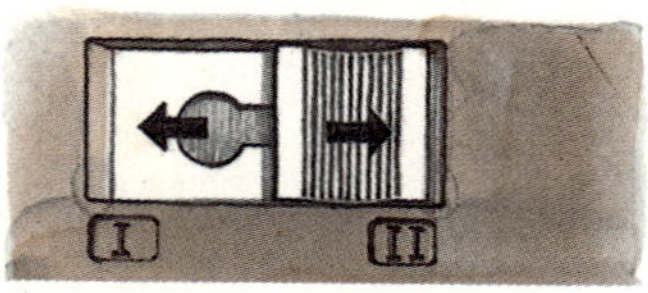

Speed selection by slide

There is quite a variation in the speed rating of a drill. It may have from one to four fixed speeds selected by a slide control or turn button, which may be converted to constantly variable speeds controlled by pressure on the trigger. A variable speed is essential if you want to use the drill to drive screws, and is also very useful when starting a hole. A reversing switch will allow the drill to withdraw screws. Fast speeds make clear cuts in wood.

When using attachments, select the speed recommended by the manufacturer.

Fitting bits

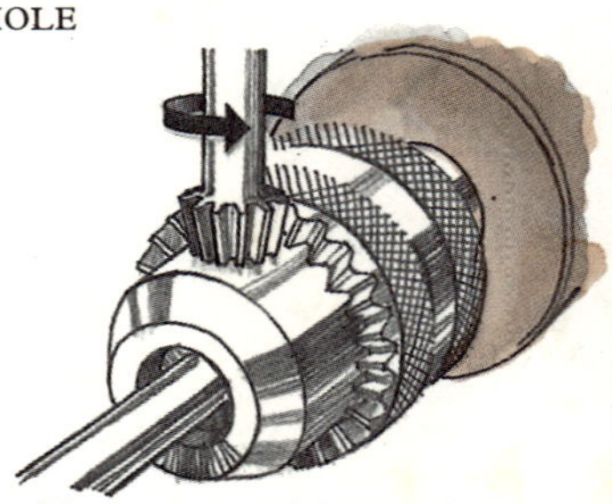

Slacken or tighten the self-centring jaws with a chuck key. Before finally tightening the jaws check that the bit is centred.

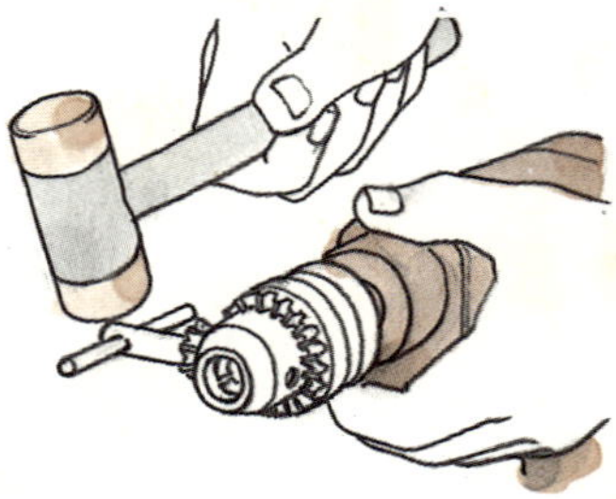

Removing the chuck
Engage the lowest speed and insert the chuck key. Holding the body of the drill firmly, strike the key with a mallet to spin the chuck rapidly and then unscrew it by hand. Some models are disconnected by using a spanner on the chuck.

OTHER FEATURES

Handgrips

Most drills have a secondary handle, which helps to steady the tool. This is particularly important with the larger drills, which could slip out of the operator's grip, if the bit becomes caught in the work. Heavy duty drills are provided with another grip at the back, where extra pressure can be applied.

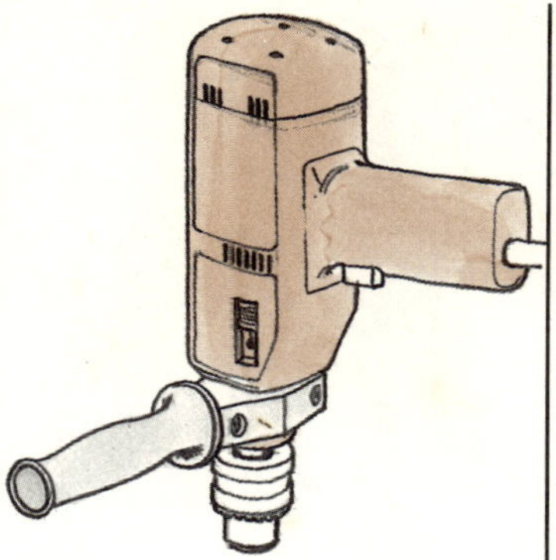

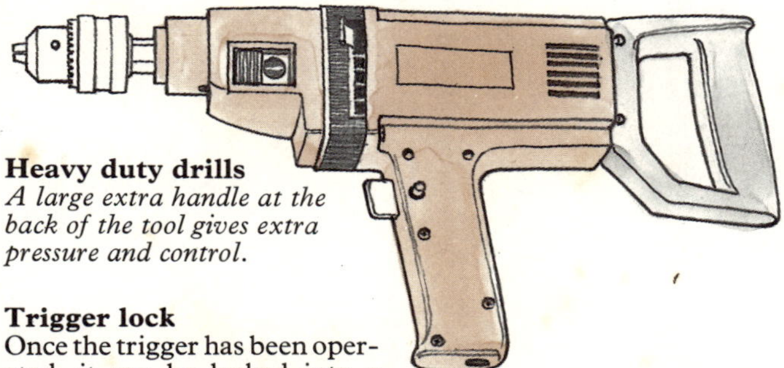

Heavy duty drills
A large extra handle at the back of the tool gives extra pressure and control.

Trigger lock

Once the trigger has been operated, it can be locked into a position for continuous running by a button, usually located to the left of the handgrip. Subsequent depression of the trigger will automatically release the button. This facility is essential if the tool is to be set up in any kind of bench attachment.

Variable speed drills either lock when the motor has reached top speed or, in a few cases, can be locked at any required speed.

Position for trigger lock

Hammer action

Some drills are fitted with a hammer action to assist when drilling concrete, stone or even hard brick. The tool will deliver 500 blows per second as the drilling progresses, which breaks up the masonry ahead of the drill tip. Even when the selector is engaged the hammer action is not activated until pressure is applied to the drill bit. Special percussion drill bits are needed for use with the hammer action.

Soft masonry such as brick or cement blocks can be drilled with standard masonry bits and the drill set on the slow speed only.

Hammer action selector

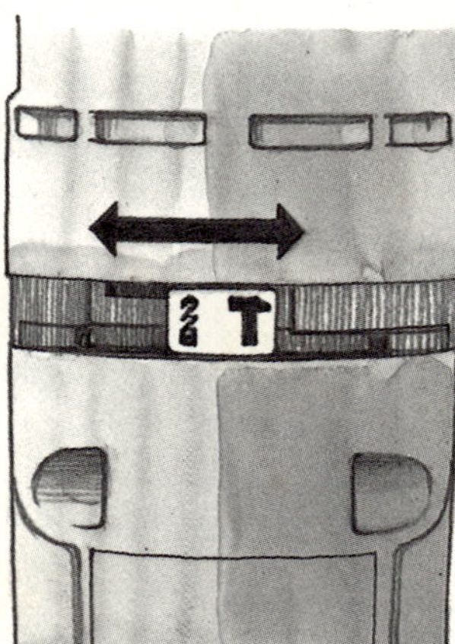

Safety factors

Before making any adjustments to the drill, disconnect it from the power supply to prevent accidental starting. Remove the chuck key before starting up the drill. Follow the safety advice given for specific attachments by the manufacturer.

Ensure that plugs are properly earthed and that your electrical circuit is fused to take the load of the drill.

Insulation
This is the international symbol for double insulation. Modern drills which are double insulated do not require earthing.

Do not pull out the plug, or carry the drill by the cable. Examine the cable regularly for signs of damage. Keep the cable away from the moving parts of of the drill when in use.

Avoid wearing loose clothing or jewellery, which could get caught up in the moving parts of the drill.

Twist Drill

OTHER NAME: Morse drill
SIZE: Diameter: up to 13mm; reduced shank drills: 13 to 18mm
MATERIAL: Steel
USE: To drill holes in various materials

The twist or Morse drill (named after its inventor), was developed to clear the swarf or waste metal from deep holes. There are two helical flutes running approximately two thirds along the length of the cylindrical drill, leaving the plain shank to fit into the drill chuck. The edges of the spirals, called the "margins", form the actual outside diameter of the bit, the rest being slightly cut away to reduce the friction on the sides of the hole. The cutting edge is known as the lip. The lip is ground to an angle of 59° for cutting metal. For practical purposes, this is also suitable for wood, although the recommended angle is approximately 45°.

Carbon steel drills are only suitable for cutting wood, whereas a high speed drill can be used to work metal as well.

Maintenance
It is important to have sharp drills for accurate work. Before using the bit, clear away wood waste which may have become packed into the flutes.

Drills need to be lubricated when drilling metal to prevent overheating, as follows: steel and wrought iron: machine oil; aluminium: paraffin; cast iron and brass: can be drilled dry.

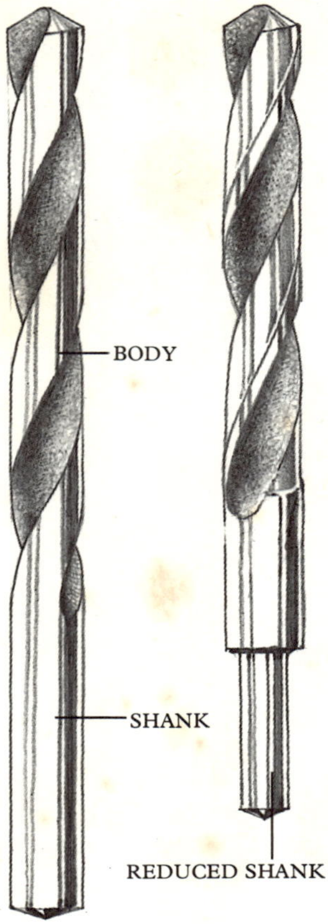

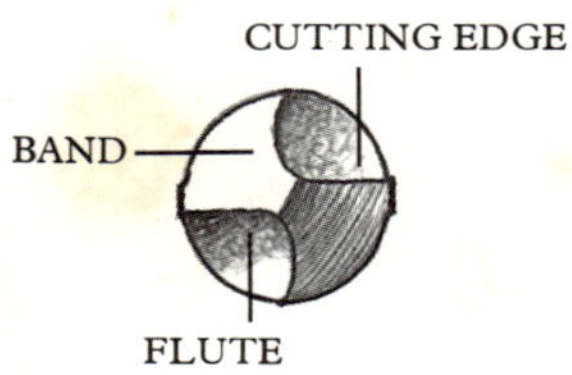

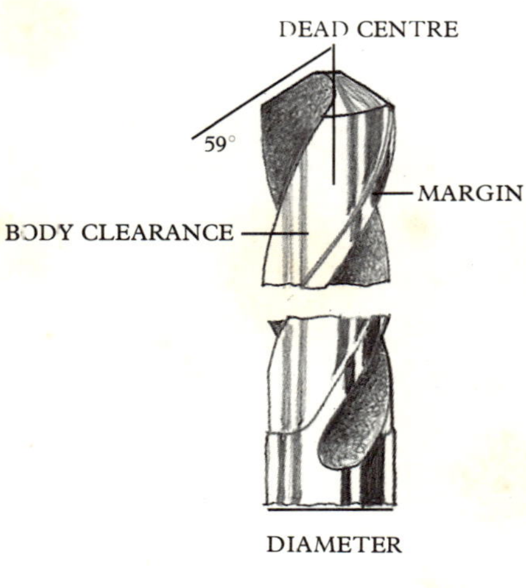

Drilling
Although twist drills can be used on wood they are more efficient for drilling metal. The workpiece must be held securely by clamps or in a vice. Mark the centre of the hole with a punch making a recess which will prevent the tip of the drill wandering off line.

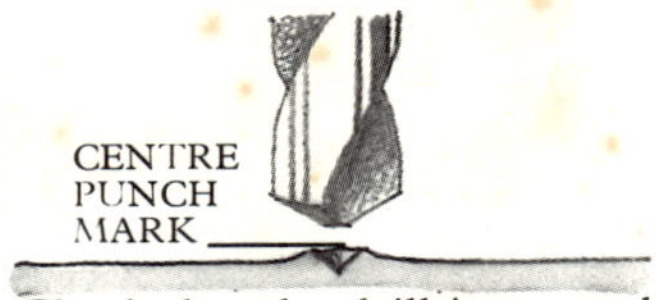

Check that the drill is centred before the body of the tool enters the work. To realign the drill, use a round nosed or diamond point cold chisel to cut a groove in the side of the depression closest to the original centre. This will encourage the drill to move in that direction until it is centred again.

Large holes must be started with a small pilot hole. The point of the larger drill will automatically follow the line of this hole. Drill very large holes with several drills gradually enlarging the pilot hole.

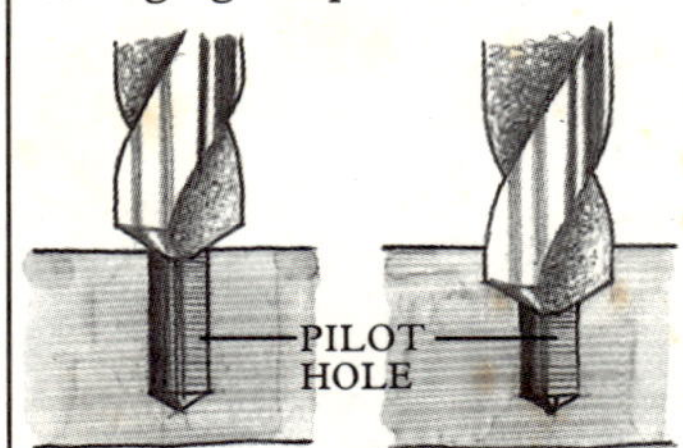

Do not force a drill to cut too fast as this will wear the drill. Try to prevent the drill suddenly emerging from the underside of the work. It is liable to catch in the resulting burrs and either break, or spin the workpiece. A slow controlled exit will not produce a large burr and will result in a clean cut.

If the drill catches as it exits when drilling thin sheet metal regrind the tip of the drill to a shallow angle. Backing up the workpiece with hardwood can prevent breaking out.

Twist drills can be used to work timber, but tend to wander in the direction of the grain. Bits with a lead point or screw are more suitable.

Dowel Bit

SIZE: Diameter: 3 to 13mm
MATERIAL: Steel
USE: To drill holes in side and end grain of wood

Dowel bits are similar in construction to the Morse drill, but they have two spurs and a centre point to prevent them following the grain and wandering off centre.

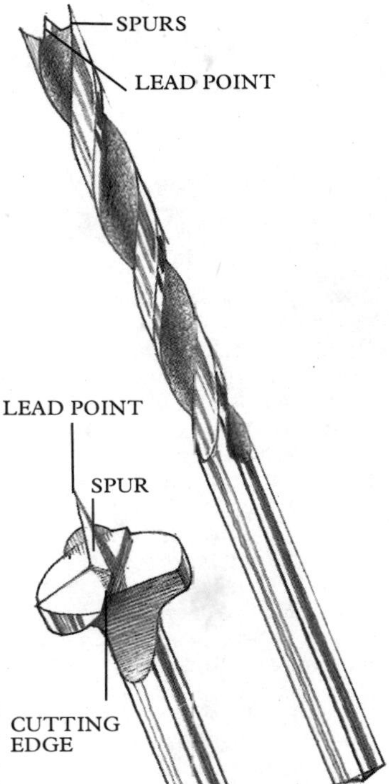

Brad Point Power Bore Bit

SIZE: Diameter 9 to 25mm
MATERIAL: Steel
USE: To drill holes in wood when used with a power drill

The long lead point of the power bore bit gives excellent location in the centre of the hole to be drilled. The shank is narrowed to fit into the chuck of the average electric drill, and the shank end has flats ground into it for positive grip in the jaws of the chuck.

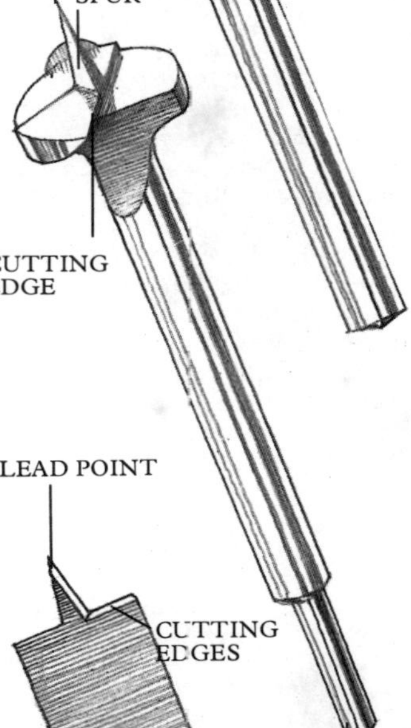

Spade Bit

OTHER NAME: Flat bit
SIZE: Diameter: 18 to 39mm
MATERIAL: Steel
USE: To drill holes in various materials when used with a power tool

The spade bit is suitable for use in both cross grain and end grain timber and works equally well in both composite boards and plastic ones. The lead point gives positive location of the bit even when drilling at an angle. In order to work efficiently, it must be run at high revs, say between 1,000 to 2,000 rpm.

Countersink Bit

SIZE: *Head diameter:* 9, 13, 15mm; *Length:* 50mm
MATERIAL: Steel
USE: To recess a hole to accept a countersunk head screw when used with a power tool

Carbon steel countersink bits are available for cutting wood only, but a high speed bit, which will cut metal, wood or plastic with equal ease, is preferable.

Both bits function in the same way.

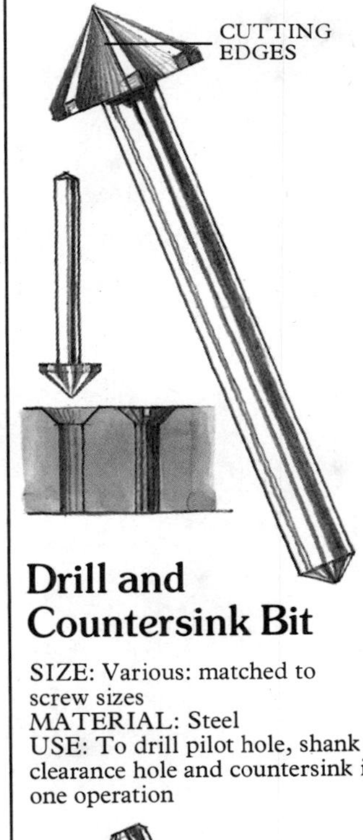

Drill and Countersink Bit

SIZE: Various: matched to screw sizes
MATERIAL: Steel
USE: To drill pilot hole, shank clearance hole and countersink in one operation

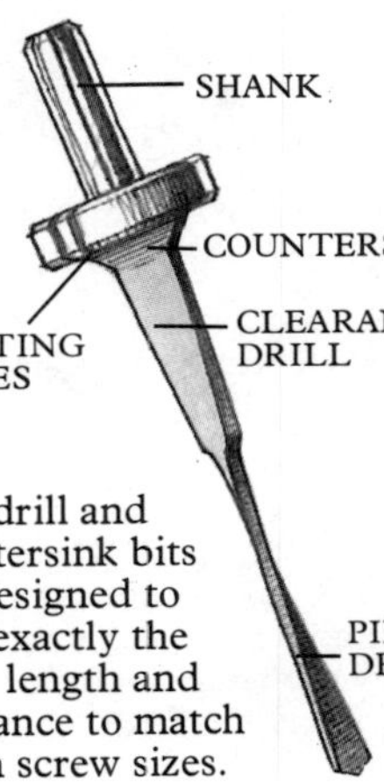

The drill and countersink bits are designed to give exactly the right length and clearance to match given screw sizes.

Drill and Counter Bore Bits

SIZE: Various: matched to screw sizes
MATERIAL: Steel
USE: To drill pilot hole, shank clearance hole and counterbore in one operation

Having drilled a pilot and clearance hole, the spurs will score the surface of the timber before counter boring to the required depth.

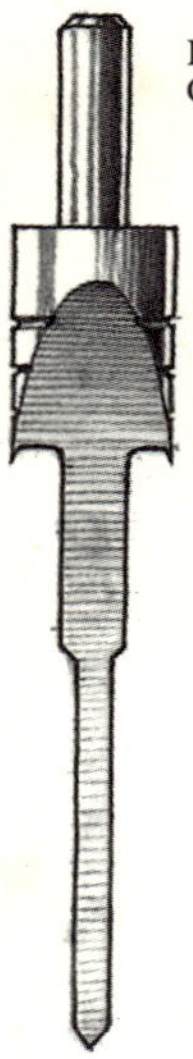

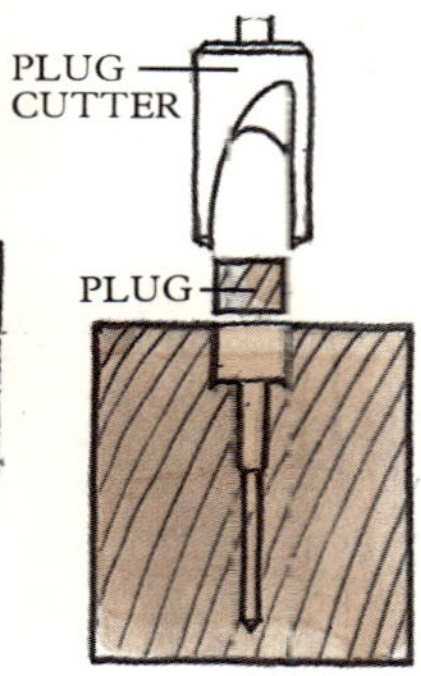

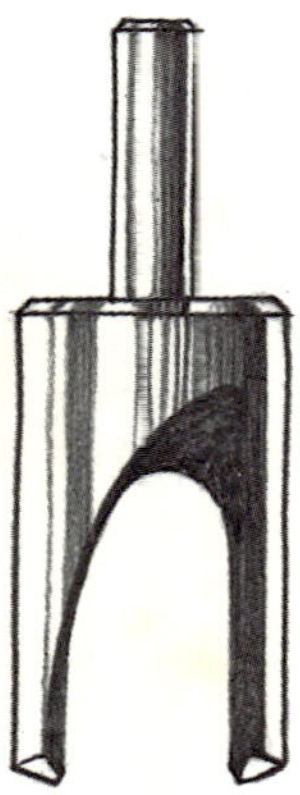

PLUG CUTTER

Plug Cutters

SIZE: Various: matched to size of counter bore bits
MATERIAL: Steel
USE: To cut wooden plugs to fit the hole cut by counter bore bits

Sometimes it is necessary to cover a counter bored screw with a wooden plug. The plug cutter makes a plug which matches the grain of the work piece and is an exact fit in the hole allowing for the glue. Plugs can be flush or button tipped.

Masonry Drill

SIZE: 3 to 25mm
MATERIAL: *Shank:* toughened steel; *Tip:* tungsten carbide
USE: To drill holes in brick, stone, concrete and ceramic tiles

Masonry bits will drill a hole which is an exact fit for wall plugs. The hard tungsten carbide tip of a masonry drill is electronically brazed to the shank with either brass or copper. The copper brazed tip is able to withstand much higher temperatures. To make a hole for wall plugs, set the electric drill at a slow speed to avoid overheating. During the operation, partially withdraw the bit occasionally to clear the spoil. It is usually necessary to drill slightly deeper than the length of the plug which will tend to pack down loose dust as it is inserted. When drilling through plaster always make sure that the hole goes right through to the solid masonry beyond.

Special percussion drills are needed when using a power tool with a hammer action on tough masonry. They have a shatter-proof tip and narrower fluting to provide maximum strength to the shank.

Glass Drill

OTHER NAME: Spear point drill
SIZE: 3 to 13mm
MATERIAL: *Shank:* toughened steel; *Tip:* tungsten carbide
USE: To drill holes in glass, mirror and porcelain

The glass drill can be used in a hand or power drill set at a slow speed. Lay the glass on a flat surface, build a wall of putty or plasticine around the intended hole and fill with turpentine, paraffin or water to cool the drill. Place the drill bit in position before applying power; a variable speed power drill is ideal for this operation. As soon as the drill point exits from the underside of the glass, reverse the workpiece and drill from the other side.

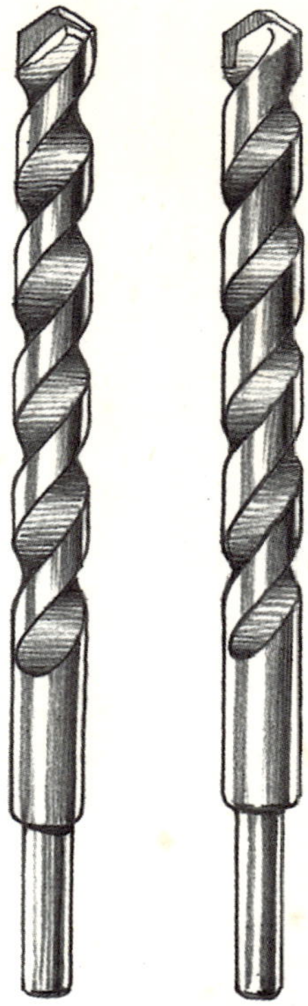

STANDARD MASONRY DRILL   PERCUSSION DRILL

CARBIDE TIP

Depth Gauge

OTHER NAME: Bit gauge
SIZE: Various
MATERIAL: Various
USE: To regulate accurately the depth of a hole being drilled

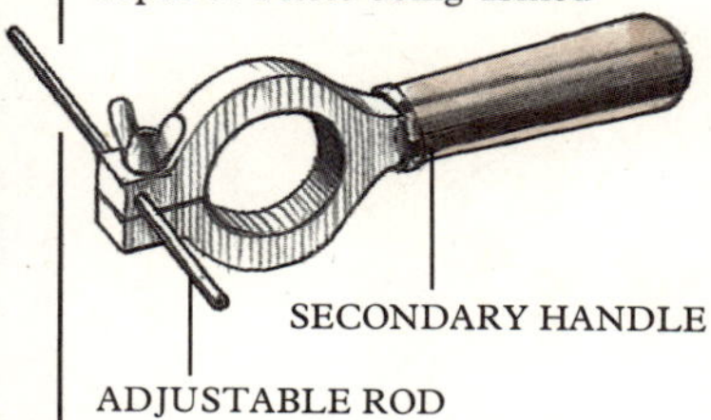

The depth gauge for a power drill is an adjustable rod attached to the body of the drill itself or to a secondary handle.

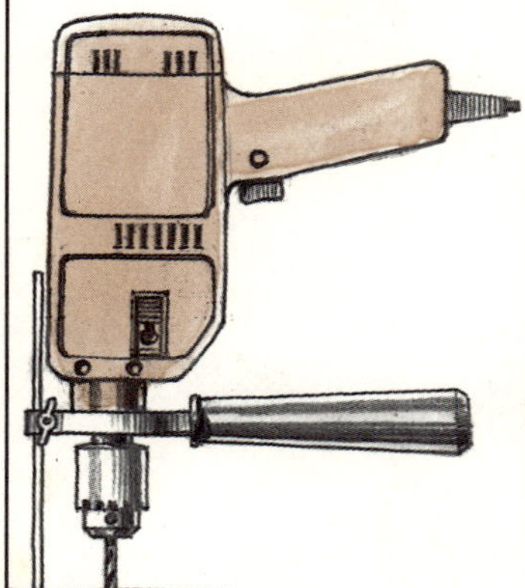

Using the gauge
Set the rod the required hole depth behind the drill tip and lock in place. When the rod comes into contact with the surface remove the drill.

Ready-made plastic gauges fit twist or masonry drills.

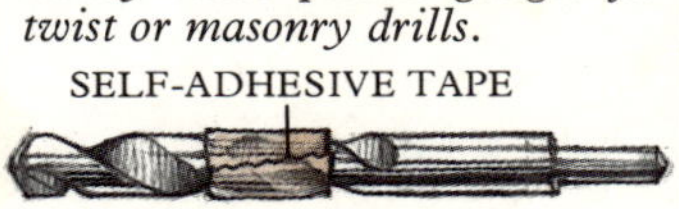

Improvising a gauge
The simplest method of marking a bit for the required depth is to wrap a piece of self-adhesive, masking or insulating tape around it as your guide.

Power Drill Extension

SIZE: 300 and 450mm
MATERIAL: Steel
USE: To extend the reach of power bore bits

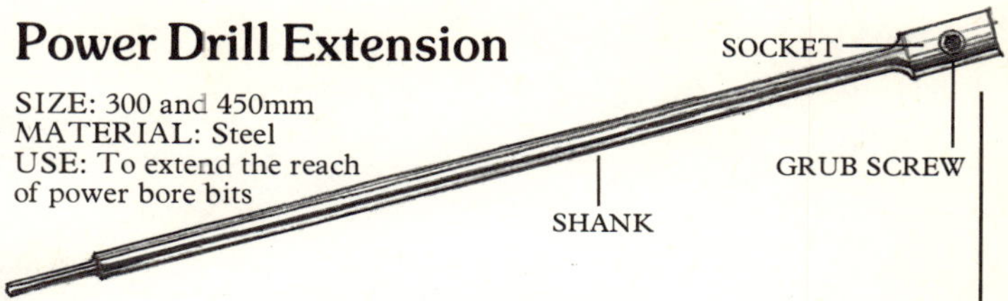

The socket of the extension takes the shank of whatever power bore bit you are using, and is secured with a set screw. The other end of the extension fits into the drill chuck.

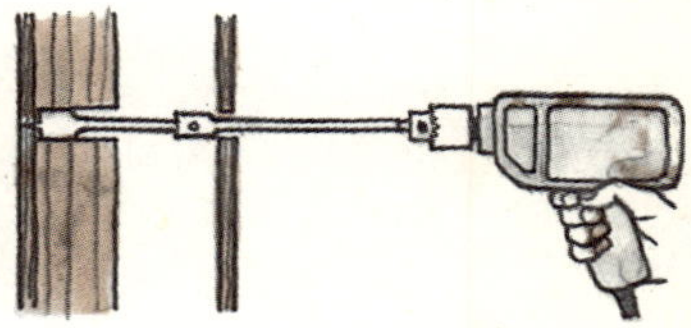

Flexible Drive

OTHER NAME: Flex shaft
SIZE: 750 to 1300mm
MATERIAL: Various
USE: To provide a flexible and portable power source

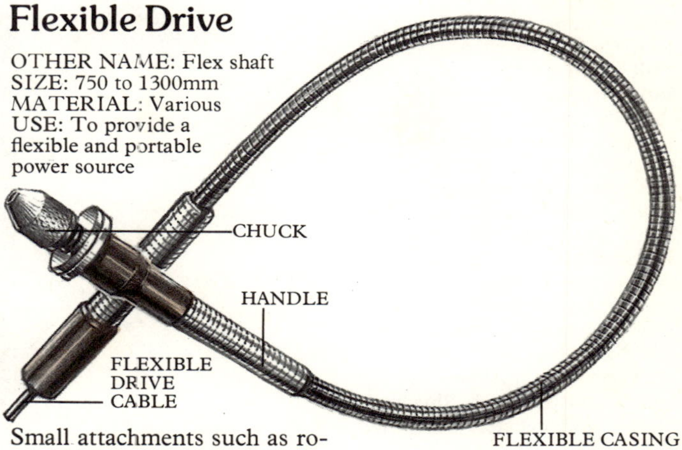

Small attachments such as rotary files and rasps, polishers and wire brushes are more easily controlled in one hand if they are fitted into a flexible drive. Power is transmitted from an electric drill through a spiral steel cable to a portable chuck. The cable is protected by a flexible steel casing.

The flexible drive also provides power in a restricted space which may be inaccessible to a power drill.

Right Angle Drive

MATERIAL: Various
USE: To provide torque to a drill bit, which is used at right angles to the power source

The right angle drive also reduces or increases the speed of the drill depending on which end of the accessory is attached to the tool. Remove the chuck from the drill, fit the right angle drive, and then fit the chuck to the other end of it.

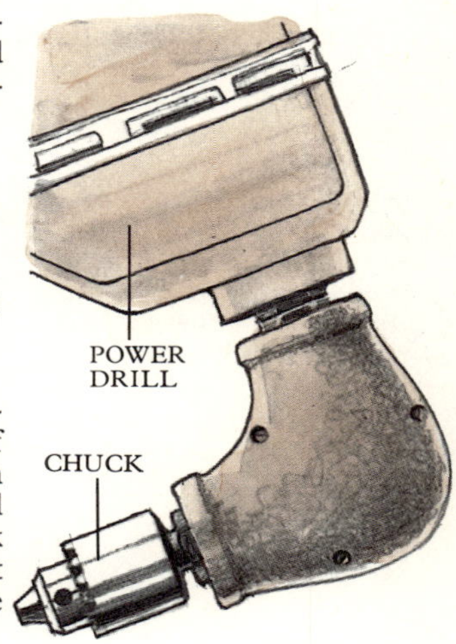

Drill Press

OTHER NAMES: Bench drill, pillar drill
SIZE: *Drilling capacity in mild steel:* 12mm, 21mm; *Depth of throat:* 150 to 250mm
MATERIAL: Various
ACCESSORIES: Drill bits, rotary rasps
ATTACHMENTS: Mortising attachment, sanding drum, routing attachment, buffing wheels
USE: To drill holes in various metals

A drill press is more accurate than a hand drill or a portable electric drill. A simple attachment will convert an electric drill into a drill press, but special purpose drill presses are sturdier, more powerful machines. Bench-standing drill presses have a heavy cast base to support the column which holds the drill head itself. The base, which can be used as a worktable, is bolted to your workbench. Above the base is another worktable which is clamped to the column. This table can be raised and lowered, pivoted sideways, and in some cases, angled. The base surface is accurately machined flat and has bolt holes for fixing workpieces or special vices to the table.

The drilling head incorporates a rear-mounted motor which drives the spindle through a series of pulley wheels and a drive belt. On top of the motor is a cone pulley, connected by a "V" belt to another, inverted cone pulley on the drive spindle. This system provides various speeds at the chuck. Some models incorporate gear wheels to provide speed changes instead of the pulley and belt system.

The chuck is fitted to the other end of the spindle. Any drill bits suitable for the portable electric drill will fit the drill press.

The whole mechanism of the drill press is protected by pressed metal covers.

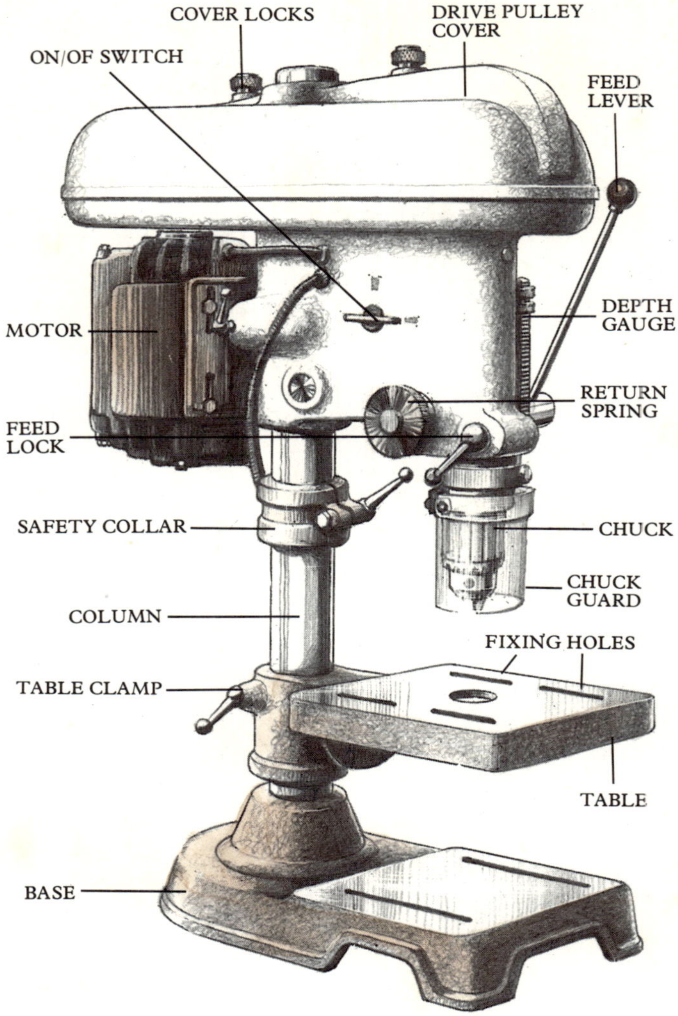

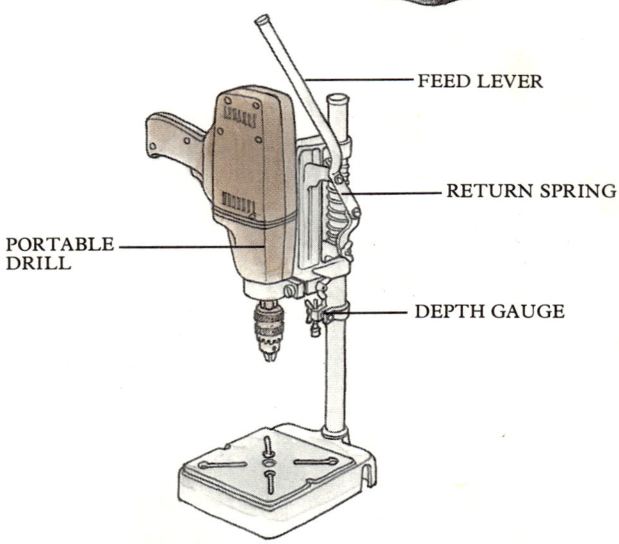

Operating the controls

Select the speed by moving the drive belt. The top position provides the fastest speed, the low position the slowest. Pull up or down on one side of the belt while turning the pulleys by hand to move the belt to the required position. To slacken the belt, move from the large pulley to the small. Metal and other hard materials need slow speeds, while a fast speed will be required for a clean finish on lumber but check with the manufacturer's instructions for precise information.

Insert the drill bit into the chuck and tighten the jaws with a chuck key. The work should be just below the point of the drill bit. Adjust the worktable by slackening the clamp lever and moving the table by hand, lining up the center hole with the drill bit. Tighten the clamp to secure the table. If you do not need the table swing it to one side. Lower the spindle and lock it in the desired position with the feed lock.

The depth of the hole is limited by the depth gauge. Align the tip of the drill with a marked line on the outside of the work and run one nut on the gauge down to meet the stop. Use the second nut as a lock nut against the first.

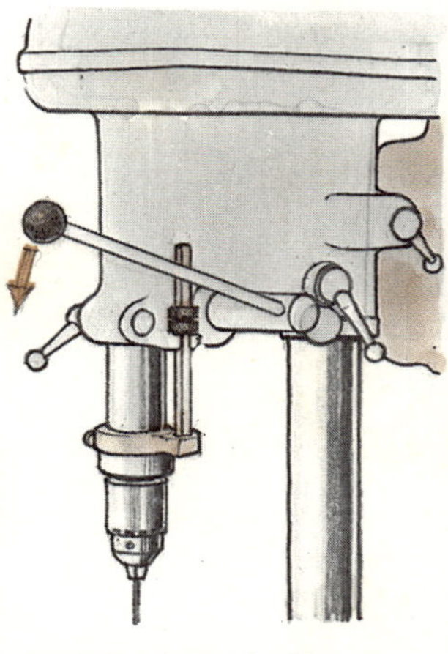

Lowering the spindle

Pull on the feed adjustment lever, which is spring-loaded to return to the rest position.

Holding the work

Hold the work securely. If the bit catches in the work, it will spin it. Be particularly careful when drilling metal, which has a greater tendency to catch. Always clamp it either in a machine vice or to the work-table. Long pieces of wood can be held against the column. Use a fence for shorter pieces, or clamp them to the table.

Using a fence

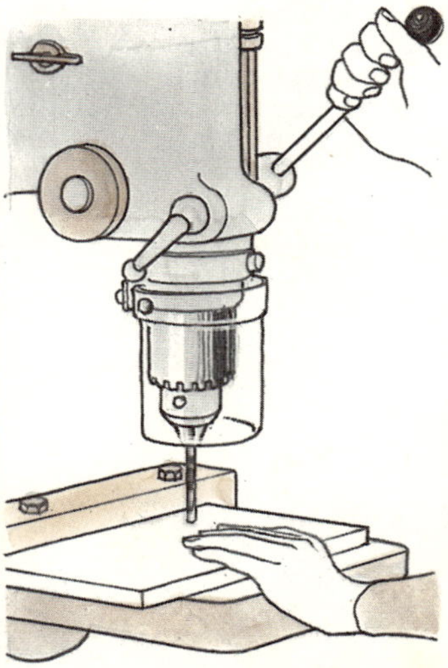

For shorter wood pieces, clamp a guide to the table. If several holes are to be drilled in a line, a fence is better than clamping as the work can then be easily moved along.

Holding round stock

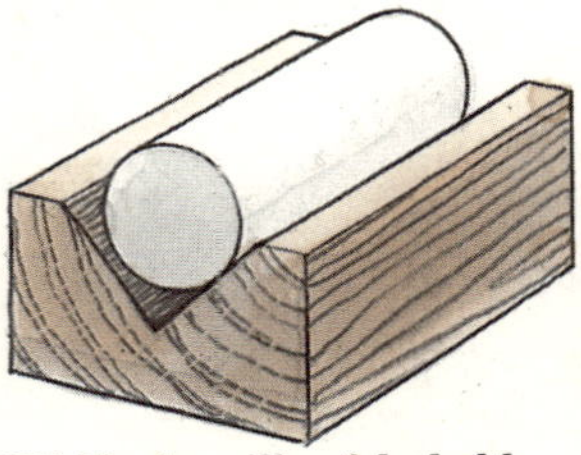

"V" blocks will safely hold pipe or round stock.

Drilling through the work

Clamp a sheet of plywood between it and the table to prevent the bit breaking out the underside of the work as it emerges. Alternatively, as soon as the drill point exits, turn the work over and drill from the other side.

Morticing attachments

A morticing attachment can be bolted just above the chuck. A square hollow chisel fits into the attachment, and a mortice bit passes up the center of the chisel into the chuck. With the motor running, work the machine as for normal drilling. As the bit removes the waste, the chisel simultaneously squares off the hole. A fence is usually provided to hold the work.

Cutting a mortice

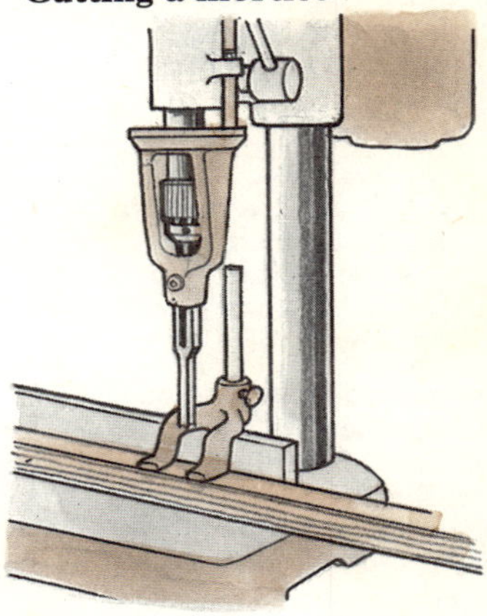

Operate the machine as you would for normal drilling, moving the work along between cuts to complete the mortice.

Other attachments

The drill press can take a router attachment (see page 153) for the range of router cutters) but many drill presses do not run fast enough for clean router work.

A drum sander has a shaft which fits in the chuck. Bolt a 18mm thick plywood sheet to the table with a hole cut in the centre so the drum can be positioned below the surface.

A buffing wheel will also fit the chuck of the drill press.

Safety factors

Insure that the chuck key has been removed before switching on the machine. Disconnect the power supply before making any adjustments. Secure the work before drilling. Do not feed the drill too quickly. Where possible, fit a transparent chuck guard.

Lathe

SIZE: *Maximum distance between centres:* 500mm to 1m; *From centre to bed:* 75 to 300mm
MATERIAL: Various
ACCESSORIES: Wood turning tools
USE: To make turned wooden objects

The lathe is used to "turn" wood into round sectioned objects such as chair legs, bowls, door knobs and so forth. The work is revolved at high speeds against the cutting edges of various wood turning tools or chisels. The basic function of all lathes is the same, although various models differ in speed and size.

If you don't do enough turning work to justify the expense of a lathe, convert an electric drill into a small bench lathe with a special attachment.

How the lathe works
Work being turned "between centres" is held between the head stock and tail stock. Both stocks are located on the lathe bed which aligns the centres. The head stock, fixed at the left hand end of the bed, houses the motor which drives the spindle. The spindle is threaded to take a chuck, face plate, or a driving centre spur which grips and turns the work. A face plate is fitted to the head stock spindle to turn bowls, trays and so on. For larger face plate work, the plate can be fitted on the other end of the spindle on some lathes.

The other end of the work is held by the tail stock which is free to move on the bed to accommodate work of various lengths. The tail stock has an adjustable spindle with a cone shaped centre point.

A tool rest is mounted on the bed at a convenient position along the work.

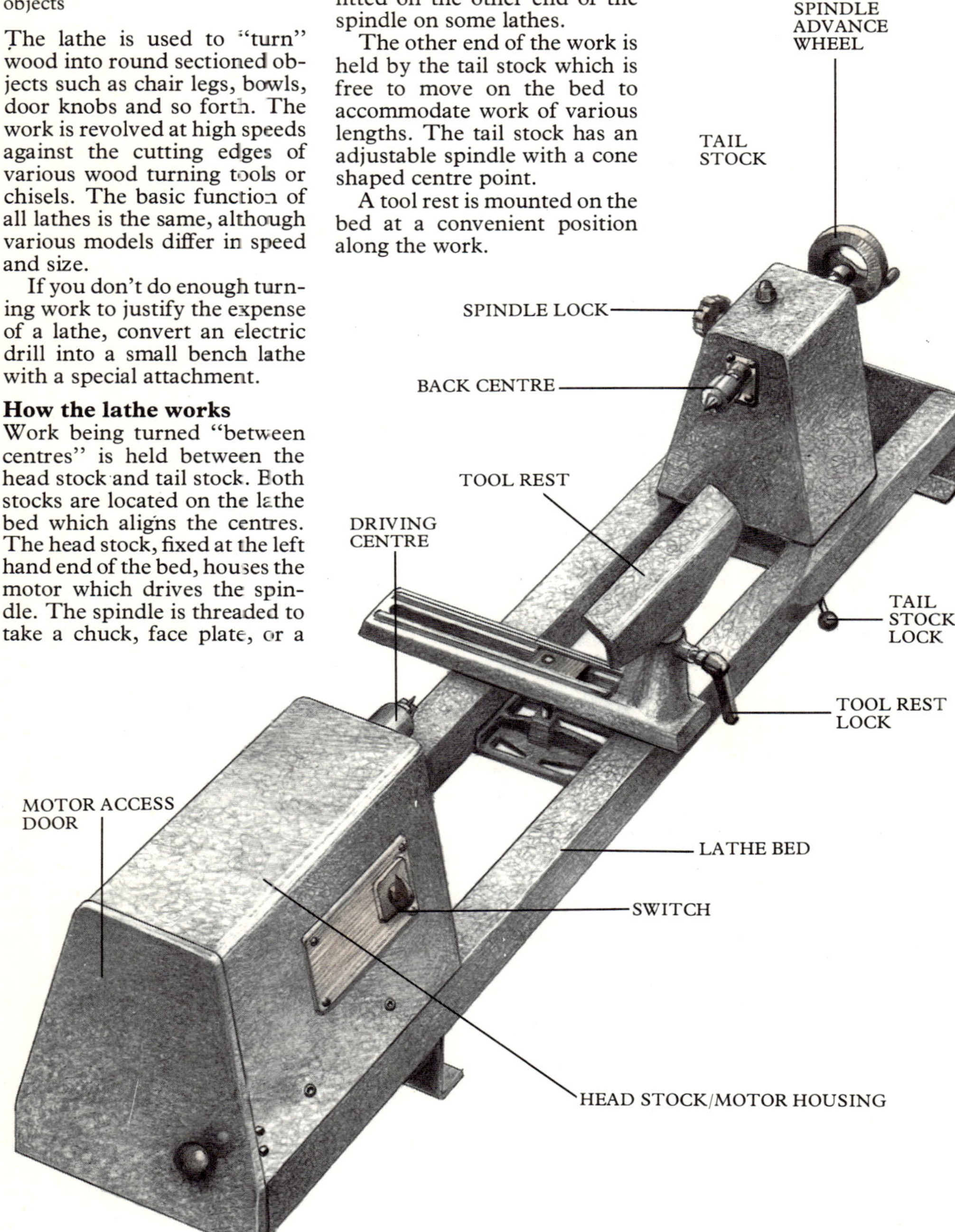

Turning between centres
Prepare the wood for turning by first cutting to length. Remember to allow an extra 12mm at each end of the workpiece to take the drive and tail stock centre. Mark the centre on each end by drawing diagonal lines. Take the point where the diagonals cross as your centre.

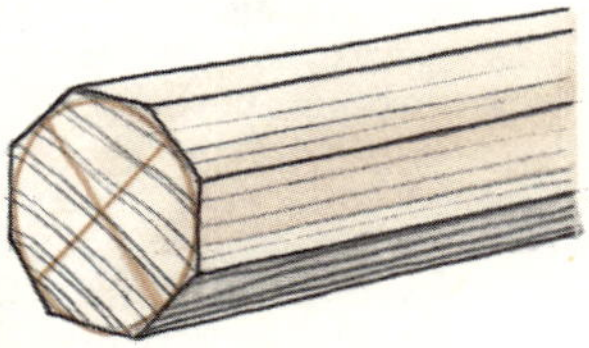

Preparing square stock
Use a compass to draw a circle on the end grain to match the maximum diameter of the workpiece. Plane off the four corners down to this line to make an octagon.

To mark the centre on round stock, use a centre finding gauge (see page 16).

Position the driving centre in one end of the work and drive the "teeth" into the end grain with a soft mallet.

Setting up the work
Remove the centre and set it up in the drive spindle. Locate the work on the drive centre and slide the tail stock to within 25mm of the other end of the work. Lock it on the bed, and turn the tail stock feed to locate the centre point in the centre of the work.
Check that the work revolves freely without being slack between the centres, and tighten the clamp on the tail stock. Grease the tail stock centre lightly to decrease friction.

Set up the tool rest 3mm from the work and 3mm below the centre line and lock it in position. Revolve the work by hand to ensure that in will not hit the tool rest.

Special cuts
Use shaped grooves, beads and coves, singly or grouped together, to make decorative effects. Files and rasps can be used as well as normal tools.

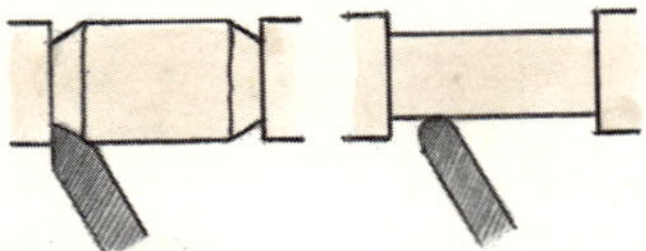

Square cut-out
Chisel two "V" cuts on the waste side of the line to the depth of the cut. Remove the waste between the cuts with a gouge. Finish with a chisel.

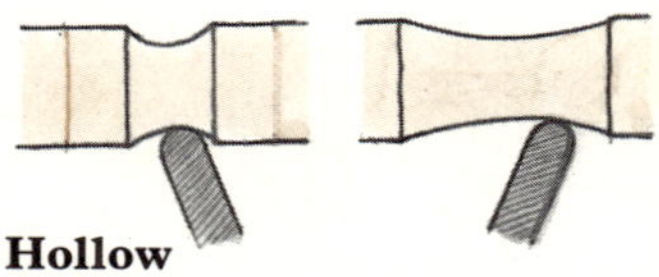

Hollow
Use a gouge. Starting at the center, swing it in an arc in both directions, making deeper and wider cuts as you progress.

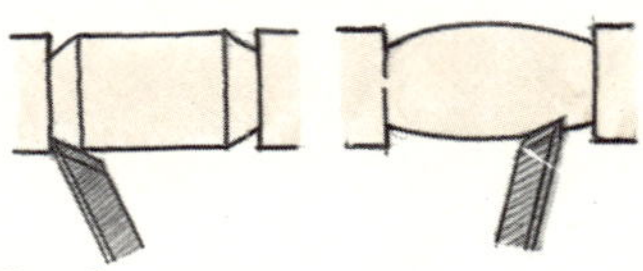

Bead
Make "V" cuts at each end. Round off the bead with a chisel, pivoting it on the rest.

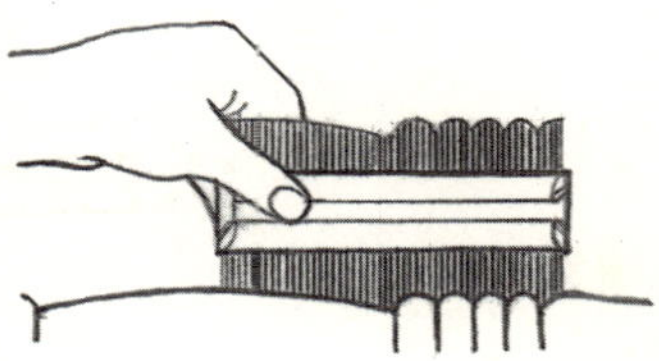

Checking the shape
Use a profile gauge or cardboard template to check a turned shape as it progresses especially on repeating patterns. Check the diameter periodically with calipers.

Wood turning tools
For information and techniques for using turning gouges, chisels and parting tools, see pages 124–128.

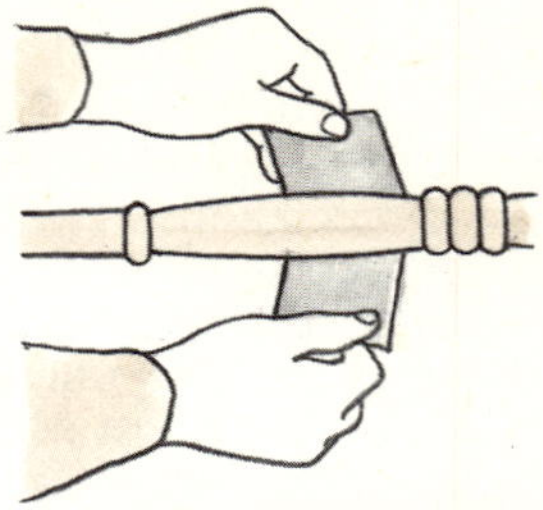

Sanding and finishing
Remove the tool rest and increase the speed of the lathe. Hold a strip of abrasive paper against the back of the work while it is spinning. Polish the work by running a cloth dampened with the finish along the work while it is spinning.

Face plate turning
Mark the centre of the work with diagonals and draw a circle to indicate the diameter of the face plate. Screw the plate to the work, centred on the circle, with short, heavy screws. Check that the screws will not hit the chisel during the turning operation.

If the screw holes would be visible on the finished work, glue a wooden plate to the underside of the workpiece to take the screws, sandwiching a layer of thick paper between. The two pieces of wood can eventually be split apart along the paper line.

Cut off the corners of the workpiece to reduce the waste before attaching the plate to the drive spindle on the lathe.

Set the tool rest parallel to the axis of the work and shape the outside profile using a template to check the shape. Finish with sand paper. Set the rest parallel with the face of the work and hollow out the inside with a gouge working from the edge inward. Smooth the surface with a round nosed chisel before finally sanding.

Safety precautions
Keep the tools sharp for better, safer work.

Stand to one side of the lathe when turning on the machine.

Never make adjustments to the lathe while it is running.

Avoid loose clothing and neckties. Tie back long hair.

Screwdrivers

The first screwdrivers appeared about the middle of the seventeenth century. In English, French and Dutch they were and are called "turnscrews" or the equivalent. In most other European languages they are known as "screw-pullers" or "unscrewers". The first use of the word "screwdriver" occurs in an order by a Philadelphia merchant to a London dealer in 1760 to supply "Cuttoes (hunting knives) . . . with screwdrivers". This American term has now superseded the old English form "turnscrew".

Types of handle

Traditional screwdriver handles swell out, forming a bulbous end, which fills the hand to provide a better grip and enable the user to provide more torque at the driving end. They are made in plastic or hardwood. The wooden variety is strengthened with a metal ferrule where the blade enters the handle, whereas plastic handles are moulded around the blade to provide a much stronger fixing.

Straight fluted handles are also made in plastic or hardwood. The fluting is presumably intended to provide even more grip, but in fact the smooth bulbous surface provides a greater area of surface contact between hand and tool. A slip-on rubber grip is available, which increases the size of the fluted handle.

There is also a very strong screwdriver with a one-piece blade and handle, formed by riveting hardwood grips to each side of the blade, which runs the length of the tool.

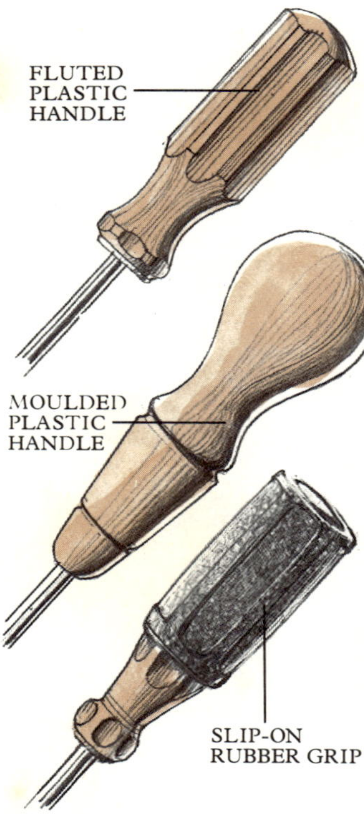

TRADITIONAL WOODEN HANDLE

ONE PIECE BLADE AND HANDLE WITH HARDWOOD GRIPS

Types of screwdriver tip

CABINET TIP, FLARED TIP

The most common screwdriver has the familiar flat tip designed to drive a slotted head screw. The end of a round or square sectioned blade is flared out and tapered by grinding down on both sides. The tip is ground square and is often narrowed by grinding back the points of the flared tip.

PARALLEL TIP

This is used on the same type of screw as a cabinet tip, but the end does not flare out. The round sectioned blade is tapered and ground square at the tip. The blade of a screwdriver with this type of tip can turn a screw at the bottom of a hole or in other restricted spaces, and is commonly used in electrical or electronic work.

PHILLIPS HEAD

This is a cross head tip formed by grinding four flutes in the end of a pointed blade to increase the grip between the tool and the screw.

POZIDRIV HEAD

This tip is similar to a Phillips head, but designed to fit into an additional square hole in the centre of the crossed slots on the screw head.

REED AND PRINCE

Another cross head tip similar to Phillips and Pozidriv, but the flutes are ground square and the tip comes to a sharp point.

OTHER TYPES OF HEAD

Several other types of screwdriver tips have been designed to provide a more positive location in the screw head. Some examples are the **CLUTCH HEAD**, **ROBERTSON** and **TORX**.

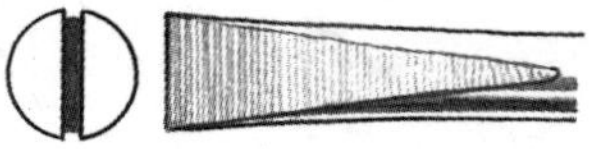

FLARED TIP

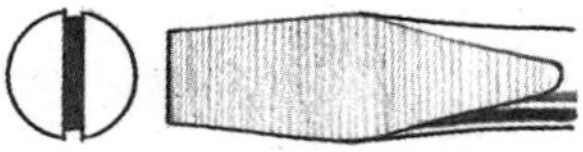

FLARED TIP
GROUND ON EDGES

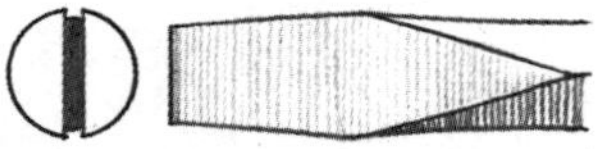

FLARED TIP ON
SQUARE BLADE

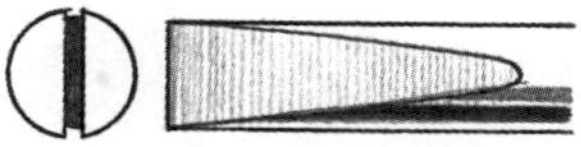

PARALLEL TIP

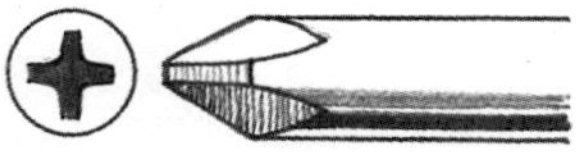

PHILLIPS

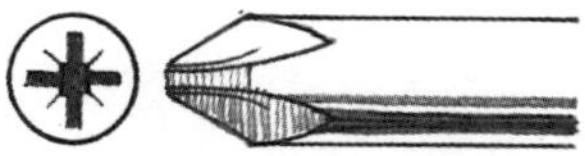

POZIDRIV

REED AND PRINCE

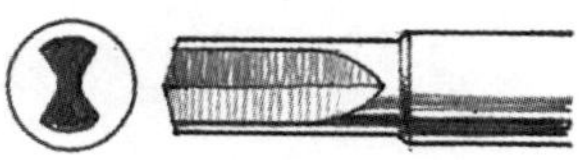

CLUTCH HEAD

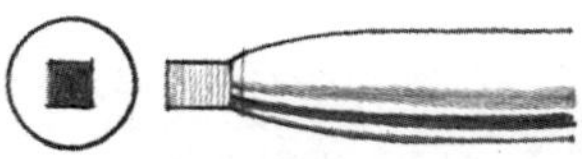

ROBERTSON

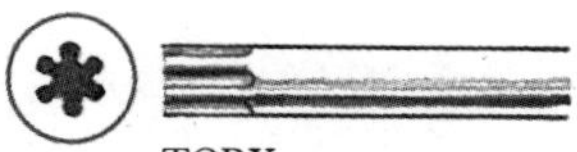

TORX

Care of screwdrivers

Choose a screwdriver which is correctly ground and the right size to fit snugly in the screw head. A rounded, chipped or undersized tip will slip and damage either the screw slot or the work itself. Similarly avoid using a tip that is too large and projects from either side of a countersunk screw. This will damage the work as the screw is driven home.

Use the correct cross head driver to fit the screw. Using a straight tip or another make of cross head can damage the screw, and once a cross head screw has been damaged it is very difficult to remove.

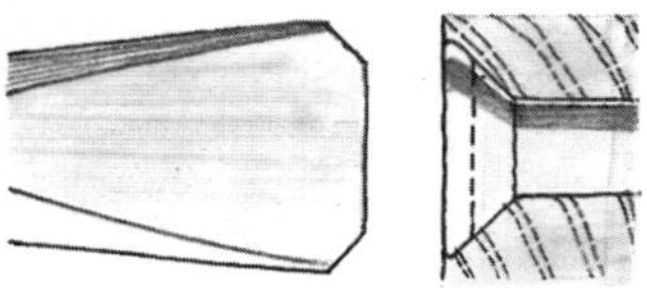

Removing a seized screw
To do this you may need a large powerful screwdriver. If the blade is too large to fit the screw head, grind the corners until the blade fits the slot.

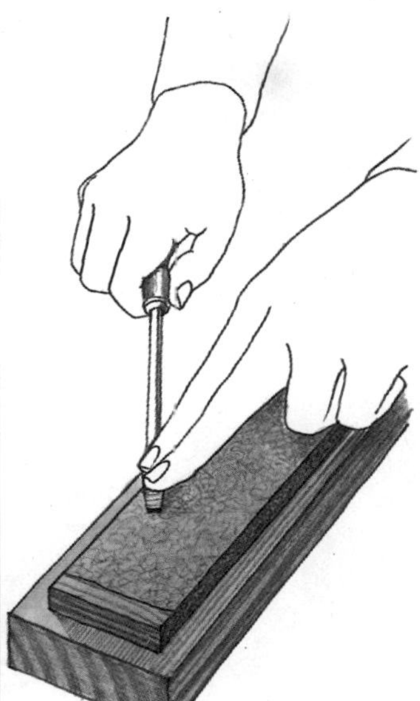

Repairing a straight edged screwdriver
Grind the side of the tip on an oilstone, keeping the blade at the correct angle.

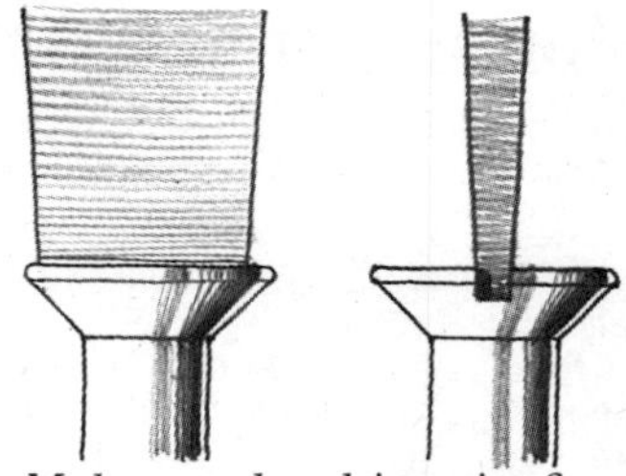

Make sure that driver tips fit properly into screw heads, as shown above.

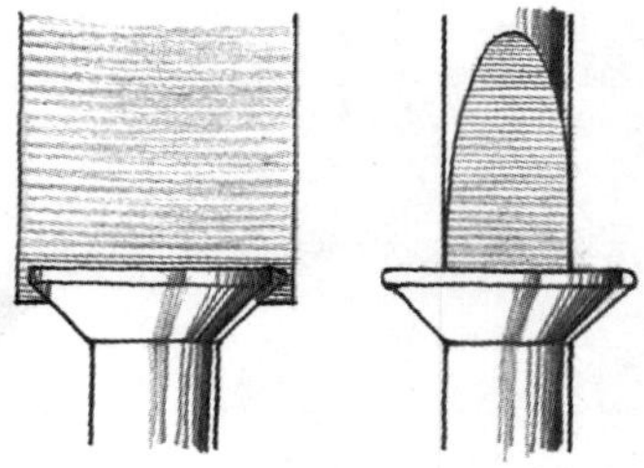

A tip that is too large (above left) will damage surrounding work; a tip that is too small will not grip the screw correctly.

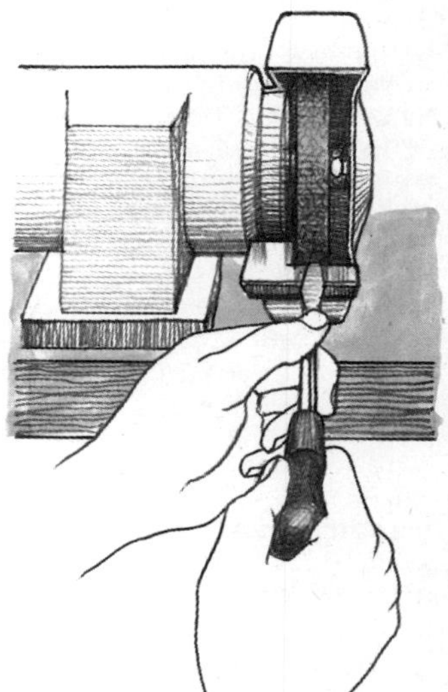

Alternative grinding method
You can regrind a straight tipped screwdriver on an emery wheel, although this is not recommended by every manufacturer.

Cabinet Screwdriver

SIZE: Blade: 75 to 250mm
MATERIAL: *Blade:* steel;
Handle: beech, boxwood
USE: To drive wood screws and slotted machine screws

The cabinet screwdriver is the woodworker's traditional driver. The hardwood handle is oval in section, swelling out to fit the palm of the hand. The cylindrical blade flattens where it enters the ferrule, whereas the blade of the present day counterpart often extends throughout the handle. The flared tip of the blade is sometimes ground back into a taper.

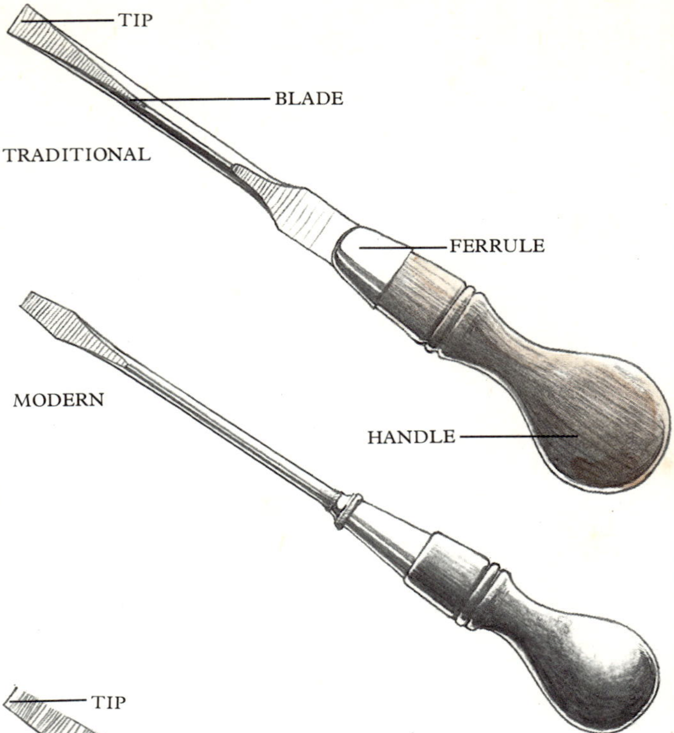

London Pattern

SIZE: Blade: 150 to 300mm
MATERIALS: *Blade:* steel;
Handle: beech
USE: To drive wood screws and slotted machine screws

The London pattern is a large screwdriver, characterized by its flat waisted blade and beechwood handle with flats on two sides. These flats were probably designed to fit the palm of the hand, and also to prevent the driver rolling off the bench. London pattern screwdrivers are not common in the average workshop today. They are normally reserved for the occasional job where considerable torque is required, which can only be supplied by a big screwdriver.

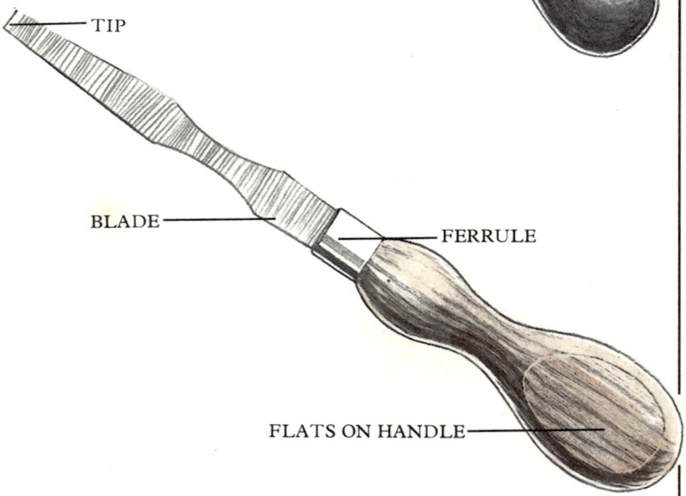

Electrician's Screwdriver

SIZE: Blade: 75 to 250mm
MATERIAL: *Blade:* steel;
Handle: plastic
USE: To drive machine screws in electrical work

The electrician's screwdriver has a long thin cylindrical blade with a parallel ground tip. The plastic handle insulates the user. Some drivers are further insulated by a plastic tube running down the length of the blade.

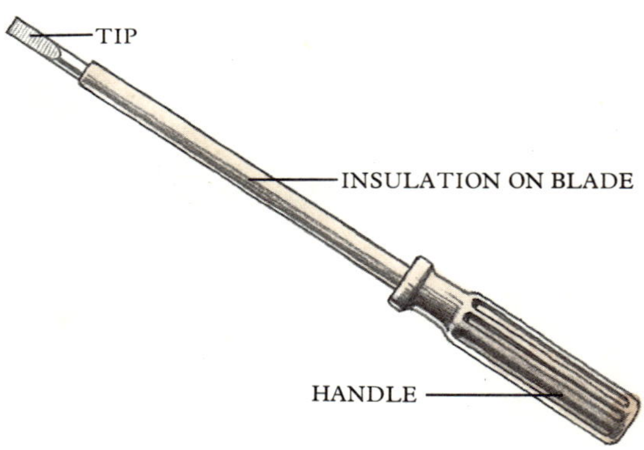

Spiral Ratchet Screwdriver

OTHER NAMES: "Yankee" ratchet screwdriver, pump screwdriver
SIZE: Extended blade length with bit: 240 to 711mm
MATERIAL: Various
ACCESSORIES: Standard bits, cross head bits, chuck adaptors, countersink bits
USE: To drive screws automatically

This tool drives screws by pressure. The spiral grooves along the length of the screwdriver blade produce a turning force at the tip when pressure is applied to the handle. The spring-loaded handle returns when pressure is released. The action is consequently much faster than that of a standard screwdriver which relies on the twisting action of the human arm, so the spiral screwdriver is very useful when a lot of screws are involved in a job.

Clockwise or counter-clockwise action can be selected by means of a thumb slide on the ferrule or the mechanism can be locked to convert the driver to a standard screwdriver action. A knurled ring at the end of the ferrule will lock the blade in the fully extended or retracted positions, where it will act like a standard ratchet driver.

A pilot hole is essential for the most efficient action, although screws can be driven unpiloted into softwood where the finish is unimportant. Take care that the bit does not slip and damage the work.

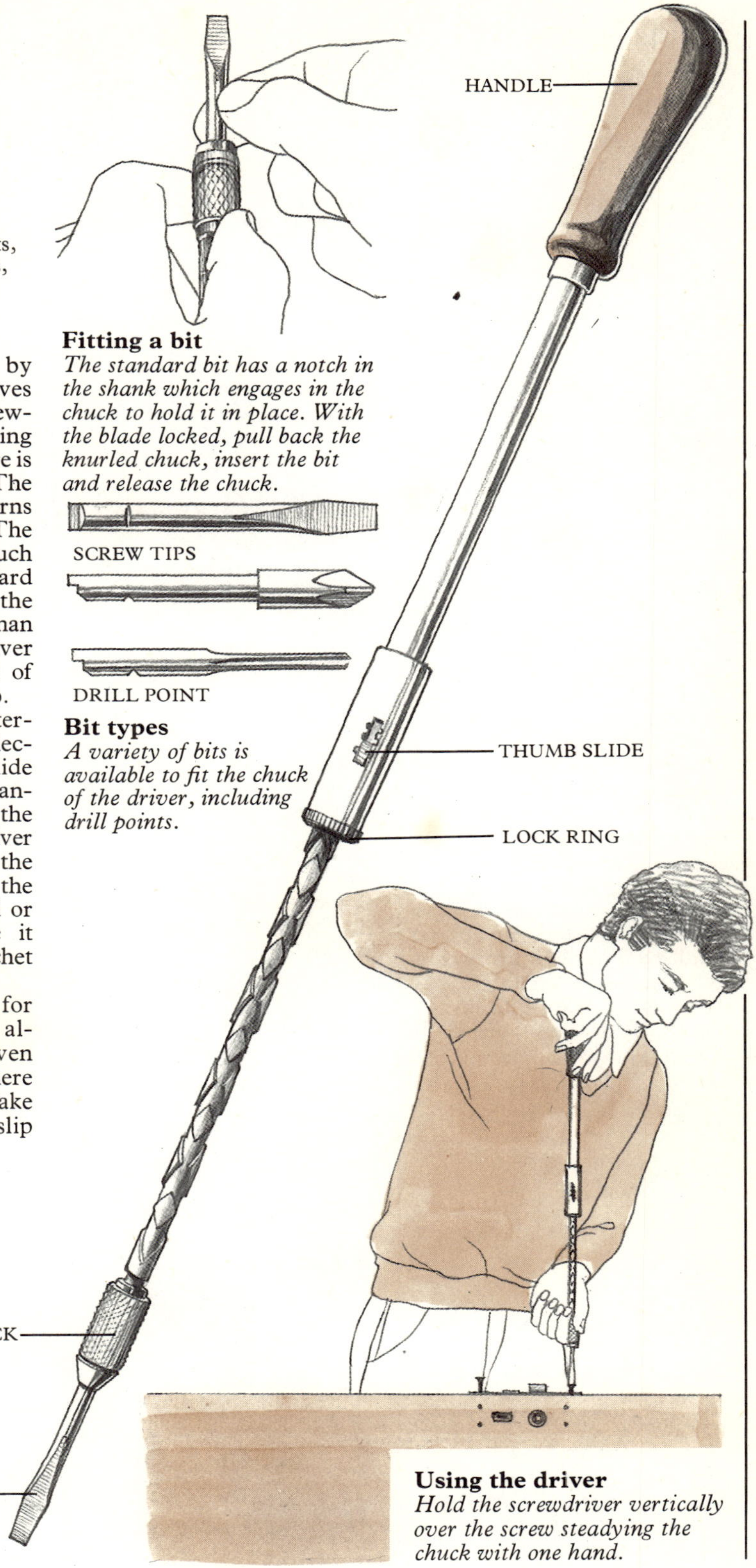

Fitting a bit
The standard bit has a notch in the shank which engages in the chuck to hold it in place. With the blade locked, pull back the knurled chuck, insert the bit and release the chuck.

Bit types
A variety of bits is available to fit the chuck of the driver, including drill points.

Using the driver
Hold the screwdriver vertically over the screw steadying the chuck with one hand.

Mains Tester

OTHER NAMES: Spark detecting screwdriver, voltage tester
SIZE: Various
MATERIAL: Various
USE: To test for the presence of an electrical current

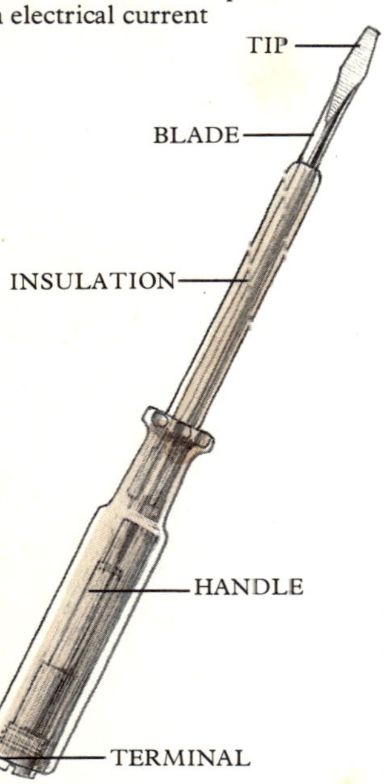

The mains tester is an electrician's screwdriver with an insulated blade and handle. By keeping a finger on the metal terminal at the end of the handle and placing the tip on a live terminal, a circuit is completed and a neon bulb in the handle lights up if electrical power is present.

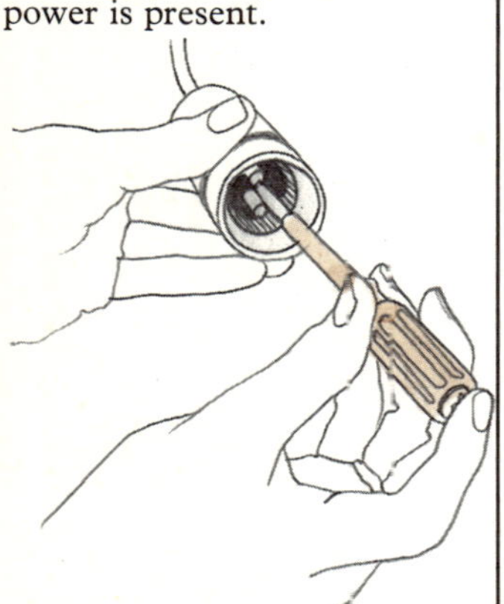

Testing voltage
Touch a live terminal with the tester's tip. A resister in the handle prevents shocks.

Stubby Screwdriver

SIZE: Blade: 25 and 38mm
MATERIAL: *Blade:* steel; *Handle:* hardwood, plastic
USE: To drive screws in restricted space

The stubby screwdriver has a short blade for use in confined spaces. Its main feature is the enlarged handle which provides enough grip to produce efficient torque. A stubby screwdriver can be fitted with a tommy bar in the handle for increased torque. Stubbys are manufactured with all the various types of tips.

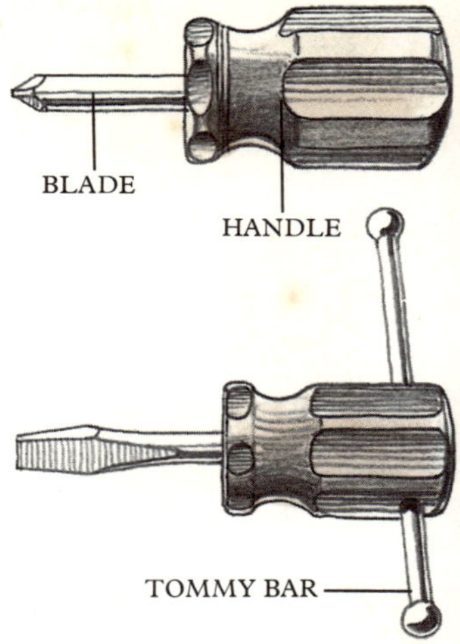

Ratchet Screwdriver

SIZE: Blade: 75 to 150mm
MATERIAL: *Blade:* steel; *Handle:* hardwood
USE: To drive screws without altering the grip

The ratchet enclosed in the ferrule of this screwdriver allows the user to drive a screw without changing his grip. A thumb slide adjusts the action to drive clockwise or anticlockwise as well as to remain fixed in either direction. The smaller sizes are fitted with a knurled ring which can be turned, using forefinger and thumb, to drive the blade when starting screws.

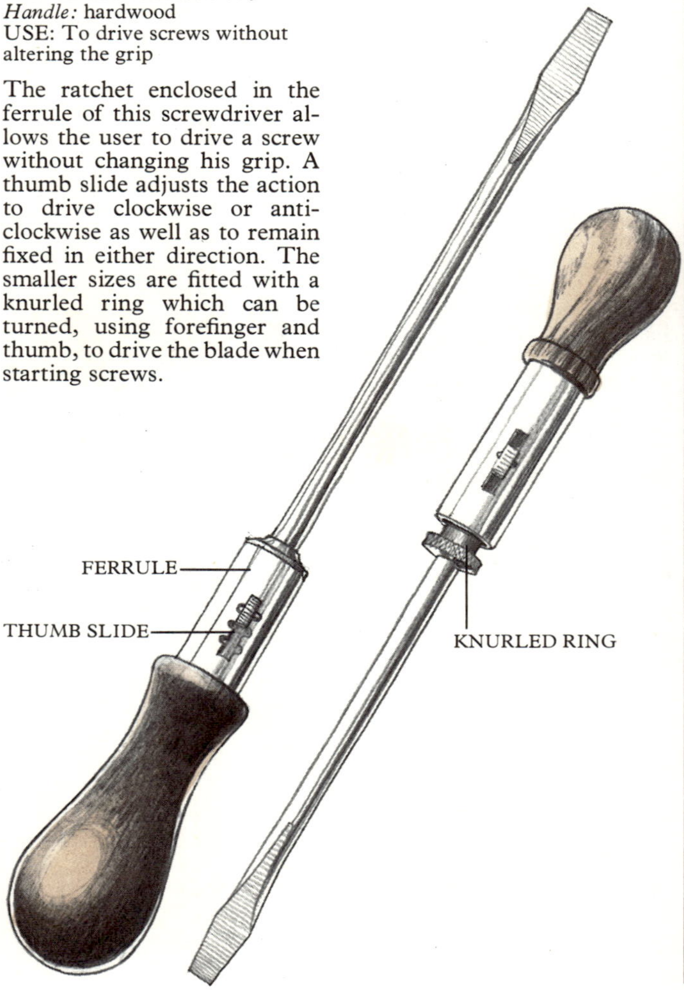

Offset Screwdriver

OTHER NAMES: Round the corner screwdriver, cranked screwdriver
SIZE: Blade: 75 to 150mm
MATERIAL: Steel
USE: To drive screws inaccessible to a standard screwdriver

The offset driver is used where there is insufficient room to use a conventional screwdriver. It is also good for applying extra torque to a stubborn screw.

The driver is simply a steel bar, either hexagonal or round in section, with the ends bent at right angles and ground to form a screwdriver tip. It is double ended and can be used for cross head or slotted head screws. In the latter case one tip is in line with the bar while the other is at right angles to it. Combination cross head and slotted head drivers are also manufactured.

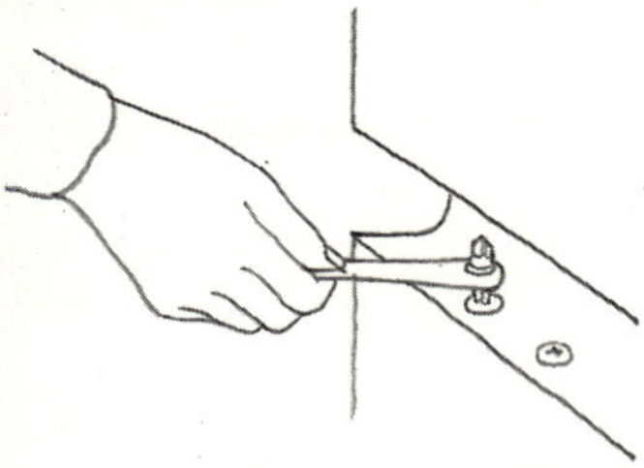

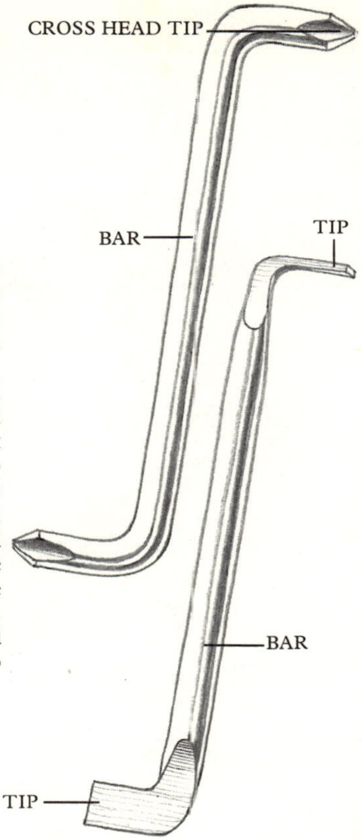

Offset Ratchet Screwdriver

SIZE: Blade: 100 to 120mm
MATERIAL: Steel
USE: To drive screws in a confined space

The offset ratchet screwdriver performs the same function as the standard offset driver with the advantage of a ratchet mechanism that allows the screw to be driven without having to remove the tip from the screw head. Clockwise or counter clockwise action can be selected by moving a lever in the stock of the tool. The drivers have two sizes of tip of either the conventional slotted head or the cross head variety; alternatively, there may be one of each head.

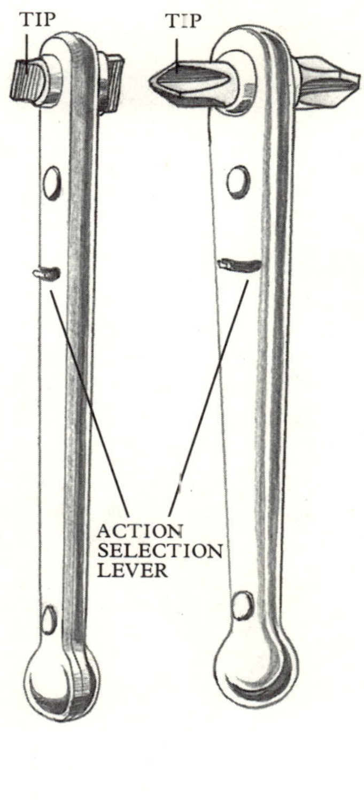

Jeweller's Screwdriver

OTHER NAME: Instrument maker's screwdriver
SIZE: *Length:* 110mm; *Blade width:* 0.6 to 2.5mm
MATERIAL: *Blade:* steel; *Body:* various
USE: To drive very small screws

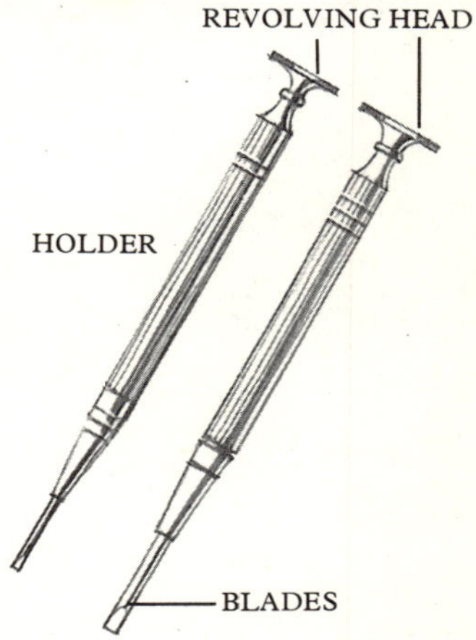

The jeweller's screwdriver is used by watchmakers, opticians, model makers, or any other kind of fine instrument maker. They are either made in sets with fixed blades or as one holder with a selection of interchangeable blades.

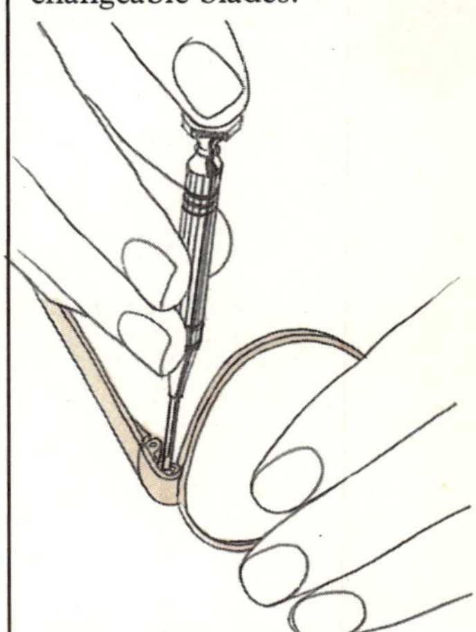

Using the driver
The driver is held vertically between fingers and thumb with the index finger resting on the revolving head. With the tip located in the screw the body is revolved while pressure is applied by the index finger.

Screwdriver Bit Holder

SIZE: *Blade:* 80mm
MATERIAL: *Shaft:* steel; *Handle:* wood, plastic
USE: To hold and drive interchangeable tips

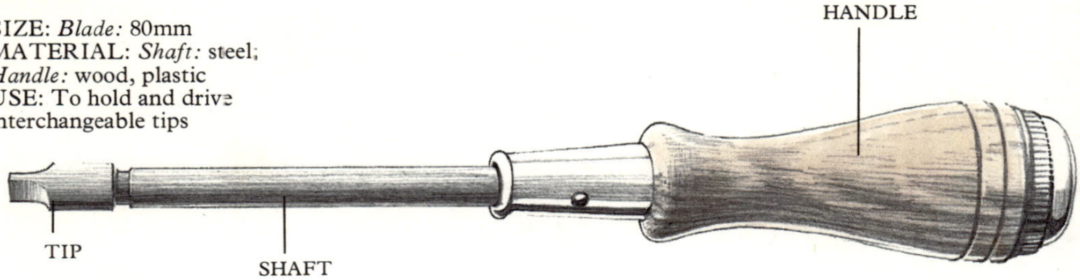

The bit holder is a screwdriver type handle fitted with a hollow ended shaft into which various screwdriver tips can be inserted.

Power Screwdriver Bit

SIZE: Various
MATERIAL: Steel
USE: To drive screws with a variable speed electric drill

Power screwdriver bits have hexagonal shafts to fit in the chuck of an electric drill and tips suitable for slotted head and cross head screws. A magnetic bit holder is available for any short hexagonal sectioned tips. (For screwdriver bits to fit hand brace see page 207).

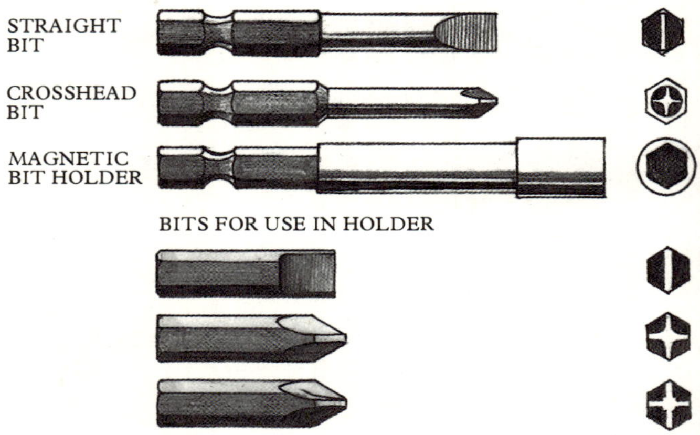

Impact Driver

SIZE: 140mm
MATERIAL: Steel
ACCESSORIES: Screwdriver bits, socket set
USE: To free tight screws or nuts

The impact driver is used to free screws or nuts which have seized. The square drive fits socket heads and, with an adaptor, drives replaceable bits for both slotted and cross head screws.

With the tool in position on the nut or in the screw head, strike the end with a hammer. Inside the handle is a mechanism which converts the blow into torque to break free a tight fitting. By twisting the handle, clockwise or counter-clockwise movement can be selected.

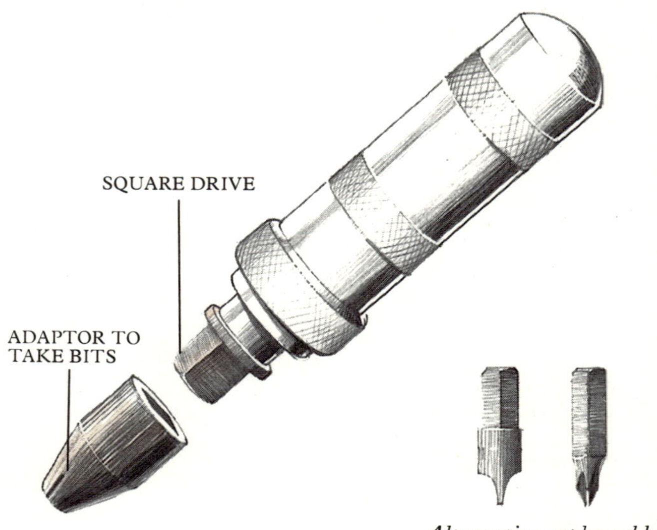

Alternative replaceable screwdriver bits

Sanders and Abrasives

The first abrasive used by woodworkers and masons was probably sand itself. An early Egyptian relief at Saqqara shows two workmen apparently rubbing down a tabletop with small blocks of stone: they would have had little difficulty in finding plenty of sand to use with them. In the Middle Ages the skin of the dogfish was used for this purpose; at Westminster, London in 1355 "a skyn called a *hundysfyshskin* for the carpenters" was bought for six old pence. This was still in use as late as 1708, when the inventory of Charles Plumbley, a cabinetmaker of Philadelphia, listed: "4 pairs of fish Skins at 10/-". A few years earlier Moxon advised finishing work with "Seal-skin or Dutch reeds".

It is not known when sandpaper (later more properly called "glasspaper"), was introduced. The earliest known reference is to an advertisement in the Boston Gazette of September 1764 for sand and emery paper, but it was not in general use until about 1800. The date given for carborundum in the Oxford English Dictionary is 1893; this material and other abrasives were widely adopted for machine sanders and grinding wheels at the beginning of the present century.

Modern abrasives are available in a variety of finishes. They can be used by hand or fitted in power tools to sand individual workpieces, large floor surfaces or small local areas.

Abrasives are available to finish a wide range of materials. There are three categories of abrasive, coarse, medium and fine, but within each grade there are progressively finer subdivisions. Apart from the size of the grain the spacing of the grain is also graded. The closely packed grains, or "closed coat" abrasives, will cut quickly but clog easily. Wide spaced or "open coat" grains are best suited for materials like paint which tend to clog abrasives quickly. Sandpaper is no longer available although the word is still used as a general term to describe all abrasive papers.

FLINT OR GLASSPAPER

This is most often confused with sandpaper because of the yellow colour of the adhesive and backing paper. It is the cheapest abrasive available, wears quickly and is used to roughly finish timber. For a finer finish, choose a better quality grit.

GARNET

This is a natural red material, which, backed with paper, is used to hand finish all types of timber including hardwood. It is harder than flint and is available in finer grades. Use it dry.

EMERY

Another natural material, this is used mainly to finish metal. It is available with paper or cloth backing. Paper backing is adequate for flat areas, but a cloth backing is much stronger especially if you are working on tightly curved sections. It can be lubricated with water.

SYNTHETIC SILICON CARBIDE

This is harder than emery and is backed by waterproof paper so that it can be used wet or dry to finish paint or metal. (It is sometimes known as "wet and dry" paper.) When rubbing down paintwork, the water and paint particles form a slurry which should be wiped off the workpiece while still wet. The abrasive itself should be rinsed periodically in water to remove any paint which is clogging the grit. Silicon carbide can also be used on bare wood, but should only be used dry.

ALUMINIUM OXIDE

Another synthetic material with paper and cloth backing which is often used to machine-sand lumber, plastics and metal.

TUNGSTEN CARBIDE

This is the hardest abrasive material. It is mainly used in sanding machines, and is therefore sold in thin metal discs or strips.

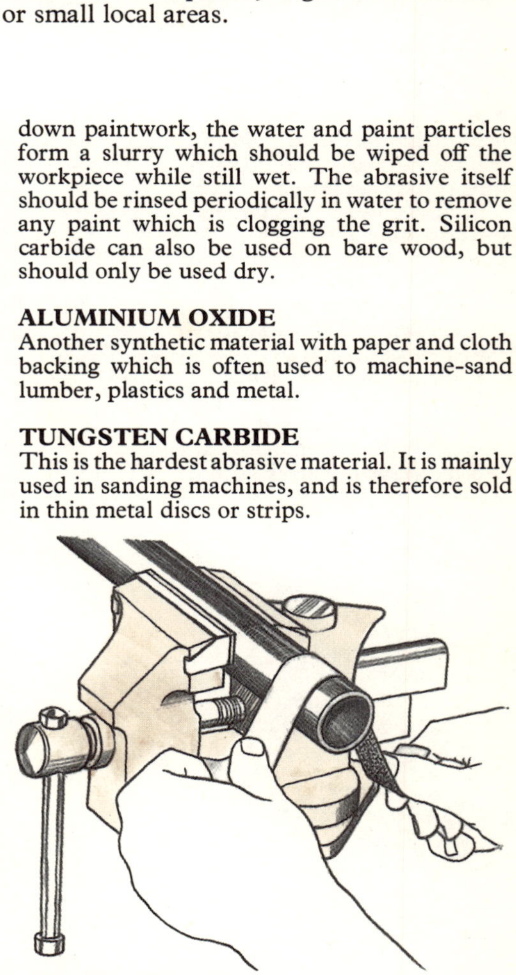

Sanding round stock
Mount the work on a vice and pull cloth-backed emery strips across the surface. Angle your strokes to cover all the pipe.

Sanding Block

SIZE: Various
MATERIAL: *Block:* cork, plastic, rubber, softwood; *Covering:* abrasive paper
USE: To finish flat surfaces

Abrasive papers used on their own will often produce uneven sanding and are likely to follow any undulations in the workpiece. Paper wrapped around a sanding block will keep a wider area of abrasive flat on the workpiece.

A quarter of a standard sheet of abrasive paper is ideal for wrapping around a sanding block. Tear the paper rather than cutting it with a knife or pair of scissors.

The simplest block is merely a rectangular piece of cork, rubber or softwood. Other, more sophisticated blocks are moulded to fit the palm of the hand and take strips or even rolls of paper ready cut to size.

Sand wood in the direction of the grain. Scratches across the grain, which may not even show when the wood is unfinished, will be exaggerated by the application of varnish or polyurethane paint.

Clogged abrasive will not cut efficiently. Remove the paper from the block and tap it firmly on the bench to remove dust. Wash clogged material from wet and dry paper.

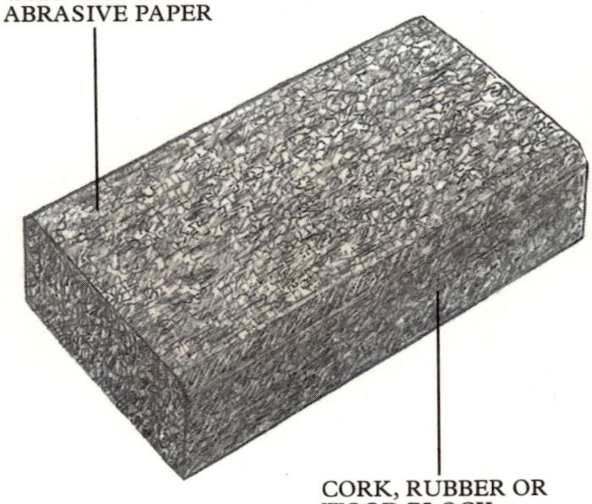

Tearing abrasive paper
Fold the sheet in half over the edge of a bench. Hold one half firmly on the bench and pull down the edge to tear off the other half.

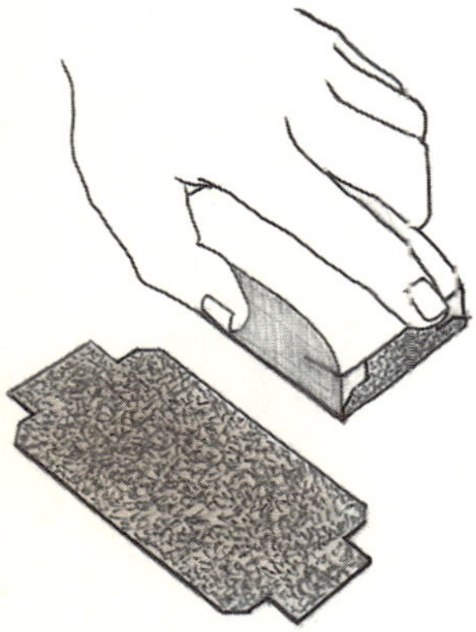

Shop bought blocks
These are shaped to the hand and supplied with abrasive paper cut to size.

Sanding edges
Keep the block flat on the work so that it will not round off the edge where it overshoots.

Belt Sander

SIZE: *Belt:* 75 and 100mm; *Capacity:* 1,150 to 1,600 surface ft. per minute
MATERIALS: Various
ACCESSORIES: Abrasive belts, dust collecting bag
USE: To sand wood and metal quickly

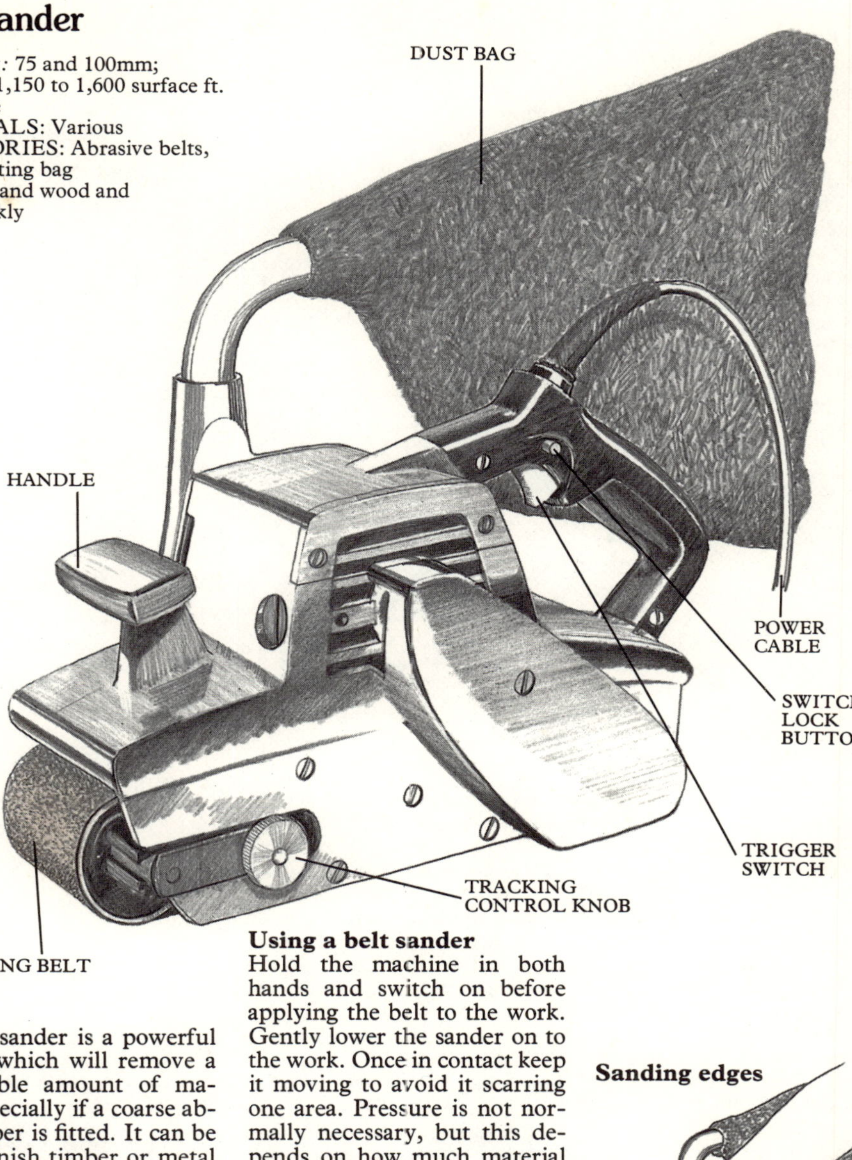

The belt sander is a powerful machine which will remove a considerable amount of material, especially if a coarse abrasive paper is fitted. It can be used to finish timber or metal and will also remove old paint or varnish.

The abrasive belt is a continuous band which is driven over two rollers to produce a non-stop sanding action. The rear roller is powered, while the front roller is adjustable for tension and tracking of the belt. A pad, known as the "platen", is mounted between the rollers and holds the belt flat on the work. If possible, choose a sander which is already fitted with an extractor and dust collecting bag.

Using a belt sander
Hold the machine in both hands and switch on before applying the belt to the work. Gently lower the sander on to the work. Once in contact keep it moving to avoid it scarring one area. Pressure is not normally necessary, but this depends on how much material you wish to remove and how quickly you want to do it.

Move the machine in a series of forward and backward strokes gradually traversing the workpiece, overlapping section by section. Lift the tool off the work before switching off.

Sand wood with the grain to produce the best finish. Sand at an angle to the grain to remove material quickly or to level a surface. Re-sand parallel to the grain and with a finer grade of abrasive to remove the cross grain scratches.

Sanding edges

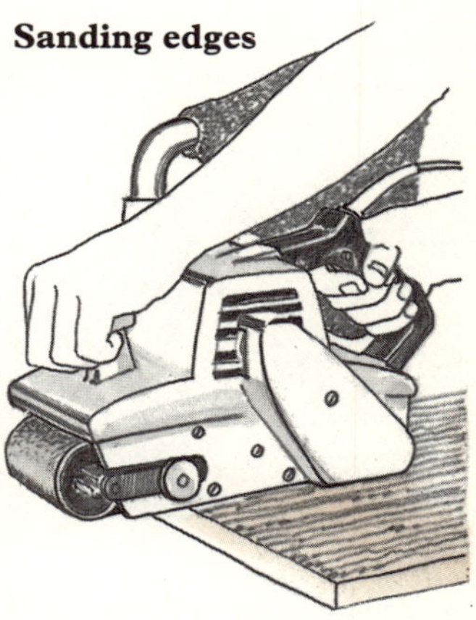

Keep the machine flat when overrunning the edge of the work to avoid rounding off.

Changing a belt

Before fitting the belt, disconnect the machine from the electrical supply. To slacken a belt, reduce the distance between the rollers by operating a lever or by resting the tool on its front roller and applying pressure. This pushes the roller back against a spring and locks it in the retracted position.

Following the feed direction arrow printed on the inside of the belt, align the belt and release the front roller to take up the tension.

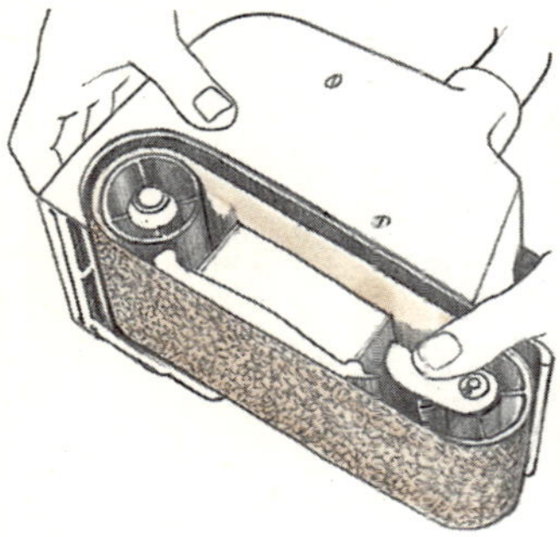

Taking up tension

To tension a new belt, release the lever on the front roller.

Tracking

The tracking of the belt can be adjusted on all machines. If the belt is not running true or parallel with the body of the machine, it may move sideways, damaging its edge. It may even run off the machine. Adjust the angle of the front roller if necessary, by switching the machine on and off momentarily between adjustments. Make final adjustments with the machine running.

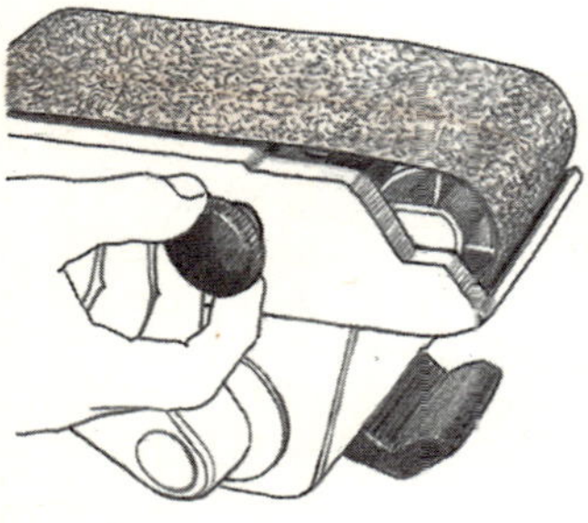

Once the new belt is fitted adjust it with the tracking adjustment knob on the side of the machine.

Disc Sander

SIZE: Diameter: 100 to 225mm
MATERIAL: Rubber, aluminium, zinc
USE: To sand wood, metal and plastics

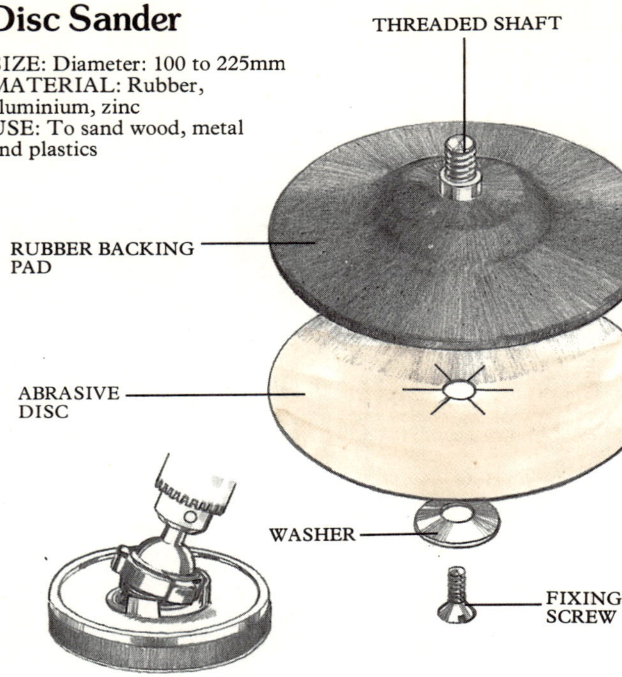

There are several models of disc sander, but they all operate in the same way. A round disc is applied to a pad which is driven in a circular motion. This produces cross grain scratches, so disc sanders are only suitable for reducing the surface or cleaning off old finishes. The simplest form of disc sander is fitted to a power drill. One pad is made of rubber, and has either a plain shank projecting from the centre, which fits into the drill chuck, or a threaded shaft which screws directly into the drill spindle.

Solid metal discs, faced with rubber, have a shank fitted to the centre with a ball joint. This enables the disc to remain flat on the work even when the drill is held at an angle. The rubber disc, on the other hand, relies on flexing to perform efficiently. Used this way the disc is more stable and consequently less likely to leave swirl marks. When using the sander keep all discs moving and apply light pressure only.

Fitting a disc

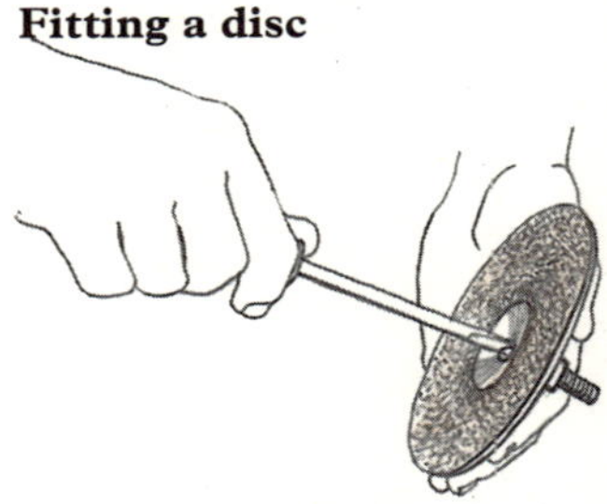

Fit the abrasive disc to the rubber pad with a screw and a shaped washer.

Using a rubber disc

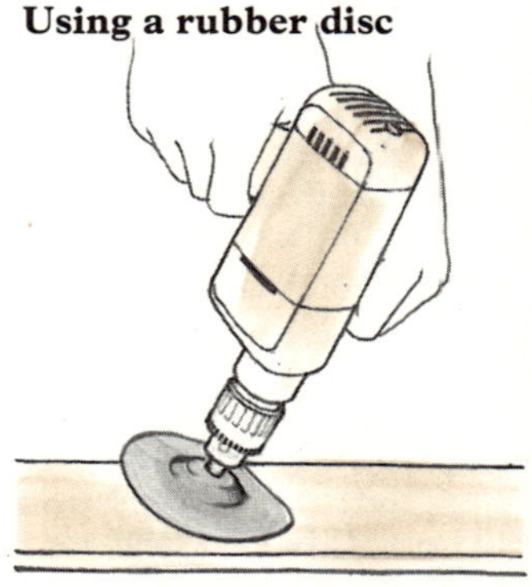

Angle the drill, flexing the top section of the rubber disc.

Abrasive discs
Abrasive discs are either made from abrasive material bonded to a paper backing or from pressed metal with tungsten carbide grains bonded to the surface. They are fitted to the backing disc with a screw thread and shaped washer which screw into the centre of the backing pad. Both washer and screw head are recessed below the working surface.

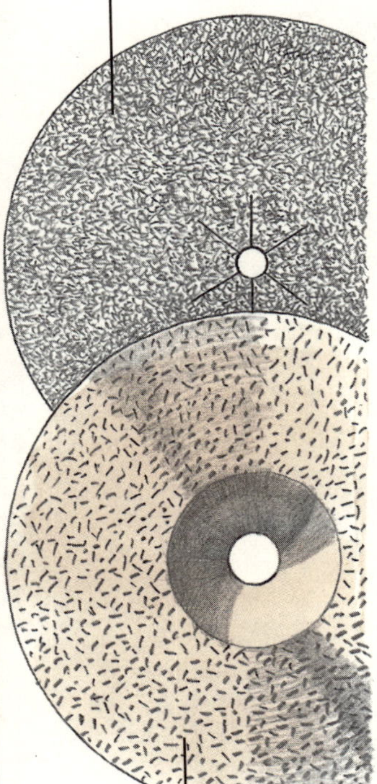

Offset sander grinder
Offset sander grinders are fitted with 175 and 225mm abrasive discs. These are industrial machines which may be worth renting for heavy duty work.

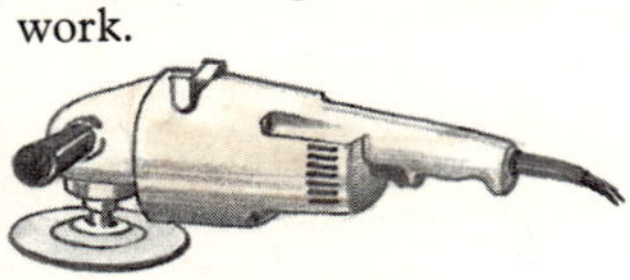

Offset sander grinder

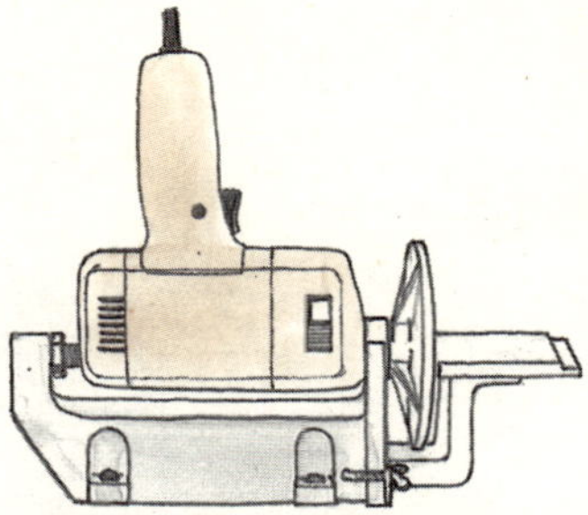

Bench mounted sanders
These can be very useful for shaping work. A small scale unit can be set up using a portable electric drill in a horizontal drill stand fitted with a work table and flat metal disc.

Gluing on discs
Hold a stick of adhesive on the surface of the metal disc while the machine is running. When the adhesive has melted and the disc surface is coated evenly, disconnect the machine and press a paperbacked abrasive disc centrally onto the backing plate of the disc.

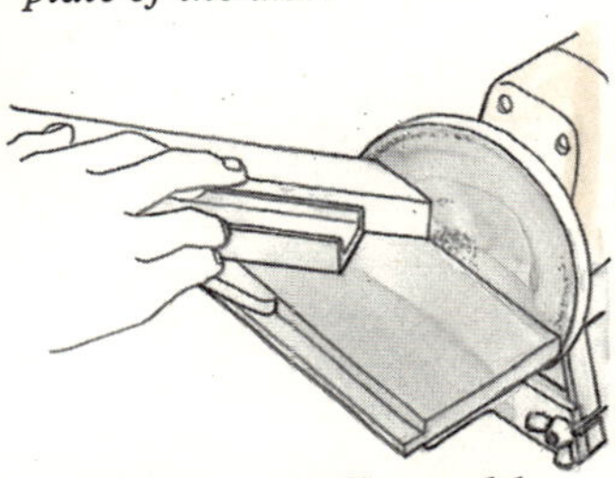

Using the sanding table
Check that the sanding table is square to the face of the disc with a try square before use. A mitre gauge runs in a groove across the table which can be set to trim ends square or at an angle. Hold the work against the downside of the disc to keep it on the table. Keep it moving to avoid uneven wear on the disc. Too much pressure is likely to burn the work.

Foam Drum Sander

SIZE: *Diameter:* 125mm; *width* 50mm
MATERIAL: *Arbor:* steel; *Drum:* particle foam
ACCESSORIES: Abrasive belt
USE: To sand flat and curved surfaces

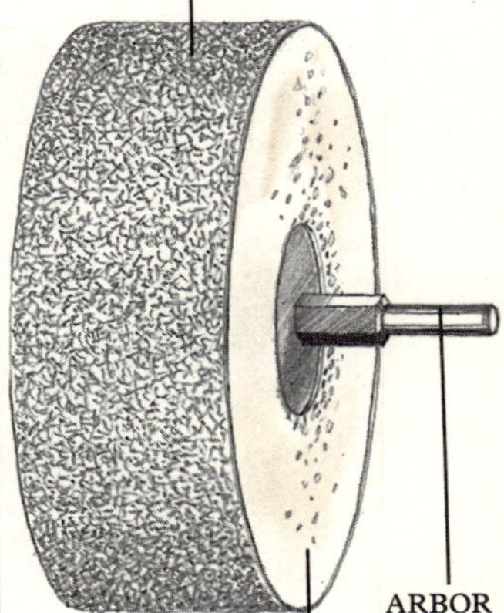

The drum is fitted with a steel arbor or shaft, which fits into the chuck of an electric drill. A continuous belt of abrasive material is slipped onto the resilient foam drum, which can shape itself to accommodate the contours of the workpiece.

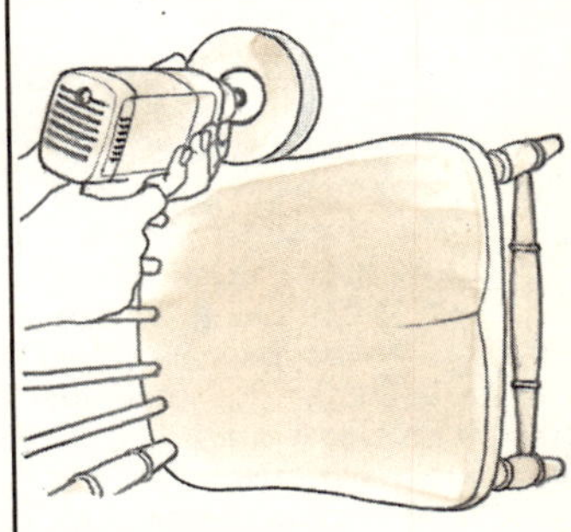

Using the drum
Use the foam drum sander to finish concave and convex shapes conveniently, as well as standard flat surfaces.

Finishing Sander

OTHER NAMES: Orbital sander, pad sander
SIZE: 100 × 100mm; 112 × 275mm; 4,000 to 14,000 orbits per minute
MATERIAL: Various
ACCESSORIES: Abrasive strips
USE: To sand a surface finally

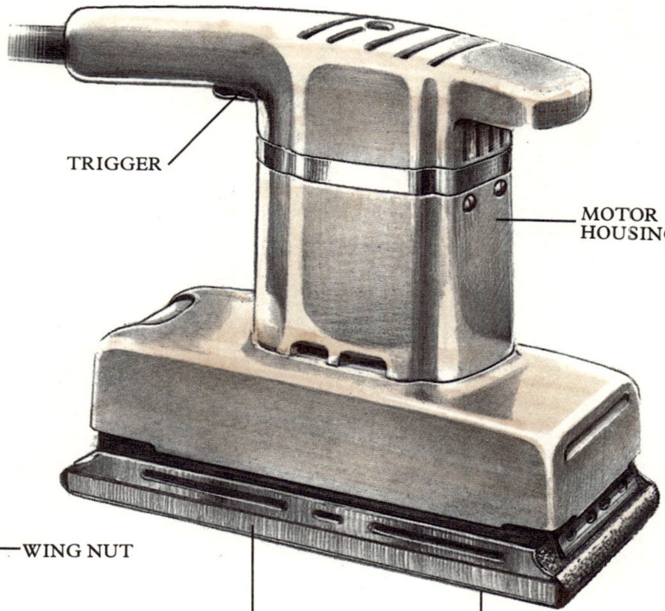

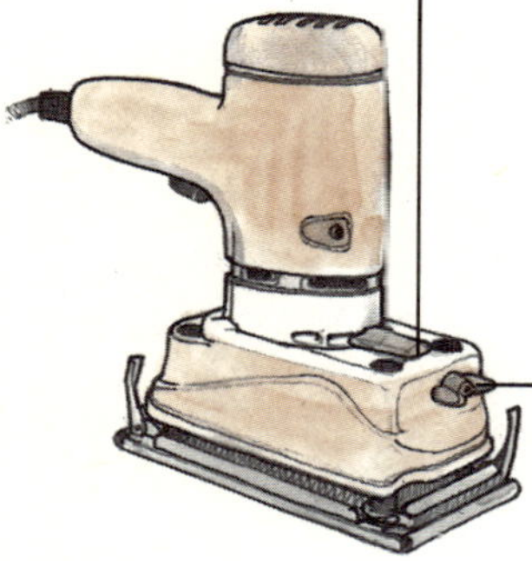

Finishing sander as a power drill attachment

The finishing sander achieves a fine smooth surface on wood by a series of tiny, high speed, orbital cuts. Some machines can be switched to an "in-line" movement for the final finish. A wide variety of sanders exist for one and two handed use as well as an attachment for an electric drill.

The finishing sander takes ready cut abrasive paper strips, which are stretched across a pad which holds them flat on the work. When using the sander work in bands parallel to the grain with the machine held at a slight angle to the direction in which it is moving. Finally finish with the machine held parallel to the grain and if possible, switched to in-line movement, while constantly moving the machine up and down the workpiece.

Fitting abrasive paper

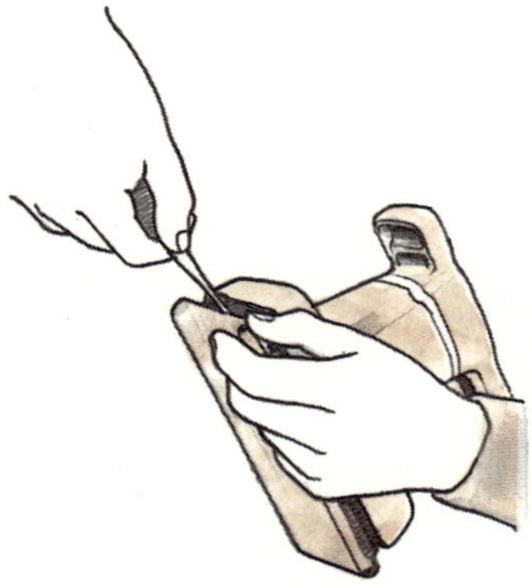

Attach one end of the strip under a spring clip or toothed roller. Stretch the paper and fit the other end the same way.

Using the sander

Work parallel to the grain, holding the machine at a slight angle to the direction of its travel. As you cover the work area, slightly overlap each sanded band as you go.

Floor Sander

SIZE: *Drum diameter:* 200 and 300mm; *disc diameter:* 200mm
MATERIAL: Various
ACCESSORIES: Abrasive paper, dust collecting bag
USE: To sand wooden floors for refinishing

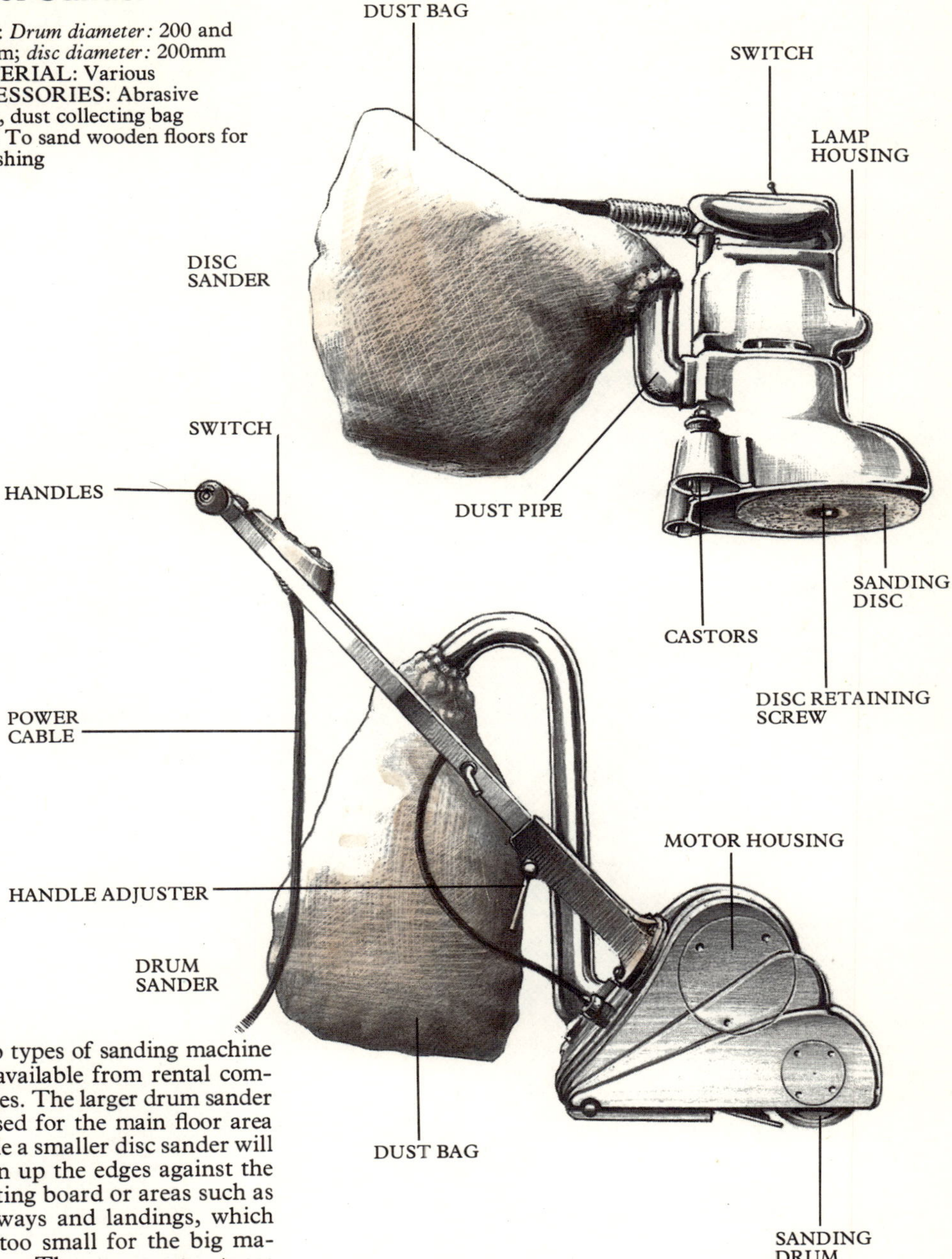

Two types of sanding machine are available from rental companies. The larger drum sander is used for the main floor area while a smaller disc sander will clean up the edges against the skirting board or areas such as hallways and landings, which are too small for the big machine. There are even types which will fit beneath radiators.

Both machines produce a considerable amount of dust. Even though they are designed to suck the dust directly into collecting bags, it is advisable to wear a face mask and if possible, seal off gaps leading to other areas of the house.

Fitting new paper to drum sanders
Floor sanders are supplied with abrasive paper in coarse, medium and fine grades. The coarse paper is used to level the surface; medium and fine are for finishing.

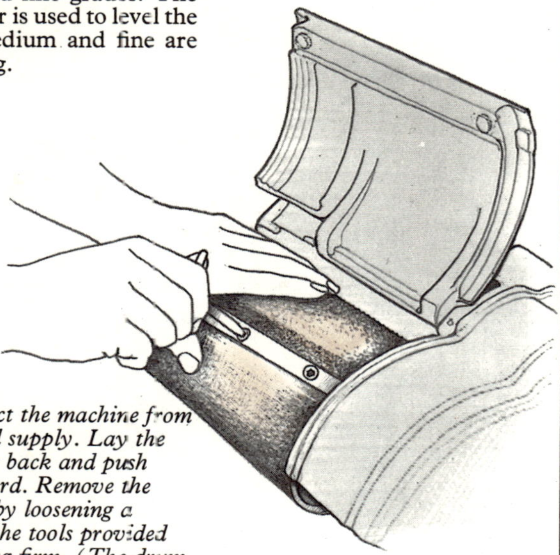

1. *Disconnect the machine from the electrical supply. Lay the sander on its back and push back the guard. Remove the worn paper by loosening a clamp with the tools provided by the renting firm. (The drum itself may be split lengthwise on some models.)*

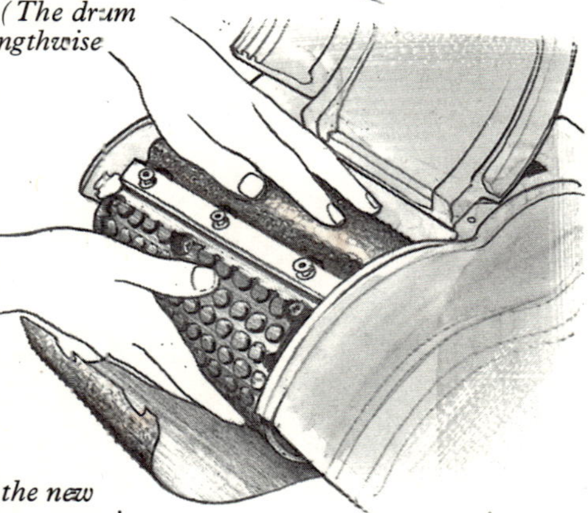

2. *Insert one end of the new paper under the clamp, wrap it around the rubber roller and insert the other end.*

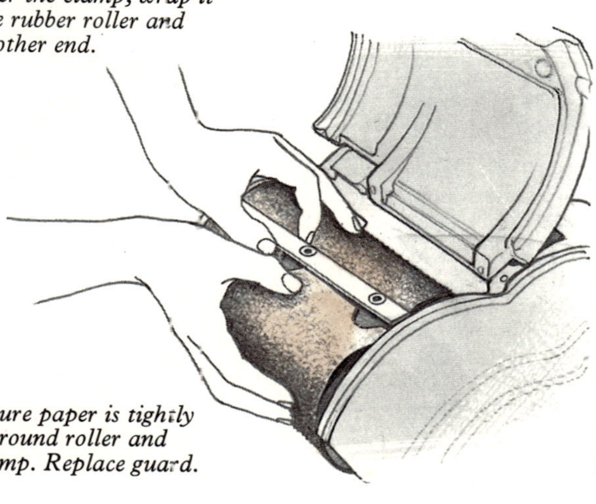

3. *Make sure paper is tightly wrapped around roller and tighten clamp. Replace guard.*

Fitting new paper to disc sanders
Coarse, medium and fine abrasive paper is also supplied for disc sanders. Disconnect the machine from the electricity supply before fitting new discs or paper. Turn the machine upside down to fit new discs.

1. *Undo the retaining clamp by turning it counter clockwise in the middle of the disc.*

2. *Remove the old disc and throw it away. Fit a new one of the appropriate coarseness and tighten the clamp once more. Turn the sander upright.*

Preparing the surface for sanding
Remove all carpet tacks, edging strips or adhesive tape from the surface. Sink all nail heads. If the gaps between the floor boards are very large, consider lifting them and closing them up before sanding.

Sweep the floor to remove loose material which might damage the machine's roller.

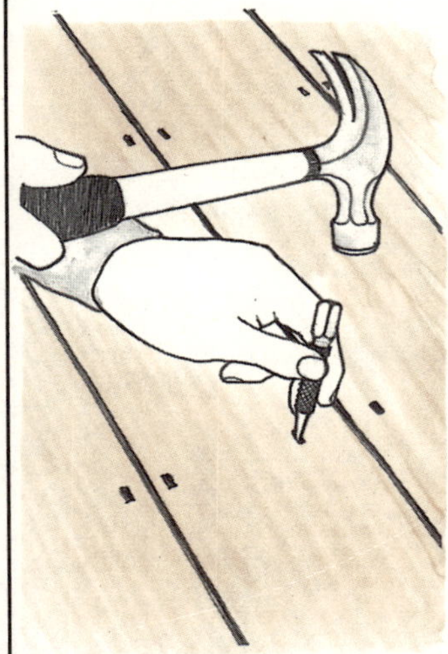

Sink all nail heads below the surface of the boards with a hammer and nail set.

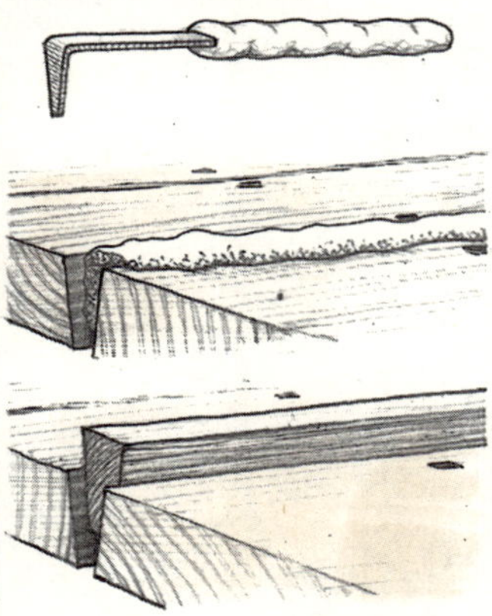

Filling wide gaps
Make a steel scraping tool, tapered to rake out the gaps between the floorboards. Either fill the gaps with papier mâché and sand it flush when it is dry, or tap in suitably tapered strips of softwood and plane them flush when in place.

Using the machines
Never switch on the drum sander while it is resting on the floor. It will either move off on its own or sand a deep mark in the floor. Tilt the machine backward to lift the roller off the floor, switch on the machine and gradually lower it.

At the end of the run, tilt the machine once more, turn it around, and sand the section parallel with and overlapping the previously sanded area.

If the boards are already flat and only require cleaning, you need only sand the floor parallel with the boards.

1. *Lower the sander. As it comes into contact with the surface, start to move the machine across the floor at an angle to the boards.*

2. *When the entire floor has been covered, sand at an opposite angle to the first. This will level any high points instead of following them.*

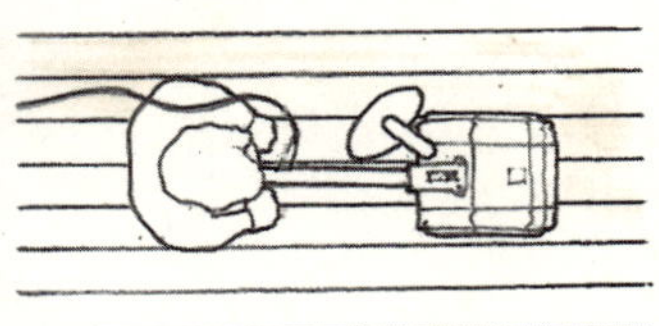

3. *Fit a medium then a fine paper to finish sanding the floor in the direction of the boards.*

Finishing off
The floor sander will not be able to clean the edges of the floor near the skirting board or get into any small or awkward corner areas. When you have done all you can with the big machine, switch to the smaller disc sander.

Vacuum the whole area to remove all loose dust before applying the chosen finish.

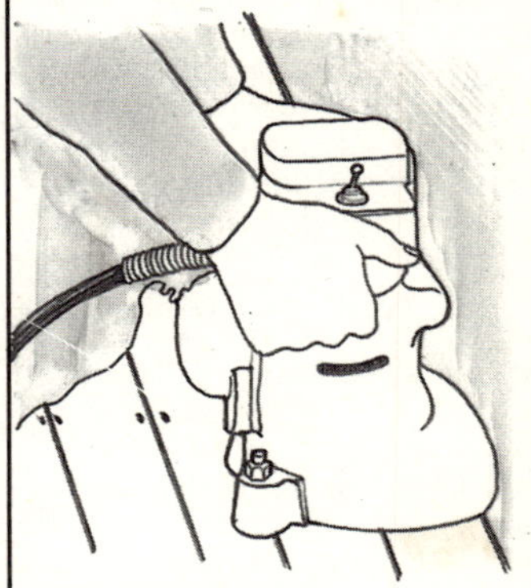

Sanding edges
Drape the cable over your shoulder to keep it away from the discs. Grip the handles and switch on the machine. Keep it moving to prevent over-sanding in one area. Take it as far into the edges as the sander housing will allow.

Sanding corners
To clean up corners, use a sanding disc in a power drill *(see page 230)**. The flexible disc should reach most corners. For even more inaccessible areas, use a scraper and sanding block.*

Oil Can

SIZE: Capacity: up to 1 litre
MATERIAL: Tinplate, plastic
USE: To apply oil to an oilstone or lubricate moving metal parts

Oil cans range from simple plastic or tinplate containers which pump the oil through the spout by squeezing the sides or base of the container, to cans which incorporate a thumb operated pump.

Pumped oil cans are more suitable for lubricating machines as they can be used at various angles and incorporate long spouts which reach into confined spaces.

The bench oil can is commonly used in the workshop to apply oil to sharpening stones. The spout is closed or opened by turning the valve.

An oil syringe is used to pump large quantities of oil into reservoirs such as a car gearbox. The flexible plastic spout means the syringe can fill through side filler holes.

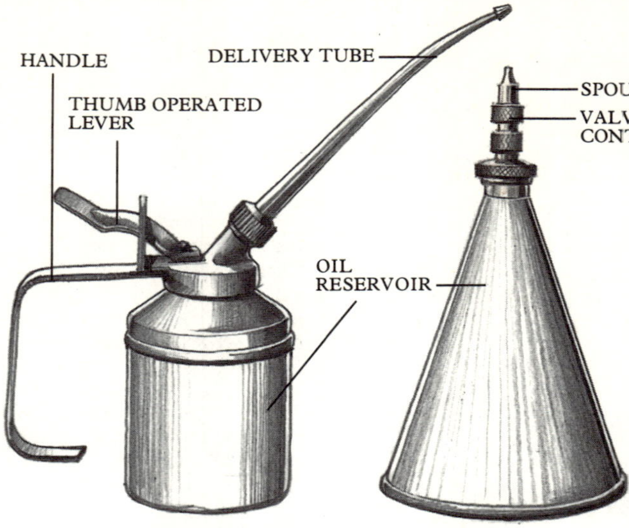

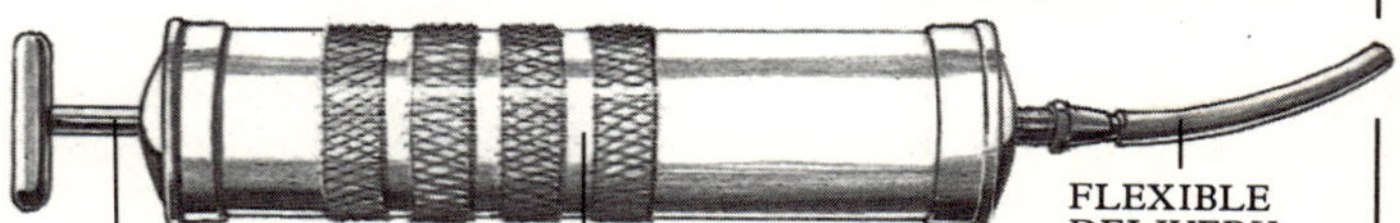

Grease Gun

SIZE: Capacity: 28 to 800gm
MATERIAL: *Handle:* steel; *Delivery tube:* steel or nylon
USE: To force grease under pressure into a bearing

You need pressure to force thick grease into the tightly fitting parts of a bearing. Small grease guns which are designed to deliver soft grease, are operated by pumping the body of the gun. Larger guns, for heavier grease, are operated by levers or triggers. The grease is either loaded as pre-packed cartridges or must be packed into the container from a can.

The nozzle of the gun fits on to a valve known as a grease nipple, which has a spring-loaded seal. Wipe the nipple clean before fitting the nozzle to keep dirt out of the bearing.

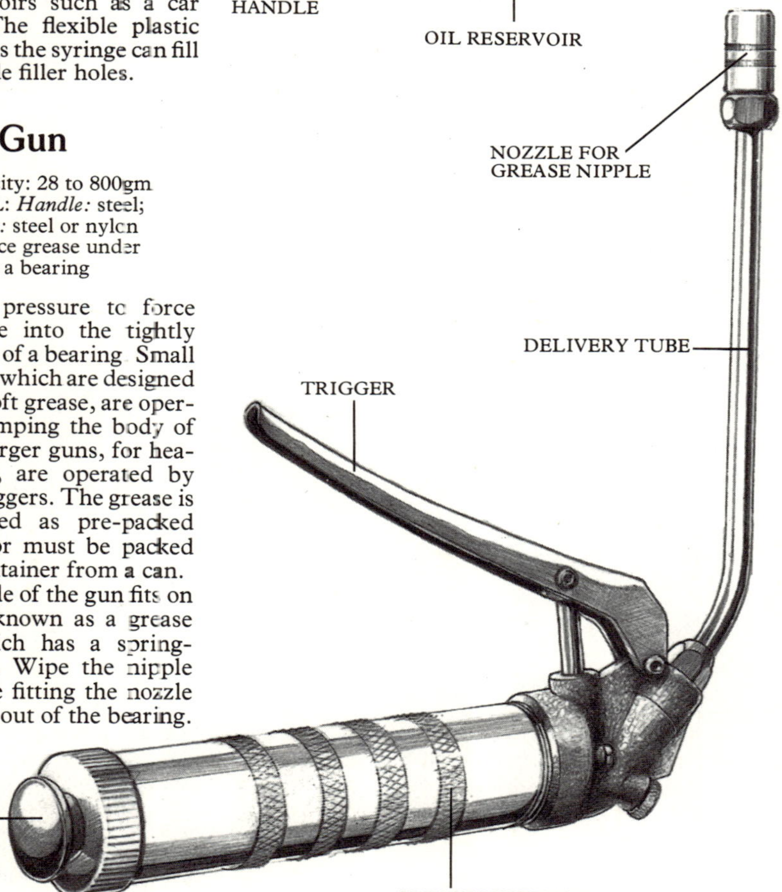

Hydrometer

SIZE: 215 to 280mm
MATERIAL: *Barrel float:* glass; *Bulb:* rubber
USE: To check the state of charge of a car battery

An hydrometer checks the charge of a battery by measuring the specific gravity of the electrolyte in the cells.

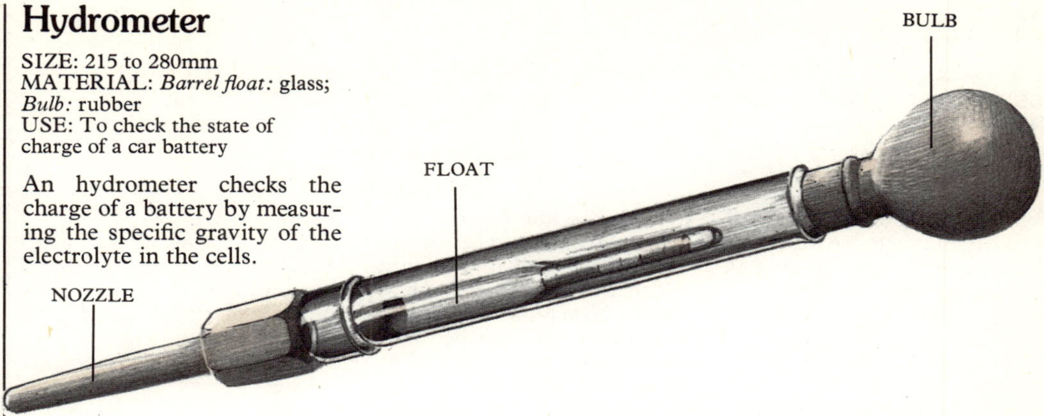

You can check the charge each month by squeezing the bulb on the hydrometer, inserting the nozzle in the cell and drawing off some of the diluted acid by slowly releasing the bulb. When the float is clear of the bottom, read off the state of charge on the float where it emerges from the electrolyte. The lower the charge in the battery, the deeper the float will sink into the electrolyte.

Some floats indicate full or half charge. A graduated scale will indicate a full charge between 1.250 and 1.350.

Once you have taken the reading, return the electrolyte to the cell and check each cell in turn. Wash out the hydrometer after use.

Circuit Tester

SIZE: To measure 6, 12, 24 volt systems
MATERIAL: Various
USE: To test the presence of electricity in a car wiring system

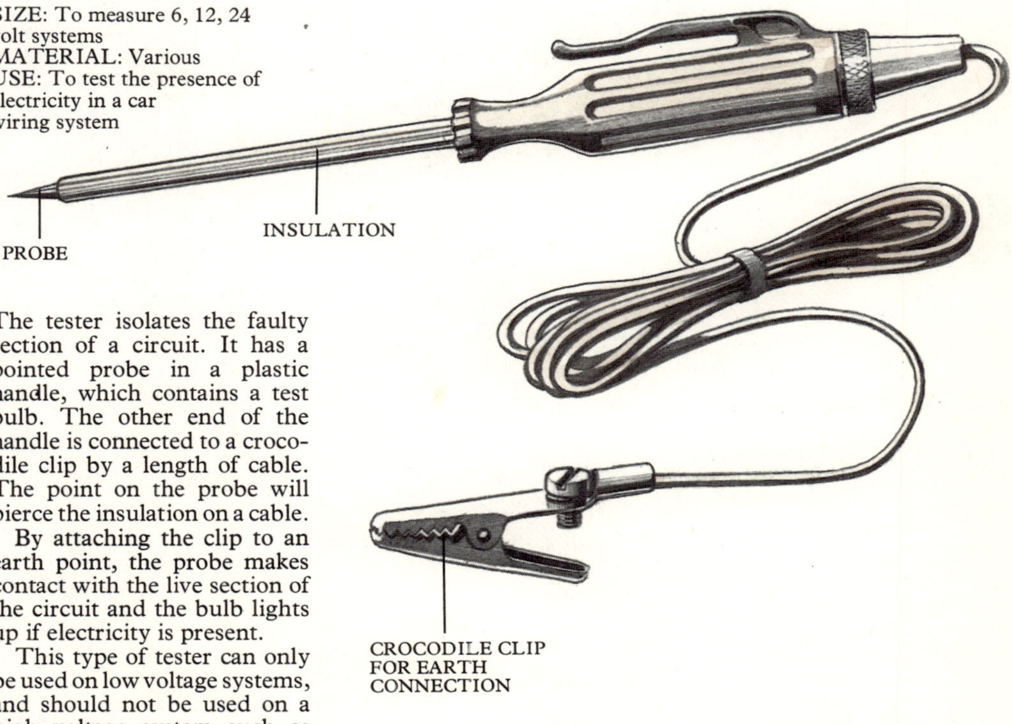

The tester isolates the faulty section of a circuit. It has a pointed probe in a plastic handle, which contains a test bulb. The other end of the handle is connected to a crocodile clip by a length of cable. The point on the probe will pierce the insulation on a cable.

By attaching the clip to an earth point, the probe makes contact with the live section of the circuit and the bulb lights up if electricity is present.

This type of tester can only be used on low voltage systems, and should not be used on a high voltage system such as house wiring.

Rasps and Files

Files originated in Egypt and have been used since the Bronze Age. Traditionally they were hand made. A file-making machine was designed by Leonardo da Vinci, but the first one was not built until 1750, and machine file-making was not established until a century later.

Files are used to smooth metal and wood, to remove burrs and local irregularities, to enlarge and finish holes and slots, to sharpen cutting tools and, with a saw set, to set saw teeth.

They are classified by their cut (how the teeth are arranged on the blade) and the degree of coarseness. This is determined by the number of teeth per 25mm and the amount of space between the rows of teeth. In general, the longer the file the coarser it is.

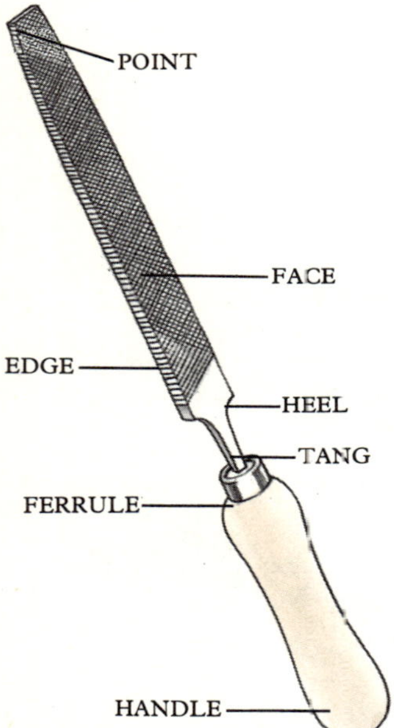

Some files have one edge uncut. This is called the "safe" edge, and can be rested against an inside work surface without damage while the other edge or edges do the filing.

File handles
Few files have handles. Handles, usually of softwood or composition, are sold separately. One handle usually fits a small range of files.

Never use a file without a handle, as the tang can be very dangerous.

Fitting the handle
Insert the tang into the handle socket. Tap the handle on the workbench until the tang is seated. Never use a hammer. Tap lightly with a mallet if the handle is difficult to get on. To remove the handle, pull it from the file while tapping the ferrule gently on the edge of the workbench.

New files
Break in new files on brass, bronze or smooth cast iron. When they have become rough on that they are ready for heavy work on hard metals. Never start a new file on work narrower than the blade. Wood files need no breaking-in.

The cuts
Files are single cut, double cut or curved tooth. Single cut files have parallel rows of teeth cut at an angle of 60° to 80° to the edge. Double cut teeth have a second set of parallel grooves cut into them, usually at an angle of 45°. The cut of the file determines its use. A single cut is used for precision work and a double cut for fast preliminary clearance.

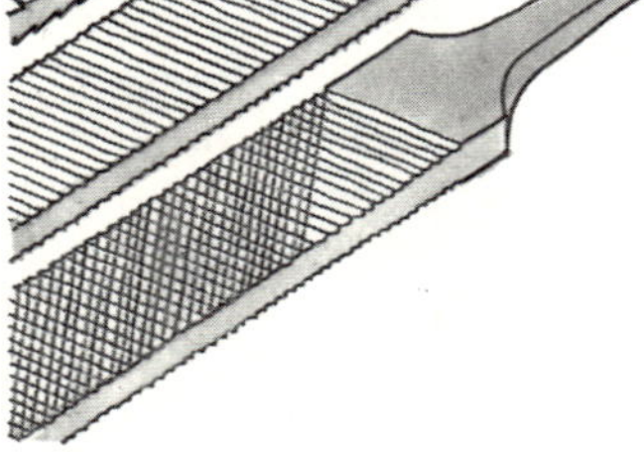

Use curved tooth files (top) on soft metal, single cut (center) for fine work and double cut (bottom) for roughing.

Maintenance
Clean files frequently and hang them in racks if you use them often or wrapped up individually if stored for a long time. Do not use them to pry things open or to strike objects as they are very brittle and break easily.

Coarseness
Whether a file is rough or smooth depends on the number of teeth per 25mm and the space left between each row of teeth. There are three generally accepted degrees of coarseness: bastard, medium coarse with 26 teeth per 25mm; second cut, medium smooth with 36 teeth per 25mm; and smooth, with 60 teeth per 25mm. Some makers provide rough and dead smooth files.

Cuts and coarseness

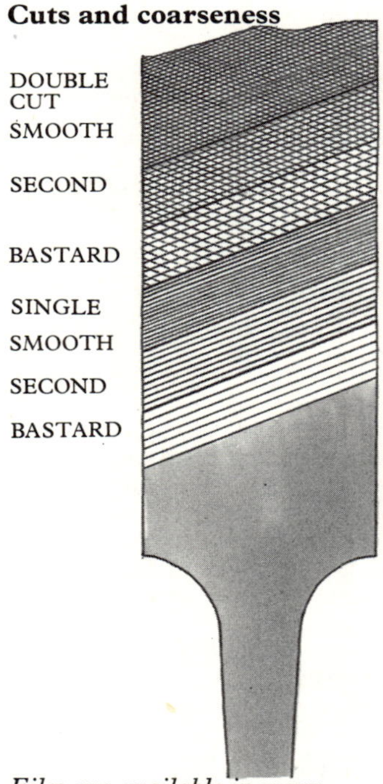

Files are available in many combinations of cut and coarseness. The most popular are shown above.

Using a file

Filing is harder than it looks, and you may need to practice on scrap or unimportant pieces before you perfect your skill. Always clamp the work, however small, in a vice, preferably at elbow level. Set it low in the vise to prevent vibration and allow the work to project slightly. Clamp large sheets to the workbench.

Never use a file without a handle. Remember that the file cuts on the forward stroke only so apply even pressure as you push the file across the work, and lift it on the return stroke. Hold the file as shown and try to keep it in a straight line. Chalk applied to the teeth of the file helps to keep them clear of any metal residue.

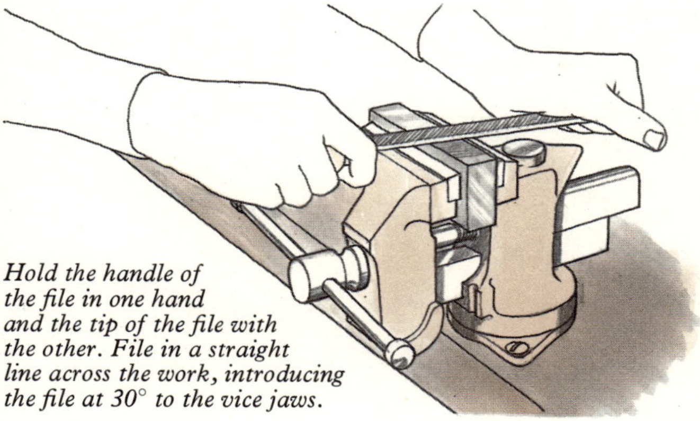

Hold the handle of the file in one hand and the tip of the file with the other. File in a straight line across the work, introducing the file at 30° to the vice jaws.

Cross filing

With large flat areas, avoid a curved surface by constantly changing the direction of the file, though not the angle of approach. Check frequently with a square edge that you are filing true. It is very easy to establish a faulty stroke.

If the work is becoming curved, you are starting the stroke too early and finishing it too late.

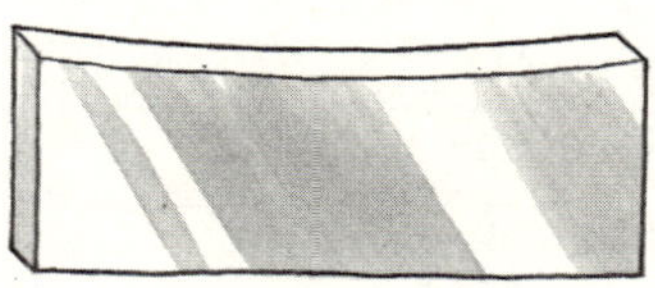

If there is a hollow, you are starting the stroke too late and finishing it too early.

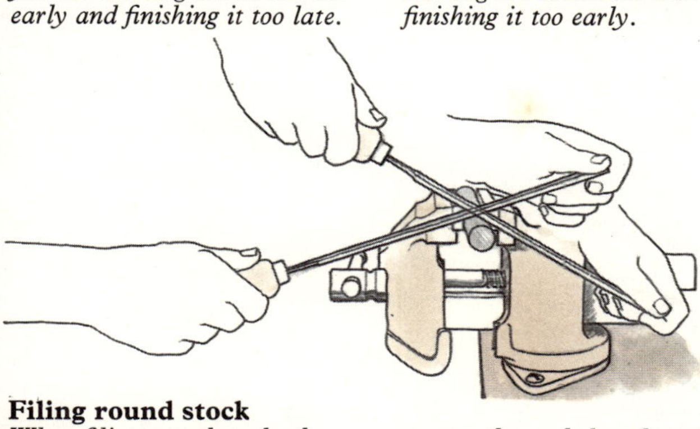

Filing round stock

When filing round stock, the ability to rock the file is an advantage, unlike filing flat work. The file must be constantly angled so that all the teeth come into contact with the work. This keeps the file even on the workpiece.

Draw filing

Draw filing puts a smooth finish on a piece, removing all cross filing marks. Use a single cut file, make sure it is clean and well chalked. Draw the file across the work toward you. For a fine finish wrap the blade in emery cloth. Do not overdo draw filing as you could unintentionally hollow the surface of the work. Use a flat file on flat surfaces and outside curves and a round or half round file for inside curves.

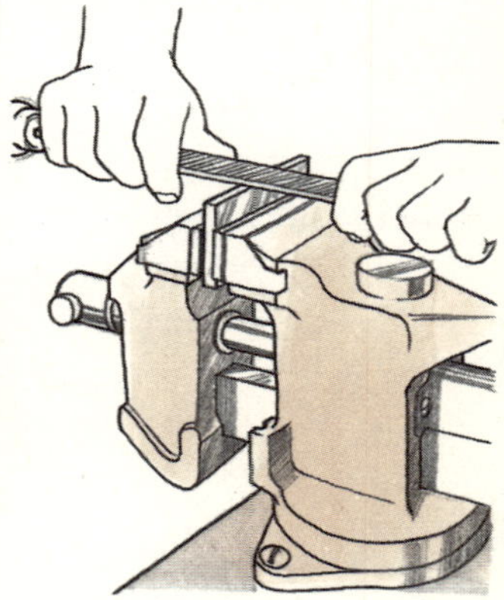

Hold the file at right angles to the work, using two hands close together to prevent snapping. Light pressure is needed for light work, heavy for rough work. You may have to use the palm of your hand rather than the fingers to guide the file over coarse material. Do not use your body weight for extra power. The file will break.

Deburring

Use a single cut file to remove burrs. Clamp the work in a vice, or to the workbench if it is large. For small areas of local burring, file across the edge.

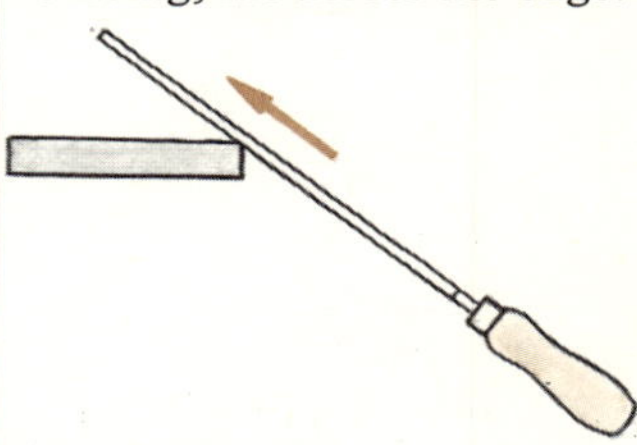

Filing long burrs

To remove a length of burr or to chamfer an edge, angle the file and push it along the length of the edge.

Cleaning
Files need to be cleaned regularly otherwise they become "pinned", or clogged with filings. Pinned files slip on and scratch the work and quickly become unusable. Clean them with a file brush or file card. The file brush has two brushes, one coarse and one fine, and incorporates a wire pick to remove stubborn bits of filing. A file card has a coarse brush and a wire scorer on the back for extracting individual filings.

When the file is clean, chalk it before you use it again. Never oil a file or strike it to remove excess filings.

Using the file brush

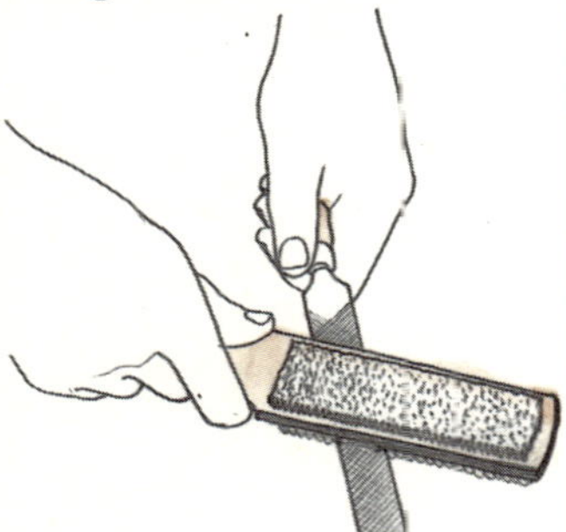

Stroke the file brush parallel to the file teeth. Remove obstinate filings with a nail or ice pick and soft metal residue with a block of end grain hardwood.

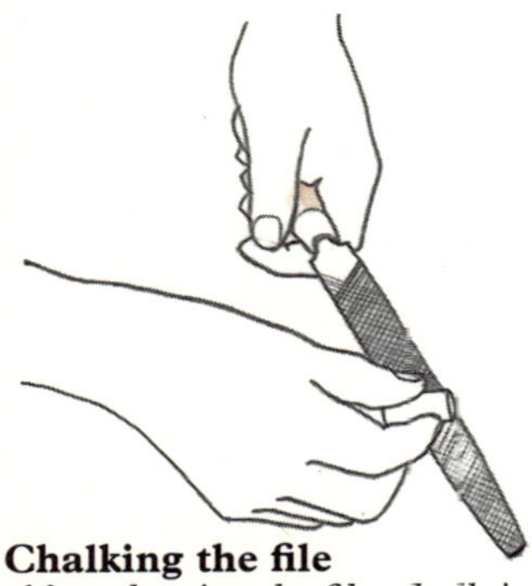

Chalking the file
After cleaning the file, chalk it before use. This fills up the gaps between the file teeth, discouraging further pinning. Make sure that the gaps are well packed with chalk.

Flat File

SIZE: 100 to 450mm
MATERIAL: Steel
USE: To file flat surfaces

The commonest file for all types of work except inside curves, the flat file tapers in both width and thickness toward the head. Single cut and double cut flat files are available, but the most general type is the double cut bastard.

Round File

SIZE: 100 to 450mm
MATERIAL: Steel
USE: To file round holes or in curved surfaces

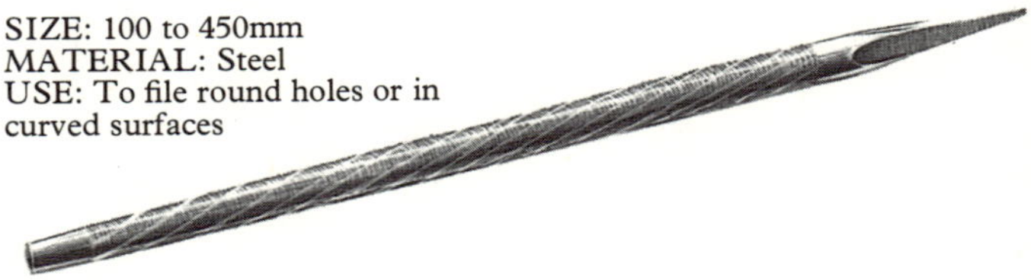

The round file tapers toward the point and is used to enlarge or smooth round openings and to finish concave surfaces. Small versions of the round file are sometimes called rat-tail files. Use the round file on small circular openings; the half round file is best for larger round areas.

Half Round File

SIZE: 100 to 450mm
MATERIAL: Steel
USE: All purpose filing

The half round file is the most useful of all the files, combining the features of both round and flat files. One side is rounded and one flat, so the tool can be used on flat, concave and convex surfaces. It also files both wood and metal. Use it for work on larger circular areas.

Hand File

SIZE: 100 to 450mm
MATERIAL: Steel
USE: General purpose filing

The hand file is slightly different from other files. It is flat in cross section but has parallel sides right up to the tip, tapering only in thickness. There is one safe and one "live" edge, and it is consequently useful for stepped work, and any general jobs where a safe edge is needed or where both sides of a corner must not be cut simultaneously. "Hand" is possibly a corruption of "handy".

Pillar File

SIZE: 75 to 200mm
MATERIAL: Steel
USE: To file narrow openings

The pillar file is a slimmer version of the hand file, with one safe edge. It is mostly used for slots and keyways. Narrow pillar files, about half the width of the standard variety, are used for very small orifices.

Square File

SIZE: 100 to 500mm
MATERIAL: Steel
USE: To file square holes or angles

The square file is used on rectangular slots, keyways and splines. Some models have three sides toothed and the fourth left "safe"; in a confined space the file can rest on its safe edge without damaging its surroundings, while the other edges do the work.

Triangular File

OTHER NAME: Three square file
SIZE: 100 to 450mm
MATERIAL: Steel
USE: To file angular stock

The triangular file has three flat sides. It is used to file acute internal angles, clean cut square corners, enlarge and clean up angular holes and sharpen serrated jaws and saw teeth (see pages 75–76).

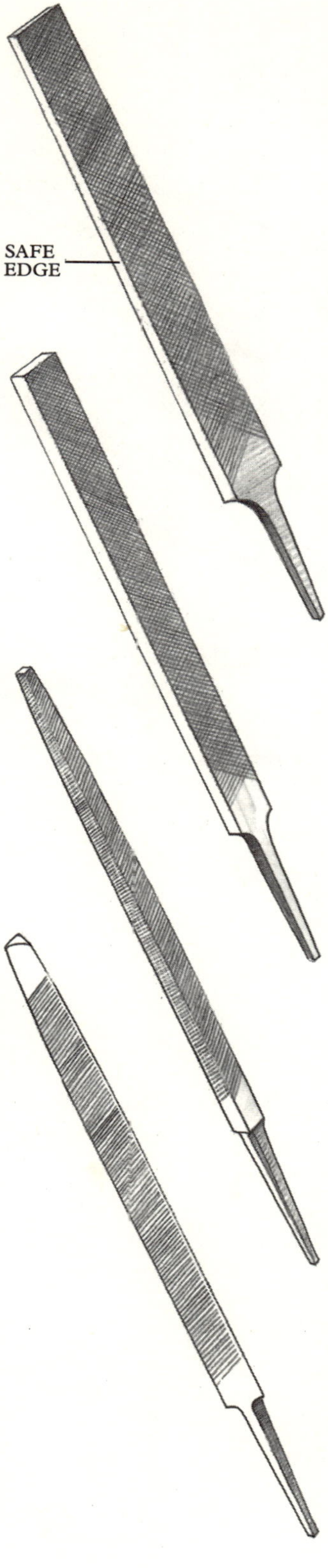

Mill File

OTHER NAME: Mill saw file
SIZE: 200 to 250mm
MATERIAL: Steel
USE: Fine work and sharpening

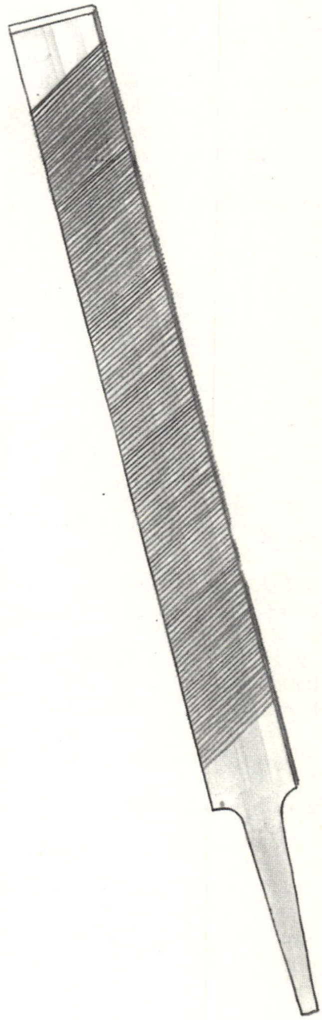

Mill files can have one or two rounded edges and often have one safe edge. They are always single cut, and are mostly used for lathe work and draw filing, but are basically all purpose fine finishing tools. They are also used to sharpen mill and circular saws, knives, lawn mower blades, axes and shears.

Needle Files

OTHER NAMES: Swiss pattern files, jeweller's files
SIZE: *Length:* 75 to 300mm; 34 to 184 teeth per 25mm
MATERIAL: Steel
USE: Precision filing

These small, delicate files are usually sold in sets. They are very accurately made, and the tangs are knurled and lengthened to make handles. Needle files are principally used for precision work on instruments or mechanisms, but they also make fine finishing tools on important work. They are also used to sharpen the fragile spurs on spur nosed drill bits and can be used to tidy up slots, square corners, notches, keyways and grooves.

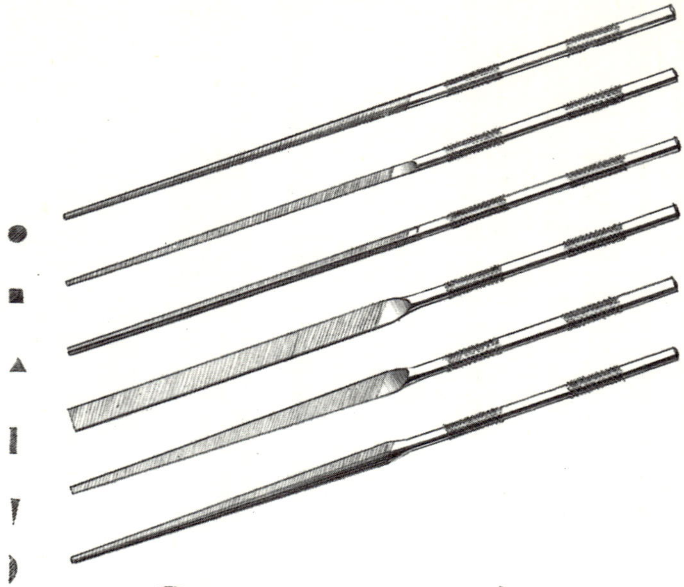

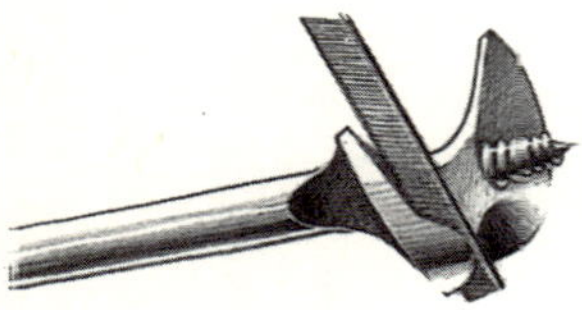

Sharpening the spur
Hold the twist of the bit firmly against the bench, tip uppermost. File inside the spur with a flat needle file. Filing outside will reduce clearance.

Sharpening the cutter
Rest the bit on the bench, lead screw down. Work a triangular needle file through the throat of the bit, filing the cutters on the underside only.

Sharpening the side wings
Hold the bit as for sharpening the cutters. Using a square needle file, file the side wings on the inside only.

Knife File

SIZE: 100 to 200mm
MATERIAL: Steel
USE: To file very acute angles

The knife file has a section like a knife blade, and tapers toward its point. It is used by tool and diemakers on work which has acute angles.

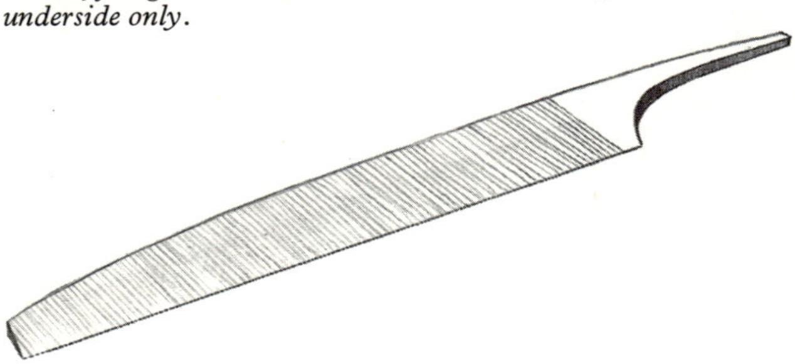

Warding File

SIZE: 100 to 200mm
MATERIAL: Steel
USE: To file locks and keys

The rectangular warding file is a small slender file, tapering to a narrow point. It is primarily a locksmith's tool, used for filing notches on keys and locks, but can be used where a thicker file would be too clumsy. It has a broad, strong blade, so can be used vigorously on edge.

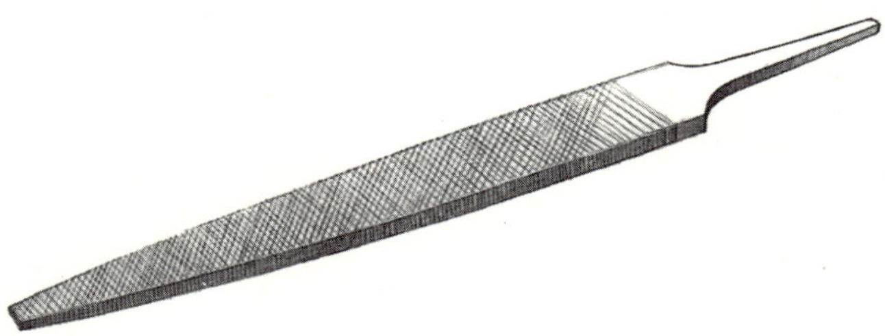

Saw File

SIZE: 75 to 250mm
MATERIAL: Steel
USE: To file saw teeth

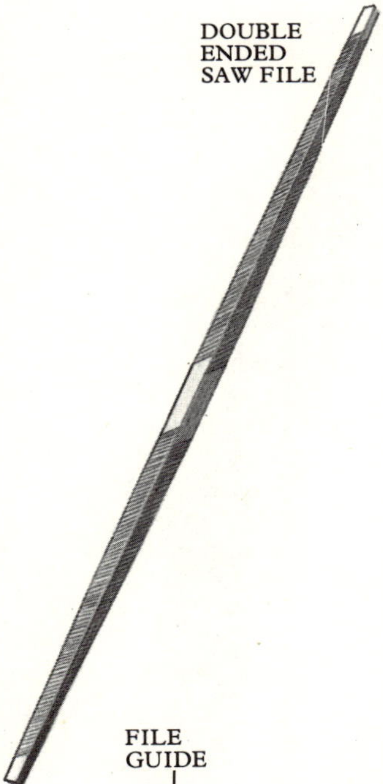

Various files are made specifically to file the teeth of the many models of saw on the market. There are taper saw files, mill saw files with two square edges, double ended saw files, cross cut saw files and chain saw files. All are available in coarse or fine grades. Use them with a saw set to keep saw teeth sharp (see page 76). Otherwise use a mill file of the correct cut.

There is also a tool on the market called a saw sharpener, which will accurately sharpen cross cut, tenon and fleam saws when used with a saw set. It is a small double ended file.

Rasps

Unlike file teeth, rasp teeth are formed individually to slice off slivers of wood quickly and easily. Rasps are mostly used on wood, but work well on soft metal (aluminium, lead), leather and bone as well. Bastard (coarse) and smooth cut are available, and the usual shapes are flat, round and half round.

Surform Round File

SIZE: 250mm
MATERIAL: *Blade:* steel; *Handle:* plastic; *Body:* aluminium
USE: To enlarge holes and shape decorative cuts

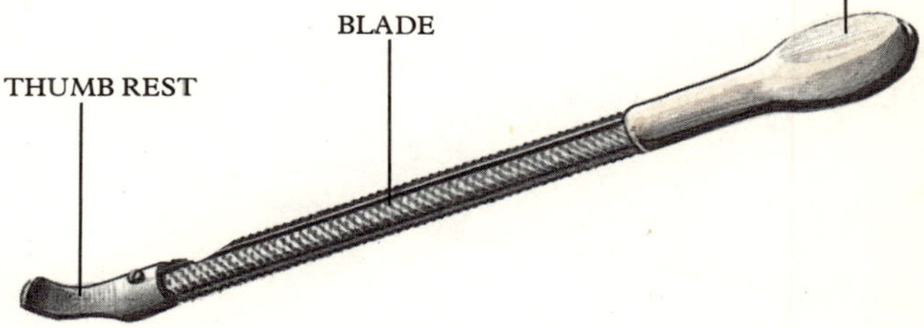

Surform tools are unique. They are hollow rasps, consisting of steel blades perforated with sharp edged holes which cut away wood rapidly. The waste is passed easily through the holes.

The round file is tube shaped and has a removable front holding piece. It can do any round file work on wood, aluminium, copper, plastics, tiles, laminated surfaces and metal no harder than mild steel. It is particularly useful for enlarging holes.

Surform Flat File

SIZE: 250mm
MATERIAL: *Blade:* steel; *Body:* aluminium; *Handle:* plastic
USE: General filing

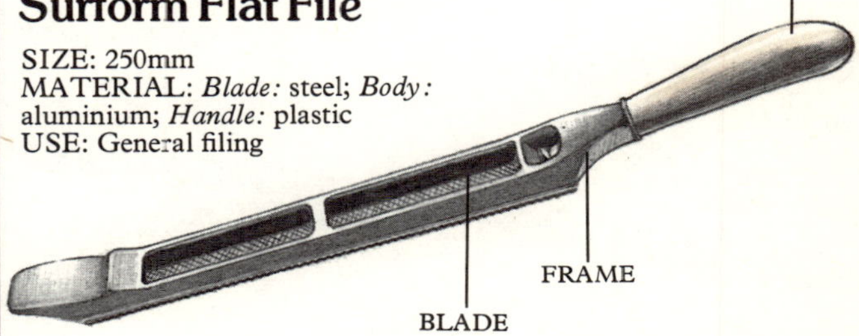

The surform flat file has the same perforated blade as the round file, and does the same job as a standard flat rasp.

Cabinet Rasp

SIZE: 200 to 300mm
MATERIAL: Steel
USE: To remove wood quickly

Cabinet rasps are the best known wood rasps. They are usually shaped like half round files with one flat and one rounded edge. There are also flat versions. Cabinet makers use them to rough file wood before finishing with a wood file or abrasive paper.

Wood File

SIZE: 200 to 350mm
MATERIAL: Steel
USE: To finish wood

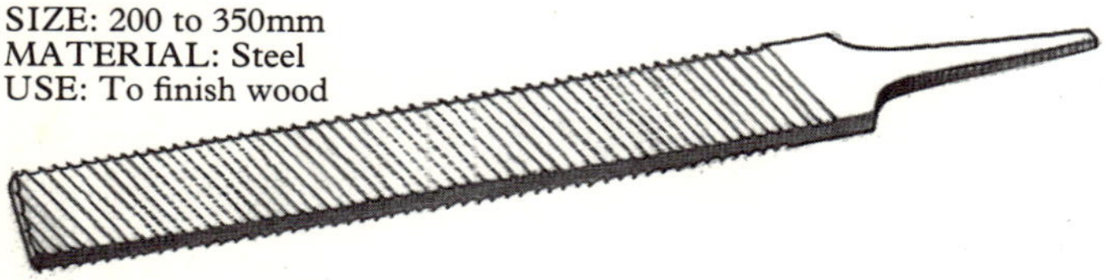

Used for wood only, the wood file is used after a rasp to smooth wooden surfaces. It has coarse file teeth.

Flat Wood Rasp

SIZE: 200 to 400mm
MATERIAL: Steel
USE: General rasping

This is exactly like a flat file in section, but is rasp cut. It can be used on flat or convex surfaces.

Round Wood Rasp

SIZE: 150 to 350mm
MATERIAL: Steel
USE: To rasp round holes or curved surfaces

This is a large, round sectioned rasp, which is used on tightly curved wood sections or circular holes. Bastard, second cut and smooth grades are available.

Half Round Wood Rasp

SIZE: 150 to 400mm
MATERIAL: Steel
USE: General rasping

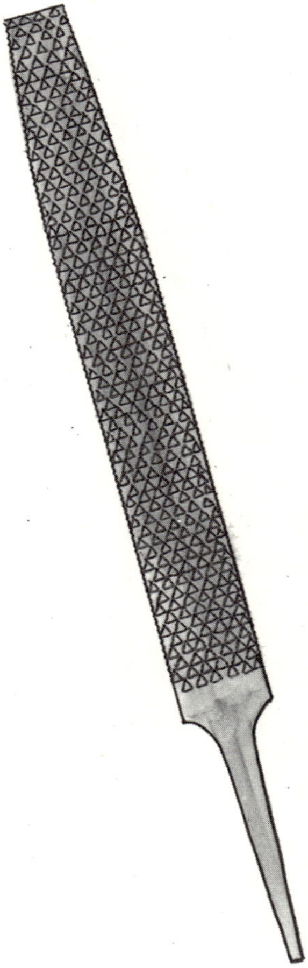

The half round rasp, like the half round file can be used on flat, concave and convex surfaces. Bastard, second cut and smooth grades are available. There is not much difference between this tool and the half round cabinet rasp.

Shoe Rasp

OTHER NAMES: Last maker's rasp; shoemaker's rasp; 4-in-hand rasp file
SIZE: 200 to 350mm
MATERIAL: Steel
USE: To file or rasp

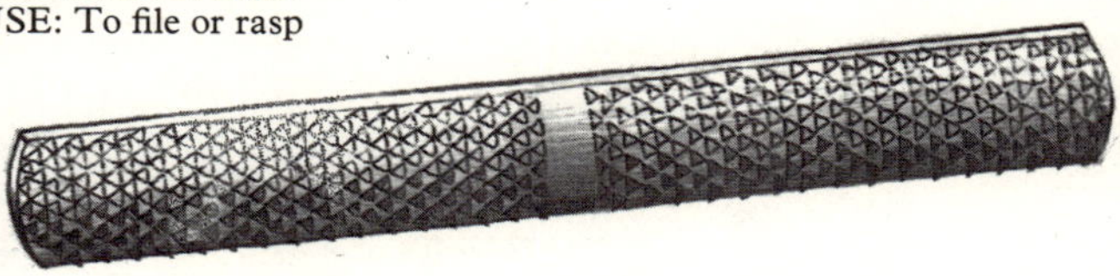

This is a versatile, double ended tool. One end has a file cut surface on each side and the other end is rasp cut. Use it on wood or leather.

Horse Rasp

SIZE: 300 to 450mm
MATERIAL: Steel
USE: Rough wood filing

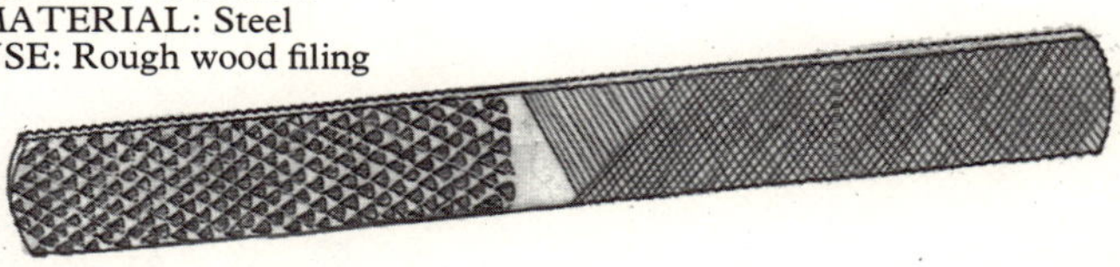

The horse rasp is the biggest and coarsest rasp there is. It is used for rough work, and normally has no tang to take a handle but is squared off at each end. Tanged versions are available up to 400mm.

Rifflers

OTHER NAMES: Woodcarver's file; woodcarver's rasp; bent rifflers
SIZE: 150 to 250mm
MATERIAL: *Handle:* hardwood; *Blade:* steel
USE: To file woodcarving

Rifflers are craftsmen's tools. They are miniature files, with the same selection of cut, coarseness and cross section, and are adapted to suit individual needs. Some are double ended, with rasp cut blades at one end and file cut at the other. Some are ready fitted with hardwood handles, and are bent at an angle of 45° to reach into the hard-to-get-at places on a woodcarving or sculpture. Diemakers have a special set of rifflers which are more substantial than woodcarving rifflers.

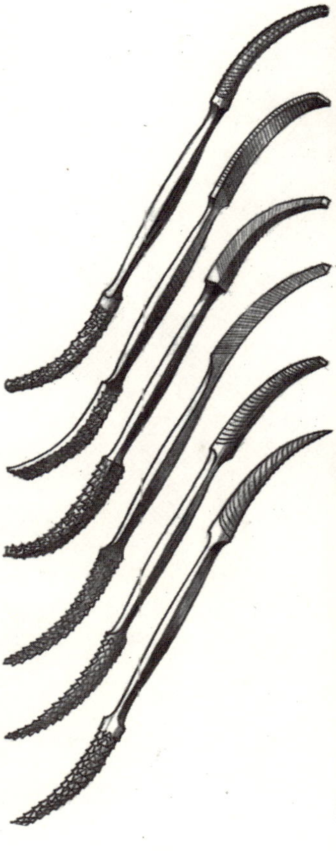

Rotary Files and Rasps

SIZE: Shank diameter: 3 to 6mm
MATERIAL: Steel
USE: To shape and file small areas

These tools are sold singly as well as in sets. The rotary files have finer teeth and can be used on both metal and wood. The coarser rasps should only be used on wood. These files and rasps come in a huge variety of shapes, cut in bastard, second cut and smooth grades. They are mounted on shanks and are used with a power driven flexible shaft tool (see page 215). Some can fit the chuck of an electric drill.

These tiny, accurate files are particularly useful for modeling work or intricate carving. They can be fitted to the miniature power drill (see page 189). The best tools for carving are called burrs.

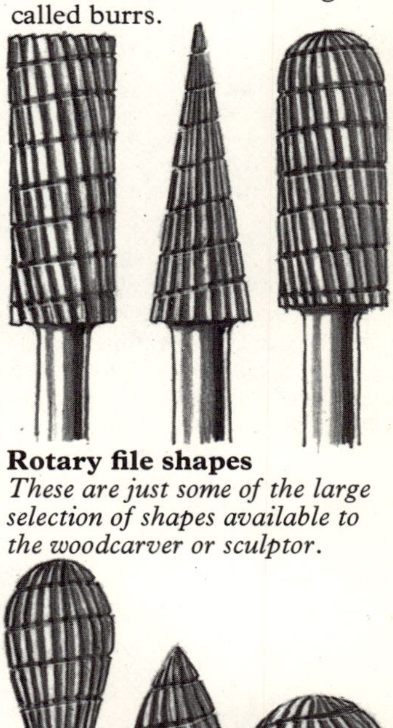

Rotary file shapes
These are just some of the large selection of shapes available to the woodcarver or sculptor.

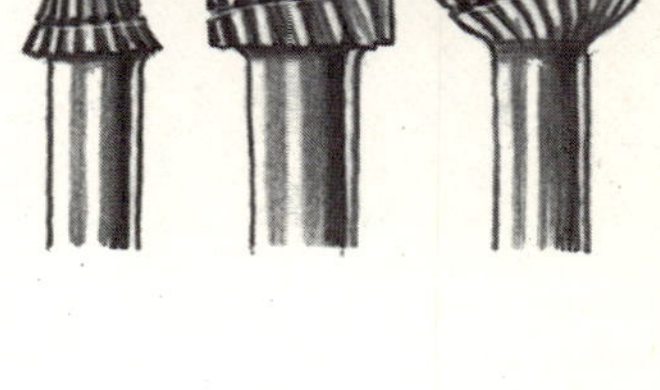

Snips and Shears

Snips or shears for cutting metal were used by the Romans and were very similar to the modern stock shears or universal snips. The earliest example so far known appears on a terracotta plaque or shop sign of a toolmaker of Ostia, near Rome, dating from the time of Hadrian, about AD 120. A much larger tool of the same type forms part of the ironwork in the Cairo Museum from Qustul in Nubia, dating from about AD 400. The Ostia plaque also shows an early form of light shears used by tailors for cutting cloth. This type continued in use right through the Middle Ages and survived as the standard pattern for sheep shears down to the nineteenth century. A pair of scissors with closed forged handles for the thumb and finger is shown in the Virgin Mary's needlework basket on a Spanish Holy Family miniature of the mid-fifteenth century.

Straight Snips

OTHER NAMES: Flat blade snips, standard snips
SIZE: 175 to 350mm
MATERIAL: Steel
USE: To make straight cuts in sheet metal

All-metal cutting snips have long handles to provide adequate leverage when cutting sheet metal. Straight snips have straight jaws in line with the handle. The handles themselves are either straight with a slight curve at the very end, or finished with scissor-like grips which make them easier to open with one hand.

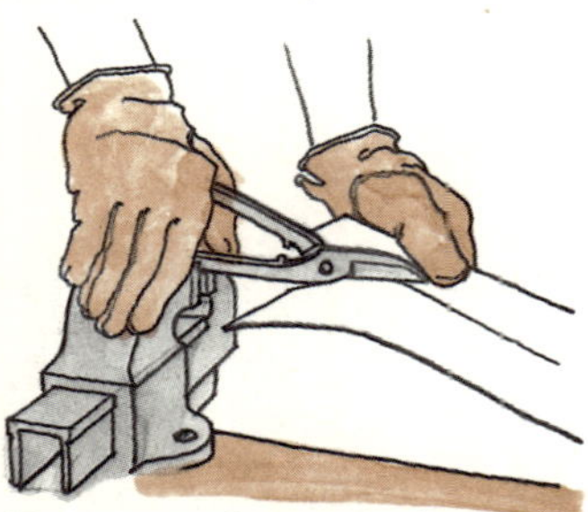

For greater leverage, clamp one handle in a vice and apply pressure to the free handle. Control the work with the other hand.

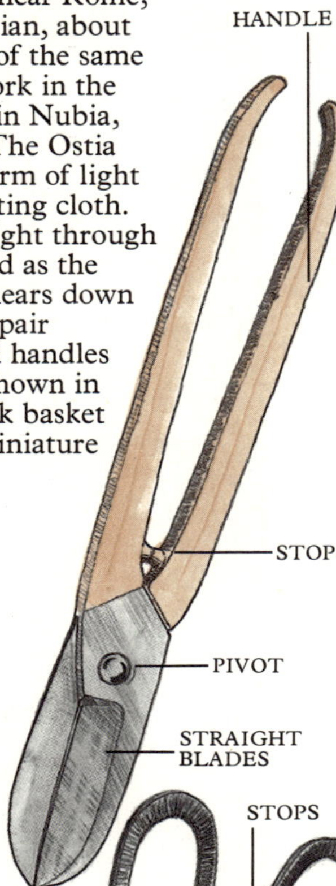

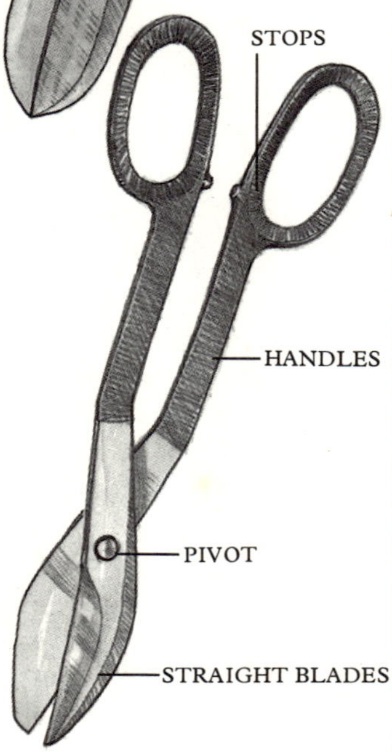

Making a straight cut
Keep the blades upright at all times to avoid the metal twisting in the jaws and causing them to spring.

Use as much of the blade length as possible for each cut, but avoid completely closing the jaws otherwise you will make a ragged cut.

You can use the edge of a bench to guide the snips when making a straight cut. Rest the work on a bench with the waste projecting over the edge and proceed with the cut in the normal way. The waste will curl away below the work as the cut proceeds.

Avoid cutting wire or sheet metal that is too thick, as it will dull the blade.

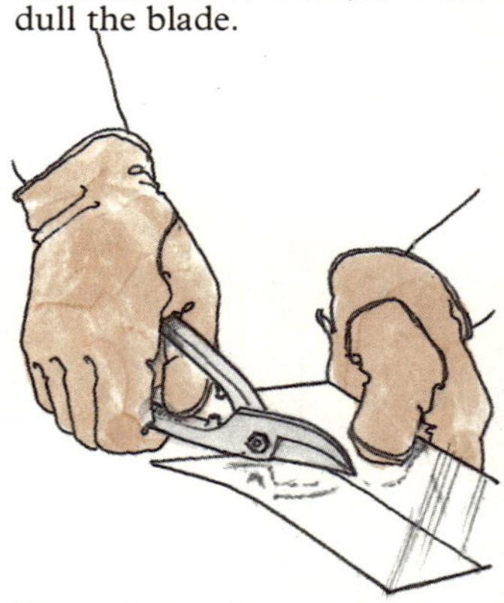

Wear gloves when cutting sheet metal with snips as a precaution against injury.

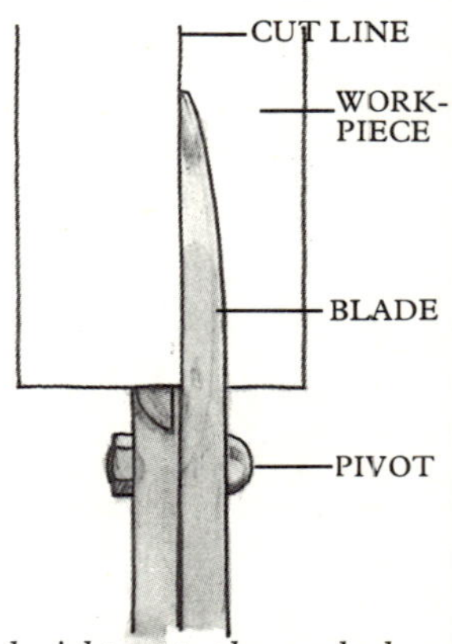

Work right up to the marked line as the tool does not remove metal when making a cut.

Making a convex cut
An outside or convex curve can be cut with straight or universal snips. Cut off as much waste as possible before cutting to the marked line. Proceed as for a straight cut.

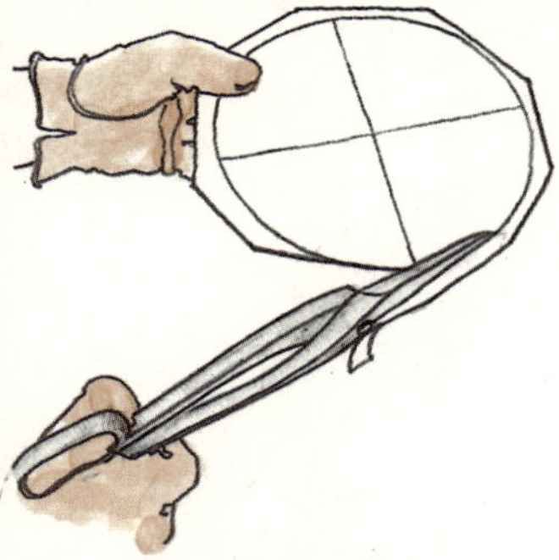

Try to keep the waste in one continuous piece. File away any burrs from the finished edge.

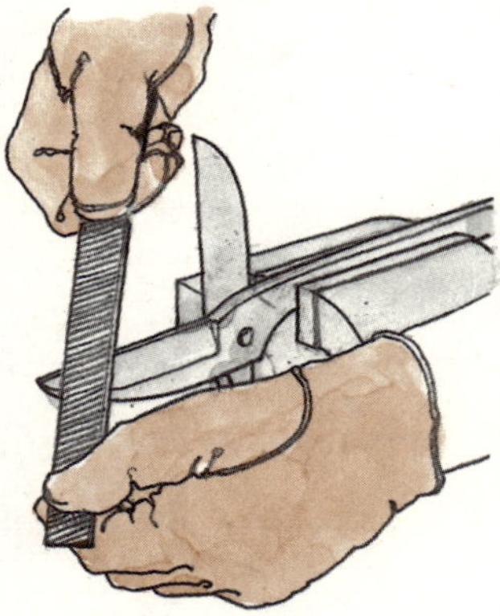

Sharpening snips
Clamp the snips in a vice with the jaws open and file the cutting edge to an angle of approximately 85°. Do not file the flat faces. Take off the burr by rubbing the flat face of each blade on an oil stone from pivot to tip. Take care not to round the cutting edge.

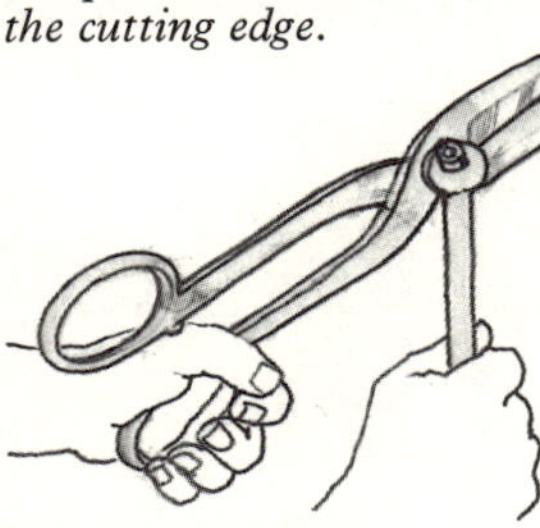

Setting the pivot
Adjust the pivot to the correct setting and oil the blade as well as the pivot itself.

Hawk's Bill Snips

SIZE: 275 to 325mm
MATERIAL: Steel
USE: To make tight internal or concave cuts in sheet metal

The exaggerated curve and bevelled blades of the hawk's bill snips make it easier to cut sharp curves without distorting the metal.

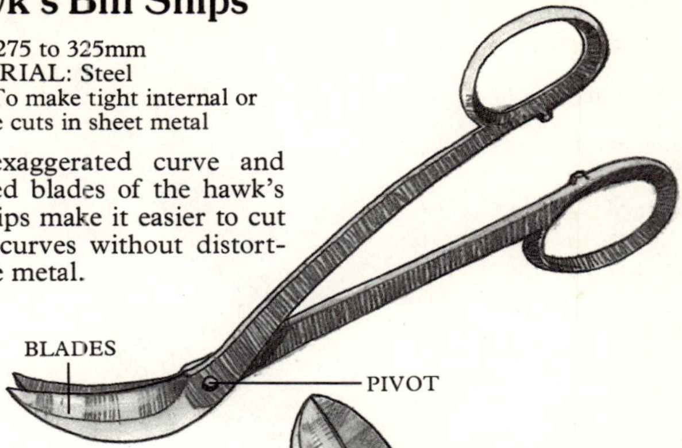

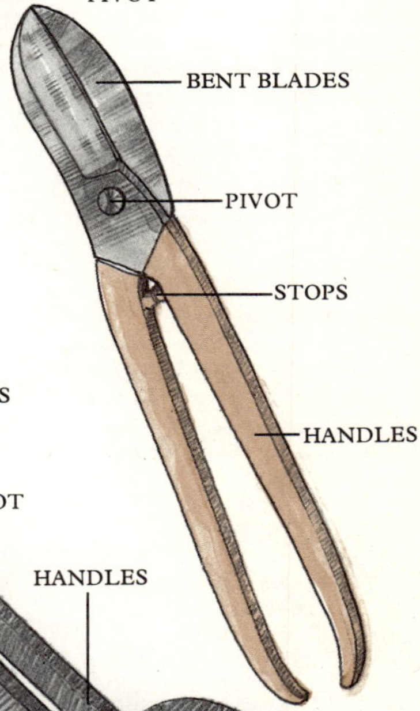

Circle Snips

OTHER NAMES: Bent blade snips, curved snips
SIZE: 175 to 350mm
MATERIAL: Steel
USE: To make internal or concave cuts in sheet metal

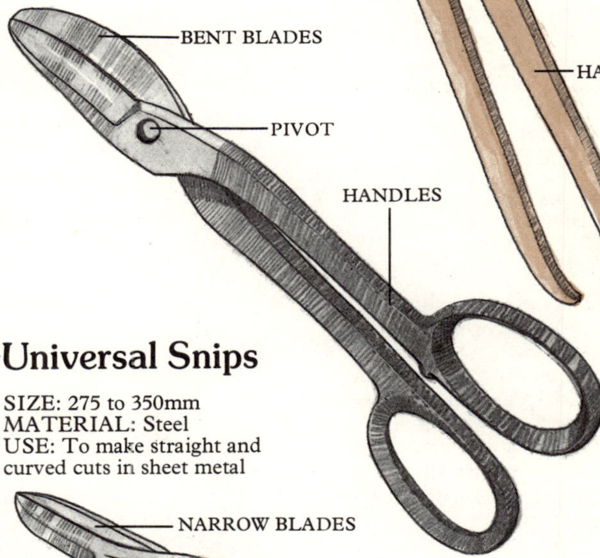

Universal Snips

SIZE: 275 to 350mm
MATERIAL: Steel
USE: To make straight and curved cuts in sheet metal

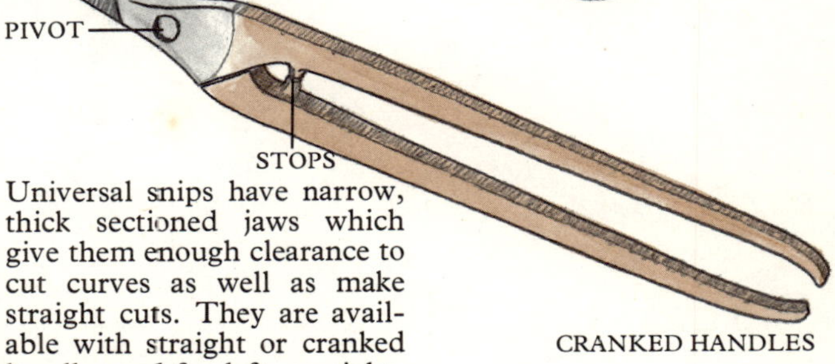

Universal snips have narrow, thick sectioned jaws which give them enough clearance to cut curves as well as make straight cuts. They are available with straight or cranked handles and for left- or right-hand use.

Double Cutting Snips

OTHER NAME: Pipe and duct snips
MATERIAL: Steel and plastic
USE: To make straight or curved cuts in sheet metal without distortion

Double cutting snips do not distort the material on either side of a cut. This makes them particularly useful when cutting through strong curved shapes such as piping or guttering which cannot be worked with conventional snips. They can also be used with special blades to cut materials which would crack or shatter if bent such as asbestos, plastic laminate, hardboard and thin plywood.

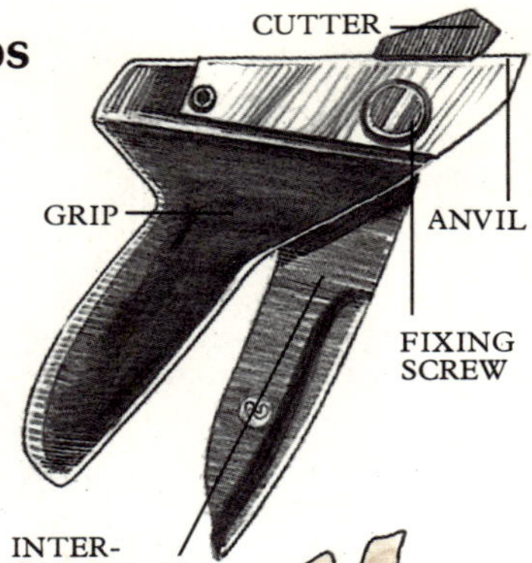

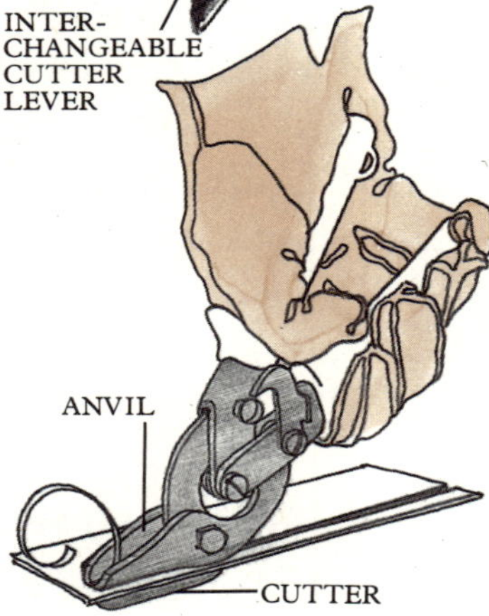

Using the cutter
A cutter passes between the two fixed blades, sometimes known as the "anvil", removing a thin strip of waste metal. Allow for this when marking out the work.

Bolt Cutters

SIZE: *Length:* 35 to 105cm; *To cut bolts:* 6 to 16mm diameter
MATERIAL: Steel
USE: To cut steel bolts and rods

Bolt cutters are available with centre cut jaws for general use or "clipper cut" jaws for close cutting at an obstruction. The compound lever action of the tool provides considerable force at the jaws which are adjustable to ensure that they meet along their entire length without a gap.

When cutting a bolt keep it as far back in the jaws as possible. A cut bolt can fly off, so use a shield to prevent injury or damage.

Replace worn cutters when necessary and keep moving parts well oiled.

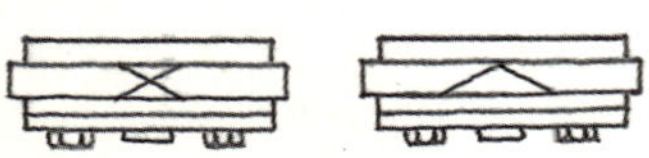

CENTRE CUT   CLIPPER CUT

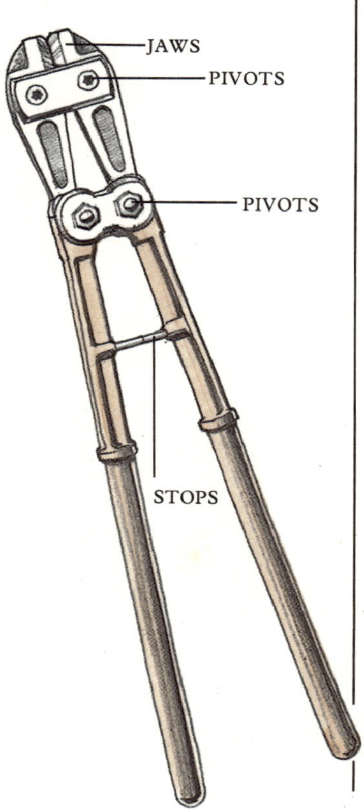

Aviation Snips

OTHER NAME: Compound action snips
SIZE: 250mm
MATERIAL: Steel and plastic
USE: To provide improved leverage when making straight or curved cuts in sheet metal

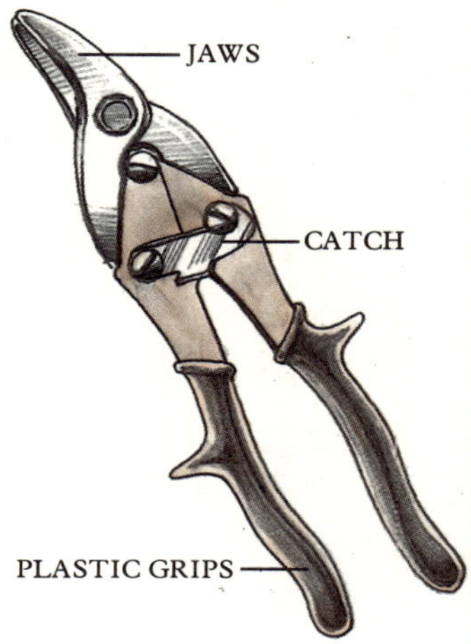

Aviation snips, originally developed for use in the aircraft industry, are made for straight cuts as well as right- and left-hand curves. Their compound lever action permits greater control as well as providing the means to cut harder material. The snips also have specially hardened jaws and comfortable plastic grips.

Making a concave cut
If the curve to be cut is very large and you want to save the waste material, cut to within 13mm of the marked line with a cold chisel before using the snips. Alternatively, cut a starting hole in the centre of the waste material and cut outward toward the line in a slow curve.

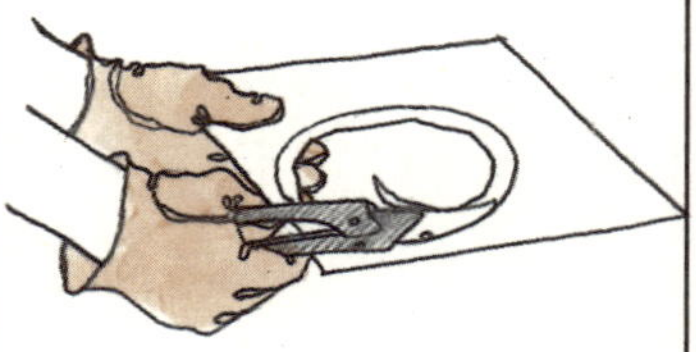

Continue the curved cut around the circle until the cut is joined up. Finish burred edges with a half round file.

Paper Hanger's Scissors

SIZE: 225 to 300mm
MATERIAL: Steel
USE: To trim wall paper

Paper hanger's scissors have very long blades which make it easier to achieve a straight cut when trimming wall paper. The scissors should be kept sharp by grinding and the cutting edge finished with an oiled slipstone.

Before the days of pre-trimmed paper, paper hangers used to rest the roll of paper in their up-turned feet and gradually unroll the free end in one hand while trimming the edge with the other.

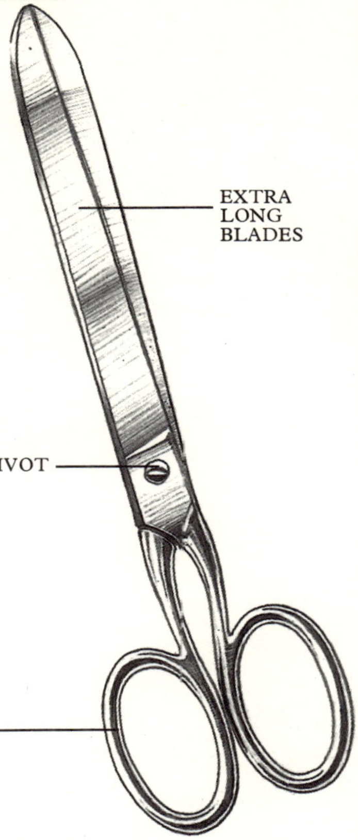

Hanging a strip of wallpaper

When cutting wallpaper to wall lengths, allow an extra 50mm top and bottom for trimming to fit.

Very expensive or traditionally made wallpapers may need to have the selvedge trimmed in the old-fashioned way.

Gently mark the ceiling or skirting board line on the paper with the point of the scissors.

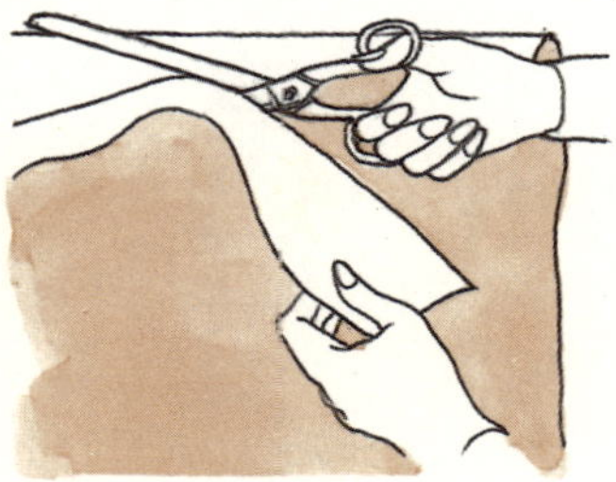

Peel back the paper, trim off the excess and brush back into place.

Pruning Shears

OTHER NAME: Secateurs
SIZE: Various
MATERIAL: *Blades:* steel; *Handles:* steel, plastic
USE: To cut back plants

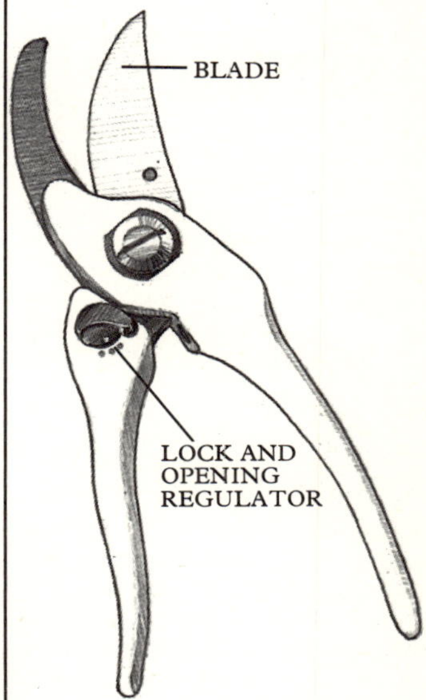

Pruning shears come in many designs, shapes and sizes. Shears can be double bladed or have one cutting blade working against an anvil. Good pruning shears have rust resistant steel blades and handles sprung to open automatically. A lock holds them in a closed position, and is sometimes incorporated with a mechanism which controls the maximum open position to suit different hand sizes.

Keep the blades in good condition by removing moisture and sap after use and applying a little oil.

Flower Shears

OTHER NAME: Flower gatherer
SIZE: 150mm
MATERIAL: *Blade:* steel; *Frame:* nylon
USE: To cut flower stems

Flower shears cut like scissors through the stems of flowers. As the blade severs the stem it is automatically held between a spring and an anvil. This allows the tool to be used with one hand which is useful when reaching into dense plant growth. A stem crusher is incorporated behind the pivot.

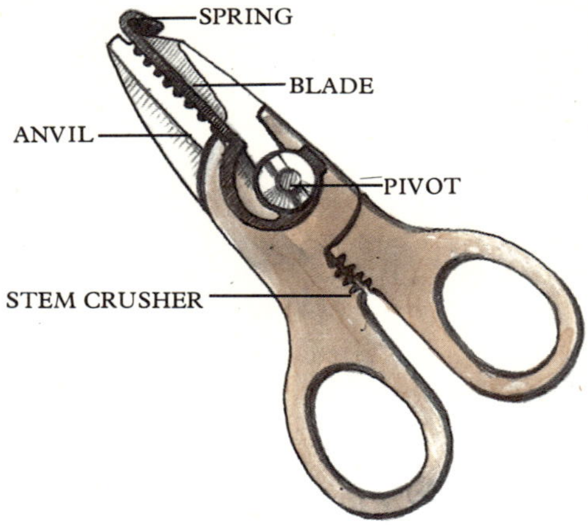

Lopping Shears

SIZE: 300 to 750mm
MATERIAL: *Blade:* steel; *Handle:* ash, steel; *Grips:* plastic
USE: To cut back shrubs or trees

Lopping shears do exactly the same job as pruning shears, but their long handles improve the reach of the user as well as increase the leverage necessary to cut through thicker material. Some lopping shears incorporate compound leverage which greatly increases their cutting power.

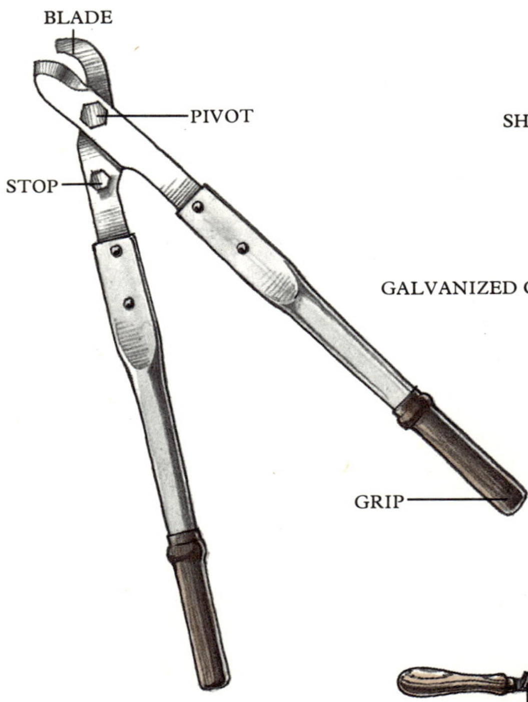

Tree Pruner

SIZE: 180 to 360cm
MATERIAL: *Cutter:* steel; *Shaft:* tubular steel, hardwood
USE: To reach and prune very high tree branches

The tree pruner cuts off high branches by remote control. At the cutting end is a hook which is placed over a branch at the point it is to be cut. At the handle end is a lever attached to the blade by a galvanized cable, which is pulled to sever the branch.

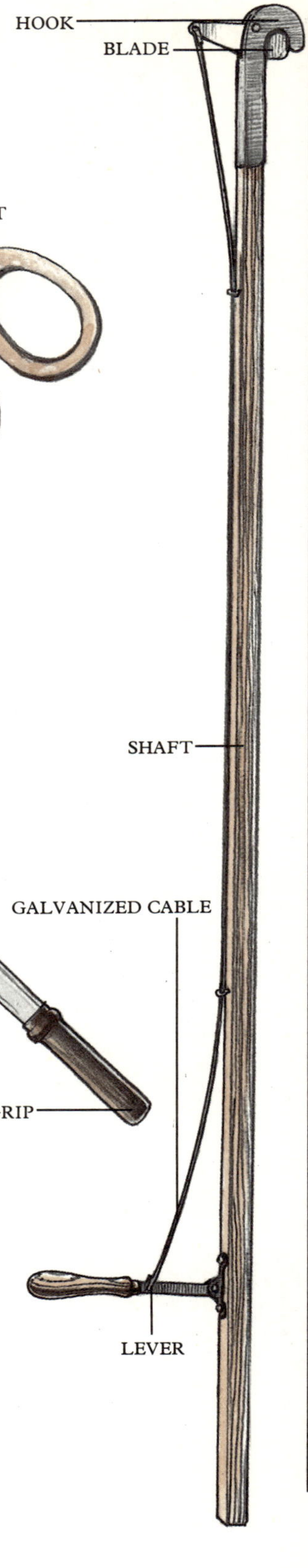

Garden Shears

SIZE: Blade length: 163 to 200mm
MATERIAL: *Blades:* steel;
Handles: hardwood, tubular steel
USE: To trim grass and hedges

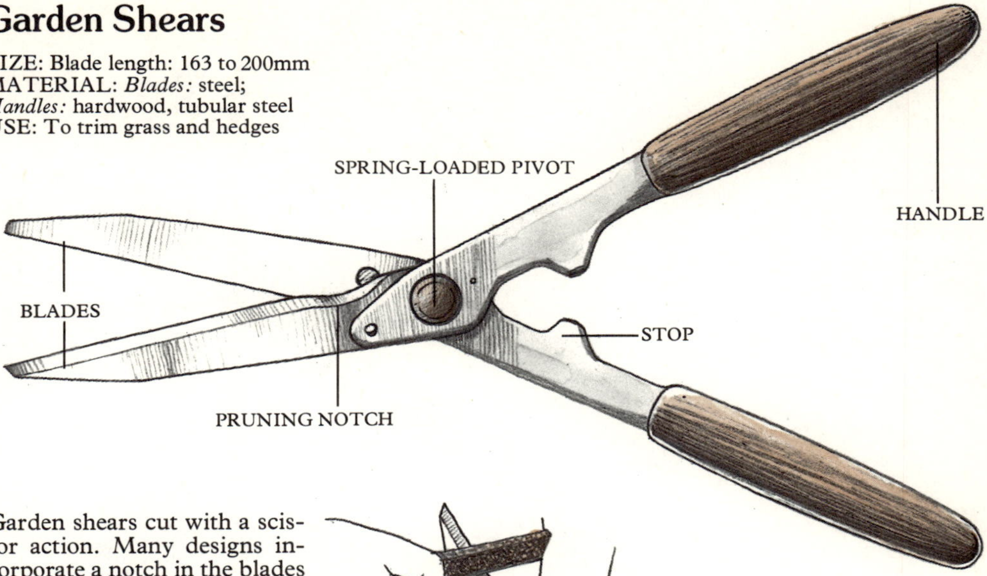

Garden shears cut with a scissor action. Many designs incorporate a notch in the blades near the pivot to retain thicker branches and cut them through with maximum leverage.

The cutting edges should press together throughout their entire length during the cut. This clearance can be adjusted on some shears by loosening or tightening the spring-loaded nut at the pivot point. In some cases, the pivot itself is spring loaded to take up this adjustment automatically.

The blades should be cleaned after use and lightly oiled to prevent rust. Clean off any accumulated rust or residue with emery cloth.

Sharpening shears
Hold the blades apart and finish the cutting edge with an oiled carborundum stone, by stroking from pivot to tip. Keep to the original angle of the cutting edge. Remove the burr by rubbing the stone flat on the inside face of the blade.

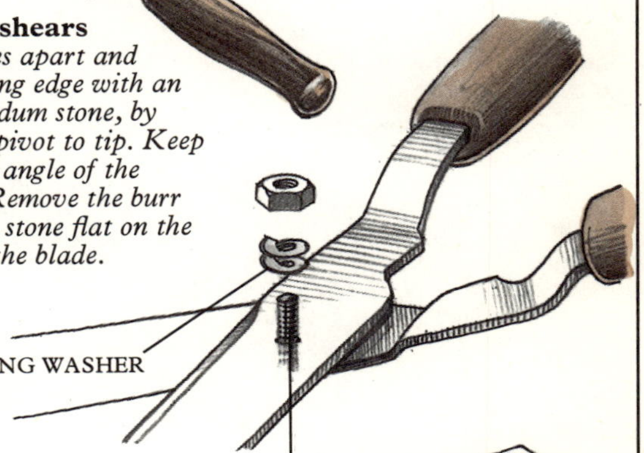

Grass Shears

SIZE: 250 to 325mm
MATERIAL: Steel
USE: To cut grass in restricted spaces

Grass shears are used with one hand to trim around trees, rocks and flower beds or in any space where a lawn mower cannot be used. A push button or catch locks the blades closed to protect the cutting edge. Clean and lightly oil the shears after use.

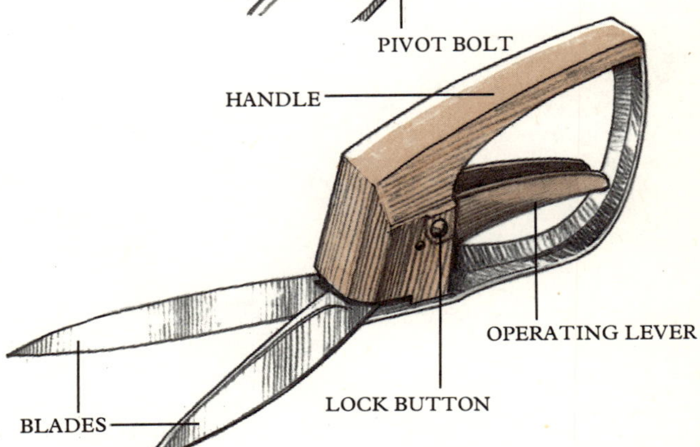

Electric Hedge Trimmer

SIZE: *Blade:* 300 to 400mm; *Speed:* approximately 3,000 to 4,000 rpm
MATERIAL: *Blades:* steel; *Casing:* plastic
USE: To trim hedges and shrubbery

Electric hedge trimmers are available as purpose-made tools or as power drill accessories. They can be powered by heavy duty outdoor extension cords or by rechargeable batteries incorporated in the casing. However powered, the motor operates one or two rows of reciprocating cutters.

When cutting with a cord fitted trimmer, keep the cord draped over your shoulder and try to work away from it. Battery charged trimmers have an unrestricted range and there is no danger of accidentally cutting through a cord.

A hedge trimmer is normally fitted with two handles: one incorporates the trigger switch and supports the main weight of the tool, while the crossbar is held in the other hand and used to sweep the tool sideways across the hedge. Double edged trimmers are preferable as they will cut in either direction as the tool is swept across the hedge; not only is the hedge cut faster, but shoots growing in different directions are picked up by the cutters on the return stroke. To cut the hedge evenly, sweep from the previously trimmed area into the uncut portion.

Remove and clean the blades regularly. As with all power tools hedge trimmers should be disconnected from the power supply before adjustment. In the case of a cordless trimmer, a safety catch should be fitted to prevent accidental starting. Do not use an electric hedge trimmer in wet conditions.

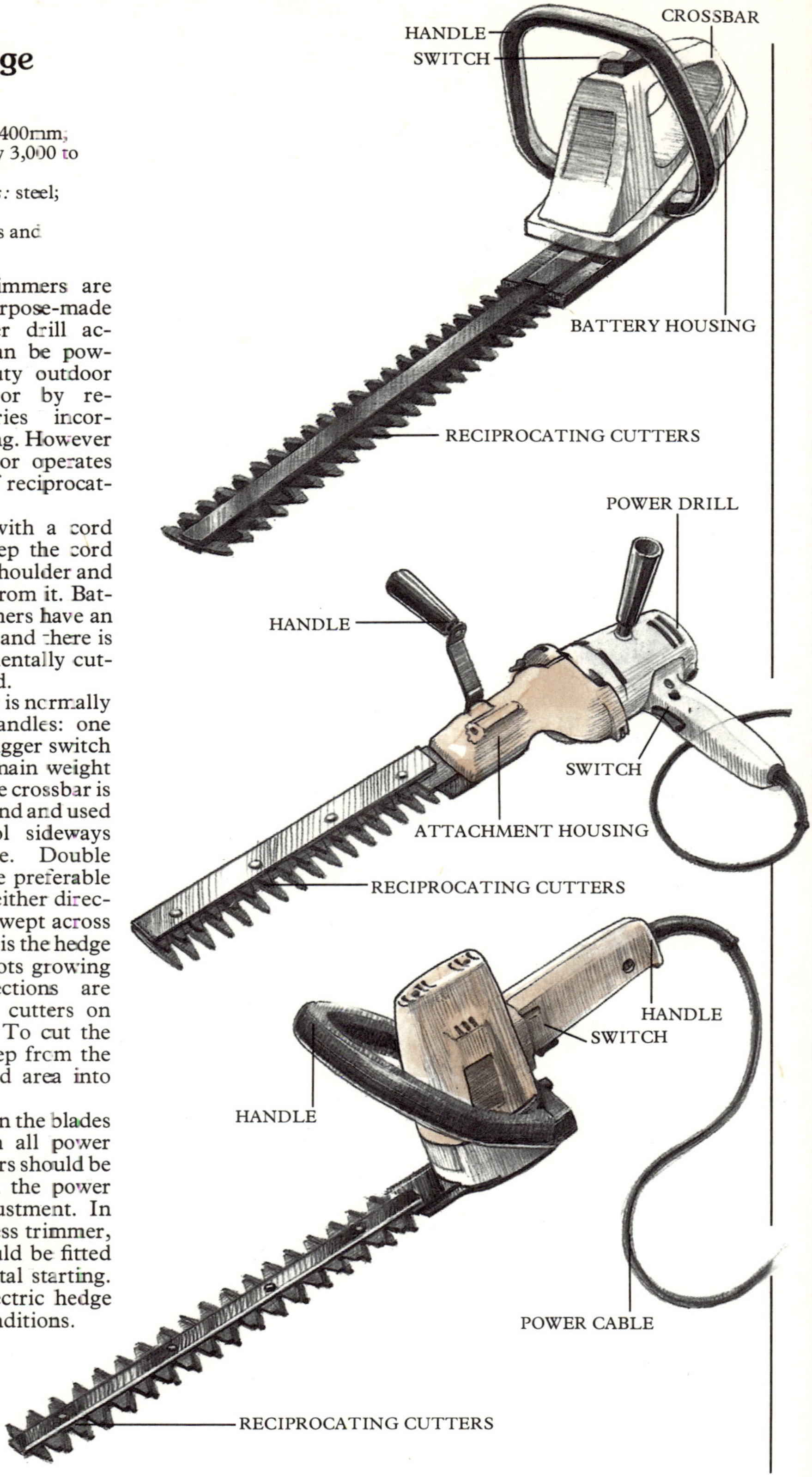

Lawn Shears

SIZE: *Length:* 900mm;
Blade: 188mm
MATERIAL: *Blades:* steel;
Shafts: tubular steel, aluminium
USE: To trim restricted areas of lawn

Lawn shears perform the same function as grass shears, trimming those parts of the lawn which are inaccessible to a mower. The extended handles allow the shears to be used while standing, and are often detachable for easy storage.

Edging Shears

OTHER NAME: Border shears
SIZE: *Length:* 900mm;
Blade: 188mm
MATERIAL: *Blades:* steel;
Handles: tubular steel
USE: To trim the edge of a lawn

Edging shears are used to trim the borders of the lawn after mowing. Some designs have detachable handles for storage.

Using shears
Edging shears (left) and lawn shears (right) take the backache out of trimming and grooming your lawn.

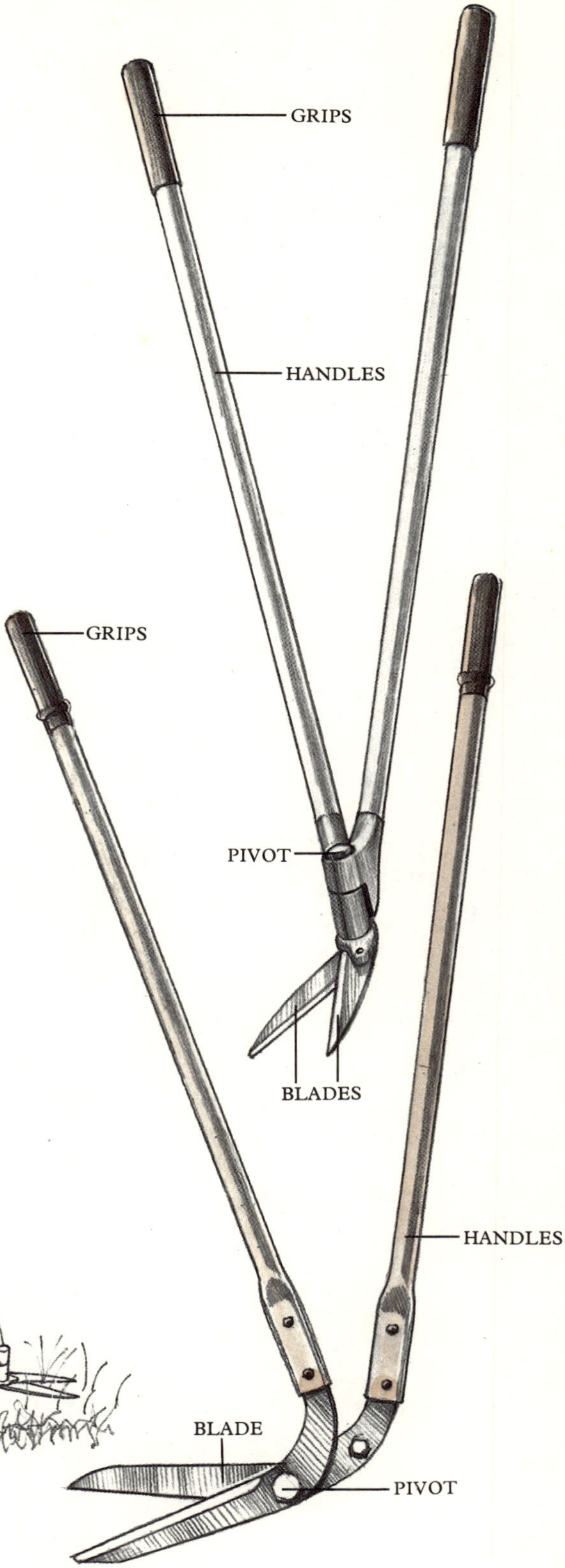

Spanners

When screws or bolts with nuts were first developed in the fifteenth century, the ring spanner was the most common tool used to work on them. The first screws had square heads, something like modern coach screws or lag bolts, but the more versatile hexagonal shape appeared quite early. By leaving one side of the "ring" open the ring spanner was adapted to work the hexagonal nut. The strength lost by opening one end was compensated for by widening the jaws, and the resultant spanner could be used for both types of nut. The great variety of adjustable spanners available at the present time are by-products of the intensive growth of machinery since the nineteenth century.

Old smith-made spanners may be of wrought iron, and some are made of cast iron which is brittle and weak under tension.

Modern light duty spanners, designed for use in awkward positions where their slendernesss is essential, are stamped from sheet metal. The majority of engineering spanners are forged from carbon steel or chrome vanadium.

Open Ended Spanner

OTHER NAMES: Open ended wrench, "C" spanner
SIZES: See page 344
MATERIAL: Alloy steel, wrought iron, cast iron
USE: To tighten or loosen nuts and bolts

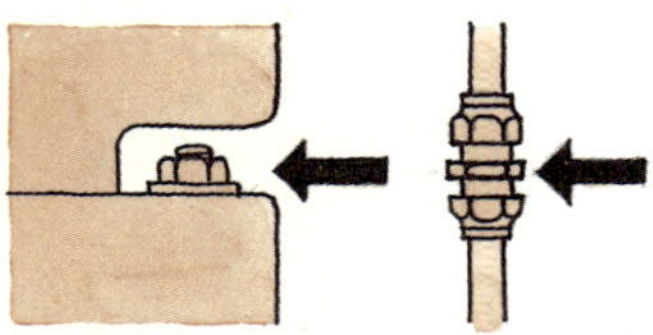

One of the most common and versatile spanners, the open ended spanner is designed to engage the nut or bolt head from the side. Although the open jaw is not as strong as the enclosed jaw of the ring spanner, it is faster to work.

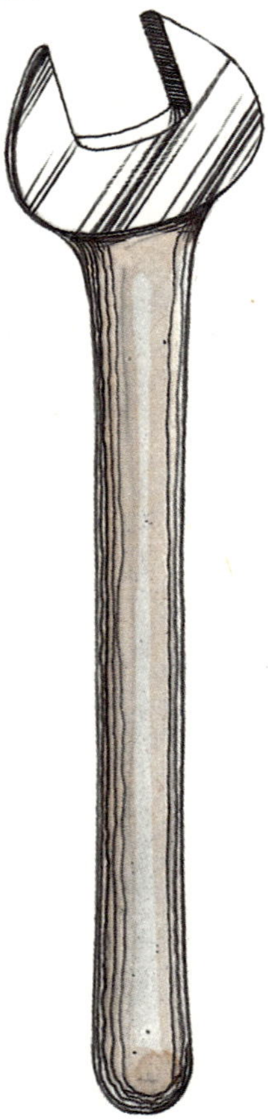

Open ended spanners

The advantages of the open ended spanner is that it can be used where there is an obstruction directly above the nut, or on pipe unions where the pipe would restrict the use of a ring spanner.

Make sure that the spanner fits snugly on the flats of a nut; a slack fitting spanner will slip and round off the corners. Normally the head of an open spanner is set at an angle of 15° to the shaft. By turning the spanner over, another set of flats is engaged which is useful in a confined space.

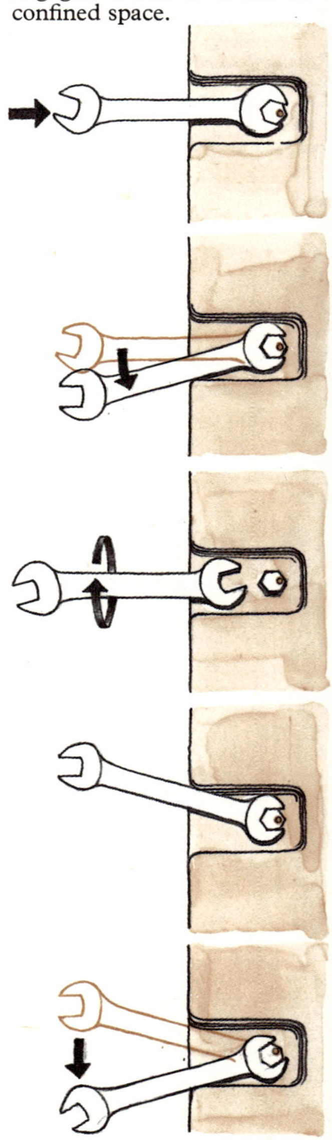

OBSTRUCTION SPANNERS
Obstruction spanners are special open ended spanners intended to make working in confined spaces easier. They sometimes have curved shafts and the head can be set at an angle of up to 90°.

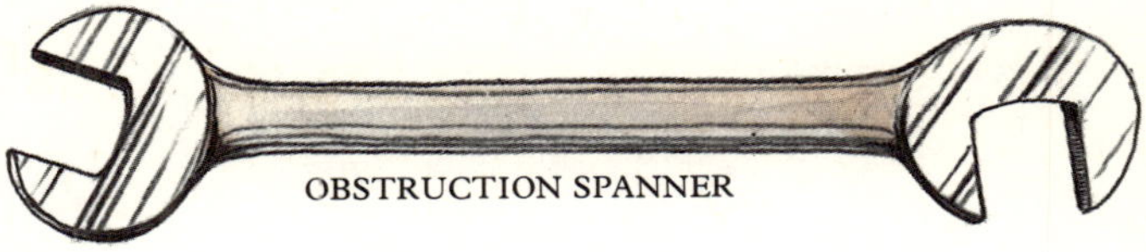

DOUBLE ENDED SPANNERS
Like most spanners, open ended spanners are often double ended. The ends are usually of consecutive sizes, each size being duplicated on one of the adjacent spanners in the set. This allows you to work on a nut and bolt head which are the same size or to tighten two lock nuts simultaneously.

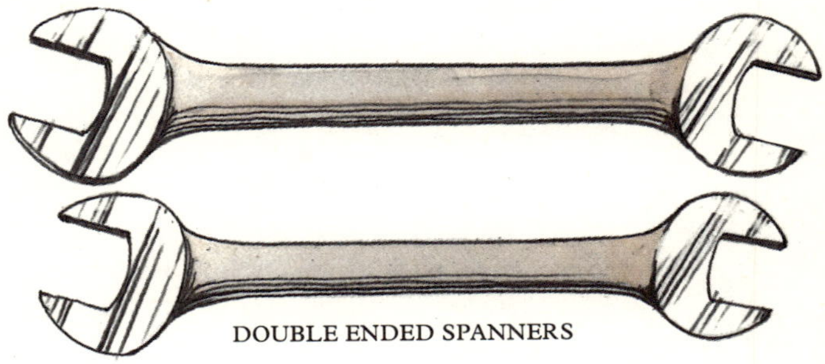

BICYCLE SPANNER
This is a multi-jawed spanner for work on the many different size nuts and bolts on a bicycle.

Ring Spanner

OTHER NAME: Box wrench
SIZE: See page 344
MATERIAL: Steel
USE: To tighten or loosen nuts and bolts

The completely enclosed head of a ring spanner is potentially stronger than any open ended spanner, but it is slower in use as it must be engaged from above and carefully aligned before it will fit. Because the ring spanner fits better, it is easier to strip a thread with it than with an open spanner. Moreover, it is also more likely to jam on a damaged nut.

The ring of the spanner contains 6 or 12 points which locate on the flats of a nut. The 12 point spanner need only be turned 30° before engaging a new set of flats and is therefore preferable when working in confined spaces. Providing the fit is good, a 12 point spanner can be used on a square nut or bolt head.

The length of a ring spanner varies in proportion to the size of the nut it is used on. This limits the amount of torque applied to smaller nuts.

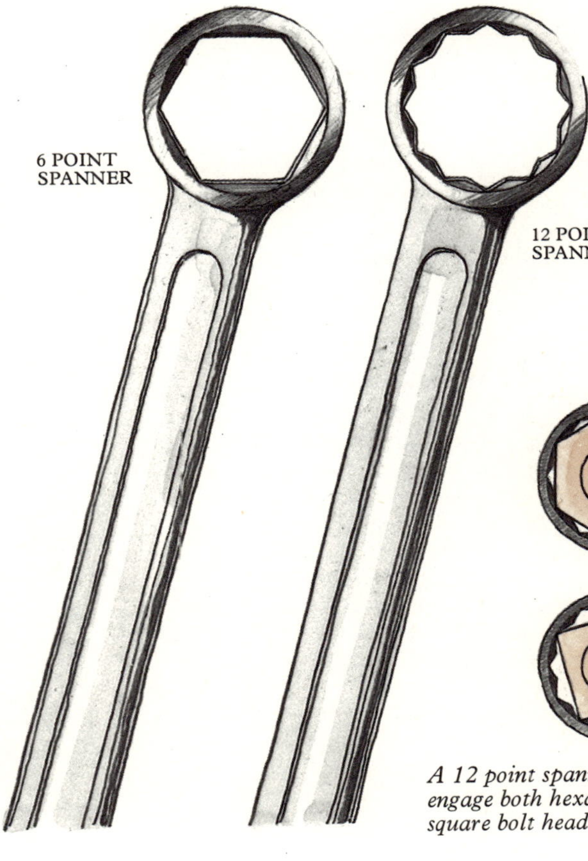

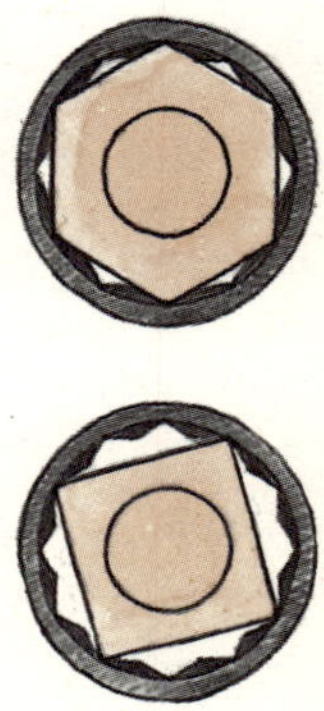

A 12 point spanner can engage both hexagonal or square bolt heads.

OFFSET SPANNER
Most ring spanners are offset or cranked to give hand clearance, and to allow the operator to reach into recesses and over obstructions.

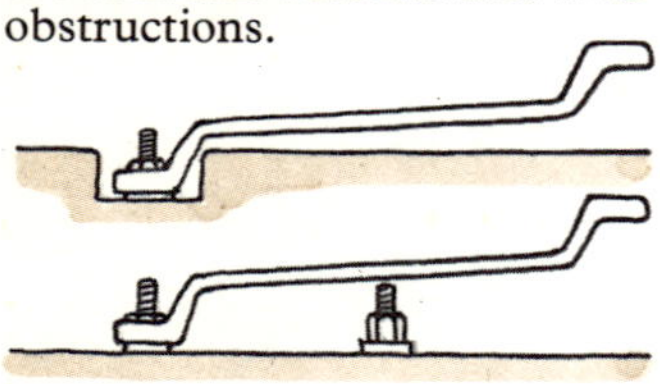

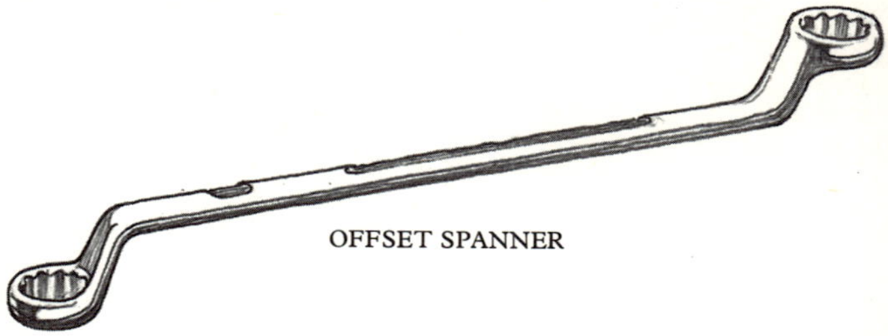

OFFSET SPANNER

MULTIPLE RING SPANNER
Intended for light work only, this is a light alloy spanner with a selection of different size "rings" conveniently grouped together in one tool.

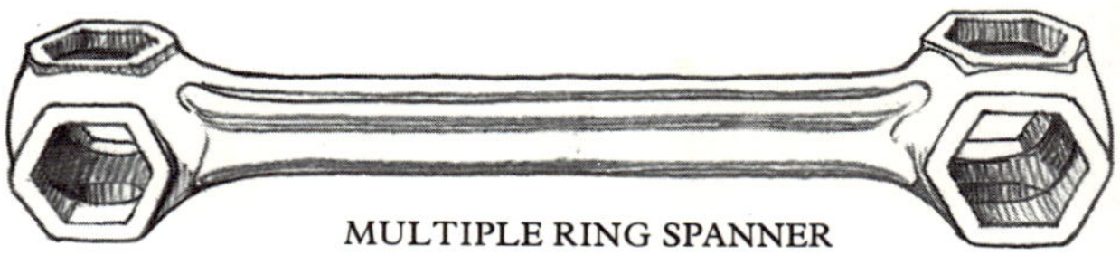

MULTIPLE RING SPANNER

SPLIT RING SPANNER
Unlike a standard ring spanner, a split ring spanner can be used on a pipe union where the pipe must pass through the jaws before they can engage the flats. It is no stronger than an open ended spanner but its better location makes it less likely to slip.

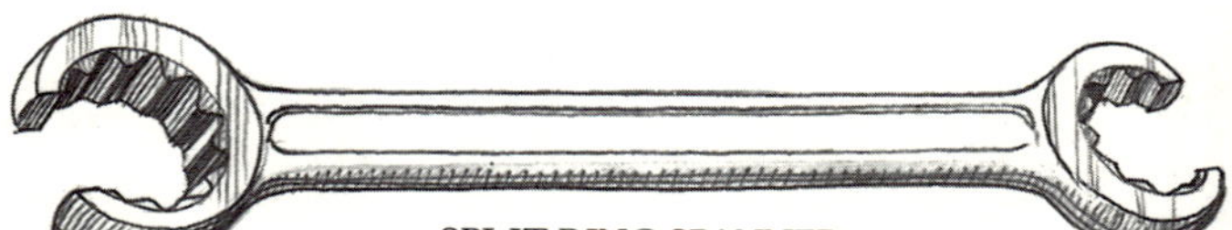

SPLIT RING SPANNER

COMBINATION SPANNER
A combination spanner is open at one end and closed at the other, both jaws being the same size. The greater strength of the ring is used to loosen the nut, which can then be quickly removed with the faster, open ended jaw.

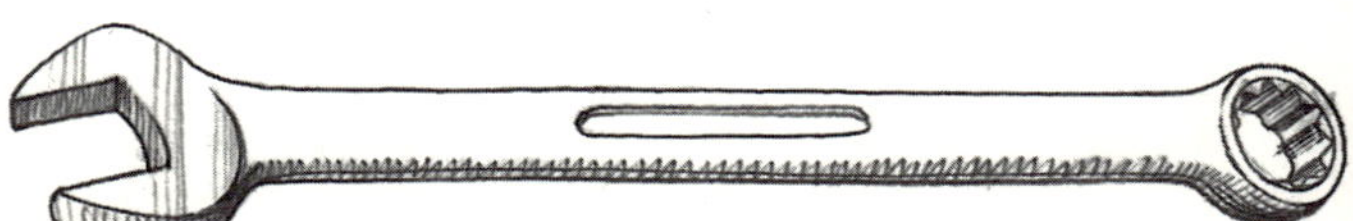

COMBINATION SPANNER

Adjustable Spanners

Adjustable spanners are usually open ended with one movable jaw. They are bulkier than equivalent fixed spanners but will fit a wide range of sizes, being infinitely adjustable between limits and therefore not confined to a particular thread system.

Like open ended spanners, adjustable spanners have their heads set at an angle to the shaft, 15° and 90° being the most common setting, although 45° are also available.

There are several different patterns which vary according to their method of adjustment.

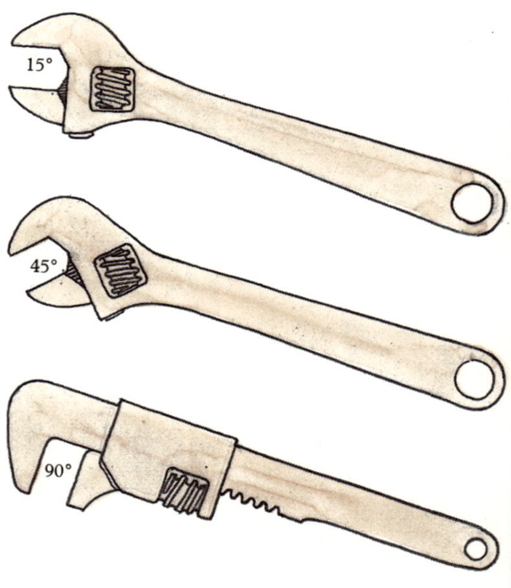

Slip Wrench

OTHER NAMES: Wedge spanner, shifting spanner
SIZE: Up to 750mm
MATERIAL: Steel, wrought iron
USE: To work nuts and bolts of any size between limits

The moving jaw of the slip wrench slides on the shaft and is held with a wedge which can be hammered tight. The tool is obsolete but still in use.

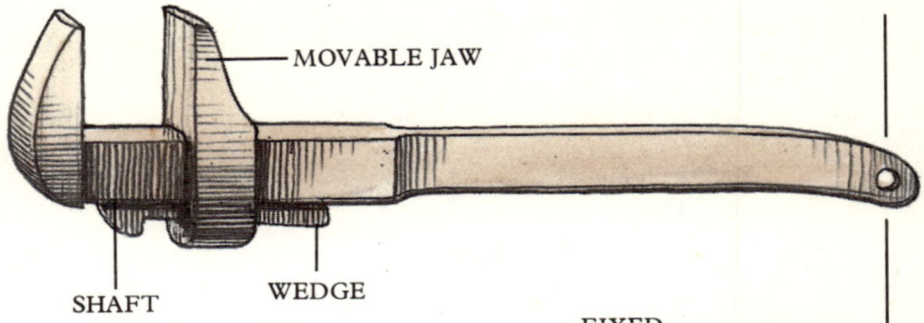

Monkey Wrench

OTHER NAMES: Screw wrench, coach wrench, bolt clam
SIZE: 150 to 450mm
MATERIAL: Steel
USE: To work nuts and bolts of any size between limits

BACK RACK WRENCH
This is like the slip wrench but has a worm screw on the moving jaw which acts on a rack on the shaft.

CENTRE SCREW WRENCH
These are also known as "King Dick" spanners, named after the original manufacturer. With this type of wrench, the moving jaw carries a threaded rod which passes through a trapped nut in the handle.

FRONT RACK WRENCH
These are the same as the back rack type but with the mechanism at the front.

FRONT SCREW WRENCH
These are like the centre screw "King Dick" type having a captive nut and screw, but set on one side.

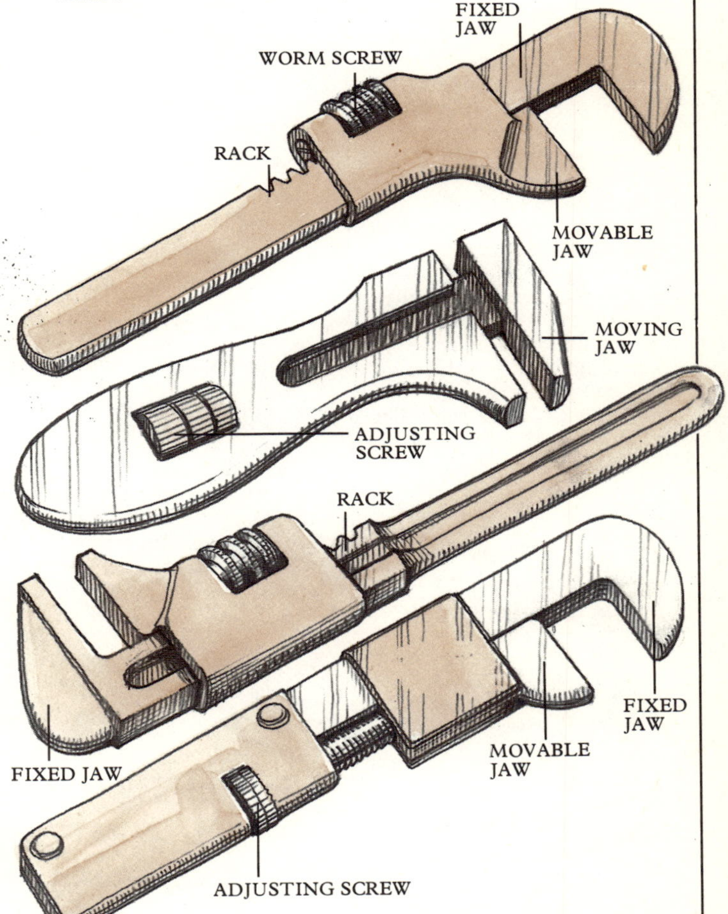

Crescent Spanner

SIZE: Up to 600mm
MATERIAL: Steel
USE: To work nuts and bolts of any size between limits

The spanner is adjusted by a captive worm screw in the handle acting against a rack on the moving jaw. Another pattern is operated by a thumb slide, located in the handle to make adjustment easy.

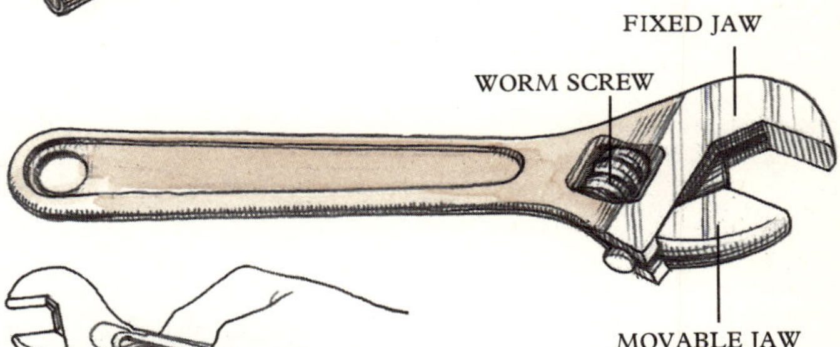

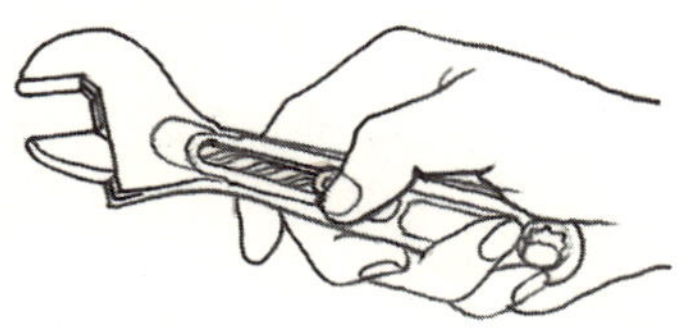

Using adjustable spanners
Adjustable spanners are inherently weaker than their solid equivalents, therefore greater care must be exercised when you use them to avoid straining the jaws, or damaging the nut or your hand. Only use an adjustable spanner when it is impossible to use a fixed one. When undoing a nut, use the largest convenient spanner, but not an over-large one as the thread could be stripped.

When fitting a spanner, make sure that the nut goes as far into the jaws as possible to prevent the tool springing off. Close the jaws onto the nut, rocking the tool slightly to help tighten the spanner.

Unlike pipe wrenches, adjustable spanners are intended for use in both directions. The jaws on some spanners are set at an angle of 15° to the shaft. By turning the spanner over you can engage the same flats on the nut for a further turn.

Points of torque reaction
The black markers show where torque reaction occurs when the spanner is pulled clockwise. The brown markers show where it occurs when the spanner is pulled anti-clockwise.

Maintenance
Clean adjustable spanners after use with a rag soaked in paraffin to remove grease. Lightly oil moving parts occasionally.

Multi-Purpose Spanner

OTHER NAME: Multi-plier
SIZE: 200mm
MATERIAL: Steel
USE: To provide the facility of spanner, pliers, screwdriver and wirecutters within a limited capacity

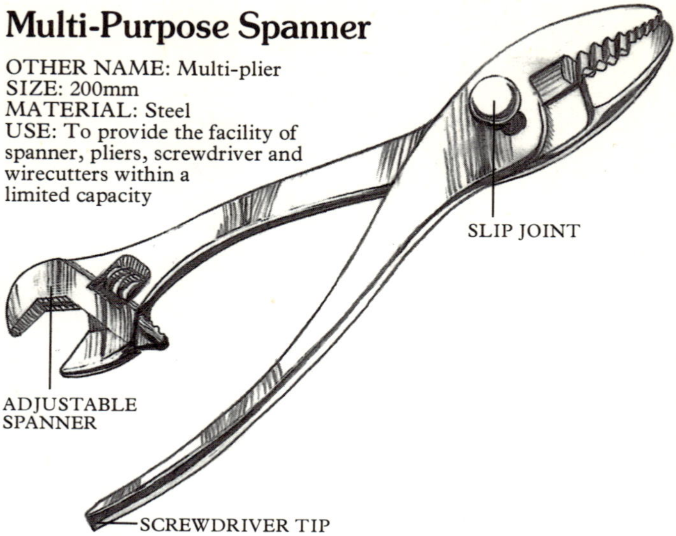

Grabber Spanner

SIZE: Jaw capacity: up to 15mm
MATERIAL: Alloy steel
USE: To work nuts and bolts of any size between limits

Unlike the normal adjustable spanner, this tool actually tightens as more force is applied to it, in much the same way as a pipe wrench.

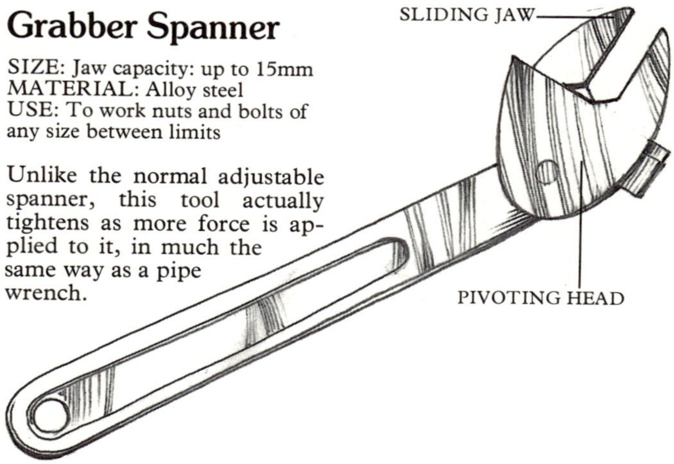

Adjustable Box Spanner

OTHER NAME: Adjustable ring spanner
SIZE: *Across flats:* 9 to 22mm; *Handle:* 213mm
MATERIAL: Steel
USE: To work nuts and bolts of any size between limits

This automatically fits different size nuts and bolts and tightens as force is applied. It grips a minimum of three flats and need not be removed between strokes.

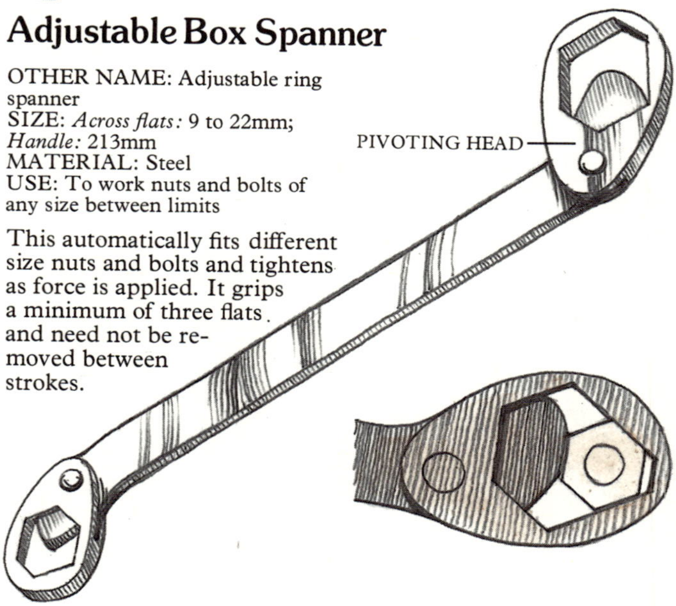

Box Spanner

OTHER NAME: Tubular wrench
SIZE: See page 344
MATERIAL: Steel
USE: To work nuts and bolts

Most box spanners are made from metal tubing and are double ended, with different sizes at each end. There are also single ended solid spanners which look like socket extensions. You can lengthen a box spanner by fitting a socket or open spanner to the other end.

A box spanner engages the nut from above, and although not as strong as a socket spanner, it is slimmer and usually deeper. It can be spun tight with the fingers and final torque applied by a tommy bar passed through the holes in the spanner. If you fit a long tommy bar, you can easily apply too much force. This will normally bend a mild steel bar but it can cause the thin walls of the spanner to override the points of the nut. Too much force can also strip the thread or even twist the body of the spanner. If the bar is centred it is less likely to bend.

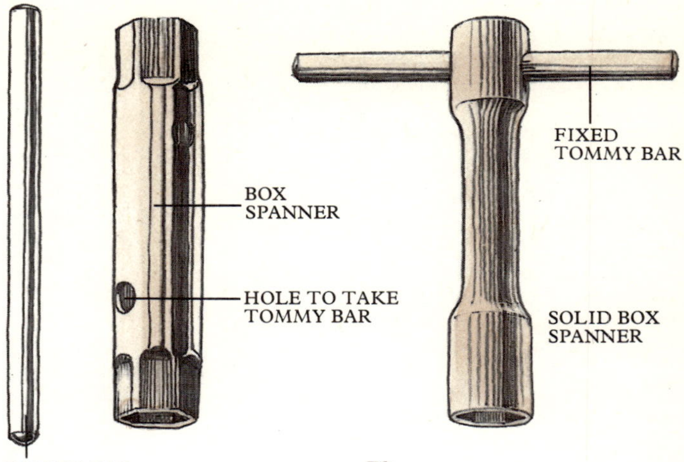

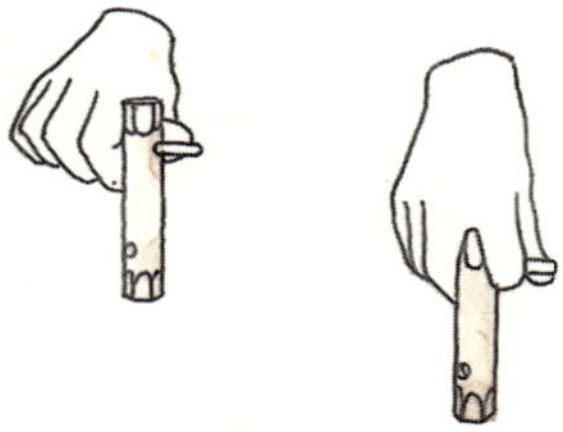

Using the spanner
Spin the spanner finger tight. For more torque, use a tommy (above) centred to avoid bending.

Extending the range
Add another box spanner (top) a socket (centre) or an open spanner (bottom).

Socket Spanner

OTHER NAME: Socket wrench
SIZE: *Square drive hole:* 6mm, 9mm, 13mm, 19mm, 25mm; *Socket end:* See page 346
MATERIAL: Steel
ACCESSORIES: Universal joint, rigid "L" bar handle, sliding "T" bar handle, ratchet handle, speed handle or brace speeder, hinged handle, extension bar, flexible extension
USE: To work nuts and bolts

The socket spanner has a boss with a square hole into which various handles can be fitted to drive the spanner. Moreover, the internal depth of the socket is limited and it may not be usable where a bolt protrudes a long way out of a nut. Special deep sockets are available for long bolts.

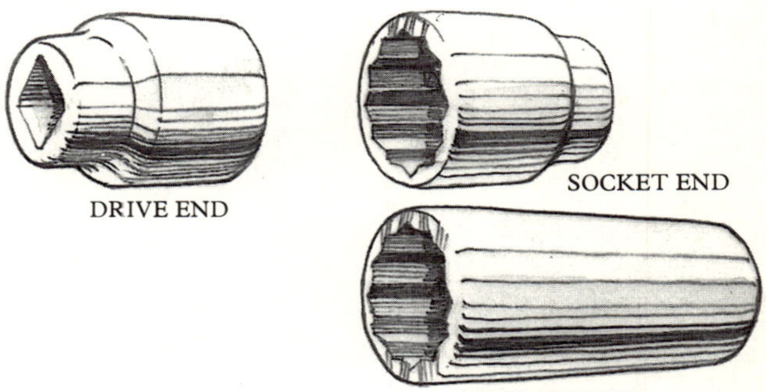

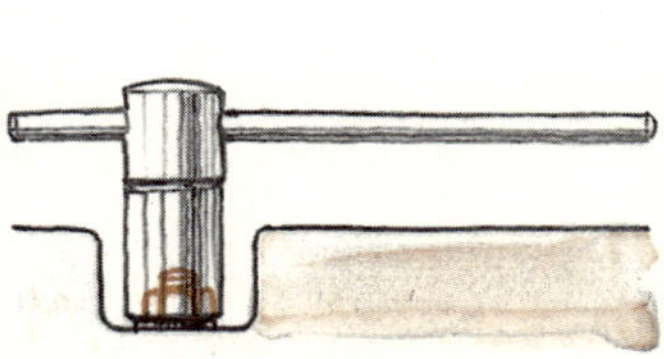

Socket spanner as box spanner
In its simplest form the spanner can be used as an offset ring spanner.

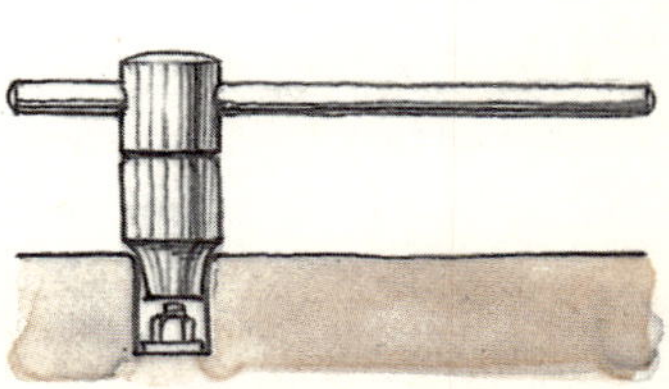

Socket spanner limits
In the smaller sizes the boss diameter may restrict access to the nut or bolt.

RIGID "L" BAR
This is the simplest handle. It can be used with either the long or the short leg of the "L" inserted in the boss to provide more force or speed.

SLIDING "T" BAR HANDLE
This carries a sliding head with a square drive. The head usually has two spring-loaded balls, one to grip the tommy bar, the other the socket.

RATCHET HANDLE
This increases operating speed because the socket does not have to be removed from the nut between strokes. The action of the handle can be reversed either by turning the wrench over or by throwing a lever.

HINGED HANDLE
This can be used at right angles to loosen a nut, and then swung to a vertical position where it can be spun between fingers. It can also be used to reach over or under obstructions.

SPEED HANDLE
A speed brace is faster than a tommy bar and has less torque.

EXTENSION BAR
This is fitted to increase the reach of the socket. Common lengths are 125mm and 250mm. It has a square drive at one end to fit the socket while the other end takes the drive of the various accessories.

UNIVERSAL JOINT
Fit a universal joint if there is misalignment between the socket and the extension bar.

FLEXIBLE EXTENSION
This is used in the same way as a universal joint to allow a nut to be worked at an angle.

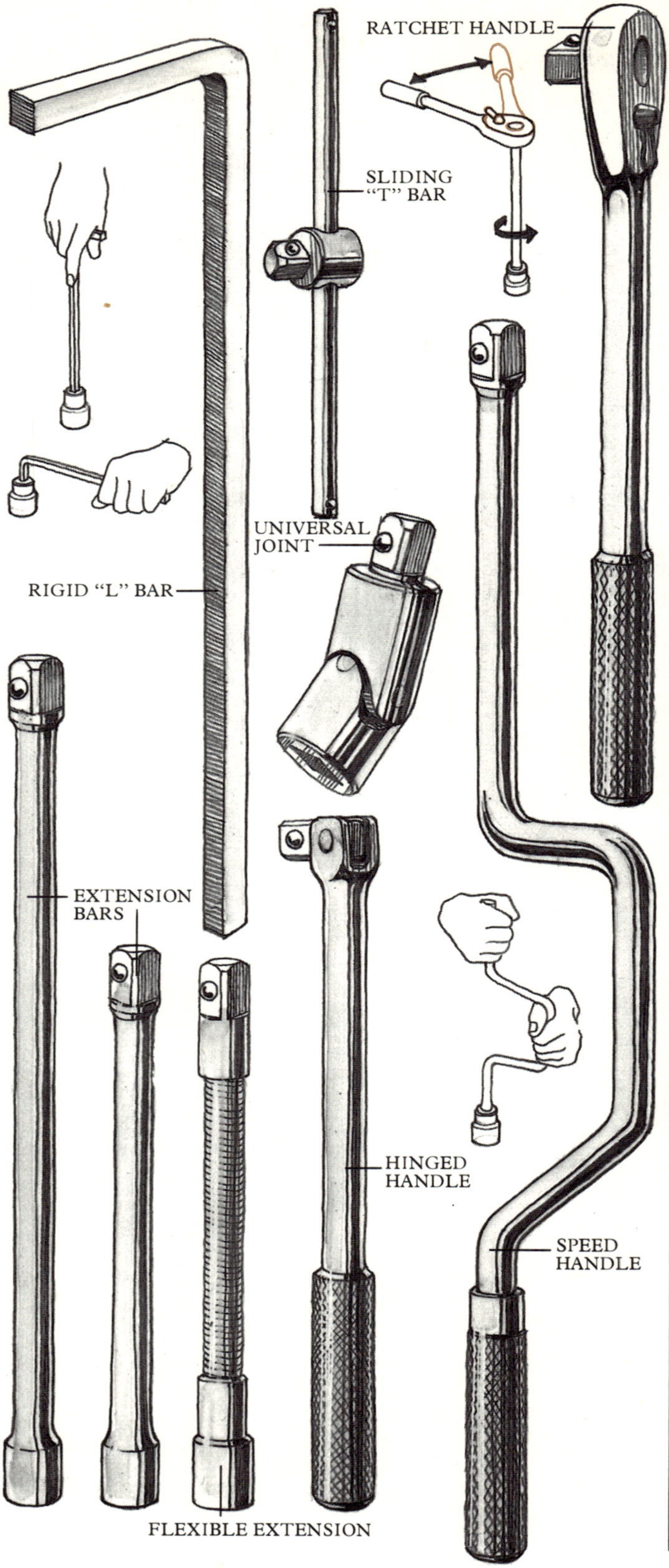

Spark Plug Spanner

OTHER NAME: Spark plug wrench
SIZE: *Single ended:* 16mm across flats or 10mm thread diameter; *Double ended:* 20mm across flats or 14mm thread diameter
MATERIAL: Steel, alloy steel
USE: To remove and replace engine spark plugs

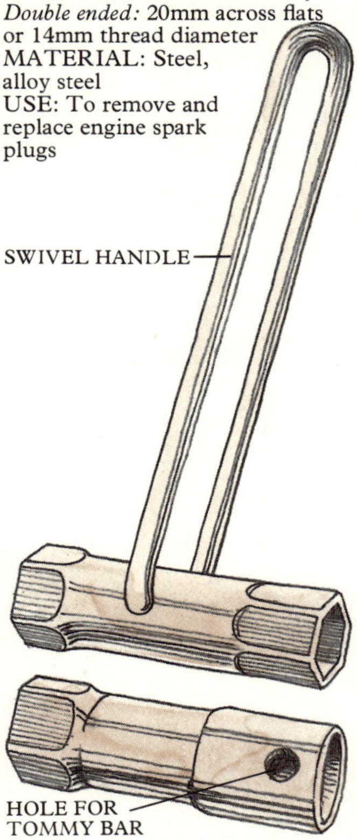

Common spark plug spanners, whether single or double ended, have either a tommy bar which passes through a hole in the spanner, or a captive swivel handle which can be used in line or at right angles.

Special socket spanners are available to fit spark plugs.

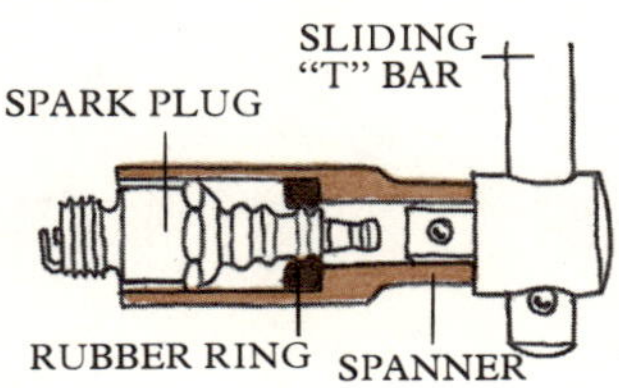

Spark plug socket spanner
These fit any of the accessories in the set. The spanner often has a rubber ring inside to grip and protect the insulator of the plug.

Capstan Wheel Nut Spanner

SIZE: See page 344
MATERIAL: Steel
USE: To tighten or loosen nuts and bolts, usually the wheel nuts of cars

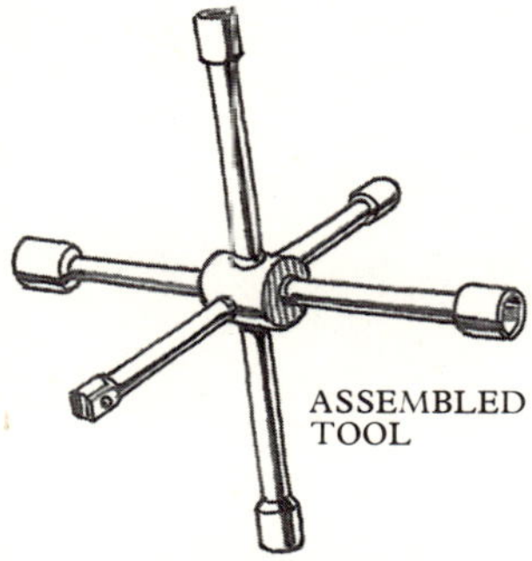

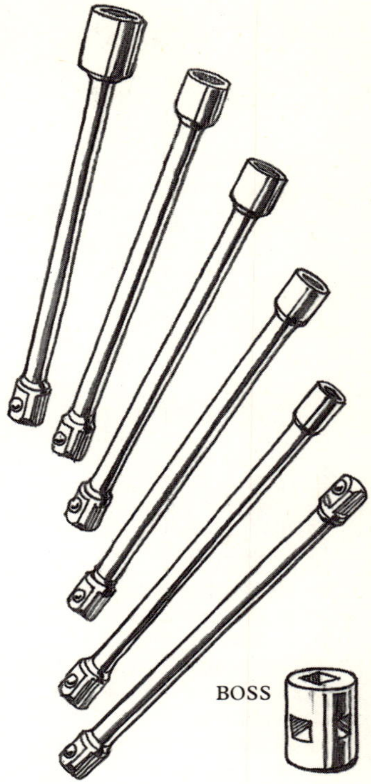

In its simplest form, the capstan wheel nut spanner comprises two double ended socket spanners welded together in the form of a cross. There are more versatile versions with a central boss into which are plugged six different spanners in the form of extension bars.

Allen Key

OTHER NAMES: Setscrew wrench, hex key, Bristol wrench
SIZE: Up to 15mm
MATERIAL: Steel
USE: To engage and turn a machine screw

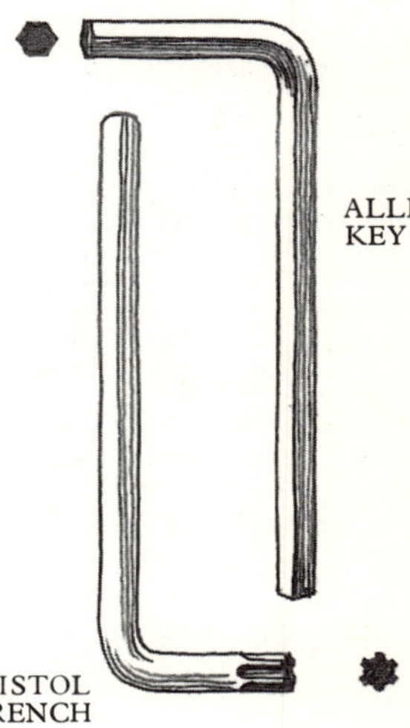

An "L" shaped hexagonal Allen key is used where the head of a bolt or machine screw is recessed in such a way that a conventional spanner cannot reach it. It fits into a hexagonal hole in the end of the screw. Either end of the key can be inserted into the screw to give greater reach and speed or greater torque.

Bristol wrenches have splines (thin radial strips) instead of flats and are normally single ended. They are used with screws slotted to match the splines.

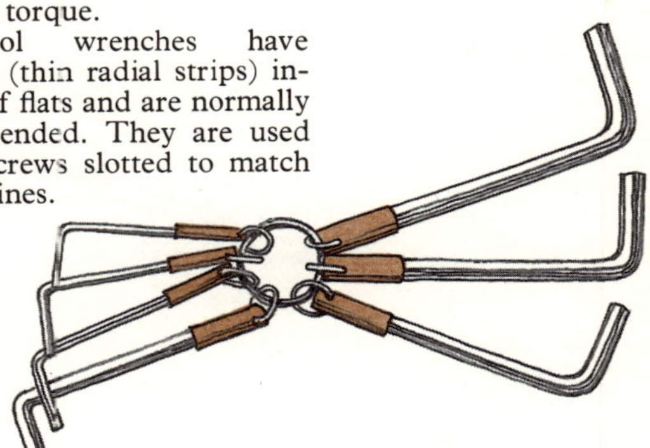

Pipe Wrenches

Although similar to adjustable spanners, pipe wrenches are intended for gripping and turning round objects such as pipework or damaged nuts. They have serrated jaws designed to provide grip on a smooth surface. Some wrenches have the serrations on each jaw angled in opposite directions to improve the grip as force is applied to the handle. Never use a pipe wrench on a good nut as the jaws will damage it. Always apply force in the direction of the opening of the jaws.

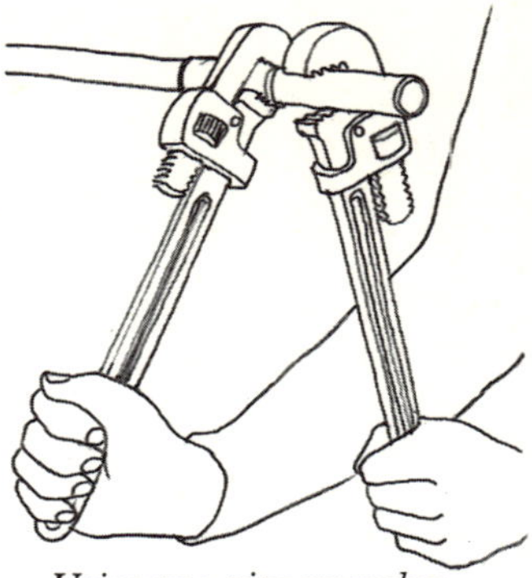

Using two pipe wrenches for more force.

Footprint Wrench

OTHER NAME: Pipe tongs
SIZE: *Length:* up to 525mm; *Jaw capacity:* up to 113mm
MATERIAL: Steel
USE: To grip round work

The name derives from the original manufacturer. The wrench has two handles with several possible positions for the pivot to accommodate a range of pipe sizes. It is tightened by squeezing the handles together.

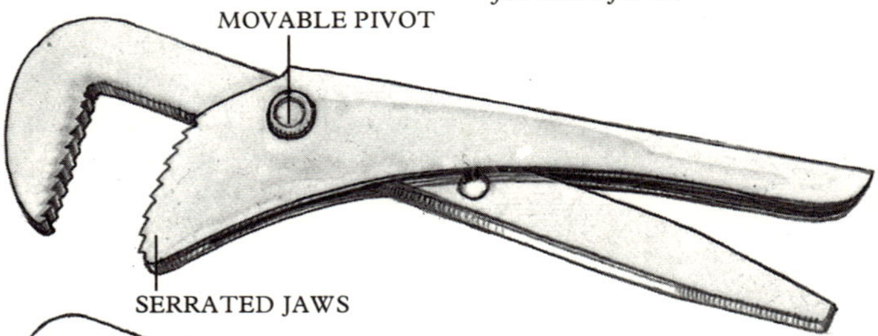

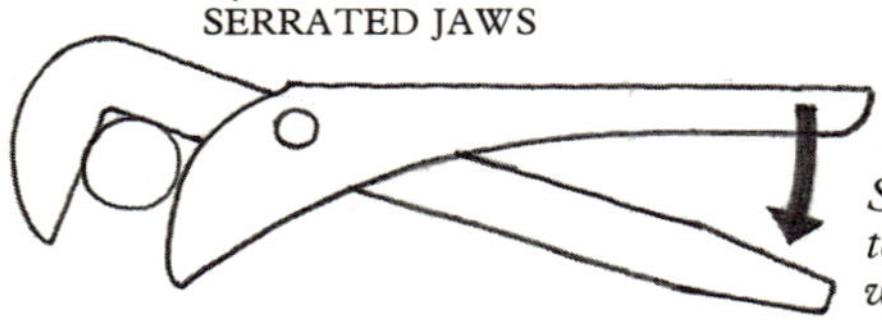

Squeeze the handles together to work the wrench.

Stilson Wrench

SIZE: 15 to 200mm
MATERIAL: Steel with hardened steel jaws
USE: To grip round work

The Stilson wrench is adjusted by means of a trapped nut working on a screw on the moving or "hook jaw". Pull on the wrench handle so that it hinges about its pivot and grips more tightly. Too much pressure may crush the pipe.

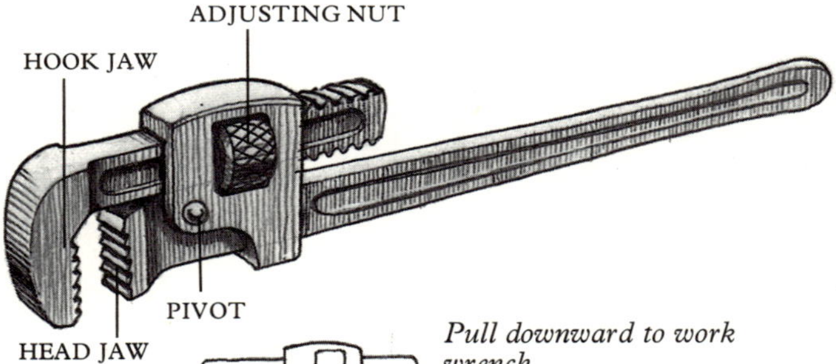

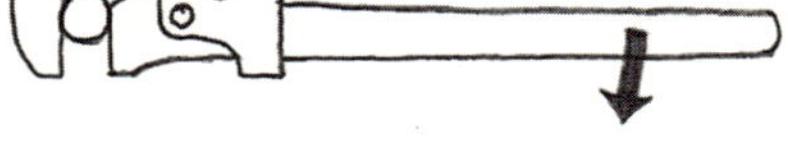

Pull downward to work wrench.

Chain Wrench

SIZE: 3 to 300mm
MATERIAL: Steel with high tensile steel chain
USE: To grip round work

A chain wrench comprises one or more serrated jaws and a length of bicycle type chain attached at one end of the jaw. The chain is wrapped around the pipe and hooked onto the other end of the jaw. When the handle is pulled, the cam action of the jaw tightens the chain and increases the grip of the wrench on the pipe.

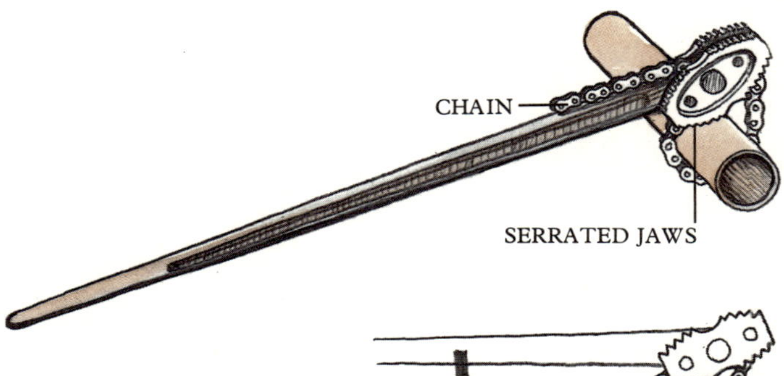

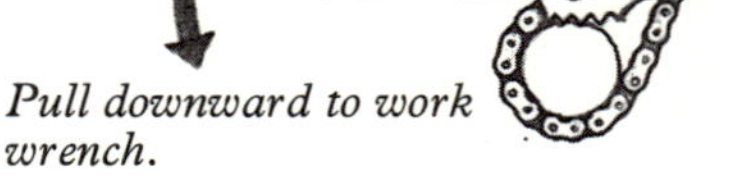

Pull downward to work wrench.

Strap Wrench

SIZE: Up to 300mm
MATERIAL: *Handle:* cast iron; *Webbing:* canvas
USE: To grip and turn round objects such as pipework where the finish is important

The strap wrench is a variation of the chain wrench, the chain being replaced by canvas webbing. There are no serrated jaws to damage the finish on something like chrome pipework. The strap is wrapped around the pipe and passed through a slot in the handle. The strap is pulled tight and friction on the pipe is increased by levering on the handle.

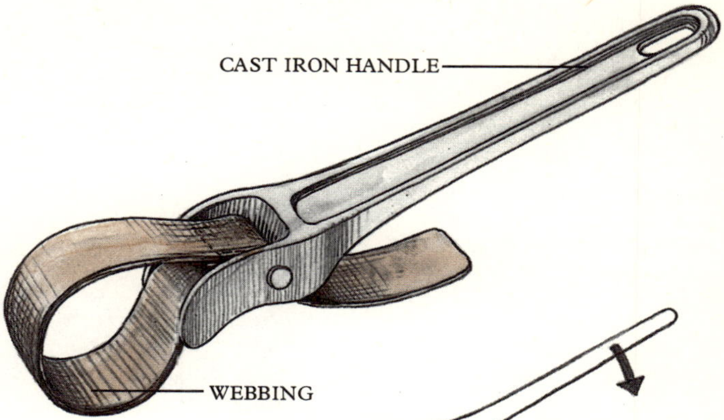

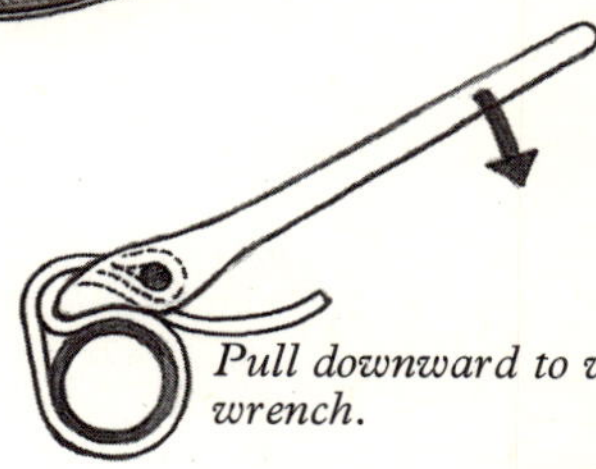
Pull downward to work wrench.

Crocodile Wrench

OTHER NAME: Bulldog wrench
SIZE: Jaw capacity: Up to 75mm
MATERIAL: Steel
USE: To grip and turn pipework, or other round objects

The crocodile pipe wrench looks like a conventional open ended wrench, with one smooth and one serrated jaw. Unlike other pipe wrenches, it does not have movable parts.

The jaws are pressed firmly over the pipe and the wrench turned away from the serrated jaw. This jaw grips the work while the smooth jaw slips, forcing the pipe further into the tapering jaws.

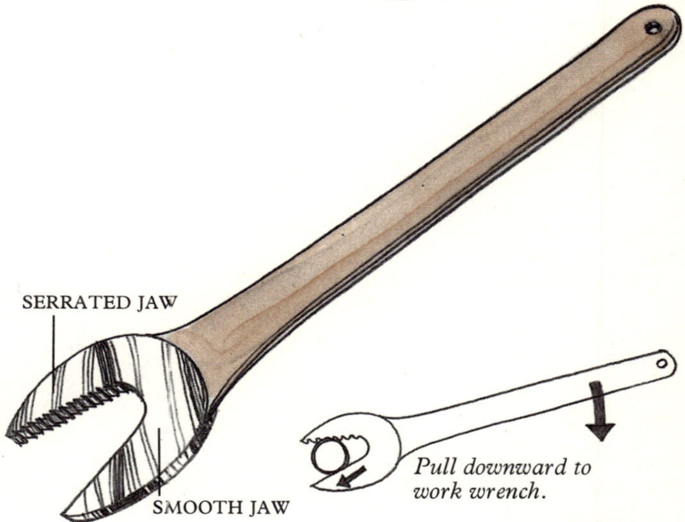

Pull downward to work wrench.

Basin Wrench

SIZE: For fittings up to 50mm across
MATERIAL: Steel
USE: To work on fittings where an ordinary wrench will not reach

This type of wrench has a Stilson type head with a long handle at right angles to it. It is designed for use in confined spaces, to work on basin nuts, flush valves and ballcocks. The jaw is reversible so that it can be used both to tighten and loosen nuts.

Possible positions of reversible jaw.

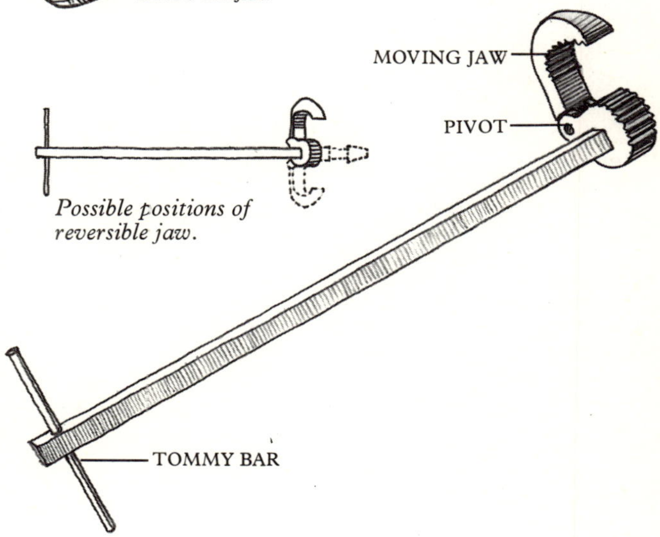

Torque Wrench

SIZE: Specified as a "torque range" for a particular tool
MATERIAL: Steel
USE: To apply an accurate pre-set force to a nut or bolt

Wrenches with a built-in torque measuring device are very useful where one or more nuts or bolts must be tightened to a pre-determined, accurate tightness, such as the cylinder head on a car engine which must be sealed to an equal pressure all around.

DEFLECTING BEAM WRENCH
This consists of a steel bar with a square drive, usually double ended, at right angles to the shaft. Attached at one end is a pointer which extends parallel to the shaft almost to the other end where it is read against a double ended torque scale. (The scale is double ended so that it can be read when the wrench is inverted or used on L/H nuts.) Beyond this is a handle. The bar bends in proportion to the torque being applied; since the pointer is not subject to this force it remains straight while the scale moves past it.

DIAL INDICATING WRENCH
With this wrench, the movement of the square drive is transmitted against spring pressure to a dial. As in the case of the deflecting beam wrench the drive is double ended.

MICROMETER OR PRE-SET WRENCH
The micrometer differs from the other two in that it does not have to be read and can, therefore, be used in difficult positions or in poor light. It is pre-set to the required torque, normally by turning a shaft which compresses a spring in the hollow handle. The spring resists the turning of the square drive until the set torque is reached. At this point the wrench "breaks" or moves freely for a few degrees giving a loud click. The micrometer does not have to be reset for another application.

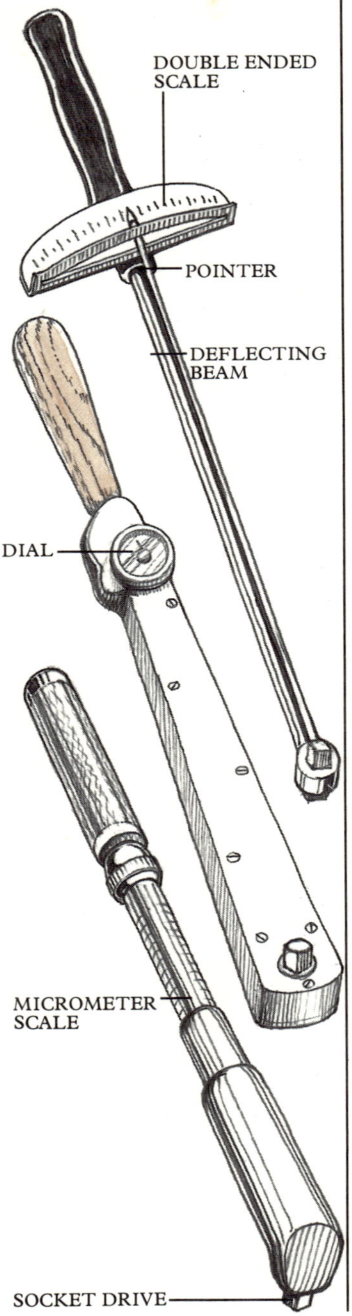

What is torque?
Torque is turning force, usually measured in ft/lbs or kg/m, that is the force used times the length of lever used to apply it. For example a 5kg pull with a 2m lever gives 10m/kg of torque.

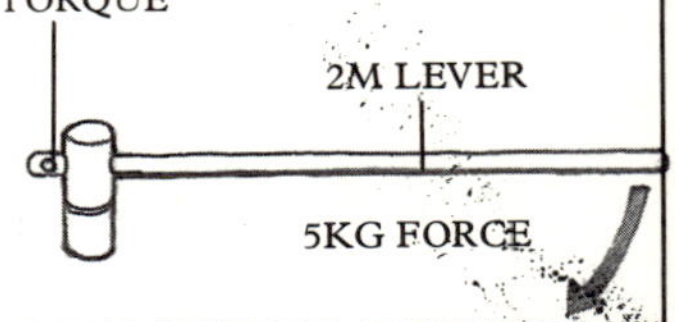

IMPROVISED TORQUE WRENCH
In the absence of a torque wrench, you can improvise with a tommy bar of known length and a spring balance. If possible use a tommy bar of 300mm length to allow the torque to read directly from the balance. If the bar is not a convenient length a correcting calculation will have to be made:

Reading on balance =

$$\frac{\text{Require torque (kg/m)} \times 100}{\text{Length of bar (cm)}}$$

Bar 30cm
Required torque 20kg/m
Reading on balance:

$$\frac{20 \times 100}{30} = 66.6\text{kg}$$

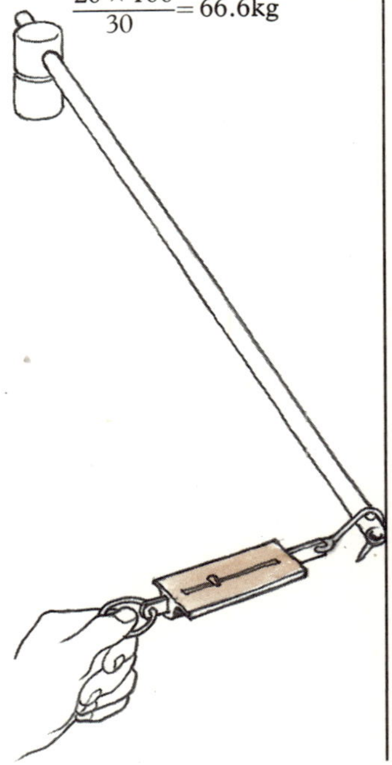

Hook and Pin Spanners

OTHER NAME: Spanner wrench
SIZE: 100 to 250mm
MATERIAL: Steel
USE: To turn special nuts or plugs

Special nuts are often made without flats but with edge notches or holes. They are used in restricted spaces or on smooth surfaces. One of their important applications is in bicycle construction. These nuts need specially designed spanners with either hooks or pins to engage and turn them. These spanners are one-directional and normally fit a particular nut, although there are adjustable hook spanners.

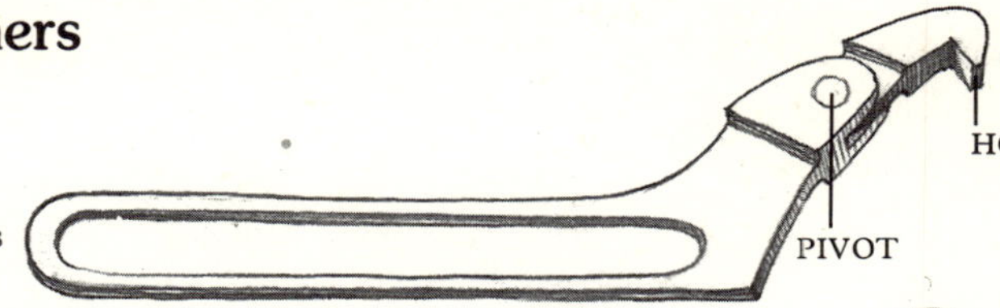

ADJUSTABLE HOOK SPANNER

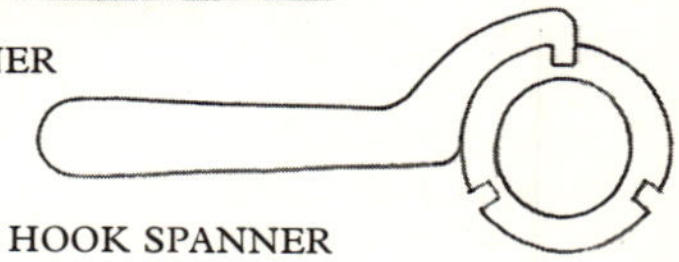

FIXED HOOK SPANNER

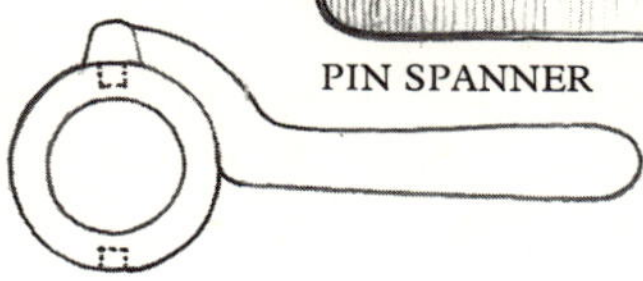

PIN SPANNER

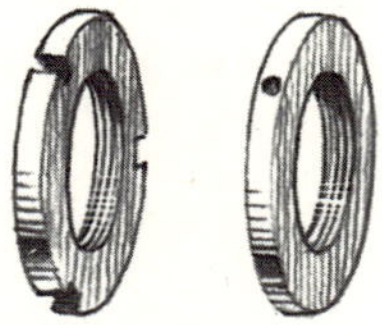

Face pin spanners
These are used to engage the drive holes in the face of threaded plugs. They usually have two pins and can be used in either direction.

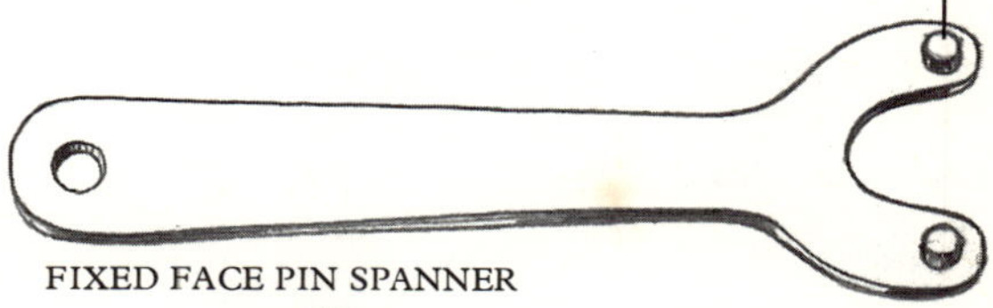

FIXED FACE PIN SPANNER

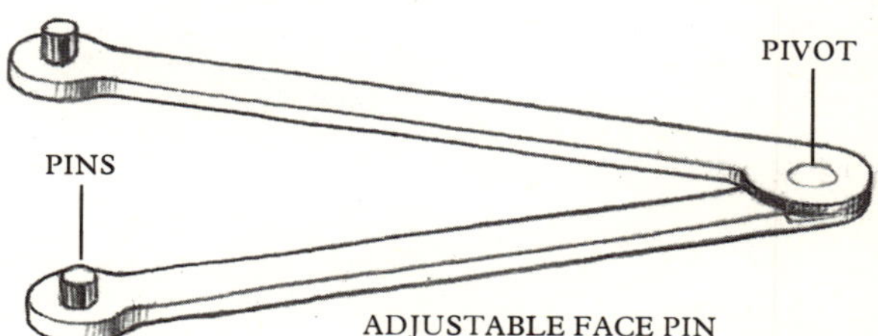

ADJUSTABLE FACE PIN SPANNER

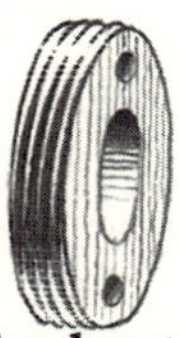

Specialized nuts
Notched or holed nuts can only be worked with hook or pin spanners.

Nut Drivers

OTHER NAME: Long shank box spanner
SIZE: *Length:* 175 to 238mm; *To fit nuts:* 4 to 16mm and up to approximately 25mm
MATERIAL: *Shank:* alloy steel; *Handle:* plastic or wood
USE: To drive nuts in like a screwdriver

The nut driver is extensively used by electricians and electronics engineers to turn smaller nuts or self tapping screws rapidly. They can be held in the end of the driver making for easy location.

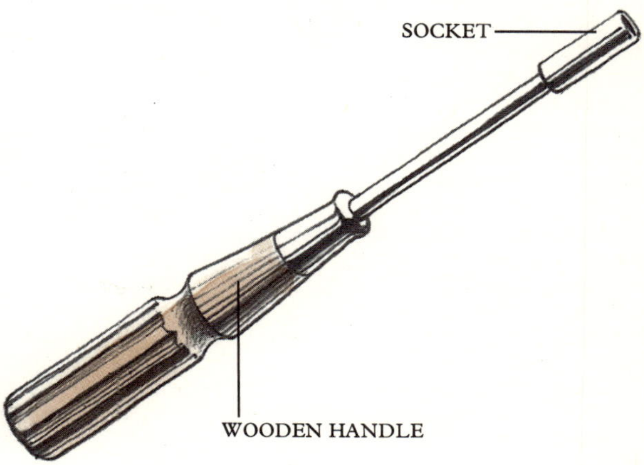

Taps and Dies

Taps and dies are tools used to cut threads for nuts and bolts. One of the earliest forms of tap was illustrated by Leonardo da Vinci toward the end of the fifteenth century. It was a set of three short square sectioned bars with the thread cut deeper on each face, mounted like a star so that each tap could be turned using the other two as handles. These were used for tapping the screw box, an early form of die, which cut the corresponding screw thread on a turned cylinder, usually made of hardwood in those days.

SCREW THREAD TYPES

When screw threads were cut with smith-made taps and dies there was no standardization, as each workshop used its own pattern. Even now there are many different screw thread types, far more than necessary, some differing from each other by only small amounts. Those most likely to be encountered are as follows:

B.A. (British Association)
Used on the small screws extensively used in electrical equipment, available in 16 sizes, Nos. 0–15 (0.236 to 0.031in.)

B.S.W. (British Standard Whitworth)
Made from $\frac{1}{4}$in. diameter upward, rising in $\frac{1}{16}$in. steps. Now obsolete, this was the first standard thread in Britain, but was found to be too coarse for some applications. The steepness of the thread gives too little clamping force in the presence of vibration. It is now used for soft or weak materials such as aluminum or cast iron or for cheaply made nuts and bolts where accuracy is not important.

B.S.F. (British Standard Fine)
This was introduced to overcome the lack of clamping force of B.S.W. and is made in the same sizes.

UNF Unified Fine, UNC (Unified Coarse)
the American equivalent of Whitworth and B.S.F. Made from $\frac{1}{4}$in., rising in $\frac{1}{16}$in. steps.

Metric Coarse
This thread is made in diameters from 1 to 300mm and is recommended for all general work.

Metric Fine
There are various fine threads for special purposes such as in machinery where vibration would loosen the fixing.

Taps

SIZE: See above
MATERIAL: Steel
ACCESSORIES: Tap wrench
USE: To cut internal screw threads as for a nut

A tap is a length of high speed steel cut with the thread form of a bolt, but having longitudinal flutes which form cutting edges and allow clearance for the swarf (metal shavings). In place of a bolt's hexagonal head the tap has a small square shaft to fit a tap wrench.

Taps usually come in sets of three. The first, and forming tap, is the "taper", which is tapered for at least half its length, sometimes down to the minor diameter at the tip. This provides an easy start to the threading operation. The "second", and "bottoming" or "plug" taps are progressively less tapered. All three cut the full thread, so that in thin plate the taper tap may be all that is necessary.

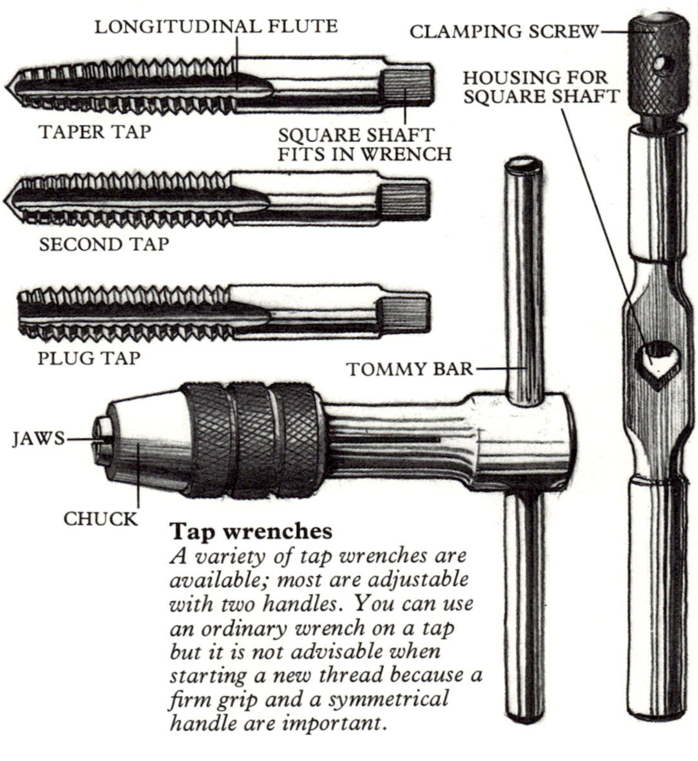

Tap wrenches
A variety of tap wrenches are available; most are adjustable with two handles. You can use an ordinary wrench on a tap but it is not advisable when starting a new thread because a firm grip and a symmetrical handle are important.

Matching a thread to a bolt
If a bolt hole has been stripped of its thread, it is necessary to match the tap to a larger bolt. If you know the thread type and size, look for the appropriately marked tap. If you do not, measure the bolt with calipers to ascertain the right diameter. Alternatively, use a screw pitch gauge. Compare the thread of the bolt with that of the tap by fitting them together: they should marry exactly. If you are in any doubt, take the bolt to be matched by a tool supplier.

Starting a threaded hole
To make a thread mark the position of the hole and centre punch it. If the work is important or is likely to be subjected to high stress, use the correct tapping drill for the tap and the material being worked. Alternatively, select a drill slightly larger than the minor diameter of the thread. If the drill is the same size or smaller than this the tapping will be stiff and the tap may break.

Fit the taper tap into the wrench and position it in the hole. Make sure you align the tap with the hole as it will be impossible to correct misalignment once cutting has begun.

For accuracy, use a lathe or drill press to start the thread Do not use the power unless you have an automatic tapping device but turn the machine by hand to avoid breaking the tap. In each case provide pressure into the work while turning. Once the thread is started it can be continued by hand.

Using a lathe

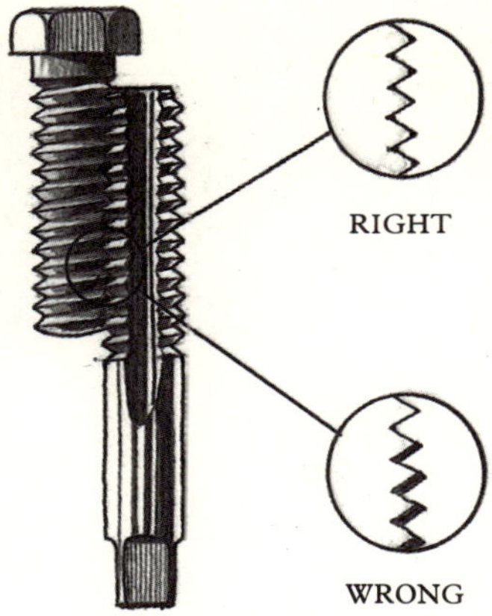

Marrying thread and bolt
Press the thread of the tap to the bolt to see that they fit flush together.

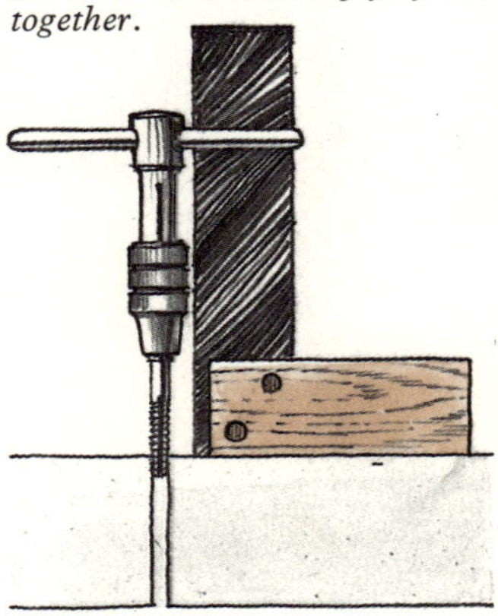

Keeping the tap straight
Use a try square to check for true in two directions at right angles.

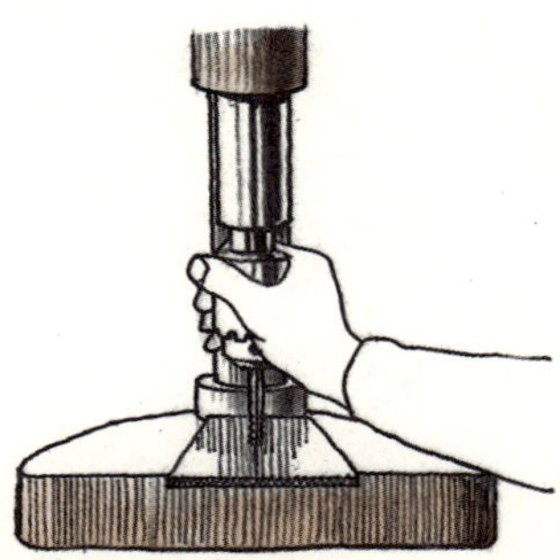

Using a drill press

Completing the thread
Use tallow or oil lubricants for steel and turpentine for copper or aluminium. Thread brass and cast iron dry.

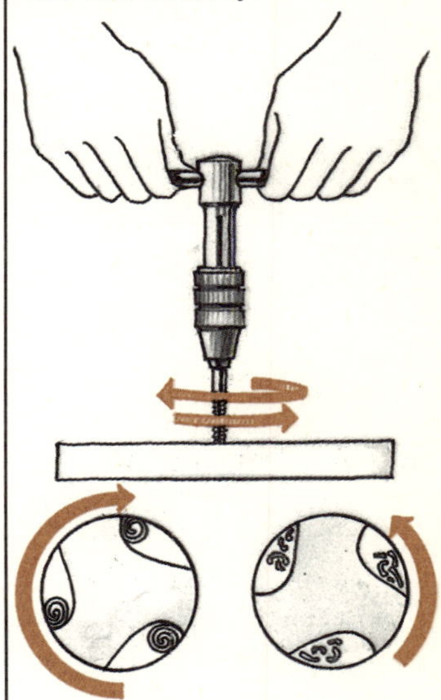

Turn the tap back $\frac{1}{4}$ turn to break the swarf then proceed with a $\frac{1}{2}$ turn back and so on.

Threading deep holes
Cut part of the thread using the three taps in sequence then start again with the taper tap and repeat the process. This will reduce the strain on the taps and lessen the chance of breakage.

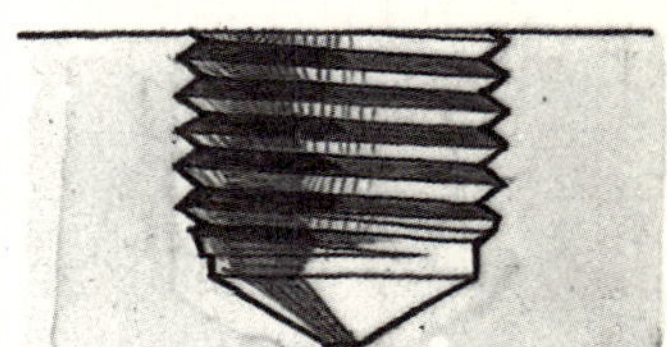

Any stopped holes should be drilled deeper than the required depth of thread because it is impossible to cut right to the bottom. Remove taps frequently to clear them of swarf. Remove swarf from the hole by shaking the work or, where this is not possible, use compressed air (wear safety glasses) or a greased rod. Take care when approaching the bottom of a hole; if you go too far, the tap can easily break.

Dies

SIZE: See page 266
MATERIAL: Steel
ACCESSORIES: Stock or handle
USE: To cut external screw threads as for a bolt

ROUND SPLIT DIE

The most common type of die is the split ring or round split die. This has a central threaded hole with a slight chamfer at one end.

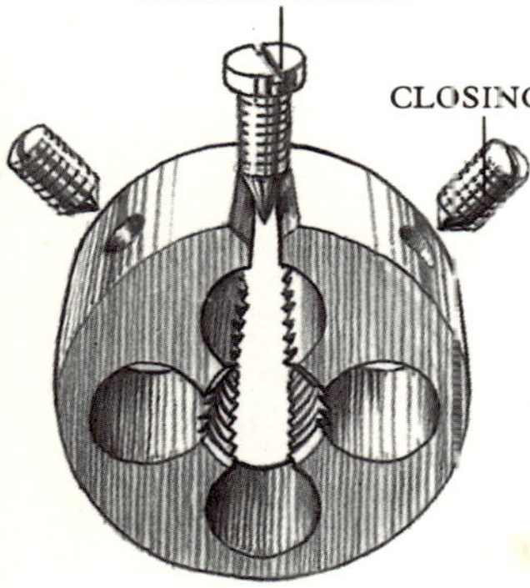

ROUND SPLIT DIE

Three or four holes grouped around the central one form cutting edges. The die is split to allow for adjusting by means of screws in the stock. To open it, the locking screws are backed off and the adjusting screw screwed in; the locking screws are then tightened to secure it. The die can be closed by backing off the adjusting screw until the natural spring of the die closes the gap. To close the die further, tighten the locking screws. This adjustment provides a good fit between nut and bolt and also allows metal to be removed in easy stages.

SPLIT DIES

The other common type of die is the split die, which consists of two rectangular jaws assembled in the stock and operated by means of a single adjusting screw. This type of die allows more adjustment than the round split die.

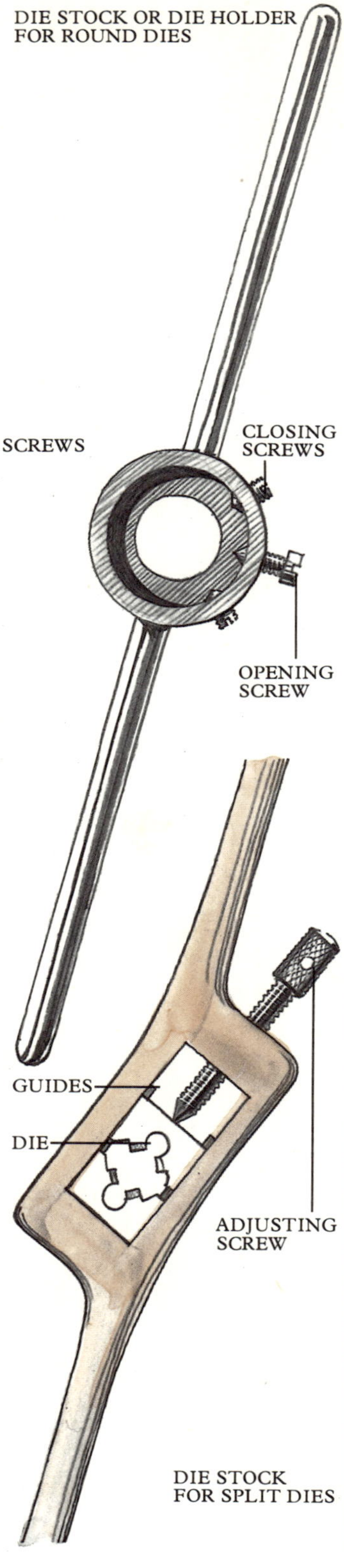

Threading a rod
First cut a 5° to 7° chamfer on the end of the rod for about $1\frac{1}{2}$ diameters. Open the die (and tighten the locking screws in the case of a split ring die) and place it on the end of the rod which must be firmly held. Press down and turn while keeping the die square to the rod. Once the die has begun to bite, no further pressure is required. Proceed a half turn forward and a quarter turn backward to break the swarf and lubricate as for tapping.

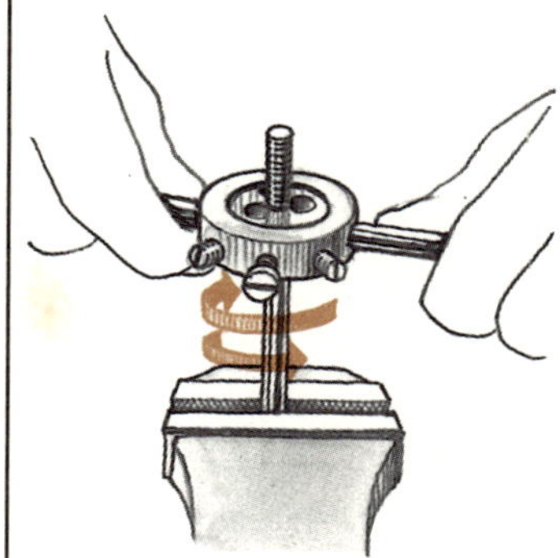

Preparing for another cut
Having completed the required length of thread, wind the die back to the beginning and tighten for another cut. Check the fit of the nut after each cut.

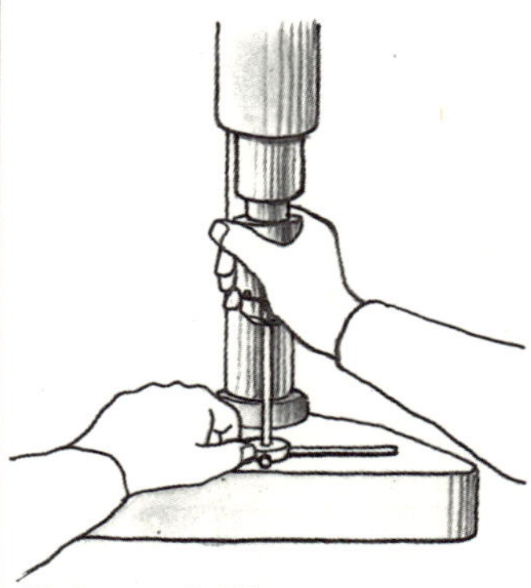

Using a drill press
Rest the die stock on the bed of the machine, chamfer uppermost, and hold firmly. Insert the rod in the chuck which should be hand turned. You can also use a lathe, fitting the work in the chuck and the die stock on a face plate.

Pipe Die

SIZE: 6 to 31mm
MATERIAL: Steel
ACCESSORIES: Diestock, guide bushing
USE: To cut a screw thread on pipework

The pipe die can be a one piece cutter made to fit a particular pipe size, or adjustable if constructed from separate jaws. You need a guide to align the die with the pipe: this can be either part of the stock itself or a separate bushing which fits into it along with the die. The cutting sequence is the same as that for normal thread cutting, with the die being lubricated every 2 to 3 turns. Some diestocks have ratchets so the tool can be used in confined spaces.

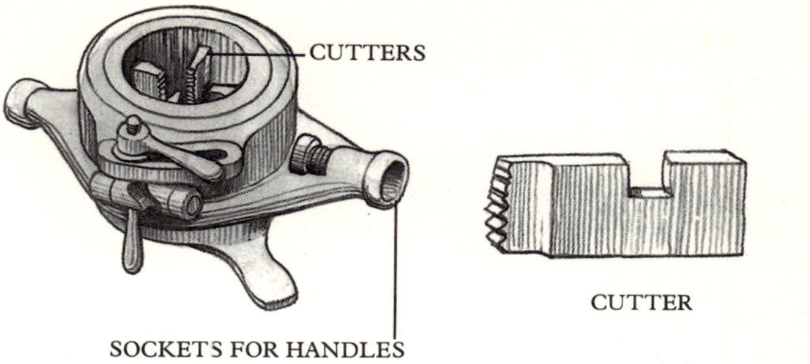

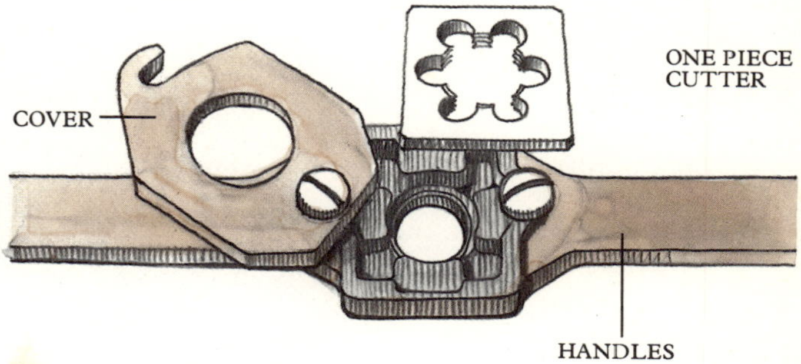

Die Nut

OTHER NAME: Rethreading die
SIZE: See page 266
MATERIAL: Steel
USE: To recut damaged or rusty machine screw threads

A die nut can be used to clean up an existing thread. It is not adjustable and must be matched to the screw thread. It can be driven by any convenient spanner.

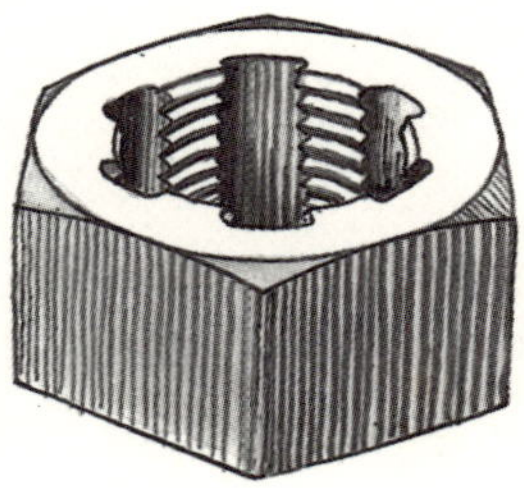

Screw Box

SIZE: To thread from 40 to 75mm diameter
MATERIAL: *Box:* wood; *Cutter:* metal
USE: To cut threads in wood

The screw box is made in two parts and is held together by screws. The cutter is mounted between the two. The first section of the box is smooth bored to act as a guide when starting the cut. With the wooden dowel held in a vice, the box is engaged on the end and turned clockwise until it begins to cut.

Internal threads are cut with a tap like those used for metal.

While now rare, wooden threads were once extensively used in hand tools such as clamps and rebate planes. Today, wooden screws are used in marking gauges.

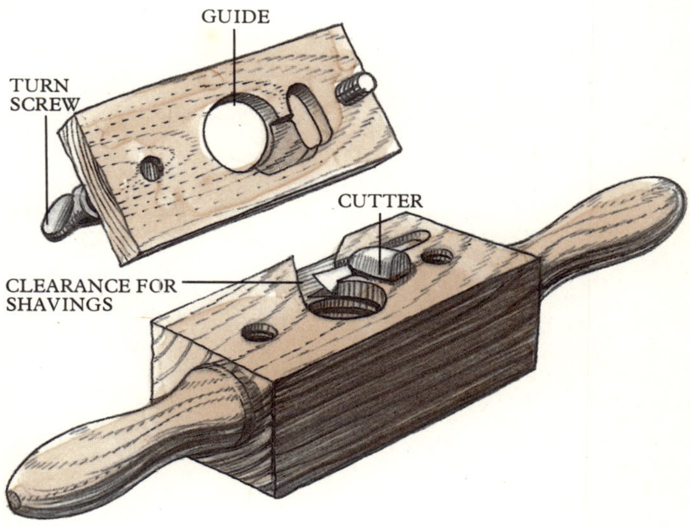

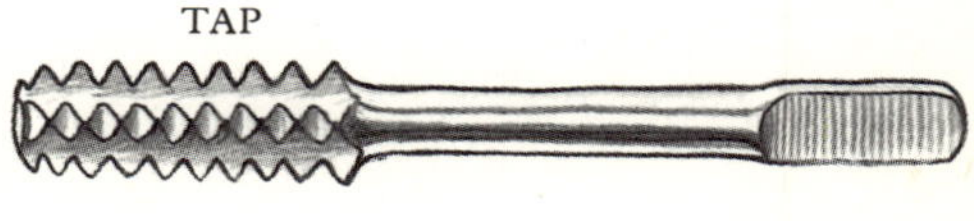

Plumbing Tools

Most plumbing tools found about the house fall into two categories: those that are used for clearing blockages and those that are needed to work with pipework. The latter tools include bending, cutting, reaming and shaping implements. Pipe wrenches, discussed in detail on pages 262–263, are specially designed for gripping round work and for reaching into awkward places.

Plunger

OTHER NAME: Force cup
SIZE: Diameter: 62 to 125mm
MATERIAL: *Cup:* rubber; *Handle:* wood
USE: To remove blockages from a toilet or sink drain

The plunger removes blockages by building up air pressure. The cup must be wide enough to completely cover the drain and make contact with the porcelain all around. A little petroleum jelly spread on the lip of the cup improves contact with the drain.

Block the overflow outlet with a wet rag before starting.

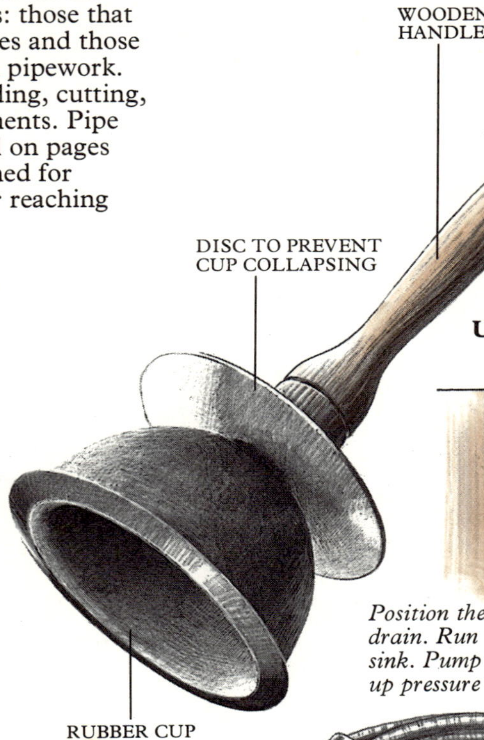

Using the plunger

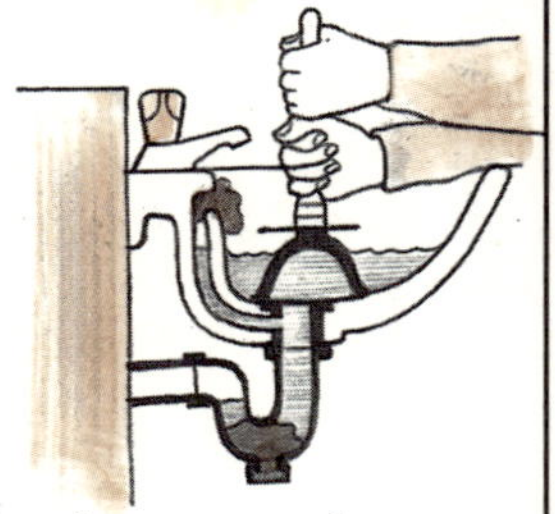

Position the cup over the open drain. Run a little water in the sink. Pump the handle to build up pressure to dislodge blockage.

Sink Waste Auger

OTHER NAMES: Drain auger, snake
SIZE: *Diameter:* 4, 6, 9, 12mm
Length: 2.4 to 30m
MATERIAL: Steel
USE: To clear blockages from the sink or drainage pipes

A sink auger is used to remove a blockage from pipework beyond the sink trap. Check first that the blockage is not in the trap before removing it and inserting the auger.

Push the hooked end of the auger into the pipe until it reaches the blockage. Tighten the clamp on the handle to grip the auger and crank the handle. This should dislodge all the blockage which can then be flushed through the system. If not, the blockage will be retained by the hook and pulled out as the auger is removed.

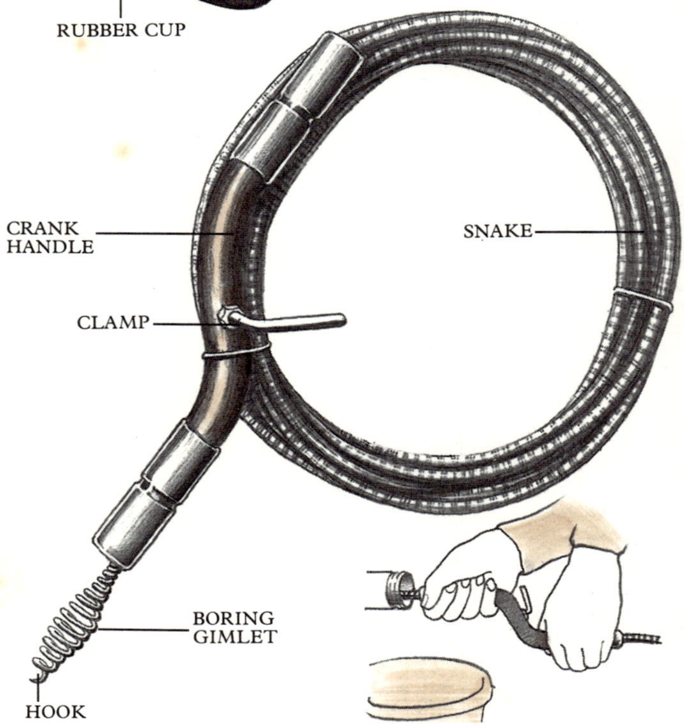

Using an auger

Toilet Auger

OTHER NAME: Closet auger
SIZE: *Diameter:* 10, 9, 12mm
Length: 900mm and 1.8m
MATERIAL: *Auger:* spring steel; *Tube:* plated steel; *Handle:* plastic, wood
USE: To remove a blockage from a toilet

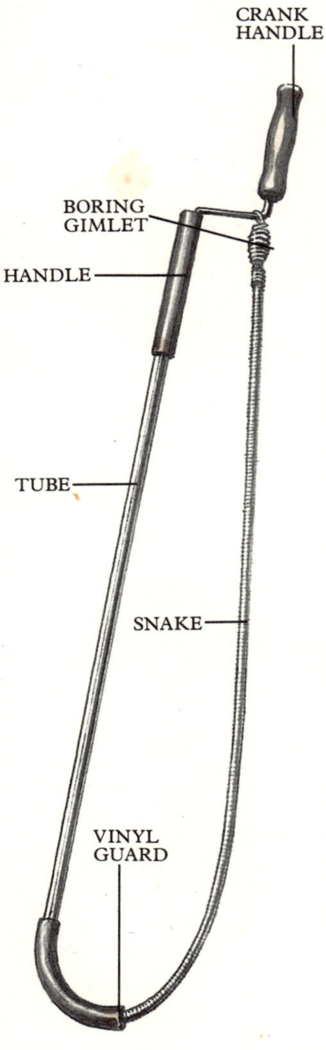

The auger and hook is fed through the toilet drainage passages until it encounters the blockage. The vinyl guard at the end of the hollow tube protects the toilet bowl from scratches. Grip one of the handles at the top of the tube and crank the other until the blockage is dislodged or pulled out.

Spring Tube Bender

OTHER NAME: Pipe bender, pipe bending spring
SIZE: To fit 6 to 15mm nominal diameter pipe
MATERIAL: Steel
USE: To support a pipe locally while it is being bent

If metal tubing or pipework is bent into a tight curve without being supported it will kink and collapse. Soft copper pipework can be bent over your knee as long as it is supported internally or externally by a coiled steel spring. Choose a bender that just fits the pipe, which is usually up to 15mm diameter, although some benders will support a pipe up to 50mm. Centre it on the proposed bend and with your thumbs on the inside of the curve, or pulling against your knee, bend the tube slightly past the required angle, easing it back afterward.

To remove an internal bending spring, place a bar in the ring at the end and turn counter clockwise while pulling. If bender is too short for the end of the spring to protrude, join a length of string to the ring.

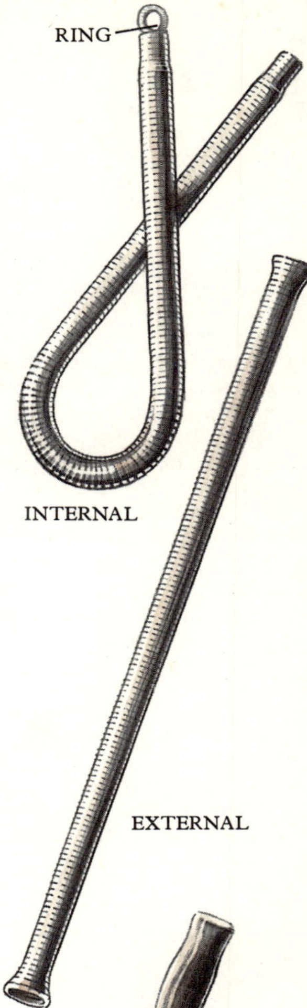

Pipe Burring Reamer

SIZE: To ream tubes with 3 to 50mm bore
MATERIAL: Alloy steel
USE: To remove the burr on a cut metal tube

The pipe reamer is available with a shank which fits into a brace or with its own tommy bar. It removes the burr from a cut tube which could otherwise encourage obstructions to build up on the inside.

Holding the tube in a vice, revolve the reamer clockwise keeping it centred in the pipe.

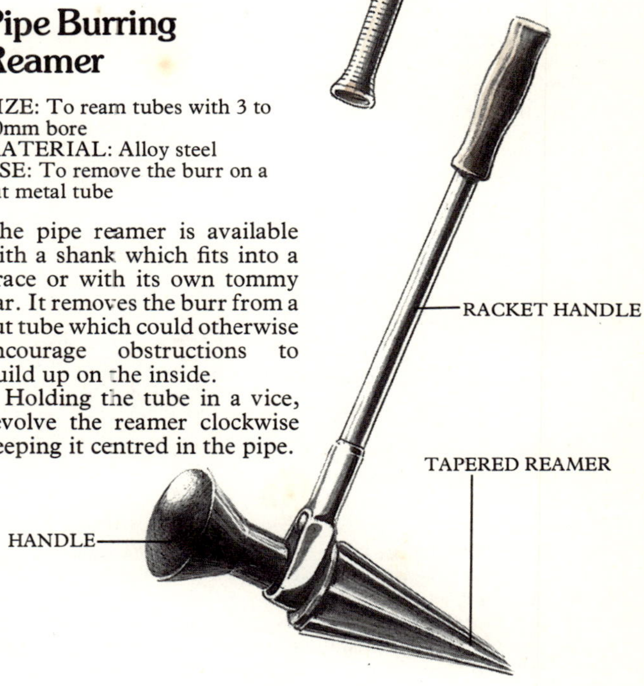

Pipe and Tube Cutter

OTHER NAME: Wheel cutter
SIZE: To cut 3 to 100mm outside diameter tube
MATERIAL: Cutters/rollers: alloy steel
USE: To cut metal pipework

Pipe cutters cut a metal tube cleanly and squarely. Tackle thin-wall tubing of brass, copper, iron or steel with a tube cutter. A pipe cutter is recommended for large-scale tubing.

The tube cutter has one fixed cutting wheel and an adjustable slide holding two guide rollers. Line the cutter up with the mark and tighten the rollers by turning the handle. Rotate the cutter while tightening the tool between each revolution until the tube is cut. Tube cutters normally have a fixed reamer for removing the burr from the inside.

The larger pipe cutters operate in exactly the same way, but they have three cutters instead of the rollers. They cut faster and are better if a complete revolution is impossible. Hold the tube in a pipe vice and lubricate the cutters with oil.

Other versions of pipe cutter are available with a plier wrench mechanism. For really large drainage pipework, there is a cutter made up by linking a series of cutter wheels to form a cutter chain.

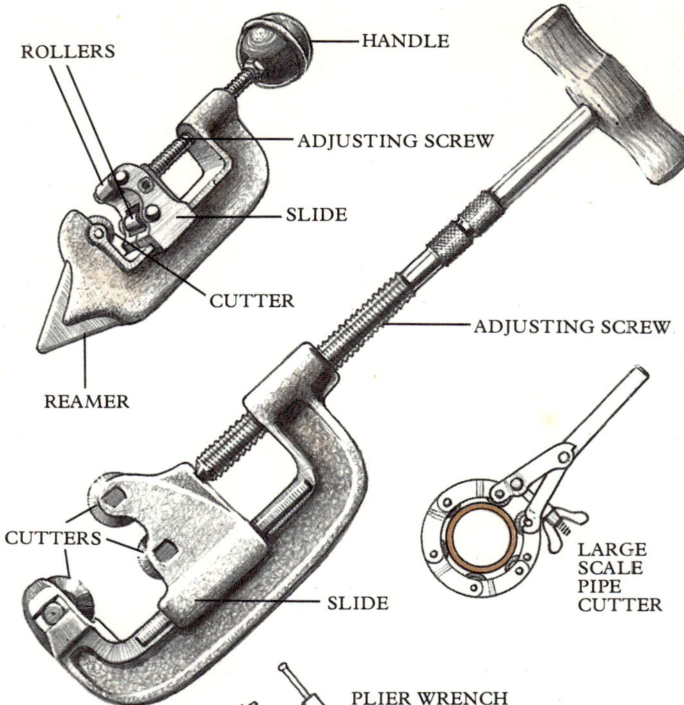

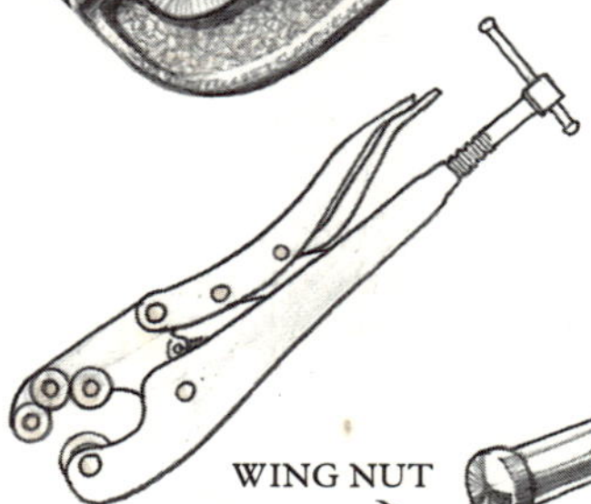

Flaring Tool

SIZE: To flare tube with 4 to 15mm outside diameter
MATERIAL: Steel and cast iron
USE: To flare the end of a tube to fit a pipe fitting

Compression fittings are used to join lengths of copper, brass or aluminium tubing. To make a water-tight seal against the fitting, the end of the tube must be accurately flared with a flaring tool. It has a split die block, which can be clamped with wing nuts around pipework of different sizes, and a yoke. This fits into the block and has a screw fed cone which flares the tube to a 45° bell shape.

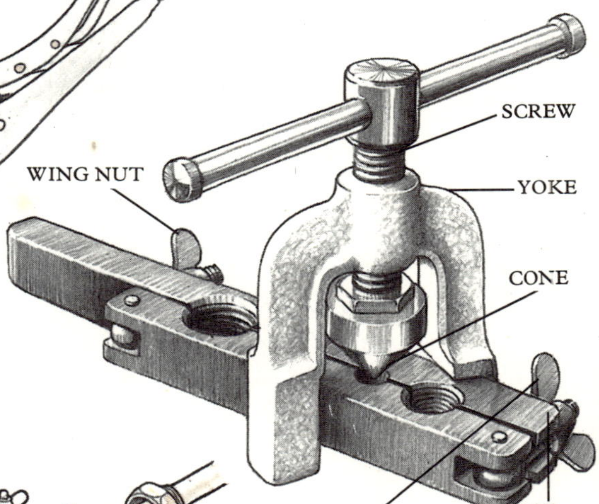

Using the flaring tool
Cut and ream the tube and slip a flange nut over the end. Clamp the tube in the flaring tool, keeping the end flush with the surface of the block. Replace the yoke and turn the screw.

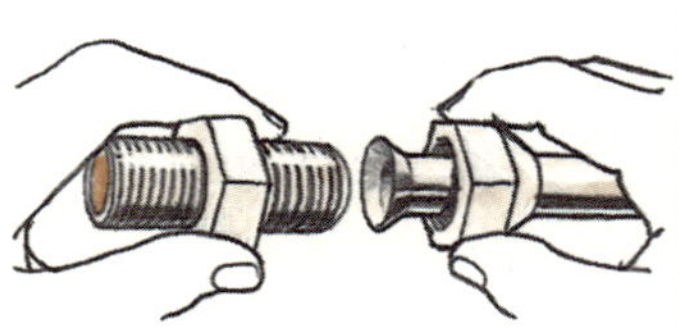

Once the tube is flared, the flange nut can pull the pipe tightly against the fitting. Check that it will fit.

Tube Bender

OTHER NAME: Pipe bender
SIZE: To bend tube with an outside diameter of 6 to 32mm
MATERIAL: Cast iron and steel
USE: To support a pipe while it is bent

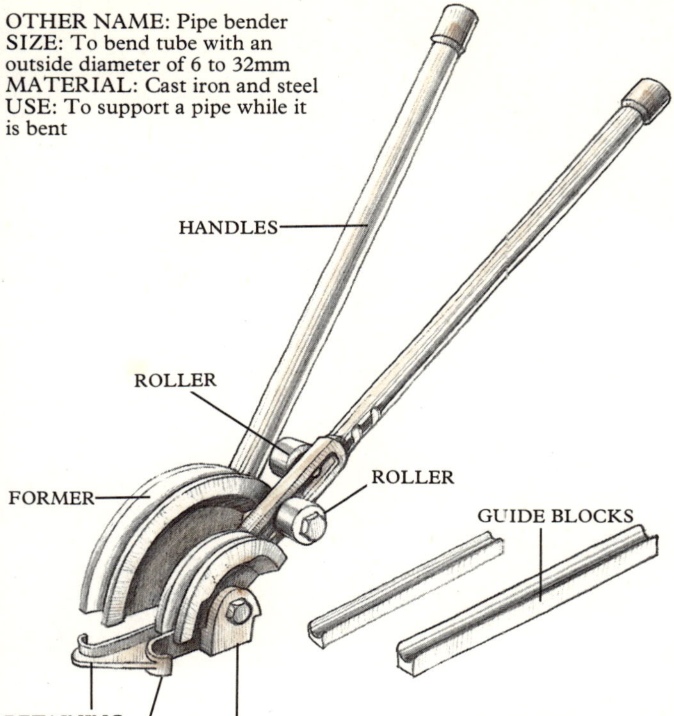

Like spring benders, the tube bender supports the walls of a tube locally while it is bent, but does it in a different way. The tube is bent over a former which is curved to the radius of the required bend and shaped to support half the wall of the tube. A separate guide block supports the upper half of the tube as it is bent. Long handles provide the necessary leverage.

Pipe benders are produced in a variety of sizes, from small domestic tools to large scale hydraulic benders for the trade. A pipe bender is an extravagance for the amount of plumbing work the average home needs, so rent if possible.

Using the tube bender

Place the straight tube in the former and under the retaining hook. Line up the marked bend with the former's shoulder.

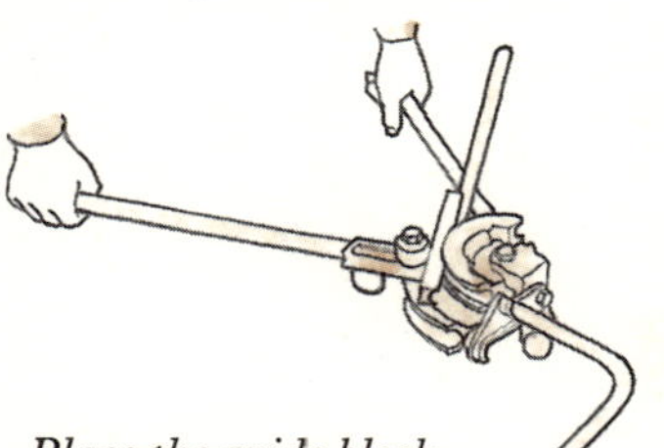

Place the guide block on top of the tube. The movable lever will take up the slack. Pull the levers in opposite directions to bend the tube over the former.

Riveter

OTHER NAME: Pop riveter
SIZE: Sets rivets of 2 to 4mm diameter
MATERIAL: Steel
USE: To rivet thin sheet material

The riveter will join any thin sheet material, but canvas or vinyl sheeting will require washers to prevent tearing.

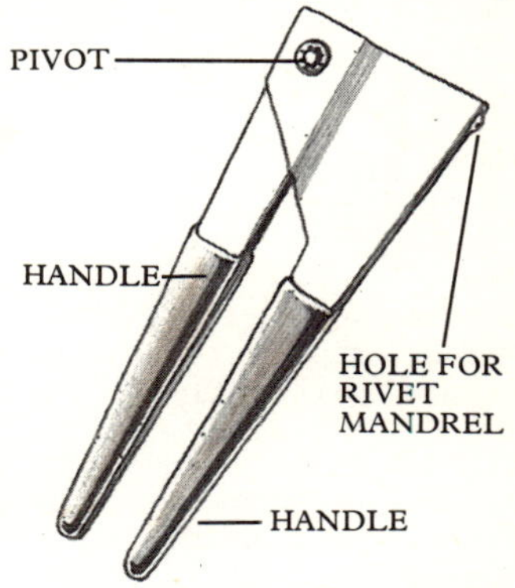

The main advantage of the riveter is that it can blind rivet: when the far side of the rivet is inaccessible, the soft head is spread against the inner face of the work.

Simple riveters take one size of rivets; swivel or exchangeable heads take various sizes.

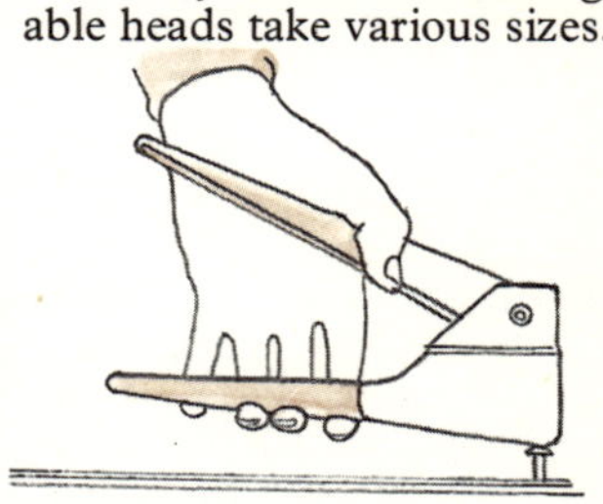

Using the riveter
Drill matching holes through two halves of joint to take rivet head snugly. Open handles; insert mandrel of rivet in riveter's head between the jaws.

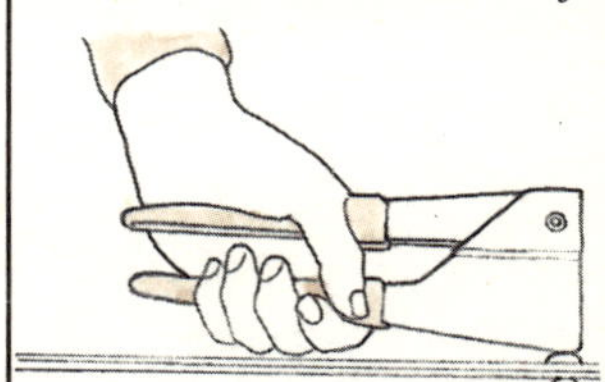

Push rivet head through hole and press hard against work to seat rivet. Squeeze handles until mandrel snaps off.

Soldering Iron

OTHER NAME: Soldering copper
SIZE: *Head weight:* 56g to 1.36kg; *Power:* 15 to 240 watts
MATERIAL: *Head:* copper; *Shaft:* steel; *Handle:* hardwood, plastic
USE: To heat metal and soft solder for joining

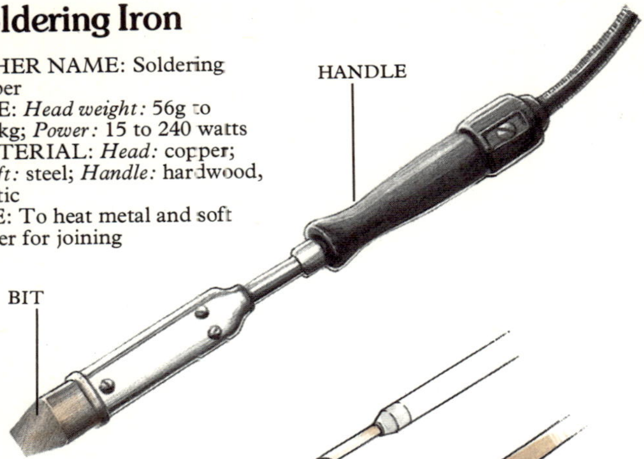

Some metals can be joined by melting soft solder, an alloy of tin and lead which solidifies when cooled. It must have a lower melting point than the metal being used for the job so that it can flow into a hot joint. A soldering iron supplies the heat. It has a copper bit or head which is fitted to a shaft and heated by electricity or a flame.

The head size and weight are important. The soldering iron must be able to heat the job to the temperature at which the solder will flow. A small soldering iron will melt the solder, but if it cannot heat the workpiece sufficiently, a poor join will result.

The shape of the head also varies depending on the job. Small soldering irons, designed to make electrical connections, have a narrow "pencil" bit for working in confined spaces. Larger irons have pointed, hatchet-shaped or tapered bits. A pointed bit provides accurate "spot" soldering, a hatchet bit is designed for soldering seams, and a tapered bit is a good all-round tool: the flat wide section will heat up a broad area, while the tool can be used on edge for a seam.

Flux

Metals to be joined must be free of the oxide film which normally coats the surface. The oxide is removed with flux.

Rosin flux is non-corrosive and is therefore ideal for electrical connections. It comes in powder or paste form and is

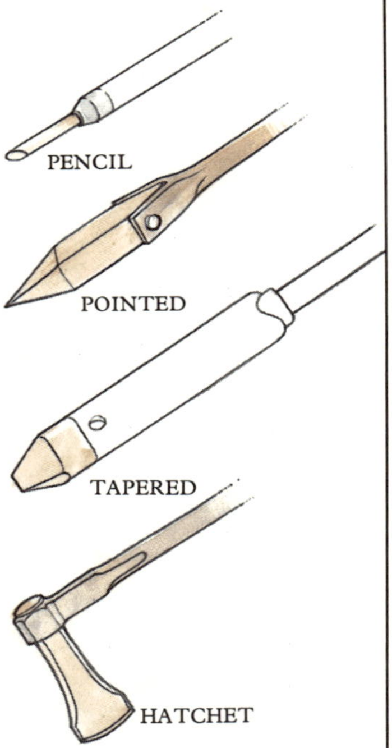

also incorporated in the core of wire solders: it melts just before the solder, and runs into the joint before it.

An active flux such as salammoniac will remove grease and dirt as well as oxide. It must be washed off in warm water after the joint is made or it will corrode the metal.

Tinning the bit

Before use, a soldering iron must be "tinned" to remove oxide from the surface and to improve its heat transferring ability. If a bit is damaged or pitted, reshape with a file. Heat up the bit and when it reaches the temperature where it will readily melt the solder, dip it in flux, and immediately apply solder to coat the metal.

Soldering a terminal

Strip off the insulation and fan the wires so that you can stroke them with a folded piece of emery cloth. Make this a pulling stroke only to avoid bending the filaments. Twist the filaments together with a pair of pliers, and tin the twisted end by applying the hot iron and cored solder.

Clean up the point of contact on the terminal with emery cloth and crimp it on to the wire with pliers.

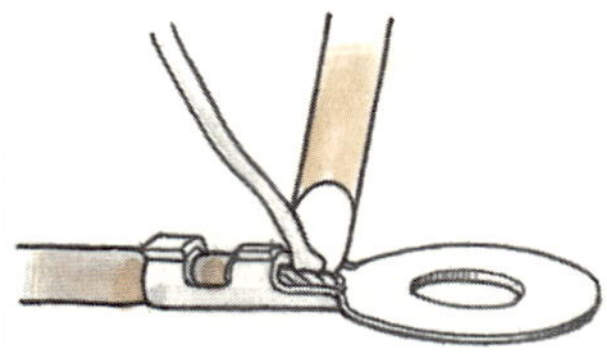

Apply the hot iron and cored solder to the junction between the wire and the fitting encouraging the solder to flow. A good connection will look smooth and wet.

Soldering a lap joint

Lap or folded joints are used to join sheets of tinplate which need a large overlap. To make a lap joint, clean up the areas of contact with wire wool or emery. Dip the stick of solder in active flux and apply it to the area. Apply a hot 125 watt soldering iron and solder to both halves of the joint. Assemble

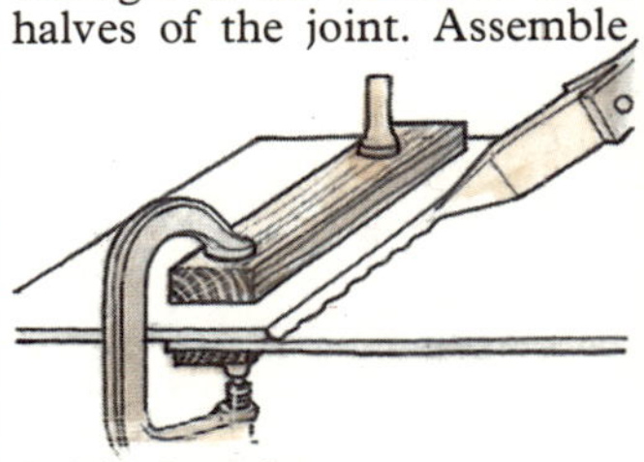

Soldering the seam
Apply a bead of flux along the seam and work along it with the iron. It must be continuous for a good joint.

the joint holding it firmly in clamps or between wooden blocks in a vice. Tack the joint as shown above.
Check the other side of the joint to see that the solder has permeated and solidified on that side. Wash the joint under running hot water.

Propane Lamp

SIZE: Burner diameter: 6 to 40mm
MATERIAL: *Tubing:* brass; *Handle:* plastic
USE: To provide a heat source for soldering and brazing

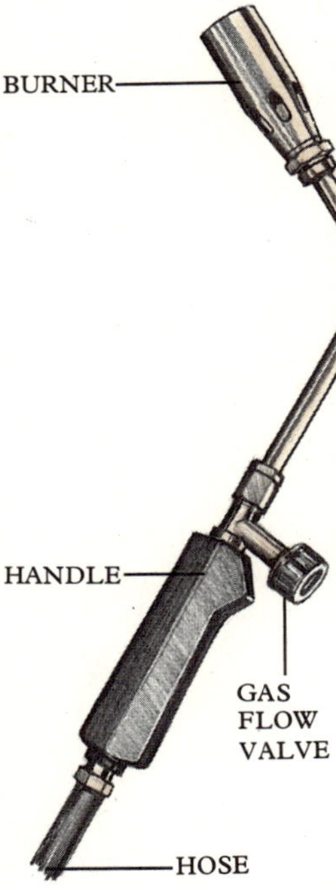

The propane lamp can be used to join metals by soft soldering, hard soldering and brazing, as well as to burn off old paint.

The propane lamp burns liquid petroleum gas which is pressurized in metal containers. Propane is the gas commonly used, as butane is used only where normal room temperature is constant.

Burners will produce a needle flame for precision soldering or a broad flame for heating pipework. A flame spreader can be attached to produce a fan shaped flame suitable for burning off old paint and varnish finishes.

The lamp is connected to the gas container by a hose. The hose connects to a large gas container through a valve or through a gas regulator which is used to maintain constant gas pressure when more than one burner is operating from the same container.

Lighting the lamp
Open the control valve to release the gas, which mixes with air drawn through air intake holes at the burner to produce a combustible mixture. Ignite the gas with a naked flame or spark and adjust the flame to the required size.

The hottest part of the flame is approximately halfway along its length. Direct this onto the work for maximum efficiency.

Soldering plumbing joints
Copper plumbing can be easily and neatly joined by soldering the joints. The plumbing connector is flared to fit over the plain end of the pipe.

How to solder joints

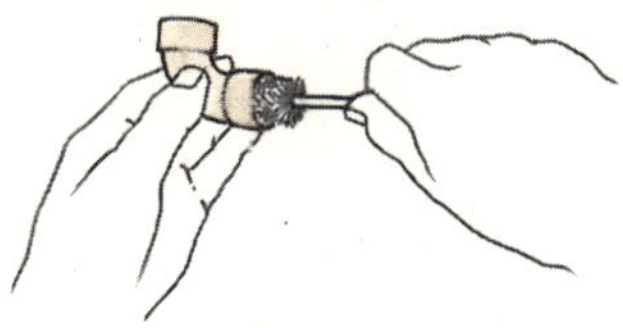

1. *Cut the tubing square; clean off the burr. Use emery or steel wool to clean inside connector and outside pipe to the depth of the flared section on connector.*

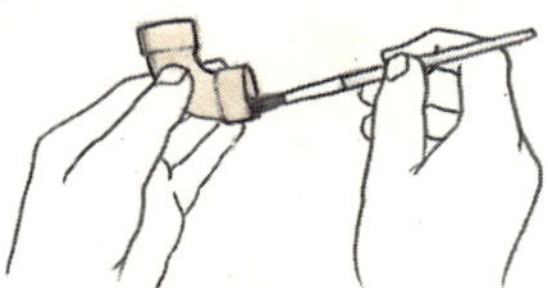

2. *Brush a non-corrosive flux, preferably a paste, on the clean metal. Insert the tubing in the connector and rotate to spread the flux. Wipe off excess flux.*

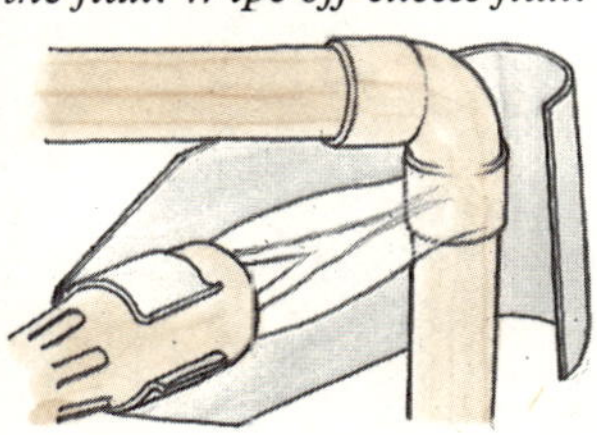

3. *Heat the joint with a propane lamp. A heat shield fixed to the end of the lamp will enclose the area and protect material behind the work.*

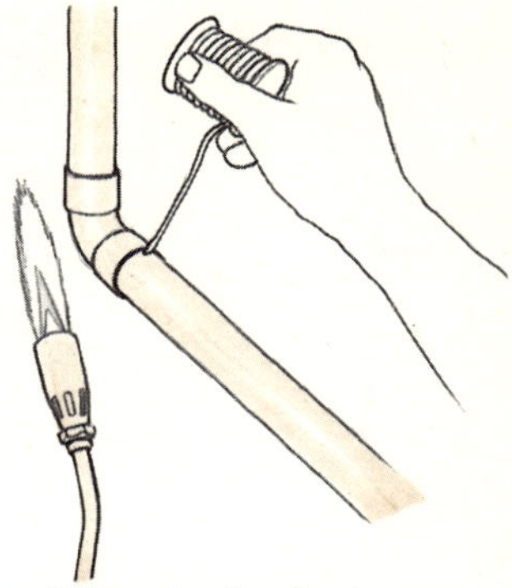

4. *When the flux begins to bubble out, remove the lamp and apply the tip of the solder to the edge of the connector where capillary action will draw the solder into the space whichever way the connector is facing. Do not apply flame to the solder itself. It is the heated metal which melts the solder, not the flame. Apply the solder to two or three places around the edge of the fitting until a line of solder shows around the entire joint.*

Solder all joints while the connector is hot. Reheating the area will soften existing joints and weaken the seal.

Brazing
Higher temperature brazing will produce stronger load-bearing joints. Wire the joint together so it does not move and use a suitable flux and brazing rod. Enclose brazing area with a firebrick furnace.

Safety factors
Check your equipment regularly for leaks.

Do not use a naked flame to check a leak. It can usually be detected by smell and confirmed by brushing on a soapy water solution which will bubble where the gas is escaping.

Keep the container away from sources of heat and discard empty containers safely. Do not throw them on to a fire.

Do not leave a burning lamp unattended. When you have finished working, turn off the supply at the container first so that all gas in the hose is burned off before disconnecting. Close the valve at the lamp and disconnect from the container before storing.

Arc Welder

SIZE: Amperage range: 30 to 250
MATERIAL: Various
ACCESSORIES: Welding rods
USE: To join metal by fusion of the workpiece

Arc welding joins metal to metal by heating the material to melting point with an intense electrical discharge in the form of an arc. The arc is produced by passing an electric current, regulated by a transformer, across an air gap between an electrode and the work. The electrode also melts, adding more molten metal to the weld, filling up any vacant space and reinforcing the joint. The outside of the electrode is covered with a flux-like coating. During the welding process some of the coating is burnt off, forming a gaseous screen to protect the molten metal from oxidation. The remaining material combines with impurities in the molten metal floating to the surface to form a coating of "slag" which is broken off when the weld finally "freezes".

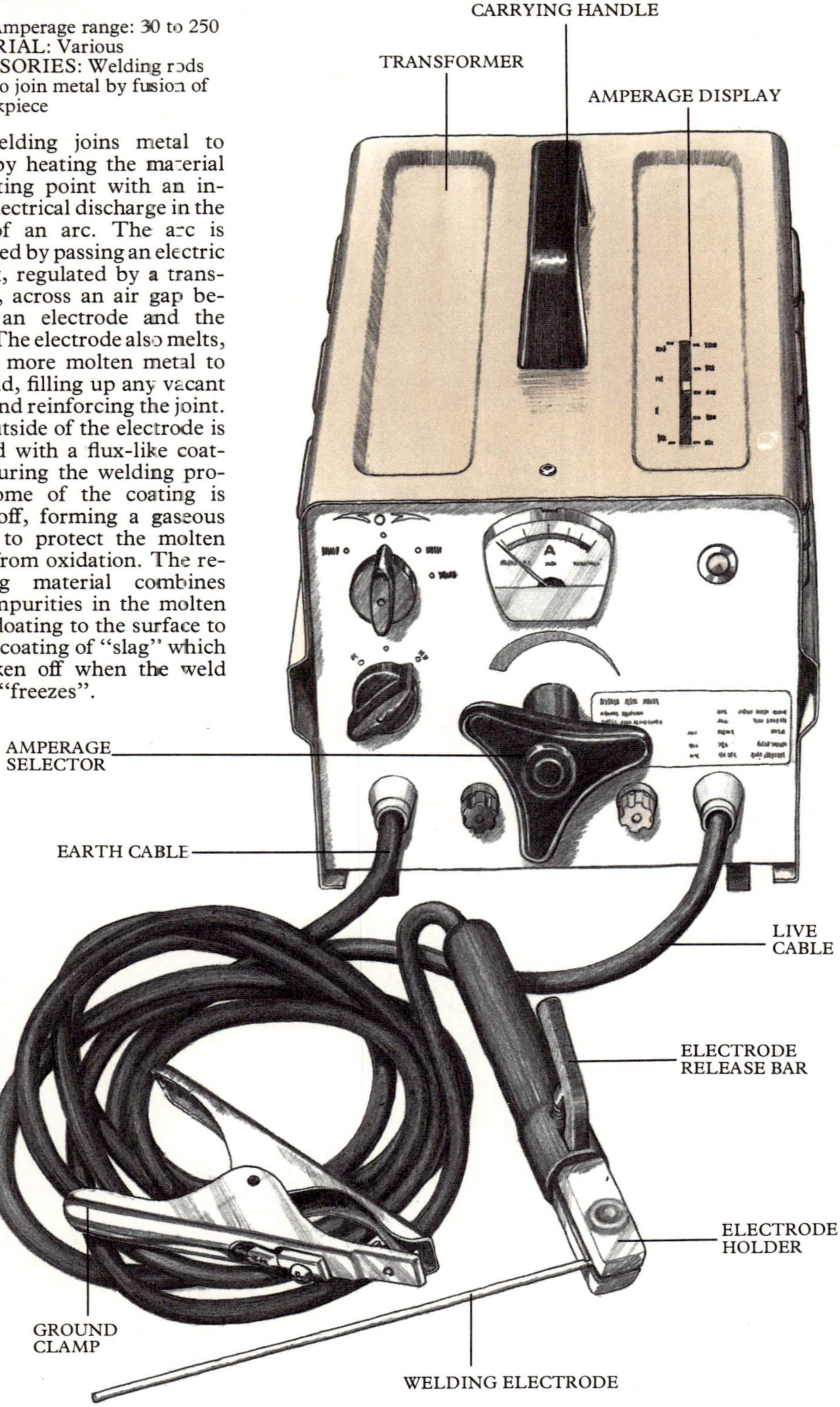

Preparing to weld

Protect yourself against the intense light produced by arc welding, as well as the inevitable shower of sparks. Use special dark glass goggles or a face mask to view the work whenever the welder is used.

Wear heavy duty leather gloves preferably with gauntlets. A leather apron stops any sparks falling on your clothes, which should be dark to avoid reflected light from the arc.

Make sure that the area surrounding the welding bench is free from inflammable material. If possible, cover the bench in 6mm sheet steel.

Setting up the equipment

The ground connection must be connected to the work, or to a metal bench top if the work is in contact with it. Insert a welding rod in the electrode holder and select the appropriate amperage recommended for the rod. The smaller transformers available to the home user will handle electrode sizes from 16 to 10 swg. Mild steel electrodes are the most common, although many alloys are used for different materials.

Clamp or wire together the workpieces to secure the joint.

Striking an arc

When the electrode is brought into contact with work and quickly lifted 3mm from the surface, a spark is produced. Either strike the work with the tip of the rod letting it bounce the required amount, or swing the tip against the work rather like striking a match, lifting it from the work as it comes into contact. If the electrode is not lifted quickly enough, the end of the rod will stick to the work producing a short circuit. Dislodge a sticking electrode as quickly as possible by moving the rod from side to side pulling it from the work.

An electrode held the correct distance from the work will crackle evenly. If held too far away, it will sound uneven and snap out completely at a certain distance from the work. At the end of the weld, lift the electrode quickly from the work to snap out the spark.

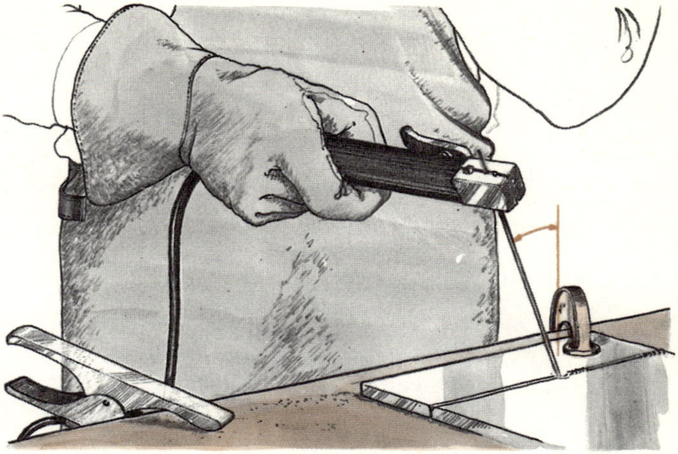

Laying a bead

The process of applying molten metal to the weld is known as "laying a bead". Hold the electrode 15° in the direction of the weld. Strike an arc and move the rod at a steady rate, maintaining the correct angle and length of arc. Move the rod as the back end of the crater fills up with the molten metal called the "puddle".

If you move it too slowly, the slag will flow in front of the molten metal and contaminate the weld, producing gas pockets. When the weld has frozen, chip off the slag with a cold chisel or a "chipping hammer", which has a cross peen and a pointed end.

Getting the bead right

A good weld will produce an evenly rippled bead which is uniform in width. Current which is too low will not penetrate the metal very far, leaving a high bead on the surface of the work. The arc will also be intermittent.

If the current is set too high, it will penetrate well, but the bead itself will be thin leaving undercuts. The arc will hiss.

If the weld is too slow, a wide bead will form, which does not fuse well at the sides. The job will also be overheated, encouraging distortion.

If the weld is too fast, it will not deposit enough metal, so an irregular narrow bead with undercuts will form.

If the arc is too long, it will produce a rough weld, splattering globules of metal along the bead. If you have any trouble maintaining an arc, even with the electrode held at the recommended distance from the work, check that the earth connection is satisfactory. Alternatively, you may need to increase the current to suit the size of the welding rod.

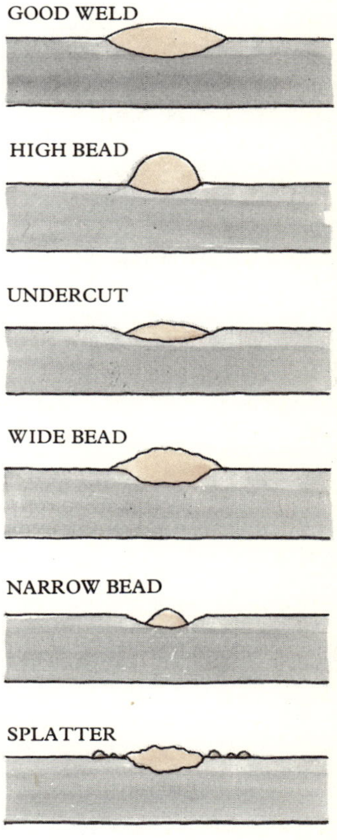

Types of joint
Practise all the various joints and techniques on scrap material before attempting to weld an actual job. Always tack-weld a job with beads about 6 to 9mm long at strategic positions along the joint to hold the work securely while you lay the main bead.

Butt joint
For thin gauge metal, 16 swg, for example, butt the edges together and tack-weld the joint. Raise the work above the bench on pieces of scrap metal, and lay a bead along the joint.

If the current is too high or the rate of travel is too slow you may burn through thin sheet metal. Set the transformer at 30 to 50 amps for this thickness of metal and use a 14 swg rod. For thicker sheets, say 18 swg metal, leave a 1.5mm gap at the joint and tack-weld both sides before laying a bead on one side to penetrate halfway through the metal. Turn the work over and lay a second bead.

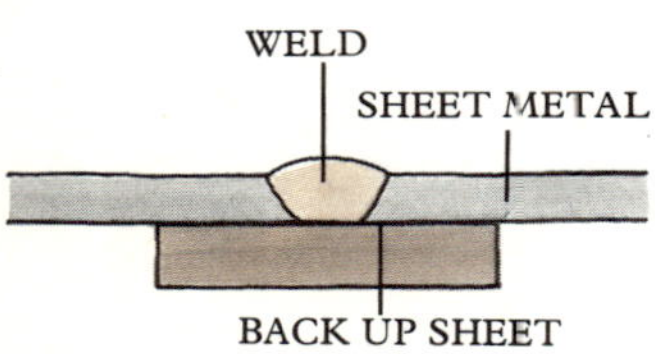

Preventing burn-through
Back up the joint with a strip of copper to absorb some of the heat of the arc. It will also leave a perfectly flat joint on the underside.

Butt jointing thick metal
On metal up to 9mm thick, bevel the edges of the plate. If the plates can be welded from both sides, bevel the underside also. Make a pass to lay a bead in the centre of the joint. Clean off the slag and lay two more beads. Finally, lay a reinforcing bead. You will need to weave the electrode from side to side as you move along the joint to achieve a wide enough bead.

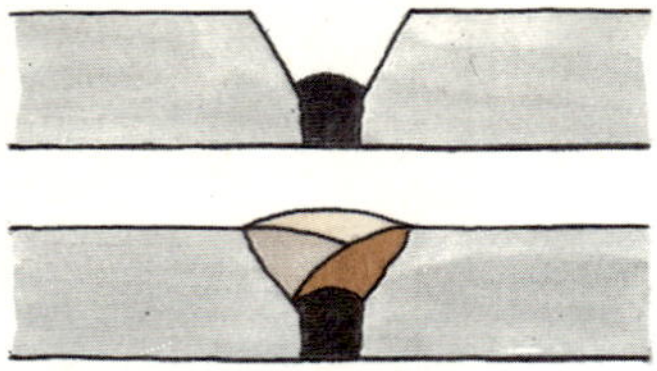

Reinforcing bead
Make four passes to butt joint really thick metal. The first pass (top) deposits the bead in the centre of the joint. It must penetrate to form a small bead on the other side. Make the second and third passes side by side to fill the gap. Finish the joint with a reinforcing bead (bottom).

Corner weld
To join on the outside of a corner, fill the right angle gap between the two edges. For thin metal lay one bead down the centre, or fill the gap with weld as for a bevelled butt joint.

Edge weld
Weave a bead across the two edges for a side by side join.

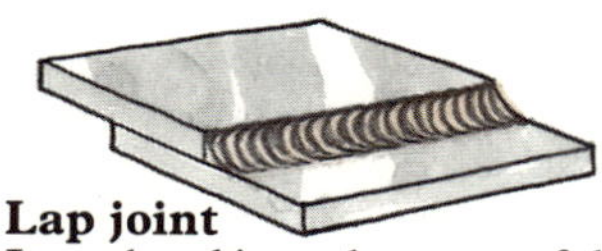

Lap joint
Lay a bead in each corner of the lap joint. Try to fill the right angle with an even bead. Do not melt too much of the top corner.

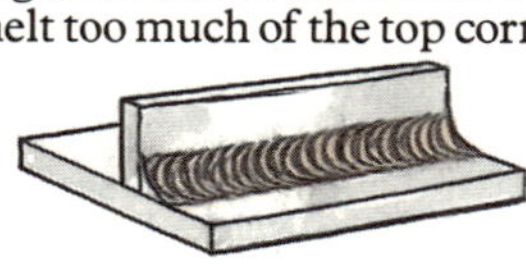

Fillet or right angle weld
Lay a single bead down the centre of the joint, keeping the electrode centred between the two halves of the joint. The thickness of the bead should be approximately that of the metal, and the surface of the bead should be nearly flat with the edges slightly curved where they meet the metal. If necessary, lay more than one bead.

Position welding
The easiest way of welding a joint is to lay it flat on the bench. Welding in this position is known as "flat welding". It is not always possible to work on the bench and it may be necessary to weld a joint *in situ.*

Vertical welding
The most difficult part of welding a vertical joint is keeping the molten metal from falling out of the puddle. The arc must be kept short and the puddle kept small to encourage the weld to freeze quickly.

For welding sheet metal over 3mm thick use the vertical-up method. Use 8 or 10 swg rods.

Lay wider beads for a large fillet or bevelled joint by weaving the rod from side to side.

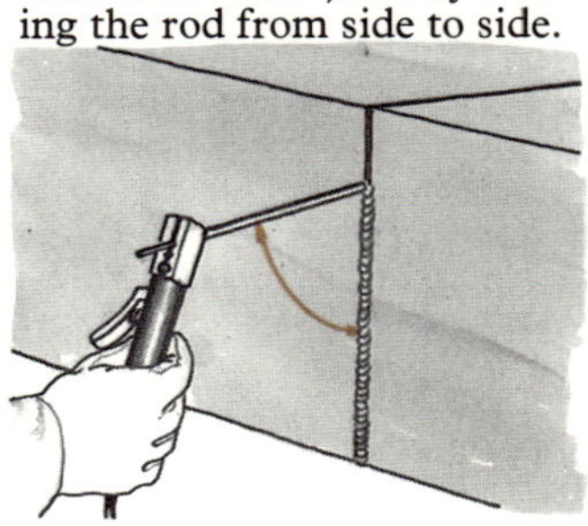

Vertical up welding
Point the electrode up slightly and strike an arc depositing a small amount of metal at the base of the joint. Quickly raise the tip with a wrist movement, which lengthens the arc before depositing more metal on that previously laid. Continue with this "whipping" motion up the entire joint.

Vertical down welding
For sheet metal up to 3mm thick work from top to bottom. Hold the electrode centrally on the joint pointing upward and lay a bead at a steady rate. Large diameter rods are difficult to control so use as small a rod as will do the job.

Horizontal and overhead welding
To prevent the bead sagging, the movement of the electrode must be slightly faster than for other positions. Make sure that falling sparks or molten metal cannot get inside your collar or gauntlets.

Needles and Skewers

Needles are extremely ancient tools, starting life about 14,000 years ago as bone, flint or thorn awls used to punch holes in animal hides. Later a notch was incorporated to carry thread, and by the Bronze Age, the eye had been developed. The Romans used bronze needles and steel needles, probably from China, were brought to Europe by the Moors in the Middle Ages.

Upholsterer's Needle

SIZE: *Length:* 100 to 400mm
Gauge: 15 to 11
MATERIAL: Steel
USE: General upholstery sewing

Upholstery needles can be round or bayonet pointed, and are usually double ended, either with two round points, two bayonet points or one of each. Use bayonet points for stitching edges of rolls. For heavy duty work use a mattress needle, a tougher version of the upholsterer's needle.

Needles are measured by gauge as well as length. The higher the gauge number, the thinner the needle.

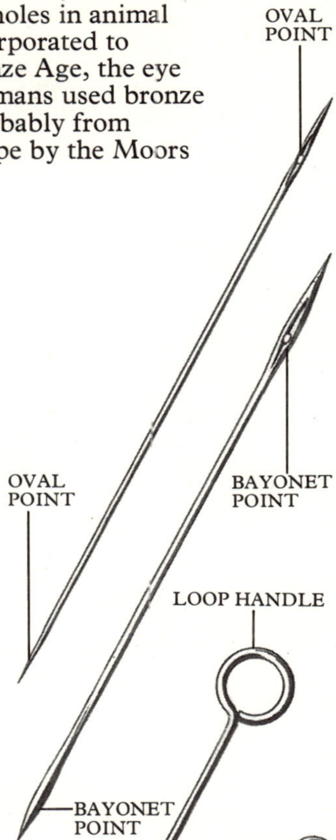

Upholsterer's Skewer

SIZE: 75 to 100mm
MATERIAL: Steel
USE: To hold upholstery temporarily in place

The skewer is used to anchor upholstery work in place while adjustments are made for fit before final tacking, sewing or gluing, or while preliminary stitching is done.

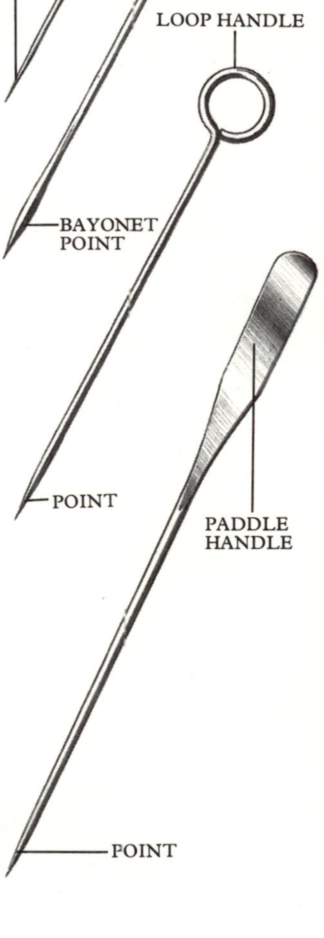

Upholsterer's Regulator

SIZE: 150 to 300mm
MATERIAL: Steel
USE: To adjust stuffing

The upholsterer's regulator is spiked at one end and paddle-shaped at the other to make it easy to hold. It is poked through the hessian covering and used to smooth out or redistribute the stuffing.

Half Circular Needle

SIZE: *Length:* 50 to 150mm;
Gauge: 17 to 14
MATERIAL: Steel
USE: For general upholstery work inaccessible to straight needles

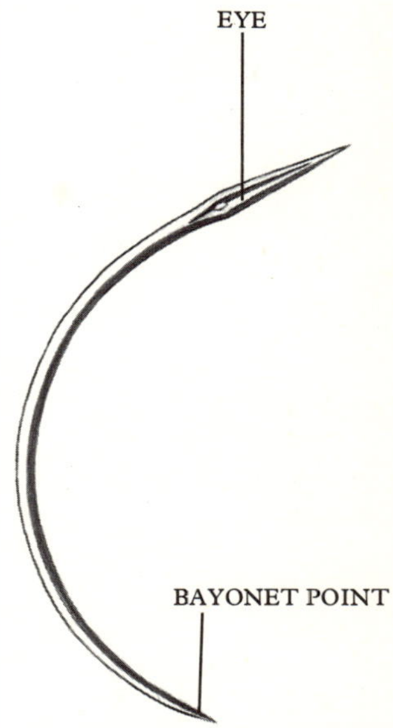

Half circular needles are the most useful, as nearly all upholstery work is done in confined places or at awkward angles. Curved needles make it easy to sew on flat or on fixed surfaces. They usually have a bayonet point.

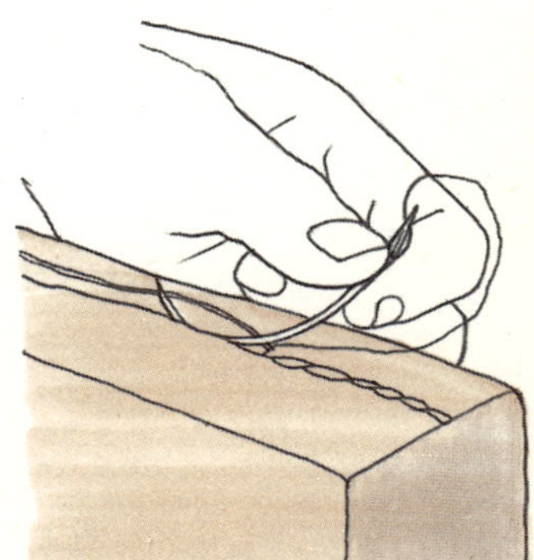

Sewing at awkward angles
The half circular needle carries the thread easily through the stitch where the material itself cannot be manipulated.

Repairing an edge tear
Half circular needles are particularly useful for repairing tears near a piped edge. The stitching technique is called "frenching".

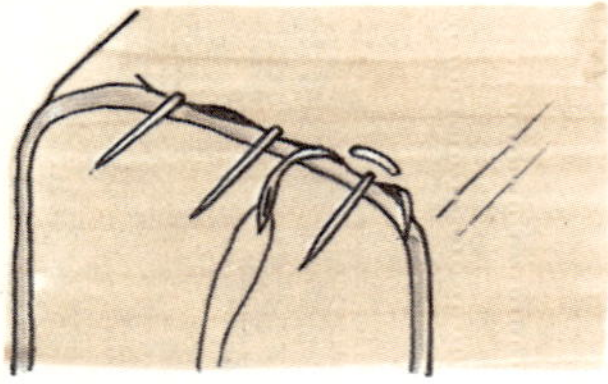

1. *Fold the far edge of the tear under 6mm. Secure the torn edge close to the piping with upholsterer's skewers. (Darning needles make a reasonable substitute.) Thread the needle with upholsterer's twine, knotted at the end.*

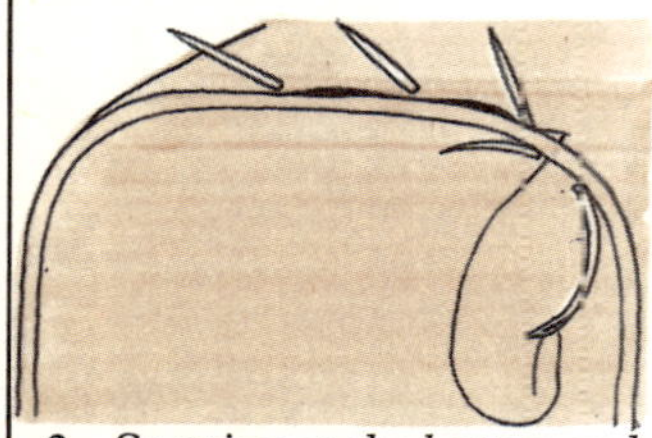

2. *Starting at the bottom end of the tear, push needle up through cover and back again.*

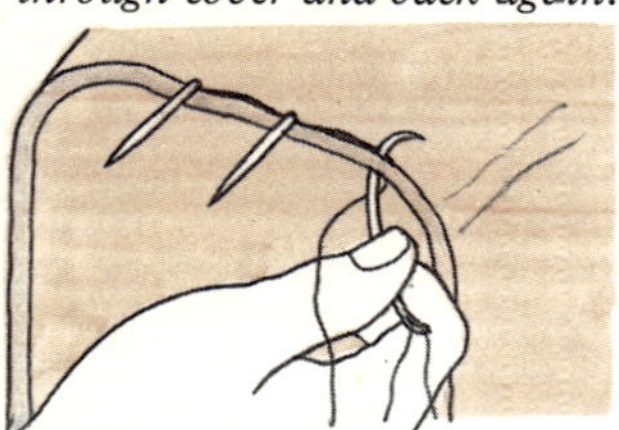

3. *Take needle back 6mm. Push it under piping to outside edge. Make another stitch through side cover just below piping.*

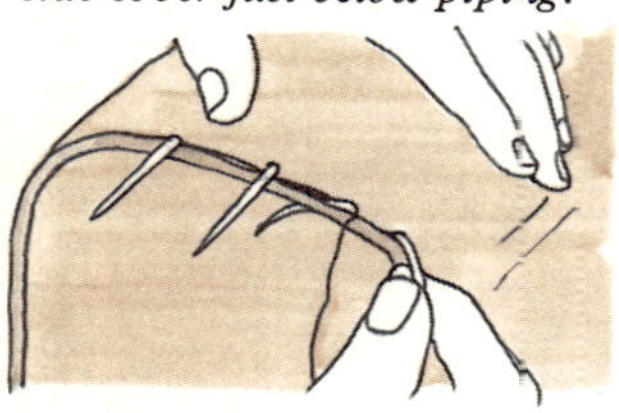

4. *Pull thread tightly to close tear. Push needle back up under piping and pull thread tight. Pass needle through the torn cover and then back under piping. Pull thread again. Continue process, removing skewers as you go, taking stitching about 12mm beyond tear.*

Sail Needle

SIZE: *Length:* 62 to 125mm;
Gauge: 18 to 6
MATERIAL: Steel
USE: To make and repair sails

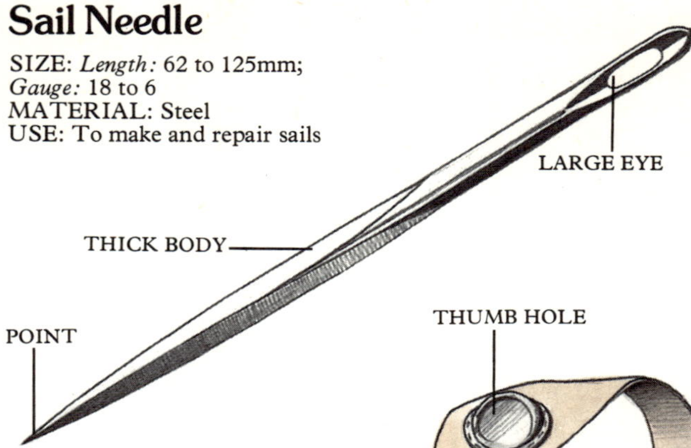

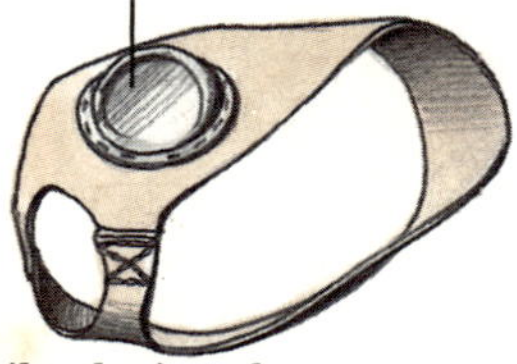

Sailmaker's palm

Sail needles are extremely strong, chunky needles with large rectangular eyes. They are used with a leather sailmaker's palm, which makes it easier to push them through canvas.

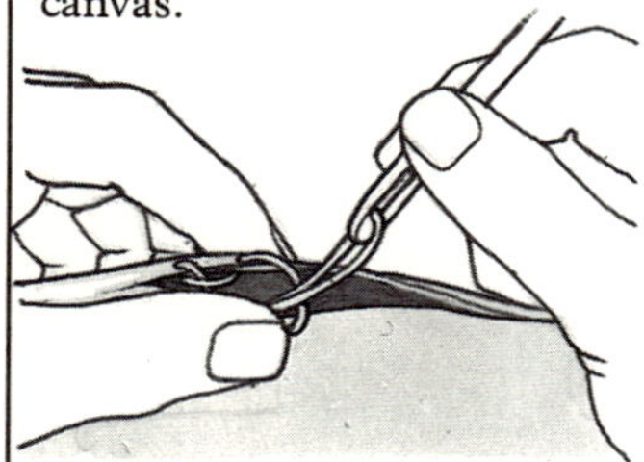

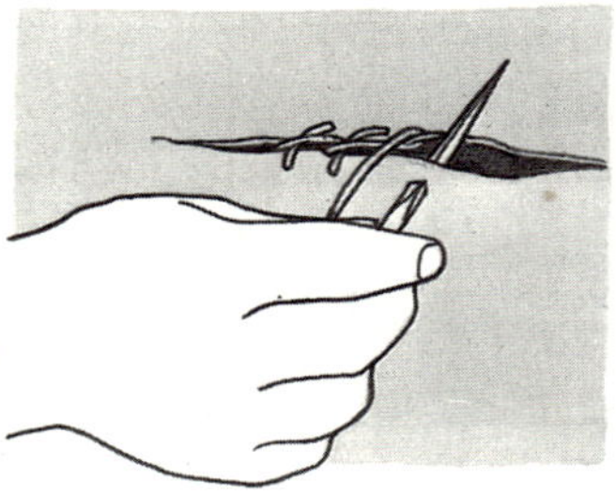

Mending a sail
Double the twine and grease it with a candle. Push the needle up one side of the tear from below, take the twine across the hole and push the needle down through the other side.

Bring the needle up through the tear, across the stitch just made and start again, continuing to the end of the tear.
Protect the repaired slit with beeswax or candle grease.

Leather Needle

SIZE: *Length:* 50 to 175mm;
Gauge: 18 to 14
MATERIAL: Steel
USE: To sew leather

The curved leather needle has a bayonet point and is used for stitching leather to make bags, shoes, saddles etc.

There are also flat leather lacing needles which have a triangular shaped eye to take lacing thongs.

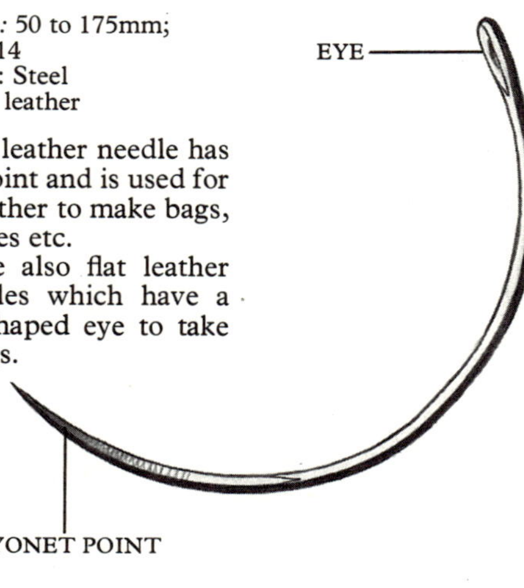

Spring Needle

SIZE: *Length:* 100 to 150mm; *Gauge:* 10
MATERIAL: Steel
USE: To attach springs to webbing

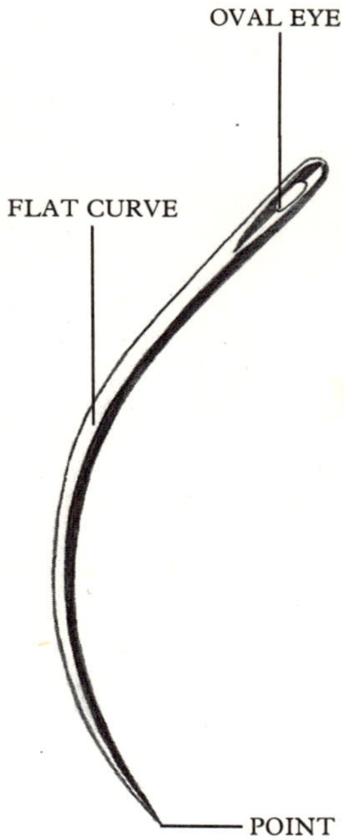

The spring needle is a stout, curved needle used to sew springs to upholstery webbing and hessian. It can also be used where a half circular needle would be the right shape but not strong enough. Use strong, six-cord spring twine for attaching springs.

Springing
Whether you are springing a new chair or repairing an old one, make sure the springs are fixed upright to the webbing and in straight lines in all directions. To avoid damage, use a blanket-covered workbench for all upholstery work.

Fixing new springs
With the chair (or stool) upside down on the bench, arrange the springs, bottoms up, roughly in position. Nail the webbing to the chair frame using the webbing stretcher (see page 201).

Lace the strips of webbing which go from front to back securely under each spring in the row. Interlace the side-to-side webbing, making sure that the strips cross over above a spring. Stitch the springs to the webbing at the junction of the two webbing strips, using three or four fixing ties for each spring, depending on the size of the spring and the dimensions of the chair itself.

After threading the webbing through the springs, pull it tight and tack to the frame.

Thread the spring needle with twine, and stitch down the first spring. Begin with a slip knot. Without tying off the threads, move on to the adjacent spring and repeat the sequence. Work from front to back and tie off the last spring with a double knot. Trim the twine.

Turn the chair upright and secure the tops of the springs. Cover with hessian, tacked to the top edges of the seat frame. Leave 25mm surplus all around. Sew the tops of the springs to the hessian as before.

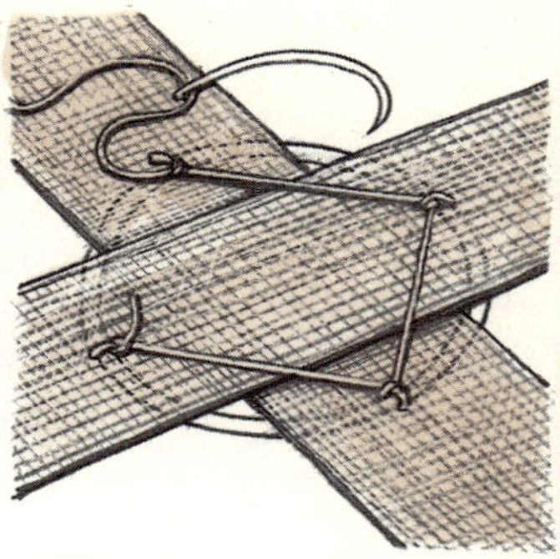

Stitching the springs
Stitch the spring at equidistant points with a half-hitch or other strong knot. At the end of the operation the spring should be anchored to both strips of webbing.

Tying springs
Larger chairs (nine springs or more) will need the springs to be additionally tied in with strong, soft twine.

Turn the chair over. Secure a length of twine to the back of the seat frame with a tack. Tie each spring with two knots. Tack the twine to the front rail. Follow the sequence below.

Do not compress the springs more than 50mm below their free-standing height, as this makes an uncomfortable seat.

Cover the springs with hessian and continue as before.

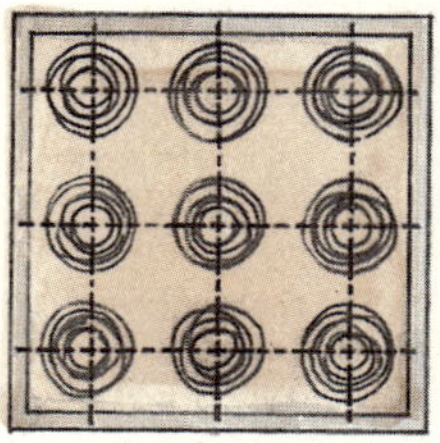

Tying sequence
Beginning with the middle row work toward the front, tying the top of each spring. Tie each side row, then work across the chair, following the same order.

Repairing springs
Turn the chair upside down and take off the hessian and webbing, using an old chisel and mallet to remove tacks. Note the position of the old springs, and replace any if necessary. Then dust the inside thoroughly and proceed as for new springs.

Brushes, Rollers and Paint Sprayers

Brushes of some kind must have been used by the cave painters of the Old Stone Age, but what they were made of is not known. To come to more recent times, the accounts for work done at Westminster in 1352, quoted by L.F. Salzman in his *Building in England* include "2 dussen graye (badger) tailes and 4 dussen quyllis whereof were made pensellis and for threde had for byndynge of the same." For St Stephen's Chapel in the same year "2½d was paid for 30 quills of peacocks and swans and squirrel tails for the painters' brushes and thread for binding the brushes and pencils and 12d for a pound of pigs' bristles."

The construction of brushes

Before being bound to the stock of the brush, the filling is "set" in pitch, resin or more commonly in vulcanized rubber, which is impervious to all the normal materials a paint brush is likely to encounter. Pitch and resin may dissolve in volatile spirit and are therefore used mainly for dry brushes such as dusting brushes or for brushes used only with water such as washing down brushes.

The ends of the filling are dipped in the setting and bound while still soft to hold them firmly in the stock. There are several ways of binding, the most familiar being the metal ferrule. This is a sheet of thin metal wrapped around the filling and riveted or pinned to the stock section of the handle. Seamless ferrules are pressed onto the filling and handle in one continuous band. On other brushes, the filling is a circular bunch of filaments, set and bound to the stock with wire or string. Each group of filaments is known as a knot. Knotted brushes can also be bound with sheet metal.

Some brushes have the filling divided into small circular bunches, bound with string or wire and set with rubber or pitch into holes drilled at regular intervals in the stock.

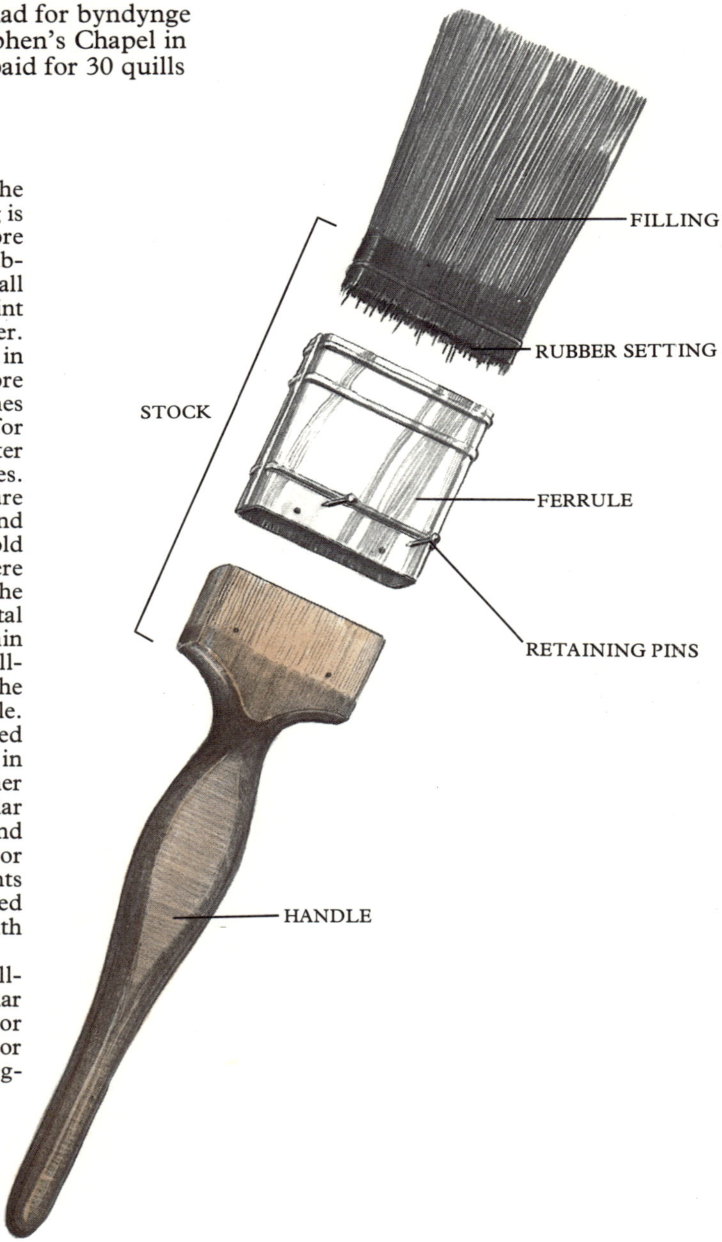

The filling
The filling is the part of the brush commonly referred to as the "bristles". This is a misnomer, now entrenched in the language, as strictly speaking, the word describes only one of the common fillings.

Bristle
Bristle filling, obtained from the coat of a boar, is used in the best quality paint brushes, and can be black, white, gray or yellow. The natural construction of bristles makes them ideal for applying paint. Each individual filament is tapered and finally splits at the end which helps when "laying off" the paint; the split ends are known as "flags". The barbed surface of the bristle enables them to retain more paint than other fillings, and a bristle brush is very resilient, springing back to its original shape when flexed. However, when used with water-based paint, brushes with bristle filling may swell out of shape.

Horsehair
Horsehair filling comes from the mane and tail of a horse. Horsehair is perfectly smooth and lacks the resilience of bristle. It is best used to bulk out a filling in combination with better quality filaments.

Oxhair
Oxhair filaments are very similar to horsehair, but somewhat coarser. Available in black, brown and white they are used for grainers and also for professional signwriting brushes.

Badgerhair
A soft yet springy filling used for softeners. They are easily recognized by the gradation of their colour from white to black.

Fibre
Fibre is a cheap, tough filling obtained from the stem of a palm tree. Its natural colour is yellowish white, but it is often dyed to match better quality filaments when used in combination with them. It is often used in washing down brushes, and wall brushes designed for rough surfaces.

Synthetic filling
Many modern paint brushes are now made with nylon or other synthetic filaments. Good quality synthetic fillings are very hard-wearing and apply paint well. The filaments are made to resemble genuine bristle, being tapered, flagged and textured to hold the paint.

Squirrel and sable
These are soft brush fillings, used in short lengths only for the thin paint brushes used for signwriting and graining.

Choosing a brush
A good quality brush is an investment as long as you clean and store it properly after use. It will hold more paint and apply it better than a cheap brush, and is less likely to shed its filaments.

Test the resilience of a new brush by stroking it against a firm surface as though you were painting. The filling should flex without spreading too much and should spring quickly back to shape.

Fan the filling with your fingers to ensure that it is solidly set and bound to the stock. Make sure that a ferruled brush is firmly attached to its handle.

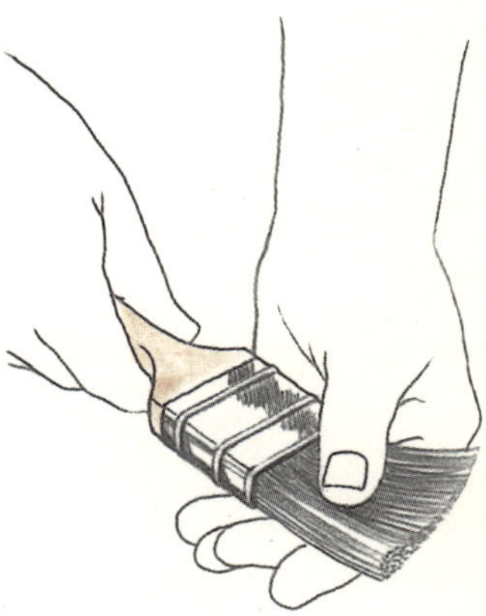

Testing the brush
Fan the brush to check that the filling is firmly set and bound securely to the stock.

Flat Paint Brush

OTHER NAME: Varnish brush
SIZE: 12 to 100mm
MATERIAL: *Filling:* bristle, fibre, synthetic, mixed; *Binding:* plated steel; *Handle:* hardwood
USE: To apply paint or varnish

Flat paint brushes are used for applying gloss or semi-matt paint to woodwork.

Do not overload your brush. If you consistently dip it too far into the paint it will begin to run down the handle filling the roots of the bristles. Such paint could be difficult to remove when cleaning the brush.

Hold the brush so that you can move your wrist easily in both directions. Apply the paint in even strokes, flexing the bristle against the surface to make the paint flow down to the tip of the brush. To spread the paint evenly, change the direction of the brush strokes frequently, finishing with light upward strokes to prevent running. Take particular care around mouldings which exert uneven pressure on the bristles squeezing out excess paint to form unwelcome runs.

Normal interior paintwork will need one undercoat which should be left for 16 hours before rubbing down lightly with fine glass paper. Apply one or two top coats as directed by the manufacturer.

Charging the brush
Dip about a third of the filling into the paint, and touch it lightly on both sides of the lip of the container to remove excess paint from the outside.

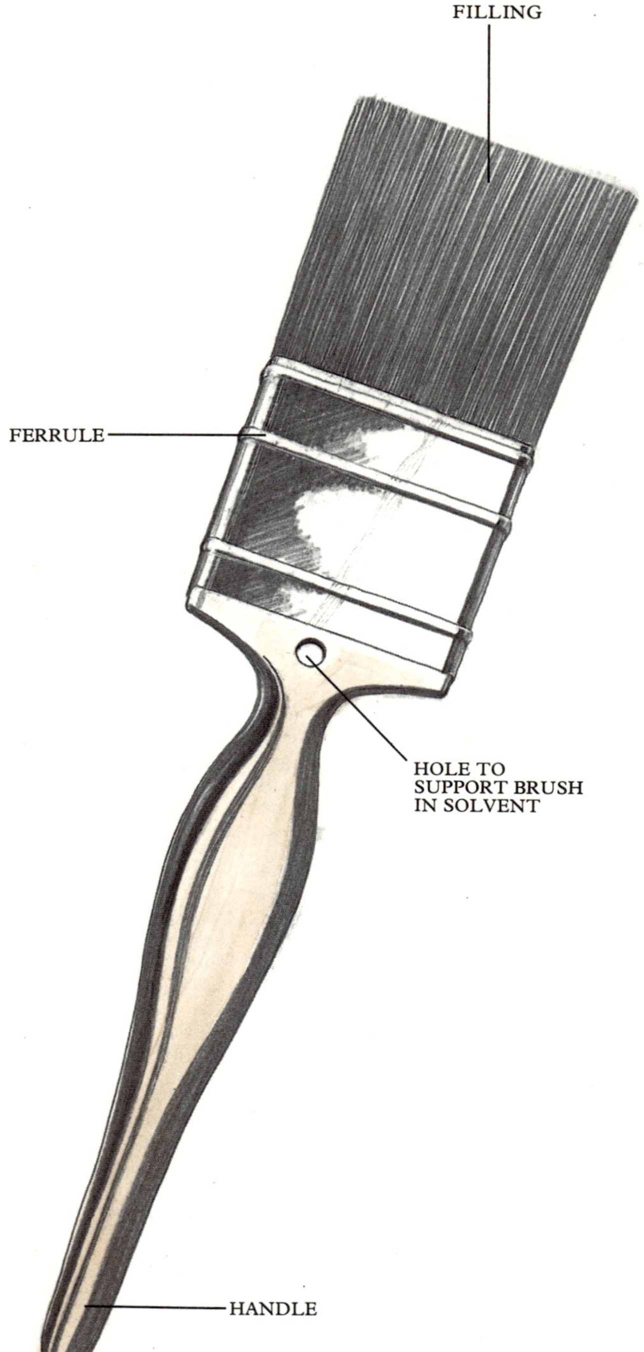

Painting doors
Painting doors is an exacting job and requires great care if you are to achieve a smooth finish. Panelled doors are particularly tricky as their mouldings encourage paint to run. Do not wear woollen clothing which might shed hairs that stick to the work. Remove all fittings from the door and wedge it in an open position.

Panelled doors
Panelled doors should be painted in the following sequence:
1. Mouldings
2. Panels
3. Centre uprights
4. Horizontal rails
5. Side rails
6. Edges
7. Frame

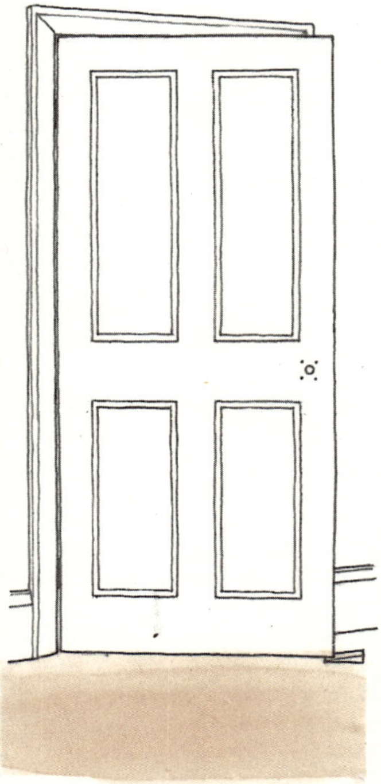

When painting any kind of door, make sure that you lay off the paint in the direction of the grain in each section of the panelled door.

Doors are usually painted with knockproof gloss paint for protection but will still need an undercoat. Apply this in the sequence shown above.

Flush doors
When painting flush doors, you must work at a reasonable speed to avoid join marks showing between sections of paint work. Start at the top. Apply paint across the top section of the door using horizontal and vertical strokes (1). Without reloading the brush, smooth out the entire section with horizontal strokes (2). Finally lay off with light vertical/upward strokes (3). Continue in the same way painting down the door (4).

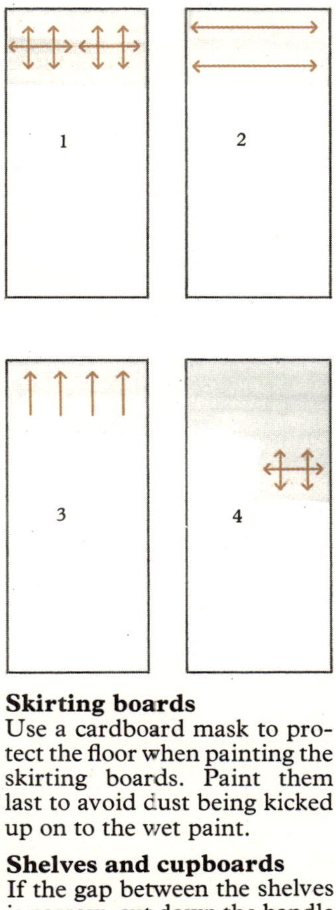

Skirting boards
Use a cardboard mask to protect the floor when painting the skirting boards. Paint them last to avoid dust being kicked up on to the wet paint.

Shelves and cupboards
If the gap between the shelves is narrow, cut down the handle of an old brush to avoid marking the paintwork. Paint the inside of a cupboard first to avoid touching doors covered with wet paint.

One Knot Paint Brush

OTHER NAME: Ground brush
SIZE: 50 to 68mm
MATERIAL: *Filling:* bristle, mixed; *Binding:* copper wire, sheet copper; *Handle:* hardwood
USE: To apply paint and varnish

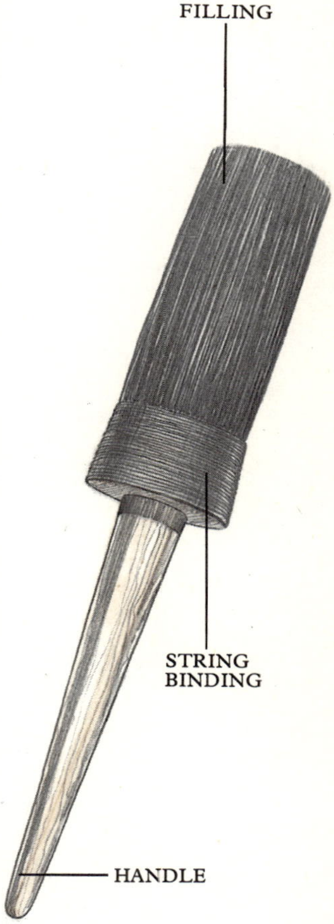

The traditional one knot brush has now been almost entirely superseded by the flat paint brush. They are however particularly good for the application of thick or heavy paint. Knotted brushes have to be "run-in" for a while before they can spread the paint evenly. Older painters would often use the brush as a duster until it was sufficiently worked in to perform well as a paint brush.

Sash Tool

OTHER NAME: Sash brush
SIZE: 15 to 25mm
MATERIAL: *Filling:* bristle; *Binding:* string, aluminium, plated steel; *Handle:* hardwood
USE: To paint window frames

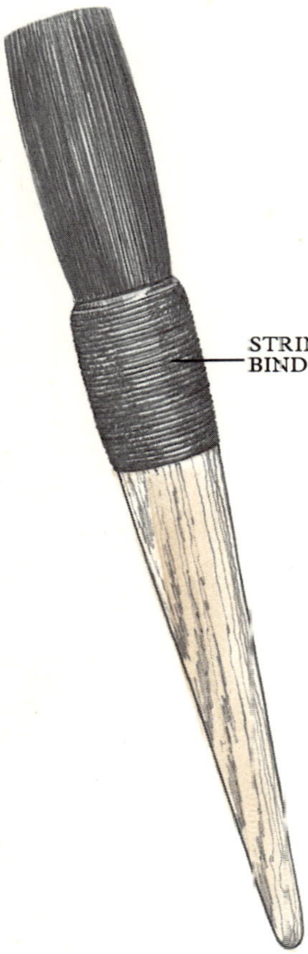

The sash tool is an old-fashioned brush which is now hardly ever used, and most manufacturers have dropped it from their catalogues. Most painters today use a standard 12 to 25mm wide flat paint brush to paint window frames.

Care of brushes
For overnight protection, suspend the brush, with the bristles up to the ferrule in a suitable solvent. For oil-based paint use turpentine or paint thinner, and for emulsion paint use clean water. Make sure that the container is deep enough to keep the bristles off the bottom. When using a chemical solvent avoid plastic containers as they might dissolve along with the paint.

Overnight soaking
Suspend the brush in a container of suitable solvent by passing a rod through the hole drilled in the brush handle.

When you have finished the job, wipe off any excess paint and soak out the brush in a container of solvent. When you have removed as much paint as you can, wash the brush in warm soapy water to remove the solvent and partially dissolved paint. Shake out the excess water and blot the filling with an absorbent rag, gently smoothing the bristles into place with the fingers.

Removing excess paint
Wipe off the brush on old newspapers to get rid of as much paint as possible before you soak the brush in solvent.

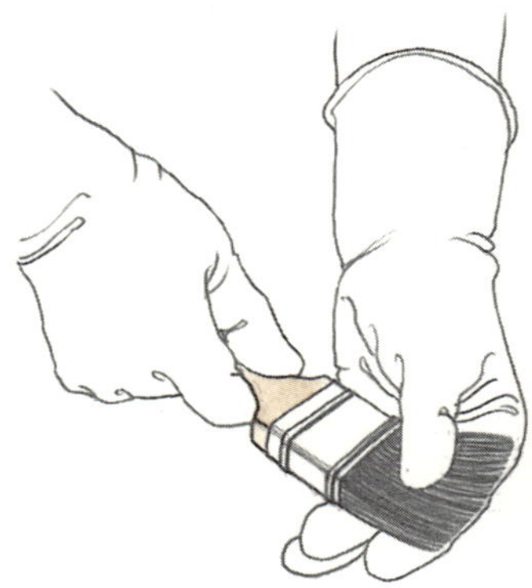

Removing dissolved paint
Work out remaining paint by squeezing and fanning out the filling with your fingers.

If you will not need to use the brushes for some time, protect the filling by wrapping it up when it is completely dry.

Long term storage

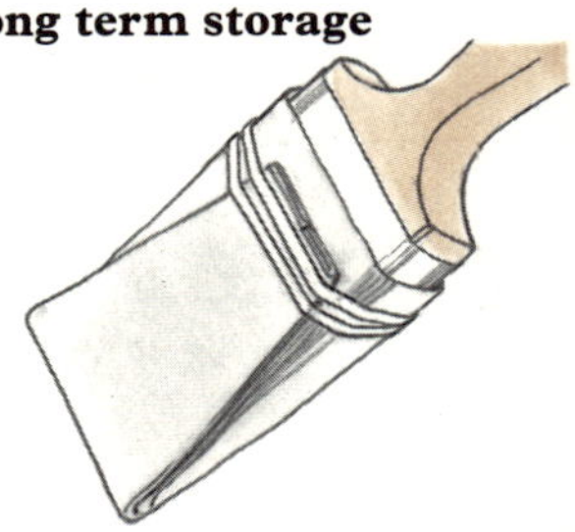

Wrap brush heads in brown paper or aluminium foil, and secure with a rubber band.

Bevelled Sash Tool

OTHER NAMES: Trim-brush, cutting-in tool
SIZE: 18mm
MATERIAL: *Filling:* bristle, synthetic, mixed; *Binding:* plated steel; *Handle:* hardwood
USE: To paint window frames

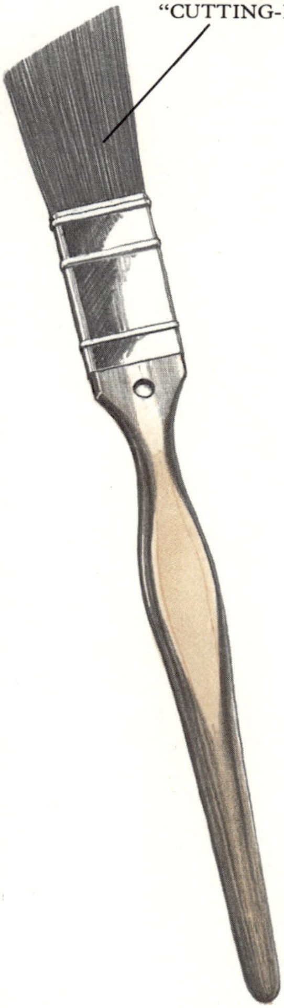

The bevelled sash tool is a small flat paint brush, with the filling trimmed to an angle. This makes it easier to paint up to the edge of window glass and into the corners of the frame.

Painting around glass
With a little practice, it is not difficult to paint right up to the glass with a slow, free-hand stroke. In fact, a slight overlapping of paint onto the glass seals the gap between putty and glass to make the frame weatherproof. If you do not feel confident, use some form of paint shield. Several commercial shields are available, but a sheet of stiff cardboard will do as well. If you do overshoot, remember that paint can be neatly removed with a razor blade when dry.

Using a paint shield

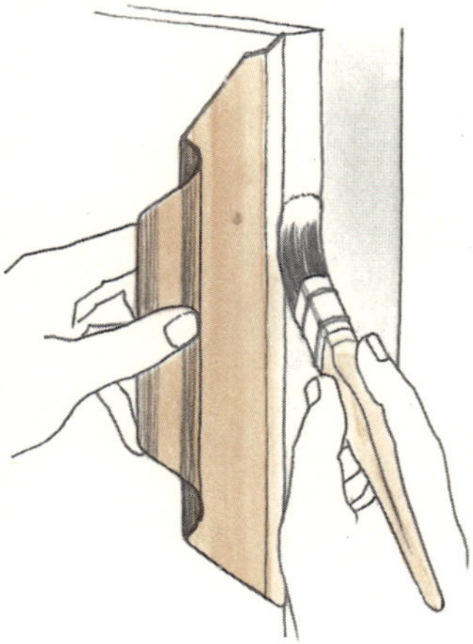

Press the paint shield into the joint between glass and frame. Hold it in place while painting.

Using masking tape

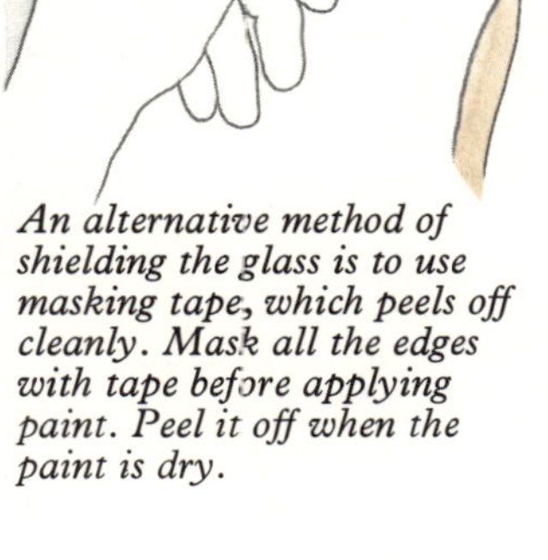

An alternative method of shielding the glass is to use masking tape, which peels off cleanly. Mask all the edges with tape before applying paint. Peel it off when the paint is dry.

Casement windows
When painting casement windows leave the stay in position to control the angle of the window. Paint it last if it is to match the window frame, or mask it with tape.

Paint as follows:
1. Rebates, where the frame meets the glass
2. Crossbars
3. Cross rails
4. Side rails and edges
5. Window frame

Fasten the window open before starting on the cross rails.

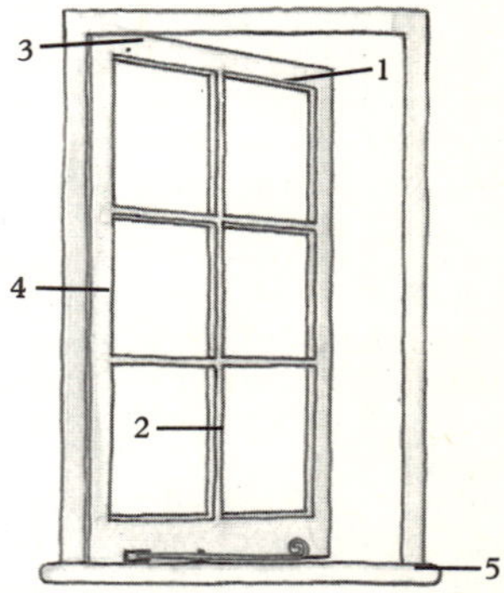

Sash windows
Open the window top and bottom and move sash cords out of the way. Paint the bottom meeting rail and as far up the vertical section of the sash as you can go. Almost close the window and paint the rest of the top sash. Paint the bottom sash followed by the frame. When the paint has dried, paint the top 150mm of the outside runners, and with the bottom sash closed, paint the whole of the inside runners.

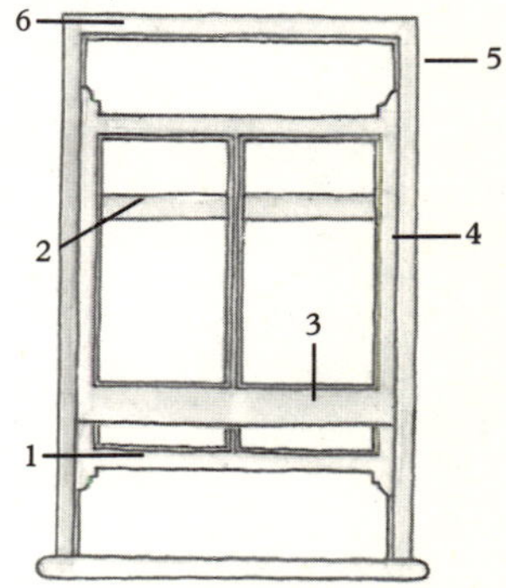

Before starting, push the bottom sash up and the top sash down to overlap by 150mm.

Wall Brush

OTHER NAMES: Distemper brush, kalsomine brush, paste brush
SIZE: 100 to 200mm
MATERIAL: *Filling:* bristle, fibre, mixed, synthetic; *Binding:* plated steel, copper wire, sheet copper; *Handle:* hardwood
USE: To paint large areas

Wall brushes come in several forms. The traditional model has two or three knots, bound with copper wire or sheet metal. The best known modern version has a one piece handle and stock and is bound like a flat paint brush. The stock extends as a wooden wedge around which bristles are grouped forming a reservoir for the paint.

Another type, sometimes called the "Dutch" pattern, has a turned handle jointed into a wooden stock. The filling is bound to the stock with a metal ferrule.

Large brushes can become very tiring to use, so do not overload your brush.

Emulsion paint will dry evenly, regardless of brush strokes. If it appears patchy when dry, apply a second coat. Gloss paint on the other hand should be laid off with light vertical strokes. Gloss paint will probably require two undercoats followed by a top coat. The unfinished edges of gloss paint-work should be "picked up" as quickly as possible before they dry out, or they may show when the job is finished.

Use a wide, soft wall brush to apply paste to wallpaper. (See page 55 for method.)

Tie a length of string across the paste bucket to support the brush between pasting sessions.

Using the wall brush

Hold the brush like a flat paint brush and then apply the paint in alternating vertical and horizontal strokes to achieve an even cover. Emulsion paint should dry evenly, but gloss paint needs more care.

Painting a wall with gloss paint

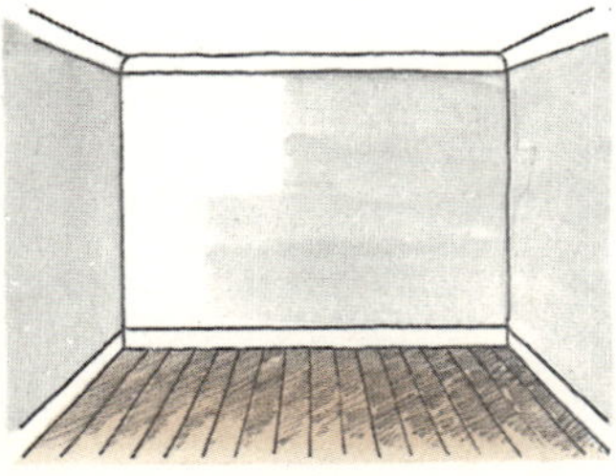

Work in vertical sections across the wall, starting from the ceiling. This blends the wet edges together. Pick up any unblended edges quickly.

Washing Down Brush

OTHER NAME: Wash down brush
SIZE: 150mm
MATERIAL: *Filling:* bristle, fiber, mixed; *Binding:* copper wire, sheet copper; *Handle:* hardwood
USE: To wash walls and ceilings

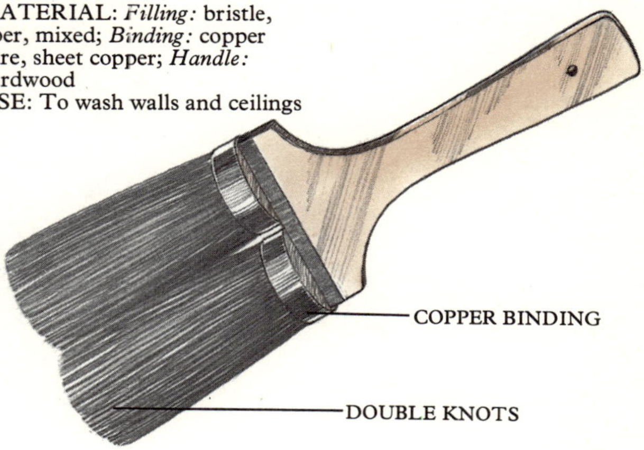

The washing down brush is used for washing off old paint work and for soaking wallpaper prior to stripping. It is traditionally a two knot brush, resembling a wall brush but with shorter, cheaper quality bristles as filling.

Worn wall brushes will make very good washing down brushes.

Paint Pad

OTHER NAME: Brush pad
SIZE: 50 × 25 to 200 × 87mm
MATERIAL: *Holder:* plastic; *Pad:* mohair covered plastic foam
USE: To apply paint

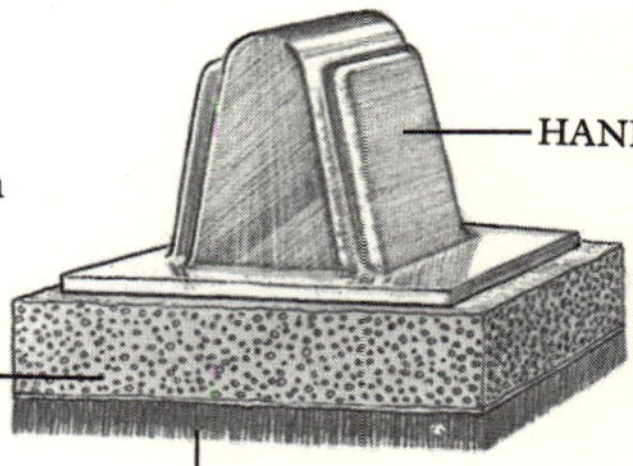

An entirely new kind of paint applicator, the paint pad has very fine mohair bristles backed up by plastic foam which is clipped into a holder. The pads apply paint quickly and evenly, achieving a very smooth finish, but they are not as versatile as a traditional paint brush.

Clean the pad's fine bristles thoroughly immediately after use. Blot excess paint onto old newspapers, and remove the pad from its holder to clean it in the appropriate solvent.

Dusting Brush

OTHER NAME: Jamb brush
SIZE: 87 to 100mm
MATERIAL: *Filling:* bristle, horsehair, fibre, mixed; *Handle/stock:* hardwood
USE: To brush down paintwork before painting

The dusting brush is designed to remove the inevitable layer of dust which accumulates after paint has been rubbed down, especially if filling has been applied to mend cracks.

Mottler

SIZE: 25 to 100mm
MATERIAL: *Filling:* hoghair, camelhair, squirrelhair; *Binding:* plated steel; *Stock:* hardwood
USE: To produce imitation wood grain effects

With the mottler a skilled grainer can move wet colour over the work to create a wood grain effect, or lift it, to leave pale, soft edged areas. The pressure across the filling is varied by the fingers to produce alternate dark and light stripes of colour.

The mottler has no handle as such; the stock doubles as handle, giving the fingers easy access to the filling.

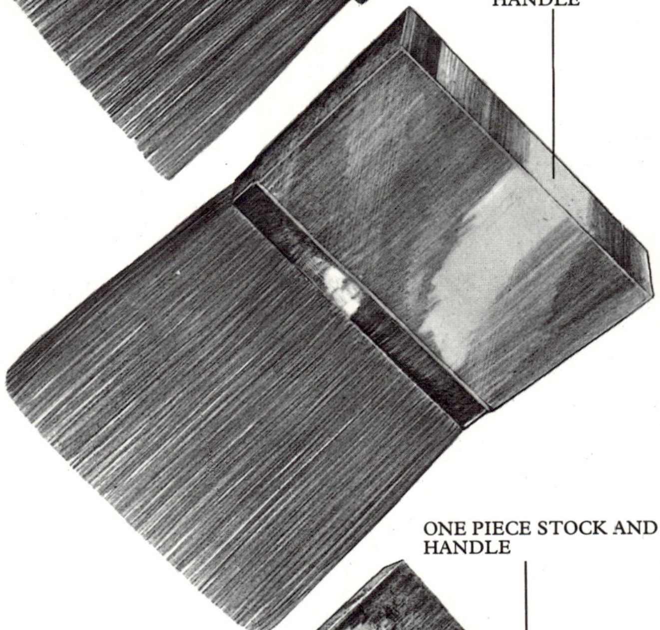

Pencil Overgrainer

SIZE: 25 to 100mm
MATERIAL: *Filling:* squirrel hair, sable; *Binding:* plated steel; *Stock:* hardwood
USE: To produce imitation wood grain effects

The overgrainer is a row of pencil brushes set into a one piece stock and handle. It is used to draw wood grain effects either by applying colour to a surface or by lifting wet colour off the work leaving lighter areas to make the pattern.

Flogger

SIZE: 100mm
MATERIAL: *Filling:* bristle; *Binding:* plated steel; *Handle:* hardwood
USE: To produce imitation wood grain effects

A flogger is made like a standard paint brush, but has longer bristles than normal.

The flat of the brush is used to strike or "flog" the wet colour to produce a patterned texture which resembles some types of wood grain.

Softener

SIZE: 62 to 100mm
MATERIAL: *Filling:* badgerhair, hoghair, skunkhair; *Stock/handle:* hardwood
USE: To produce imitation wood grain effects

Once the hard edge lines have been drawn on the work with a fine brush, a grainer softens the edges by stroking the colour with a softener. The whole graining may be softened, or a graduated band produced by leaving one edge sharp while softening the other.

Stippling Brush

SIZE: 100 × 75 to 200 × 150mm
MATERIAL: *Filling:* bristle; *Stock/handle:* hardwood
USE: To produce a texture on a painted surface

Stipplers are used to texture wet paint. A well-textured surface hides many structural irregularities as well as obscuring the brush marks. The ends of the bristles do the actual work as the stippler strikes the wall.

Keep the brush square to the work at all times, but keep on changing the angle of approach to achieve an even texture. Work in overlapping bands.

Stencilling Brush

SIZE: Diameter: 10.5 to 38.5mm
MATERIAL: *Filling:* horsehair, bristle; *Binding:* plated steel; *Handle:* hardwood
USE: To apply paint through a stencil

Using a stencil is the easiest method to paint a motif on a surface, especially if it is to be a repeat pattern.

Cut the shape from thick paper or thin cardboard, lay it flat on a surface, and stipple with a stenciling brush. Do not move the stencil until the motif has been completed.

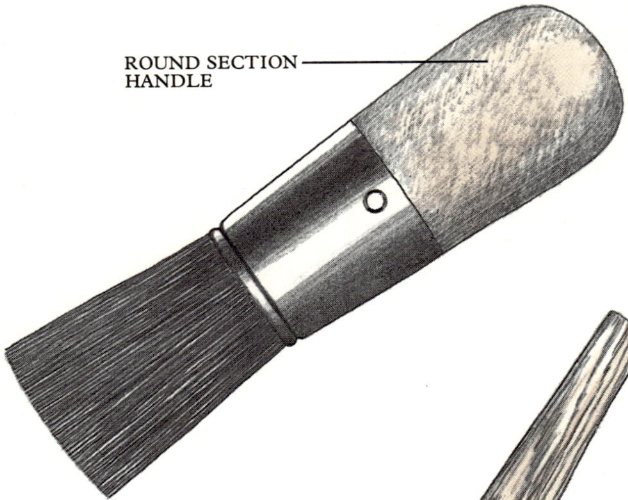

Using the stencil

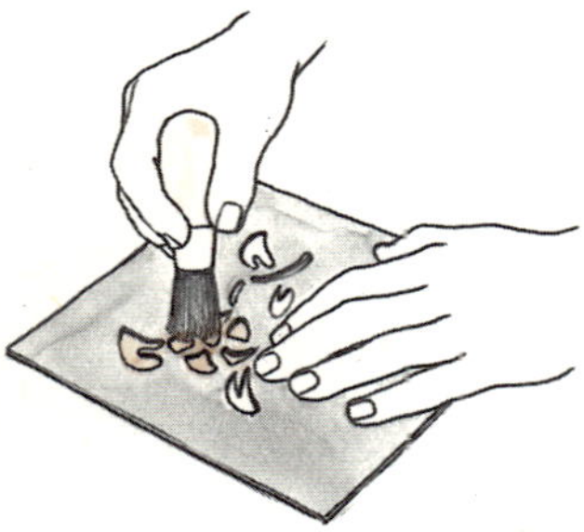

Lightly strike the surface through the stencil with the ends of the bristles, which carry the paint.

Lining Tool

OTHER NAME: Lining fitch
SIZE: *Width:* 6 to 37mm; *Thickness:* 4.5 to 7.5mm
MATERIAL: *Filling:* bristle, horsehair; *Binding:* plated steel; *Handle:* hardwood
USE: To paint straight lines

Painted straight lines are often needed either as decoration or to emphasize a particular area.

The lining tool is specially designed for use with a straight edge. The filling is bound in a rectangular ferrule and is cut at an angle at the end. The paint used should flow easily so that a line can be drawn in one pass, but not be so fluid that it begins to run.

Line up a straight edge, bevel side down, and run the brush against it. Keep the brush upright throughout.

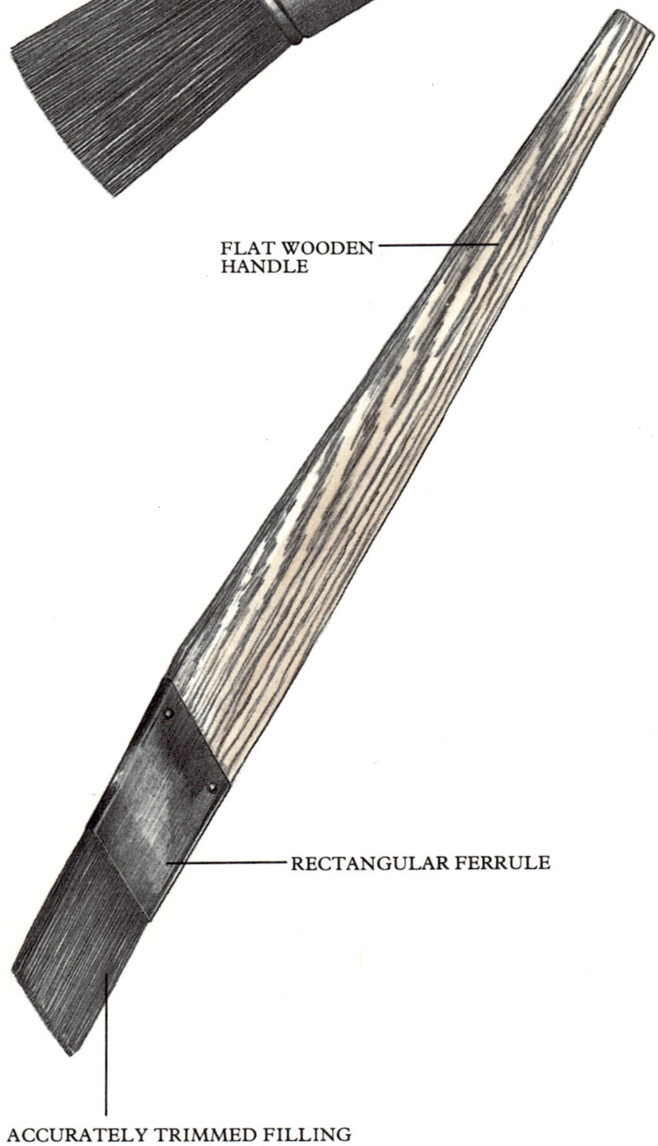

Fitch

SIZE: *Diameter:* 3 to 19.5mm; *Width:* 4.5 to 29.5mm
MATERIAL: *Filling:* bristle; *Binding:* plated steel; *Handle:* hardwood
USE: To paint fine detail

A fitch is used to paint small details or narrow window frames. It is available with round sectioned filling and ferrule, or with the ferrule crimped to flatten the filling.

Crevice Brush

OTHER NAME: Radiator brush
SIZE: 25 to 50mm
MATERIAL: *Filling:* bristle, mixed, synthetic; *Binding:* plated steel; *Handle:* steel, hardwood
USE: To paint in confined spaces

The crevice brush has the bound filling mounted at an angle on a long handle. It is used to apply paint in confined or awkward spaces, such as behind radiators, which could not be reached with a normal paint brush.

Tar Brush

SIZE: Diameter: 45 to 46mm
MATERIAL: *Filling:* bristle; fibre; mixed; *Binding:* plated steel, iron; *Handle:* hardwood
USE: To apply thick paints

The tar brush has a round splayed filling bound either to a short turned handle or to a pole-like handle, up to 1.2m long. It is used to apply pitch-like rust proofing paint to metal surfaces.

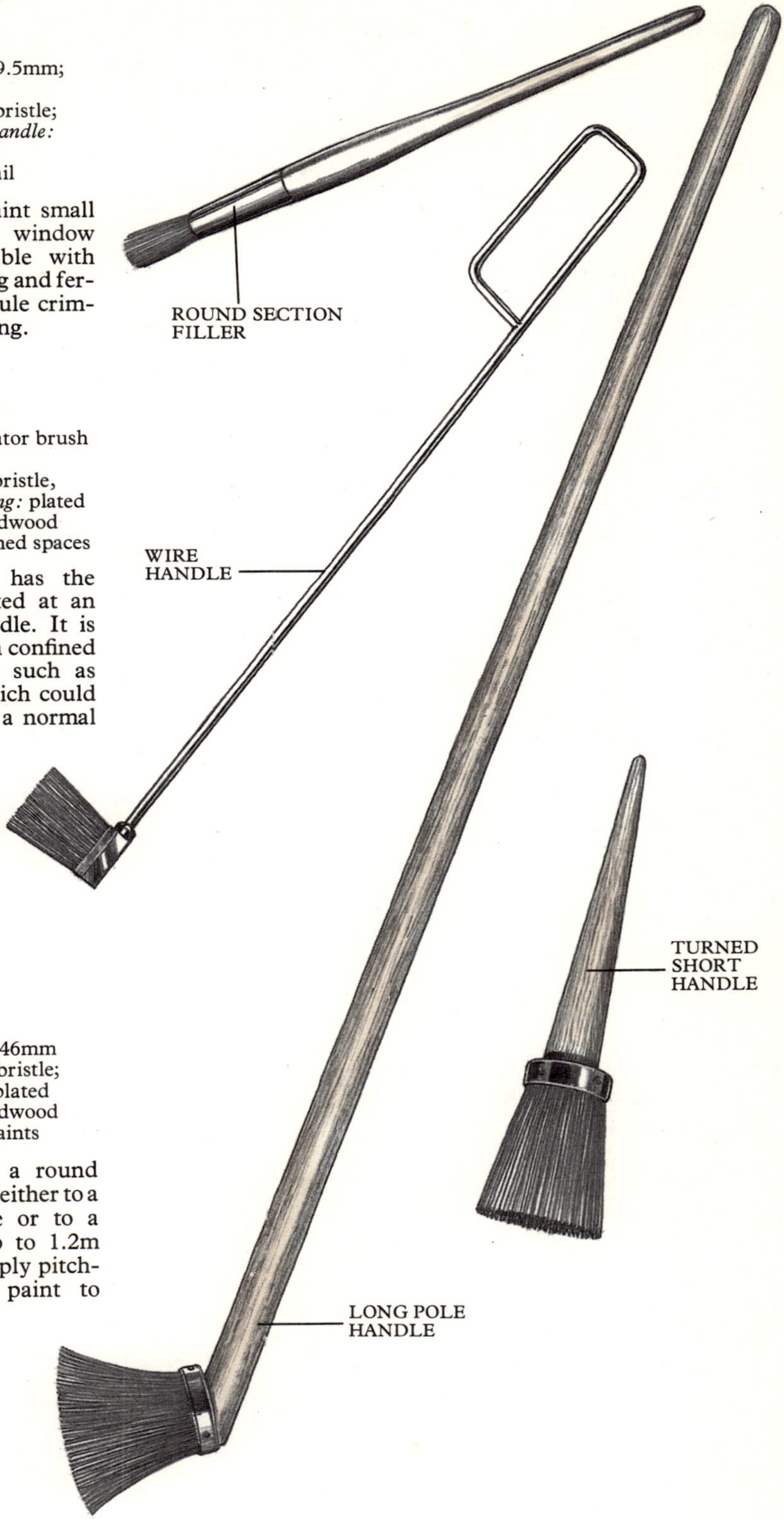

Smoothing Brush

OTHER NAME: Paper hanger's brush
SIZE: Width: 187 to 250mm
MATERIAL: *Filling:* bristle; *Handle:* hardwood
USE: To smooth pasted wallpaper on to the wall

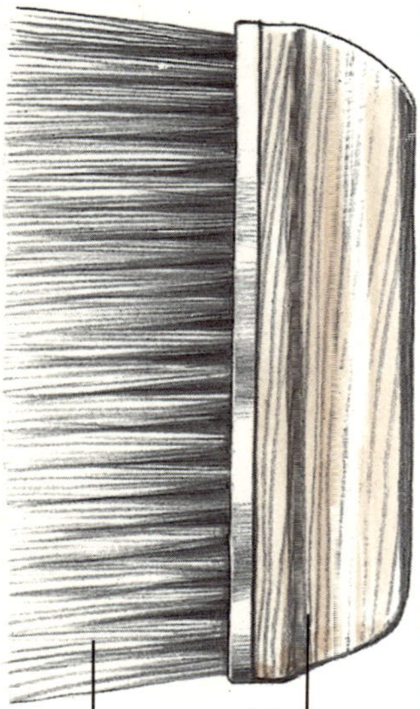

The smoothing brush gives wallpaper a professional finish. Align the strip of paper with a plumbed line or butt it against the previous strip. Brush out lightly by hand, before using the brush. Use the edge of the brush to tap paper into corners.

Using the brush

Work the brush systematically from the centre of the strip outward, smoothing out creases or air bubbles.

Paint Roller

SIZE: 175 to 337mm
MATERIAL: *Sleeve:* lambswool, mohair, polyurethane foam, man-made fibre; *Cage:* steel and plastic; *Handle:* hardwood, plastic
USE: To apply paint over large areas

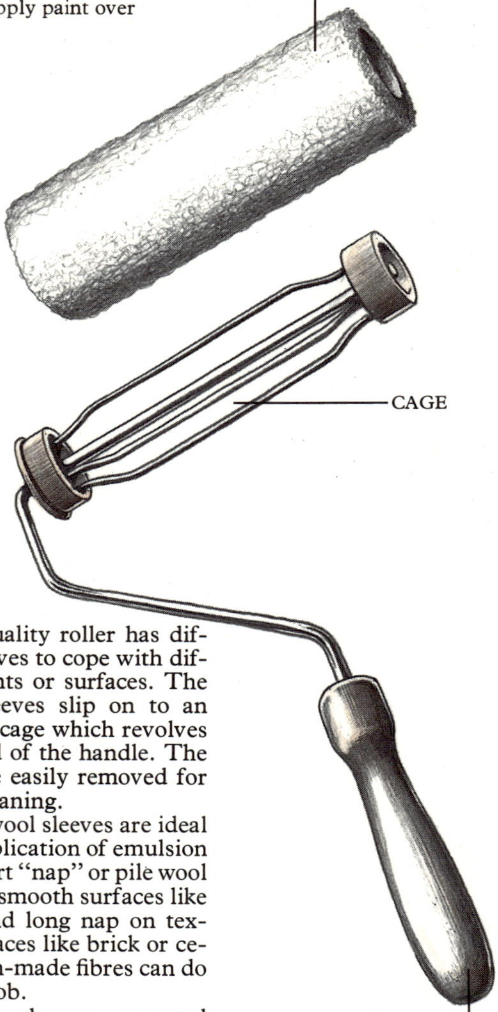

A good quality roller has different sleeves to cope with different paints or surfaces. The hollow sleeves slip on to an open wire cage which revolves on the end of the handle. The sleeves are easily removed for regular cleaning.

Lambswool sleeves are ideal for the application of emulsion paint. Short "nap" or pile wool is used on smooth surfaces like plaster, and long nap on textured surfaces like brick or cement. Man-made fibres can do the same job.

Mohair sleeves, covered with a very fine pile, are best for applying gloss paint.

Plastic foam rollers can be used with any paint, but are not as long lasting as the better quality rollers.

Rollers are charged by being rolled in paint poured into a special shallow metal or plastic tray. The roller is run on the sloping, textured surface of the tray to distribute the paint evenly over the sleeve. A metal tray may rust unless carefully washed and dried after use.

Special rollers

A long extension handle can be attached to some rollers to enable you to paint the ceiling while standing on the floor. Short rollers are useful to apply paint in restricted spaces. Shaped rollers are available for painting into corners.

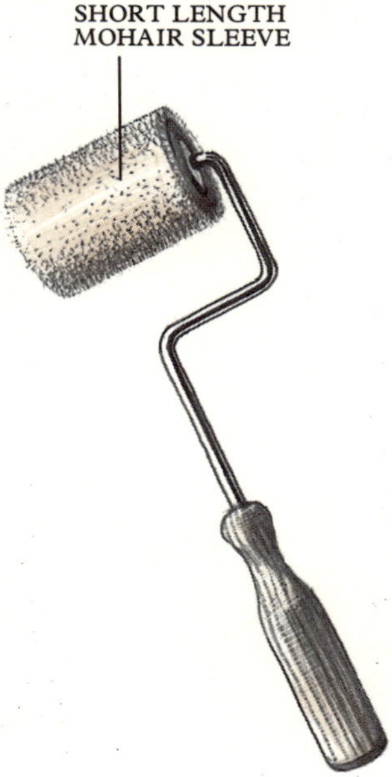

Painting ceilings and walls

If the walls and ceiling are to be the same colour, rollers can be used throughout (except around the light fixtures). If you are using different colours, paint the edges of the ceiling with a brush before taking over with a roller. Work the roller in bands across the ceiling picking up the unfinished edges as quickly as possible. Do not let the roller spin at the end of a stroke as it might splatter paint. Paint the walls in the same way.

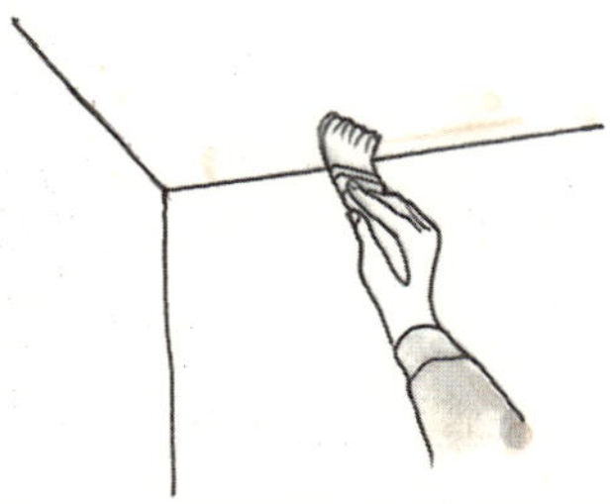

Preliminary brushwork
Starting near the window, paint the edges, corners and around light fixings where the roller cannot go.

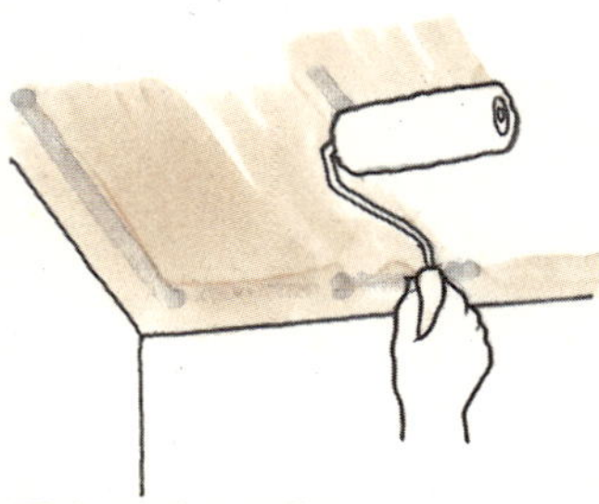

Using the roller
Now switch to the roller, painting in one direction only.

Before the paint has a chance to dry take the roller across at right angles for even coverage. Pick up any unfinished edges.

Care of rollers

Removing excess paint
Roll out excess paint on to newspaper. Pour any paint left in the tray back into the can and wipe it out with a solvent-soaked rag.

Cleaning the sleeve
Pour the solvent into the tray and soak the roller. Wash both in warm soapy water, massaging the sleeve with your fingers to remove partially dissolved paint.

Drying and storing
Squeeze out the water from the sleeve and dry it with an absorbent rag. For long term storage wrap the sleeve in brown paper or foil.

Clean paint from the handle and cage and dry them with rags especially if you are about to use the roller immediately with a new colour.

Seam Roller

OTHER NAME: Butt roller
SIZE: Width: 25 to 50mm
MATERIAL: Hardwood
USE: To press down the edges of pasted wallpaper

Use the seam roller to press down the butt-jointed edges of wallpaper to make sure that they are firmly stuck down. Wipe off any paste after use.

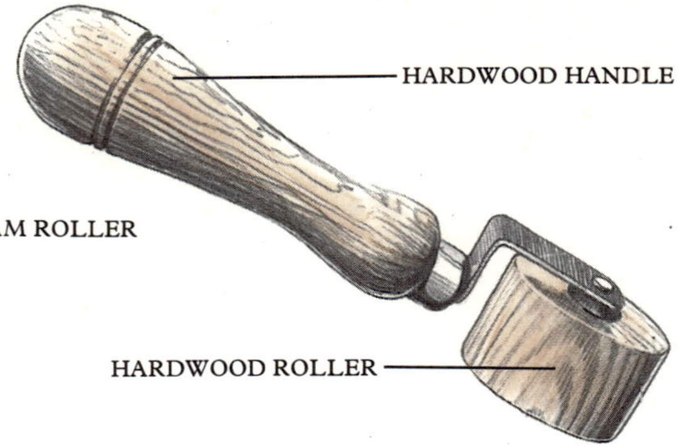

Smoothing Roller

SIZE: 87 to 175mm
MATERIAL: *Roller:* rubber, felt; *Handle:* hardwood
USE: To smooth down pasted wallpaper

A smoothing roller is used to roll out excess air and paste from paper pasted on the wall and to press the paper firmly onto the wall.

Rollers made from hard rubber are for general use, while rollers made from discs of felt mounted on a centre core are best for delicate, especially flock-covered, paper.

Do not use a roller on embossed paper.

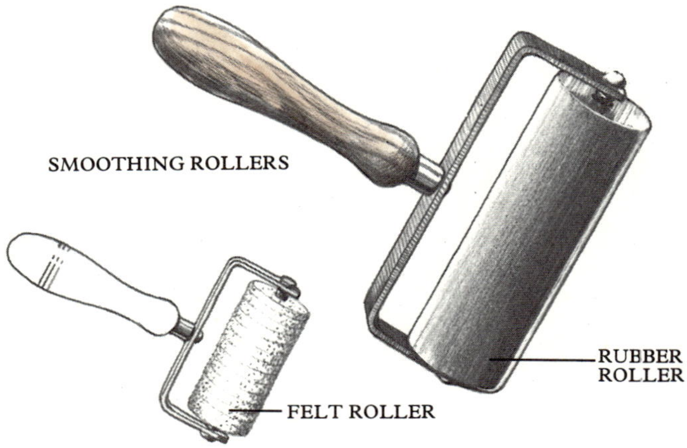

Scratch Brush

OTHER NAME: Welder's wire brush
SIZE: 275 to 337mm
MATERIAL: *Bristles:* steel wire; *Handle/stock:* hardwood
USE: To clean off flaking material

Scratch brushes are used to remove dirt, rust, or flaking paint from metal to take it back to the firm bright surface before it is treated for rust and repainted as required.

Some scratch brushes have a scraper fitted to the end of the stock to remove the loosened material from walls.

You can also use wire brushes to score the surface of vinyl wallpapers just before soaking them for stripping.

Rotary Wire Brushes

SIZE: *Wheel diameter:* 25 to 300mm; *Cup brush diameter:* 12 to 150mm; *End brush diameter:* 4.5 to 28mm
MATERIAL: Brass, steel
USE: To clean off flaking material and score metal

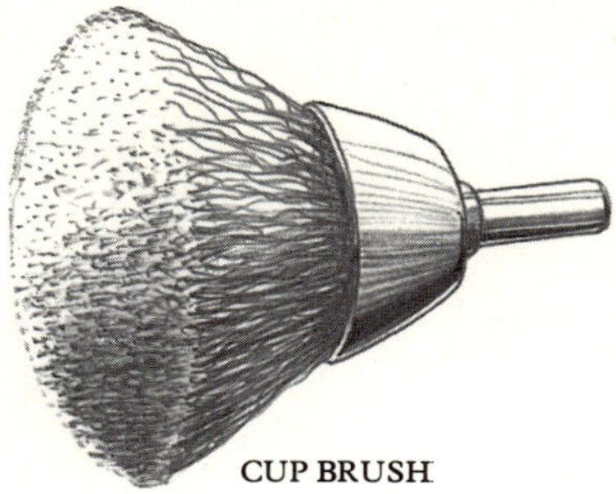

CUP BRUSH

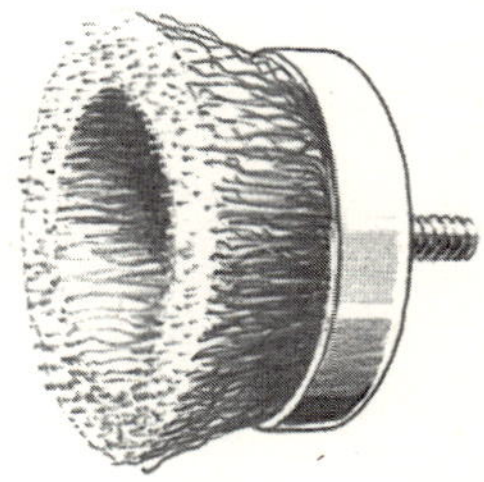

HOLLOW FACED CUP BRUSH

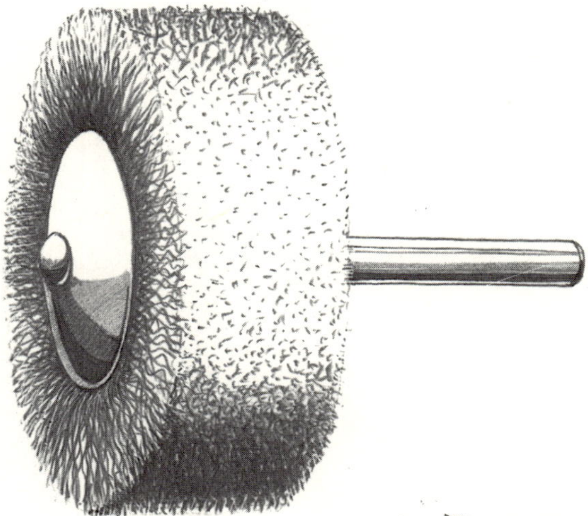

WHEEL BRUSH

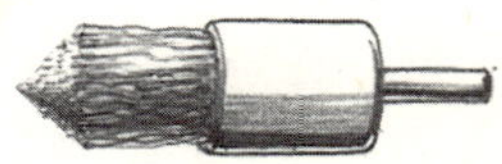

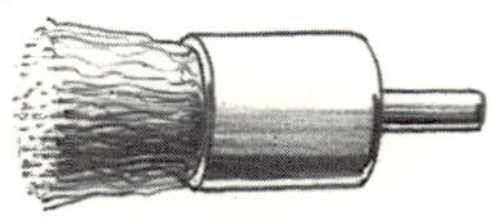

END BRUSHES

Coarse and fine rotary wire brushes are available in an enormous range of shapes and sizes. They are attached to a power drill and used to clean off flaking material or clean up metal, usually to provide a key for painting.

Wheel brushes should be used on a fixed, bench-mounted drill. If you cannot take the work to the drill, use a cup brush, available flush or hollow faced, attached to a free drill. End brushes are used to clean up metal in more confined spaces, and can be fitted in a flexible drive connected to a power drill. They are made in various lengths, with straight and flared bristles, and with flat or pointed ends.

Using the cup brush
Use cup brushes free-hand in the drill to clean up metal fixtures. Hold the drill firmly to prevent the action of the brush spinning it off the work.

Using the wheel brush
Use wire wheels with the drill mounted in a bench stand. With the wheel revolving toward you, hold the work against the brush slightly below centre.

Paint Sprayer

SIZE: 0.05 to 0.5cm per minute
MATERIAL: Various
USE: To apply flat even coats of paint

A paint sprayer produces a fine layer of paint which is generally more even than paint applied any other way, and also dries quickly. There are airless or compressed air sprayers.

Airless sprayers
These are probably the most convenient for domestic use. They are self-contained units fitted with an electric pump which forces the paint at high pressure through a small hole, breaking it up into a fine spray. The width of the spray cone and the delivery of paint can be adjusted to suit the painting of wide flat areas or small objects. The spray pattern is produced by the shape of the nozzle.

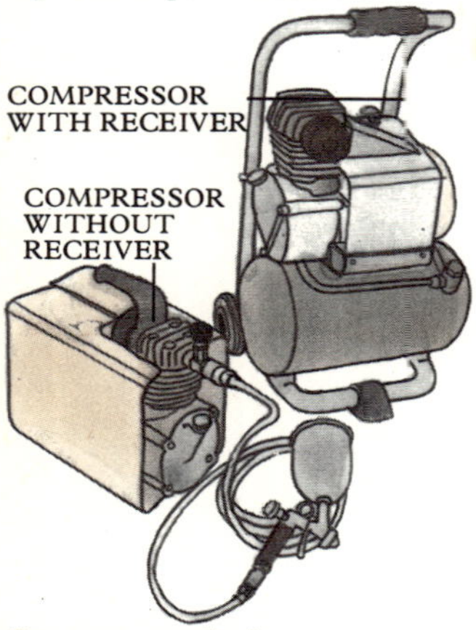

Compressed air sprayers
In these types, the paint is mixed with compressed air to atomize it. A compressor takes in air and compresses it either with a piston in a cylinder, a diaphragm or rotating blades. Compressors vary enormously in size and are driven electrically or by gasoline.

Some machines supply the compressed air directly to the gun. Others store it in a metal tank called a receiver, which delivers air to the gun as required and is topped up by the compressor when the pressure in the gun drops below functioning level.

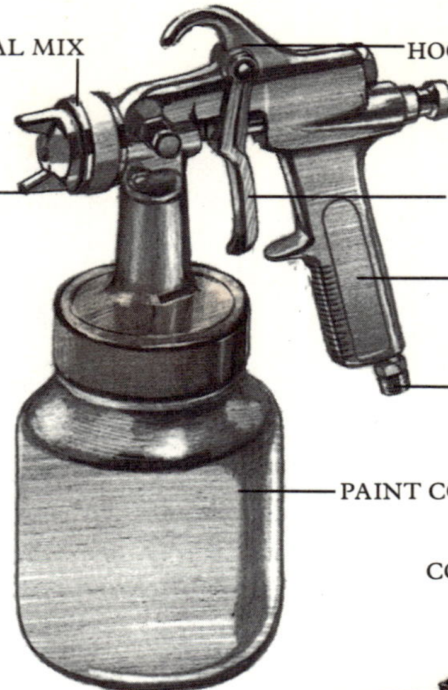

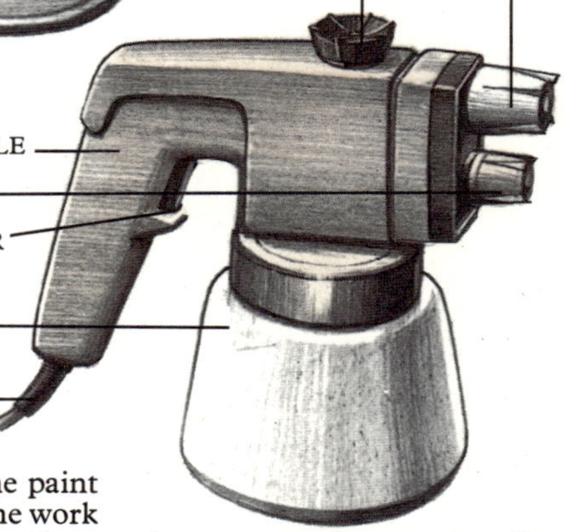

Bleeder guns
A spray gun delivers the paint and compressed air to the work in the required proportions and controls the shape of the spray cone. In a bleeder gun, the compressed air may flow continuously through the gun, being bled off to relieve the pressure from the air hose and compressor when the gun is not in use. Non-bleeder guns have a valve which shuts off air as the trigger is released.

How spray guns work
As the trigger is depressed, it withdraws a needle from the outlet of the fluid tip where the paint comes out of the gun. The fluid tip is mounted with the air cap which directs the compressed air into the stream of paint. Air caps can be either internally or externally placed. The internal mix cap combines the paint and air before they are released from the gun. It can be used with low pressure equipment, but the cone pattern cannot be controlled and it does not produce such a fine spray. With the external mix cap, the paint comes out from a central hole and is mixed with air from surrounding holes. This type of cap also has projecting horns which direct air from side portholes to produce a fan pattern.

Paint delivery
The paint is delivered by gravity, suction or pressure feed. Gravity fed guns simply have a container mounted on top of the gun. Suction fed guns have a specially designed air cap which produces a low vacuum at the fluid tip so that the paint is delivered by atmospheric pressure from a container slung underneath the gun. Pressure fed guns have a similar container, but the paint is forced out by compressed air. The container may be slung underneath the gun or be floor standing.

Preparation for spraying
Protect areas adjacent to the surface being painted. Use masking tape to give a straight edge to the painted area, with newspaper covering the area behind the line. For large areas, tape, staple or weight down plastic sheets.

Ventilate interiors and extinguish naked flames. Wear goggles and a face mask.

Consistency of paint
It is a good idea to thin paint before spraying. It will be less likely to clog the fluid tip and will smoothe out after it is applied. Add the appropriate solvent and stir thoroughly to a smooth consistency that runs easily from the end of the stirring stick. Old paint which has developed a skin should be strained through cheesecloth in order to remove any lumps or particles.

Common faults
Spitting
Spitting is caused by dried out packing around the fluid needle valve. This allows air to enter the fluid passage ways, or dirt to seep between the fluid tip seat and body. Lubricate the dry packing with one or two drops of oil. Clean the fluid tip and seat and the body of the gun with a rag dampened with thinner. Replace the tip.

Spattering
An uneven, speckled application is caused by too much pressure on the paint or inefficient atomization. Adjust the sprayer accordingly.

Uneven pattern
A spray pattern that is heavy on one side or deflects to one side, is probably the result of uneven pressure produced by a blockage in an air hole. Clean with a rag dipped in thinner or clear with a fibre bristle.

Cleaning the spray gun
Pour any remaining paint from the container and spray the appropriate thinner through the gun until it comes out clear. Wipe the container clean with a rag dampened with solvent. Dismantle the air cap and fluid tip and wipe clean making sure that all holes are clear.

Using the gun
Using waste paint, adjust the gun to produce the desired shape and density of spray. Turn the air control screw clockwise to produce a narrow cone or counter clockwise to spread the cone. As the cone is increased, the fluid control screw must be adjusted to increase the paint flow. The fan pattern gives maximum coverage. It is produced by the position of the air cap horns. Set horizontally they will make a vertical fan. Set vertically, they produce a horizontal fan.

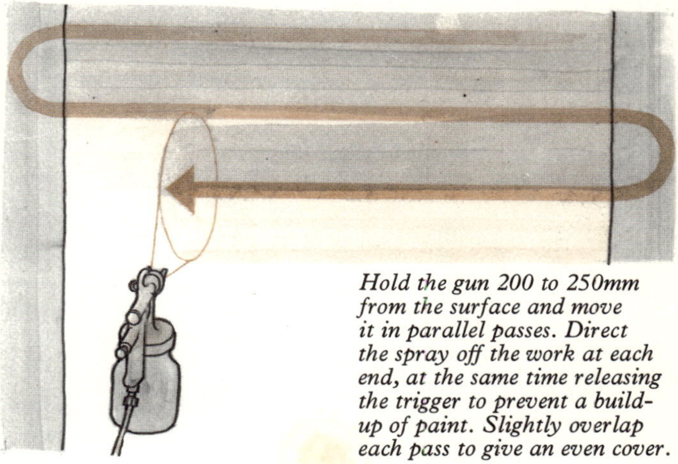

Hold the gun 200 to 250mm from the surface and move it in parallel passes. Direct the spray off the work at each end, at the same time releasing the trigger to prevent a build-up of paint. Slightly overlap each pass to give an even cover.

Right way

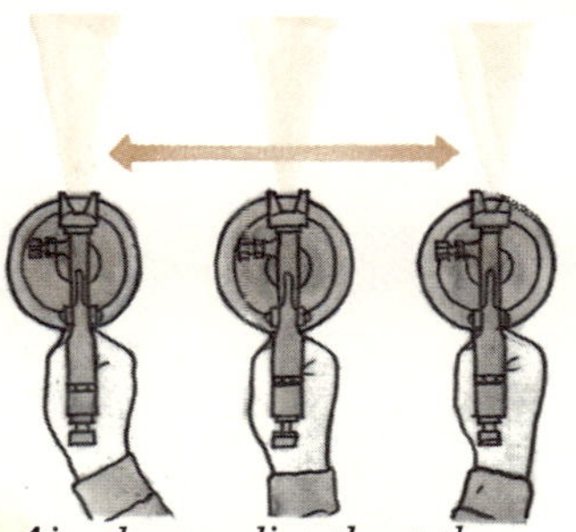

Aim the gun directly at the wall, keeping it the same distance throughout the pass.

Wrong way

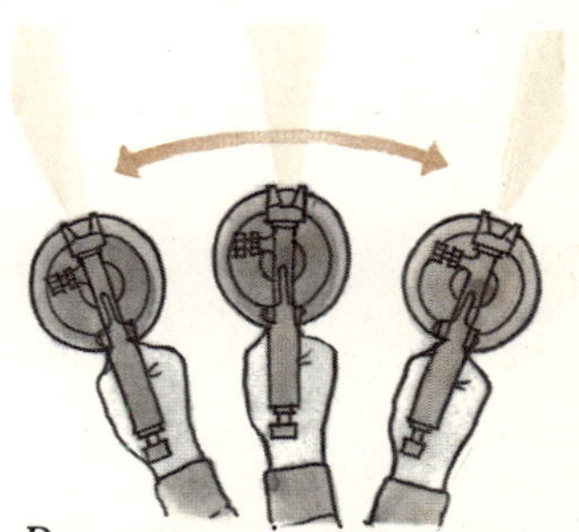

Do not spray in an arc: you will produce light coverage at each end of the sweep.

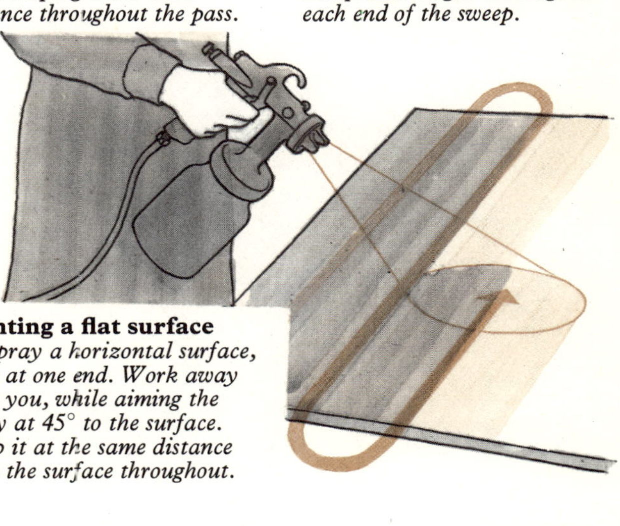

Painting a flat surface
To spray a horizontal surface, start at one end. Work away from you, while aiming the spray at 45° to the surface. Keep it at the same distance from the surface throughout.

Ladders

The Old Testament story of Jacob's dream shows that ladders must have been in use in the Middle East during the Bronze Age or even earlier, as the Tower of Babel could hardly have been built without them. They have changed little since, except for getting lighter, longer, safer and extensible.

Single Ladder

SIZE: 1.8 to 7.9m
MATERIAL: **Wooden:** *Stiles:* softwood; *Rungs:* hardwood
Metal: aluminium alloy
ACCESSORIES: Ladder brackets, ladder stays, safety feet
USE: To provide access to a high worksite

The wooden single ladder is made of two straight grain uprights called "stiles", which are joined by "rungs" which act as steps when the ladder is leaned against a wall. The stiles are made of a variety of softwoods, while the rungs are made of hardwood. The rungs of the better quality ladders are tenoned through the stiles and wedged from the outside to form a strong joint. As an extra precaution, metal reinforcing rods are stretched across the underside of the rungs.

A pole ladder has semi-circular stiles cut from one straight length of timber. This type of ladder is normally a fixture on a scaffold erection.

Aluminium ladders are lighter than the equivalent wooden ladders and will not warp or crack. The stiles are a hollow box section. The rungs are ribbed to provide grip.

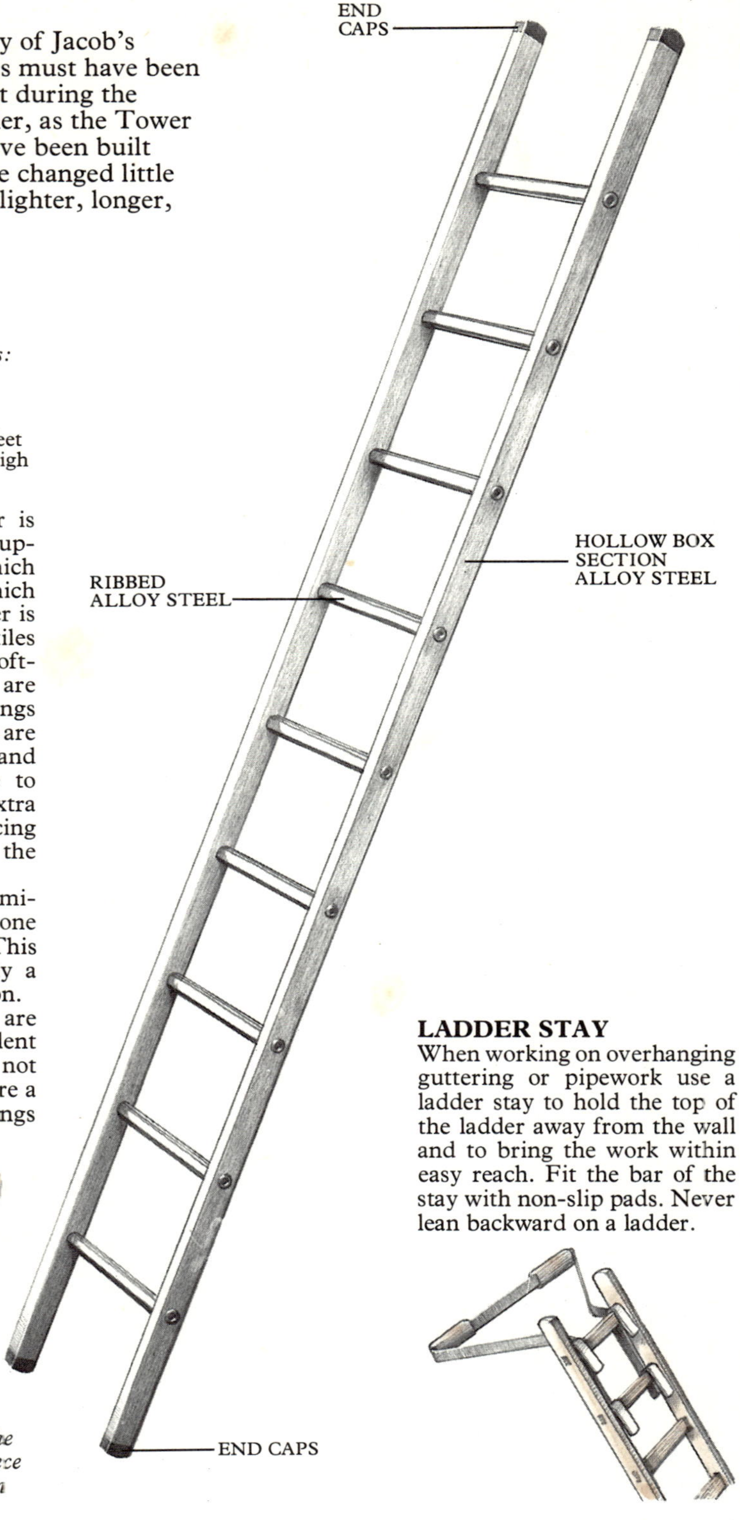

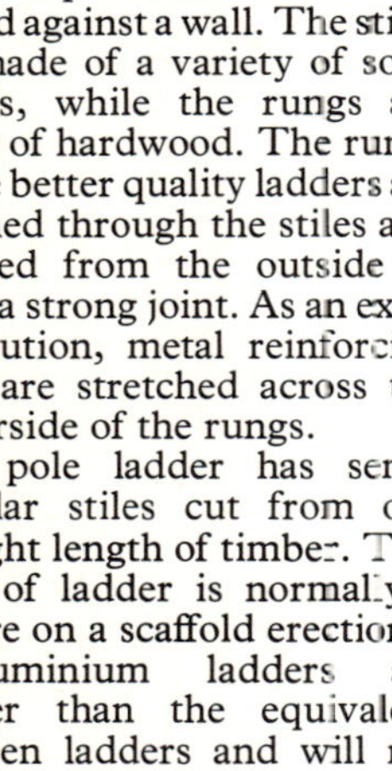

Pole ladder
The semi-circular stiles of the pole ladder, cut from one piece of wood, give equal spring on both sides of the ladder.

LADDER STAY
When working on overhanging guttering or pipework use a ladder stay to hold the top of the ladder away from the wall and to bring the work within easy reach. Fit the bar of the stay with non-slip pads. Never lean backward on a ladder.

LADDER BRACKETS

Ladder brackets are used in the construction of a work platform. Stand two ladders at the same angle so that scaffold boards stand evenly. The brackets either hook on the front of the ladders or hang underneath them. Simple brackets are fixed at an angle, while the better versions are adjustable. All brackets are wide enough to take two boards. Use a third ladder to get to the platform.

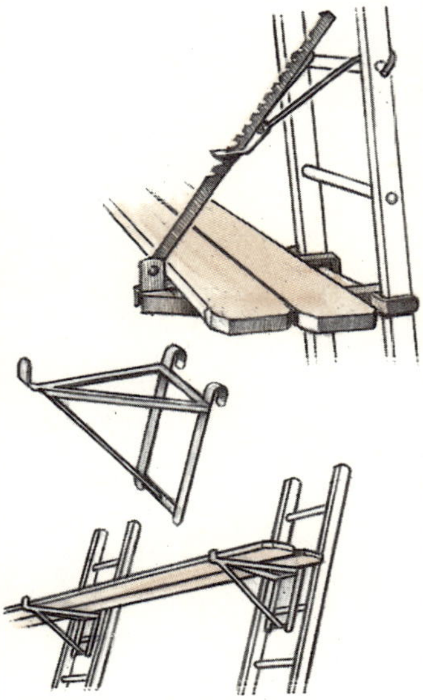

SAFETY FEET

Aluminium ladders are normally fitted with rubber or plastic non-slip end caps. You can also buy special feet for wooden ladders in use on potentially slippery surfaces. The feet are either rubber pads or, where the surface is suitable, textured to grip the ground.

Extension Ladder

SIZE: *Closed height:* 1.8 to 6.1m; *Extended height:* 5.4 to 10.9m
MATERIAL: **Wooden:** *Stiles:* softwood; *Rungs:* hardwood; **Metal:** aluminium alloy
ACCESSORIES: Ladder brackets, ladder stays, safety feet
USE: To provide access to a high worksite

An extension ladder is a combination of two or three sections sliding one inside the other to form a ladder of varying height. Metal brackets hold the sections of ladder together while hooks on the bottom of one section locate on the rungs of the lower section. They are either extended by hand or, after a certain length, are fitted with a rope and pulley system to extend the upper sections. The sections are constructed like a single ladder.

The rungs of overlapping sections should align to maintain a constant tread height. No section should be extended more than three quarters of its actual length.

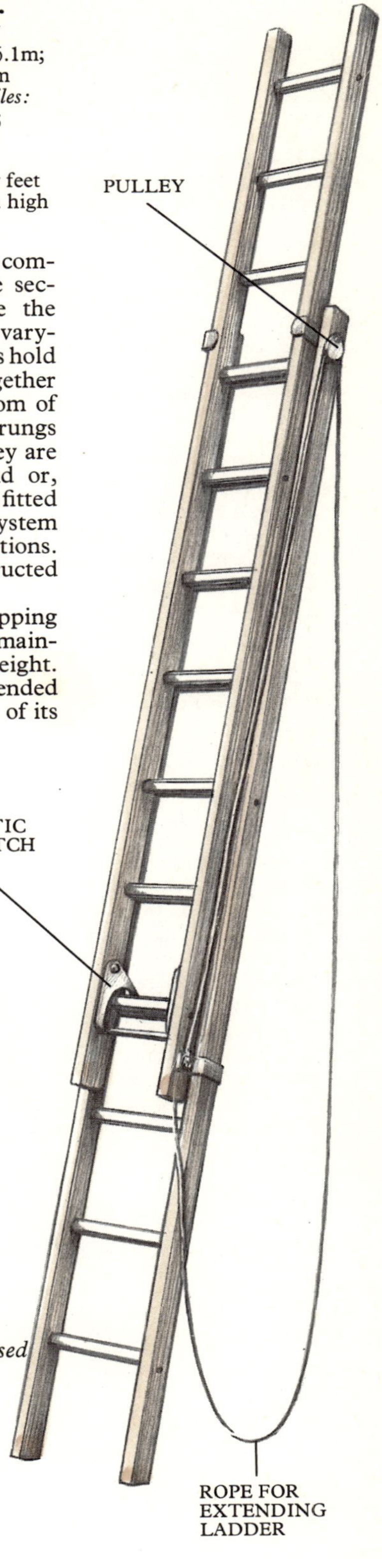

Reinforcements
The stiles on wooden ladders are reinforced on the underside with a recessed steel cable.

Trestle

OTHER NAME: Painter's trestle
SIZE: Height: 900m to 4.2m
MATERIAL: Softwood
USE: To support scaffold boards

Trestles are designed to be used in pairs to support scaffold boards in order to construct a work platform to reach the ceiling or high walls.

The cross bars on one half of the trestle are staggered with those on the other half. This gives you a greater choice of platform height while keeping the weight of the trestle down.

The top of the stiles are cut at an angle to form a stop when the trestle is fully opened, but secondary ropes or stays are sometimes fitted below.

The trestle should be able to support two boards side by side. Make sure that the boards overhang the cross bars by a safe amount.

Scaffold Board

OTHER NAME: Scaffold plank
SIZE: *Length* 1.5 to 4.2m; *Width:* 150 to 200mm
MATERIAL: Softwood
USE: To make work platforms

Scaffold boards are used with trestles or step ladders to form work platforms above the ground. They are cut from straight grained, knot-free softwood. The ends are bound with metal strip to protect them from damage.

Always make sure that the boards are secure, and if in doubt, clamp or tie them in position. Double up on the boards when bridging a span greater than 1.5m.

Step Ladder

OTHER NAME: Builder's steps
SIZE: 5 to 16 treads
MATERIAL: Softwood, aluminium alloy
USE: Indoor ladder

Step ladders, made in wood or metal, are self supporting, having a frame hinged to the back of the ladder. Instead of rungs they have wide steps which lie horizontally when the ladder is fully opened. The hinged sections are fitted with ropes or folding stays to prevent them sliding open further than the optimum position. A platform at the top of the ladder carries tools or paint cans.

Safety factors
Inspect step ladders before use paying particular attention to the condition of the steps, stays and hinges. Make sure that the steps are fully opened and on even ground before climbing on them.

Do not lean or stretch too far out on the step ladder, as it can easily fall sideways.

If you must erect a step ladder in front of a door, either lock it or give plenty of warning to other members of the household.

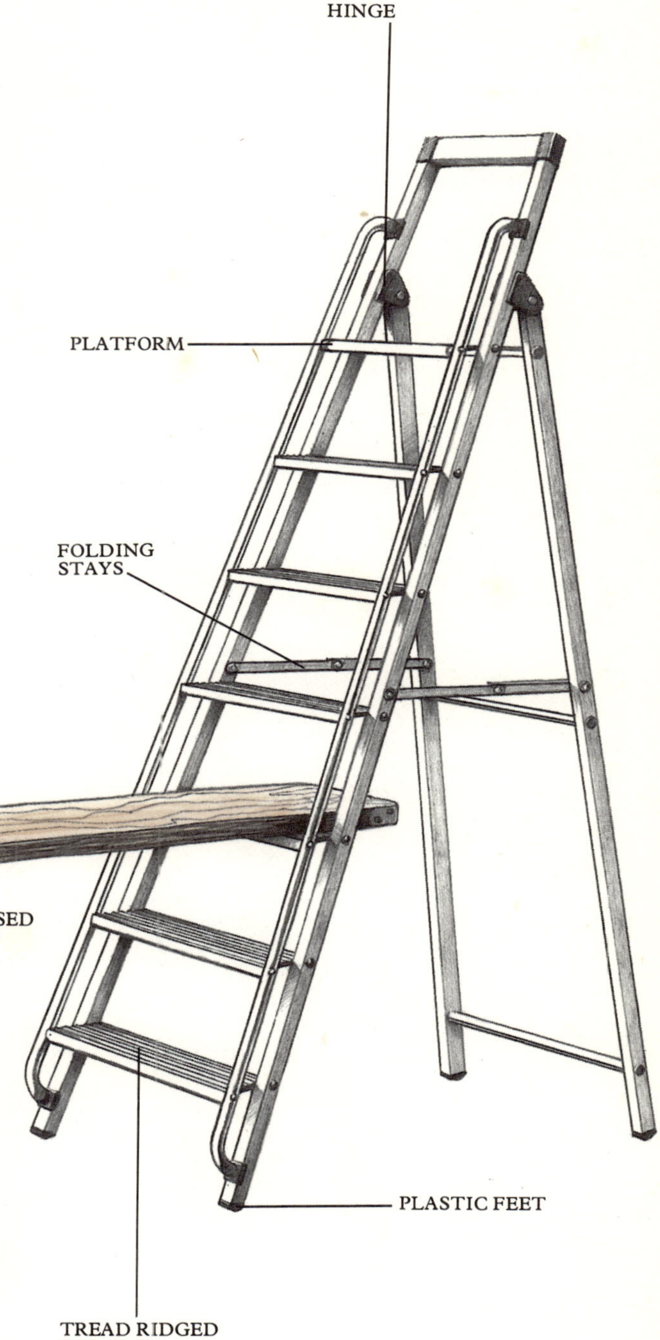

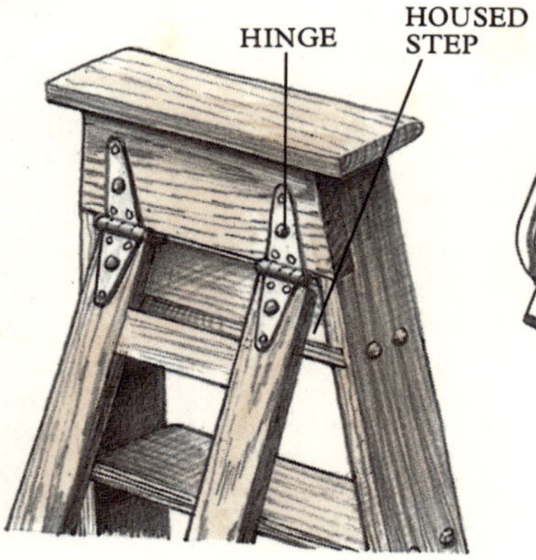

Wood ladder construction
Hinges are screwed to the ladder back while the heads are housed in the wood and further secured by gluing and nailing.

Multi-Purpose Ladder

SIZE: *Closed height:* 1.3 to 1.9m; *Maximum extended height:* 4.2 to 6.5m
MATERIAL: Tubular steel, aluminium alloy
USE: To do the jobs of an extension ladder, step ladder and trestle

There are now several multi-purpose ladders on the market, which combine the functions of different types of ladder and are adjustable to stand on a flight of stairs.

They will perform as a pair of step ladders, which in some cases are adjustable in height. They can be used as a pair of trestles to support a scaffold board. All designs are capable of being converted to an extension ladder.

Each half of the system can be adjusted independently so that the ladder will stand securely on a flight of stairs. The addition of scaffold boards allows you to reach the sides of the stairwell without moving the ladder. Whenever you construct a platform over a staircase, make sure that it is safe before using it. If necessary, remove the stair carpet and screw wooden blocks to the treads to secure the foot of the ladder. Clamp or lash the scaffold board securely to the ladder if it does not seem secure.

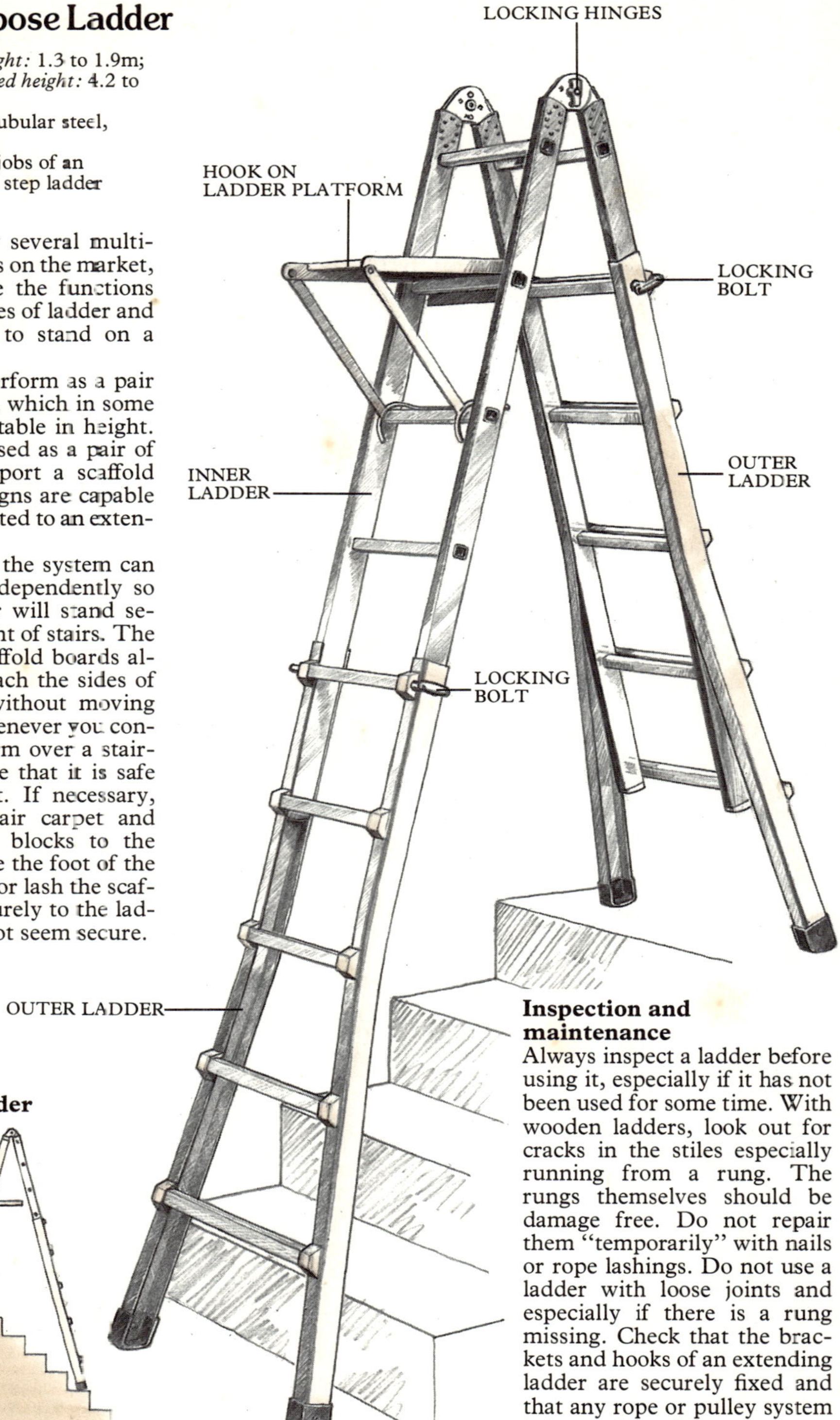

Using the ladder

Position the scaffolding board on the rungs at one end and the stair tread at the other.

Inspection and maintenance

Always inspect a ladder before using it, especially if it has not been used for some time. With wooden ladders, look out for cracks in the stiles especially running from a rung. The rungs themselves should be damage free. Do not repair them "temporarily" with nails or rope lashings. Do not use a ladder with loose joints and especially if there is a rung missing. Check that the brackets and hooks of an extending ladder are securely fixed and that any rope or pulley system is in good condition.

Painting a ladder may obscure faults, but a coat of clear matt lacquer will preserve it.

Carrying a ladder
Carry the ladder held upright, one hand hooked under a rung and the other hooked over another. Alternatively, carry it on your shoulder with your hand

passing through the ladder and gripping a rung. Support the ladder with the other hand.

Erecting a ladder
At the site, support the foot of the ladder against the wall and gradually raise it to the vertical by walking towards the wall.

Move the foot out from the wall for a distance the quarter of the length of the ladder. Make sure the ladder is upright and not resting against guttering or window glass.

Pulling out the foot

The foot should be extended one quarter of the ladder's length.

Extending ladders
You will need help to erect an extending ladder. Support the ladder from behind and hold it away from the wall while each section is extended. Avoid rubbing the ladder against the wall which will damage both the surface and the ladder. If the ladder extends beyond a staging, it should project at least 900mm above the level.

Securing the ladder
Secure the base of the ladder to prevent it slipping. If it is on soft or loose ground, rest it on a

board to spread the load and screw a wood piece to the board to support the ladder's foot.

Even on firm ground, it is advisable to fix safety feet, especially if the surface is slippery, and guy ropes should still be used if necessary. As a last resort support the foot of the ladder with bags of sand.

Preventing movement
Tie the ladder back to a firm fixing on the wall or to tent pegs driven into the ground to prevent it slipping sideways.

Safety factors
Wear well-fitting shoes, not rubber boots, and check that there is no grease, mud or sand on the soles before ascending the ladder. Face the wall when going up or down the ladder.

Never stand higher than the fourth rung from the top so you can always hold on with at least one hand. Resist the temptation to overstretch, keeping the main weight of your body squarely on the ladder.

Roof Ladder

OTHER NAME: Cat ladder
SIZE: 3 to 6.7m
MATERIAL: Softwood, aluminium alloy
USE: To gain access to a sloping roof

A roof ladder provides access and spreads the load over fragile materials.

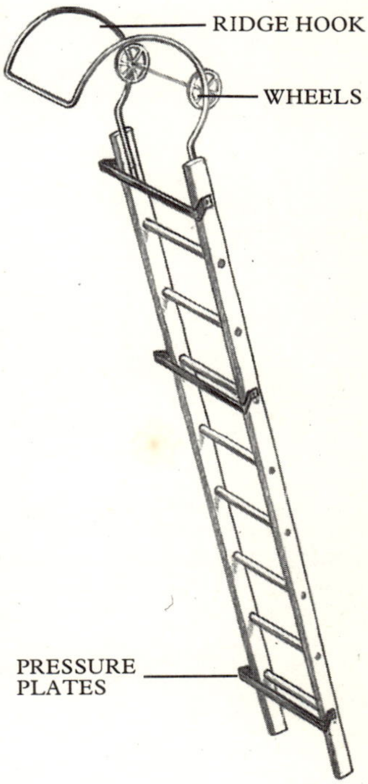

Stow your tools between the rungs of the ladder to prevent them slipping off the roof.

Using the roof ladder
Turn the ladder on its back and run it up the roof on its wheels. At the top, turn it over and place the hook over the ridge.

Scaffolding System

SIZE: 1.8 to 4.2m
MATERIAL: Galvanized steel, aluminium alloy
USE: To construct a working tower

The easiest system of scaffolding for a home user incorporates prefabricated tubular metal frames. They plug together in rectangular frames and are braced diagonally to form a rigid structure. The system can be used to build structures from a simple mobile platform to paint a ceiling, to a tower which will reach the roof of a large house.

The base can be fitted with metal base plates. Place wooden boards under the base plates on soft ground. Alternatively, locking castors can be plugged into the frame so that the tower can be moved from one location to another without dismantling. Do not, however, move the platform if someone is standing on it.

The work platform is made from boards supplied with the system, which have locating boards on the underside to fit inside the frame. "Toe" boards fit all around the platform to prevent tools being accidentally kicked off.

Interlocking frames

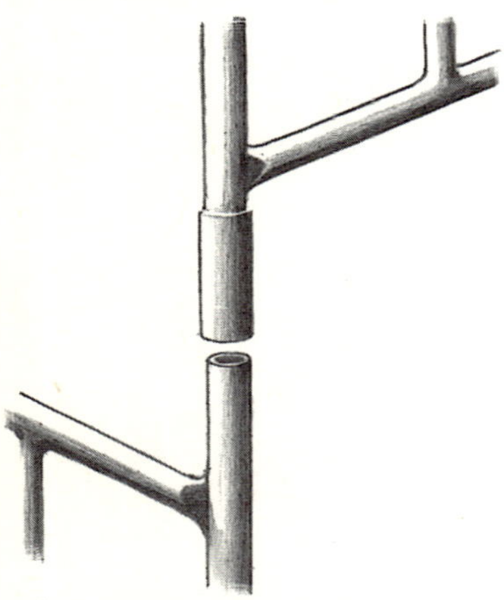

A joint system which fits the top of the frame over *the lower prevent rain water collecting in the joint.*

Building Tools

Down to the sixteenth century the hod was a wicker basket for carrying mortar. The brick hod was first mentioned in 1532 at Westminster, when helves (long handles) of ash timber were bought for hods, hammers and mattocks. The hawk was originally a wooden platform for mixing mortar; the hand hawk is a plasterer's tool. Masons' trowels have changed very little down the ages, but special types were developed for bricklaying, after the Great Fire of London (1666) had destroyed all the wooden houses, and for internal and external decoration on plasterwork from the eighteenth century onward.

Brick Hod

SIZE: *Weight:* 2.3 to 3.2kg; *Handle length* 1m
MATERIAL: *Pan:* aluminium alloy; *Handle:* ash
USE: To carry bricks

A brick hod has a three sided metal pan which is used to carry bricks from the stack to the worksite. It is carried with the base of the pan resting on one shoulder and one hand resting on the long handle to steady the tool.

Hawk

OTHER NAME: Plasterer's hawk
SIZE: 250 × 250 to 350 × 350mm
MATERIAL: Softwood, aluminium alloy
USE: To carry plaster or mortar to the wall

A hawk is a square sheet of softwood or satin-finish aluminium fitted with a straight wooden handle in the centre of the underside.

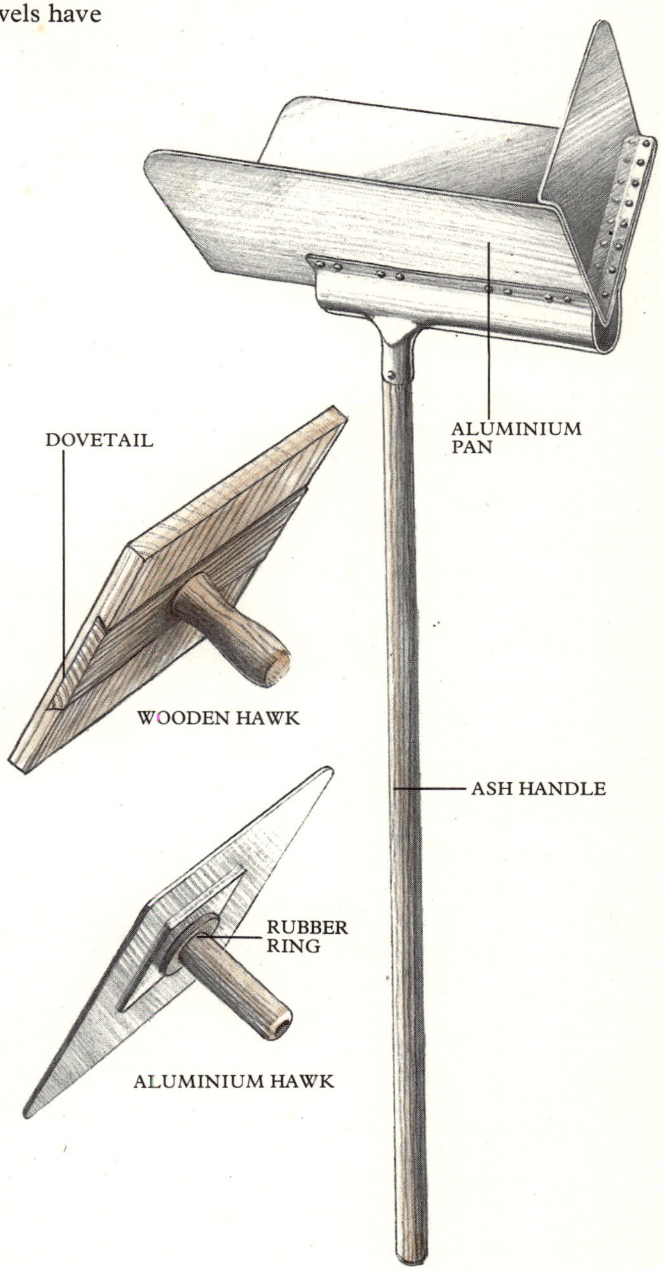

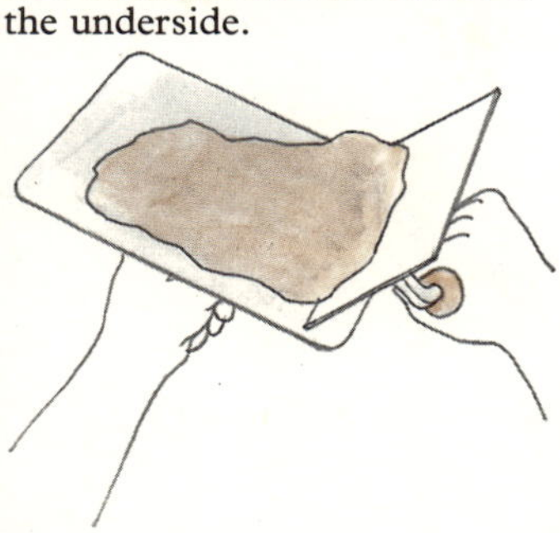

Using the hawk
Tip the hawk toward an upturned trowel, and lift and scoop plaster from the surface. Return the hawk to the horizontal to keep the rest of the plaster from falling off.

Brick Trowel

OTHER NAME: Mason's trowel
SIZE: Blade length: 162 to 300mm
MATERIAL: *Blade:* steel; *Handle:* hardwood, plastic, leather
USE: To apply mortar when building with bricks or blocks

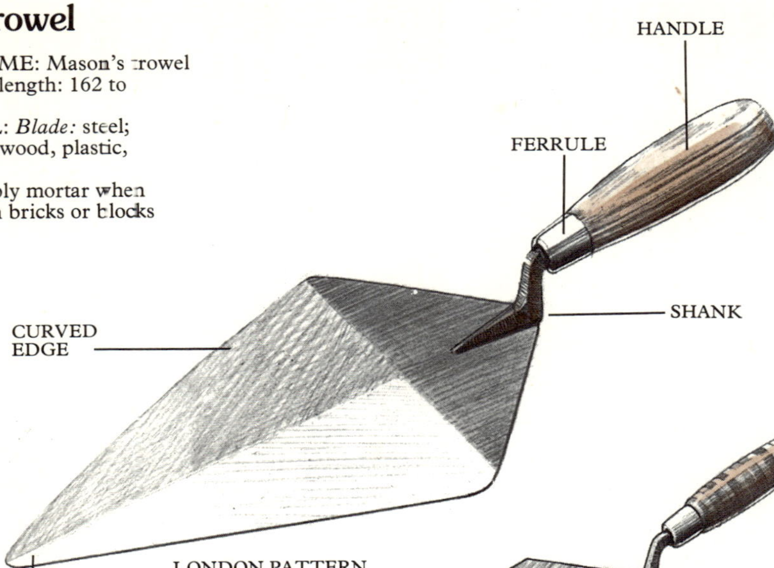

LONDON PATTERN

CANADIAN PATTERN

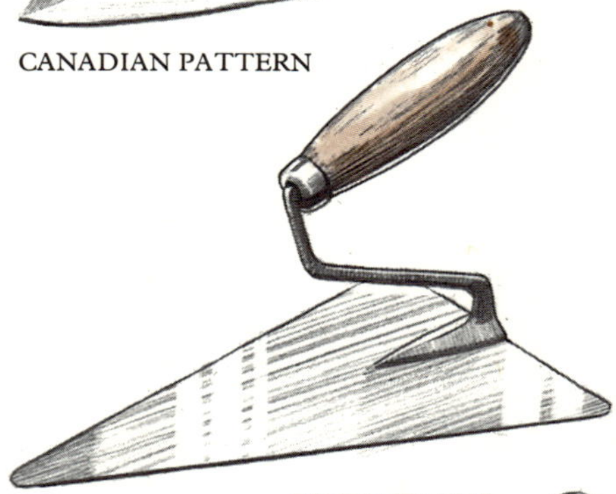
CONTINENTAL PATTERNS

The brick trowel is a traditional tool which has developed into many various shapes and sizes. The most common tool here as well as in the USA is the "London" pattern trowel which has a flat, roughly triangular blade, which angles back at the "heel" to meet the tang or shank. The "narrow" or standard width blade is useful when extra mortar is required such as when laying building blocks.

The blade is made for right- and left-handed masons being flat on one side for lifting the mortar from a board. The curved edge is hardened for cutting bricks. The handle is set at an angle to balance the tool while keeping the mason's hand clear of the mortar. It is round in section and is sometimes capped with metal for tapping the bricks into place.

The "Canadian" pattern trowel is curved on both edges and has a more flexible toe.

European masons favor a shorter, wider blade which is square across the heel and either completely triangular or has a blunt pointed toe.

Picking up mortar

Mortar is mixed up on a flat plywood board and is lifted from this board, a trowel load at a time, for spreading on to the brick course. A full trowel load is sufficient for approximately three to four bricks.

1. *Hold the trowel with your thumb resting on top of the handle. This balances the tool most comfortably in the hand.*

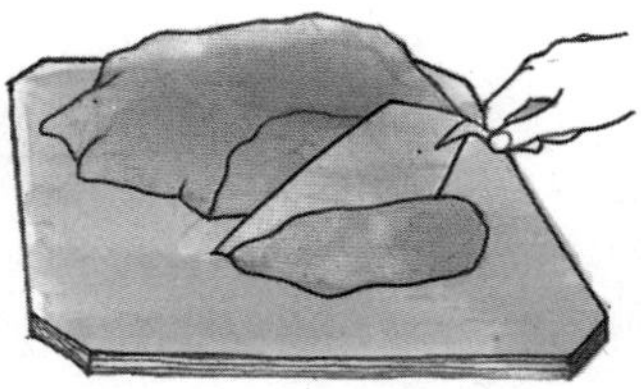

2. *Slice off a trowel load of mortar and pull it behind you.*

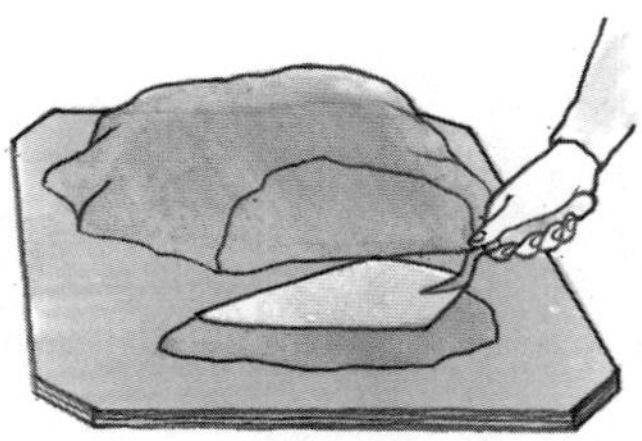

3. *Using the back of the trowel, shape the load into a roughly triangular mound.*

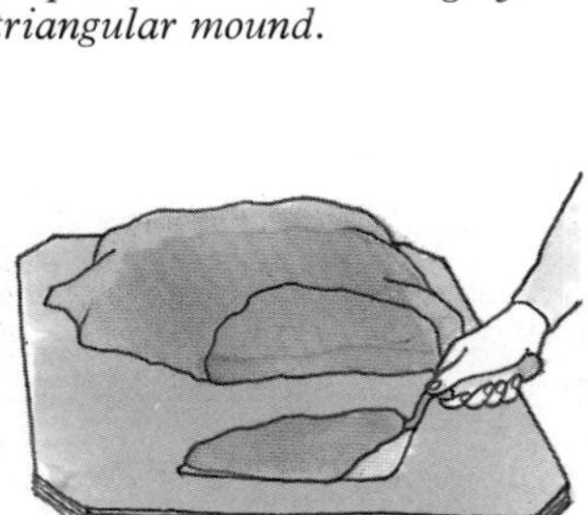

4. *With the flat of the blade on the board, slide the trowel under the mortar, seating it firmly on the blade with a slight jerk of the wrist.*

Using a trowel

Hold the edge of the blade over the center of the wall. Move the trowel backward, tilting it to slide the mortar gradually from the blade, leaving an even bed of mortar approximately 25mm thick on the surface.

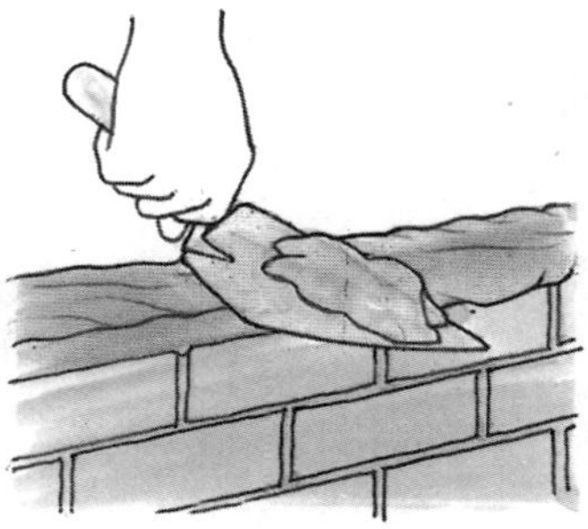

Cut off excess mortar that protrudes from the wall after each application, by holding the blade of the trowel against the wall with the face uppermost but angled slightly outward. Slice along the length of the wall to cut and lift the mortar cleanly from the bricks. Use the mortar to fill uneven areas in the mortar bed, or return it to the mortar board.

The bed must be "furrowed" to allow enough movement to position the bricks. Run the toe of the trowel backward along the bed gently tapping a shallow depression in the center.

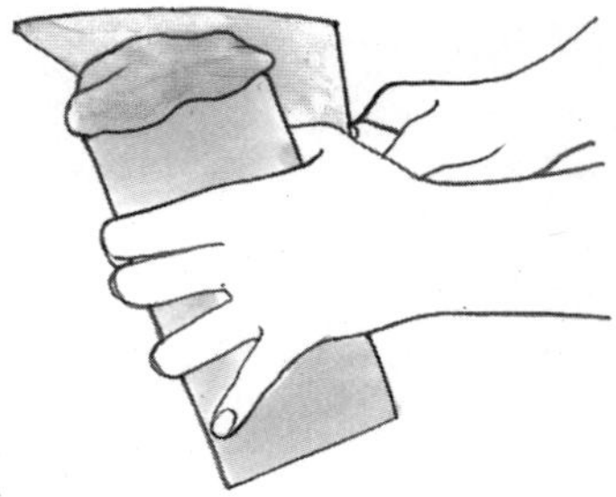

"Butter" the end of the brick with the mortar before it is laid against its neighbour. Smooth an even 12mm thick layer of mortar on the end of brick with the point of the trowel.

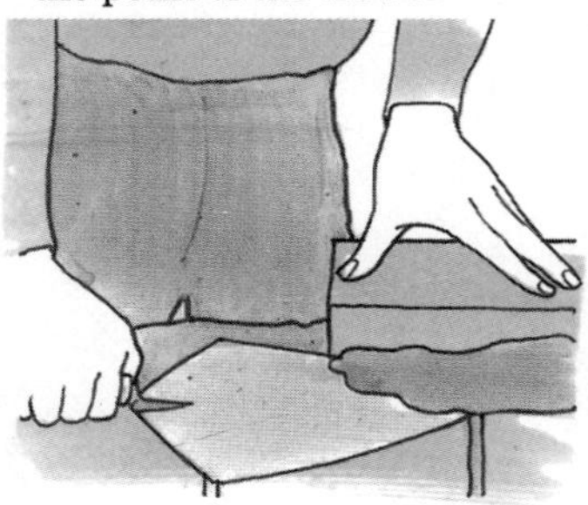

Position the brick in line with the rest of the course pressing it into the mortar bed and against its neighbour making a joint about 12mm thick.

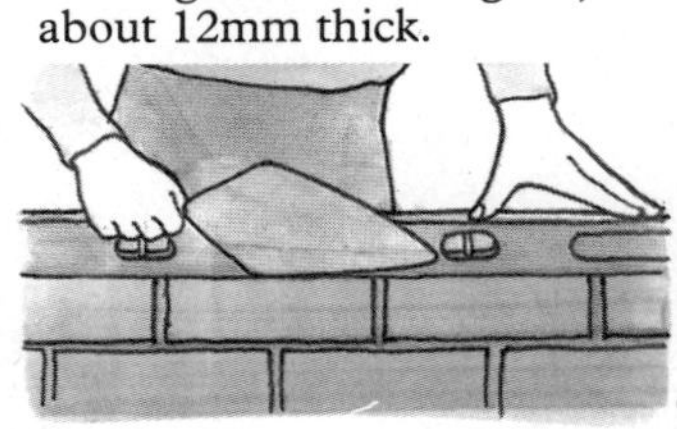

Lay other bricks to cover the bed and tap them into line. Rest a builder's level on top of the bricks for a horizontal check, then plumb the two end bricks against the wall face.

Line up the level on the edge of the two bricks and tap the remaining bricks in or out until they are aligned.

Plasterer's Trowel

OTHER NAME: Metal float, laying-on-trowel, finishing trowel
SIZE: 100 × 250 to 118 × 275mm
MATERIAL: *Blade:* steel; *Handle:* hardwood, plastic
USE: To apply plaster scratch coats, and finish the top coat with a smooth texture

The plasterer's trowel or metal float is a flat rectangular sheet of steel with a single or double hang handle fitted centrally down the back face. For most do-it-yourselfers a general purpose trowel is sufficient for both applying and finishing the material. Some professionals prefer a "laying-on" trowel, with its slightly thicker blade, for applying the material and a "finishing trowel" with a more flexible blade to finish the surface smoothly.

Patching large areas
Surfacing a large area with plaster is a skilled job requiring considerable experience with the tools and materials to achieve a first class result. Patching areas of loose plaster is not so demanding, as the sound areas of plaster act as a guide for levelling the new.

Removing loose plaster
Using a club hammer and cold chisel hack off loose plaster. Then rake out the joints to a depth of about 6mm to "key" the plaster, and brush loose debris from the wall. Dampen the wall to encourage the fresh material to stick.

Using the trowel
Lift the plaster from the hawk on to the trowel and then apply it to the wall with an even stroke. Hold the trowel at a slight angle to apply pressure to spread the material evenly.

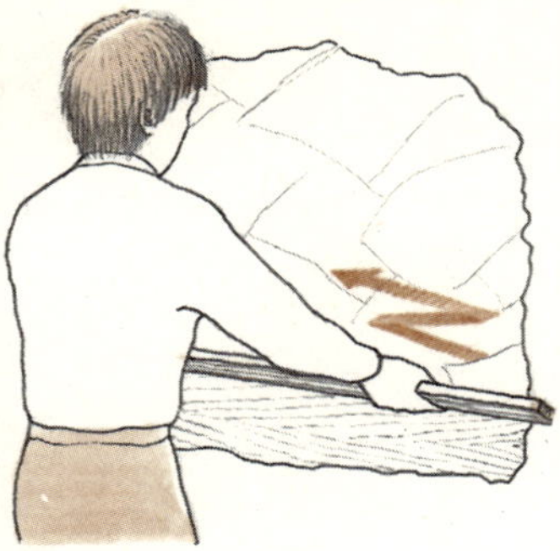

Levelling the surface
If the area is larger than the trowel, use a stout, straight edged wood piece to level the surface. Hold the straight edge at bottom of the patch so that it spans from one sound area to the next. Move it up and across the wet plaster with a sawing motion levelling off the material as you do so. Smooth any uneven areas with a trowel. When the surface glaze dries out, smooth the patch with a wet trowel.

Plastering a wall
First fix your own guides to establish the thickness of the material. Pin 4mm furring strips or "screeds" to the wall at 1.5m centres. Use a builder's level to plumb the strips. The first or scratch coat is cement and sand mixed in a proportion of 1 to 4 with water.

Dampen the wall and apply the scratch coat from the bottom of the wall filling between two strips at a time. Level the area with a steel trowel and then use a straight edge across the strips. Complete one bay, finish the surface with a wooden float, and work along wall.

About four hours later the material should be firm enough to key the surface for the top coat. Drive nails through a furring strip to make a scratching tool. Drag it across the surface leaving a series of 3mm marks.

Remove the strips and fill in with the mix using a pointing trowel. After a day, wet the wall and apply the plaster top coat about 3mm thick. Polish the surface with a steel trowel.

Margin Trowel

SIZE: 50 × 100 to 50 × 125mm
MATERIAL: *Blade: steel;*
Handle: hardwood
USE: To apply plaster in confined spaces

The margin trowel is like a pointing trowel but has a flat rectangular blade. It is used by plasterers to apply and smooth material in areas where a larger trowel would be inconvenient.

Gauging Trowel

SIZE: Blade length: 150 to 200mm
MATERIAL: *Blade:* steel;
Handle: hardwood
USE: To apply plaster in confined spaces

The gauging trowel is used by plasterers in the same way as a margin trowel. It is preferred by some professionals for general applications, such as mixing small quantities of quick setting plaster.

Angle Trowel

OTHER NAME: Plasterer's twitcher
SIZE: 100 × 62 with 25mm sides
MATERIAL: *Blade:* steel;
Handle: hardwood
USE: To finish the internal curve on a plaster moulding

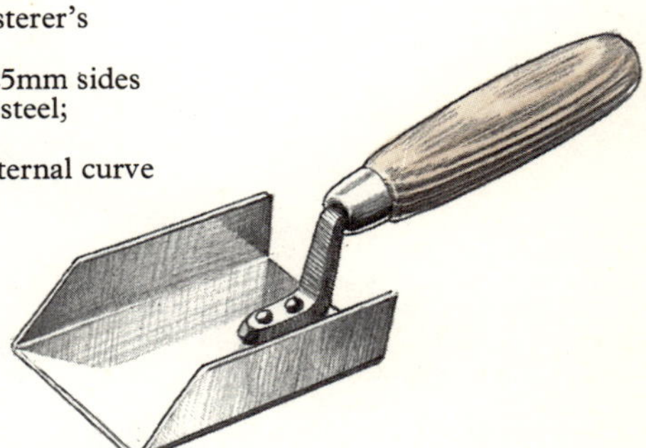

The angle trowel has a flat blade with the edges turned up at right angles. It is used by plasterers to smooth the surface of the material when working into a corner.

Cove Trowel

SIZE: 150 × 75, 275 × 75mm
MATERIAL: *Blade:* steel;
Handle: hardwood
USE: To finish the internal curve on a plaster moulding

The cove trowel is like a plasterer's trowel, but the rectangular blade is bent into a curve across its width. It is used to smooth the internal curve of the decorative plaster mouldings sometimes found between ceilings and walls.

Corner Trowel

SIZE: *Blade length:* 87mm;
Sides: 50mm
MATERIAL: *Blade:* steel;
Handle: hardwood
USE: To finish plaster corners

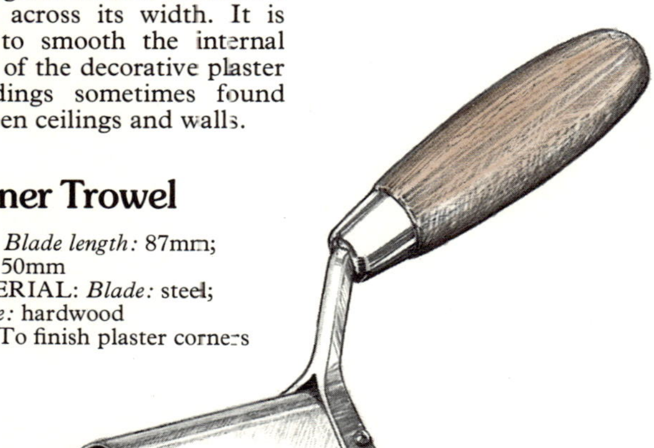

Once the plaster has been applied with a plasterer's trowel the corner is finished with the corner trowel. This trowel has a steel blade bent to form an internal or external angle of 90°. The ridge between the two halves of the blade forms either a radius or a square edge depending on the required finish.

Repairing a damaged corner

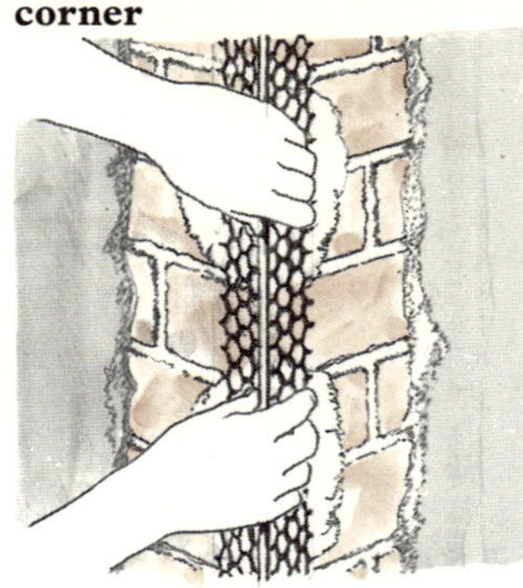

1. *To repair extensive damage on external corners, cut back plaster to the brickwork and apply a metal corner bead to strengthen the corner. The beading has expanded metal wings which are stuck to the wall with dabs of wet plaster.*

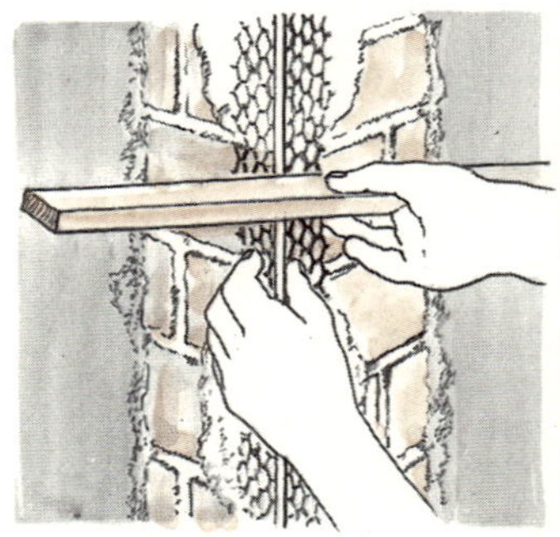

2. *Plumb edge with a builder's level and check with a straight edge that the nose of the bead is flush with the sound plaster.*

3. *When the beading is firmly fixed, apply plaster to the area with a plasterer's trowel and finally smooth the corner with a corner trowel dipped in water.*

Edging Trowel

OTHER NAME: Edger
SIZE: 62 × 175 to 112 × 275mm
MATERIAL: *Blade:* steel; *Handle:* hardwood
USE: To finish the edge of concrete work

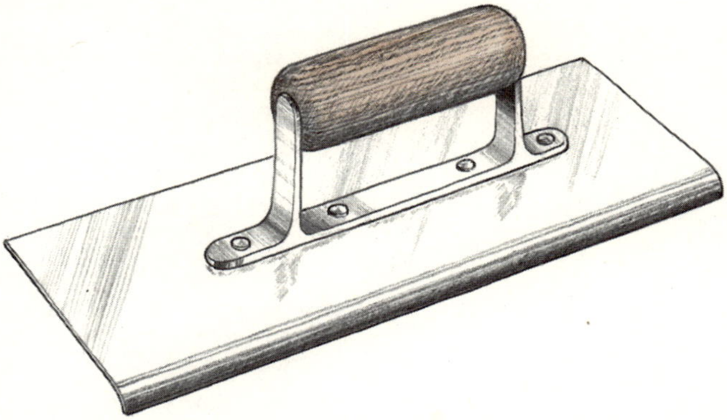

The edging trowel is a floor trowel with one long curved edge. It is used to round off the corners of concrete work.

Flooring Trowel

OTHER NAME: Concreting trowel
SIZE: *Concreting trowel:* 112 × 275mm; *Flooring trowel:* Length: 350 to 450mm
MATERIAL: *Blade:* steel; *Handle:* hardwood
USE: To apply and finish mortar or concrete on a floor

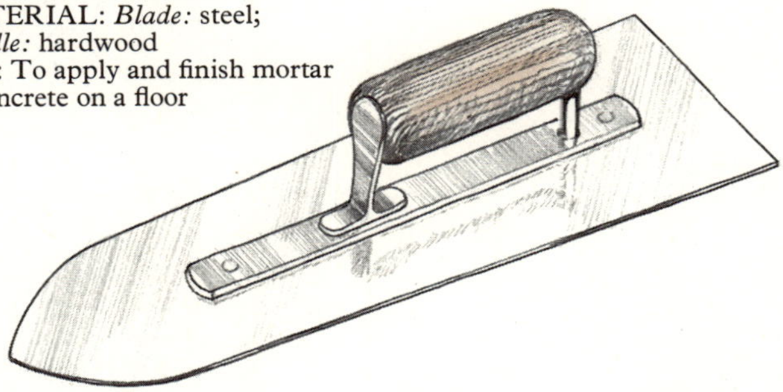

The concreting trowel is similar to a plasterer's trowel but has a heavy gauge steel blade for greater rigidity when working with aggregates. Use it as you would a plasterer's trowel.

Another type of flooring trowel has a much longer blade than normal, which tapers slightly from heel to toe. The toe is pointed for working into corners. The greater surface area of the blade is useful when floating a large floor to a finished smooth texture.

Repairing a concrete floor

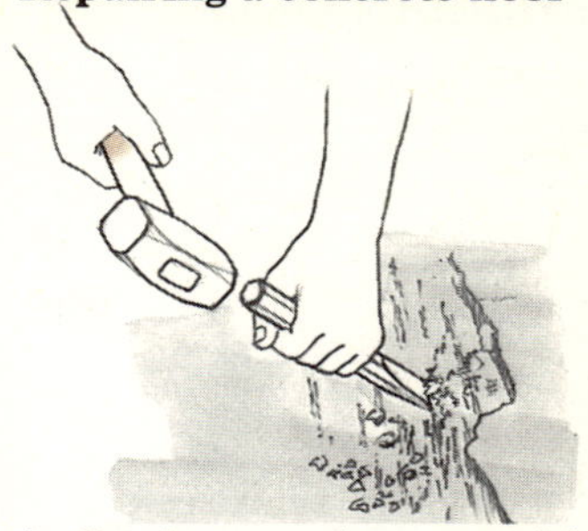

1. *Break up any loose material with a cold chisel to a depth of about 25mm. Use the chisel to undercut the second concrete as a key for the new material.*

2. *Dampen the surface and apply a paste of cement powder and water. Before the paste dries, fill with a concrete mix of 1 part cement, to 2 parts sand and 2 parts fine aggregate. With a concreting trowel push mix well into undercut edges.*

3. *If the surface is uneven after trowelling, use a straight edge to level the surface.*

4. *Finish with a wooden float for a textured finish or a flooring trowel for a smooth one.*

Pointing Trowel

SIZE: Blade length: 75 to 200mm
MATERIAL: *Blade:* steel;
Handle: hardwood
USE: To apply mortar to the joints between bricks

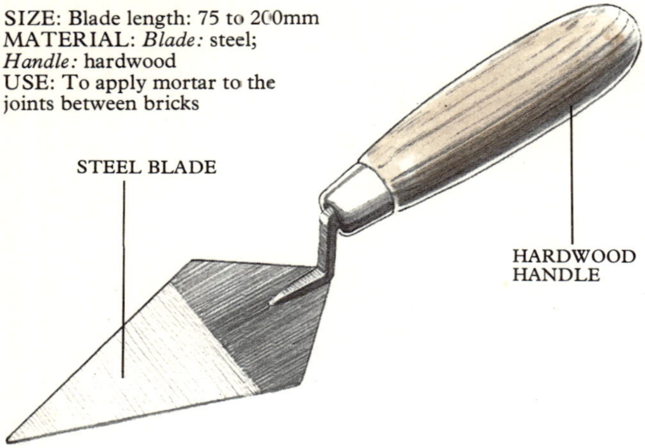

The pointing trowel is shaped and constructed like a brick trowel but is much smaller and has a symmetrical blade. It is one of several tools used to finish the mortar joints between bricks and to apply new mortar to a joint where the old mortar is crumbling.

Repointing
Repairing a crumbling brick joint is known as repointing.

1. *Rake out the loose mortar with a cold chisel to a depth of 12mm. Brush out any loose material and dampen the wall.*

2. *Pick up a roll of fresh mortar from the hawk on the back of a pointing trowel.*

3. *Press it into the vertical joints first, followed by the top and bottom horizontal joints.*

Ready for shaping
When the mortar is just hard enough to take the impression of a thumb without sticking, it is ready to be shaped in a number of ways.

Flush joints
You can make a rough flush joint by rubbing the brickwork with hessian, but a flat bladed jointer ("slicker") produces a better finish.

Raked joints
A flat bladed jointer is also used to produce a raked or recess joint which is not suitable for exposed brickwork.

Weather joint
Form the vertical joints first, angling in either directions, but making sure they are all angled the same way. Form the horizontal joints sloping from top to bottom. Use a straight edge to guide the edge of the jointer to cut off the excess mortar from the bottom.

Concave joint
To make this joint use the convex jointer. It is available, like the slicker, with a chisel-like handle and short blade, or with a double hang handle fitted to a longer ski-like blade turned up at the front. These longer bladed tools are particularly good for finishing the horizontal joints, while the curved front end is ideal for working the vertical joints. The curved section should be slightly wider than the joint.

"V" joint
This is made with the "V" jointer which looks like the convex jointer, but has a deeper, sharply angled blade.

Grapevine joint
This is a decorative flat joint with a deeply impressed shadow line in the centre. It is made with the grapevine jointer which has a central rib.

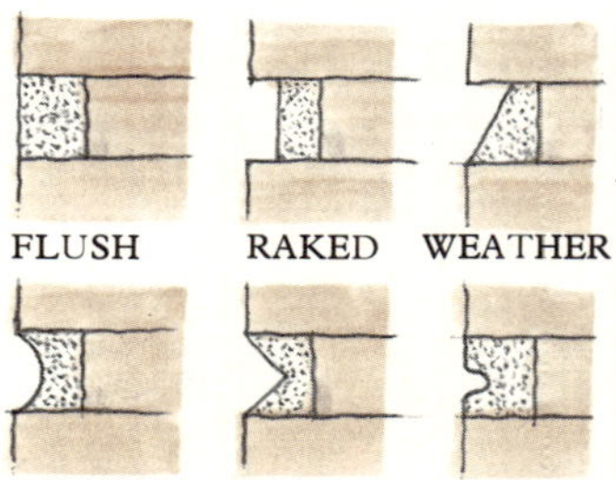

Jointer

OTHER NAMES: Slicker, striking tool, striking iron, brick jointer
SIZE: Blade length: 125 to 300mm
MATERIAL: *Blade:* steel; *Handle:* hardwood
USE: To finish the mortar joints between bricks

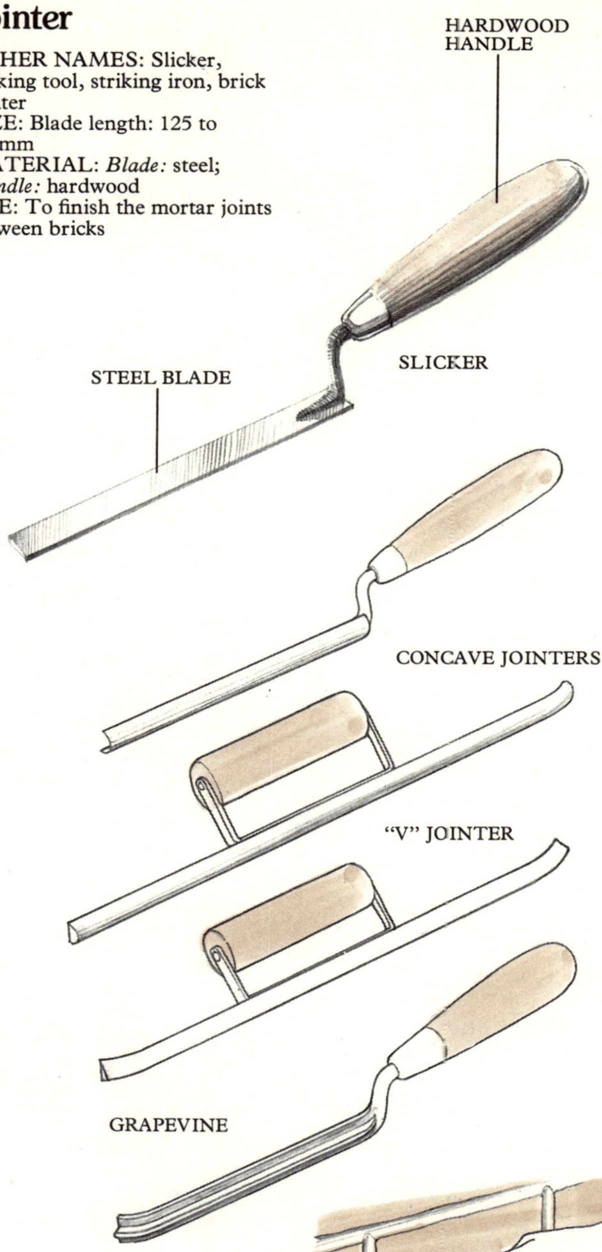

The mortar joints between bricks must be formed in order to make them weatherproof and to improve the appearance of the brickwork. When the mortar is almost dry it is pressed into the required shape. Several jointer tools are available to produce the required joint.

Using a jointer
Work along the vertical joints, first to impress the pattern or angle in the soft mortar.

Wooden Float

OTHER NAME: Skimmer float
SIZE: 125 × 275mm
MATERIAL: *Face:* softwood; *Handle:* hardwood
USE: To finish the surface of concrete or plaster with a fine texture

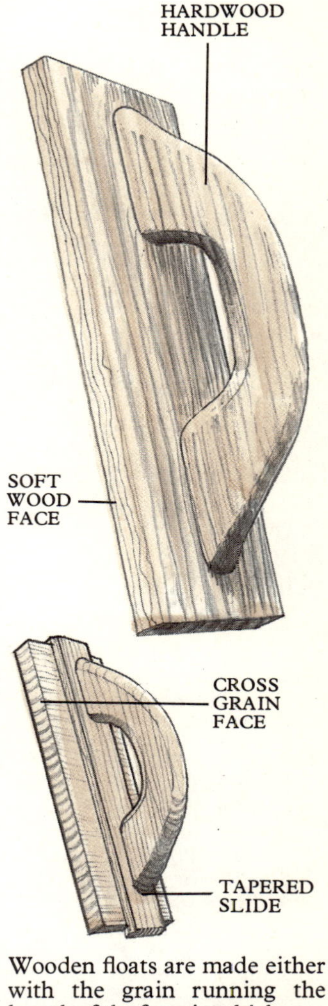

Wooden floats are made either with the grain running the length of the face, in which case the shaped wooden handle is fixed directly to it, or with the grain running across the face. A cross grained float has the handle fitted to a tapered slide, which is dovetailed.

Wooden floats are used to finish or "float" plaster or concrete surfaces producing a finely textured matt surface. Keep face flat while sweeping tool lightly across surface.

Serrated Edge Trowel

OTHER NAMES: Mastic trowel, adhesive trowel, notched trowel
SIZE: Blade length: 112 × 275mm
MATERIAL: *Blade:* steel; *Handle:* hardwood
USE: To spread ceramic tile adhesive

The serrated edge trowel is used to spread adhesive over large areas for operations such as covering a floor with ceramic tiles. There are two types of blades for the trowel which can be bolted to the frame. One blade has small "V" serrations all around, while the other is deeply notched on one side and end, leaving the other edges straight for normal trowelling operations.

Cover about 1 square metre of the floor with adhesive at a time. Holding the blade of the trowel at an angle to the floor, drag it through the adhesive to spread it across the floor to the stipulated thickness.

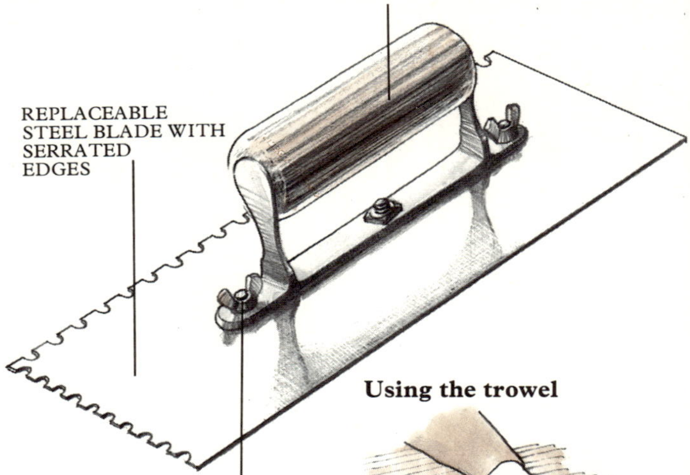

Using the trowel

Moving the trowel in one direction only, raise regular parallel lines to give the required amount of adhesive cover to the area.

Rubber Float

SIZE: 125 × 275mm
MATERIAL: *Face:* softwood surfaced with rubber; *Handle:* hardwood
USE: To apply grout to floor tiles

The rubber float is like a normal wooden float, but is surfaced with rubber. It is used to apply the grout which seals the joints between floor tiles. It is also useful for grouting a large area of wall tiles.

Hold the tool at an angle and sweep it across the surface working the grout into the joints from all angles. Finally wipe off the excess grout from the surface of the tiles with a damp sponge.

Floats can be surfaced with other materials such as plastic foam, cork and carpet. Surfaces of this type are used to texture plaster surfaces to give a decorative finish.

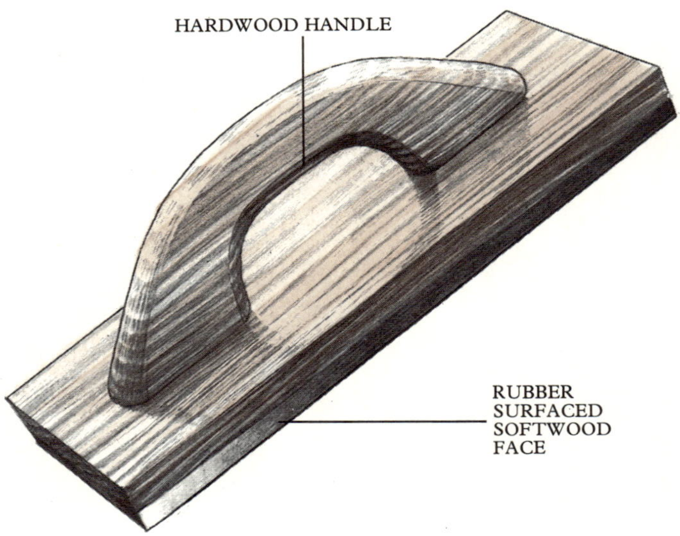

Caulking Gun

OTHER NAME: Mastic gun
SIZE: Length: 600mm
MATERIAL: Steel, zinc and aluminium
USE: To apply a waterproof sealant to joints around door and window frames; to fill cracks

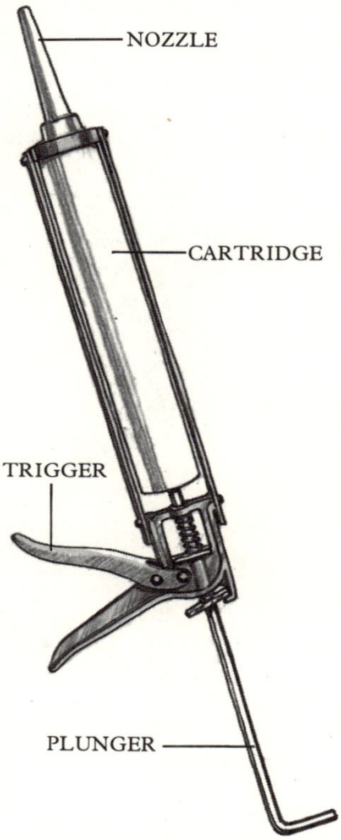

A caulking gun takes standard cartridges of mastic, a flexible, oil or latex based sealant used to seal gaps.

Cartridges of adhesive can be used in the gun to apply glue for wall panelling.

Always hold the gun at 45° to the direction of movement.

Using the gun

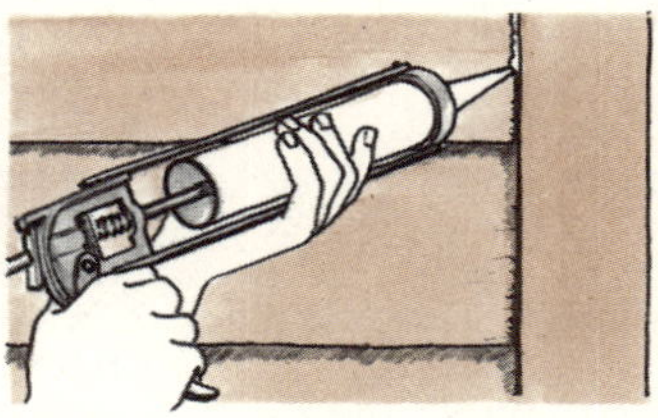

Squeeze the trigger to eject a stream of caulking material from the nozzle.

Concrete Mixer

SIZE: Domestic use: Capacity 42 to 84 cubic litres
MATERIAL: Various
USE: To mix concrete

Small concrete mixers, available from rental companies, are invaluable when a lot of concrete must be mixed for laying floors, paths, driveways and so on. They are petrol or electrically driven, the latter being the less noisy.

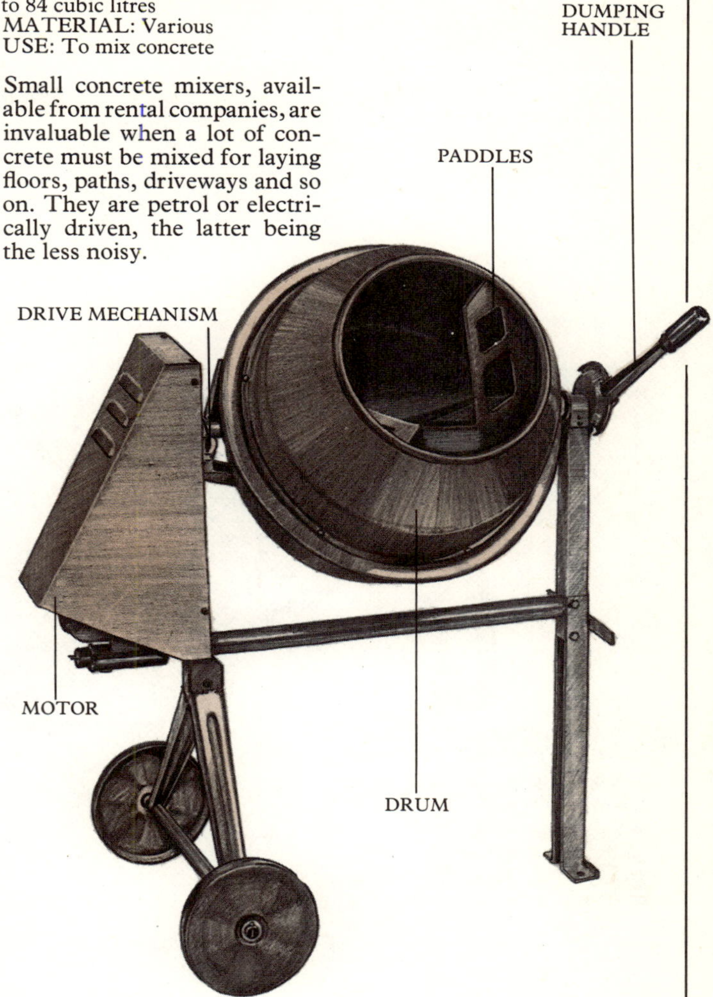

Measure out the ingredients demanded by the required mix, and with the mixer running, load the coarse aggregate into the drum. Load the sand and let it combine with the aggregate. Add the dry cement, letting the ingredients mix thoroughly. Gradually add water until the mix reaches the required consistency letting it mix for about 2 to 3 minutes. Tip mix into a wheelbarrow.

When you have finished with the mixer wash out the drum by spinning coarse aggregate and water in it. Finally hose out the drum and any spilled concrete from the outside.

Wheelbarrow

OTHER NAMES: Contractor's wheelbarrow, concrete barrow
SIZE: Capacity: 84 to 112 cu. ltr
MATERIAL: Steel
USE: To carry loads of mortar, concrete or rubble about the worksite

A strong tubular steel framed barrow is essential to move materials around a work site. Barrows are available with solid and pneumatic tires.

When a loaded barrow must stand for some time, relieve the strain on the tire by supporting the frame in front of the wheel on a brick.

Crow Bar

SIZE: 1.5m
MATERIAL: Steel
USE: To lever heavy weights

A crow bar is a length of 28mm diameter steel rod, pointed at one end and chisel shaped at the other.

Insert one end of the crow bar under the object being moved, and wedge a strong block of wood or masonry under the bar as a fulcrum. Press down on the bar to lever the object out of its place.

Rope Pulley

OTHER NAME: Block and tackle
SIZE: Lifting capacity: 178 to 406kg
MATERIAL: *Line:* sisal, nylon, steel; *Blocks:* various
USE: To lift heavy weights

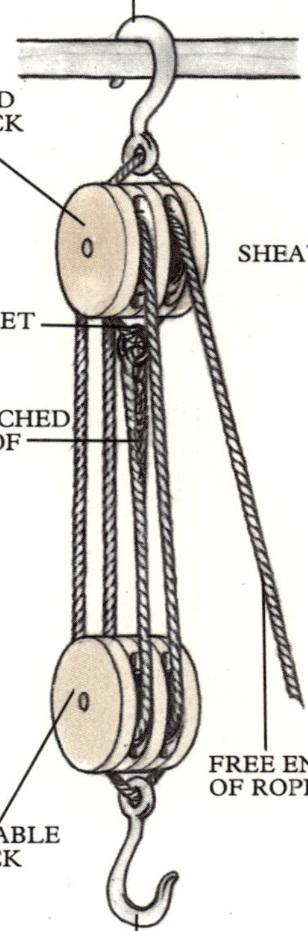

The rope pulley system is a series of blocks and lines used together to lift heavy weights. The more times the rope passes over a wheel or "sheave" in a block, the greater the mechanical advantage and therefore the lifting power. The tackle is held above the weight being lifted by a hook attached to the top, fixed block. This fixing must be secure for efficient and safe lifting. A hook on the lower, movable block is fitted to the weight, which is lifted by pulling on the free end of the rope. If the weight is to be held clear of the ground, tie off the rope securely.

Chain Hoist

OTHER NAMES: Chain blocks, block and tackle
SIZE: Lifting capacity: 254 to 1524kg (available up to 10 tonnes)
MATERIAL: Steel
USE: To lift heavy weights

The chain hoist is used like a rope pulley, but it can lift heavier weights. The power is transmitted to the load through a series of gears or through a double chain wheel.

Chain wheel hoist
The chain wheel assembly has two wheels, one slightly smaller than the other, shaped to prevent the chain slipping. A continuous length of chain passes over the wheels to form two loops. The movable hook hangs from a wheel in one of the loops. If one side of the other loop is pulled, the chain will pass through the whole system, gradually raising or lowering the hook. The load remains at rest in any position without having to be tied off.

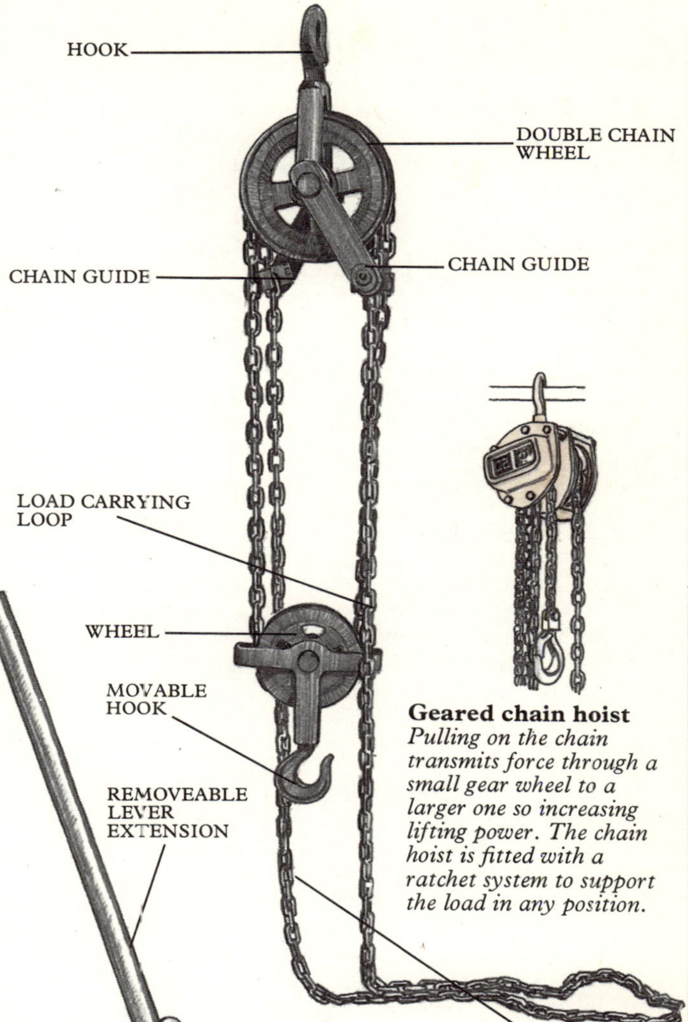

Geared chain hoist
Pulling on the chain transmits force through a small gear wheel to a larger one so increasing lifting power. The chain hoist is fitted with a ratchet system to support the load in any position.

Winch

SIZE: Pulling capacity: ½ to 5 tonnes
MATERIAL: *Jaws/cable/hooks:* steel; *Casing:* aluminium, plastic
USE: To pull heavy weights

The winch is used mainly to uproot tree trunks, or pull heavy weights such as boats or other vehicles but it can be used just as successfully to lift weights vertically.

A lever on the winch activates self-energizing jaws which grip and pull the cable. Open the jaws to pass the cable through the machine. A hook at the other end of the cable is located in a sling which passes around the load. The fixed hook on the winch locates on a similar sling which passes around an anchor point. Pull the cable through the winch by hand to take up the slack, and lock the jaws on to it.

A second lever passes the cable in the opposite direction to take the load off the machine so that the jaws can be opened to retrieve the cable.

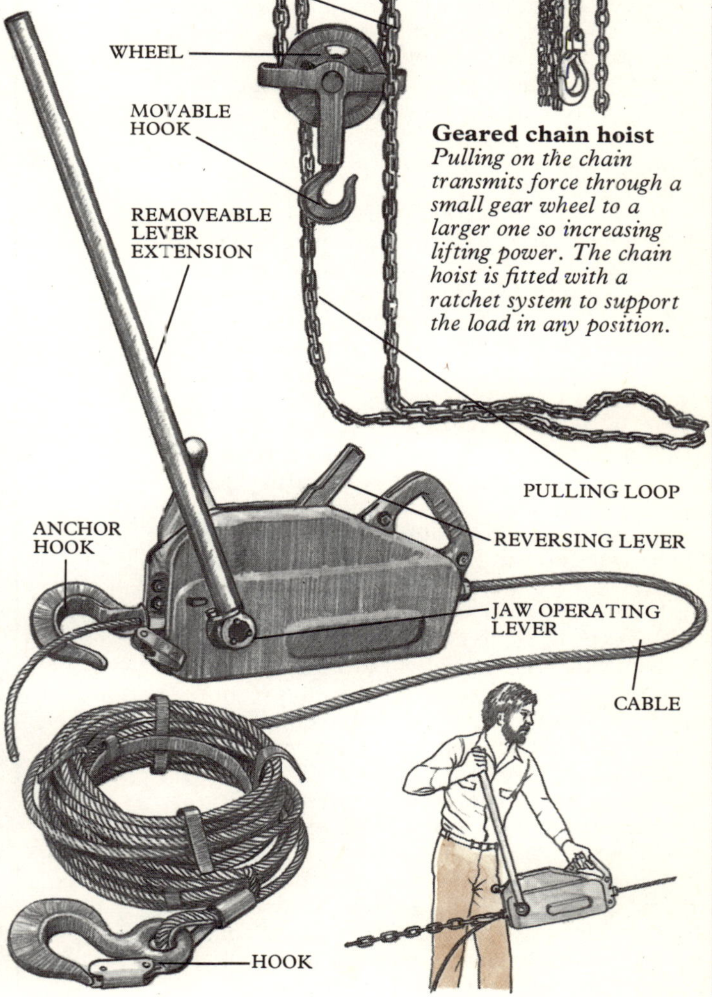

Axes and Hatchets

Like the hammer, the axe is an ancient tool, among the first used by man. It developed over a long period from about 8000 to 2000 BC. The first heads were of flint or other hard stone, fixed to wooden or bone handles, either let in directly or fitted into a slot in a knee-shaped bend and lashed with thongs. The earliest copper axe heads followed the same pattern. With the discovery of the bronze casting process, the heads were made with a slot to fit over the end of the bent handle. It took some time for Bronze Age smiths to realize that a more efficient tool would be produced by making a hole in the head itself to take the handle. Axes constructed this way eventually appeared in Eastern Europe about 2500 BC. Oddly enough the Egyptians never adopted this obvious solution for securing the axe head but preferred the old-fashioned method of attaching the head with thongs. Other notable carpenters of the period, the Cretans and Myceneans, introduced a special tool, the double axe, which also became a religious symbol. It was not known in Europe after the Roman period but re-emerged about 1840 in Maine, USA, where it was used for felling trees.

With the introduction of iron, axes became more specialized. The Romans developed a full range of felling, hewing and general purpose axes and about this time the smiths discovered that iron could be transformed into steel by working it with the charcoal from the forge and that this, when tempered, gave a sharper and more effective tool.

Once the basic construction had been perfected, the axe diversified even further to suit the special requirements of crafts, such as ship-building and barrel-making. During the Middle Ages, different tradesmen developed their own patterns, each type having regional variations according to the kind of work done and the local wood available.

Over the last two centuries, the number of specialized and regional variants has dwindled. However, a revitalizing contribution from America was the long handled, wedge headed felling axe, indispensable to pioneers. Whereas most earlier European axes were flat backed, this had a heavy poll which gave more weight and therefore more momentum to the woodman's swing.

The difference between an axe and a hatchet is primarily one of size. A large, heavy headed tool wielded with both hands is an axe; hatchets are always used with one hand and usually have lighter heads and straight handles.

Axe heads
Head shapes vary according to the function of the axe. They can be wedge shaped, flat backed, curve edged, with or without lugs or even equipped with vocational extras, like the spike on a fire axe. However, the basic elements are the same and the Kent axe head (below) incorporates most of the features found on any modern axe.

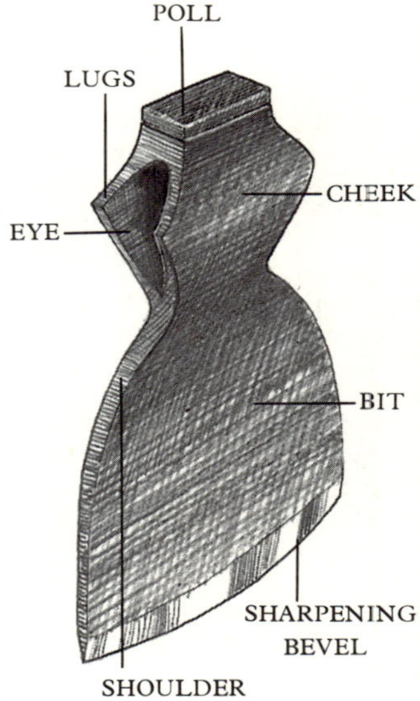

How it works
An axe cuts with a cutting and splitting action. The sharp edge of the bit makes the initial cut and the weight of the thick wedge drives in after it to open up the cut. The heavier the head, the greater the cutting force. The angle at which the cutting edge is ground will to some extent be determined by the wood being cut.

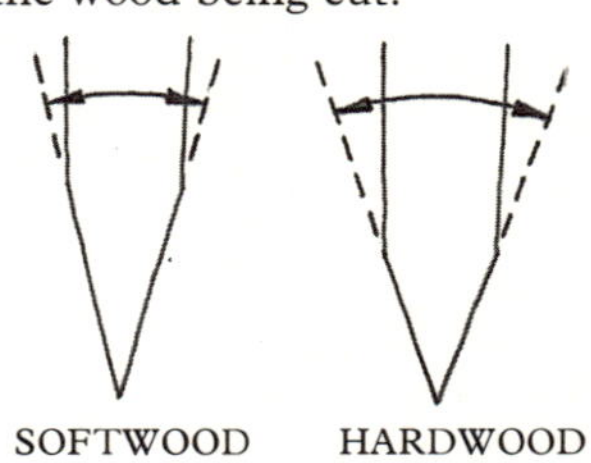

The angle of the edge
A fine narrow edge will suit softwoods but will soon become blunt if used on hardwoods, which need a chunkier, wider angled edge.

Handles, Shafts and Hafts

Axe and hatchet handles are commonly made from hickory or ash. Both woods are strong and springy due to their long fibres, and can withstand and absorb the shocks incurred during use.

Some modern hatchets are now made with tubular steel handles with a hammer-like grip to absorb the shock. These handles are made as an integral part of the hatchet and should last the tool's lifetime.

Handle shapes have traditionally been a matter of personal preference. Before mass production, craftsmen would make their own. These were often straight, being a simpler shape to make, and usually oval in section for comfortable handling and greater directional control. Straight handle axes are still available while hatchets, being one handed tools often have straight, hammer like handles.

The most common axe handle today, used also for hatchets, is the "fawnfoot" pattern. This beautifully curving shape, thought to have evolved in America for the felling axe, has a wide shoulder and a slim, elliptical section. The end has a pronounced swelling resembling the foot of a fawn complete with toe and heel. This is a safety feature which prevents the axe from slipping dangerously through the hand.

Fitting a new shaft

A wooden axe handle is fitted to the head through the waisted, elliptical hole known as the eye. The tapered end of the handle is spread and held in place with a wedge. To replace a broken handle, remove the broken end from the eye using a chisel. Make a saw cut lengthways across the top end of the new shaft and cut a slim hardwood wedge to fit. Drive the handle into the head until it is a tight fit, then drive in the wedge. Cut off any projecting waste flush with the axe head. Additional metal wedges can be driven in across the eye.

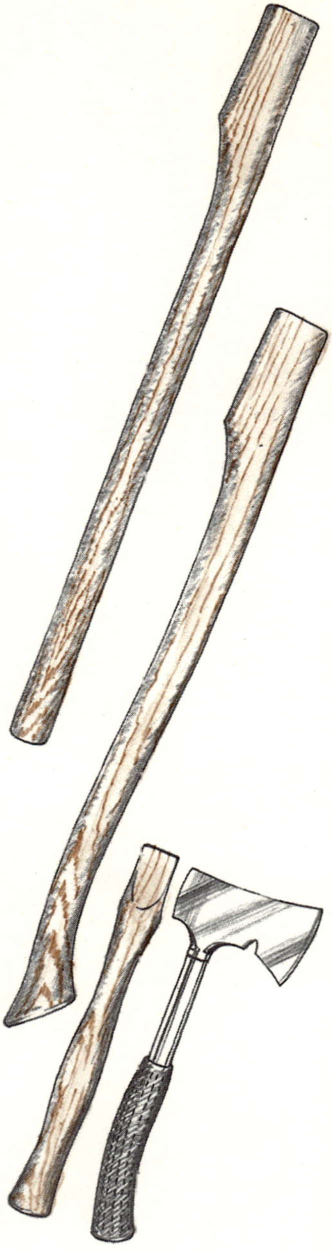

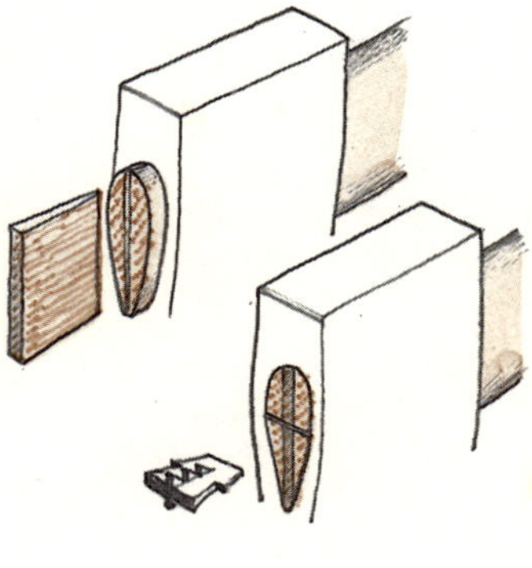

Kent Axe

OTHER NAME: Broad hatchet
SIZE: *Head:* 1kg; *Handle:* 450mm
MATERIAL: *Head:* steel; *Handle:* hickory
USE: General purpose

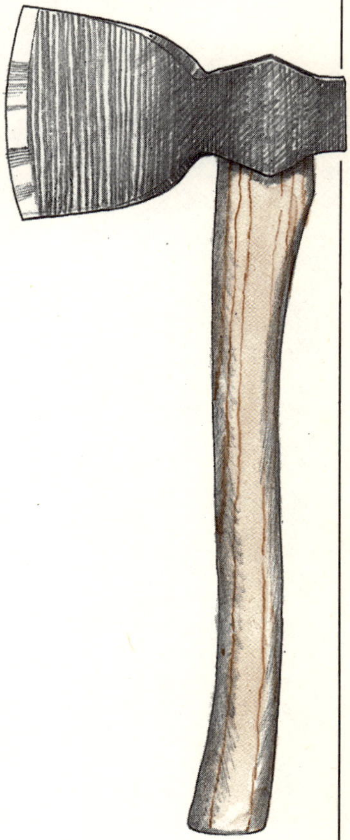

A number of English axes were named after the counties in which they were developed and used but the Kent axe is the only surviving pattern. Although there are a number of variations of the Kent pattern, most have a symmetrical blade with a curved cutting edge, curved shoulders, pointed lugs in front and behind the eye, and a flat poll. The handle is usually the fawnfoot type but a straight, hammer type handle can be fitted to the smaller versions.

Hunter's Hatchet

OTHER NAME: Canada hatchet
SIZE: *Head:* 500 to 700g;
Handle: 350 to 400mm
MATERIAL: *Head:* steel;
Handle: ash or hickory
USE: To trim and shape timber

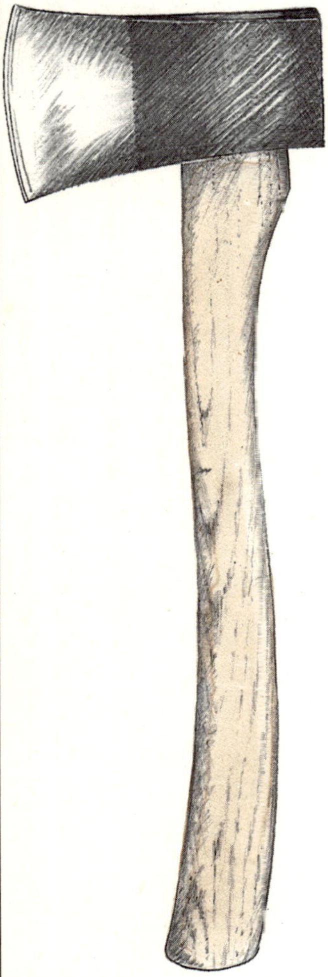

The hunter's hatchet has a light, wedge type head and a slightly curved handle with a straight foot. The Canada hatchet has a similar head, but is fitted with a fawnfoot handle.

Half Hatchet

OTHER NAMES: Shingle hatchet; lathing hatchet
SIZE: *Head:* 500 to 800g;
Handle: 300 to 325mm
MATERIAL: *Head:* steel;
Handle: hickory or steel tube with vinyl grip
USE: To trim and nail shingles or lathes

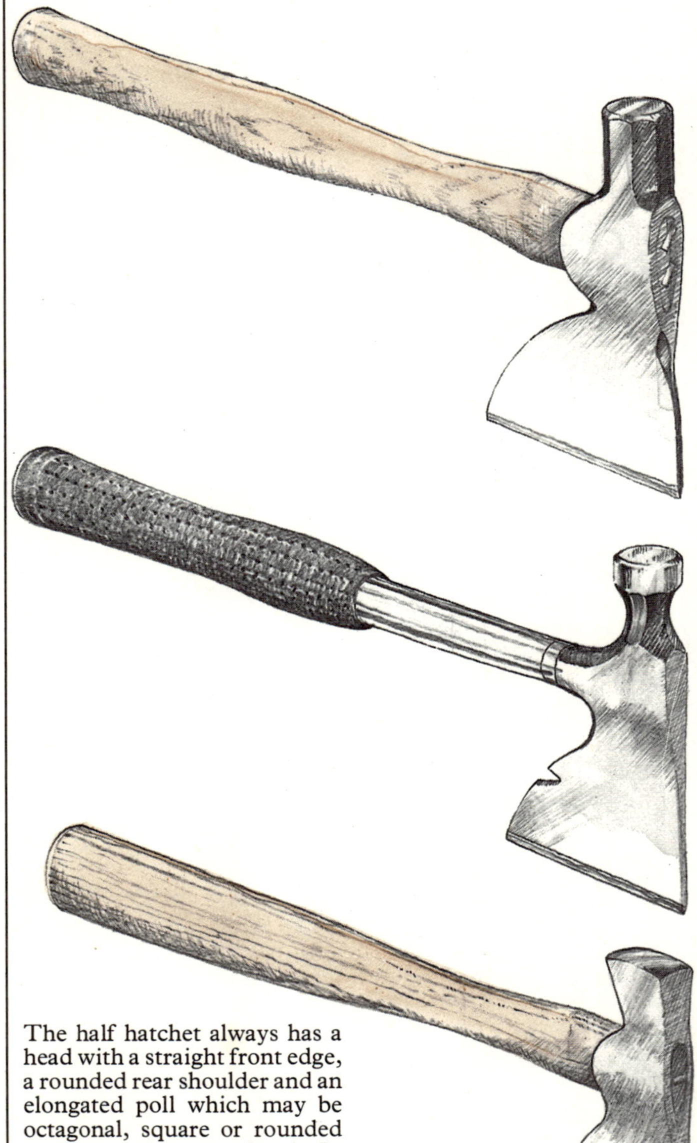

The half hatchet always has a head with a straight front edge, a rounded rear shoulder and an elongated poll which may be octagonal, square or rounded to form a hammer head. In some cases the curved shoulder is notched to form a nail puller. The flat front edge enables the head to be used close to a corner as when fixing lathes near a ceiling.

Wedge Felling Axe

OTHER NAMES: American axe, square axe, Yankee axe
SIZE: *Head:* 1 to 2.75g; *Handle:* 675 to 900mm
MATERIAL: *Head:* steel; *Handle:* hickory
USE: To fell trees or cut a "mouth" for the felling saw

Felling axes are the largest type of axe. The head weight and handle length usually reduce in proportion to maintain a well balanced tool.

The wedge pattern, said to have come to prominence in the USA, is now the most widely used type for felling and general work. It has a thick short head with a single wedge shaped bit and is noted for its large flat poll. The cheeks are extra thick, swelling out about 50mm up from the cutting edge which has a cutting bevel on each side. Its stocky shape and concentrated weight make this pattern comparatively easy to use – its steadier and therefore more accurate to swing. There are many regional variations – Kentucky wedge, Canadian wedge, etc.

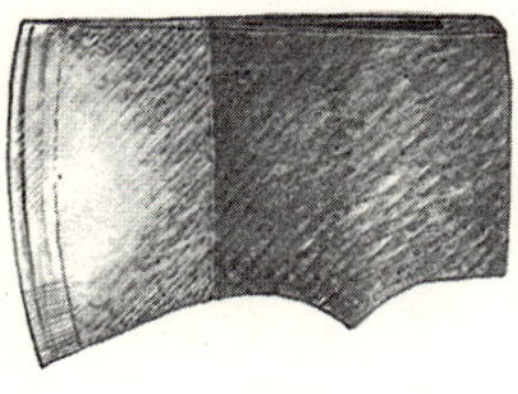

JERSEY WEDGE

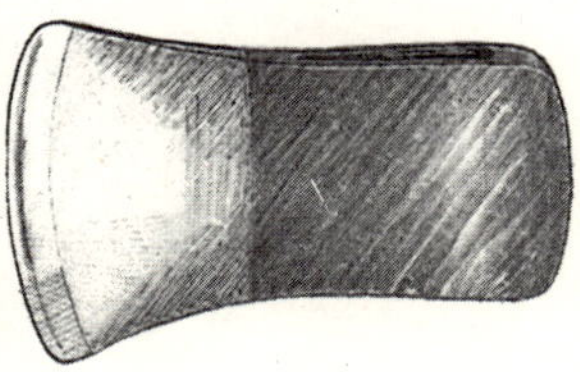

MICHIGAN WEDGE

KENTUCKY WEDGE

Kent Felling Axe

OTHER NAMES: English felling axe, trimming axe, rounding axe
SIZE: *Head:* 1.45 to 2.75kg; *Handle:* 700 to 900mm
MATERIAL: *Head:* steel; *Handle:* hickory
USE: To fell, lop and top trees

This axe has a straight front edge, single flared shoulder, and pointed lug behind the eye. It has a longer, slimmer head than the American wedge and a square poll.

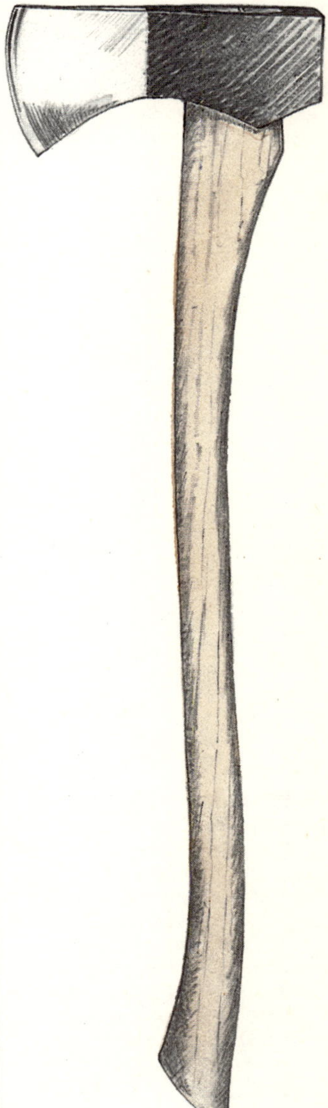

Double Bit Axe

SIZE: Head: 1.45kg
MATERIAL: *Head:* steel; *Handle:* hickory
USE: To fell, lop and top trees

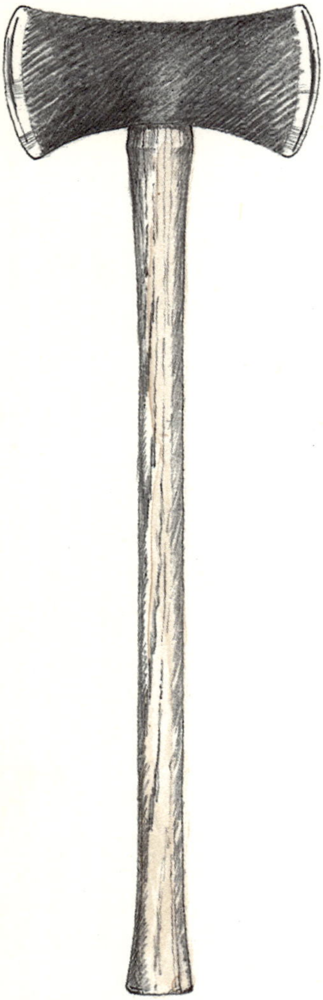

This axe has a wedge type head with two cutting edges and is, in effect, two axes in one. Because the two edges share the work, it does not need sharpening so often. It can also be ground to different cutting bevels for various types of work.

The axe is fitted with a straight, symmetrical handle which allows it to be gripped either way round. It is most commonly known in the USA, where it has been irreverently called the Methodist Axe because it is two faced.

Using a felling axe
The felling axe is designed to be used with two hands, one gripping the handle close to the foot end, the other sliding up and down the handle during the swing. The swing should be a natural movement using the whole body, legs apart and slightly flexed to give good stability, and the feet firmly placed.

Downward cut
Lift the axe with the sliding hand under the head. Pull this arm back, lifting the axe head up and away from the tree, at the same time twisting your body. Your fixed hand, holding on to the front of the handle, will pass across your body and at maximum lift will be about level with your shoulders.

As the stroke is made, this hand and arm pulls the axe across the body, with the sliding hand following through, guiding the tool. Both hands should meet at the bottom of the stroke. A slight jerk should free the blade from the cut and the process can then be repeated.

Upward cut
An upward cut is made in a similar way but the axe is pulled back in a low arc with the body bent away from the tree.

Take care to avoid a glancing blow which could cause the blade to skid off the tree.

Slater's Axe

SIZE: Length: approximately 400mm
MATERIAL: *Head:* steel; Handle: ash
USE: To trim and cut slate

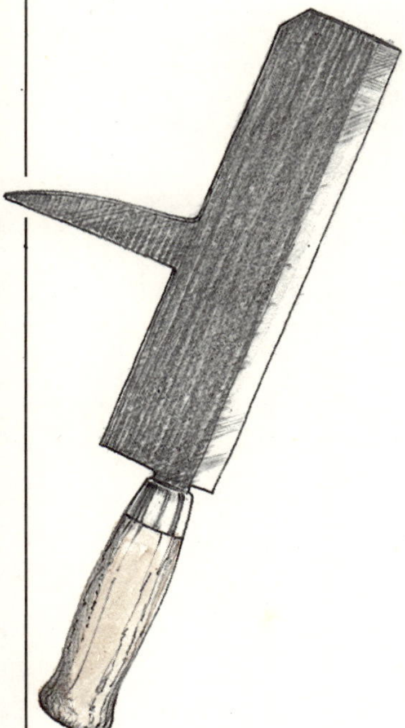

The slater's axe has a rectangular shaped bit about 250mm long. It is fitted by means of a tang to a 150mm round section handle that is parallel with the cutting edge. A flat spike, curving slightly backward toward the handle projects from the back edge of the bit near the center. The spike is for punching nail holes into slates.

To trim slate, support the roughly shaped piece on a straight edged flat block. With the edge of the slate overhanging the block, make a series of cuts with the axe using the straight edge as a guide. On finishing the first side, turn the slate 90° and trim the second side. Continue until all sides are straight and square.

Side Axe

OTHER NAMES: Broad axe, hewing axe
SIZE: Head: 1.5 to 3kg
MATERIAL: *Head:* steel; *Handle:* ash or hickory
USE: To trim, shape and dimension timber

A side axe was widely used by the medieval builder but is uncommon now. It is short handled and easily manoeuvred in a small space. Only one edge of the bit is bevelled for cutting, as the blade is used flat against the work. It belongs to the broad axe family, and so has a curved cutting edge wider than the depth of the head. Side axes are sometimes fitted with specially cranked handles which offset the grip and provide generous knuckle clearance.

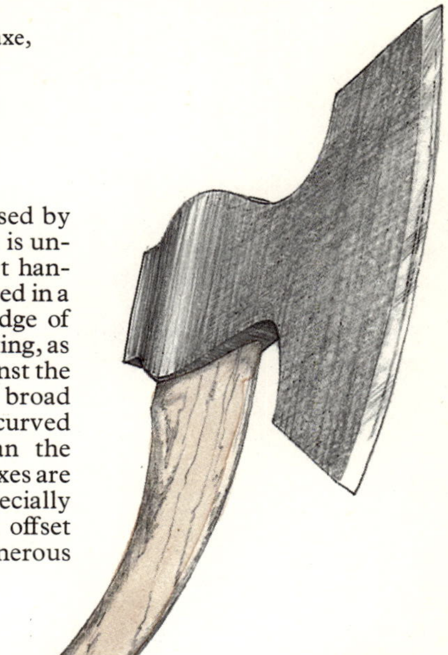

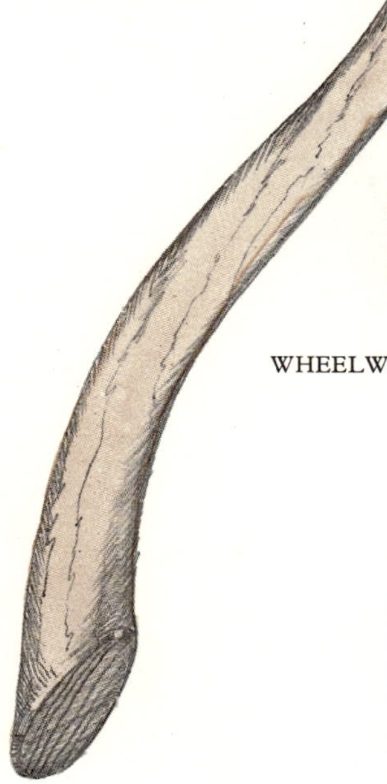

Alternatively, the eye of the axe is set off-centre to throw the handle out at an angle from the line of the cutting edge. A number of trades used side axes in various forms, and these were known as coopers' axes, coachmakers' axes, and wheelwrights' axes. In each case they were used for shaping components such as barrel staves or wheel spokes.

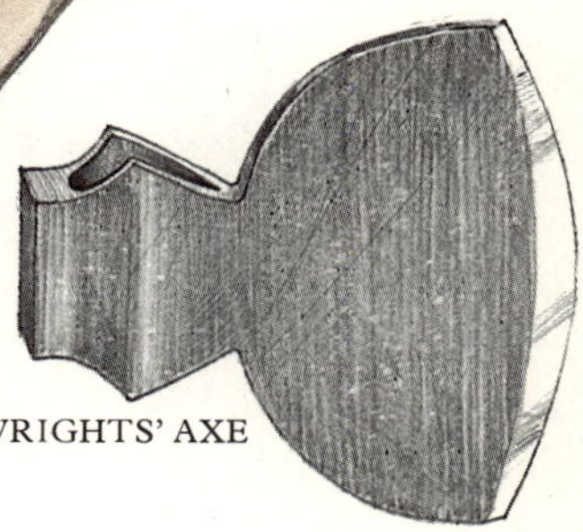

WHEELWRIGHTS' AXE

COACHMAKERS' AXE

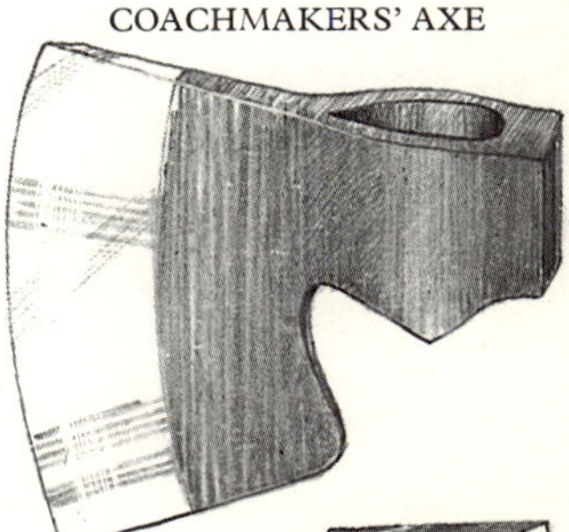

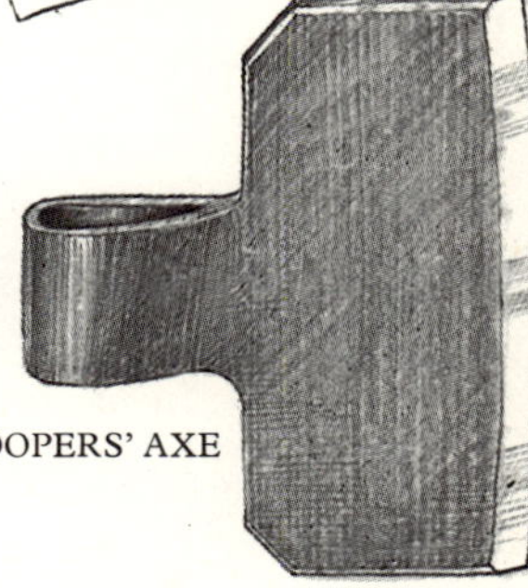

COOPERS' AXE

Adze, Hooks and Scythe

The history of the adze follows very closely that of the axe. The heads were made of the same materials and the shape was similar. However the fixing to the handle had to be modified to bring the cutting edge at right angles to it instead of being in the same plane. For this reason the adze is still known as the "cross-axe" in some countries.

The Cretans of the Late Bronze Age had double bladed adzes and the axe-adze, with an axe on one side and an adze on the other. Roman carpenters thought very highly of the axe-adze, indeed no Roman carpenter or military engineer would be seen without one. It still survives as the grubbing mattock.

One problem with the adze is that in normal use it is difficult to keep the head rigid on the handle. The Cretans first solved this by providing a deep socket; the socket is now made square and the eye tapered so that the head can be easily removed for grinding and sharpening.

Adze

SIZE: *Cutting edge width:* 75 to 137mm; *Head weight:* 1.4 to 2kg
MATERIAL: *Head:* steel; *Handle:* hickory
USE: To trim and shape the surface of large sections of wood

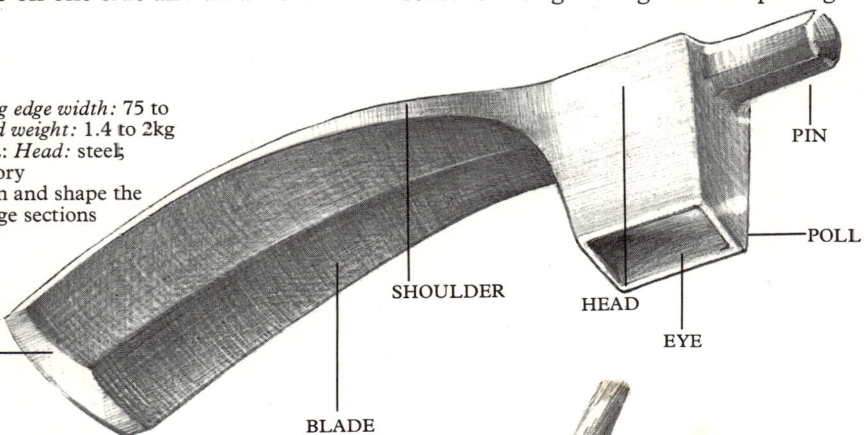

The cutting edge of the adze blade is at right angles to the line of the handle and is ground on the back surface only. The longitudinal curve of the blade is matched to the arc of the swing of the tool using the traditional curved handle. The adze head eye is squared and tapered so that the head is automatically tightened during the swing, but can be removed for sharpening by slipping it along the handle.

Different shaped heads are available. The carpenter's, shipbuilder's and curved blade adze heads, in use for centuries, are still available in modern tool catalogues.

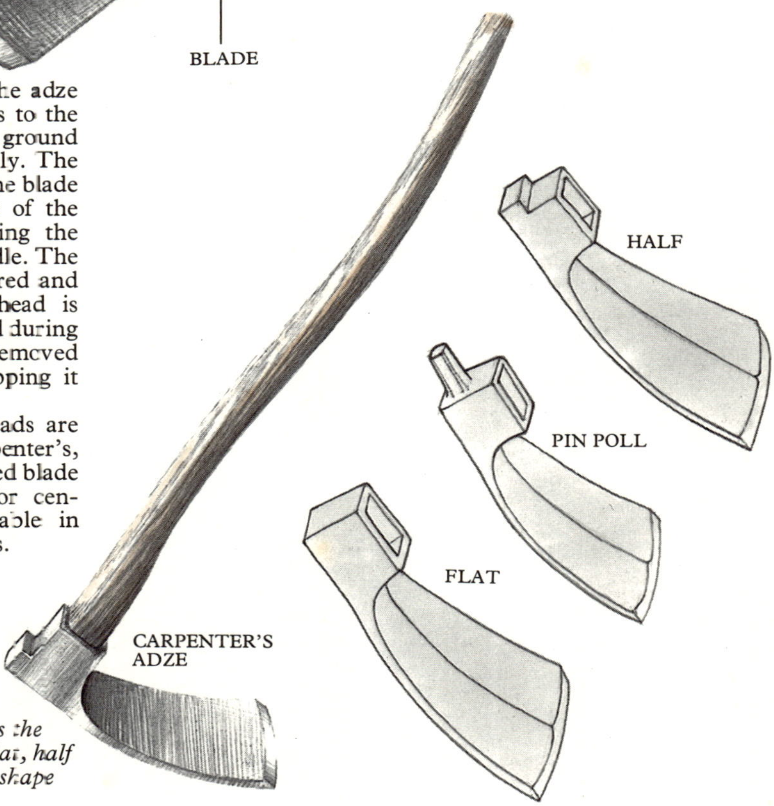

Carpenter's adze
This is almost flat across the blade and may have a flat, half or pin poll. It is used to shape flat sections of wood.

SHIPBUILDER'S ADZE
This tool is like the carpenter's adze but it has a flared cutting edge 137mm wide.

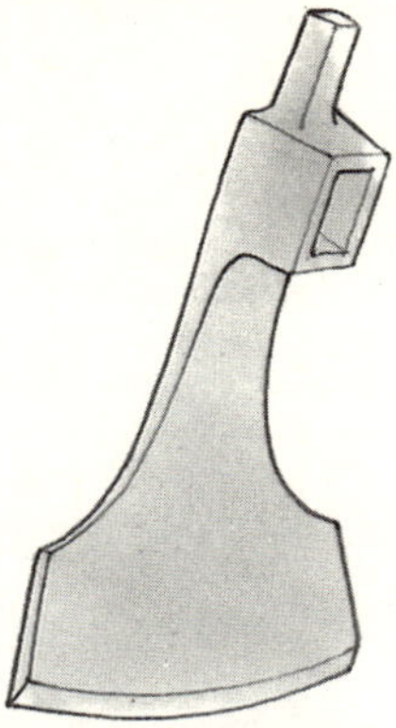

Curved blade adze
This tool has a curved, gouge type head with a blade curved in both directions. It is used to cut hollows such as the traditional wooden seat of the "Windsor" chair.

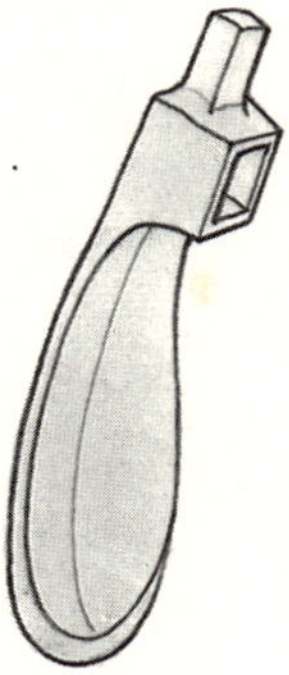

Using the adze
Stand on or astride the workpiece and swing the adze backward and forward with a pendulum action. The thigh controls the depth of the swing by acting as a stop against the swinging arm. In skilled hands an adze can remove a considerable amount of wood or produce fine shavings when finishing the surface.

Froe

OTHER NAMES: Riving axe, cleaving iron, rending axe
SIZE: Blade length: approximately 375mm
MATERIAL: *Blade:* steel; *Handle:* hickory
USE: To split timber along the grain

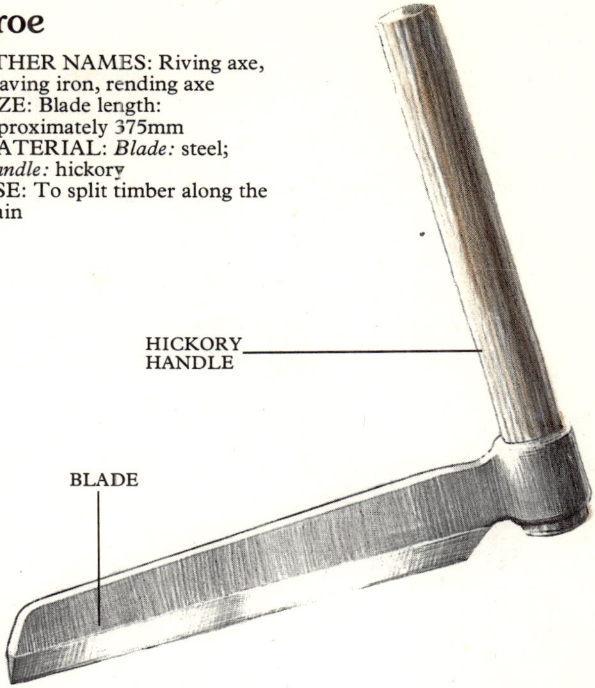

The froe is used to split wood along the grain. It is much quicker to split lumber along the grain than to saw it. It was already in common use in Roman times where it was used chiefly to split oak roofing shingles. The tool is still in use for this purpose as well as to split timber for planks, wheel spokes or simply firewood.

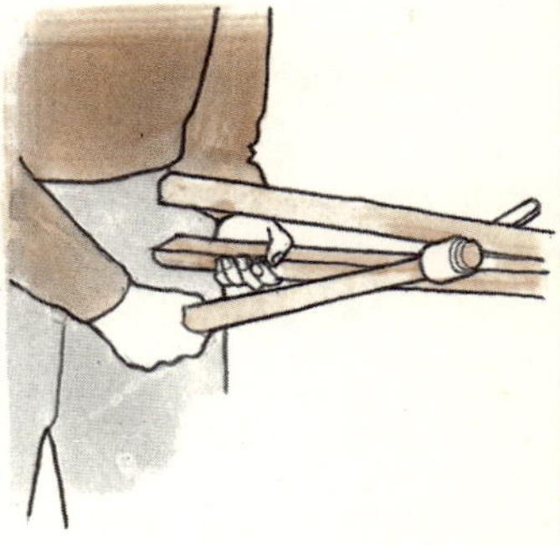

Using the froe
Drive the wedge shaped blade into the end grain of the timber with a wooden mallet or froe club. Use the handle, extending at right angles to the blade, as a lever to twist the blade, extending the split lengthwise. If the timber resists splitting, drive the blade further with the mallet, and lever once more.

Bill Hook

SIZE: Blade length 225 to 250mm
MATERIAL: *Blade:* steel; *Handle:* ash
USE: To cut and lay hedges and split branches

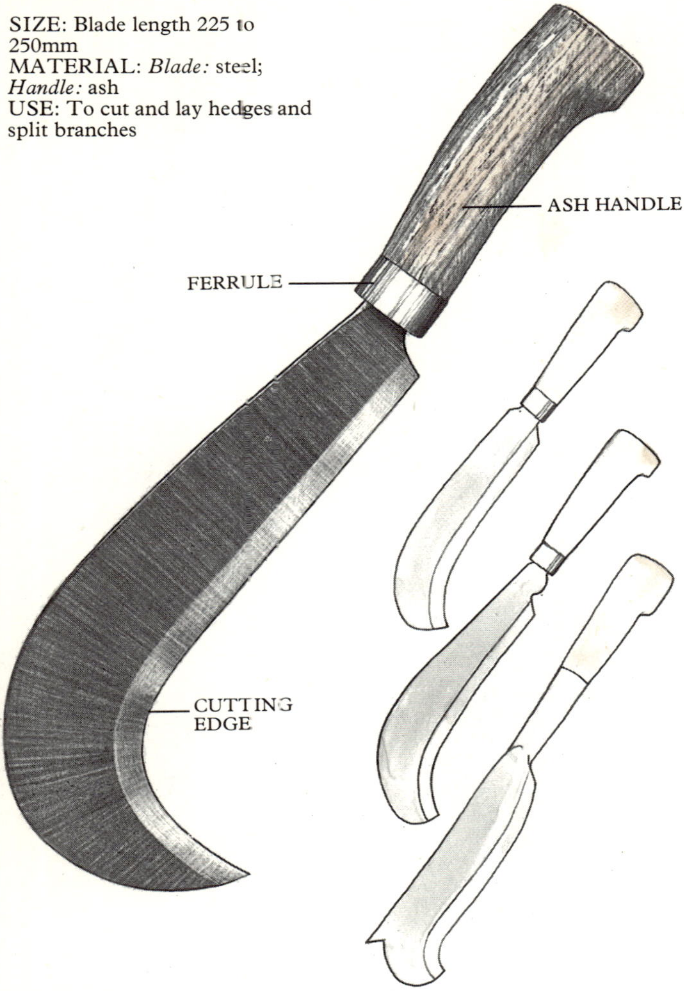

The bill hook is a wide bladed knife fitted with a straight handle, used to chop wood, to split thin branches, to make hurdles and to lay hedges. There is still a variety of "hooks" available from modern catalogues, which are derived from patterns developed many years ago by local craftsmen.

The tang of the blade passes right through the hardwood handle and is riveted over. The swelling at the end of the handle prevents the tool slipping out of the hand when it is swung with a chopping action.

Sharpen the cutting edge of the bill hook with a slipstone or use a scythe stone.

Laying a hedge

To make a strong hedge, thin out every five years leaving the strong bushes every 300mm. Trim off branching and cut the the stem of the bush halfway through, near the ground with a downward angled stroke. Bend the bush to a flat angle, facing uphill, locating it under its neighbor to secure it. When a row of bushes are cut and bent, interweave stakes with them.

Country people in Britain use the bill hook to lay hedges and make lightweight fencing.

Cut stakes out of the hedge leaving strong bushes about a foot apart. Bend each tree trunk over and half cut near the base. Force it down nearly horizontal but do not break.

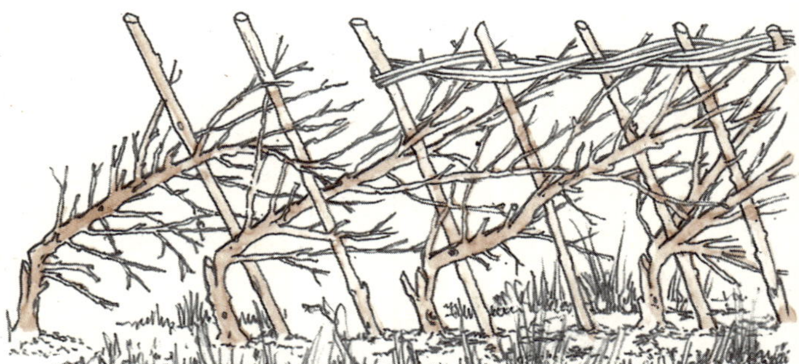

Interweaving stakes
Try to push part of each horizontal trunk under its neighbour, always working uphill. Drive in the stakes at right angles to the trunks making sure they are interwoven with the trunks. Secure the tops with split willow and hazel.

Making a wooden fence
You can make lightweight fencing by driving sharpened stakes every 225mm into the ground or into a prepared length of wood and interweaving them with split, pliable willow, hazel or holly branches. The bill hook is used to sharpen the stakes and to split the "withies". Start the cut in the end of the branch and twist the blade to propagate the split along the grain. The resulting strip is woven between the stakes and at the end, is twisted before returning it along the row to prevent it breaking at that point.

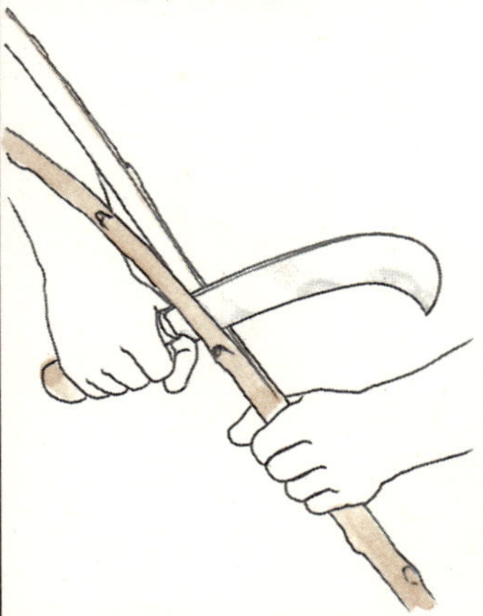

Splitting the withies
Use the bill hook to split willow, holly or hazel branches to make weaving strips.

Weaving the strips
After splitting the withies, weave each strip through the upright stakes.

Slashing Hook

OTHER NAME: Brushing hook
SIZE: *Blade length:* 225 to 350mm; *Handle length:* 550 to 800mm
MATERIAL: *Blade:* steel; *Handle:* ash
USE: To cut back hedges and undergrowth

Slashing hooks are fitted with long handles so that the head can be swung with considerable force when clearing undergrowth and thinning out hedges. They have similar blades to the bill hook and are also available in a wide variety of locally produced shapes, including a sickle-like blade.

Clearing overgrown hedges
Use the slasher to control "runaway" hedges but remove undergrowth with a shorter-handled hook.

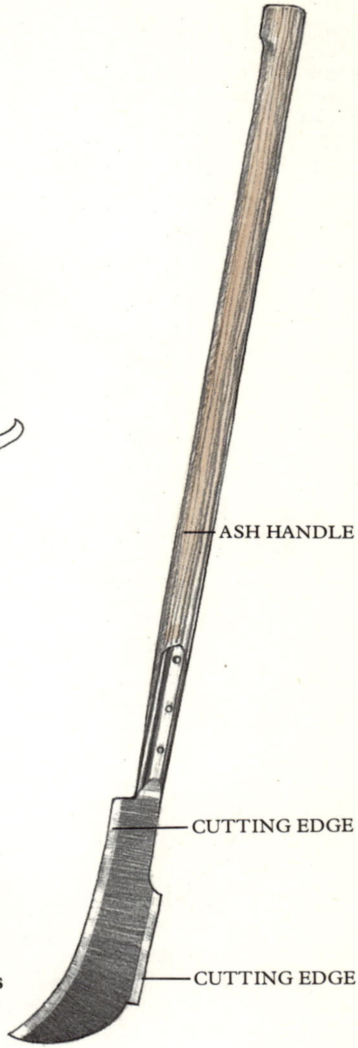

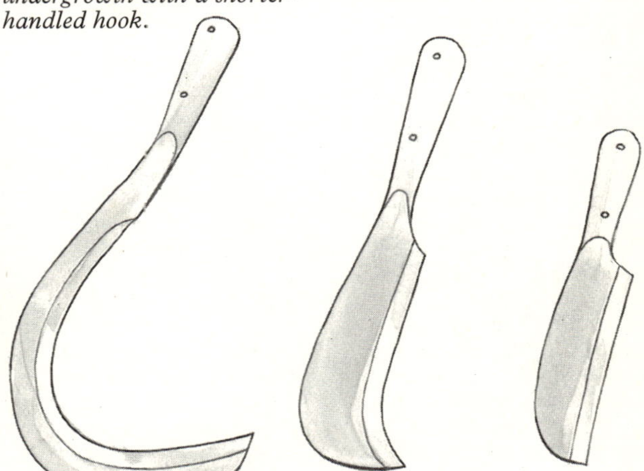

Scythe

SIZE: *Blade:* 600mm to 1m;
Snath: 1.4m
MATERIAL: *Blade:* steel;
Snath: hickory, aluminium alloy
USE: To cut weeds and long grass

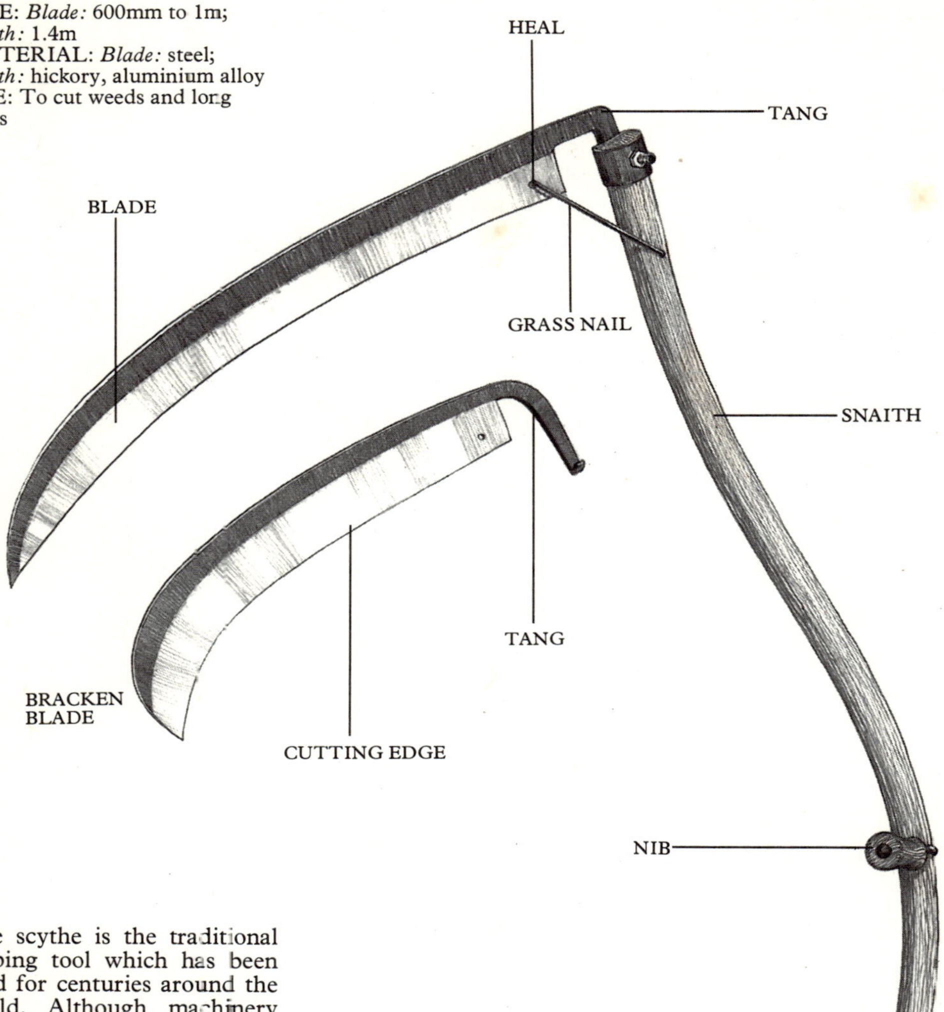

The scythe is the traditional reaping tool which has been used for centuries around the world. Although machinery has taken over the scythe's reaping role, it is still useful for cutting down extensive areas of long grass, weeds or bracken. The long, slightly curving blade, sharpened along one edge has a right angled tang which fits into a metal collar on the end of the elegantly curving shaft or snath. Other names for the shaft are snade, snead, sneathe and batt. The handles, known as nibs, hand pins or doles are fitted at an angle which suits the user. The grass nail, a rod which is stretched across from the snath to the blade, prevents grass lodging between the heel of the blade and the snath.

Using the scythe
Sweep the scythe across and in front of you. Adopt a steady rhythm. Experienced countrymen should be able to mow up to an acre per day.

Sickle

OTHER NAMES: Reaping hook, bagging hook, grass hook
SIZE: Blade length: 450 to 650mm
MATERIAL: *Blade:* steel; *Handle:* hardwood, tubular steel, aluminium alloy
USE: To cut long grass and weeds

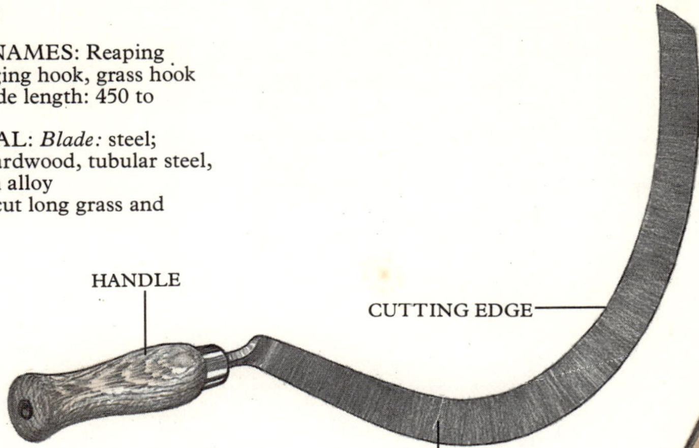

Sickles are curved knives which are still used to cut long grass or weeds in areas which are difficult to clear with machinery or even a scythe. The handle is angled upward so that the blade is swept parallel with the ground.

Using the sickle

With a natural sweeping movement of the hand and wrist, slice sideways through the grass. Hold back overhanging growth with a stick.

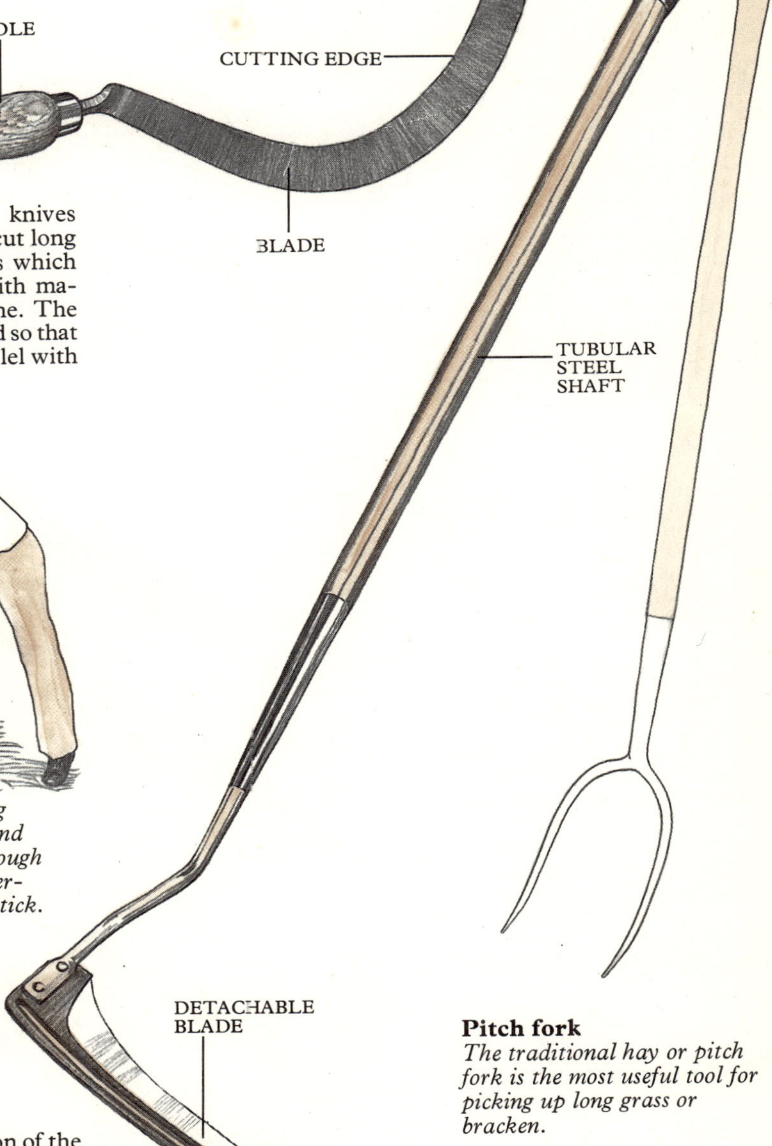

Grass hook
This is a modern version of the sickle, and it is a cross between the sickle and scythe. It has a slightly curving blade which can be fitted with a short, handle or with a tubular steel shaft up to 800m long.

Pitch fork
The traditional hay or pitch fork is the most useful tool for picking up long grass or bracken.

Digging Tools

The principal tool of the Neolithic farmers was the hoe, which had a stone head lashed to the handle, like the woodworkers' adze of the time. Down to the Middle Ages shovels for shifting earth or mixing mortar were made of solid wood, but spades for digging were shod with iron, usually costing about four times as much as the spade itself. The grubbing mattock is a direct descendant of the Roman soldier-carpenter's axe-adze, which also fathered the pickaxe. Digging forks and hand forks came later.

Pickaxe

OTHER NAME: Pick
SIZE: *Weight:* 2.2, 3, 4.5kg; *Handle:* 900mm
MATERIAL: *Head:* steel; *Handle:* hickory, good quality ash
USE: To break up solid materials

Pickaxes have one pointed tip, which is used to hack through concrete and other very hard surfaces. The chisel (or spade) tip is used for chipping up softer materials, like asphalt, or compacted soil. A lightweight 1.8kg pickaxe with a 650mm handle is handy for garden use. Heads and handles can be bought separately.

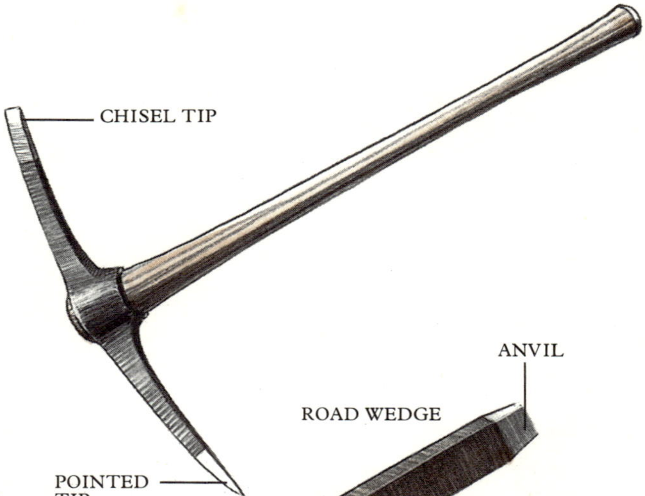

Road Wedge and Tongs

SIZE: *Wedge:* 450 × 43mm; *Tongs:* 600mm
MATERIALS: Steel
USE: To break up tough surfaces

These tools are used on surfaces too rugged to be broken up with a pickaxe, or to make a start before getting to work with a pickaxe. One person holds the wedge, with the point against the surface, in the tongs, while another strikes it with a heavy hammer. These tools are now generally superseded by power tools.

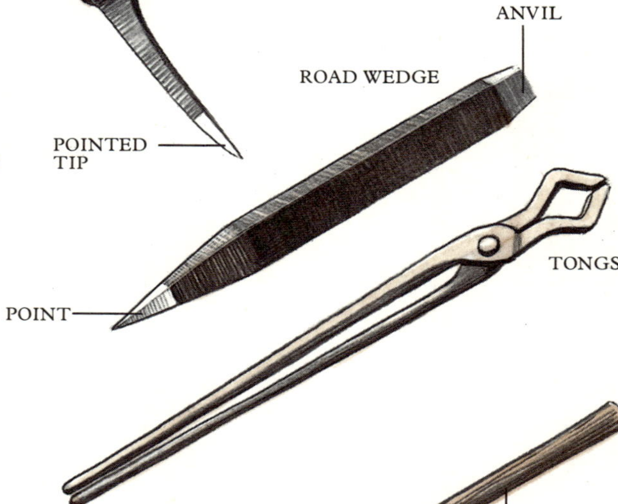

Grubbing Mattock

SIZE: *Weight:* 2.2kg; *Handle:* 900mm
MATERIAL: *Head:* steel; *Handle:* hickory, good quality ash
USE: To grub out tree roots

The chisel tip of the grubbing mattock is used to break the ground up around the roots and split and hack out the remains of the stump below ground. The wider blade loosens and prises out roots.

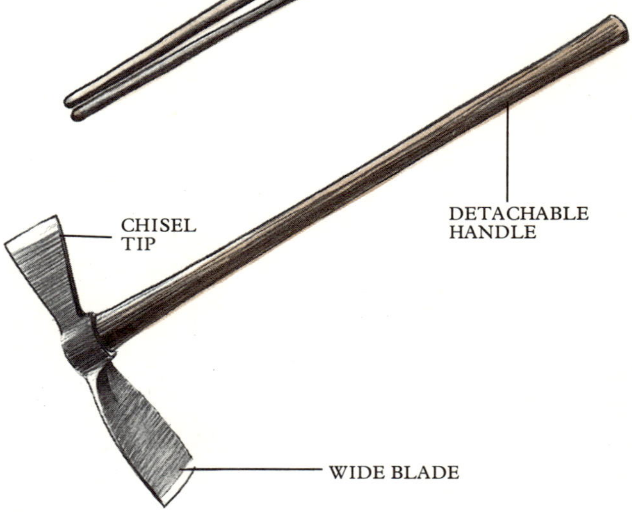

Post Hole Digger

OTHER NAMES: Post hole borer, post hole auger
SIZE: *Blades:* 150mm; *Shaft:* 1.2m
MATERIAL: Steel
USE: To make holes in the ground to take fence supports

The most effective version of the post hole digger is a borer which is pushed into the soil and twisted like a corkscrew. The blades, mounted horizontally on a steel bit, cut rapidly through the soil which is carried up to the surface by their action, leaving the hole clear.

Tree Planting Tool

OTHER NAMES: Draining tool, trenching tool
SIZE: *Blade:* 412 × 137mm
MATERIAL: *Blade:* alloy steel; *Handle:* wood or strengthened plastic; *Shaft:* wood
USE: To plant trees

The length of the blade makes it easier to dig to a good depth for tree planting, particularly where you do not want to disturb the surrounding ground too much. The long tapering blade shape makes it possible to dig out a deep, straight-sided hole suitable for fence posts. It is also used for drainage trenches and channels.

Shovel

SIZE: 275 × 212mm; 306 × 250mm; 412 × 350mm
MATERIAL: *Head:* steel; *Shaft:* hardwood, tubular alloy steel
USE: To shift gravel, manure, sand, cement, coal

Shovels are made in different shapes – taper mouth, round mouth and square mouth. The taper mouth is a dual purpose shovel used for shifting loads and for digging. The round mouth is used for shovelling up heavy material like rubble, and is also sometimes used for digging. The square mouth shovel is chiefly used for shifting sand and cement, particularly in concrete making, when the straight edge of the head can be used to mix the constituents together.

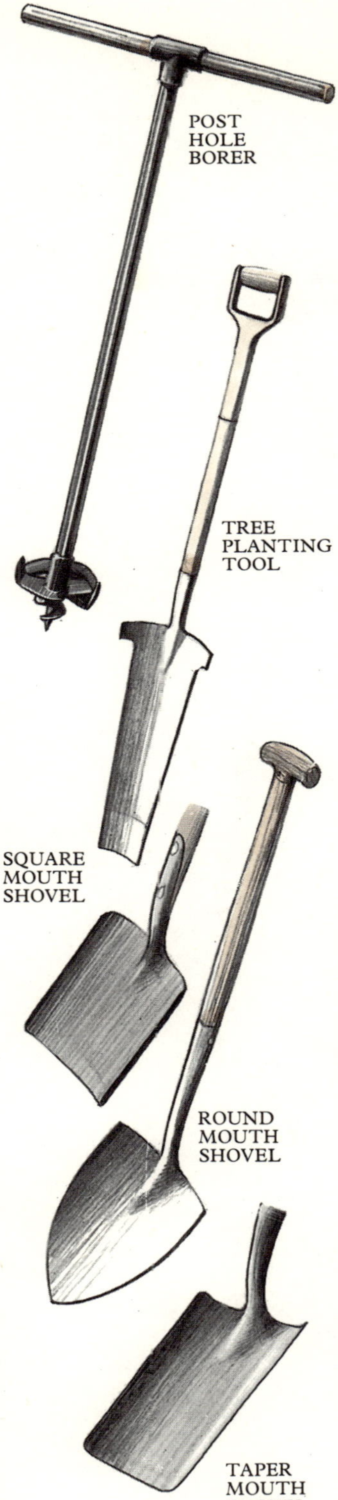

Border Spade

SIZE: 225 × 167mm
MATERIAL: *Blade:* alloy steel, stainless steel; *Handle:* moulded plastic, hardwood; *Shaft:* aluminium alloy, hardwood
USE: Light digging

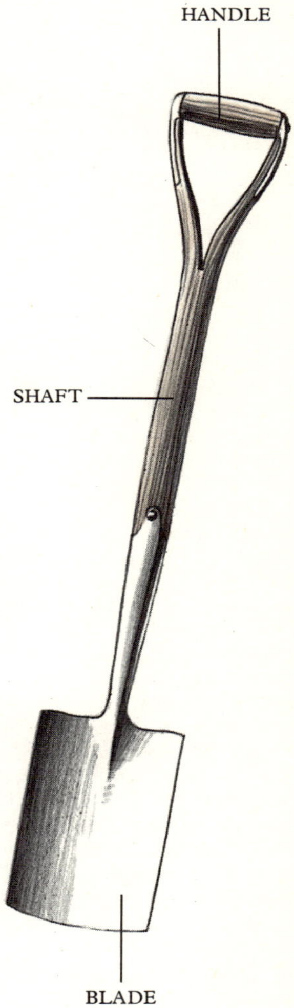

Border spades are useful when digging in restricted plots or among established plants. Being lighter in weight they are often suitable for the elderly or disabled gardener, but can be used wherever light digging only is needed.

Digging Spade

SIZE: 187 × 287mm, 162 × 262mm
MATERIAL: *Blade:* alloy steel, stainless steel; *Handle:* moulded plastic, hardwood; *Shaft:* hardwood
USE: Heavy digging

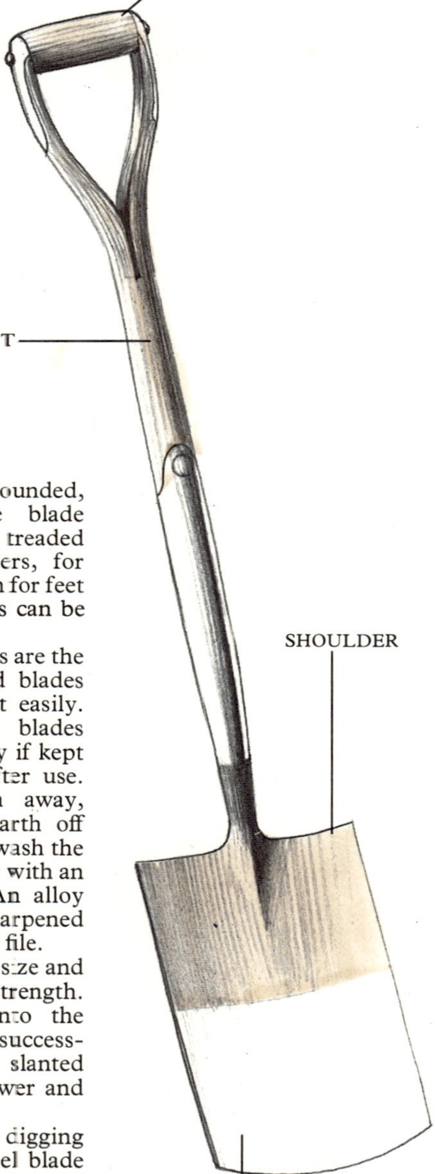

Digging spades have rounded, pointed and square blade shapes. Some have treaded (turned over) shoulders, for comfort and protection for feet and footwear. Handles can be D- or T-shaped.

Stainless steel spades are the best as their polished blades cut into the soil most easily. However, alloy steel blades will perform efficiently if kept clean and polished after use. Before storing them away, scrape all clogging earth off with a piece of wood, wash the blade, and wipe it over with an oily rag when dry. An alloy steel blade can be sharpened when necessary with a file.

Choose a spade of a size and weight to suit your strength. Thrust the spade into the ground vertically for successful deep digging. A slanted blade produces shallower and slower digging.

A variation of the digging spade has an alloy steel blade with four large points to provide a strong cutting action in heavy soil such as clay. This makes it particularly useful for people who are setting out a brand new garden.

Terrex Spade

OTHER NAME: Automatic spade
SIZE: Blade 200 × 100mm
MATERIAL: Alloy steel
USE: Assisted digging

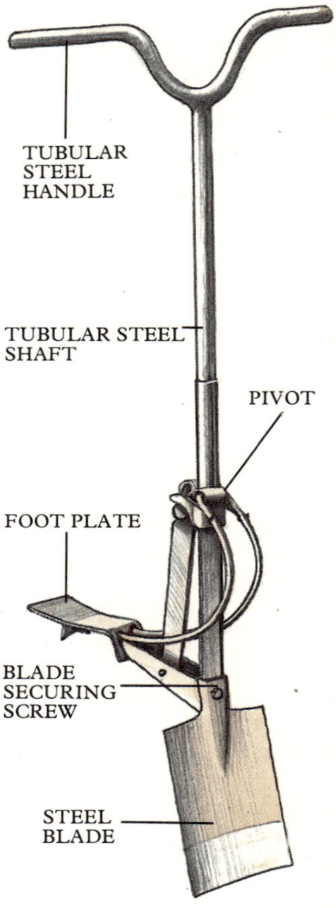

With this spade the earth is lifted and turned by a spring and lever action which eliminates unpleasant bending and the physical effort of lifting the soil. The digger only has to push the blade into the ground with the foot plate and lever the handle backward slightly. It is popular with elderly or disabled gardeners and is also a time saver for the able-bodied, enabling them to dig a much larger area of ground at one time than they could with a conventional digging spade. There is an optional fork head attachment.

Digging Fork

OTHER NAMES: Garden fork; graip
SIZE: *Prongs:* 200 × 300mm, 187 × 287mm, 175 × 275mm, 162 × 275mm, 162 × 262mm; *Junior size:* 850mm; *Length:* 975mm × 1m; *Junior:* 125 × 175mm
MATERIAL: *Prongs:* stainless steel, alloy steel; *Handle:* toughened plastic, wood; *Shaft:* aluminium alloy, hardwood
USE: To break up dug over soil

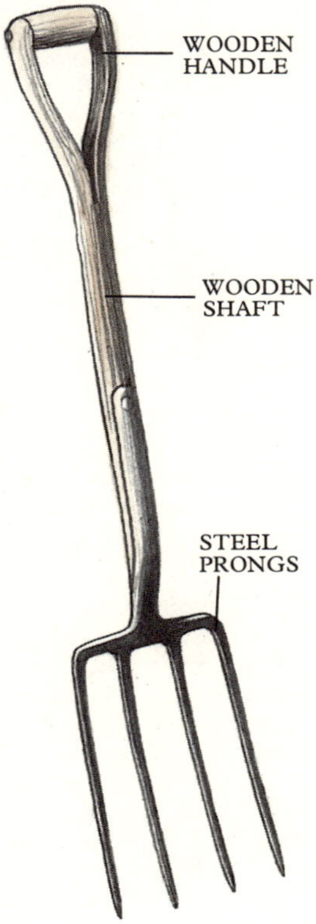

The fork is used after ground has been dug over with a spade to loosen and break up the soil even more. It is particularly useful on heavy soils which tend to stay in large clods after digging. You can also use it for lawn aeration – thrusting the prongs repeatedly as deeply as possible into the turf. It is ideal for lifting plants, as the prongs are less likely to damage the root system, and can be used for spreading and forking over manure and compost and for forking in fertilizers.

Forks are available with T- or D-shaped handles.

Border Fork

SIZE: *Prongs* 225 × 137mm; *Overall length* 912mm
MATERIAL: *Prongs:* steel; *Handle:* wood, plastic; *Shaft:* aluminium alloy, plastic
USE: To break up dug-over soil

The small, light border fork is used in confined places or crowded borders and for loosening weeds growing intermingled in clumps of perennials. Fork lightly through the clump without disturbing established flowers.

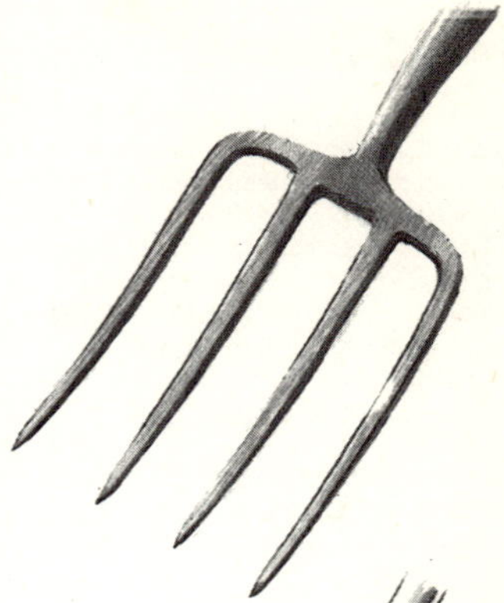

Potato Fork

OTHER NAME: Light plantation fork
SIZE: *Prongs* 312 × 187mm; *Shaft:* 750 to 800mm
MATERIAL: *Prongs:* alloy steel; *Handle:* plastic, wood; *Shaft:* wood
USE: To lift root crops

The flat faced prongs of the potato fork are designed for strength and to avoid damaging the crop. The fork can also be used to spread compost.

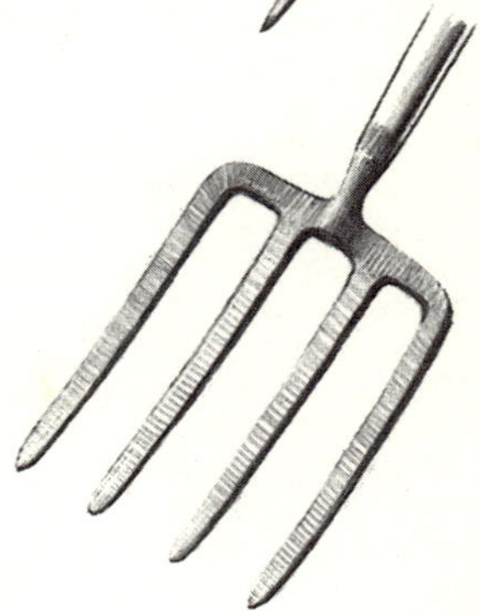

Long Handled Weed Fork

SIZE: *Head:* 75 × 118mm; *Shaft:* 750mm, 1.2, 1.3, 1.4m
MATERIAL: *Head:* steel; *Shaft:* tubular steel, aluminium alloy, wood
USE: To weed

The long handled fork is particularly useful when weeding wide flower beds or at the back of planted borders. The shorter shafted ones are used on rockeries and raised beds.

Hand Fork

OTHER NAME: Weed fork
SIZE: *Head:* 75 × 118mm; *Handle:* 125 × 300mm
MATERIAL: *Head:* steel; aluminium alloy; *Handle:* wood, aluminium alloy, plastic, nylon
USE: To loosen soil

The hand fork is used among small plants. The prongs are usually flat, but some types are twisted once. These are presented edge on, for use in heavily compacted soil.

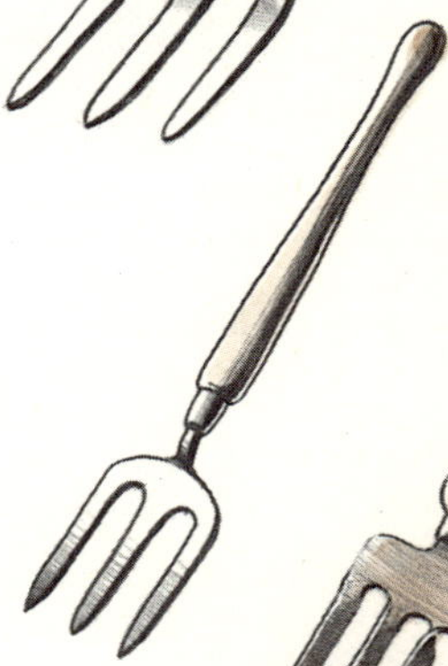

Hand Trowel

OTHER NAME: Garden trowel
SIZE: *Blade length* 125mm; *Blade width:* 50 to 125mm; *Handle:* 125 to 300mm
MATERIAL: *Blade:* stainless steel, alloy steel, strengthened aluminium alloy; *Handle:* wood, plastic sleeved aluminium plastic, nylon
USE: To plant seedlings

Wide bladed trowels are the best for planting, as the blade makes a good sized hole in the soil. The narrower bladed trowels are good for planting bulbs and small seedlings. Trowels are useful for potting up and seedbox work in the greenhouse.

Two variations of the hand trowel are the fine trowel and fine point. The fine trowel has an offset head which helps to keep the hand above the soil surface, making work easier in damp or heavy conditions. The fine point is specially designed for delicate work with house plants. It is useful too, for separating and thinning seedlings and making furrows in a seedbed or seedbox.

Some hand trowels are graduated with planting depths on the blade and have a retractable measuring tape in the handle.

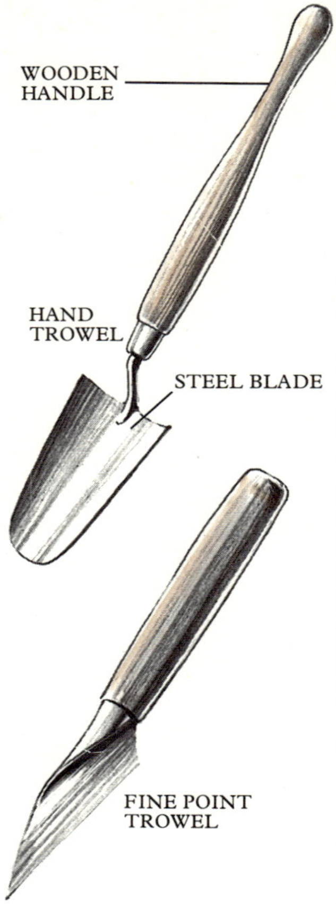

Daisy Grubber

OTHER NAME: Lawn weeder
SIZE: *Head:* 150mm; *Handle:* 125mm
MATERIAL: *Prongs:* alloy steel; *Handle:* wood
USE: To pull weeds from a lawn

The daisy grubber pulls up well rooted weeds that spoil a lawn. Push the two prongs into the ground as deeply as possible under the weed. Lever the grubber backward, using the tempered steel "elbow" as a fulcrum and tear up the weed by its roots.

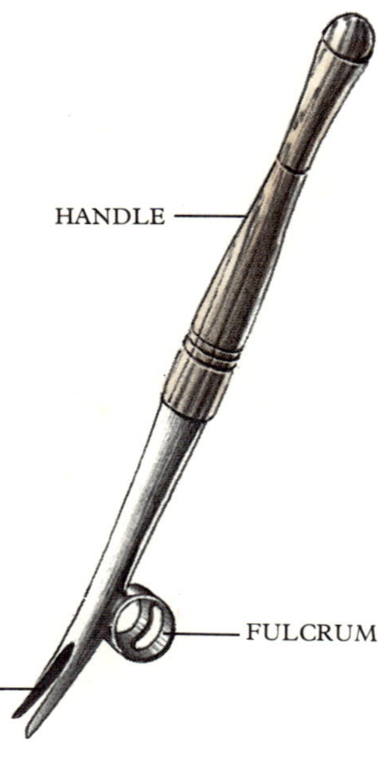

Dibber

OTHER NAME: Dibble
SIZE: Various
MATERIAL: Alloy steel, wood
USE: To make planting holes

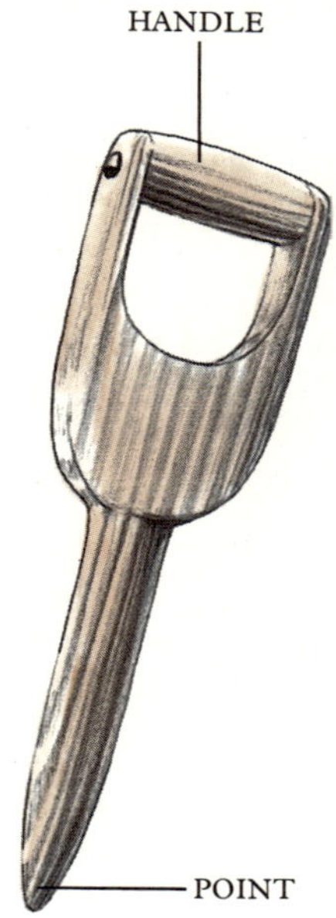

The simplest dibbers are about 150 to 200mm long with a D handle and are made of wood shaped to a point. Dibbers of steel and wooden dibbers with steel tips are also available. Some are graduated for guiding the depth of planting. Hollowed, steel dibbers, called bulb planters, are manufactured up to 75mm diameter. Many gardeners make their own dibbers from the handles of supermarket spades or forks.

There are also dibbers designed to make a series of prespaced holes simultaneously. They are plastic floats carrying a number of pointed studs, which are pressed into the soil in seed trays, levelling the earth at the same time as they create the seed holes. This speeds up seed sowing and also regulates spacing and depth.

Make sure a dibber is not too sharply pointed, otherwise an air space may be left beneath a transplanted seedling. This can fill with water and can cause root decay.

Draw Hoe

OTHER NAMES: Swan necked hoe, drag hoe
SIZE: *Length:* 1.3 to 1.6m; *Blade:* from 50mm
MATERIAL: *Head:* alloy steel, stainless steel; *Shaft:* plastic sleeved aluminium alloy, hardwood
USE: To break up soil, weed, mulch, turn up earth

Draw hoe blades come in a variety of shapes, but the most common are either straight, curved along the bottom or triangular. The neck between blade and socket can be short or long. Long necks are often curved, giving the hoe its name "swan necked".

Draw hoes are pulled through the soil toward the user, as he moves forward. They go more deeply in the soil than Dutch hoes. Alternatively, they can be used with a chopping action to break up the surface of the soil and hack out tough weeds.

The side of the blade can be used to make seed drills in prepared soil and the blade itself can be pulled through the soil to make trenches.

ONION HOE
Onion hoes are short-handled, draw hoes. They are swan necked, with 150mm half moon shaped blades. They are used for weeding in thick growth.

ITALIAN HOE
The general purpose, or Italian hoe, is a variation of the draw hoe. The forged steel blade is fixed directly to a short hardwood handle (1 to 1.2m). Used with a chopping action it clears overgrown plots quickly, but can also be used for breaking up soil and doing more delicate weeding and planting.

DOUBLE HOES
These combine the features of a draw hoe and a two or three pronged cultivator. They come in a range of sizes, including a small hand model with a 50mm wide blade and 900mm hardwood shaft for use in confined areas like rockeries and raised beds. A pointed blade version is useful for drawing seed drills.

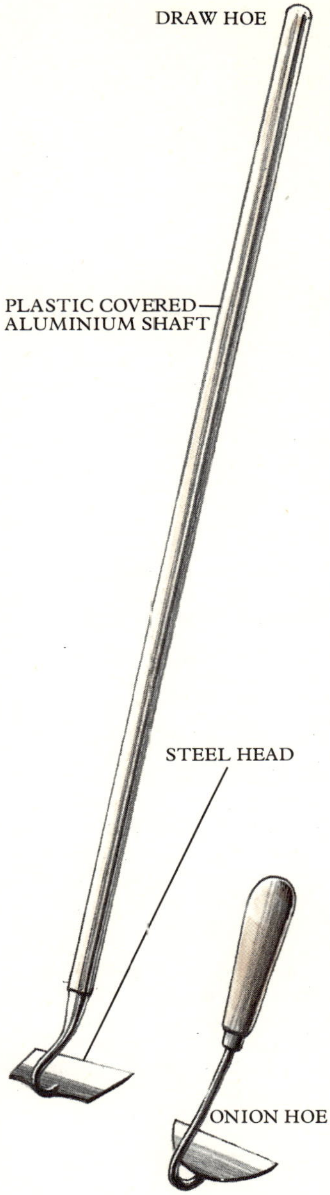

ITALIAN HOE

DOUBLE HOE

Fork Hoe

OTHER NAME: Canterbury hoe
SIZE: *Length:* 1 to 1.5m; *Head:* 200 × 112mm
MATERIAL: *Head:* alloy steel; *Shaft:* hardwood
USE: To break down turned soil, weed and turn up earth

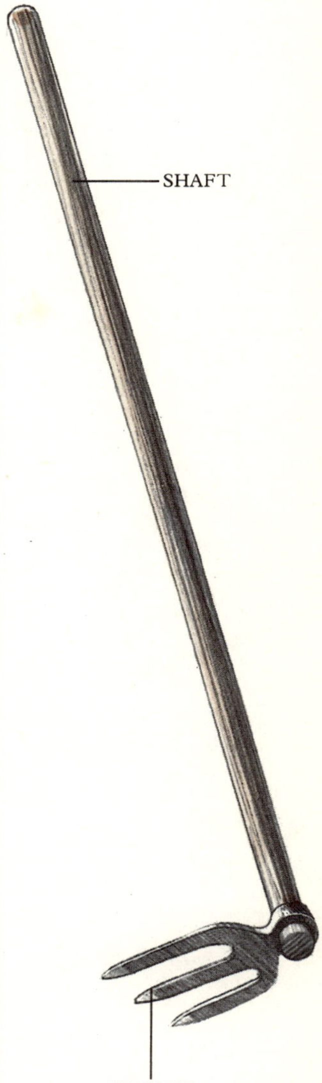

This hoe is a variation of the draw hoe and is used in the same way. It has a pronged head and combs the soil in the manner of a rake, but can penetrate to greater depth.

Dutch Hoe

OTHER NAMES: Push hoe, thrust hoe, scuffle hoe
SIZE: *Length:* 1.4 to 1.6m; *Blade width:* 100 to 150mm
MATERIAL: *Head:* alloy steel, stainless steel; *Shaft:* plastic, sheathed aluminium alloy, hardwood
USE: To weed and loosen soil

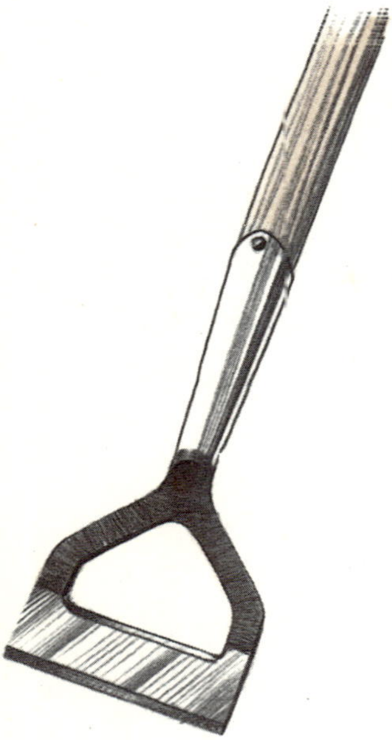

The Dutch hoe is used to keep down weeds between rows of crops and around bushes. It can also be used for mulching and working in fertilizers.

The hoe is used with a forward movement, sliding the blade just beneath the soil surface, cutting the roots of weeds and loosening the soil surface. The user moves backward as he works so that the hoed ground is not trampled.

Ideally, a hoe should reach to the user's ear level when held upright. Stainless steel hoes move most effortlessly through the ground and are easy to clean. After use, adhering soil should be scraped off all implements with a piece of wood. They should be washed clean and wiped over with an oily rag when dry.

Scuffle Hoe

OTHER NAME: Push-pull hoe, swoe
SIZE: *Length:* 1.4 to 1.6m; *Blade:* 100 to 150mm
MATERIAL: *Head:* alloy steel, stainless steel; *Shaft:* aluminium alloy, hardwood
USE: To weed and loosen soil

Scuffle hoes are double edged to allow a backward and forward hoeing motion. They can be diamond shaped, or have a double pointed blade.

The swoe is a further variation with three bevel ground edges, making it possible to hoe around plants without shifting your stance.

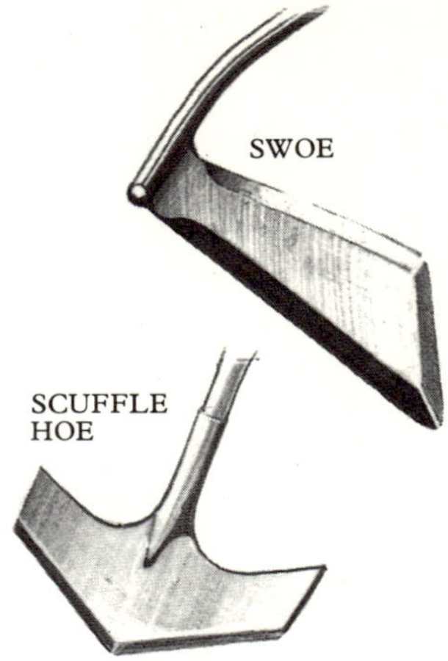

Leaf Rake

OTHER NAMES: Spring tine, rake, bamboo rake, wire rake
SIZE: *Length:* 1.4 to 1.5m; *Tines:* 15 to 24
MATERIAL: *Head:* bamboo, spring steel; *Shaft:* bamboo, aluminium, hardwood
USE: To comb out and gather up moss, dead grass and leaves

This fan-shaped rake with long, curved, flexible tines commonly made of bamboo or steel wire glides over the lawn without penetrating the soil. Used regularly it improves the quality of the grass as clogging moss, dead grass, decaying matter and the flowering heads are teased out, allowing air to reach the grass roots and permitting better drainage. It is also used to gather up grass clippings and leaves.

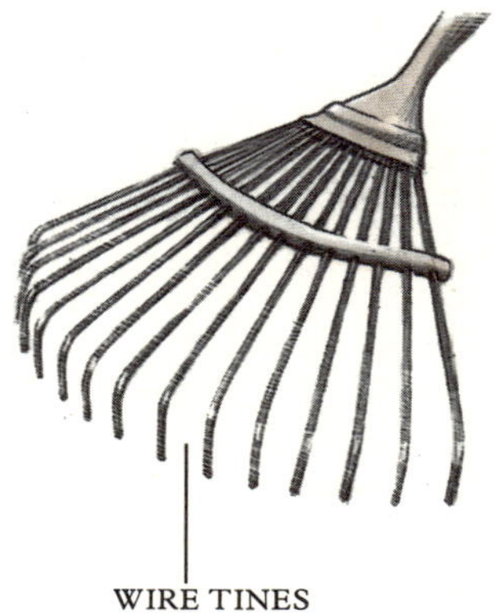

Lawn Rake

SIZE: *Length:* 1.4 to 1.5m; *Head width:* 575mm to 1m
MATERIAL: *Head:* alloy steel; *Shaft:* aluminium alloy, hardwood
USE: To collect grass cuttings

This wide headed rake has curved tines mounted on a straight rear bar. Its width makes it a speedy and efficient gatherer and it is therefore particularly useful for large lawns.

It has shorter tines than a leaf rake and can be used for levelling prepared seed beds.

Garden Rake

SIZE: *Length:* 1.3 to 1.6m; *Tines:* 10 to 16
MATERIAL: *Head:* stainless steel, alloy steel, wood; *Shaft:* plastic sleeved aluminium alloy, hardwood
USE: To prepare soil for planting

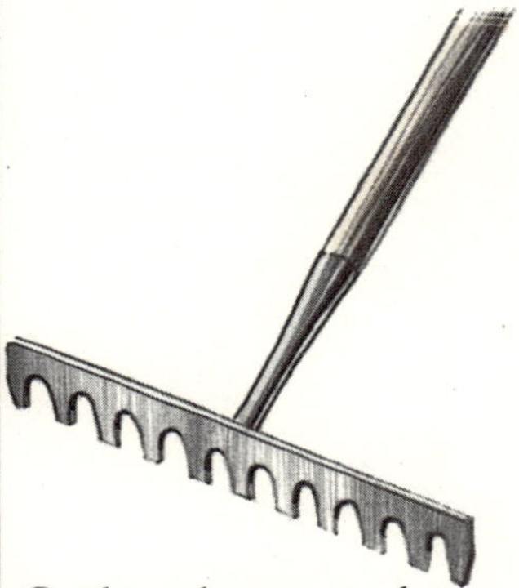

Garden rakes are used to prepare the fine tilth needed in seed beds, combing through the top centimetres of soil, breaking down lumps and removing stones and debris. The back of the head is used to make shallow seed drills, the soil being raked back after planting. Flat to the ground, the rake head is used to tamp down the soil firmly over sown drills. When sowing seed broadcast, soil is raked in one direction, the seed scattered and the soil raked again in the opposite direction to cover the seed.

Rakes are also used for leveling plots of earth, spreading gravel on paths, and working fertilizer and dressings into the topsoil. Wooden headed rakes are good for breaking up turned soil and clearing rubbish.

An upright rake should reach to the user's ear level, allowing the gardener to work without undue bending.

Small garden rakes are manufactured with 5 to 8 tines and 900mm shafts. These are used by children, and for work in confined spaces, like rockeries and raised beds.

Stainless steel heads are expensive, but are easy to use and rust resistant. The polished tines slip through heavy soil with less clogging.

Cultivator

SIZE: *Head width:* 50, 87, 100, 150 and 250mm; *Handle:* 250, 900mm 1.3, 1.5m
MATERIAL: *Prongs:* alloy steel; *Handle:* hardwood
USE: To break up and aerate topsoil quickly

The smaller headed cultivators are used in confined spaces, like rockeries and raised beds. The larger heads break up soil more quickly than the conventional hoe or rake. Some have removable prongs allowing a range of head size. Some models have heavy sharecutters on the prongs for very rugged work. A variation incorporates a blade for cutting down weeds, which can be worked out with the prongs when the tool is turned over.

They are either used with a chopping motion, like draw hoes, but with the user moving backward, as in dutch hoeing, or are pulled through the soil like a plough.

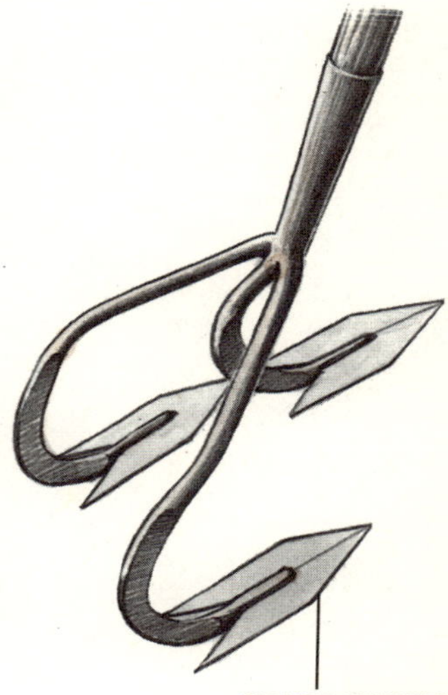

Rotary Cultivator

OTHER NAMES: Spin tiller, soil miller
SIZE: *Head width:* 150mm; *Length:* 1.6m
MATERIAL: *Head:* cast iron, alloy steel; *Handle:* hardwood
USE: To rake and weed simultaneously

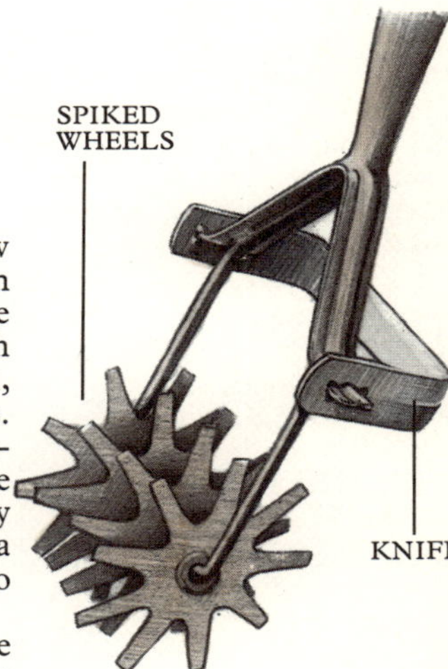

The rotary cultivator has a row of spiked wheels to break down the soil to a fine tilth, and some models have a rear knife which controls the working depth, cutting off the roots of weeds. The tool is also useful for hoeing between plants and can be used with one hand. On heavy soils it is best to go over the area twice, leaving a day or two between each tilling.

Some variations incorporate a battery of pronged blades mounted on a drum. These stir up the soil as the drum rotates, while a wide scuffle knife, fixed on the drum, cuts the roots of the surface weeds to a depth of 25mm.

Protective Clothing

Safety Helmet

OTHER NAME: Hard hat
SIZE: 162 to 200mm
MATERIAL: Fibreglass, plastic
USE: To protect the head

A one piece moulded, impact-resistant helmet protects the wearer against an accidental blow to the head. The safety helmet is fitted with a webbing harness which fits the head, leaving a gap between the helmet and the head to cushion any impact. Never wear a helmet without the harness.

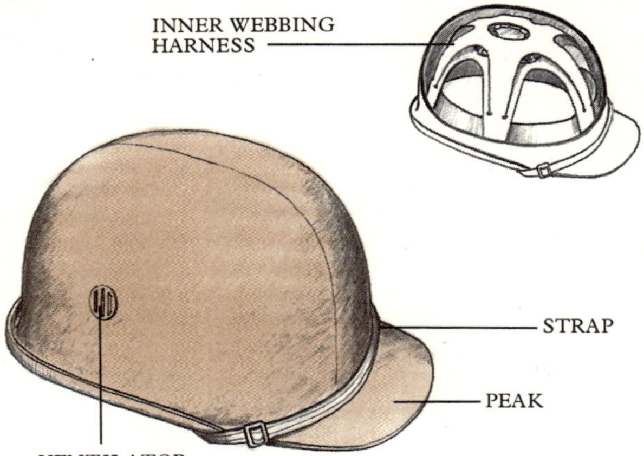

Ear Protectors

OTHER NAME: Ear muffs
SIZE: Weight 255g
MATERIAL: Foam filled plastic
USE: To protect the ears against high frequency noise

Ear protectors are foam or sometimes liquid-filled plastic cups, which fit snugly over each ear. A padded spring steel head band holds the cups against the ears. Each cup is lined with soft foam pads to seal against the side of the head. Ear protectors can be worn under a safety helmet.

Plastic or rubber plugs, which fit into the ear are quite efficient protectors and can be worn along with the earmuffs for added protection.

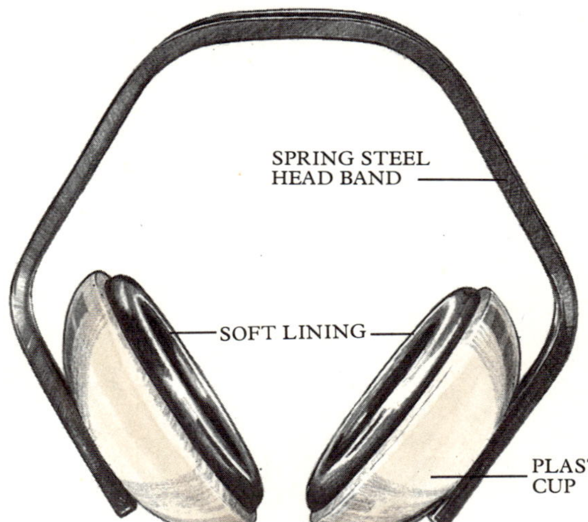

Face Mask

SIZE: Weight: under 14g
MATERIAL: Aluminium and cotton gauze
USE: To prevent the inhalation of dust or sprayed paint

The face mask is made from a pad of cotton gauze faced with thin aluminium sheet, which is easily shaped to fit the wearer's face. It has elastic straps which hold the mask against the nose and mouth, preventing inhalation of the dust particles and paint-laden air produced by spraying. The face mask will not protect you against toxic fumes for which respirators incorporating appropriate filters must be worn.

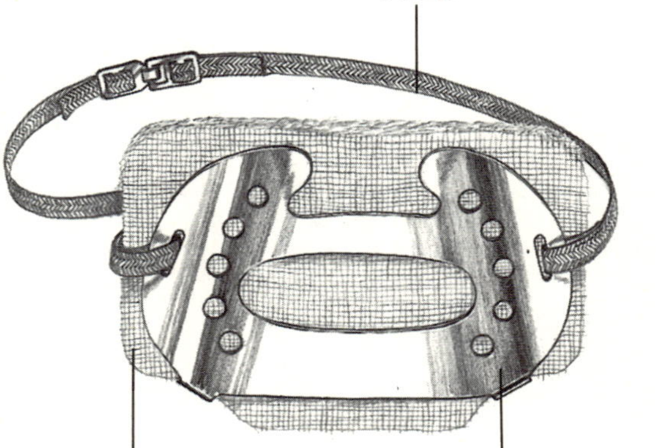

Eye Protectors

OTHER NAMES: Goggles, spectacles, face mask
SIZE: *Lens diameter:* 150mm; *Face mask screen size:* 150 to 200mm
MATERIAL: Plastic, toughened glass
USE: To protect the eyes against flying debris and harmful liquids

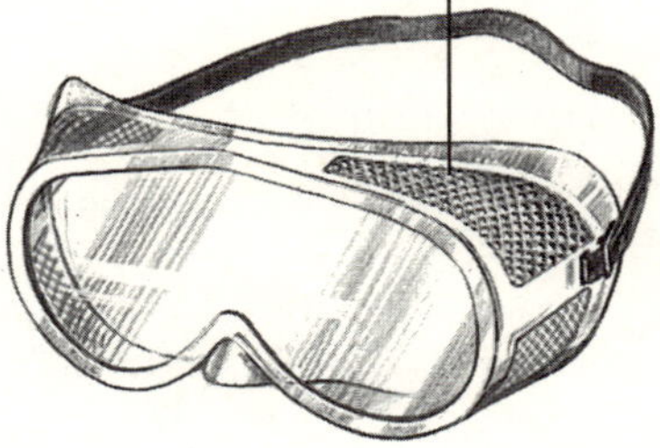

When grinding, chiseling masonry or doing any job that generates flying debris, it is essential to protect the eyes. Lightweight, clear spectacles are available with toughened, impact-resistant lens. They are comfortable to wear, even for prolonged periods. Choose a model with side screens or wraparound lens.

Goggles provide even more protection as they fit flush against the face and some can be worn over normal spectacles. They are more suitable where liquids are involved or when working in dust-laden air. Some goggles are ventilated to reduce perspiration and condensation. Green, anti-glare lenses can be fitted to some models, but these are not strong enough protection against the intense light produced during welding.

For complete protection, use a clear face screen which covers the whole face while wrapping around the sides. It is attached to a spark or splash deflector, which protects the forehead and is fitted with an adjustable harness to fit any size.

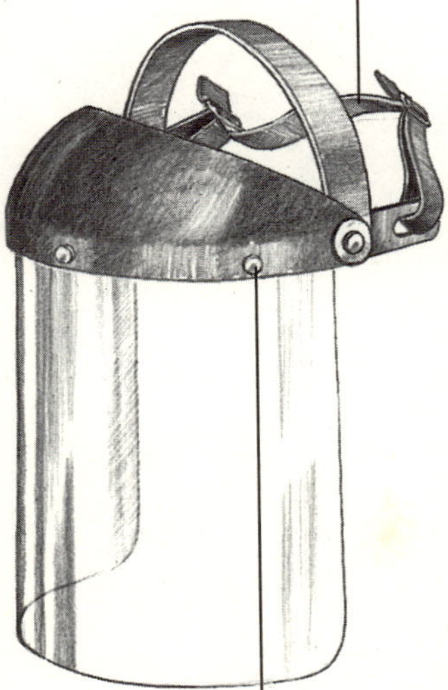

Welder's Face Mask

OTHER NAMES: Welder's hand screen, welding goggles, head screen
SIZE: Lens 106 × 81mm and 103 × 50mm
MATERIAL: Fibreglass, resin impregnated fibre
USE: To protect the eyes when welding

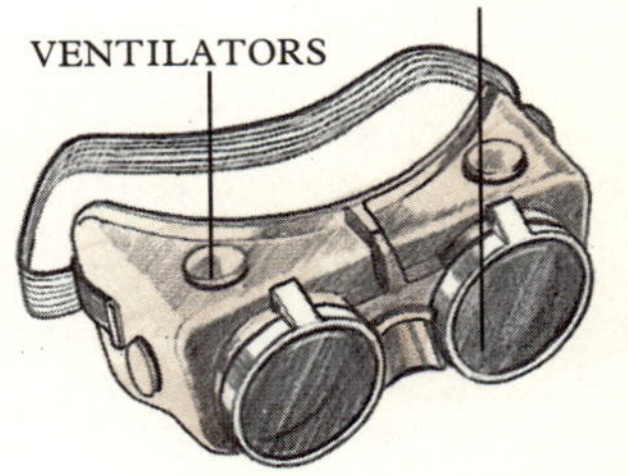

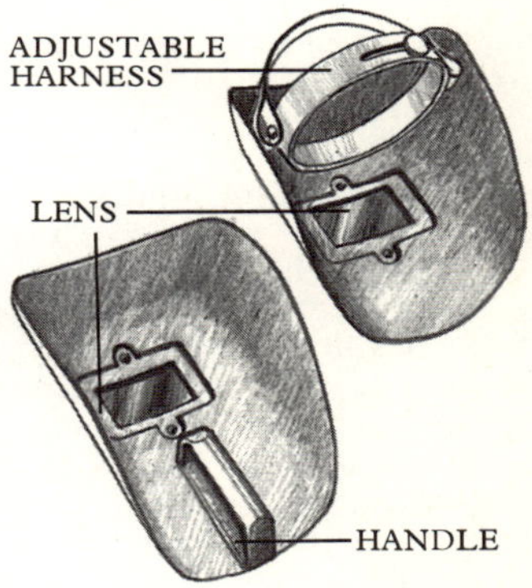

During the welding process the eyes must be protected against the intense light by a dark lens. This lens is expensive and is therefore protected from breakage and weld spatter by clear glass. The lens may be incorporated in goggles, a hand screen or head screen. The hand screen provides complete face protection being held with one hand while the work is carried on with the other. Its main advantage lies in the fact that it is easily removed for inspection of the work. Alternatively, a head screen which is attached to an adjustable harness can be worn, leaving both hands free. The screen itself hinges upward so you can easily move it to view the work.

Some welders wear clear goggles under the screen for protection while chipping.

Gloves and Gauntlets

SIZE: Various
MATERIAL: Cotton twill, asbestos, leather, rubber, plastic
USE: To protect the hands against burns

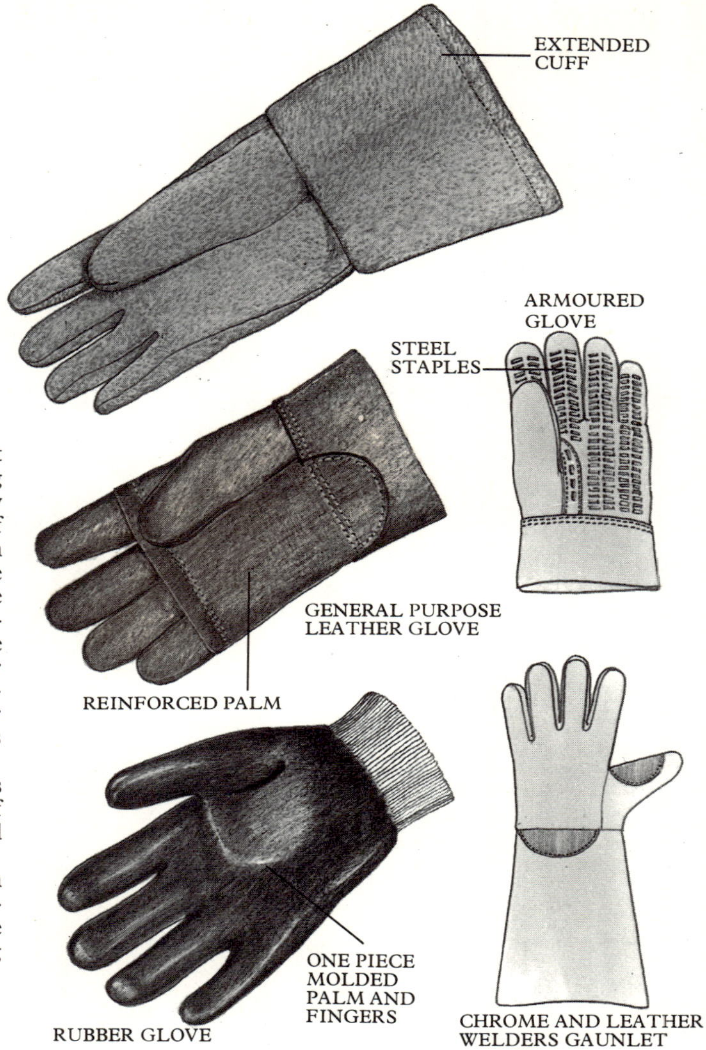

General purpose gloves protect the hands when handling rough or sharp materials. They are sometimes made entirely of leather or may be backed with cotton twill to improve the ventilation. The cuffs may be elasticated or extended to protect the wrists. Some gloves are armoured with steel staples for added protection. Heavy rubber gloves which extend over the wrists protect the hands from chemicals and cement.

Most heat-resistant welder's gloves or gauntlets are made of heavy leather or canvas and felt-lined asbestos.

Only wear gloves when operating machinery if absolutely necessary, and take care to prevent them getting caught in the moving parts.

Welder's Apron

SIZE: Length 950mm to 1m
MATERIAL: Leather
USE: To protect the welder against flying sparks and molten metal

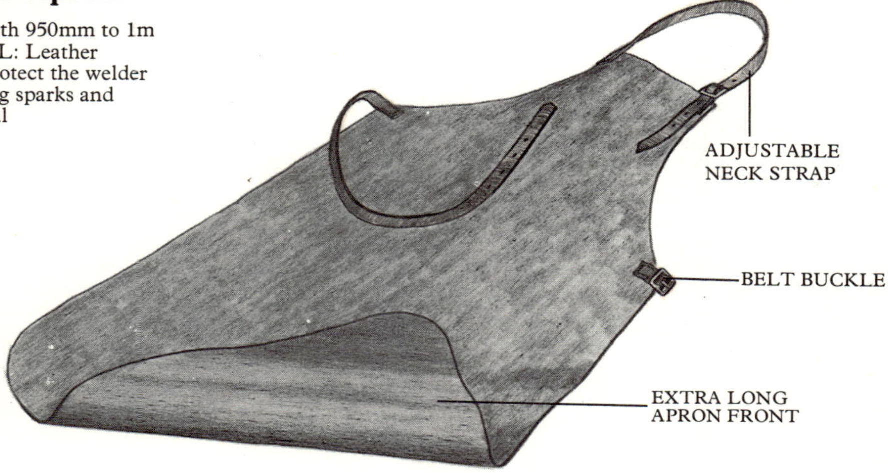

Glossary

Across the grain In a direction at or nearly at right angles to the grain of the workpiece.

Alloy Steel Steel alloyed with other elements to modify its mechanical properties. Each alloying element has a different effect on the properties of carbon steel. Nickel increases toughness; chromium increases hardness; molybdenum eliminates temper brittleness and permits higher tempering temperatures after quenching; vanadium and chrome together give high impact resistance; manganese combats the effects of sulphur; silicon increases the strength of steel used for springs; tungsten increases hardness and resistance to tempering.

Anvil Blunt or striking end of centre punch; fixed flat surface of a measurement instrument such as a micrometer.

Arris Sharp edge where two surfaces of the workpiece meet.

Back iron Steel plate screwed to the front of the cutting iron to break the shaving and reduce chatter of cutter. Usually known as the cap iron; other names: top or break iron.

Batten A strip of wood fixed to workpiece to act as a guide for a tool.

Bead A narrow, half round molding.

Bench plane Plane with flat bottom or sole, used mostly on the bench for squaring up workpieces.

Bevel Sloping edge of workpiece; tool to mark or check this.

Bifurcated Divided into two pointed or sharpened forks.

Bit Working part of drill; soldering iron; head or cutting edge of axe; cutting iron of a plane.

Blank Metal component cut to shape by pressure or stamping.

Bolster Thickening of the shank of a chisel to provide a bearing for the (usually) ferruled handle; type of cold chisel.

Bronze Age The period from about 2500 BC to 500 BC.

Burr Cutting edge of scraper produced by turning up edges with hard steel rod or the back of gauge; the rough edge produced cutting or boring metal.

Butt Flat surface of head of an axe; axe poll.

Cam Eccentric projection on rotating shaft or wheel which results in a reciprocating movement on a roller or other component in contact with it.

Casting Component produced by liquid solidifying in a mould.

Chamfer Flat surface formed by taking off the arris, leaving a bevel. A part of both surfaces should remain intact. A chamfer may be continuous or stopped.

Chuck Tool or bit holder on lathe, brace or drill.

Composite board Man-made sheet material manufactured by gluing together various materials such as wooden blocks, veneers, chips and fibres, plastics, asbestos, metals, papers, plaster, cork etc.

Concave Curved toward the observer.

Convex Curved away from the observer.

Counterbore Hole bored to admit the head of a screw or bolt which is intended to be sunk below the surface of the material.

Countersink To chamfer around the upper part of a hole, made with a coneshaped bit, to bring the head of a countersunk screw or bolt flush with or slightly below the surface.

Cranked A bar or shaft or shank of a tool bent at right angles in alternate directions in the same plane.

Cutting iron The working part of a plane iron, ground and honed to a sharp cutting edge; sometimes called the cutter or cut iron.

Dado A groove worked with or across the grain; groove worked across the grain with a dado grooving plane; panelling or other finish (European only).

Dimensioning Bringing down to the required size.

Dowel A round pin, usually of wood, acting as an inserted tenon to form a joint; rods of various diameters used for cutting into dowels.

Egyptian Period From about 3000 BC to 300 BC.

End grain Ends of wood fibres exposed after a cross cut.

Face edge Edge of workpiece made straight and square.

Face side Principal squared surface of workpiece.

Fillister Rebate plane with fixed or moving fence.

Forging Metal component produced by heating and hammering.

Frog Adjustable part of the stock of a metal plane on which the cutting iron or bit is bedded.

Flute A narrow, rounded channel.

Grain Arrangement of the wood fibres along the length of a workpiece; texture or arrangement of crystals in metal.

Greek Period Civilization of the Eastern Mediterranean from about 800 BC to AD 2000.

Gullet The notch between the teeth of a saw produced by the file.

Housing Form of woodwork joint in which one piece is fitted into a groove or rebate in the other. The groove or rebate may be continuous right across the workpiece or stopped at one or both ends to conceal the joint; the other piece being notched accordingly.

Included angle Angle formed by the opposing faces of a point, as on a punch or drill.

Infeed The side at which work is fed into the cutter or a machine.

Injection moulding Method of producing castings by squirting hot plastic into a water-cooled mould.

Inlay Ornament composed of shaped pieces of thin coloured wood or other materials, let into a contrasting wooden ground or base.

Integral Of handle, etc., shaped from the solid material of the tool or component itself.

Iron Age In Europe and the Near East, the period from about 1000 BC to the Roman period.

Jaws Seizing or holding members of a tool or machine.

Kerf Width of groove or slit produced by the action of a saw; the slit itself.

Knurled Ridged or milled surface on curved heads of metal screws or sides of a chuck.

Marquetry Overall ornament composed of patterns of coloured veneers glued to the surface of the workpiece.

Middle ages Period from about AD 1000 to the discovery of America in 1492.

Mitred joint A mitred joint is formed when two pieces of identical cross section are butted together and the line of the joint bisects the angle formed by the pieces. This is usually a right angle or 90°, and the angle of the miter is thus 45°.

Nicker Spur or spur-cutter.

Offset Set to one side.

Outfeed The side from which work is withdrawn from the cutter of a machine.

Parallax Apparent displacement of an object or a graduation on a scale due to a change of position of the observer.

Paring Removing thin shavings of material with continuous pressure applied to the work with a chisel, drawing knife, etc.

Pawl A device attached to a mechanism to allow rotation in one direction only.

Pilot hole Small hole, drilled as a guide to larger boring tool.

Pitch Advance of thread in one complete revolution of screw; bed angle of plane or bit; slope of roof; rake angle of saw teeth.

Poll The butt of an axe.

Pressing Component produced by pressing in a machine called a press.

Rebate A stepped cut made at the edge of a board so that another piece can be fitted to make a joint.

Rack Bar or part of a machine carrying teeth geared to a toothed wheel or worm, transferring circular motion of wheel or screw into rectilinear movement of the bar.

Rake angle The angle (to the vertical) of the forward edge of saw teeth.

Ratchet Part of tool or machine provided with teeth, which engages with a loose pivoted cog or pawl, in order to confine movement to one or other direction.

Roman period From about 300 BC to AD 400.

Scribing Shaping one workpiece (i.e. moulding) to fit exactly to the shape of another where they meet.

Section Usually a drawing, made as if the object has been cut through, the view being at right angles to the surface.

Shaft Handle of axe, hammer or other tool with a head.

Shank Stem or straight part of a tool nearest the handle.

Shank clearance Upper part of a hole for a screw to admit the unthreaded part of the shank.

Shim Thin collar or slip of metal used as packing.

Short grain Fault in sawn timber where direction of grain is at sharp angle to the surfaces of the workpiece (also called wild grain); potentially weak section of a joint given insufficient support by the surrounding long grain strength of the wood.

Skiving Sheet of split leather; the action of splitting thin leather.

Sole Working surface of a plane.

Spanner sizes Spanner sizes are specified in different ways depending on the thread type of the nut they are intended to fit.
BA (British Association) spanners are classified by the thread gauge. number: Nos 0.15 (0.236″ –0.031″).
BSW & BSF (British Standard Whitworth & British Standard Fine) are classified by the thread diameter of the bolt not the size of the head. A given spanner will fit nuts of the same size of both types of thread, however the BSF nut will fit a larger thread than the BSW, therefore the spanner will have two sizes on it e.g. 1/4 BSW 5/16 BSF.
UNF, UNC (Unified Fine and Coarse) spanners are marked in AF sizes. For example 9/16 AF refers to the across flats measurement of the nut which is 9/16 in. METRIC spanners are marked in millimetres and measured across the flats of the nuts they fit (except sparking plug spanners which are measured by thread diameter): ADJUSTABLE SPANNERS are classified by their overall length.

Spigot The male end of a pipe or rod wich is fitted into the enlarged end of another pipe or seating.

Spoil Waste formed when drilling masonry.

Spur The sharpened point of a scribing cutter on a plane or spiral (twist) bits and augers.

Step off Marking series of measurements on workpiece with dividers.

Stock Body or handle of tool holding working part or parts.

Stone Age Period during which most tools were made of stone, roughly down to about 2000 BC in Europe.

Stopped Method of finishing chamfer with chisel cuts; rebate or groove not running the full width or length of the workpiece.

Swarf Metal filings or shavings produced by drilling or planing.

Tempering Steel which is hardened by rapid cooling in water (quenching) from a full red heat is usually too brittle to use for cutting tools. The hardness is reduced (tempered) by heating again to a suitable temperature and then cooling. This gives a tough steel, the hardness depending on the temperature of the reheating.

Thread The spiral ridge of a screw; one complete turn of this, as the unit of measurement or pitch: e.g. six threads per inch.

Throat Aperture behind mouth of plane, etc.

Thumb gauge Home-made tool consisting of a short strip of wood with a notch at the end. Used with a pencil for marking a line parallel to the edge of the workpiece when a marking gauge would be unsuitable, for example, when chamfering.

Toe The front end of a plane stock.

Tolerance Allowable or acceptable variation in the dimensions of part of machine or workpiece.

Torque Measure of the force of rotation or twisting on a tool or machine expressed in foot/pounds or kilogram/meters.

True To make the surface of a workpiece accurately straight, level, and square to another surface.

Tungsten steel Hard steel alloy incorporating tungsten.

Universal joint Connection between rotating parts of tool or machine allowing transfer of rotation in any direction.

Vernier A small adjustable scale attached to and sliding in contact with the main scale of graduation; it enables readings to be taken on the latter to a fraction (usually a tenth) of a division. It is named after its inventor Pierre Vernier (1580-1637).

Wild grain See short grain.

Workpiece Piece of material or component which is being processed.

Worm Thread of screw or the screw itself.

Index

A

B

C

D

Italic numbers indicate text and illustration.

ACKNOWLEDGMENTS

The authors are grateful to:
W. L. Goodman for his historical contributions and advice, Black & Decker, Record Ridgway Tools, Ridgely Trimmer Co., Stanley Tools for their generous loan of tools as artists' reference, J. T. Batchelor, Black & Decker, Buck & Hickman, James Neill, Parry & Son, Record Ridgway Tools, Ridgely Trimmer Co., Spear & Jackson, Alec Tiranti, Wilkinson Sword, Woodfit for their cooperation in supplying reference material and technical information.

And the following individuals and companies for their assistance in the production of this book: Jenny Barling, Bill Brooker, Amy Carroll, Paul Chilvers, Viv Croot, Elizabeth Driver, Nick Frewing, Adam Hardy, Robin Harris, Ron Harris, Shirley Harris, Glen M. Hasker, Stuart Jackman, Kent Drawing Publications Ltd., Debbie Mackinnon, Alf Martinson, Bridget Morley, Dennis O'Grady, Jean O'Grady, Ron Pickless, Ken & Christine Robinson, B. Sayers – Diamond Arts, Venner Artists, Charley Watson.

SOME USEFUL ADDRESSES

Abrafiles
Abrasive Tools Ltd.,
Abrium Works, Colne Road,
Twickenham, Middx.

Bosch power tools
Beaver Engineering Ltd.,
Greenhills Road, Taliaght,
Co. Dublin, Eire

Power tools
Black & Decker Ltd.,
Cannon Lane, Maidenhead,
Berkshire SL6 3PD

General hand and power tools
Buck & Hickman,
Head Office, 100 Queen Street,
Sheffield S1 2DW

General hand and power tools
Buck and Ryan Ltd.,
101 Tottenham Court Road,
London W1P 0DY

Power tools
Burgess Power Tools Ltd.,
Sapcote, Leicester, LE9 6JW

Rotary rasps, power tool accessories
Ceka Works Ltd.,
Pwllheli Gwynedd, N. Wales

Leather working tools
D. A. Friend Ltd.,
28 & 29 Bond Street,
Brighton BN1 1RD

Ladders
Gravity-Randan Ltd.,
Slinford, Horsham,
Sussex RH13 7RD

Workmate, power and hand tools
Mate Tools Ltd.,
Brewery Road, Hoddesdon,
Herts EN11 8HH

Slevert gas torches
Wm. A. Meyer Ltd.,
P.O. Box 562, 9/11 Glenddon Road,
London SW16 2AV

Plumbers and builders tools
Monument Tools Ltd.,
Monument Works, 22-24 Balham Hill,
London SW12 9EB

Engineering hand tools
James Neill Ltd.,
Napier Street, Sheffield, S11 8HB

General hand tools
A. Oakden & Sons Ltd.,
86-90 Curtain Road,
London EC2A 3AB

Machine tools
Parry & Son Ltd.,
325-329 & 333 Old Street,
London EC1

Masonry drills and chisels
John M. Perkins & Smith Ltd.,
Braunston, Nr. Daventry, Northants

Measuring devices, general hand tools
Rabone Chesterman Ltd.,
Whitmore Street,
Birmingham B18 5BD

General hand tools
Record Ridgway Tools Ltd.,
Parkway Works, Sheffield S9 3BL

Painting and decorating tools
The Ridgely Trimmer Co., Ltd.,
117-119 Clerkenwell Road,
London EC1R 5DA

Garden, agricultural and builder's tools
Spear & Jackson Ltd.,
St. Pauls Road, Wednesbury,
Staffordshire WS10 9RA

General hand tools
Stanley Tools Ltd,
Woodside, Sheffield S3 9PD

Carving tools
Henry Taylor Tools,
The Forge, Lowther Road,
Owlerton, Sheffield S6 2DR

Garden tools
Wilkinson Sword Ltd.,
Sword House, Totteridge Road,
High Wycombe, Bucks HP13 6EJ

Power tools
Wolf Electric Tools Ltd.,
P.O. Box 379, Hangar Lane,
London W5 1DS

General hand tools
Woodfit Ltd.,
Whittle Low Mill, Chorley,
Lancs PR6 7HB

BIBLIOGRAPHY FOR HISTORICAL NOTES

Bergeron, H.: *L'Art du Tourneur,* Paris, 1816
Bieler, K.: *An der Hobelbank,* Braunschweig, 1951
Diderot, D.: *Encyclopedie,* Paris, 1765
Feldhaus, F. M.: *Die Säge,* Berlin, 1921
Felibien, A.: *Principes de l'Architecture,* Paris, 1676
Goodman, W. L.: *History of Woodworking Tools,* London, 1964; *Woodwork,* Oxford, 1962; *British Planemakers from 1700,* Needham Market, 1978
Gorecki, S.: *Stolarstwo,* Warsaw 1956
Greber, J. M.: *Geschichte des Hobels,* Zürich, 1956; *David Roentgen,* Neuwied, 1948
Heurtematte, J.: *Cours de Technologie du Bois,* Paris, 1948
Hummel, C. F.: *With Hammer in Hand,* Winterthur, Del. 1968
Jacobi, L.: *Das Romerskastell Saalburg,* Homburg, 1897
Kolchin, B. A.: *Chernoi Mettallurgie v Drevnoi Rusi,* Moscow, 1953
Kuksov, V. A.: *Stolyarnoe Delo,* Moscow, 1958
Lenkiewisz, V.: *Technologia Ciesielstwa,* Warsaw, 1959
Mercer, H. C.: *Ancient Carpenters' Tools,* Doylestown, Penna, 1929
Moxon, J.: *Mechanick Exercises,* London, 1683
Nicholson, P.: *Mechanical Exercises,* London, 1812
Roberts, K. D.: *Wooden Planes in 19th Century America,* Fitzwilliam, N.H., 1975
Roubo, J. A.: *L'Art du Menuisier,* Paris, 1769
Salaman, R. A.: *Dictionary of Tools,* London, 1975
Salzman, L. F.: *Building in England,* Oxford, 1952
Smith, R.: *Key to the Manufactories of Sheffield,* Sheffield, 1816